HANDBOOK OF PSYCHOLOGY AND SEXUAL ORIENTATION

HANDBOOK OF PSYCHOLOGY AND SEXUAL ORIENTATION

EDITED BY

CHARLOTTE J. PATTERSON

ANTHONY R. D'AUGELLI

OXFORD
UNIVERSITY PRESS

OXFORD
UNIVERSITY PRESS

Oxford University Press is a department of the University of Oxford. It furthers the University's
objective of excellence in research, scholarship, and education by publishing worldwide.

Oxford   New York
Auckland   Cape Town   Dar es Salaam   Hong Kong   Karachi
Kuala Lumpur   Madrid   Melbourne   Mexico City   Nairobi
New Delhi   Shanghai   Taipei   Toronto

With offices in
Argentina   Austria   Brazil   Chile   Czech Republic   France   Greece
Guatemala   Hungary   Italy   Japan   Poland   Portugal   Singapore
South Korea   Switzerland   Thailand   Turkey   Ukraine   Vietnam

Oxford is a registered trademark of Oxford University Press in the UK and certain other countries.

Published in the United States of America by
Oxford University Press
198 Madison Avenue, New York, NY 10016

Library of Congress Cataloging-in-Publication Data
Handbook of psychology and sexual orientation/edited by Charlotte J. Patterson, Anthony R. D'Augelli.—1st ed.
p. cm.
Includes bibliographical references and index.
ISBN 978–0–19–976521–8
1. Sexual orientation – Psychological aspects.   2. Sex (Psychology)   3. Age (Psychology)   4. Bisexuals.
I. Patterson, Charlotte.   II. D'Augelli, Anthony R.

HQ23.H3296 2012
155.3 – dc23
2012007188

3 5 7 9 8 6 4
Printed in the United States of America
on acid-free paper

CONTENTS

PREFACE

A tremendous outpouring of psychological research on sexual orientation has occurred in recent years and interested readers are now hard-pressed to keep up with the pace of scholarship in this field. Until now, there has been no single volume that would provide readers with an overview of this burgeoning area of scholarship. Our aim with the current volume is to present authoritative, research-based reviews of work in key areas of the psychology of sexual orientation. As such, this volume will, we hope, serve as the single most up-to-date scholarly treatment of its subject, and become a primary resource for the many researchers—including a new generation of young investigators—who are continuing to advance our understanding in this field.

This book continues our set of volumes on the general theme of lesbian, gay, and bisexual identities, framed by current psychological theory and research, all of which have been published by Oxford University Press. The first, *Lesbian, Gay and Bisexual Identities over the Lifespan* (1995), examined the nature of individual lesbian, gay, or bisexual lives as they change from adolescence through adulthood and the later years. The second, *Lesbian, Gay and Bisexual Identities and Families* (1998), reviewed research on sexual orientation and families of origin as well as research on families that lesbian, gay, and bisexual people create. The third book, *Lesbian, Gay and Bisexual Identities and Youth* (2001), addressed a crucial part of the lifespan in much more detail; this book considered sexual orientation and youth in terms of biological processes, family and peer relationships, and interactions with schools and with the larger community. With the foundation provided by our earlier volumes, and with the great increase in research in this area over the past decade, the time is now right for the emergence of this *Handbook of Psychology and Sexual Orientation.*

The first part of the book explores concepts of sexual identity and perspectives on sexual identities. The first chapter, "Concepts of Female Sexual Orientation" by Lisa M. Diamond, describes research and theory on bisexual, lesbian, and other sexual identities and their formation among women. The second, "Gay Male Identities, Desires, and Behaviors," by Jeffrey T. Parsons and Christian Grov, explicates processes of identity formation in the context of men's diverse sexual desires and practices. Sari H. Dworkin, in the third chapter, reviews theory and research on bisexual identities. Research and controversies surrounding transgender identities are presented by Francisco J. Sánchez and Eric Vilain. Alexander K. Hill, Khytam Dawood, and David A. Puts review research exploring possible biological foundations of sexual orientation in Chapter 5. The final chapter in this section, by Gary J. Gates, offers demographic perspectives on sexual orientation.

In the second section, authors explore developmental issues relevant to sexual orientation across the life course. In Chapter 7, Margaret Rosario and Eric W. Schrimshaw offer a summary of knowledge on "The Sexual Identity Development and Health of Lesbian, Gay, and Bisexual Adolescents" from an ecological perspective. The next chapter, by Bertram J. Cohler and Stuart Michaels, focuses on developments in the years of early adulthood. Andrew J. Hostetler presents an overview of "Sexual Orientation, Middle Adulthood, and Narratives of Transition and Change" in Chapter 9. The final chapter in this section, called "Sexual Orientation and Aging in Western Society," and is authored by Arnold H. Grossman, John A. Frank, and Michael J. McCutcheon.

The third part of the book focuses on different domains of life experience. Jonathan J. Mohr and Ruth E. Fassinger describe research and theory on sexual orientation, careers, and work. "Same-Sex Romantic Relationships" is the title of Chapter 12, by Adam W. Fingerhut and Letitia Anne Peplau. In the next chapter, Jane M. Simoni, Laramie Smith, Keren Lehavot, Karen Fredriksen-Goldsen, and Karina L.Walters explore what is known about sexual orientation and women's health. This is followed by a chapter on gay men's health, written by Amy L. Herrick, Mark S. Friedman, and Ron Stall. Mental health issues are taken up by Susan D. Cochran and Vickie M. Mays in Chapter 15. The final chapter in this section concerns "Sexual Orientation and Family Lives" and is written by Charlotte J. Patterson.

The final section of the book takes up communities and contextual issues. Stacey S. Horn begins this section with her chapter on "Attitudes toward Sexual Orientation." This is followed by a chapter on "Minority Stress and the Health of Sexual Minorities" by Ilan H. Meyer and David M. Frost. In the third chapter, Kimberly Balsam and Tonda Hughes review research on "Sexual Orientation, Vicitimization, and Hate Crimes." Bianca D. M. Wilson and Gary W. Harper present an overview of work relevant to "Race and Ethnicity among Lesbian, Gay, and Bisexual Communities." Finally, Chapter 21, the last chapter in the book, by Esther D. Rothblum, focuses on "Lesbian, Gay, Bisexual, and Transgender Communities."

We hope that the chapters in this book will find many varied uses and readers. The chapters are intended to provide clear and updated overviews of research areas, which we hope will be valuable both to students and to scholars. We hope this volume will contribute to the education of younger researchers and scholars, so that they will be able to build on what has already been learned.

The book is therefore intended for an audience of advanced undergraduate students, graduate students, and faculty in the fields of developmental, social, clinical, community, and counseling psychology. Those in professional practice as counselors, social workers, and therapists will also, we hope, find this book useful. In addition, the book should be helpful to those in related fields, such as sociology, anthropology, education, human sexuality, LGBTQ studies, family studies, sexuality, and gender studies. We also hope that the book may prove valuable to professionals in fields such as law, nursing, psychiatry, and education who seek current social science knowledge on sexual orientation and human development.

We want to express appreciation to our contributors, who have labored mightily over drafts and revisions of the chapters in this volume. We are grateful to Sarah Harrington, our editor at Oxford University Press, for the remarkable blend of enthusiasm, tact, and patience with which she has guided this project. We also want to offer thanks to the many friends, relatives, and colleagues who helped and supported us in many ways as we worked together to assemble and edit this volume. We also thank all those lesbian, gay, bisexual, and transgender individuals who have participated over the years in research that is described in this volume; without their willingness to share information about their lives, none of the research described in this volume would have been possible.

Finally, we note with sadness that one of our contributors, Bertram J. Cohler, died on May 9, 2012, after a battle with cancer. Bert was the William Rainey Harper Professor in the Department of Comparative Human Development at the University of Chicago, where he had taught for more than 40 years. An advocate of the life-course approach to understanding human development, Bert pioneered narrative approaches to the study of gay and lesbian lives. He brought uncommon brilliance and special warmth to all he did. We remember him fondly, will miss him greatly, and dedicate this volume to his memory.

CONTRIBUTORS

Kimberly Balsam
Palo Alto University

Susan D. Cochran
UCLA Fielding School of Public Health

Bertram J. Cohler[†]
University of Chicago

Khytam Dawood
Penn State University

Lisa M. Diamond
University of Utah

Sari H. Dworkin
California State University–Fresno

Ruth E. Fassinger
JFK University

Adam W. Fingerhut
Loyola Marymount University

John A. Frank
New York University

Karen Fredriksen-Goldsen
University of Washington

Mark S. Friedman
University of Pittsburgh

David M. Frost
Columbia University

Gary J. Gates
Williams Institute, UCLA

Arnold H. Grossman
New York University

Christian Grov
Brooklyn College

Gary W. Harper
University of Michigan

Amy L. Herrick
University of Pittsburgh

Alexander K. Hill
Penn State University

Stacey S. Horn
University of Illinois at Chicago

Andrew J. Hostetler
University of Massachusetts at Lowell

Tonda Hughes
University of Illinois

Keren Lehavot
University of Washington

[†] Bert Cohler unfortunately passed on May 9, 2012, before this book went to press.

Vickie M. Mays
UCLA

Michael J. McCutcheon
New York University

Ilan H. Meyer
UCLA

Stuart Michaels
NORC at the University of Chicago

Jonathan J. Mohr
University of Maryland

Jeffrey T. Parsons
Hunter College

Charlotte J. Patterson
University of Virginia

Letitia Anne Peplau
UCLA

David A. Puts
Penn State University

Margaret Rosario
The City University of New York–City College and
    Graduate Center

Esther D. Rothblum
San Diego State University

Francisco J. Sánchez
UCLA School of Medicine

Eric W. Schrimshaw
Columbia University

Jane M. Simoni
University of Washington

Laramie Smith
University of Connecticut

Ron Stall
University of Pittsburgh

Eric Vilain
UCLA School of Medicine

Karina L. Walters
University of Washington

Bianca D. M. Wilson
UCLA

I

Concepts, Theories, and Perspectives

Concepts of Female Sexual Orientation

LISA M. DIAMOND

"The male model of sexual orientation has been rejected in women."

(Mustanski, Chivers, & Bailey, 2002, p. 127)

Sexual orientation has historically been conceptualized as a trait-like predisposition to experience sexual attractions for one sex or the other, akin to an erotic "compass" (Bailey, 2009). This compass is generally thought to have a biological basis, to operate in a stable fashion, and to channel all markers of erotic interest (sexual attractions, fantasies, behaviors, and even romantic affection) in the same direction over the life course. Numerous studies have supported this overall model by documenting a consistent set of early-developing behavioral and cognitive markers among individuals with same-sex orientations, such as childhood "feelings of differentness," gender atypicality, and same-sex attractions and fantasies (McClintock & Herdt, 1996; Phillips & Over, 1992; Savin-Williams, 1996, 1998). Additionally, researchers have amassed substantial evidence of genetic, endocrinological, and anatomical correlates of same-sex orientations (reviewed in Mustanski et al., 2002).

With the exception of Kinsey's seminal research on women (Kinsey, Pomeroy, Martin, & Gebhard, 1953), much of the foundational research in support of the "compass" model has been conducted with predominantly or exclusively male samples, given that openly identified gay/bisexual men have historically been easier to identify and sample (Sell & Petrulio, 1996). Originally, this was not considered a substantive problem, given that sexual orientation was implicitly presumed to operate similarly for women and men. For example, most early inquiries into the origin and basis of sexual orientation did not even bother to differentiate between its manifestations in men versus women, treating it instead as a superordinate phenomenon (Adler, 1967; de Cecco, 1981; Futuyma & Risch, 1983; Harry, 1984; Storms, 1980).

Yet over the years, research documenting pervasive gender differences in the development and expression of same-sex sexuality have called this presumption into question. To provide some of the most salient examples, adult women appear particularly likely to report sizable discrepancies among their attractions, romantic feelings, and sexual behaviors; to report a markedly late and abrupt onset of same-sex sexuality, often after heterosexual marriage (Cassingham & O'Neil, 1993; Walsh, 2010); and to report fluctuations in their attractions, behaviors, and identities over time, sometimes triggered by single relationships (see reviews in Bailey, Dunne, & Martin, 2000; Baumeister, 2000; Diamond, 2003b, 2007, 2008; Hyde, 2005; Mustanski et al., 2002; Peplau, 2001; Peplau & Garnets, 2000). Most, if not all, of these findings appear attributable to two core phenomena: Women's propensity for *nonexclusive* rather than exclusive same-sex sexual attractions and behavior and women's capacity for *fluidity* in their attractions over time and across different situations.

As these phenomena have emerged repeatedly in ever larger, more diverse, and more representative samples (Bailey et al., 2000; Garofalo, Wolf, Wissow, Woods, & Goodman, 1999; Kirk, Bailey, Dunne, & Martin, 2000; Laumann, Gagnon, Michael, & Michaels, 1994; Mosher, Chandra, & Jones, 2005; Remafedi, Resnick, Blum, & Harris, 1992; Savin-Williams, 2006; Wichstrom & Hegna, 2003), researchers have increasingly rejected the presumption that female and male sexual orientation are "two sides of the same coin," and have argued instead that female sexual orientation has fundamentally unique mechanisms and manifestations (Chivers, Rieger, Latty, & Bailey, 2004; Hyde, 2005; Mustanski et al., 2002). The specific nature of these mechanisms and manifestations, however, remains unclear. Some have gone so far as to argue that female sexual orientation, as it is typically understood, might not even *exist* (Bailey, 2009), whereas others have argued that it unfolds and operates in a less rigidly deterministic fashion (Peplau, 2001), or interacts dynamically with a general propensity for erotic plasticity (Baumeister, 2000; Diamond, 2007). In essence, it is time to reconsider the nature and development of female sexual orientation: Do women really lack an erotic compass? Or do they simply have a different type of compass; or perhaps more than one? To answer these questions, we must carefully assess the distinctive features of female same-sex sexuality and consider their implications for modeling the nature and development of female sexual orientation. This is the aim of the present chapter. After reviewing the state of current research on these directions, I outline some of the most provocative and promising directions for future research.

NONEXCLUSIVE SEXUAL ATTRACTIONS

Arguably the most distinguishing feature of female sexual orientation is that women's sexual attractions are more likely to be nonexclusive (i.e., directed to both sexes, in varying degrees) than to be exclusively directed to the same sex (I use the term "nonexclusive" instead of "bisexual" because the latter term tends to connote equal degrees of attraction to each sex, whereas "nonexclusive" better captures the experiences of individuals who may be predominantly—but not exclusively—drawn to one sex or the other). This fact runs directly counter to the long-standing presumption (long known to be false among scientists, but stubbornly persistent at the level of conventional wisdom) that sexual orientation has only two forms: exclusive homosexuality and exclusive heterosexuality. Reflecting this view, researchers studying the nature of sexual orientation have historically excluded individuals claiming nonexclusive patterns of attraction, sometimes for the sake of methodological clarity and sometimes because such individuals were simply not considered to be the "prototypical types" of homosexuals (Burr, 1996; Rust, 2000; Whisman, 1993, 1996). Yet numerous surveys using large, random, representative samples have shown that the opposite is true when it comes to women: The prototypical type of woman with same-sex attractions *also* experiences

other-sex attractions (Bailey et al., 2000; Garofalo et al., 1999; Kirk et al., 2000; Laumann et al., 1994; Mosher et al., 2005; Remafedi et al., 1992; Savin-Williams, 2006).

These studies show that researchers have historically underestimated the prevalence of nonexclusive attractions among both women and men, but the error is far larger among women, given that women are more likely than men to experience nonexclusive attractions. For example, one large-scale representative study of American adults (Mosher et al., 2005) found that 6% of American men and nearly 13% of American women were attracted to both sexes, whereas 1.5% of men and 0.8% of women were exclusively attracted to the same sex. Similar results have been found internationally: Analyses of the self-reported sexual attractions of 3000 twins in the Australian Twin Registry (Bailey et al., 2000) found that 8% of men and women reported some degree of same-sex attractions and of these individuals, 75% of men and over 90% of women *also* reported experiencing other-sex attractions. A random representative sample of New Zealanders (Dickson, Paul, & Herbison, 2003) found that approximately 6.8% of men and 18% of women reported some degree of attraction to the same sex, but only 1.2% of men and 0.8%, as above of women were exclusively attracted to the same sex. Hence, directly contrary to the conventional wisdom that lesbians represent the most common "types" of sexual minorities and bisexuals are unusual exceptions, the data show that *bisexuals* are the most common type of sexual minority women, and lesbians represent the exceptions.

The specific distribution of attractions to both sexes also warrants attention. In every large-scale representative study, the single largest group of women with same-sex attractions report predominant—but not exclusive—*other-sex* attractions. In the study by Laumann et al. (1994) these women accounted for 62% of all women reporting any same-sex attractions, whereas those with exclusive same-sex attractions constituted only 7% of women with same-sex attractions (in men these percentages were, respectively, 40% and 38%). We might think of such individuals as "Kinsey 1s" or "mostly heterosexuals." On the Kinsey scale, zero represents exclusive heterosexuality and 6 represents exclusive same-sex sexuality. Hence, individuals who consider themselves "Kinsey 1s" can be viewed as possessing the minimum degree of same-sex attraction that nonetheless rules out complete heterosexuality.

What is particularly interesting about the prevalence of these individuals from study to study is that they have historically been treated with the *most* skepticism and denigration from scientists and laypeople alike. When it comes time to eliminate questionable cases from research samples, Kinsey 1s are the first to go (e.g., Bos, Sandfort, de Bruyn, & Hakvoort, 2008; Rahman, 2005; Thompson & Morgan, 2008). To some degree, this reflects appropriate scientific skepticism about measurement. Self-report measures of same-sex attraction and desires are already notoriously vague, as discussed in more depth below. Hence, when individuals describe weak or inconsistent interest in the same sex (manifested as a "1" on the Kinsey scale or as the endorsement of an altogether vague and poorly operationalized category such as "mostly straight"), social scientists have well-placed reservations about interpreting these reports.

The problem, however, is that this vaguely defined category of "mostly, but not completely, straight" women appears to represent the *majority* of women with same-sex attractions. In the study by Mosher et al. (2005), for example, fully 10% of American women described their attractions as "mostly other-sex," whereas only 3.4% endorsed "both sexes," "only same-sex," or "mostly same-sex." Among men, this difference was not as stark (3.9% endorsing "mostly other-sex" compared to 3.2% endorsing the other categories). Similar gender differences have emerged from other studies. Fergusson and colleagues (2005) found in a large New Zealand birth cohort that 12% of women but only 4–5% of men described their attractions as predominantly other-sex and described their identity as "mostly heterosexual." In another survey using a New Zealand birth cohort, Dickson and colleagues' (Dickson et al., 2003) found that 14% of women but only 4% of men described themselves as currently attracted to the same sex (Dickson et al., 2003). In a random, representative survey of American adolescents, nearly 11% of young women described their romantic attractions as "mostly heterosexual but somewhat attracted to people of the same sex," whereas only about 4% of male adolescents endorsed this description (Udry & Chantala, 2006). In a sample of nearly 2000 Montréal high school students, over 9% described their sexual identity as either "unsure" or "heterosexual with same-sex attraction," and 69% of these students were female; in contrast, only 3% of students

described themselves as gay, lesbian, or bisexual (Zhao, Montoro, Igartua, & Thombs, 2010). In one of the only systematic studies of "mostly straight" individuals, Thompson and Morgan (2008) found although "mostly straight" women show diverse patterns of current and prior attractions and behavior, they nonetheless appear to represent a distinct subtype of nonheterosexual women, with erotic profiles falling somewhere between bisexuality and exclusive heterosexuality.

Are such women really "gay enough" to include in studies of sexual orientation, or do they simply represent a group of unusually open-minded heterosexuals (sometimes called "heteroflexibles," Essig, 2000; Savage, 2002), whose high prevalence can be attributed to the growing visibility and cultural tolerance of same-sex sexuality over the past several decades? Does it matter whether they act on their attractions? Even if they *do* act on their attractions, how much should we parse their motives? These questions hearken back to a longstanding distinction between *constitutional* versus *facultative* same-sex sexuality (Bell, Weinberg, & Hammersmith, 1981). Constitutional same-sex sexuality is attributable to a stable and enduring same-sex orientation, whereas facultative same-sex sexuality is attributable to situational factors such as "play, exploration, lack of opposite-gender partners, hazing, initiation rituals, intoxication, sexual frustration, prostitution, boredom, opportunism, curiosity, and mistakes" (Muscarella, 1999, p. 9). For example, women who pursue same-sex activity in the safe and relatively tolerant environment of college, but resume exclusive heterosexual behavior afterward, have been called "LUGs," or "lesbians until graduation" (Davis, 1999; Kyrakanos, 1998; Rimer, 1993).

It could be argued that if "LUGs" and "mostly straight" women represent examples of facultative same-sex sexuality, then we can legitimately exclude them from investigations of "constitutional" sexual orientation. The problem, however, is that we have no reliable basis on which to know what distinguishes "constitutional" from "facultative" forms of female same-sex sexuality (see also Savin-Williams, 2009), or whether this distinction even makes sense for women. In fact, it is not even clear what might constitute the definitive test of constitutional same-sex sexuality: One likely candidate is stability in same-sex attraction and behavior over time, yet even this remains ambiguous. How much consistency, and over how long a period? The inconvenient reality (as noted by Kirkpatrick, 2000) is that social behaviors are *always* jointly determined by "a range of constitutional propensities interacting with a range of facultative opportunities" (2000, p. 390), rendering the entire consitutional/facultative distinction (and, of course, its implied basis in the familiar nature/nurture dichotomy) overly simplistic. Furthermore, if women's constitutional desires are typically nonexclusive, then this grants an even larger role to situational, environmental, and interpersonal factors in "pushing and pulling" her erotic profile in one direction or another (Diamond, 2006). Depending on life circumstances, two women might possess similar degrees of "constitutional" same-sex desires, but one might end up a "Kinsey 4" while the other ends up a "heteroflexible" Kinsey 1. Without knowing exactly *why* their sexual trajectories diverge, we have no basis to consider the latter "less authentically gay" than the former, or to exclude "mostly straight" women from research on female sexual orientation. Rather, a growing body of psychophysiological research on female sexual arousal suggests the critical importance of *including* such women in studies of same-sex and other-sex sexual arousal, as I review below.

Nonspecific Sexual Arousal

All of the aforementioned findings on women's nonexclusive attractions are based on self-report questionnaire data, which have known limitations when it comes to stigmatized topics such as same-sex desire. Perhaps, for example, the appearance of greater numbers of women than men with nonexclusive patterns of attraction is due to the fact that men perceive greater stigma attached to bisexuality than do women, and are therefore less likely to report nonexclusive attractions. The only way to rule out this possibility is to use measures of sexual attraction that do not rely on self-report. A fascinating series of studies has done just that (Chivers & Bailey, 2005; Chivers et al., 2004; Chivers, Seto, & Blanchard, 2007) and have provided robust evidence that women's capacity for nonexclusive patterns of attraction is also manifested in nonexclusive patterns of genital arousal. Chivers and colleagues call this pattern "nonspecific" arousal, and contrast it with the highly gender-specific patterns of genital arousal among men. The methodology for these studies involves continuous measurement of blood flow to the genitals (a well validated marker

of sexual arousal) while participants view erotic film clips. Chivers' team compared four different groups: self-identified gay men, self-identified heterosexual men, self-identified lesbian women, and self-identified heterosexual women. Respondents viewed videos of women having sex with women, men having sex with men, and men having sex with women.

The results showed that gay men were most physiologically and subjectively aroused by the male–male videos, whereas heterosexual men were most physiologically and subjectively aroused by the female–female videos. Women, however, showed a completely different pattern. First, there was much lower correspondence between women's genital responses and their *self-reported ratings* of arousal, a finding that has emerged in other similar studies (reviewed in Chivers et al., 2007). Notably, these discrepancies take multiple forms: In some cases, women report much greater subjective than genital arousal. In other cases, they show the opposite pattern, and the direction of the discrepancies does not correspond systematically to women's self-described sexual identity (making it unlikely that such discrepancies simply represent self-presentation biases). Yet perhaps most importantly, on average women had roughly equivalent genital responses to the different sexual videos. Importantly, this was not equally true for each and every woman: Some lesbians showed substantially more arousal to the female–female videos and some heterosexual women showed substantially more arousal to the male–male videos. On average, however, women's responses were "nonspecific," in that they did not show high sensitivity to the gender of the actors. Notably, women's *self-reported* arousal, measured simultaneously using a continuous scale, was more in line with their self-described identities: lesbians *reported* the greatest arousal to the female–female video and heterosexual women *reported* the greatest arousal to the female–male video.

Notably, this was not the first psychophysiological evidence for nonspecific patterns of arousal (for a detailed review of this body of research, see Chivers & Bailey, 2007) but it was arguably the most rigorous to date, and since that time the findings have been replicated numerous times (Chivers et al., 2007; Suschinsky, Lalumiere, & Chivers, 2009). Furthermore, studies using other psychophysiological measures of sexual arousal, such as electroencephalograms, functional magnetic resonance imaging, and the length of time that individuals look at erotic pictures have yielded parallel findings of gender-specific sexual interest and arousal in gay and heterosexual men but not in lesbian or heterosexual women (Costa, Braun, & Birbaumer, 2003; Costell, 1972; Hamann, Herman, Nolan, & Wallen, 2004; Wright & Adams, 1999).

Of course, genital and neurobiological measures do not necessarily provide "truer" measures of sexual orientation than do individuals' own subjective feelings: In fact, discrepancies between physiological and self-reported arousal have generated considerable research and debate in their own right (Chivers & Bailey, 2007; Chivers, Seto, Lalumiere, Laan, & Grimbos, 2010; Laan & Janssen, 2007; Suschinsky et al., 2009). But such findings dovetail with the extensive evidence reviewed above: Regardless of whether they identify as heterosexual, lesbian, or bisexual, women appear to possess a greater propensity to experience sexual attraction and arousal for both sexes than do men. Intriguingly, as pointed out by Chivers and colleagues (Chivers et al., 2007), Goy and Goldfoot noted over 30 years ago (1975) that in many different mammalian species, bisexuality is an intrinsically dimorphic trait that develops (through prenatal hormonal pathways) in *either* the male or the female of a species, but never both. This suggests the provocative possibility that in humans, women are "the more bisexual sex," whereas males are more likely to be exclusively heterosexual or homosexual (see also Bailey, 2009; Rieger, Bailey, & Chivers, 2005). Of course, numerous cultural factors might produce the very same phenomenon, such as the greater cultural acceptability of female–female intimacy more generally (reviewed in Diamond, 2003b), but the animal data suggest the possibility that there might *also* be a biological component to this gender difference. We revisit the potential implications of this notion toward the end of the chapter.

CHANGE OVER TIME

Historically, researchers have presumed that sexual orientation shows fundamental continuity in its expression over time (reviewed in Diamond, 2008). Although this is generally true for most individuals, some studies have found that a number of individuals—more often women than men—report notable shifts in same-sex attractions, behaviors, and identities over time (Golden, 1996;

Kinnish, Strassberg, & Turner, 2005; Kitzinger & Wilkinson, 1995; Weinberg, Williams, & Pryor, 1994). The most convincing evidence comes from longitudinal data. For example, Pattatucci and Hamer (1995) collected 18-month follow-up data from 175 lesbian, bisexual, and heterosexual women recruited from lesbian/gay/bisexual organizations. The authors averaged respondents' Kinsey ratings of sexual attraction, fantasy, behavior, and found that over the 18-month assessment period, about 20% changed their Kinsey classification. Stokes and his colleagues (Stokes, Damon, & McKirnan, 1997; Stokes, McKirnan, & Burzette, 1993) followed 216 bisexual men over a 1-year period, and found that over 45% changed Kinsey ratings. Longer follow-ups were conducted by Weinberg and colleagues (1994), who assessed change over a 5-year interval among, gay, lesbian, bisexual, and heterosexual men and women; approximately two-thirds reported changes of one point or more in their sexual attractions, and 85% reported changes of one point or more in their sexual behavior. Dickson, Paul, and Herbison (2003) sampled a cohort of approximately 1000 New Zealanders born in the early 1970s. They found that over a 5-year period, nearly 30% of the men and 45% of the women who reported *ever* having experienced same-sex attractions underwent a shift in their attractions between age 21 and 26. My own longitudinal research has found that over a 10-year period, approximately two-thirds of sexual-minority women changed their sexual identity labels, with between 25% and 30% changing labels within each 2- to 3-year period (Diamond, 2008). A similar percentage of respondents (in this case, a sample of 156 urban, predominantly ethnic-minority youth) reported identity changes over an 18-month period (Rosario, Schrimshaw, Hunter, & Braun, 2006).

Such findings concord with the evidence for shifts in same-sex and other-sex sexuality among individuals in other cultures (Blackwood, 2000; Herdt, 1984; Murray, 2000), suggesting that some degree of flexibility in sexual desire and behavior may simply represent a general property of human nature [Freud, (1905) 1962; Money, 1990]. Notably, however, studies consistently find larger and more frequent changes in self-reported sexual attractions and behavior among women than among men (e.g., Diamond, 2003a, 2005b; Kinnish et al., 2005; Savin-Williams & Ream, 2007; Weinberg et al., 1994). In light of the consistent gender differences, several researchers have argued that women's sexuality may be intrinsically more "plastic" or "fluid" than men's (Baumeister, 2000; Diamond, 2008; Peplau, 2001), meaning that women's desires are particularly sensitive to situational or interpersonal factors, making it possible for a woman to develop sexual desires and to enjoy sexual behaviors that run counter to her overall orientation. It bears noting that these models presume that such changes are *not* artifacts of distorted reporting (potentially brought about by force or social pressure), but are experienced by women themselves as authentic erotic experiences. In essence, sexual fluidity suggests that women's orientation provides less of a constraint on her lifetime pattern of desire and behavior than is the case for men.

Female sexual fluidity provides a possible explanation for the fact that women have historically been more likely than men to ascribe a role for choice, circumstance, chance, and change in their sexual orientation and identity over the life course (Golden, 1996; Whisman, 1996). Gagnon (1990), for example, observed over many years of research on female and male sexuality that women's participation in same-sex sexuality sometimes appeared to come about "by accident," significantly shaped by nonsexual factors. Beginning with the feminist movement of the 1970s and extending decades afterward, researchers have observed that women's immersion in feminist politics, coupled with the development of strong same-sex friendships and exposure to lesbian–gay–bisexual peers, often proved to be powerful triggers for new and unexpected same-sex attractions and fantasies (Cass, 1990; Golden, 1987, 1994; Shuster, 1987). The contemporary context provides an altogether different set of gender-specific environments that provide potential triggers for same-sex sexuality. In particular, the past decade has witnessed a notable increase in television and film portrayals of heterosexually identified women engaging in experimental same-sex behavior, usually with few negative social consequences (reviewed in Diamond, 2005a; Thompson, 2007). The phenomenon has become common enough to give rise to its own descriptor: *heteroflexibility* (Essig, 2000; Savage, 2002). Along the same lines, Morgan and Morgan–Thompson (Morgan & Thompson, 2007; Thompson & Morgan, 2008) have noted that many contemporary young women use the identity term "mostly straight" or "bicurious" to denote the fact that they are open to the possibility of same-sex contact,

even if they consider their basic orientation to be heterosexual.

In fact, many heterosexually identified women have been observed to pursue (and to report enjoying) such contact, just as many *lesbian*-identified women have been observed to pursue (and to report enjoying) sporadic other-sex contact (Bell et al., 1981; Diamond, 2003a, 2005b, 2008; Rust, 1992; Weinberg et al., 1994). Of course, such "cross-orientation" behaviors are sometimes observed among gay and heterosexual men as well (reviewed in Kirkpatrick, 2000), yet among men they are typically attributed to sexual release or the unavailability of preferred partners. Among women, in contrast, a common impetus for these encounters is an intense emotional bond (see Diamond, 2003b), and in fact numerous sexual-minority women have reported that their feelings for women are triggered or enhanced by feelings of emotional connection (Blumstein & Schwartz, 1990; Cass, 1990; Esterberg, 1994; Gramick, 1984; Nichols, 1987; Weinberg et al., 1994). In extreme examples of this phenomenon, some women report having fallen in love with one—and only one—woman, and experiencing same-sex desires for her alone (Blumstein & Schwartz, 1990; Cass, 1990; Diamond, 2000). Other women report that their desires are not so much directed toward *women* at all, but rather to "the person and not their gender" (Diamond, 2002, 2008; Golden, 1987).

Over the past 30 years, many researchers have invoked generalized notions of female sexual fluidity in attempting to explain such phenomena (Blumstein & Schwartz, 1990; Golden, 1996; Kitzinger & Wilkinson, 1995; Rich, 1980), and in recent years the possibility of a fundamental gender difference in sexual fluidity has received increasingly rigorous theoretical and empirical attention (Baumeister, 2000; Diamond, 2007, 2008). Given that changes in same-sex and other-sex sexuality have also been observed in men (Dickson et al., 2003; Kinnish et al., 2005; Rosario et al., 2006; Savin-Williams & Ream, 2007; Stokes et al., 1997; Stokes et al., 1993; Weinberg et al., 1994), the degree to which fluidity is a particularly distinctive feature of *female* sexuality remains a topic of active debate (Hyde & Durik, 2000). For example, Blumstein and Schwartz argued that "there are few absolute differences between male and female sexuality. What differences we observed are primarily the result of the different social organization of women's and men's lives in various cultural contexts" (Blumstein & Schwartz, 1990, p. 307). Other researchers, similarly, have argued that the appearance of a distinctively female capacity for fluidity might reflect the influence of female sexual socialization. For example, the pervasive social and cultural forces that have long controlled and suppressed female sexuality may have distorted women's awareness of their own sexual feelings and identities, channeling them rigidly toward heterosexuality with few opportunities to express and experiment with same-sex desires (Baumeister & Twenge, 2002; Fine, 1988; Laumann & Mahay, 2002; Tolman & Diamond, 2001; Ussher, 1993; Welles, 2005). These social and cultural influences certainly complicate our task of understanding and modeling female sexual orientation, and must be taken into account as we embark on the next generation of research on these questions.

RETHINKING FEMALE SEXUAL ORIENTATION

With these complexities in mind, how might we begin the task of building new models of female sexual orientation? One provocative possibility suggested by Bailey (2009) is that women might not *have* sexual orientations (to the degree that sexual orientation is defined as a fixed, gender-specific pattern of sexual arousal). This notion provides a compelling (if rather sweeping) explanation of the extant data on women's propensity for nonexclusive and fluid sexual attractions, and concords with Goy and Goldfoot's (1975) aforementioned observation that many mammalian species have one "bisexual" (or "unoriented") sex. At the same time, however, the extant data (reviewed earlier) on women's sexual fluidity have revealed considerable *variation* among women regarding the degree of nonexclusivity and/or nonspecificity in their attractions and behaviors. If women have no sexual orientation, then why do some women seem so much more "oriented" than others? Bailey's resolution to this problem is to argue that the majority of women (i.e., heterosexual and bisexual women) lack a sexual orientation, and that lesbians (who appear to have more gender-oriented patterns of desire) represent an exception.

But there might be a way to revise models of sexual orientation to account for *both* "oriented" and "unoriented" women. Specifically, we might imagine that female sexual orientation is comprised of two orthogonal dimensions: One dimension represents the degree of "genderedness" of a woman's desires (i.e., the degree to which a woman's desires are oriented to one gender over the other) and the other dimension represents the direction of this targeting (same-sex versus other-sex). Hence, the appropriate question to ask when assessing a woman's sexual orientation might not be "Heterosexual, lesbian, or bisexual?," as is currently presumed, but instead "First, how much does gender matter?" (*gender* denoting, in this case, an individual's observable presentation as male versus female). Second, to the degree that gender matters, which gender is preferred? Historically, scientific conceptualizations of sexual orientations have focused only on the second question, assuming that the answer to the first question was uniformly "yes" and that sexual desire is always "about" gender. Yet the experiences of women who claim to be attracted to "the person, not the gender" suggest that we should revisit this assumption. Some of the variability in women's sexual fluidity may be attributable to variability in the degree to which gender organizes and directs women's desires on a basic level. For some women, sexuality might be "gender neutral," in which case a host of other factors (emotional intimacy, sex drive, mood, personality similarity or difference) might determine the partners she finds most attractive and the sexual encounters she finds most appealing. This is certainly not a new notion. Ross and Paul (1992) argued that gender-neutrality in sexuality might explain bisexuality more generally. For Weinberg et al. (1994), gender-neutrality represented a subtype of bisexuality, rather than a defining feature. They described a subset of their bisexually identified respondents as possessing an "open gender schema," meaning that they were capable of responding sexually to a broad range of traits and characteristics, regardless of gender. Interestingly, they observed that men with "open gender schemas" were typically heterosexually identified men who sought periodic same-sex contact for purposes of sexual release, whereas women with "open gender schemas" reported that their desires were typically sparked by their emotional connection with a specific individual. Of course, this gender difference is sure to exhibit considerable variability: Some men with open gender schemas may be strongly motivated to seek sexual contact for reasons of emotional connection, whereas some women with open gender schemas may be strongly motivated to seek sexual contact for reasons of sexual release, novelty, and variability. Yet extant findings suggest that the latter pattern is generally more characteristic of men, and the former pattern is more characteristic of women.

The fact that women's sexual desires are frequently triggered by emotional factors was also noted by Blumstein and Schwartz (1990), who argued that conventional models of sexual orientation failed to account for the experiences of women "whose fundamental sexual desire seems to be produced within the context of a relationship, rather than by an abstract preference for women or men" (p. 356). They concluded that these women's sexuality was less focused on physical, bodily characteristics, and more frequently triggered by love, admiration, affection, and companionship. Although Blumstein and Schwartz's study focused on bisexuality, it bears emphasizing that not all individuals with "gender-neutral"patterns of attraction characterize themselves as bisexual (Diamond, 2008; Savin-Williams, 2005). To the contrary, some explicitly reject conventional sexual identity labels, or adopt alternative labels such as "queer" or "pansexual," in an attempt to better represent the gender-neutral nature of their attractions (Berenson, 2002; Bower, Gurevich, & Mathieson, 2002; Hollander, 2000; Horner, 2007; Savin-Williams, 2005).

This raises the inevitable question of why some women experience their nonexclusive attractions as gender-neutral, whereas others do not. We know remarkably little about the gradual "gendering" of children's erotic impulses more generally (Gagnon, 1990). Although children engage in both solitary self-stimulation and partnered sex play from an early age (reviewed in Diamond & Savin-Williams, 2009), "gender of partner" does not appear to emerge as a discernible preference until 9 or 10 (McClintock & Herdt, 1996). As Gagnon argued (1990, p. 199), "During the ages of 12 to 17 the gender aspects of the 'who' in the sexual scripts that are being formed are not fixed.... A deeper complication is that it is not obvious whether it is the gender aspects of the 'who' that have provoked the nascent desire or even if the desire is linked to a 'who' at all." Perhaps then, an orientation toward person-centered attractions represents a more substantiated form of this gender-neutrality, in which our sexual scripts remain fundamentally open with regard to the "gender aspects of the 'who.'" Notably, Liben and Bigler (2008) have argued that there is

considerable variation in children's degree of gender salience (i.e., the degree to which they reflexively attend to gender more generally), and that children with low levels of gender salience may be less likely to exhibit a rigidly homosexual or heterosexual orientation. According to this framework, low gender salience (as an individual difference dimension) might facilitate the development of an open gender schema with regard to sexual desires.

Another (albeit speculative) possibility is that most individuals begin life with a relatively open gender schema, but that this schema becomes increasingly gender targeted as a function of normative gender socialization (toward greater gender saliency, in Liben and Bigler's terms) and especially during sexual maturation (as a function of the individuals' underlying sexual orientation). Perhaps for males, then, the most common deviation from the standard heterosexual pathway is the substitution of a same-sex "compass" for the standard other-sex "compass." For females, instead, the most common deviation from the standard heterosexual pathway might be *the failure of a gender-based compass to develop.* In such cases, women's patterns of sexual arousal might remain fundamentally nonspecific, and their patterns of conscious, subjective *attraction* might come to depend on a host of nongendered cues, such as emotional intimacy and personality.

This need not suggest that *all* women with same-sex attractions follow such a trajectory. Lesbians with relatively exclusive same-sex attractions might follow a developmental trajectory more similar to that of gay men (i.e. the development of a same-sex compass rather than the failure of a compass to develop). Several studies suggest that lesbians are qualitatively distinct from both bisexual and heterosexual women in that they show more male-typical patterns of "gender specificity" (i.e., consistent and exclusive targeting toward one gender) and stability in their sexual arousal and attractions (Chivers & Bailey, 2007; Chivers et al., 2007; Diamond, 2005b; Diamond & Fagundes, 2012; Suschinsky et al., 2009; Worthington & Reynolds, 2009). Perhaps, then, there may be four forms of sexual orientation in women, with different underlying causes and developmental trajectories: Heterosexual, Bisexual, Lesbian, and *Nongendered.* Women in the latter group might resemble women in *any of the other groups* at different stages of the life course, depending on a variety of cultural, situational, and interpersonal circumstances. This may be why "Kinsey 1s" who identify as heterosexual are not necessarily misrepresenting themselves when they profess their heterosexuality. As Chivers and colleagues cautioned, we cannot presume that a woman with a nonspecific pattern of sexual arousal is fundamentally bisexual; making such a simplistic and erroneous presumption "overlooks the complexity and multidimensionality of female sexuality" (2007, p. 1119).

The complication is that *arousal* and *desire* are not equivalent constructs, despite the fact that they are often used interchangeably in discussions of sexual orientation. A woman who becomes genitally *aroused* in response to both same-sex and other-sex stimuli may not necessarily experience conscious sexual *desires or fantasies* for both men and women. Should we consider her bisexual on the basis of her genital responses, or should we grant greater weight to her subjective experiences of desire and attraction? At the present time, there is no empirical basis on which to make this determination. Bailey (2009) argues that sexual arousal is the most reliable indicator of sexual orientation (at least among men), while acknowledging that many others researchers would grant a broader role for subjective desire and/or romantic affection. A major problem in discerning which aspect of sexual experience provides the most reliable indicator of sexual orientation is the lack of research on how different components of sexual experience (arousal, desire, attraction, motivation, fantasy, etc.) relate to one other, both at a single moment in time and also over the life course (Chivers & Bailey, 2007; Chivers et al., 2010; Diamond, 2008; Igartua, Thombs, Burgos, & Montoro, 2009; Laan & Janssen, 2007; Laumann et al., 1994; Savin-Williams & Ream, 2007; Suschinsky et al., 2009). Hence, a recurring obstacle for our understanding of the nature of female and male sexual orientation is our limited conceptualization of *sexual desire* more generally.

THE DESIRE PROBLEM

The twin constructs of sexual desire and sexual attraction require far more scientific attention from scholars of sexual orientation than they have received to date. Although these constructs are fundamental to defining and modeling sexual orientation, there has been little attempt to validate individuals' self-reports of these experiences and to determine which types of experiences should be considered the most reliable indices of sexual orientation. It is somewhat surprising that although researchers studying sexual orientation have taken great pains to carefully assess how often individuals experience same-sex versus other-sex attractions, the relative balance between them, and the age at which they first emerged, they rarely ask respondents *what they mean* by the word "attraction" or "desire," and the full range of thoughts, feelings, and physical experiences that comprise an individual's erotic phenomenology (for an exception, see Tolman, 2002). Contrary to the notion that desire is a relatively straightforward experience, individuals describe startlingly diverse experiences when asked to provide examples of "desire/attraction" (Tolman, 2002). In my own longitudinal research (Diamond, 2008), I found that women's descriptions of sexual desire and attraction ranged from specific genital sensations (*tightness in my groin; wetness*) to full-body physical sensations (*warm all over; high energy, fluttery feeling in my belly; a sort of chemical connection*) to psychological states (*liking to look at their face or body; longing for nearness; not caring about their personality; wanting to have sex*). It is not clear whether these experiences reference the same underlying phenomenon, whether they have similar origins, and whether any of them constitute reliable or valid indicators of a women's sexual "compass." On this point, it bears noting that my respondents expressed their own doubts about what constituted desire or attraction, especially in cases in which they experienced differences between the subjective quality of their desires for women versus men. Some women described attractions to one gender as more/less "automatic;" "clear," "all-encompassing," "cognitive," "fleeting," "intimidating," "motivating," "intimate," "lasting," "powerful," "emotional," "pleasurable," "heartfelt," or "electrifying" (Diamond, 2008). One possibility is that such phenomenological differences correspond to differences between "constitutional" and "facultative" desires, such that desires that indicate an individual's erotic "compass" are experienced as relatively more "automatic," "powerful," and "motivating," whereas facultative desires (emanating from one's capacity for sexual fluidity) are experienced as relatively more "fleeting," "heartfelt," or "emotional." Yet at the present time, there is no empirical evidence for such a distinction, and also no empirical or theoretical basis for understanding *why* certain attractions have a different subjective phenomenology than do others.

We know that both biological and environmental factors contribute to the subjective experience of sexual desire (reviewed in Tolman & Diamond, 2001), but we do not yet know how to reliably disentangle these influences. As Laumann and Mahay pointed out, "We must all *learn* what to regard or understand as being sexual or nonsexual" (Laumann & Mahay, 2002, p. 44, emphasis added). Biological factors (such as pubertal maturation) give rise to certain physical sensations, but environmental factors give meaning to these experiences, both on a cognitive and physical level. In other words, culture and society teach us not only what "sexual" *means*, but what it feels like, and these determinations will vary widely as a function of norms, expectations, socialization practices, opportunities for different types of intimate experiences, etc. Without understanding the intersection between all of these factors, we cannot distinguish between women whose same-sex desires emanate from a stable, biologically driven erotic "compass," and those whose same-sex desires emanate from a broad female capacity for sexual fluidity.

Is such a distinction worth making? Earlier, I noted that although there is a long history of distinguishing between "constitutional" and "facultative" forms of same-sex sexuality (Bergler, 1954; Defries, 1976; Goode & Haber, 1977), going back even to Freud [(1905) 1962, p. 138], this distinction is overly simplistic and problematic. This does not mean, however, that we should treat all women with same-sex attractions as equivalent. Perhaps, instead, we need to explore new typologies of same-sex sexual orientation that rely *not* on notion of "constitutional/authentic" and "facultative/inauthentic" desire, but seek to chart more rigorously the relative influence of different factors on a woman's same-sex and other-sex desires. Consider, for example, the aforementioned findings of Chivers and her colleagues (2004). Although all women showed relatively "nonspecific" genital responses, the self-identified lesbians emerged as a distinct group, showing more gender-specificity in their sexual arousal than did the heterosexual women, although less than was observed among men. My own longitudinal research has found that women who *consistently* identified as lesbian over the course of many years were less likely to report that their desires were based on "the person and not the gender," and less likely to report sizable changes in their attractions, than lesbians who

eventually switched to bisexual or unlabeled identities (Diamond, 2005b).

Might this suggest that there is something fundamentally different—and perhaps, more essentially "oriented"—about the most exclusive and stable lesbians (i.e., those who experience practically all of their attractions for women, and who have experienced little change in this pattern), compared to women with more nonexclusive patterns of same-sex attraction? In one attempt to answer this question, Kim Wallen and I examined whether women with different histories of lesbian and bisexual identification showed different patterns of change in their motivation to act on same-sex desires as a function of ovulation (Diamond & Wallen, 2010). It has been well documented that women's sexual motivation shows different degrees of biological and environmental influence across the menstrual cycle. Specifically, researchers (going back to Beach, 1976) have distinguished between female *proceptivity* (i.e., motivation to initiate sexual activity) and female *arousability* (i.e., capacity to become aroused to sexual stimuli). As reviewed by Wallen (1995), proceptivity peaks around the time of ovulation, when women are most likely to conceive, and is manifested in increased sexual initiation, sexual activity, and orgasms; these changes are directly tied to the increased estrogen levels that accompany ovulation.

Evolutionarily speaking, an ovulatory increase in proceptivity makes sense, as it ensures that women are motivated to seek out sexual activity when they are most likely to conceive. In contrast, arousability is independent of hormonal status, and depends instead on situational factors such as exposure to sexual stimuli or direct sexual solicitation (reviewed by Wallen, 1995). We reasoned that because proceptivity specifically motivates reproductive behavior, it should be highly sensitive to "gender of target." Hence, to the degree that sexual orientation represents an early-developing, biologically based "compass" targeting sexual motivation toward partners of a particular gender, this compass should specifically target proceptivity. In contrast, arousability ought to be a more variable system, with the consequence that women may experience a range of sexual desires and behaviors with a variety of partners. Perhaps, then, women with "fluid" patterns of same-sex sexuality (such as "mostly straight" women) are those whose same-sex desires are primarily due to arousability, whereas women with stable, near-exclusive same-sex desires (i.e., long-standing lesbians) are those whose same-sex desires stem from a same-sex oriented proceptivity. On a day-to-day basis, these two types of women might be indistinguishable from one another. But during ovulation, when proceptivity increases as a function of changing estrogen levels, women with a robust same-sex "compass" should experience significantly *greater* motivation for same-sex contact. This should not be the case for women who lack such a compass, and whose same-sex desires are primarily attributable to arousability.

This was exactly what we found. We measured women's same-sex and other-sex sexual motivation and their estrogen levels over a 10-day period, and we found that during women's peak estrogen levels (around which time of ovulation is most likely to occur) women who had consistently identified as lesbian since 1995 reported a significant increase in their motivation to act on same-sex desires. This increase was significantly larger than that observed among women who had consistently identified as bisexual since 1995, and among women who had given up their lesbian or bisexual identities in favor of unlabeled or heterosexual identities since 1995. This pattern of findings is consistent with the notion that there are distinct (and potentially biologically based) subtypes of sexual-minority women whose same-sex desires might be influenced by different processes. At the same time, it bears noting that this was a preliminary study with numerous limitations. The sample is small and relatively self-selected, comprising a group of women who have been long-term participants in a longitudinal study of sexual identity development and who were willing to endure the intrusive, time-intensive nature of the study procedures. Another limitation is our inability to identify the specific mechanism through which a gender-specific form of sexual motivation would increase as a function of rising estrogen levels. Although the linkage between estrogen levels and sexual motivation has long been established (reviewed in Wallen, 2001), the specific biopsychological processes through which a *gender-targeted* form of sexual desire might be linked to changes in estrogen levels is as yet unknown. These questions call for more substantive attention in future studies conducted with larger and more diverse sample of sexual-minority *and* heterosexual women. Nonetheless, these findings suggest that closer investigation of

cyclic variation in women's same-sex and other-sex desires may provide a new way to consider whether different subtypes of lesbian, bisexual, and "mostly heterosexual" women have different "types" of same-sex desire, with different underlying determinants. Investigating this possibility may prove important in developing more accurate models of female sexual orientation.

CONCLUSIONS

Much work remains to be done in understanding the nature and dynamics of female sexual orientation. Scientists now have at our disposal an increasingly reliable body of data charting the diverse manifestations and developmental trajectories of same-sex sexuality, in our own culture as well as others (Bailey et al., 2000; Dickson et al., 2003; Garofalo et al., 1999; Kirk et al., 2000; Laumann et al., 1994; Mosher et al., 2005; Remafedi et al., 1992; Savin-Williams & Ream, 2006; Wichstrom & Hegna, 2003). Of all of the preconceptions about sexual orientation that we have come to question and revise over the years, one of the most important is the presumption that female and male sexual orientation are parallel phenomena, with the same origins and outcomes. To the contrary, women's greater propensity for nonexclusive, fluid patterns of attraction suggests the possibility that the underlying determinants of female same-sex sexuality may be quite different from those for men, requiring different explanatory models. This is not to suggest that men's sexuality is fundamentally rigid—as noted earlier, there is considerable evidence that some men exhibit change and fluidity in their sexual desires and behaviors as well (Dickson et al., 2003; Kinnish et al., 2005; Rosario et al., 2006; Savin-Williams & Ream, 2007; Stokes et al., 1993, 1997; Weinberg et al., 1994). However, among women these phenomena appear to be more common, perhaps even *normative*. Our task now is to determine why this is the case and to chart the implications of this gender difference for models of female and male sexual orientation as well as *human* sexuality more generally.

REFERENCES

Adler, K. A. (1967). Life style, gender role, and the symptom of homosexuality. *Journal of Individual Psychology, 23,* 67–78.

Bailey, J. M. (2009). What is sexual orientation and do women have one? In D. A. Hope (Ed.), *Nebraska Symposium on Motivation: Contemporary perspectives* on lesbian, gay, and bisexual identities (Vol. 54, pp. 43–63). Lincoln: University of Nebraska Press.

Bailey, J. M., Dunne, M. P., & Martin, N. G. (2000). Genetic and environmental influences on sexual orientation and its correlates in an Australian twin sample. Journal of Personality and Social Psychology, 78, 524–536.

Baumeister, R. F. (2000). Gender differences in erotic plasticity: The female sex drive as socially flexible and responsive. Psychological Bulletin, 126, 247–374.

Baumeister, R. F., & Twenge, J. M. (2002). Cultural suppression of female sexuality. Review of General Psychology, 6, 166–203.

Beach, F. A. (1976). Sexual attractivity, proceptivity, and receptivity in female mammals. Hormones and Behavior, 7, 105–138.

Bell, A. P., Weinberg, M. S., & Hammersmith, S. K. (1981). Sexual preference: Its development in men and women. Bloomington: Indiana University Press.

Berenson, C. (2002). What's in a name? Bisexual women define their terms. Journal of Bisexuality, 2, 9–21.

Bergler, E. (1954). Spurious homosexuality. Psychiatric Quarterly Supplement, 28, 68–77.

Blackwood, E. (2000). Culture and women's sexualities. Journal of Social Issues, 56, 223–238.

Blumstein, P., & Schwartz, P. (1990). Intimate relationships and the creation of sexuality. In D. P. McWhirter, S. A. Sanders, & J. M. Reinisch (Eds.), Homosexuality/heterosexuality: Concepts of sexual orientation (pp. 307–320). New York: Oxford University Press.

Bos, H. M. W., Sandfort, T. G. M., de Bruyn, E. H., & Hakvoort, E. M. (2008). Same-sex attraction, social relationships, psychosocial functioning, and school performance in early adolescence. Developmental Psychology, 44, 59–68.

Bower, J., Gurevich, M., & Mathieson, C. (2002). (Con)tested identities: Bisexual women reorient sexuality. In D. Atkins (Ed.), Bisexual women in the 21st century. New York: Haworth.

Burr, C. (1996). A separate creation: The search for the biological origins of sexual orientation. New York: Hyperion.

Cass, V. (1990). The implications of homosexual identity formation for the Kinsey model and scale of sexual preference. In D. P. McWhirter, S. A. Sanders, & J. M. Reinisch (Eds.), Homosexuality/heterosexuality: Concepts of sexual orientation (pp. 239–266). New York: Oxford University Press.

Cassingham, B. J., & O'Neil, S. M. (1993). And then I met this woman. Freeland, WA: Soaring Eagle Publishing.

Chivers, M. L., & Bailey, J. M. (2005). A sex difference in features that elicit genital response. Biological Psychology, 70, 115–120.

Chivers, M. L., & Bailey, J. M. (2007). The sexual psychophysiology of sexual orientation. In E. Janssen (Ed.), The psychophysiology of sex. (pp. 458–474). Bloomington: Indiana University Press.

Chivers, M. L., Rieger, G., Latty, E., & Bailey, J. M. (2004). A sex difference in the specificity of sexual arousal. Psychological Science, 15, 736–744.

Chivers, M. L., Seto, M. C., & Blanchard, R. (2007). Gender and sexual orientation differences in sexual response to sexual activities versus gender of actors in sexual films. Journal of Personality and Social Psychology, 93, 1108–1121.

Chivers, M. L., Seto, M. C., Lalumiere, M. L., Laan, E., & Grimbos, T. (2010). Agreement of self-reported and genital measures of sexual arousal in men and women: A meta-analysis. Archives of Sexual Behavior, 39, 5–56.

Costa, M., Braun, C., & Birbaumer, N. (2003). Gender differences in response to pictures of nudes: A magnetoencephalographic study. Biological Psychology, 63, 129–147.

Costell, R. M. (1972). Contingent negative variation as an indicator of sexual object preference. Science, 177, 718–720.

Davis, A. (1999). Confessions of a LUG. Flagpole Magazine Online, October 25, 1999.

de Cecco, J. P. (1981). Definition and meaning of sexual orientation. Journal of Homosexuality, 6, 51–67.

Defries, Z. (1976). Pseuodohomosexuality in feminist students. American Journal of Psychiatry, 133, 400–404.

Diamond, L. M. (2000). Passionate friendships among adolescent sexual-minority women. Journal of Research on Adolescence, 10, 191–209.

Diamond, L. M. (2002). "Having a girlfriend without knowing it:" The relationships of adolescent lesbian and bisexual women. Journal of Lesbian Studies, 6, 5–16.

Diamond, L. M. (2003a). Was it a phase? Young women's relinquishment of lesbian/bisexual identities over a 5-year period. Journal of Personality and Social Psychology, 84, 352–364.

Diamond, L. M. (2003b). What does sexual orientation orient? A biobehavioral model distinguishing romantic love and sexual desire. Psychological Review, 110, 173–192.

Diamond, L. M. (2005a). "I'm straight, but I kissed a girl": The trouble with American media representations of female-female sexuality. Feminism and Psychology, 15, 104–110.

Diamond, L. M. (2005b). A new view of lesbian subtypes: Stable vs. fluid identity trajectories over an 8-year period. Psychology of Women Quarterly, 29, 119–128.

Diamond, L. M. (2006). The evolution of plasticity in female-female desire. Journal of Psychology and Human Sexuality, 18, 245–274.

Diamond, L. M. (2007). A dynamical systems approach to female same-sex sexuality. Perspectives on Psychological Science, 2, 142–161.

Diamond, L. M. (2008). *Sexual fluidity: Understanding women's love and desire*. Cambridge, MA: Harvard University Press.

Diamond, L. M., & Fagundes, C. P. (2012). Emotion regulation in close relationships: Implications for social threat and its effects on immunological functioning. In L. Cambell & T. J. Loving (Eds.), *Close relationships: An interdisciplinary perspective* (pp. 83–106). New York: Springer.

Diamond, L. M., & Savin-Williams, R. C. (2009). Adolescent sexuality. In R. M. Lerner & L. Steinberg (Eds.), *Handbook of Adolescent Psychology, 3rd edition* (pp. 479–523). New York: Wiley.

Diamond, L. M., & Wallen, K. (2010). Sexual-minority women's sexual motivation around the time of ovulation. *Archives of Sexual Behavior, 38*, 417–426.

Dickson, N., Paul, C., & Herbison, P. (2003). Same-sex attraction in a birth cohort: prevalence and persistence in early adulthood. *Social Science & Medicine, 56*, 1607–1615.

Essig, L. (2000, November 15). Heteroflexibility. *Salon.com*.

Esterberg, K. G. (1994). Being a lesbian and being in love: Constructing identities through relationships. *Journal of Gay and Lesbian Social Services, 1*, 57–82.

Fergusson, D. M., Horwood, L. J., Ridder, E. M., & Beautrais, A. L. (2005). Sexual orientation and mental health in a birth cohort of young adults. *Psychological Medicine, 35*, 971–981.

Fine, M. (1988). Sexuality, schooling, and adolescent females: The missing discourse of desire. *Harvard Educational Review, 58*, 29–53.

Freud, S. [(1905) 1962]. *Three essays on the theory of sexuality* (J. Strachey, Trans.). New York: Basic Books.

Futuyma, D. J., & Risch, S. J. (1983). Sexual orientation, sociobiology, and evolution. *Journal of Homosexuality, 9*, 157–168.

Gagnon, J. H. (1990). Gender preference in erotic relations: The Kinsey scale and sexual scripts. In D. P. McWhirter, S. A. Sanders, & J. M. Reinisch (Eds.), *Homosexuality/heterosexuality: Concepts of sexual orientation* (pp. 177–207). New York: Oxford University Press.

Garofalo, R., Wolf, R. C., Wissow, L. S., Woods, E. R., & Goodman, E. (1999). Sexual orientation and risk of suicide attempts among a representative sample of youth. *Archives of Pediatrics and Adolescent Medicine, 153*, 487–493.

Golden, C. (1987). Diversity and variability in women's sexual identities. In Boston Lesbian Psychologies Collective (Ed.), *Lesbian psychologies: Explorations and challenges* (pp. 19–34). Urbana: University of Illinois Press.

Golden, C. (1994). Our politics and choices: The feminist movement and sexual orientation. In B. Greene & G. M. Herek (Eds.), *Lesbian and gay psychology:*

Theory, research, and clinical applications (pp. 54–70). Thousand Oaks, CA: Sage.

Golden, C. (1996). What's in a name? Sexual self-identification among women. In R. C. Savin-Williams & K. M. Cohen (Eds.), *The lives of lesbians, gays, and bisexuals: Children to adults* (pp. 229–249). Fort Worth, TX: Harcourt Brace.

Goode, E., & Haber, L. (1977). Sexual correlates of homosexual experience: An exploratory study of college women. *Journal of Sex Research, 13*, 12–21.

Goy, R. W., & Goldfoot, D. A. (1975). Neuroendocrinology: Animal models and problems of human sexuality. *Archives of Sexual Behavior, 4*, 405–420.

Gramick, J. (1984). Developing a lesbian identity. In T. Darty & S. Potter (Eds.), *Women-identified women* (pp. 31–44). Palo Alto, CA: Mayfield.

Hamann, S., Herman, R. A., Nolan, C. L., & Wallen, K. (2004). Men and women differ in amygdala response to visual sexual stimuli. *Nature Neuroscience, 7*, 411–416.

Harry, J. (1984). Sexual orientation as destiny. *Journal of Homosexuality, 10*, 111–124.

Herdt, G. (1984). *Ritualized homosexuality in Melanesia*. Berkeley: University of California Press.

Hollander, G. (2000). Questioning youths: Challenges to working with youths forming identities. *School Psychology Review, 29*, 173–179.

Horner, E. (2007). Queer identities and bisexual identities: What's the difference? In B. A. Firestein (Ed.), *Becoming visible: Counseling bisexuals across the lifespan.* (pp. 287–296). New York: Columbia University Press.

Hyde, J. S. (2005). The genetics of sexual orientation. In J. S. Hyde (Ed.), *Biological substrates of human sexuality* (pp. 9–20). Washington, DC: APA Press.

Hyde, J. S., & Durik, A. M. (2000). Gender differences in erotic plasticity—Evolutionary or sociocultural forces? Comment on Baumeister (2000). *Psychological Bulletin, 126*, 375–379.

Igartua, K., Thombs, B. D., Burgos, G., & Montoro, R. (2009). Concordance and discrepancy in sexual identity, attraction, and behavior among adolescents. *Journal of Adolescent Health, 45*, 602–608.

Kinnish, K. K., Strassberg, D. S., & Turner, C. W. (2005). Sex differences in the flexibility of sexual orientation: A multidimensional retrospective assessment. *Archives of Sexual Behavior, 34*, 173–183.

Kinsey, A. C., Pomeroy, W. B., Martin, C. E., & Gebhard, P. H. (1953). *Sexual behavior in the human female*. Philadelphia: W.B. Saunders.

Kirk, K. M., Bailey, J. M., Dunne, M. P., & Martin, N. G. (2000). Measurement models for sexual orientation in a community twin sample. *Behavior Genetics, 30*, 345–356.

Kirkpatrick, R. C. (2000). The evolution of human homosexual behavior. *Current Anthropology, 41*, 385–413.

Kitzinger, C., & Wilkinson, S. (1995). Transitions from heterosexuality to lesbianism: The discursive production of lesbian identities. *Developmental Psychology, 31*, 95–104.

Kyrakanos, J. (1998). LUGgin' It. *InsideOUT Magazine, 9.*

Laan, E., & Janssen, E. (2007). How do men and women feel? Determinants of subjective experience of sexual arousal. In E. Janssen (Ed.), *The psychophysiology of sex.* (pp. 278–290). Bloomington: Indiana University Press.

Laumann, E. O., Gagnon, J. H., Michael, R. T., & Michaels, F. (1994). *The social organization of sexuality: Sexual practices in the United States.* Chicago: University of Chicago Press.

Laumann, E. O., & Mahay, J. (2002). The social organization of women's sexuality. In G. M. Wingood & R. J. DiClemente (Eds.), *Handbook of women's sexual and reproductive health* (pp. 43–70). New York: Academic/Plenum.

Liben, L. S., & Bigler, R. S. (2008). Developmental gender differentiation: Pathways in conforming and nonconforming outcomes. *Journal of Gay & Lesbian Mental Health, 12*, 95–112.

McClintock, M. K., & Herdt, G. (1996). Rethinking puberty: The development of sexual attraction. *Current Directions in Psychological Science, 5*, 178–183.

Money, J. (1990). Agenda and credenda of the Kinsey scale. In D. P. McWhirter, S. A. Sanders, & J. M. Reinisch (Eds.), *Homosexuality/heterosexuality: Concepts of sexual orientation* (pp. 41–60). New York: Oxford University Press.

Morgan, E. M., & Thompson, E. M. (2007). Young women's sexual experiences within same-sex friendships: Discovering and defining bisexual and bi-curious identity. *Journal of Bisexuality, 6*, 7–34.

Mosher, W. D., Chandra, A., & Jones, J. (2005). *Sexual behavior and selected health measures: Men and women 15–44 years of age, United States, 2002.* Advance data from vital and health statistics, no. 362. Hyattsville, MD: National Center for Health Statistics.

Murray, S. O. (2000). *Homosexualities.* Chicago: University of Chicago Press.

Muscarella, F. (1999). The homoerotic behavior that never evolved. *Journal of Homosexuality, 37*, 1–18.

Mustanski, B. S., Chivers, M. L., & Bailey, J. M. (2002). A critical review of recent biological research on human sexual orientation. *Annual Review of Sex Research, 13*, 89–140.

Nichols, M. (1987). Lesbian sexuality: Issues and developing theory. In Boston Lesbian Psychologies Collective (Ed.), *Lesbian Psychologies* (pp. 97–125). Urbana: University of Illinois Press.

Pattatucci, A. M. L., & Hamer, D. H. (1995). Development and familiality of sexual orientation in females. *Behavior Genetics, 25*, 407–420.

Peplau, L. A. (2001). Rethinking women's sexual orientation: An interdisciplinary, relationship-focused approach. *Personal Relationships, 8*, 1–19.

Peplau, L. A., & Garnets, L. D. (2000). A new paradigm for understanding women's sexuality and sexual orientation. *Journal of Social Issues, 56*, 329–350.

Phillips, G., & Over, R. (1992). Adult sexual orientation in relation to memories of childhood gender conforming and gender nonconforming behaviors. *Archives of Sexual Behavior, 21*, 543–558.

Rahman, Q. (2005). Fluctuating asymmetry, second to fourth finger length ratios and human sexual orientation. *Psychoneuroendocrinology, 30*, 382–391.

Remafedi, G., Resnick, M., Blum, R., & Harris, L. (1992). Demography of sexual orientation in adolescents. *Pediatrics, 89*, 714–721.

Rich, A. (1980). Compulsory heterosexuality and lesbian existence. *Signs, 5*, 631–660.

Rieger, G., Bailey, J. M., & Chivers, M. L. (2005). Sexual arousal patterns of bisexual men. *Psychological Science, 16*, 579–584.

Rimer, S. (1993, June 5). Campus lesbians step into unfamiliar light. *New York Times*, p. A2.

Rosario, M., Schrimshaw, E. W., Hunter, J., & Braun, L. (2006). Sexual identity development among lesbian, gay, and bisexual youths: Consistency and change over time. *Journal of Sex Research, 43*, 46–58.

Ross, M. W., & Paul, J. P. (1992). Beyond gender: The basis of sexual attraction in bisexual men and women. *Psychological Reports, 71*, 1283–1290.

Rust, P. C. R. (1992). The politics of sexual identity: Sexual attraction and behavior among lesbian and bisexual women. *Social Problems, 39*, 366–386.

Rust, P. C. R. (2000). Criticisms of the scholarly literature on sexuality for its neglect of bisexuality. In P. C. R. Rust (Ed.), *Bisexuality in the United States: A reader and guide to the literature* (pp. 5–10). New York: Columbia University Press.

Savage, D. (2002, May 11). Heteroflexible. *The Stranger.com, 11.*

Savin-Williams, R. C. (1996). Memories of childhood and early adolescent sexual feelings among gay and bisexual boys: A narrative approach. In R. C. Savin-Williams & K. M. Cohen (Eds.), *The lives of lesbians, gays, and bisexuals: Children to adults* (pp. 94–109). Fort Worth, TX: Harcourt Brace.

Savin-Williams, R. C. (1998). *"… And then I became gay": Young men's stories.* New York: Routledge.

Savin-Williams, R. C. (2005). *The new gay teenager.* Cambridge, MA: Harvard University Press.

Savin-Williams, R. C. (2006). Who's gay? Does it matter? *Current Directions in Psychological Science, 15*, 40–44.

Savin-Williams, R. C. (2009). How many gays are there? It depends. *Nebraska Symposium On Motivation. Nebraska Symposium On Motivation, 54*, 5–41.

Savin-Williams, R. C., & Ream, G. L. (2006). Pubertal onset and sexual orientation in an adolescent national probability sample. *Archives of Sexual Behavior, 35*, 279–286.

Savin-Williams, R. C., & Ream, G. L. (2007). Prevalence and stability of sexual orientation components during adolescence and young adulthood. *Archives of Sexual Behavior, 36*, 385–394.

Sell, R. L., & Petrulio, C. (1996). Sampling homosexuals, bisexuals, gays, and lesbians for public health research: A review of the literature from 1990 to 1992. *Journal of Homosexuality, 30*, 31–47.

Shuster, R. (1987). Sexuality as a continuum: The bisexual identity. In Boston Lesbian Psychologies Collective (Ed.), *Lesbian Psychologies* (pp. 56–71). Urbana: University of Illinois Press.

Stokes, J. P., Damon, W., & McKirnan, D. J. (1997). Predictors of movement toward homosexuality: A longitudinal study of bisexual men. *Journal of Sex Research, 34*, 304–312.

Stokes, J. P., McKirnan, D., & Burzette, R. (1993). Sexual behavior, condom use, disclosure of sexuality, and stability of sexual orientation in bisexual men. *Journal of Sex Research, 30*, 203–213.

Storms, M. D. (1980). Theories of sexual orientation. *Journal of Personality and Social Psychology, 38*, 783–792.

Suschinsky, K. D., Lalumiere, M. L., & Chivers, M. L. (2009). Sex differences in patterns of genital sexual arousal: Measurement artifacts or true phenomena? *Archives of Sexual Behavior, 38*, 559–573.

Thompson, E. M. (2007). Girl friend or girlfriend?: Same-sex friendship and bisexual images as a context for flexible sexual identity among young women. *Journal of Bisexuality, 6*, 47–67.

Thompson, E. M., & Morgan, E. M. (2008). "Mostly straight" young women: Variations in sexual behavior and identity development. *Developmental Psychology, 44*, 15–21.

Tolman, D. L. (2002). *Dilemma of desire: Teenage girls and sexuality.* Cambridge, MA: Harvard University Press.

Tolman, D. L., & Diamond, L. M. (2001). Desegregating sexuality research: Combining cultural and biological perspectives on gender and desire. *Annual Review of Sex Research, 12*, 33–74.

Udry, J. R., & Chantala, K. (2006). Masculinity-femininity predicts sexual orientation in men but not in women. *Journal of Biosocial Science, 38*, 797–809.

Ussher, J. M. (1993). The construction of female sexual problems: Regulating sex, regulating woman. In J. M. Ussher & C. D. Baker (Eds.), *Psychological perspectives on sexual problems: New directions in theory and practice* (pp. 9–40). New York: Routledge.

Wallen, K. (1995). The evolution of female sexual desire. In P. R. Abramson & S. D. Pinkerton (Eds.), *Sexual nature/sexual culture* (pp. 57–79). Chicago: University of Chicago Press.

Wallen, K. (2001). Sex and context: Hormones and primate sexual motivation. *Hormones and Behavior, 40*, 339–357.

Walsh, C. (Ed.). (2010). *Dear John, I love Jane: Women write about leaving men for women.* Berkeley, CA: Seal Press.

Weinberg, M. S., Williams, C. J., & Pryor, D. W. (1994). *Dual attraction: Understanding bisexuality.* New York: Oxford University Press.

Welles, C. E. (2005). Breaking the silence surrounding female adolescent sexual desire. *Women & Therapy, 28*, 31–45.

Whisman, V. (1993). Identity crisis: Who is a lesbian anyway? In A. Stein (Ed.), *Sisters, sexperts, queers: Beyond the lesbian nation* (pp. 47–60). New York: Penguin.

Whisman, V. (1996). *Queer by choice: Lesbians, gay men, and the politics of identity.* New York: Routledge.

Wichstrom, L., & Hegna, K. (2003). Sexual orientation and suicide attempt: A longitudinal study of the general Norwegian adolescent population. *Journal of Abnormal Psychology, 112*, 144–151.

Worthington, R. L., & Reynolds, A. L. (2009). Within-group differences in sexual orientation and identity. *Journal of Counseling Psychology, 56*, 44–55.

Wright, L. W., Jr., & Adams, H. E. (1999). The effects of stimuli that vary in erotic content on cognitive processes. *Journal of Sex Research, 36*, 145–151.

Zhao, Y., Montoro, R., Igartua, K., & Thombs, B. D. (2010). Suicidal ideation and attempt among adolescents reporting "unsure" sexual identity or heterosexual identity plus same-sex attraction or behavior: Forgotten groups? *Journal of the American Academy of Child & Adolescent Psychiatry, 49*, 104–113.

2

Gay Male Identities, Desires, and Sexual Behaviors

JEFFREY T. PARSONS AND CHRISTIAN GROV

In this chapter we review seminal research and theory regarding gay men's identities, their desires, and their sexual behavior. First we discuss the emergence of the gay identity and describe how meanings of the "gay community" have changed in response to fluid social/political climates, HIV, and technology. Next we discuss the role of desire in gay men's sexual partnerships and behaviors, focusing on masculinity, penis size, and semen/ejaculation. Third, we elaborate on the array of sexual behaviors in which gay men engage and describe the various types of relationships that are common within gay partnerships. Finally, we conclude by positing future directions for research with gay men, focusing on the measurement of sexual orientation and the role that social policy can play in improving the lives of gay men.

WHEN A COMMON, MARGINALIZED, EXPERIENCE BECOMES A THRIVING COMMUNITY

A "community" is defined as a unified body of individuals with a common history, or common social, economic, or political interests. Ironically, the gay "community," also often called the lesbian, gay, bisexual, transgendered community (or "communities"), is an amalgamation of ages, races and ethnicities, economic backgrounds, religious beliefs, and political views. Yet, one of the unifying factors connecting lesbian, gay, bisexual, and transgender communities is adoption of an identity as a member of these communities (Nardi & Schneider, 1998). "Identification" as a gay person need not be via a public announcement. We may admit to ourself that we are gay, but not disclose this to others, and still be considered gay. This would be in contrast to individuals who have sex with people of the same sex, but self-identify as heterosexual. For the purposes of this chapter, we do not consider heterosexually identified men who have sex with men (MSM) to be "gay" (Jeffries, 2009; Siegel, Schrimshaw, Lekas, & Parsons, 2008).

Identification as someone who is gay requires that both individuals and larger social groups have an understanding of what this classification means. In essence, social meaning must be attached to the term "gay," and this definition must be shared by members adopting the identity for themselves, in addition to others (i.e., those who are not gay, but understand what "gay" means). Greenberg (1990) identified this process as the *construction* of homosexuality. Given that, societies' definitions of "gay" have shifted throughout history—as has the tolerance/acceptance of same-sex sexual behavior. In all, the idea of a gay *community* is a relatively new concept, originating after the Industrial Revolution (D'Emilio, 1983).

Homosexuality Then and Now

Although the idea of a gay "community" and identity as a gay person is relatively new, homosexual behavior and sexual attraction between members of the same sex have both been documented throughout history, and across many cultures (cf. Duberman, Vicinus, & Chauncey, 1990; Greenberg, 1990). For example, Hubbard's (2003) sourcebook contains a collection of literary works from ancient Greece and Rome and documents homosexual relationships in ancient plays, oratory, philosophy, and art. Plutarch (1973), a Greek historian (born 46 CE), wrote of the Sacred Band of Thebes, an army consisting of same-sex couples. Hercules was rumored to have had many male lovers. In addition, same-sex sexual behavior and attraction have been documented cross-culturally, including among Siberian shamans (Harvey, 2003), Native American two-spirit medicine men (Jacobs, Thomas, & Lang, 1997), African tribesmen (Murray & Roscoe, 1998), and Chinese emperors (Hinsch, 1992).

Williams (1999) noted that between 200 BCE and 200 CE, Roman males could engage in certain sexual acts, particularly insertive or "active" acts with persons of any gender without having their masculinity called into question. Often, the act was not considered perverse if it was with someone who was younger, if the act was with a member of a lower class (e.g., slaves, prostitutes), or if the act was insertive (as noted). During this time, sexuality was not categorized into homosexual and heterosexual, but rather contextualized by its appropriateness based on one's own desires and sexual positioning. For example, being receptive or wishing to give pleasure with your mouth was considered demasculinizing whether the behavior was with a man or a woman (Williams, 1999).

Throughout history, homosexual behavior has been regarded in many ways, ranging from abhorrent to revered (Wolf, 2004). The idea of a gay community and identifying oneself as "gay" is a concept that emerged, as D'Emilio (1983) proposed, as a result of the Industrial Revolution and the spread of capitalism throughout Europe and the United States. The Industrial Revolution brought major changes in agriculture, manufacturing, mining, and transportation. The growth of industrial and financial centers was the root of urbanization, concentrating people in huge numbers. Many young adults moved away from their families. Those living in urban centers encountered a new-found sense of anonymity that had not previously existed. Living apart from one's family proved to be an ideal circumstance in which to explore new sexual practices. And, in spite of a new-found sense of anonymity, the sheer concentration of people within urban centers allowed those with marginalized interests to meet, congregate, discuss, and mobilize. These were the roots of the modern gay community, and the subsequent invention of a gay "identity."

Political Movements Shaping Gay Identity and Gay Community

With the growth in the visibility of, what some perceived to be, "perverse" sexual behavior between members of the same sex came the sanctioning, legislating, medicalization, and criminalization of homosexuality. These included the passage and enforcement of sodomy laws and, as medicine grew in the nineteenth and twentieth centuries, the classification of homosexuality as a diagnosable mental disorder. In tandem, social views concerning homosexuality continued to shift. As gay, lesbian, bisexual, and transgender communities continued to grow in urban pockets across the globe, so did these communities' strength, political power, and ability to mobilize in response to antigay violence and legislation. It is well documented that the Mattachine Society and the Daughters of Bilitis of the 1950s and the Stonewall Riots of 1969—which kicked off what is often regarded as the modern gay rights movement in the 1970s—represent a solidifying series of events that established visible and politically organized gay communities on a global landscape. In 1973, the American Psychiatric Association removed homosexuality from the *Diagnostic and Statistical Manual of Mental Disorders* (*DSM*) as a classified mental disorder. It could be argued that in the United States, the 1970s represented the first decade in which the assertion of a positive gay identity was possible. There was, of course, a dramatic shift with the discovery of HIV in the early 1980s.

Before the virus that causes AIDS was discovered, the illnesses many gay men were suffering from were believed by some to be retribution for immoral behavior (Shilts, 1987). Lack of research, medicine, and political action to provide treatment and services for people with HIV paved the way for political and social movements. Once again, urban lesbian, gay, bisexual, and transgender communities (re)organized; however, this time it was in response to a devastating illness. For many, being "gay" meant being impacted in some way by the HIV/AIDS epidemic. Now that we are more than three decades into the epidemic, younger generations of gay men are removed from the panic, fear, and mobilization that occurred in the 1980s and 1990s. The discovery of antiretroviral medications in the mid-1990s has transformed HIV seropositivity from a terminal diagnosis into a chronic/managed illness. Some have proposed that gay communities are experiencing fatigue around HIV prevention/awareness. Meanwhile, young gay men today are coming of age in a time when HIV is considered a "chronic" disease. Despite the tens of thousands of gay men who died from AIDS in the 1980s and early 1990s, HIV was no longer a *defining* feature of gay identity at the beginning of the twenty-first century. These changes have occurred in tandem with cultural shifts in views of homosexuality.

Specifically, the political and social landscape of homosexuality shifted again the late 1990s and 2000s. Television shows such as *Will and Grace*, MTV's *The Real World*, and *Queer Eye for the Straight Guy* featured prominent gay characters. Same-sex marriage emerged onto the political landscapes of many European countries, and many states in the United States took up the issue. In 1993, the Hawaii State Supreme Court ruled that same-sex couples should have the right to marry, but, in 1998, Hawaii voters approved a constitutional amendment banning same-sex marriage. In 2003, Massachusetts legalized same-sex marriage and the U.S. Supreme Court decision *Lawrence v. Texas* overturned all of the remaining state sodomy laws. In 2010, the U.S. Congress voted to overturn the nearly two-decade old policy preventing gays and lesbians from being out in the military. In 2011, President Obama concluded that the Defense of Marriage Act (DOMA), a 1996 federal law that defined marriage as only between a man and woman, could not be defended. Although the political landscape for lesbian, gay, and bisexual issues remains polarizing, these events are examples of how gay people moved toward being accepted members of society. Some could argue this has resulted in the "mainstreaming" of homosexuality.

Beyond "Gay" Identity

With the increased public acceptance of homosexuality have come remarkable transitions in gay identity (i.e., what it means to be gay). We could argue that the various historical, political, and social events of the past 50 years have created "cohort effects" for those gay men coming of age. For example, some research suggests that individuals are coming out—accepting their identity as gay and publically disclosing it to family, friends, peers, school officials—at earlier ages than in past decades (Grov, Bimbi, Parsons, & Nanín, 2006), but with mixed results. Savin-Williams (2006) found that many lesbian, gay, and bisexual teens are open about their sexual identities and are psychosocially well adjusted. Meanwhile, others have noted that the *context* in which someone comes out (and the subsequent social/emotional support that is received) is directly related to that person's psychosocial well being and physical health (Centers for Disease Control and Prevention, 2005, 2009a; Friedman, Marshal, Stall, Cheong, & Wright, 2008).

Savin-Williams identified a unique phenomenon among younger gay adults, in which many are reluctant to categorize their sexuality at all. With the "mainstreaming" of homosexuality throughout the United States, have we begun to see a backlash against "defining" oneself as gay? Researchers have noted that many youth eschew the label gay in favor of descriptions such as "queer," "same gender loving," "in the life," "one of the children," and "in the family" (Battle, Cohen, Warren, Fergerson, & Audam, 2002). In addition, these terms are used more often among persons of color in response to the belief that the term gay evokes the perception of a white-dominated gay community. Utilization of different terminology clearly presents challenges to defining what exactly "gay" means and who this label actually describes.

The Internet has also played a powerful role in gay identity development. Studies suggest that the Internet has become the most common medium through which gay men meet partners, both for casual sex and for long-term relationships (Grov, Parsons, & Bimbi, 2007; Liau, Millett, & Marks, 2006). Trend data (1993–2002) found younger MSM were more likely than older men to meet their first male partners online and less likely to meet them in public places (Bolding, Davis, Hart, Sherr, & Elford, 2007). Rosser et al. (2008) noted how MSM's transition to sex-seeking on the Internet may be correlated with the decline of gay infrastructure, visibility, and community identification across gay communities. This is not to suggest that the Internet has caused this decline, but research indicates there has been a clear shift in how gay men communicate with each other when navigating their sexuality and sexual discourse (Zablotska, Holt, & Prestage, 2012).

Two decades ago, in order to socialize with and meet other men, gay men congregated in public spaces such as gay bars/clubs, bathhouses, and community groups (such as lesbian, gay, bisexual, and transgender community centers). Today, gay men engage in chatting (instant messaging) on gay-themed websites such as manhunt.net, gay.com, and adam4adam.com and more traditional social networking websites such as facebook.com. Meanwhile, mobile technology has placed the Internet in men's pockets with mobile email, text messaging (including sending photos and video over text), and social network applications installed on telephones. For example, in 2010 Grindr emerged as a popular application on a vast array of mobile platforms (iPhone/iPod Touch/iPad/Blackberry/

Android). Based on someone's GPS location, a man could locate other men (e.g., Grindr users) in their proximity—colloquially dubbed a modern "gay-dar" (a play on the word "radar"). Historically, younger adults have often been the first to adapt new technologies. The Internet and the mobile world are likely to play seminal roles in young gay men's identity and the identity development process. Perhaps instead of young gay men congregating at Gay–Straight Alliances and other community groups, it may be that they are more likely today to navigate their sexuality in a virtual environment. The full impact of these emerging technologies has yet to be realized and thus remains an important area for consideration when trying to understand sexual identity today and in the future.

Desire: The Quest for Masculinity?

For gay men, traditional masculinity (as opposed to femininity) is often a desired trait. In general, gay men not only prefer men who describe themselves as masculine, but not one participant in a study of gay male personal ads looking for sexual partners listed masculinity as an *undesired* trait in a partner (Bailey, Kim, Hills, & Linsenmeier, 1997). In contrast, when undesired partner traits were listed, they were always feminine traits. Masculinity was also the number one trait sought out in advertisements for preferred partners of gay men. Masculinity though is sometimes conflated with heterosexuality among gay men, and conversely femininity with homosexuality. For example, some gay men will indicate in personal ads that they are looking for "straight acting" partners, or will specify "no fems" to articulate clearly their desire for masculinity and their resistance to femininity (Clarkson, 2006). It has been suggested that such gay men want to achieve "hegemonic masculinity" or a culturally normative ideal of male behavior in order to overcome negative stereotypes about effeminate gay men (Eguchi, 2009).

Sometimes masculinity is expressed among gay men through the sexual role they take during anal sex (Carrier, 1977; Weinrich, Grant, Jacobson, Robinson, & McCutchan, 1992), with masculinity being associated with the insertive partner (the "top") and femininity being associated with the receptive partner (the "bottom"). Wegesin and Meyer-Bahlburg (2000) found consistency between sexual role self-label and actual sexual behavior—"tops" engaged in more frequent insertive anal acts and "bottoms" engaged in more frequent receptive

anal acts. However, it has also been suggested that self-labels of sexual behavior among gay men vary by culture (Magana & Carrier, 1991). A 2010 study in San Francisco found that Asian/Pacific Islander gay men were more likely to prefer being a bottom (rather than a top) and African-American men were more likely to prefer being a top (rather than a bottom) (Wei & Raymond, 2011). Interestingly, however, there were no racial differences in actual reported anal sex practices, suggesting that sexual role preference and sexual behavior are not always consistent. A study of Latino MSM in New York City found that the majority of men reported being sexually "versatile" (Carballo-Dieguez et al., 2004). However, men in this study also reported taking an active or passive sexual role based on the perception of masculinity in their partner. This suggests that even self-identified versatile gay men may modify their sexual practices depending on the perceived masculinity or femininity of a sexual partner. Further to that point, it is likely that individual identities as top, versatile, or bottom may be fluid over time.

So, from where does such a strong desire and preference for masculinity and the perceived sexual roles of those who are more masculine/feminine come? "Gay men are not free to invent new objects of desire…choice of object is structured by gender order" (Connell, 1992, p. 747). According to Dowsett et al. (2008), "Gay men are still male after all; male bodies have certain similarities; and all men have learned similar ways of thinking about bodies and pleasure" (p. 130). The ideals of hegemonic masculinity shape gay men as much as they shape heterosexual men. In other words, gay men are no more affected by hegemonic masculinity than straight men are; both groups are working toward the same ideal and structuring of the gender order (Sanchez, Greenberg, Ming Liu, & Vilian, 2009).

Although gay men's desire may be shaped and guided by the ideals of hegemonic masculinity they are by no means bound to those definitions. Social pressures compel gay men to value masculinity and devalue femininity. However, many gay men are sexually versatile (Hart et al., 2003; Wei & Raymond, 2011) and willing to sexually play both "masculine" and "feminine" roles—both sexually and behaviorally. Our community-based data found 37% self-identified as versatile, compared with 33% as tops and 25% as bottom (Grov, Parsons, & Bimbi, 2010a). Masculinity being valued is not inherently a problem, especially since it can be seen as a form of resistance against gay stereotypes, as long as femininity is not devalued.

A Man's Worth: Bigger Is Not Always Better

Though it is well known that men's genitalia come in many shapes and sizes, larger penis size has been equated with a symbol of power, fertility, stamina, masculinity, and social status (Bogaert & Hershberger, 1999; Bordo, 1999; Connell, 1987, 1995; Drummond & Filiault, 2007; Lehman, 1998; Paley, 2000; Pope, Phillips, & Olivardia, 2000; Stulhofer, 2006). It is no surprise that researchers have found that most men are unsatisfied with their penis size, wishing it were larger (Lever, Frederick, & Peplau, 2006). With few exceptions (e.g., Drummond & Filiault, 2007; Grov et al., 2010a; Harding & Golombok, 2002), much of this research is based on heterosexual populations.

We reported on community-based data from 1065 New York City MSM (Grov et al., 2010a). Our study noted that penis size was positively related to satisfaction with size and inversely related to lying about penis size to others. Men who rated themselves as having smaller than average penises rated themselves lower on multiple measures of psychosocial well being (including higher gay-related stigma and poorer satisfaction with their lives as gay individuals). Finally, the size of the penis was related to sexual positioning. Men with self-reported smaller than average penises were significantly more likely to identify as "bottoms" and men with above average penis sizes were significantly more likely to identify as tops. As we have noted, taking the insertive role is perceived to be a more masculine act; thus, those with bigger penises were more likely to assume the "masculine" role sexually. The direction of this relationship further supports notions of the cultural value of having a large penis and the presumed masculine penetrative role these men are socially—and sexually—scripted to enact (Drummond & Filiault, 2007). Our findings suggest the question, "To what extent are men with below average penises being socially-sexually-scripted into anal receptive roles?" Does their perception of having a smaller than average penis devalue these men's sexual potential, socially coercing them into sexual roles they may not have otherwise assumed? The same could be asked of men who think they have larger than average penises.

Barebacking and Semen Play/Exchange

Research suggests many gay men want an intimate connection with their sexual partners, as do heterosexual men. These can include skin-to-skin contact in the context of anal sex and, sometimes, the exchange of semen—both of which significantly increase the risk for HIV and sexually transmitted infection (STI) transmission. Barebacking, or intentionally having anal sex without a condom, has been growing in popularity among MSM, perhaps because many no longer fear HIV as they once did (Berg, 2009; Carballo-Dieguez & Bauermeister, 2004; Crossley, 2004). There is a large literature on barebacking suggesting that intimacy plays a major role in many men's decision to engage in barebacking; the absence of a physical barrier between partners is perceived to be more intimate and erotic (Halkitis, Parsons, & Wilton, 2003; Parsons & Bimbi, 2007; Shernoff, 2006). Other variables may include the eroticization of risky behavior.

An important component of bareback sex is *intentionality*. A person who does not use a condom in the "heat of the moment" but otherwise planned to use a condom would be described as having unprotected sex, but not necessarily as having engaged in "bareback" sex. Thus it is necessary to distinguish the two. Our community-based data with gay and bisexual men in New York City estimates that between 10% and 13% self-identify as barebackers. In contrast, a much larger proportion report having engaged in unprotected anal intercourse with a casual male partner (between 19% and 39%) but may not adopt the barebacker label (Grov et al., 2007; Grov, Parsons, & Bimbi, 2008, 2010b; Parsons & Bimbi, 2007). These data indicate that a majority of men are *not* barebackers; most use condoms with casual sex partners. Nevertheless, these findings highlight the importance of recognizing that some gay men perceive condoms to be a barrier to intimacy and pleasure, and that some gay men eroticize risky sexual acts. Certainly, the probability for HIV and STI transmission in the context of unprotected anal sex (whether intentional or not) can be mitigated if both partners are in a mutually monogamous relationship and both have identical HIV/STI results (e.g., if both men are HIV positive or both are HIV negative).

In a similar vein, semen/ejaculation is perceived by some gay men as a very important aspect of their sexual experience. Achieving orgasm with ejaculation is often a critical component for both partners, though there are certainly many men who may engage in sexual behavior without achieving orgasm themselves, and yet feel fully satisfied (however, typically only if their partner was able to achieve orgasm). Semen can carry symbolic meaning (and thus symbolic power) for some men, representing (1) successful completion of sexual behavior, and (2) sexual power, virility, strength, and masculinity (Reynolds, 2007). Given this, it is no surprise that some individuals enjoy engaging in semen exchange in the context of their sexual behaviors. This may include ejaculating onto one's partner (on the body, buttocks, or genitals), into one's partner (mouth or anus), or engaging in various forms of semen sexual play. Such behaviors can include snowballing (ejaculating into a partner's mouth and then erotically kissing to exchange semen between mouths), felching (ejaculating into a partner's rectum and then using your mouth to pull the semen from his rectum), or using a partner's semen as lubrication for masturbation. Our community-based data found that 7% had engaged in felching and 20% had engaged in snowballing at one point in their lives (Grov et al., 2010b). Thus, a significant minority of gay men do report engaging in these behaviors, which can be seen as stemming from a desire for semen exchange in the context of men's sexual encounters. Each of these behaviors introduces opportunities for HIV transmission, and thus men who engage in semen exchange face challenges in navigating these risks. We explore the behavioral repertoires of gay men further in the next section.

Sexual Behavior: Common and Uncommon

The sexual behaviors of gay men are as diverse as the people who comprise the gay community. In this section we discuss some of the various sexual behaviors in which gay men engage. First, it is notable that not all gay men are sexually active with other male partners. For a variety of reasons, some gay men limit their sexual behavior to masturbation or nothing at all. Although not sexually active with other men, these men may maintain their desire for members of the same sex and thus are still considered gay (i.e., not "asexual"). Second, it is particularly alarming that so few young gay men receive relevant and accurate information about gay male sexuality from family, peers, or schools. One study in Los Angeles found that young gay men often

have little information about HIV and STIs prior to initiation of anal sex (Kubicek, Bever, Weiss, Iverson, & Kipke, 2010).

Since the introduction of HIV/AIDS, the majority of studies examining the sexual behaviors of gay men now use the broader category MSM. By categorically including bisexual and other MSM (who might not identify as bisexual) with gay men, it becomes a challenge to understand fully the specific sexual behaviors of gay-identified men. Furthermore, because most of the research related to gay male sexual behaviors has an HIV/AIDS focus, it is difficult to develop an accurate picture of gay male sexuality that is independent of an emphasis on condoms or HIV risk reduction. Nonetheless, below we describe patterns of gay male sexual behaviors, relying on both published and unpublished data, and often needing to report data from studies in which gay men were a subgroup of MSM.

The United States National Health and Nutritional Examinations Surveys (NHANES), a population-based sample of men and women ages 18–59 collected from 2001 to 2006, found that of the 4319 men surveyed, 5.2% reported ever having sex with a man and 2.5% reported at least one male sex partner in the past year (Xu, Sternberg, & Markowitz, 2010). The 2002 National Survey of Family Growth (NSFG) (Mosher, Chandra, & Jones, 2005) is a national household sample in which a variety of sexual behavior data are collected. Among the 4928 men (ages 15–44), 2.3% self-identified as homosexual, 1.8% as bisexual, 90% as heterosexual, and 3.9% as "something else." Further illustrating the lack of concordance between identity and behavior, 1.6% reported having only male sexual partners in the past year, and 2.9% reported any male sexual partner in the past year. Lifetime rates of oral or anal sex with another male were 6.0%, with 5.7% reporting any oral sex with another male and 3.7% reporting any anal sex with another male. Most recently, the National Survey of Sexual Health and Behavior (Herbenick et al., 2010; Reece et al., 2010a) found that of the 2936 adolescent and adult males in the nationally representative sample, 112 (3.8%) identified as gay and 72 (2.4%) as bisexual.

As can be seen from the NSFG data, men are more likely to report oral sex with other men than anal sex. Other studies focused specifically on gay or gay/bisexual men confirm this finding. An Internet-based survey of 428 gay/bisexual male college students assessed lifetime rates of engagement in specific sexual behaviors (Lindley, Nicholson, Kerby, & Lu, 2003). The majority (66%) reported being exclusively sexually attracted to males and an additional 22.4% were primarily attracted to males. Lifetime rates of a variety of sexual behaviors revealed that 96.2% of the men had received oral sex (but this may have been from a male or a female partner), 94.8% had performed oral sex on a male partner, 66.5% had engaged in insertive anal sex, and 58.0% had engaged in receptive anal sex. With regard to sexual behaviors with female partners, 28.3% reported penile–vaginal sex and 23.9% reported performing oral sex on a female.

The men who identified as gay in NHANES reported a median of 17.7 lifetime male sexual partners. Similarly, the lifetime number of male sexual partners reported by gay/bisexual college student males in the Lindley et al. (2003) study was 16.8, although this significantly differed as a function of age; respondents aged 25 and older (who reported 30 lifetime male sexual partners) were different from those aged 18–24 (who reported 6.22 lifetime male sexual partners). These men reported an average of 2.82 male sexual partners in the past 3 months.

Project EXPLORE (Koblin et al., 2003) was a study of 4925 HIV-negative MSM from six U.S. cities enrolled in 1999–2001. As part of eligibility, men reported engaging in anal sex with one or more male sexual partners in the past year and could not report a monogamous relationship for two or more years with an HIV-negative partner. Men reported a median of seven male sexual partners in the past 6 months, and 42% reported 10 or more partners. Although nearly half (49%) of participants reported being involved in a primary relationship, only 7% of the sample reported having only one male partner, suggesting a considerable amount of sex outside of a "primary" relationship. A study of over 20,000 gay and bisexual men from a popular Internet-based networking site for men found that 18.5% were in a monogamous sexual relationship, 23.9% were engaged in sexual relationships with more than one person, and 40.7% reported being sexually active but not in a relationship (Jozkowski et al., 2010).

Limiting a discussion of gay male sexual behavior to oral and anal sex, however, fails to recognize the full repertoire of sexual activities. For example, mutual masturbation and rimming are behaviors engaged in by significant numbers of gay men. A study of 189 MSM in Boston found that 75% reported mutual masturbation in the past year and 54% reported rimming (Reisner, Mimiaga, Skeer, & Mayer, 2009). A 2010 national sample of gay men via the Internet found that nearly half (48.9%) of gay men reported using vibrators, for both partnered and solo sexual activities (Reece et al., 2010b).

Furthermore, some gay men also engage in what has been described as kinky or "fetish" sexual behavior. Some use the term "fetish" colloquially to describe a nonnormative sexual behavior, but note that a true "fetish" has specific diagnostic criteria outlined the *DSM*. As such, we will use the term "kink." There is limited published data on the prevalence of various kink behaviors among gay men. Our community-based data of men in New York City (Grov et al., 2010b) found the prevalence of kink behaviors as follows: 60% group sex; 56% anal play (broadly defined); 40% exhibitionism, photography, or voyeurism; 33% watersports (urine exchange); 30% bondage and domination; 21% fisting (hand/fist in anus); 21% sadism and/or masochism; and 8% breath play, asphyxiation. We have previously noted the prevalence of snowballing (20%) and felching (7%). Some of these behaviors may put men at risk for HIV or STI transmission, whereas others could be used as alternative behaviors and actually reduce one's your risk (e.g., exhibitionism and voyeurism poses no risk for HIV transmission). Although the majority of gay men we studied did not report engaging in these kinky behaviors, it is clear that many have expanded their sexual repertoires beyond oral and anal sex. Some data suggest that men who engage in these behaviors are more likely to display symptoms of sexual compulsivity (Grov et al., 2010b), engage in anal sex without condoms, and be HIV positive (Moskowitz, Seal, Rintamaki, & Rieger, 2011). This is certainly an area worth further exploration.

Variety in Relationships

Significant research on gay male relationships began in the early 1980s, with *American Couples* being the first large survey study to examine same-sex couples in comparison to opposite-sex couples (Blumstein & Schwartz, 1983). Most of the early studies focused on differences between heterosexual and same-sex relationships. However, McWhirter and Mattison's (1984) *The Male Couple: How Relationships Develop* really brought the study of gay male relationships into the forefront of discussions of gay male sexuality, particularly in terms of their identification of the various stages of gay male relationships and what happens when partners are in discrepant stages, a common experience in relationship development (Mattison & McWhirter, 1987; McWhirter & Mattison, 1984).

Data from our 2008 community-based survey indicated that 45.4% of gay men were currently in a relationship with another man, the average length of which was 6.8 years. Of those in a relationship, 50.6% described a mutually monogamous agreement, whereas 21.3% reported having sex with other people "as a couple" in the past 3 months. Although these patterns and agreements may not mirror patterns within heterosexual relationships, researchers have consistently found that gay male couples have as much love, happiness, and satisfaction in their relationships as do heterosexual and lesbian couples (Kurdek, 1998; Peplau & Fingerhut, 2007).

What sets gay male relationships apart from others is the variety of forms they take, especially in their likelihood of departing from the practice of monogamy. Gay male couples have repeatedly been found to be more accepting of nonmonogamy than are lesbian or heterosexual couples. In the *American Couples* study (Blumstein & Schwartz, 1983), only 36% of gay men reported that sexual monogamy in a relationship was important (compared to 84% of heterosexual wives, 75% of heterosexual husbands, and 71% of lesbians). Furthermore, whereas 28% of lesbians, 26% of heterosexual husbands, and 21% of heterosexual wives reported sex outside the relationship, 82% of the gay men in relationships reported extradyadic sex at some point in their relationship. It should be noted, however, that these research studies were conducted before the HIV/AIDS epidemic and when relationships might not have been as common.

More recent research suggests less nonmonogamy than in the time before HIV/AIDS, but still high rates of open relationships among gay male couples. Research still suggests that typically more than half of gay men in relationships have some sort of "open" aspect to them (Appleby, Miller, & Rothspan, 1999; Hickson et al., 1992; Hoff & Beougher, 2010; Peplau, Cochran, & Mays, 1997). The majority of these open relationships have some restrictions in their agreements that have been decided upon by the couple (Hoff et al., 2009), although Hoff and Beougher (2010) report, in their study of 39 gay male couples in San Francisco, that 56.4% reported breaking their agreement at some point. In 2010 we

asked a community-based sample of gay and bisexual men about 13 different rules they may have developed with their partner to navigate non-monogamy. The 5 most commonly endorsed rules were as follows: condoms must be used for anal sex (62.5%), we must tell our outside partners that we are in a relationship (47.1%), we are not allowed to spend the night with an outside sex partner (39.4%), we don't have sex with people we know (e.g., our friends, my boyfriend's friends) (38.5%), and there are certain people who are "off limits" (34.6%) (Grov, Starks, Rendina, & Parsons, in press). Men in open relationships cite sexual variety and personal independence as being the important reasons why they chose an open relationship (Blasband & Peplau, 1985). Kurdek (1991) in his longitudinal study of couples found that monogamy was positively related to relationship satisfaction for all types of couples, except for gay men. Couples with a monogamy agreement also tend to be in relationships that are less than 1 year old (Prestage et al., 2008).

For couples in these open relationships, outside sex is not perceived as an act of cheating and may instead reflect emotional monogamy (Bonello & Cross, 2010; Lasala, 2004). Some gay male couples in the Hoff and Beougher (2010) study reported being open only with regard to having threesomes as a couple. In 2008, Dr. Sarit A. Golub, a member of our research group, coined the term "monogam*ish*" to describe situations such as this, in which the relationship is neither monogamous nor open, but closer to monogamy than not, and our recent research has confirmed this unique relationship arrangement and suggests gay men in monogamish relationships report low levels of sexual risk and high levels of relationship satisfaction (Parsons et al, in press).

Although gay male relationships may come in a variety of forms, the benefits of being in a relationship are clear (Kurdek, 1998; Peplau & Fingerhut, 2007). There are no significant differences in the quality of open versus closed relationships and 93% of men in relationships say they are in love with their partner (Blasband & Peplau, 1985). For couples in open relationships, however, those with explicit rules about sex outside of the relationship are more satisfied than those without rules (Ramirez & Brown, 2010). Couples with agreements for outside sex are benefitted by providing boundaries for the relationship and fulfilling their sexual needs as a couple (Hoff & Beougher, 2010). More importantly, compared to single men, gay men in same-sex relationships, regardless of agreements about outside sex, report increased levels of self-esteem over time. This is particularly true if the relationship is prolonged as opposed to being short and episodic (Bauermeister et al., 2010).

Future Directions: Measuring Sexual Orientation Today

It is difficult to obtain an accurate picture of gay male sexuality and sexual behavior in light of the challenges found in obtaining representative samples of gay men. And what does it mean to be a gay man? Is it dependent on self-identification? Is it dependent on having had sex with another man? And how can we obtain samples of men who will report accurate behaviors when same-sex behaviors and gay identity remain stigmatized, despite decades of the gay rights movement?

Researchers are beginning to conceptualize sexual orientation in the same way that race and ethnicity are categorized as basic demographic variables. However, such measurement has not become standard. One study (Sell, Kates, & Brodie, 2007) found that in a probability telephone sample of 30 cities, only 2.6% of the over 14,000 households contacted refused to answer a screening question on sexual orientation. However, because of the discordance between gay identity and same-sex behavior, it is critical to assess both sexual identity and sexual behavior.

The HIV and AIDS epidemic had a profound impact on gay men's sexuality. Emerging out of the epidemic has been a tremendous body of public health research and overall infrastructure centered on understanding, preventing, and treating HIV. It is understood that HIV transmission is attributable to behavior, not sexual identity. As a result, our understanding of HIV has created a dialogue whereby gay men are described by their *behavior* as MSM, and not their *identity* as gay. The focus on behavior is beneficial as it contextualizes HIV transmission. Meanwhile the term "MSM" has permeated a variety of scientific fields (beyond public health) including sociology, anthropology, psychology, etc. Nevertheless, some have expressed concerns that terms such as MSM are problematic because they "obscure social dimensions of sexuality; undermine the self-labeling of lesbian, gay, and bisexual people; and do not sufficiently describe variations in sexual behavior"(Young & Meyer, 2005, p. 1144). In addition, terms such as MSM combine individuals

who are gay identified with those who are not gay identified (but may have sex with men). Although this amalgamation of individuals shares a common behavior, non-gay-identified MSM may have completely different social, mental health, and psychological needs. In essence, HIV prevention—the chief field for which the term MSM was created to serve—cannot possibly be tailored for MSM when it includes such a broad array of individuals defined solely by their behavior. Have our efforts to create a neutral term that we could use to epidemiologically classify those at risk (and thus develop prevention, care, and research) actually created a hindrance to progress in HIV prevention? And what use is this term to other scientific disciplines that have embraced "MSM" in their own discourse? Certainly, we cannot answer these questions and rather use this opportunity to illustrate the complex ways in which sexual identify, desire, and behavior intertwine within psychological and public health discourse.

Recommendations

As the social acceptance of homosexuality continues to increase we are likely to see a greater number of individuals exploring their sexuality, sexual identity, and "coming out" during developmental periods that are on par with heterosexual peers who are also exploring their own sexuality and sexual identity. Many gay men no longer wait until their 20s, 30s, or later to adopt a gay identity and disclose it to others. This process seems likely to continue on its current trajectory so that many boys can come out during middle and high school. If so, middle and high schools will be charged with creating social and emotional atmospheres that are more supportive of gay adolescents.

In addition, an increase in HIV infections among young gay men, particularly black and Hispanic men, suggests a major need to understand this population better and to identify new ways to prevent HIV transmission (Centers for Disease Control and Prevention, 2009b; Mustanski, Newcomb, Du Bois, Garcia, & Grov, 2011). In 2006, young MSM aged 13–29 comprised 37.8% of the new infections among MSM (10,850 of 28,720) (Centers for Disease Control and Prevention, 2008). Many variables influence the risk of HIV transmission. Considerable research has noted the connection between homophobia and HIV transmission (Francis & Mialon, 2010; Nakamura & Zea, 2010; Newcomb & Mustanski, 2011; Ross,

Simon Rosser, Neumaier, & Positive Connections Team, 2008; Shoptaw et al., 2009; Smolenski, Ross, Risser, & Simon Rosser, 2009). Although the exact pathways through which homophobia affects HIV transmission are not clear, evidence of its connection suggests a need for action in this area. One mechanism of action would be to change existing social policies that promote homophobia and the further isolation of sexual minorities. Some examples include the DOMA, state bans on same-sex marriage, and state bans on adoptions by lesbian and gay adults. Efforts to improve the lives of gay men and prevent further transmission of HIV should undertake a comprehensive approach, focused on individual, community, and structural level factors.

Finally, we have noted the difficulty in counting gay men in the United States (see also Gates, Chapter 6, this volume). We suggest that sexual orientation be included in the U.S. Census and all surveys being conducted by the Department of Health and Human Services. The 2010 Census included questions to identify same-sex *couples*, but had no way to identify single lesbians, gays, or bisexual people. A clearer sense of the number of gay men in the United States will aid in allocating appropriate resources and services (mental health, health services, and HIV and STI prevention). In this way, it will support future research on gay male sexual desires, sexual behaviors, and sexual identities.

REFERENCES

Appleby, P., Miller, L., & Rothspan, S. (1999). The paradox of trust for male couples. *Personal Relationships, 6,* 81–93.

Bailey, J., Kim, P., Hills, A., & Linsenmeier, J. (1997). Butch, femme, or straight acting? Partner preferences of gay men and lesbians. *Journal of Personality and Social Psychology, 73,* 960–973.

Battle, J., Cohen, C., Warren, D., Fergerson, G., & Audam, S. (2002). *Say it loud: I'm Black I'm Proud; Black Pride Survey 2000.* New York: The Policy Institute of the National Gay and Lesbian Task Force.

Bauermeister, J. A., Johns, M. M., Sandfort, T. G., Eisenberg, A., Grossman, A. H., & D'Augelli, A. R. (2010). Relationship trajectories and psychological well-being among sexual minority youth. *Journal of Youth and Adolescence, 39,* 1148–1163.

Berg, R. C. (2009). Barebacking: A review of the literature. *Archives of Sexual Behavior, 38,* 754–764.

Blasband, D., & Peplau, L. A. (1985). Sexual exclusivity versus openness in gay male couples. *Archives of Sexual Behavior, 14,* 395–412.

Blumstein, P., & Schwartz, P. (1983). *American couples: Money, work, sex.* New York: William Morrow & Co.

Bogaert, A. F., & Hershberger, S. (1999). The relation between sexual orientation and penile size. *Archives of Sexual Behavior, 28,* 213–221.

Bolding, G., Davis, M., Hart, G., Sherr, L., & Elford, J. (2007). Where young MSM meet their first sexual partner: The role of the Internet. *AIDS and Behavior, 11,* 522–526.

Bonello, K., & Cross, M. C. (2010). Gay monogamy: I love you but I can't have sex with only you. *Journal of Homosexuality, 57,* 117–139.

Bordo, S. (1999). *The male body: A new look at men in public and private.* New York: Farrar, Straus & Giroux.

Carballo-Dieguez, A., & Bauermeister, J. (2004). "Barebacking": Intentional condomless anal sex in HIV-risk contexts: Reasons for and against it. *Journal of Homosexuality, 47,* 1–16.

Carballo-Dieguez, A., Dolezal, C., Nieves, L., Diaz, F., Decena, C., & Balan, I. (2004). Looking for a tall, dark, macho man...sexual-role behaviour variations in Latino gay and bisexual men. *Culture, Health & Sexuality, 6,* 159–171.

Carrier, J. M. (1977). "Sex role preference" as an explanatory variable in homosexual behavior. *Archives of Sexual Behavior, 6,* 53–65.

Centers for Disease Control and Prevention. (2005). Sexually transmitted disease surveillance, 2004 Retrieved May 16, 2006, from http://www.cdc.gov/std/stats04/default.htm.

Centers for Disease Control and Prevention. (2008). Subpopulation estimates from the HIV incidence surveillance system—United States, 2006. *Morbidity and Mortality Weekly Report, 57,* 985–989.

Centers for Disease Control and Prevention. (2009a). *HIV and AIDS among gay and bisexual men.* Retrieved March 25, 2011, from http://www.cdc.gov/hiv/topics/msm/resources/factsheets/msm.htm.

Centers for Disease Control and Prevention. (2009b). *HIV/AIDS and young men who have sex with men.* Atlanta: Centers for Disease Control and Prevention; National Center for Chronic Disease Prevention and Health Promotion; Division of Adolescent and School Health. Retrieved from http://www.cdc.gov/healthyyouth/sexualbehaviors/pdf/hiv_factsheet_ymsm.pdf.

Clarkson, J. (2006). "Everyday Joe" versus "Pissy, Bitchy, Queens": Gay masculinity on StraightActing.com. *The Journal of Men's Studies, 14,* 191–207.

Connell, R. W. (1987). *Gender and power: Society, the person, and sexual politics.* Palo Alto, CA: Stanford University Press.

Connell, R. W. (1992). A very straight gay: Masculinity, homosexual experience, and the dynamics of gender. *American Sociological Review, 57,* 735–751.

Connell, R. W. (1995). *Masculinities.* Berkeley: University of California Press.

Crossley, M. (2004). Making sense of "barebacking": Gay men's narratives, unsafe sex and the "resistance habitus." *British Journal of Social Psychology, 43,* 225–244.

D'Emilio, J. (1983). Capitalism and gay identity. In A. Snitow, C. Stansell, & S. Thomson (Eds.), *Powers of desire: The politics of sexuality* (pp. 100–113). New York: Monthly Review Press.

Dowsett, G., Williams, H., Ventuneac, A., & Carballo-Dieguez, A. (2008). "Taking it like a man": Masculinity and barebacking online. *Sexualities, 11,* 121–142.

Drummond, M. J. N., & Filiault, S. M. (2007). The long and short of it: Gay men's perceptions of penis size. *Gay and Lesbian Issues and Psychology Review, 3,* 121–129.

Duberman, M. B., Vicinus, M., & Chauncey, G. (Eds.). (1990). *Hidden from history: Reclaiming the gay and lesbian past.* New York: Plume.

Eguchi, S. (2009). Negotiating hegemonic masculinity: The rhetorical strategy of "straight-acting" among gay men. *Journal of Intercultural Communication Research, 38,* 193–209.

Francis, A. M., & Mialon, H. M. (2010). Tolerance and HIV. *Journal of Health Economics, 29,* 250–267.

Friedman, M. S., Marshal, M. P., Stall, R., Cheong, J., & Wright, E. R. (2008). Gay-related development, early abuse and adult health outcomes among gay males. *AIDS and Behavior, 12,* 891–902.

Greenberg, D. F. (1990). *The construction of homosexuality.* Chicago: University of Chicago Press.

Grov, C., Bimbi, D. S., Parsons, J. T., & Nanín, J. E. (2006). Race, ethnicity, gender, and generational factors associated with the coming-out process among gay, lesbian, and bisexual individuals. *Journal of Sex Research, 43,* 115–121.

Grov, C., Parsons, J. T., & Bimbi, D. S. (2007). Sexual risk behavior and venues for meeting sex partners: An intercept survey of gay and bisexual men in LA and NYC. *AIDS Behavior, 11,* 915–926.

Grov, C., Parsons, J. T., & Bimbi, D. S. (2008). In the shadows of a prevention campaign: Sexual risk in the absence of crystal methamphetamine. *AIDS Education and Prevention, 20,* 42–55.

Grov, C., Parsons, J. T., & Bimbi, D. S. (2010a). The association between penis size and sexual health among men who have sex with men. *Archives of Sexual Behavior, 39,* 788–797.

Grov, C., Parsons, J. T., & Bimbi, D. S. (2010b). Sexual compulsivity and sexual risk in gay and bisexual men. *Archives of Sexual Behavior, 39,* 940–949.

Grov, C., Starks, T. J., Rendina, H. J., & Parsons, J. T. (in press). Rules about casual sex partners, relationship satisfaction, and HIV risk in partnered gay and bisexual men. *Journal of Sex and Marital Therapy.*

Halkitis, P. N., Parsons, J. T., & Wilton, L. (2003). Barebacking among gay and bisexual men in New York City: Explanations for the emergence of intentional unsafe behavior. *Archives of Sexual Behavior, 32,* 351–357.

Harding, R., & Golombok, S. E. (2002). Test-retest reliability of the measurement of penile dimensions in a sample of gay men. *Archives of Sexual Behavior, 31,* 351–357.

Hart, T. A., Wolitski, R. J., Purcell, D. W., Gomez, C., Halkitis, P., & Team, T. S. (2003). Sexual behavior among HIV-positive men who have sex with men: What's in a label? *Journal of Sex Research, 40,* 179–188.

Harvey, G. (Ed.). (2003). *Shamanism: A reader.* New York: Routledge.

Herbenick, D., Reece, M., Schick, V., Sanders, S. A., Dodge, B., & Fortenberry, J. D. (2010). Sexual behavior in the United States: Results from a national probability sample of men and women ages 14–94. *The Journal of Sexual Medicine, 7,* 255–265.

Hickson, F. C., Davies, P. M., Hunt, A. J., Weatherburn, P., McManus, T. J., & Coxon, A. P. (1992). Maintenance of open gay relationships: Some strategies for protection against HIV. *AIDS Care, 4,* 409–419.

Hinsch, B. (1992). *Passion of the cut sleeve.* Los Angeles: University of California Press.

Hoff, C., & Beougher, S. C. (2010). Sexual agreements among gay male couples. *Archives of Sexual Behavior, 39,* 774–787.

Hoff, C., Deepalika, C., Beougher, S., Darbes, L., Dadasovich, R., & Torsten, N. (2009). Serostatus differences and agreements about sex with outside partners among gay male couples. *AIDS Education and Prevention, 21,* 25–38.

Hubbard, T. K. (Ed.). (2003). *Homosexuality in Greece and Rome: A sourcebook of basic documents.* Berkeley: University of California Press.

Jacobs, S.-E., Thomas, W., & Lang, S. (Eds.). (1997). *Two-Spirit people: Native American gender, identity, sexuality, and spirituality.* Champaign, IL: University of Illinois.

Jeffries, W. L. (2009). Sociodemographic, sexual, and HIV and other sexually transmitted disease risk profiles of non homosexual-identified men who have sex with men. *American Journal of Public Health, 99,* 1042–1045.

Jozkowski, K., Rosenberger, J. G., Schick, V., Herbenick, D., Novak, D. S., & Reece, M. (2010). Relations between circumcision status, sexually transmitted infection history, and HIV serostatus among a national sample of men who have sex with men in the United States. *AIDS Patient Care and STDs, 24,* 465–470.

Koblin, B. A., Chesney, M. A., Husnik, M. J., Bozeman, S., Celum, C. L., Buchbinder, S., et al. (2003). High-risk behaviors among men who have sex with men in 6 US cities: Baseline data from the EXPLORE Study. *American Journal of Public Health, 93,* 926–932.

Kubicek, K., Bever, W. J., Weiss, G., Iverson, E., & Kipke, M. D. (2010). In the dark: Young men's stories of sexual initiation in the absence of relevant sexual health information. *Health Education and Behavior, 37,* 243–263.

Kurdek, L. A. (1991). Correlates of relationship satisfaction in cohabiting gay and lesbian couples. *Journal of Personality and Social Psychology, 61,* 910–922.

Kurdek, L. A. (1998). Relationship outcomes and their predictors: Longitudinal evidence from heterosexual married, gay cohabiting, and lesbian cohabiting couples. *Journal of Marriage and the Family, 60,* 553–568.

Lasala, M. C. (2004). Monogamy of the heart: Extra-dyadic sex and gay male couples. *Journal of Gay & Lesbian Social Services, 15,* 1–24.

Lehman, P. (1998). In an imperfect world, men with small penises are unforgiven. *Men and Masculinities, 1,* 123–137.

Lever, J., Frederick, D. A., & Peplau, L. A. (2006). Does size matter? Men's and women's views on penis size across the lifespan. *Psychology of Men and Masculinity, 7,* 129–143.

Liau, A., Millett, G., & Marks, G. (2006). Meta-analytic examination of online sex-seeking and sexual risk behavior among men who have sex with men. *Sexually Transmitted Disease, 33,* 576–584.

Lindley, L. L., Nicholson, T. J., Kerby, M. B., & Lu, N. (2003). HIV/STI associated risk behaviors among self-identified lesbian, gay, bisexual, and transgender college students in the United States. *AIDS Education and Prevention, 15,* 413–429.

Magana, J. R., & Carrier, J. M. (1991). Mexican and Mexican American male sexual behavior and spread of AIDS in California. *Journal of Sex Research, 28,* 425–441.

Mattison, A., & McWhirter, D. (1987). Stage discrepancy in male couples. *Journal of Homosexuality, 14,* 89–99.

McWhirter, D., & Mattison, A. M. (1984). *The male couple: How relationships develop.* Upper Saddle River, NJ: Prentice-Hall.

Mosher, W. D., Chandra, A., & Jones, J. (2005). Sexual behavior and selected health measures: Men and women 15–44 years of age, United States, 2002. *Advance data from Vital and Health Statistics, 362.*

Moskowitz, D. A., Seal, D. W., Rintamaki, L., & Rieger, G. (2011). HIV in the leather community: Rates and risk-related behaviors. *AIDS and Behavior, 15,* 557–564.

Murray, S. O., & Roscoe, W. (Eds.). (1998). *Boy-wives and female husbands.* New York: Palgrave.

Mustanski, B., Newcomb, M. E., Du Bois, S. N., Garcia, S. C., & Grov, C. (2011). HIV in young men who have sex with men: A review of epidemiology, risk and protective factors, and interventions. *Annual Review of Sex Research, 48,* 218–253.

Nakamura, N., & Zea, M. C. (2010). Experiences of homonegativity and sexual risk behaviour in a sample of Latino gay and bisexual men. *Culture Health and Sexuality, 12,* 73–85.

Nardi, P. M., & Schneider, B. E. (Eds.). (1998). *Social perspectives in lesbian and gay studies: A reader.* New York: Routledge.

Newcomb, M. E., & Mustanski, B. (2011). Moderators of the relationship between internalized homophobia and risky sexual behavior in men who have sex with men: A meta-analysis. *Archives of Sexual Behavior, 40,* 189–199.

Paley, M. (2000). *The book of the penis.* New York: Grove/ Atlantic, Inc.

Parsons, J. T., & Bimbi, D. S. (2007). Intentional unprotected anal intercourse among sex who have sex with men: barebacking—from behavior to identity. *AIDS and Behavior, 11,* 277–287.

Parsons, J. T., Starks, T. J., Du Bois, S. N., Grov, C., & Golub, S. A. (in press). Alternatives to monogamy among gay male couples in a community survey: Implications for mental health and sexual risk. *Archives of Sexual Behavior.* doi: 10.1007/s10508-011-9885-3

Peplau, L. A., Cochran, S. D., & Mays, V. M. (1997). A national survey of the intimate relationships of African American lesbians and gay men: a look at commitment, satisfaction, sexual behavior, and HIV disease. In B. Greene (Ed.), *Ethnic and cultural diversity among lesbians and gay men* (pp. 11–38). Thousand Oaks, CA: Sage.

Peplau, L. A., & Fingerhut, A. (2007). The close relationships of lesbians and gay men. *Annual Review of Psychology, 58,* 405–424.

Plutarch. (1973). *The age of Alexander: Nine Greek lives.* Harmondsworth: Penguin.

Pope, H. G., Phillips, K. A., & Olivardia, R. (2000). *The Adonis complex: The secret crisis of male body obsession.* New York: Free Press.

Prestage, G., Jin, F., Zablotska, I., Grulich, A., Imrie, J., Kaldor, J., et al. (2008). Trends in agreements between regular partners among gay men in Sydney, Melbourne and Brisbane, Australia. *AIDS and Behavior, 12,* 513–520.

Ramirez, O., & Brown, J. (2010). Attachment style, rules regarding sex, and couple satisfaction: A study of gay male couples. *The Australian and New Zealand Journal of Family Therapy, 31,* 202–213.

Reece, M., Herbenick, D., Schick, V., Sanders, S. A., Dodge, B., & Fortenberry, J. D. (2010a). Sexual behaviors, relationships, and perceived health among adult men in the Unites States: Results from a national probability sample. *The Journal of Sexual Medicine, 7,* 291–304.

Reece, M., Rosenberger, J. G., Schick, V., Herbenick, D., Dodge, B., & Novak, D. S. (2010b). Characteristics of vibrator use by gay and bisexually identified men in the United States. *Journal of Sexual Medicine, 7,* 3467–3476.

Reisner, S. L., Mimiaga, M. J., Skeer, M., & Mayer, K. H. (2009). Beyond anal sex: Sexual practices associated with HIV risk reduction among men who have sex with men in Boston, Massachusetts. *AIDS Patient Care and STDs, 23,* 545–550.

Reynolds, E. (2007). "Pass the cream, hold the butter": Meanings of HIV positive semen for bugchasers and giftgivers. *Anthropology and Medicine, 14,* 259–266.

Ross, M. W., Simon Rosser, B. R., Neumaier, E. R., & Positive Connections Team. (2008). The relationship of internalized homonegativity to unsafe sexual behavior in HIV-seropositive men who have sex with men. *AIDS Education and Prevention, 20,* 547–557

Rosser, B. R. S., West, W., & Weinmeyer, R. (2008). Are gay communities dying or just in transition? Results from an international consultation examining possible structural change in gay communities. *AIDS Care, 20,* 588–595.

Sanchez, F., Greenberg, S., Ming Liu, W., & Vilian, E. (2009). Reported effects of masculine ideals on gay men. *Psychology of Men & Masculinity, 10,* 73–87.

Savin-Williams, R. C. (2006). *The new gay teenager.* Cambridge, MA: Harvard University Press.

Sell, R. L., Kates, J., & Brodie, M. (2007). Use of a telephone screener to identify a probability sample of gays, lesbians, and bisexuals. *Journal of Homosexuality, 53,* 163–171.

Shernoff, M. (2006). Condomless sex: gay men, barebacking, and harm reduction. *Social Work, 51,* 106–113.

Shilts, R. (1987). *And the band played on. Politics people and the AIDS epidemic.* New York: St. Martin's Press.

Shoptaw, S., Weiss, R. E., Munjas, B., Hucks-Ortiz, C., Young, S. D., Larkins, S., et al. (2009). Homonegativity, substance use, sexual risk behaviors, and HIV status in poor and ethnic men who have sex with men in Los Angeles. *Journal of Urban Health, 86 (Suppl 1),* 77–92.

Siegel, K., Schrimshaw, E. W., Lekas, H. M., & Parsons, J. T. (2008). Sexual behaviors of non-gay identified non-disclosing men who have sex with men and women. *Archives of Sexual Behavior, 37,* 720–735.

Smolenski, D. J., Ross, M. W., Risser, J. M. H., & Simon Rosser, B. R. (2009). Sexual compulsivity and high-risk sex among Latino men: The role of internalized homonegativity and gay organizations. *AIDS Care, 21,* 42–49.

Stulhofer, A. (2006). How (un)important is penis size for women with heterosexual experience? *Archives of Sexual Behavior, 35,* 5–6.

Wegesin, D., & Meyer-Bahlburg, H. F. L. (2000). Top/bottom self-label, anal sex practices, HIV risk and gender role identity in gay men in New York City. *Journal of Psychology and Human Sexuality, 12,* 43–62.

Wei, C., & Raymond, H. F. (2011). Preference for and maintenance of anal sex roles among men who have sex with men: Sociodemographic and behavioral correlates. *Archives of Sexual Behavior, 40,* 829–834.

Weinrich, J. D., Grant, I., Jacobson, D. L., Robinson, S. R., & McCutchan, J. A. (1992). Effects of recalled childhood gender nonconformity on adult genitoerotic role and AIDS exposure. HNRC Group. *Archives of Sexual Behavior, 21,* 559–585.

Williams, C. A. (1999). *Roman homosexuality: Ideologies of masculinity in classical antiquity.* Oxford: Oxford University Press.

Wolf, S. (2004). The roots of gay oppression. *International Socialist Review, 37.* Available at http://www.isreview.org/issues/37/gay_oppression.shtml.

Xu, F., Sternberg, M. R., & Markowitz, L. E. (2010). Men who have sex with men in the United States: Demographic and behavioral characteristics and prevalence of HIV and HSV-2 infection: Results from National Health and Nutrition Examination Survey 2001–2006. *Sexually Transmitted Diseases, 37,* 399.

Young, R. M., & Meyer, I. H. (2005). The trouble with "MSM" and "WSW": Erasure of the sexual-minority person in public health discourse. *American Journal of Public Health, 95,* 1144–1149.

Zablotska, I. B., Holt, M., & Prestage, G. (2012). Changes in gay men's participation in gay community life: Implications for HIV surveillance and research. *AIDS and Behavior, 16,* 669–675.

3

Bisexual Identities

SARI H. DWORKIN

There has been a proliferation of research on bisexuality over the past 10 years. Much of the research has consisted of doctoral dissertations, although there has also been an increase in research on bisexuality done by seasoned researchers. One exciting development is that in contrast to the previous scholarly literature much of the current research has focused specifically on bisexual populations and has not generalized from findings on lesbians and gay populations. Thus, the overall quality of the research literature on bisexuality has improved in recent years.

DEMOGRAPHICS

Research on bisexuality is challenging due to definitional problems as well as methodological concerns. A helpful starting place is to estimate how many people self-identify as bisexual. Gates (2011) reviewed nine population surveys conducted during the past 10 years. Five were done in the United States. Studies done in the United States estimate that 3.5% of adults identified as lesbian, gay, or bisexual. That is equivalent to approximately eight million adults, split about evenly between lesbian/ gay and bisexual adults. A nationally representative probability study done in 2010 (Herbenick et al., as cited in San Francisco Human Rights Commission, 2011) on 5042 male and female respondents found that 3.1% self-identified as bisexual and 2.5% self-identified as lesbian or gay. In the majority of population studies, more women identify as bisexual than lesbian. Among men, more identify as gay than bisexual. Herbenick and colleagues (2010) reported that among 818 adolescent respondents 4.9% self-identified as bisexual and 1.0% self-identified as lesbian or gay. Thus, bisexuality is more common than sometimes believed, especially among women (for further discussion, see Gates, Chapter 6, this volume).

Early research on bisexuality was conducted in the context of dichotomous heterosexual/homosexual concepts, making it difficult to identify bisexual individuals. Over time, research shifted to a multidimensional framework (Dodge, Reece, & Gebhard, 2008; Fox, 1996; Firestein, 1996, Rust, 2000). Because many scholars did not believe at the outset that bisexuality was anything more than a phase, early researchers were forced to argue for bisexuality as a valid sexual identity or sexual orientation. Now that bisexuality is more widely recognized as a valid identity/orientation, researchers have moved to consider attitudes, identities, health issues, multicultural issues, and the intersections of these aspects.

ATTITUDES TOWARD BISEXUALITY

The belief that bisexuality is a phase and not a separate, valid identity is, unfortunately, still very popular. The research suggests that heterosexual people distrust those who identify as bisexual. In fact, this view may be shared by lesbian and gay individuals, as well.

Scales developed by Mohr and Rochlen (1999) and Mulick and Wright (2002) have been used to assess attitudes of heterosexual, lesbian, and gay populations toward bisexual people. These authors found that heterosexual, lesbian, and gay people endorse negative statements about bisexual persons with surprising frequency. Eliason (1997, 2001) assessed the attitudes of heterosexual college students and found that these students had more negative attitudes about bisexual men than about lesbian women or gay men.

In the context of a larger study, Herek (2002) assessed heterosexual individuals' attitudes toward bisexual men and women (among others). Bisexual people were rated more negatively than any other group assessed. Attitudes were measured toward religious, racial, ethnic, and political groups as well as toward injection drug users. The only group rated less favorably than bisexuals was the injection drug users. Heterosexual women rated bisexual individuals lower than homosexual individuals of either gender. Heterosexual men rated gay or bisexual men lower than they rated women regardless of sexual identity. Another study later replicated this pattern of findings when assessing African-Americans' attitudes toward homosexuality and bisexuality (Heath & Goggin, 2009).

In their review of attitudinal research on bisexuality, Israel and Mohr (2004) concluded that homonegativity is a key element in the negative attitudes of heterosexuals toward bisexual people. They also noted that heterosexual individuals tend to agree that bisexuality is not a legitimate identity and that bisexual persons cannot be trusted. Such views also extend to attitudes toward bisexual people in relationships. Spalding and Peplau (1997) found that heterosexual individuals were likely to endorse statements such as "bisexual people are less likely to be monogamous" and "bisexual people are more likely to infect others with a sexually transmitted disease," but also such as "bisexuals are more likely to give their partners sexual satisfaction." Galupo (2007) found that negative attitudes such as these also had a negative impact on friendships among bisexual, lesbian, and heterosexual women.

The ways in which others see bisexual people can affect how bisexual persons see themselves. This, in turn, can influence the emotional and physical well-being of bisexual individuals. In short, negative attitudes toward bisexual people have an impact on their mental and physical health throughout the lifespan.

LIFESPAN DEVELOPMENT

The scholarly literature on sexual minority adolescents and young adults has focused on developmental issues, sexual behavior, and physical and mental health issues (see Rosario and Schrimshaw, Chapter 7, this volume). Most of the research has used samples that combined bisexual, lesbian, and gay participants. Sexual orientation of young adults has sometimes been assessed via measures of sexual attraction, sexual behavior, or gender of partner rather than on self-identification. A key concept of much of this literature is the reaction to minority stress (see Meyer and Frost, Chapter 18,

this volume), which reflects the internalization of stigma, oppression, and rejection (Scott, 2007).

Findings suggest that minority stress often leads to greater risk-taking behaviors among lesbian, gay, and bisexual youth and young adults as compared to their heterosexual counterparts. Lesbian, gay, and bisexual adolescents and young adults score higher for anxiety and depression, victimization, and abuse (Eisenberg & Wechsler, 2003; Hershberger & D'Augelli, 2000), and also higher for sexually transmitted diseases (Lindley, Nicholson, Kerby, & Lu, 2003) than do their heterosexual peers.

Some research has examined bisexual youth separately from lesbian and gay youth. This research has yielded similarities and differences among the bisexual as compared to lesbian and gay youth. In a study of young and middle-aged adults, Jorm and colleagues (2002) found that bisexual people scored highest on assessments of psychological distress such as depressive symptoms, and on risky behaviors such as alcohol abuse. The bisexual participants also had the highest self-reported life problems (e.g., less support from family members and more financial problems). In a sample of men who reported having sex with men, Paul and colleagues (2002) found that the largest numbers of suicide attempts were reported by bisexual men. In another study of high school students from two different states, Robin and colleagues (2002) found that bisexual adolescents (identified via self-reports about sexual behavior) had the highest suicide rates and exhibited the most risky health behaviors of any group, including both heterosexual and homosexual adolescents. Udry and Chantala (2002) conducted a large-scale study of adolescents in the United States and found that bisexual individuals of both genders exhibited more high-risk behaviors (e.g., substance abuse and delinquency) and reported more psychological distress than did heterosexual or other sexual minority youth.

Sheets and Mohr (2009) studied university students who considered themselves bisexual. They reported that lack of support from family members and friends was associated with depressive symptoms, life dissatisfaction, and negative feelings about a person's sexual orientation. Those with more support from family members reported fewer depressive symptoms and greater life satisfaction.

A few studies have been conducted to assess the mental health of bisexual adults. Dodge and Sandfort (2007) reviewed research that compared bisexuals to lesbians, gay men, and heterosexual individuals. They were able to find only five studies conducted between 1994 and 2004 that did not collapse bisexuals into the lesbian/gay sample. Warner and colleagues (2004) examined gay men, lesbians, and bisexual men and women in England and Wales. They found that bisexual men showed more psychological distress than gay men but there was no difference between lesbians and bisexual women. Dodge and Sandfort (2007) also reviewed HIV risk studies and found that most of the studies described men who had sex with men rather than men who self-identified as bisexual; those who engaged in bisexual behavior were at higher risk than were other men.

Dodge and Sandfort (2007) call for more research that separates bisexuals from other groups and also includes bisexual women. When bisexual individuals have been studied separately from lesbian and gay people, Dodge and Sandfort (2007) noted elevated distress among bisexual people. In contrast to the negative findings of the studies reviewed by Dodge and Sandfort (2007), Firestein (2007a, 2007b) suggested that the findings to date are not entirely consistent. On balance, however, most investigators have reported greater psychological distress among bisexuals as compared to other individuals (Rothblum & Factor, 2001; Saphira & Glover, 2000; Silverschanz, 2004).

After reviewing the limited research on aging bisexual people, Dworkin (2006) discussed some issues relevant to many older bisexual people: isolation, concerns about available communities (heterosexual, lesbian, gay), financial planning, housing, health, and retirement. In the United States, financial planning poses particular challenges because, for instance, same-sex bisexual couples are not recognized by the law in many jurisdictions. This can result in many difficulties (for example, with Social Security, which is a federal program). Baron and Cramer (2000) pointed out the isolation, need for social support, and negativity from the general population that older bisexual individuals face. Keppel (2002) and Keppel and Firestein (2007) noted that in addition to issues already discussed, older bisexual people may need to explore age-related changes in sex and sexuality, something many mental health professionals are uncomfortable exploring with seniors.

The challenges that bisexual people face throughout their lifespan can affect the development of

their bisexual identities. For example, experiences with stigma may delay identity development. The next section explores identity issues.

BISEXUAL IDENTITY MODELS

Development of Bisexual Identities

The first bisexual identity model was that of Weinberg, Williams, and Pryor (1994). This model was based on their research in San Francisco in the 1980s and it included four stages: initial confusion, finding and applying the bisexual label, settling into the identity, and then continued uncertainty. The fourth stage reflected the difficulty of maintaining a bisexual identity in social contexts that allowed for nothing but homosexuality or heterosexuality. In their follow-up study with the same participants, Weinberg and his colleagues reported that bisexual identities were relatively consistent over a 15-year period (Weinberg, Williams, & Pryor, 2001).

Bradford (2004) also developed a model for bisexual identity development. This model emphasized how internalized binegativity affects the maintenance of a positive bisexual identity, and reflected how attitudes toward bisexuality have changed in recent years. Her four stages are questioning reality, inventing the identity, maintaining the identity, and transforming reality. This model replaced "continued uncertainty" with "the importance of support and community" for maintaining a positive bisexual identity.

Bisexual identity development models must take into account the historical context. Today's adolescents and young adults often do not use the terms heterosexual, bisexual, homosexual, or even gay and lesbian. Today's youth often use labels such as "bicurious," "fluid," "queer," "questioning" or they may refuse labels altogether (Entrup & Firestein, 2007). For instance, Hoburg et al. (2004) found that about a third of the university students in their study who identified as heterosexual also indicated that they had same-sex attractions. Thus, labels may vary across historical periods and cultural groups.

Consistent with the recognition that historical context is important, Baron and Cramer (2000) emphasized that when working with older bisexual individuals, it is necessary to consider "combined effects of 'ableism,' ageism, heterosexism, homophobia, racism, and sexism" (p. 207). It is important to recognize that today's older bisexual individuals were born at a time in history when nonhetero-sexuality remained hidden (Baron & Cramer, 2000; Greene, 2001; Keppel & Firestein, 2007).

Research has reported that bisexual persons often come out at older ages than do lesbian or gay people (Fox, 1995, 1996). Given the historical and cultural context in which older bisexuals grew up, coming out as bisexual at middle age or older could well cause a coming out crisis (Baron & Cramer, 2000). For older bisexual people in heterosexual marriages, the recognition of a bisexual identity can be problematic. Weinberg, Williams, and Pryor (2001) noted that the men in their study reported feeling pressure to identify as heterosexual. About 20% of the sample adopted exclusively lesbian or gay identities later in life. Women reported that this was because they were tired of dealing with men, and the men reported that identifying as gay allowed for a larger pool of male partners. In contrast, Dworkin (2006) suggested that adherence to feminism and liberal politics might have given some older bisexual women the freedom to identify as bisexual. For men (and for some women) a bisexual identity allows more freedom to be sexually adventurous (Dworkin, 2006). Once a bisexual identity is adopted, questions about the stability of that identity can create important challenges to identity maintenance.

Sexual Orientation and Self-Identification

As stated earlier,Weinberg, Williams, and Pryor (2001) interviewed a group of bisexual women and men that had previously been interviewed more than 10 years earlier. They found that bisexual identities remained constant over time. Russell and Seif (2002) also reported that for self-identified bisexual women, sexual identities were stable over time. Only 5% of the women who self-identified as bisexual during the first set of interviews reported shifting to another identity later in subsequent years.

Diamond (2000) (see Diamond, Chapter 1, this volume) interviewed a group of young sexual minority women about their sexual desires, identities, and behaviors over time. Over the early years of the study, there was evidence of considerable fluidity in sexual attractions and behaviors for some women. Ten years later, Diamond (2008) interviewed these women again. She found that more women identified as bisexual or unlabeled at the end than at the beginning of the 10-year period. In addition, Diamond (2008) found that bisexual

women's same-sex/other-sex attractions were relatively stable over the 10 years of the study (see also Amestoy, 2001).

Identifying as bisexual is difficult given the prevailing beliefs and attitudes. Sometimes these difficulties inspire bisexual persons to be more visible (Bower, Gurevich, & Mathieson, 2002; Ochs, 2007; Parker, Adams, & Phillips, 2007). There is increasing recognition today that self-identification does not operate in isolation from the other factors such as gender, race-ethnicity, and culture that affect identity. The next section addresses these multicultural issues and their impact on sexual identities among bisexual individuals.

MULTICULTURAL ISSUES

Gender

Most cultures of the world not only dichotomize sexual identity but also, and to even a greater extent, dichotomize gender into "male" and "female." For purposes of this chapter gender will refer to the biological sex of women and men. (For a discussion of trangender issues see Sanchez and Vilain, Chapter 4, this volume.) Gender role will be used to refer to behaviors played out as either masculine or feminine according to the compulsory heterosexuality and sexism of the culture (Pennington, 2009). Sexism affects the ways in which bisexuality manifests in men and women. For instance, Rust (2000, p. 209) states that for heterosexual individuals, "gender is the deal breaker," by which she means that both a person's intelligence and his or her physical characteristics may play into attraction for bisexual women, but the desired partner need not be somebody of the opposite sex. For bisexual people, the partner's gender is not the deal breaker; other characteristics may be more important.

Bisexuality is often seen as a departure from compulsory heterosexuality because bisexuality moves outside of dichotomous categories (Fassinger & Arseneau, 2007; Rust, 2000). An important question is whether or not bisexuality relies on traditional gender role categories. In a study of 20 bisexual individuals (six men and 14 women) Pennington (2009) examined this question. The women and the men subscribed to traditional beliefs such as "women are more emotional" and "men are more logical." The participants were aware of using traditional gender role characteristics in describing themselves and others. They stated that they did not accept these traditional notions even though they described themselves and others using them. This study sought to examine whether gender role performance of the bisexual individual changed with same-sex and other-sex partners. Results showed that women exhibited more gender role flexibility both within and between relationships than did men.

Potocyniak (2007) contrasted the issues of bisexual men with those of bisexual women. There is greater stigma for men than for women who do not fall on one side or the other of the heterosexual/homosexual dichotomy. Potoczniak (2007) suggested that the gay male community endorses "the dichotomous, monosexual, and essentialist nature of sexual orientation" (p. 125). Empirical research tends to suggest that bisexual men are indeed more stigmatized than bisexual women, making sexual identification as a nonheterosexual man more difficult for men. Regardless of how a man identifies in terms of sexual identity, men tend to be more sexually active than women, and may have more opportunities to engage sexually with both sexes (Bronn, 2001). Anonymous sexual relationships that are engaged in by some men also make disclosure of sexual identity unnecessary. All of this makes identification as bisexual more challenging for men than for women.

Research suggests that women are more fluid and flexible than men in their sexual behavior, regardless of their sexual identities (Rust, 2000). Some women who identify as lesbian have sex with and are in relationships with men, and some women who identify as heterosexual have relationships with women. Explanations for these phenomena (e.g., Dworkin, 2002; Firestein, 2007a; Rust, 2000) reflect the socialization of men and women. For example, it is easier for women to show affection for both women and men. The basis for identifying one way or another seems different for men than for women. For men this identity is often based on sexual behavior, whereas for women it is based on factors such as emotional attachment and relationship quality. Some view identity as an integration of sexual feelings with sexual behaviors, with the expectation that the two will be consistent. Such consistency may, however, be more true of men than women. Rust (2000) termed this psychological expectation of consistency a "masculinist" definition (p. 215). In fact, Rust (1996) found that whereas men usually select a single descriptor when asked about their sexual identities, bisexual women often choose more than one descriptor when given the opportunity to do so.

It is important to note that what may appear to be acceptance of bisexuality may not always be genuine, and that pseudoacceptance of bisexuality can be exploited (Fahs, 2009). As Fahs (2009) has cautioned, "women's sexuality shifts in response to changing social trends and pressures more readily than men's sexuality, which can be particularly dangerous in a patriarchal climate" (p. 425). In her qualitative study of 40 women, Fahs (2009) reported evidence of what she called "performative bisexuality." Performative bisexuality occurs when women in heterosexual relationships have sex with another woman in front of the male partner for his sexual enjoyment. Fahs reported that younger women participated in performative bisexuality in public (e.g., in bars) and older women did it in private (e.g., in homes). She noted that "pressure to perform as bisexual appeared for heterosexual-identified women and for bisexual and lesbian-identified women, though heterosexual women reported more pressure from their sexual partners whereas bisexual and lesbian women reported feeling pressure from men who were strangers and/or nonpartners" (Fahs, p. 439). Fahs (2009) found such performative bisexuality disturbing and remarked that

> compulsory heterosexuality, however challenged by increasing acceptance of, and performance of, bisexual behavior, is still alive and well. This fact is notable in women's descriptions of minimizing the significance of their same-sex feelings, attractions, behaviors, and experiences, and it exists when describing the ways in which same-sex sexual eroticism often requires the literal and figurative presence of men in the sexual exchange. Women may engage in same-sex sexual behavior, but this often occurs in the presence of men, with men's approval, and for men's sexual arousal. Women are classically heterosexual even when performing as bisexual. (p. 445).

Thus, the work of Fahs (2009) provides examples of the pseudoacceptance of bisexuality, in which bisexuality is based on behavior rather than identity. Sexual identity is, of course, multifaceted. Gender influences sexual identities as well as sexual behaviors, and so do race, ethnicity, and culture.

Race, Ethnicity, and Culture

Most scholarly writing about bisexuality among people of color starts from racial/ethnic identity development models and models of sexual identity development, and discusses issues that bisexual persons of color may face (Stanley, 2004; Wilson, 2008). To integrate these issues, Chun and Singh (2010) proposed a model of intersecting identity development among bisexual youth of color. As they wrote, "This model represents a dynamic conceptualization of the fluidity with which the identities of sexually fluid youth of color may continually evolve in response to changes within the microsystem (e.g., primary social support and youth resilience) and the macrosystem (e.g., sociopolitical context) of their lives" (Chun & Singh, 2010, p. 430). Collins (2000) theorized a four-stage model (questioning/confusion, refusal/suppression, infusion/exploration, and resolution/acceptance) based on a study of 15 Japanese-American adults. Recently, King (2011) decided to empirically test this model with a qualitative study of six college students who identified as multiracial/biracial and bisexual. King's results provided little support for Collins' (2000) model. The participants in her study instead described separate sexual and racial developmental processes, and enumerated ways in which these processes were affected by external factors such as social context. The participants did not recall having ever adopted identities as "final," instead expecting their identities to continue to grow and change. Thus, the Collins (2000) model was not supported by King's (2011) findings.

It is important to recognize that when working with ethnically and racially diverse bisexual persons, sociohistorical relationships play a role (San Francisco Human Rights Commission, 2011). Multiple group membership affects identification and the salience of particular aspects of identification (Dworkin, 2002). There are real differences within racial/ethnic communities such as within African-American communities, Latino communities, and Asian-American communities, and these must be understood (Collins, 2007; Ferrer & Gomez, 2007; Israel, 2004; Scott, 2007). Early developmental models for self-identification as gay or lesbian were linear in nature and had as their final stage acceptance and commitment to disclosure of a lesbian or gay identity. This approach is not consistent with the experiences of many racially and ethnically diverse people who have felt the need to hide their sexual orientation due to homophobia, biphobia, and sexism in their ethnic communities and due to racism in lesbian, gay, and bisexual communities (San Francisco Human Rights Commission, 2011).

Black American bisexual men face added discrimination due to the myth that they are spreading HIV/AIDS and other sexually transmitted diseases in both the heterosexual and gay/lesbian communities. Actual studies have found such infection rates to be low (Malebranche, 2008; San Francisco Human Rights Commission, 2011). Coming out is difficult, especially given the stereotypes and myths that are prominent in some ethnic communities. In such contexts, visibility might result in ostracism and even violence (Scott, 2006). In addition, sexual identities other than heterosexual ones may be seen as essentially white in character. If so, any black who identifies as bisexual cannot be an authentic black (Wilson & Miller, 2002).

The influence of race, ethnicity, and culture on bisexual identity development needs more empirical research. Theoretical models can guide this research, but empirical studies are needed. As King (2011) has emphasized, such research should include longitudinal studies.

Disability

Although the intersection of disability and sexual identity is recognized as an important area for study, there is very little research on lesbian and gay issues and disability and even less on bisexuality and disability. Cheng (2009) reviewed some theories about gender and sexuality, including social constructionist theory, feminist and gender theory, queer theory, and resistance theory. Cheng described the first two as marginalizing disabled people. According to Cheng (2009), feminist and gender theories consider all of the intersections of identity and specifically place an emphasis on women's oppressive status. The disabled can be seen as weaker and therefore feminine. Queer theory focuses on how able-bodied ideology and heterosexual ideology affect disabled queer people. It also examines the oppression faced by both the disabled and by lesbian, gay, and bisexual people. Finally, Cheng (2009) suggested that resistance theory examines how individuals live their daily lives and how the community responds to their daily lives. Other researchers also describe models of disability and add overviews of the experiences of disabled lesbian and gay persons (Castanda & Peters, 2000; Coffman, 2007; Schulz, 2009). Much of the work to date is anecdotal. Coffman (2007) stated that bisexual disabled people face issues similar to lesbian and gay disabled people. In addition, however, it may be harder to find romantic partners and to assert the right and the ability to behave in sexual ways, given that a common myth proclaims that disabled people are not interested in sexuality.

The dependence of disabled people on caregivers can magnify issues faced by lesbian, gay, and bisexual disabled persons, especially when the caregivers are negative toward bisexuals or homosexuals (Dworkin, 2000; Fassinger & Arseneau, 2007). Schulz (2009) pointed out that much of the psychological literature about sexuality and disability operates from a heterosexist assumption. Caregivers, like the rest of society, often fall victim to heterosexist expectations.

One study of young lesbian and gay people with intellectual disabilities in Sweden confirmed the existence of heterosexist assumptions among parents, school personnel, and staff of group homes, recreational environments, and short-term homes (Lofgren-Martenson, 2009). The author noted that the youth themselves also anticipated heterosexual bias, possibly due to the difficulty for mentally challenged people to be in places in which same-sex behavior would be acknowledged. This might even be a more important factor for disabled youth whose personal preferences might be bisexual in their character.

There have been a few attempts to look at the intersection of disability and sexuality (Schulz, 2009). These few studies have been conducted in exclusively heterosexual frameworks (e.g., with women married to disabled men). Furthermore, the research is interpretive and anecdotal. Future research needs to examine sexual identity, disability, and their intersections among both men and women (Schulz, 2009).

Religion/Spiritual Issues

Religion can be a major conflict for those acknowledging a lesbian and gay sexual identity (Ritter & Terndrup, 2002). Any such conflicts are likely to be similar for any bisexuals who choose same-sex relationships, but little is yet known about such issues. Lingwood (2010) argued that bisexual persons as other religiously oppressed persons have turned away from organized religion and tend to take traditions and practices and beliefs from many different religious traditions, but much of this argument was based on anecdotal evidence. More research is clearly needed in this area.

SUMMARY AND CONCLUSIONS

Research on bisexuality is constantly evolving. Early studies were based on dichotomous (i.e., heterosexual/homosexual) frameworks. More recently, a multidimensional understanding of bisexuality has emerged. Increasingly, researchers have recognized bisexual people as a unique group, different from lesbians, gay men, and heterosexual people. Negative attitudes about bisexual people add to the overall level of minority stress experienced by bisexual people.

Developmental research has revealed some of the different stresses experienced by bisexual persons at different periods across the lifespan. Bisexuality imposes challenges at every age. Bisexual women and men appear to internalize negative messages about bisexuality to some degree, and this often manifests in the performance of risky behaviors and the experience of negative emotional states. Cohort effects mean that midlife and older bisexual people of today have issues that might not be faced by younger bisexual individuals. Future research should consider both developmental and cohort issues.

The current multidimensional approach to research on bisexual populations emphasizes the intersectionality of identities. It also emphasizes the differential salience that different identities may have for bisexual persons at different times of their life and within different communities. There are differences between men and women as to how they experience and manifest bisexual identities. Sexism may foster a pseudoacceptance of bisexuality through pressure for women to participate in performative bisexuality. Men and women base their identities on different characteristics such as sexual behavior for men and relationships for women. Women tend to be more fluid than men in their behavior as well as in their identities. Demographic studies have revealed that women are more likely than men to identify as bisexual.

In addition, bisexuality will be different for African-Americans, Asian-Americans, Latinos/Latinas, Native Americans, biracial persons, and multiracial persons. Multiple identities, based both on race/ethnicity/culture and on sexual minority status, pose unique challenges for bisexual persons in terms of visibility and acceptance by others and the development of a positive bisexual and racial/ethnic/cultural identity. Empirical research is necessary to understand the development of multiple identities.

Research on disability and religious differences is sparse and mostly anecdotal. It nevertheless seems clear that disabled bisexual persons face oppression due to their disabilities as well as their sexual identities. Their reliance on caregivers poses challenges to their recognition of bisexual identities and to their access to information about bisexuality. Religious traditions appear to have the greatest impact on bisexual people who are in same-sex relationships.

Does life in a heteronormative environment adversely affect the health of bisexual people? Many studies have reported risky behaviors and high psychological distress among bisexual compared to lesbian, gay, and heterosexual people. Future research must study bisexual persons as a separate group from gay and lesbian people. Research should be designed to study models of identity development. In this regard, longitudinal studies could be helpful. Future studies should also examine issues encountered by bisexual persons of color. An important topic here is the integration of multiple identities.

In conclusion, this is an exciting era for work on bisexuality. It is no longer necessary to defend bisexuality as a legitimate orientation. Research is beginning to focus on bisexual individuals and on bisexuality as unique in many ways from lesbian, gay, and heterosexual orientations, identities, and behaviors. As researchers continue to study these issues in the years ahead, we can expect considerable progress in the understanding of bisexuality.

REFERENCES

Amestoy, M. M. (2001). Research on sexual orientation labels' relationship to behaviors and desires. *Journal of Bisexuality, 1*(4), 91–113.

Baron, A., & Cramer, D. W. (2000). Potential counseling concerns of aging lesbian gay, and bisexual clients. In R. M. Perez, K. A. DeBord, & K. J. Bieschke (Eds.). *Handbook of counseling and psychotherapy with lesbian, gay, and bisexual clients* (pp. 207–223). Washington, DC: APA Press.

Bower, J., Gurevich, M., & Mathieson, C. (2002). (Con)Tested identities: Bisexual women reorient sexuality. In D. Atkins (Ed.), *Bisexual women in the twenty-first century* (pp. 23–52). Binghamton, NY: Harrington Park Press.

Bradford, M. (2004). The bisexual experience: Living in a dichotomous culture. *Journal of Bisexuality, 4*(1/2), 7–23.

Bronn, C. D. (2001). Attitudes and self-images of male and female bisexuals. *Journal of Bisexuality, 1*(4), 5–9.

Castanda, R., & Peters, M. (2000). Ableism: Introduction. In M. Adams, W. J. Blumenfeld, R. Castaneda, H. W. Hackman, M.L. Peters, & X. Zuniga (Eds.), *Readings for diversity and social justice* (pp. 319–323). New York: Routledge.

Cheng, R. P. (2009). Sociological theories of disability, gender, and sexuality: A review of the literature. *Journal of Human Behavior in the Social Environment, 19*(1), 112–122.

Chun, K. Y. S., & Singh, A. A. (2010). The bisexual youth of color intersecting identities development model: A contextual approach to understanding multiple marginalization experiences. *Journal of Bisexuality, 10*, 429–451.

Coffman, S. L. (2007). Disability and bisexuality: Confronting ableism at the intersection of gender and queer desire. In B. A. Firestein (Ed.), *Becoming visible: Counseling bisexuals across the lifespan* (pp. 186–201). New York: Columbia University Press.

Collins, J. F. (2000). Biracial-bisexual individuals: Identity coming of age. *International Journal of Sexuality & Gender Studies, 5*(3), 221–253.

Collins, J. F. (2007). Counseling at the intersection of identities: Asian/Pacific American bisexuals. In B. Firestein (Ed.), *Becoming visible: Counseling bisexuals across the lifespan* (pp. 229–245). New York: Columbia University Press.

Diamond, L. M. (2000). Sexual identity, attractions, and behavior among young sexual-minority women over a 2-year period. *Developmental Psychology, 36*(2), 241–250.

Diamond, L. M. (2008). Female bisexuality from adolescence to adulthood: Results from a 10-year longitudinal study. *Developmental Psychology, 44*, 5–14.

Dodge, B., Reece, M., & Gebhard, P. H. (2008). Kinsey and beyond: Past, present, and future considerations for research on male bisexuality. *Journal of Bisexuality, 8*, 175–189.

Dodge, B., & Sandfort, T. G. M. (2007). A review of mental health research on bisexual individuals when compared to homosexual and heterosexual individuals. In B. A. Firestein (Ed.), *Becoming visible: Counseling bisexuals across the lifespan* (pp. 28–51). New York: Columbia University Press.

Dworkin, S. H. D. (2000). Individual therapy with lesbian, gay, and bisexual clients. In R. M. Perez, K. A. DeBord, & K. J. Bieschke (Eds.). *Handbook of counseling and psychotherapy with lesbian, gay, and bisexual clients* (pp. 157–181). Washington, DC: APA Press.

Dworkin, S. (2002). Biracial, bicultural, bisexual: Bisexuality and multiple identities. *Journal of Bisexuality, 2*(4), 93–107.

Dworkin, S. D. (2006). The aging bisexual: The invisible of the invisible minority. In D. Kimmel, T. Rose, & S. David (Eds.), *Lesbian, gay, bisexual, and transgender aging: Research and clinical perspectives* (pp. 36–52). New York: Columbia University Press.

Eisenberg, M. E., & Wechsler, H. (2003). Social influences on substance-use behaviors of gay, lesbian, and bisexual college students: Findings from a national study. *Social Science & Medicine, 57,* 1913–1923.

Eliason, M. J. (1997). The prevalence & nature of biphobia in heterosexual undergraduate students. *Archives of Sexual Behavior, 26*(3), 317–325.

Eliason, M. (2001). Bi negativity: The stigma facing bisexual men. *Journal of Bisexuality, 1*(2/3), 137–154.

Entrup, L., & Firestein, B. A. (2007). Developmental and spiritual issues of young people and bisexuals of the next generation. In B. A. Firestein (Ed.), *Becoming visible: Counseling bisexuals across the lifespan* (pp. 89–107). New York: Columbia University Press.

Fahs, B. (2009). Compulsory bisexuality?: The challenges of modern sexual fluidity. *Journal of Bisexuality, 9,* 431–449.

Fassinger, R. F., & Arseneau, J. R. (2007). "I'd rather get wet than be under that umbrella": Differentiating the experiences and identities of lesbian, gay, bisexual, and transgender people. In K. J. Bieschke, R. M. Perez, & K. A. DeBord (Eds.), *Handbook of counseling and psychotherapy with lesbian, gay, bisexual, and transgender clients* (pp. 19–49). Washington, DC: American Psychological Association.

Ferrer, L., & Gómez, L. A. J. (2007). Counseling bisexual Latinos: A minority within a minority. In B. Firestein (Ed.), *Becoming visible: Counseling bisexuals across the lifespan* (pp. 246–267). New York: Columbia University Press.

Firestein, B. A. (1996). Bisexuality as paradigm shift: Transforming our disciplines. In B. A. Firestein (Ed.), *Bisexuality: The psychology and politics of an invisible minority* (pp. 263–291). Newbury Park, CA: Sage Publications.

Firestein, B. A. (2007a). Cultural and relational contexts of bisexual women: Implications for therapy. In K. J. Bieschke, R. M. Perez, & K. A. DeBord (Eds.), *Handbook of counseling and psychotherapy with lesbian, gay, bisexual, and transgender clients* (pp. 91–117). Washington, DC: American Psychological Association.

Firestein, B. A. (2007b). Cultural and relational contexts of bisexual women. In B. A. Firestein (Ed.), *Becoming visible: Counseling bisexuals across the lifespan* (pp. 127–152). New York: Columbia University Press.

Fox, R. C. (1995). Bisexual identities. In A. R. D'Augelli & C. J. Patterson (Eds.), *Lesbian, gay, and bisexual identities over the lifespan: Psychological perspectives* (pp. 48–86). New York: Oxford University Press.

Fox, R. C. (1996). Bisexuality in perspective: A review of theory and research. In B. A. Firestein (Ed.), *Bisexuality: The psychology and politics of an invisible minority* (pp. 3–50). Newbury Park, CA: Sage Publications.

Galupo, M. P. (2007). Sexism, heterosexism, and biphobia: The framing of bisexual women's friendships. *Journal of Bisexuality, 6*(3), 35–45.

Gates, G. J. (2011 April). How many people are lesbian, gay, bisexual, and transgender. Los Angeles CA: The Williams Institute, UCLA School of Law.

Greene, B. (2001). Older lesbians' concerns and psychotherapy: Beyond a footnote to the footnote. In F. K. Trotman & C. M. Brody (Eds.), *Psychotherapy and counseling with older women* (pp. 161–174). New York: Springer.

Heath, J., & Goggin, K. (2009). Attitudes towards male homosexuality, bisexuality, and the Down Low lifestyle: Demographic differences and HIV. *Journal of Bisexuality, 9,* 17–31.

Herbenick, D., Reece, M., Schick, V. Sanders, S. A., Dodge, B., & Fortenberry, J. D. (2010). Sexual behavior in the United States: Results from a national probability sample of men and women aged 14–94. *Journal of Sexual Medicine, 7,* 255–265.

Herek, G. M. (2002). Heterosexuals' attitudes toward bisexual men and women in the United States. *Journal of Sex Research, 39,* 264–274.

Hershberger, S. L., & D'Augelli, A. R. (2000). Issues in counseling lesbian, gay, and bisexual adolescents. In R. M. Perez, K. A. DeBord, & K. J. Bieschke (Eds.), *Handbook of counseling and psychotherapy with lesbian, gay, and bisexual clients* (pp. 225–247). Washington, DC: American Psychological Association.

Hoburg, R., Konik, J., Williams, M., & Crawford, M. (2004). Bisexuality among self-identified heterosexual college students. *Journal of Bisexuality, 4,* 25–36.

Israel, T. (2004). Conversations, not categories: The intersection of biracial and bisexual identities. *Women & Therapy, 27,* 173–184.

Israel, T., & Mohr, J. J. (2004). Attitudes toward bisexual women and men: Current research, future directions. *Journal of Bisexuality, 4,* 117–134.

Jorm, A. F., Korten, A. E., Rodgers, B., Jacomb, P. A., & Christensen, H. (2002). Sexual orientation and mental health: Results from a community survey of young and middle aged. *British Journal of Psychiatry, 188,* 423–427.

Keppel, B. (2002). The challenges and rewards of life as an outspoken bisexual elder. *OutWord, 8,* 1, 6.

Keppel, B., & Firestein, B. A. (2007). Bisexual inclusion in issues of GLBT aging: Therapy with older bisexuals. In B. A. Firestein (Ed.), *Becoming visible: Counseling bisexuals across the lifespan* (pp. 164–185). New York: Columbia University Press.

King, A. R. (2011). Are we coming of age? A critique of Collins's proposed model of biracial-bisexual identity development. *Journal of Bisexuality, 11,* 98–120.

Lindley, L. L., Nicholson, T. J., Kerby, M. B., & Lu, N. (2003). HIV/STI associated risk behaviors among self-identified lesbian, gay, bisexual and transgender college students in the United States. *AIDS Education and Behavior, 15,* 413–429.

Lingwood, S. (2010). Bi Christian Unitarian: A theology of transgression. *Journal of Bisexuality, 10,* 31–43.

Lofgren-Martenson, L. (2009). The invisibility of young homosexual women and men with intellectual disabilities. *Sexuality and Disability, 27,* 21–26.

Malebranche, D. J. (2008). Bisexually active black men in the United States and HIV: Acknowledging more than the "down low." Retrieved June 1, 2011 from http://works.bepress.com/david_malebranche/11.

Mohr, J. J., & Rochlen, A. B. (1999). Measuring attitudes regarding bisexuality in lesbian, gay male, and heterosexual populations. *Journal of Counseling Psychology, 46,* 353–369.

Mulick, P. S., & Wright, L. W., Jr. (2002). Examining the existence of biphobia in the heterosexual and homosexual populations. *Journal of Bisexuality, 2,* 45–64.

Ochs, R. (2007). What's in a name? Why women embrace or resist bisexual identity. In B. Firestein (Ed.), *Becoming visible: Counseling bisexuals across the lifespan* (pp. 72–87). New York: Columbia University Press.

Parker, B. A., Adams, H. L., & Phillips, L. D. (2007). Decentering gender: Bisexuality identity as an expression of a non-dichotomous worldview. *Identity: An International Journal of Theory and Research, 7,* 205–224.

Paul, J. P., Catania, J., Pollack, L., Moskowitz, J., Canchola, J., Mills, T., Binson, D., & Stall, R. (2002). Suicide attempts among gay and bisexual men: Lifetime prevalence and antecedents. *American Journal of Public Health, 92,* 1338–1345.

Pennington, S. (2009). Bisexuals "Doing Gender" in romantic relationships. *Journal of Bisexuality, 9,* 33–69.

Potoczniak, D. J. (2007). Development of bisexual men's identities and relationships. In K. J. Bieschke, R. M. Perez, & K. A. DeBord (Eds.), *Handbook of counseling and psychotherapy with lesbian, gay, bisexual, and transgender clients* (pp. 119–145, 2nd ed.). Washington, DC: American Psychological Association.

Ritter, K. Y., & Terndrup, A. I. (2002). *Handbook of affirmative psychotherapy with lesbians and gay men.* New York: The Guilford Press.

Robin, L., Brener, N. D., Donahue, S. F., Hack T., Hale, K., & Goodenow, C. (2002). Associations between health risk behaviors and opposite-same-and both-sex sexual partners in representative samples of Vermont and Massachusetts high school students. *Archives of Pediatrics and Adolescent Medicine, 156,* 349–355.

Rothblum, E. D., & Factor, R. (2001). Lesbians and their sisters as a control group: Demographic and mental health factors. *Psychological Science, 12,* 63–69.

Russell, S. T., & Seif, H. (2002). Bisexual female adolescents: A critical analysis of past research, and results from a national survey. *Journal of Bisexuality, 2,* 73–94.

Rust, P. C. (1996). Managing multiple identities: Diversity among bisexual women and men. In B. A. Firestein (Ed.), *Bisexuality: The psychology and politics of an invisible minority* (pp. 53–83). Thousand Oaks, CA: Sage.

Rust, P. (2000). Bisexuality: A contemporary paradox for women. *Journal of Social Issues, 56,* 205–221.

San Francisco Human Rights Commission. (2011, March 19). Bisexual Invisibility: Impacts and recommendations. Retrieved from http://www.sfhrc.org/Modules/ShowDocument.aspx?documentid=989.

Saphira, M., & Glover, M. (2000). New Zealand national lesbian health survey. *Journal of the Gay and Lesbian Medical Association, 4,* 49–56.

Schulz, S. L. (2009). Psychological theories of disability and sexuality: A literature review. *Journal of Human Behavior in the Social Environment, 19,* 58–69.

Scott, R. L. (2006). Promoting well-being: An ecology of intervening with African American bisexual clients. *Journal of Bisexuality, 6,* 65–84.

Scott, R. L. (2007). Addressing social invalidation to promote well-being for multiracial bisexuals of African descent. In B. Firestein (Ed.), *Becoming visible: Counseling bisexuals across the lifespan* (pp. 207–228). New York: Columbia University Press.

Sheets, R. L., & Mohr, J. J. (2009). Perceived social support from friends and family and psychosocial functioning in bisexual young adult college students. *Journal of Counseling Psychology, 50,* 152–163.

Silverschanz, P. (2004). Sexual minority women and mental health: A review of the research 1992–2002. Unpublished manuscript.

Spalding, L. R., & Peplau, L. A. (1997). The unfaithful lover: Heterosexuals' perceptions of bisexuals & their relationships. *Psychology of Women Quarterly, 21,* 611–625.

Stanley, J. L. (2004). Biracial lesbian and bisexual women: Understanding the unique aspects and interactional processes of multiple minority identities. *Women & Therapy, 27,* 159–171.

Udry, J. R., & Chantala, K. (2002). Risk assessment of adolescents with same-sex relationships. *Journal of Adolescent Health, 31,* 84–92.

Warner, J., McKeown, E., Griffin, M., Johnson, K., Ramsay, A., Cort, C., & King, M. (2004). Rates and predictors of mental illness in gay men, lesbians, and bisexual men and women: Results from a survey based in England and Wales. *British Journal of Psychiatry, 185,* 479–485.

Weinberg, M. S., Williams, C. J., & Pryor, D. W. (1994). *Dual attraction.* New York: Oxford University Press.

Weinberg, M. S., Williams, C. J., & Pryor, D. W. (2001). Bisexuals at midlife: Commitment, salience, and identity. *Journal of Contemporary Ethnography, 30,* 180–208.

Wilson, P. A. (2008). A dynamic-ecological model of identity formation and conflict among bisexually-behaving African-American men. *Archives of Sexual Behavior, 37,* 694–809.

Wilson, B. D. M., & Miller, R. L. (2002). Strategies for managing heterosexism used among African American gay and bisexual men. *Journal of Black Psychology, 28,* 371–391.

4

Transgender Identities: Research and Controversies

FRANCISCO J. SÁNCHEZ AND ERIC VILAIN

Over the past decade, transgender people in the United States have been increasingly present in the cultural mainstream. For instance, the *Oprah Winfrey Show* repeatedly highlighted transgender issues and several popular television series have included transgender characters (e.g., *Ugly Betty* and *Nip-Tuck*). In 2008, Stu Rasmussen became the first openly transgender person to be elected mayor of a U.S. city (Silverton, OR). In 2009, Dylan Orr and Amanda Simpson became the first openly transgender presidential appointees (in the U.S. Department of Labor and the U.S. Commerce Department, respectively). Consequently, public awareness of transgender people has been increasing.

This heightened awareness has been beneficial to the transgender community. Not only are role models becoming more visible, but there is also a growing interest in better serving the community. For instance, the American Medical Association (2008) voted to support health insurance coverage of transgender people and to oppose any discrimination by insurance companies regarding transition-related treatments. Employers are increasingly providing employment protection based on gender identity or expression, and many are providing coverage for transition-related treatments (Human Rights Campaing, 2011). The Obama Administration added gender identity as a protected class within the federal Equal Employment Opportunity policies (Knowlton, 2010). Thus, important entities are taking steps to include transgender people within the American family.

At the same time, the number of reported crimes perpetrated against transgender people has risen (Stotzer, 2008). Unfortunately, the perpetrators are sometimes relatives of the victim who have difficulty accepting their transgender family members (Grossman, D'Augelli, Howell, & Hubbard, 2005). Even within the lesbian, gay, and bisexual community, transgender people often feel excluded and discriminated against, especially by gay men (Devor & Matte, 2004; Stone, 2009).

Nevertheless, the transgender community has become more mobilized. For instance, there are national groups that lobby political officials and educate the public (e.g., the National Center for Transgender Equality and the International Foundation for Gender Education) and transgender-specific festivals are becoming more common (e.g., *TransUnity Pride* in Los Angeles and *Translations: The Seattle Transgender Film Festival*). The Internet has also played a major role in helping people connect with one another (Shapiro, 2003). Consequently, fewer transgender people struggle alone today than did in earlier generations.

Even though the transgender community has become more visible, the field of psychology has been slow to include the experience of transgender people. Although many well-intended psychologists attempt to openly include transgender issues under the rubric of multicultural and social justice issues, some have warned against practitioners using treatments and interventions that lack empirical support (e.g., Beutler, 2009; Lilienfeld, 2007). Only within the past 5 years has the American Psychological Association (APA)—the largest association of organized psychology in the United States—directly addressed transgender issues (APA Task Force, 2008).

In this chapter, we seek to provide an overview of scientific understanding of transgender issues, drawing from empirical articles published in peer-reviewed journals. Specifically, we briefly summarize biological and psychological research aimed at understanding the development of a transgender identity, and we highlight four controversies that have caused tension among psychologists while straining the relationship between the profession and the transgender community. Although we discuss some issues related to clinical treatments, we do not provide guidelines for treatment, but instead refer readers to other sources on this topic. Our focus is on Western societies (mainly the United States); thus, we do not include any of the limited research conducted on other groups of transgender people (e.g., the *fa'afafine*; Vasey & VanderLaan, 2010). Before addressing these topics, we will provide some brief definitions.

DEFINITIONS

People in the transgender community may identify in a variety of ways including transsexual, cross-dresser, and intersex [see Bockting (2008) for a discussion of various descriptors]. Here we provide some key definitions as used in this chapter:

- *Birth sex* refers to the sex assigned to a baby at birth (Vilain, 2000).
- *Gender identity* is a person's psychological sense of maleness or femaleness (Stoller, 1968).
- *Transgender* is an "umbrella term" that refers to people whose gender identity and/or gender expression differ in important ways from their birth sex (Davidson, 2007).
- *Transsexual* refers to a person who lives or desires to live full-time as a person opposite to their birth sex; often the person takes drastic steps to alter his or her anatomy and physiology so that it is congruent with his or her identity (APA Task Force, 2008).
- *Cross-dresser* is a person who dresses in clothing customary for the opposite-sex; cross-dressing does not necessarily mean that a person is a transsexual or that he or she is doing it for sexual reasons (Brown et al., 1996).
- *Intersex* refers to conditions characterized by atypical sexual development resulting from genetic, chromosomal, or hormonal anomalies (Vilain, 2000).

TRANSSEXUALISM

A keyword search of the terms "transgend*" and "transsex*" on *PubMed* yielded 3188 peer-reviewed articles, and on *PsycINFO* yielded 2806 peer-reviewed articles (as of May 30, 2012)—a large number given the proportion of the population that they represent. Few articles, however, address the psychological well-being and the positive aspects of transgender people. That is, most studies have focused on etiology and psychopathology. Furthermore, most research has focused on male-to-female (MTF) transsexuals. Although this work is important, it presents a very limited view of the experience of being transgender (Hill, 2005).

In terms of prevalence, no epidemiological study of transsexualism has been conducted in the United States. The American Psychiatric Association (2000) estimates that 1 in 30,000 males are MTF transsexual and 1 in 100,000 females are female-to-male (FTM) transsexual. These estimates are markedly lower than figures from population-based studies conducted in Europe and Asia. For instance, a study in the Netherlands found a prevalence of 1 in 11,900 for MTF transsexualism and 1 in 30,400 for FTM transsexualism (Bakker, van Kesteren, Gooren, & Bezemer, 1993). In Singapore, the prevalence was reported as being 1 in 2900 for MTF transsexualism and 1 in 8300 for FTM transsexualism (Tsoi, 1988).

The development of a transsexual identity is complex. Most transsexuals report feeling "different" since early childhood (Mason-Schrock, 1996; Morgan & Stevens, 2008). Once a person assumes a transsexual identity, he or she may take several steps to alter the body so that it is congruent with his or her gender identity (e.g., taking cross-sex hormones). Several factors can influence the decision to transition from one sex to the other including family of origin, economic barriers, current surgical practices, and personal choice. Many transsexuals only do partial treatments (e.g., FTM transsexuals who take all the physical steps except having a phalloplasty; Cohen-Kettenis & Pfäfflin, 2010).

Although many transsexuals seek medical and mental health services, as of this writing no major professional organization within the United States (e.g., APA, American Medical Association, and American Academy of Pediatrics) has adopted practice guidelines to aid in the transition from one sex to the other. However, the World Professional Association for Transgender Health (WPATH) has devised standards of care to provide clinical guidance for health professionals who are working with transgender people (WPATH, 2011). For instance, WPATH recommended that transsexuals be at the age of majority before commencing hormone therapy and surgery, and that they live in the gender role congruent with their identity for 12 continuous months before undergoing genital surgery.

Although some objected to previous versions of these standards (e.g., Jacob, 2007), as of this writing, it is unclear how the new standards are being received by healthcare providers.

MTF TRANSSEXUALS

As previously mentioned, most studies on transgender people have focused on MTF transsexuals. This may be in part because the prevalence of MTF transsexualism is greater than for other members of the transgender community. Here we highlight trends that have been noted in this subgroup and theories about their developmental trajectory.

There are two distinct periods of life during which most MTF transsexuals begin their transition—a bimodal trend not seen among FTM transsexuals (Nieder et al., 2011). The first period occurs in childhood or adolescence, and the second period occurs at mid-life. Several characteristics are common—though not exclusive—within these two groups of MTF transsexuals in the United States (see Table 4.1; Nuttbrock et al., 2011). Those who transition earlier in life are typically members of racial or ethnic minority groups, come from lower socioeconomic backgrounds, report more stereotypically feminine occupational interests, are sexually attracted to men, and have a relatively easy time "passing" as a woman (i.e., a stranger may not realize that the person is a transsexual). Those who transition later in life are typically white (non-Latino), come from middle-class backgrounds, report more stereotypically masculine occupational interests, are

sexually attracted to women before transitioning (though some may identify as asexual or bisexual), report a history of marriage and having children (Maguen, Shipher, Harris, & Welch, 2007), and have mixed results "passing" as a woman (Smith, van Goozen, Kuiper, & Cohen-Kettenis, 2005).

The empirical literature may refer to MTF transsexuals by one of several dichotomous labels (Blanchard, 1985; Burns, Farrell, & Brown, 1990; Smith et al., 2005). These terms are presented in the bottom row of Table 4.1 for readers unfamiliar with such usage. It should be noted, however, that some find such categorical labels—especially the homosexual versus nonhomosexual label relative to birth sex—as offensive (Lane, 2008).

In noting the differences between these two groups, Blanchard (1989, 1991, 2005) reported that the etiology for these groups might differ. Specifically, late transitioners may experience a type of paraphilia termed *autogynephilia* (or self-woman-love) rather than gender dysphoria. We will discuss this controversial concept later in this chapter.

Some members of the Los Angeles transgender community have offered an alternative explanation regarding why MTF transsexuals come out at different periods in their lives (V. Ortega, personal communication, July 16, 2009). Given that early transitioners typically come from lower socioeconomic backgrounds and from racial/ethnic minority groups, they may not feel the pressure to adhere to traditional ideals regarding success in the United States. Thus, they have less to lose by coming out

TABLE 4.1. CHARACTERISTICS COMMONLY NOTED AMONG MALE-TO-FEMALE TRANSSEXUALS WHO TRANSITION EARLIER VERSUS LATER IN LIFE

	Transition Earlier in Life	Transition Later in Life
Life stage during which female identity is fully adopted	Childhood/adolescence	Middle adulthood
Race/ethnicity	Not White	White (non-Latino)
Stereotypical interests	More feminine than masculine	More masculine than feminine
Sexual attraction pretransition	Attracted to men	Attracted to women
Can pass as a woman?	Yes	No
Terms that may be associated with the group in the literature[a]	Early-onset Core group Homosexual transsexual Primary transsexual	Late-onset Noncore group Nonhomosexual transsexual Secondary transsexual

Note. These characteristics are common—though not exclusive—within these two groups of MTF transsexuals in the United States (see Nuttbrock et al., 2011).
a = Some of the terms are considered offensive (Lane, 2008)

at an early age and/or they are already used to feeling marginalized in the United States. In contrast, because late transitioners are typically white (non-Latino), come from more affluent families, and tend to hold high-status jobs (e.g., businessmen and engineers), there is far more privilege for them to lose by identifying as transsexual. Although this explanation has not been empirically evaluated, it is possible that demographic variables and cultural values contribute to the decision to disclose a transsexual identity.

EMPIRICAL RESEARCH ON TRANSSEXUALISM

Most transgender research has concentrated on transsexuals—specifically MTF transsexuals. In this section, we will review the research on the development of a transsexual identity by first focusing on biological research and then focusing on psychological research.

Biological Research

Some researchers have examined biological factors that may contribute to a transsexual identity. Three specific lines of research include hormone studies, genetic studies, and brain studies. Below is a brief review of the limited biological research. Interested readers can find further details in Sánchez, Bocklandt, and Vilain (2009).

The first line of research has focused on the influence of sex hormones (i.e., androgens and estrogens). The main hypotheses are that transsexuals (1) have atypical levels of sex hormones during fetal development that "organized" the body and brain differently, and/or (2) have atypical levels of circulating sex hormones during adulthood that affected their gender identity. Falsifying the first hypothesis (i.e., manipulating human fetuses) would be difficult and unethical. The closest approximation has been to study people who were exposed to atypical levels of sex hormones *in utero*—specifically women with congenital adrenal hyperplasia who were exposed to high levels of androgens. Studies of such women, however, have found that the majority of them do not experience gender dysphoria (Dessens, Slijper, & Drop, 2005).

Studies testing the latter hormonal hypothesis have reported inconsistent findings. Early reports found atypical levels of sex hormones in MTF transsexuals (Starká, Spiová, & Hynie, 1975) and FTM transsexuals (Spiová & Starká, 1977). However, several other studies failed to replicate the findings (e.g., Meyer, Webb, Stuart, Finkelstein, Lawrence, & Walker, 1986; Spijkstra, Spinder, & Gooren, 1988). Furthermore, reports on a higher incidence of polycystic ovarian syndrome—which is associated with an excessive amount of androgen—among FTM transsexuals have been inconsistent (cf. Baba et al., 2007; Mueller, Gooren, Naton-Schötz, Cupisti, Beckmann, & Dittrich, 2008). Overall, support for a hormonal hypothesis is extremely sparse and limited to FTM transsexuals.

The second line of biological research has focused on genetic influences. Unlike many behavioral traits, transsexualism does not cooccur within families at rates high enough to employ traditional methods such as genetic-linkage analysis (Green, 2000)—an approach that traces the inheritance of genes. Nevertheless, candidate genes (genes suspected of contributing to a trait) have been examined, including genes that play a role in "masculinizing" the brain, in biochemically modifying androgens, and in moderating the concentration of sex hormones (e.g., Hare et al., 2009; Henningsson et al., 2005). Findings have been notably inconsistent. Large-scale studies are underway, but no genes have as yet been pinpointed.

The third line of biological research has focused on brain structure and function. Brain autopsy studies conducted in the Netherlands found that the size and neuronal density of specific brain regions in six MTF transsexual looked more like female than male controls (Kruijver et al., 2000; Zhou et al., 1995); however, these findings were criticized because the transsexual participants had been on estrogen therapy for numerous years (Hulshoff Pol et al., 2006). Subsequently, magnetic resonance imaging (MRI) studies conducted on transsexuals before receiving any hormonal treatment have found differences when compared to controls. For instance, specific brain regions in transsexuals have been found to be more similar to the brain regions in people of the opposite birth sex [e.g., the putamen in MTF transsexuals (Luders et al., 2009) and the distribution of white matter in FTM transsexuals (Rametti et al., 2011)]. These preliminary findings suggest that there may be distinct neuroanatomy associated with a transsexual identity.

Overall, the biological mechanisms involved in the development of gender identity have yet to be identified. Although there are promising preliminary findings from genetics and neuroscience, these findings would need to be replicated in larger samples before confidence could be placed in them. Advances in scientific technology may contribute to a greater understanding of the biological influences on gender identity.

Psychological Research

Psychological studies have yielded few if any significant results in identifying factors that may influence the development of a transgender identity. Many of the unsubstantiated theories for a transgender identity development mirror the theories that were once used to explain homosexuality (e.g., McCord, McCord, & Thurber, 1962).

First, some hypothesized that a cross-gender identity may be the result of the person's parent of the same birth sex being absent during childhood (Green, 1971; Stoller, 1979) or an enmeshed relationship with the parent of the opposite sex (Green, 1974). However, studies testing these hypotheses have yielded inconsistent results, including observations of more distant relationships between transgender children and their fathers (Buhrich & McConaghy, 1978; Cohen-Kettenis & Arrindell, 1990), more "affiliative" relationships between transgender children and their fathers (Newcombe, 1985), no difference in the relationships between transgender children and both parents (Bullough, Bullough, & Smith, 1983), and no adverse effects of an absent parent (Stevens et al., 2002). Even though the studies have their limitations, it appears that transsexuals may come from families that are similar to families in the general population (Docter, 1988; Prince & Bentler, 1972).

A second hypothesis is that transsexuals were forced or encouraged to behave in gender-atypical ways as children. For example, if parents had wished for a boy, then they may have treated their daughter like a boy (Ball, 1967). There are a few reports of transsexuals recounting that their parents encouraged them to behave in gender-atypical ways (Schott, 1995), that their parents had wished for an opposite-sex child before the birth (Buhrich & McConaghy, 1978), or that their parents had punished them by requiring them to wear clothing of the opposite sex (Prince & Bentler, 1972). However, such reports are uncommon and no causative link between such parental behavior and a transsexual identity has ever been established.

A third hypothesis is that a transgender identity is the result of childhood abuse (e.g., as a dissociative coping mechanism; Devor, 1994). Numerous studies have found that transgender adults recall being emotionally, physically, and sexually abused at higher rates than the general population (e.g., Gehring & Knudson, 2005; Koken, Bimbi, & Parsons, 2009). Nonetheless, it is difficult to determine causation in these cross-sectional studies.

Overall, psychological theory and research have been less than successful at identifying factors that contribute to the development of a transsexual identity. This failure to substantiate psychological theories regarding the emergence of a transgender identity may actually have ruled out the idea that such identities are the result of a problem within the person or the environment. This does not mean that environmental factors do not play a role. Rather, their influence is either minimal or dependent on the presence of specific biological predispositions.

CONTROVERSIES

The relationship between psychology and members of the transgender community has been affected by many factors. Four specific controversies that have strained that relationship include gender identity disorder as a diagnosable mental disorder, the description of autogynephilia among MTF transsexuals, the treatment of childhood gender nonconformity, and the proposition that transsexualism is an intersex condition.

Gender Identity Disorder as a Diagnosis

Transsexuals who wish to transition from one sex to the other usually work within the existing medical system. Consequently, physicians and mental health professionals historically served as providers as well as gatekeepers to treatment. Although some transsexuals find other ways to receive treatment (e.g., purchasing hormones from unauthorized vendors and seeking treatment overseas), many seek treatment within the medical system. Currently, as part of this treatment, transsexuals are often diagnosed with Gender Identity Disorder (GID) to receive care.

The full criteria for GID can be found in the fourth edition of the *Diagnostic and Statistical Manual of Mental Disorders* (*DSM–IV–TR*; American Psychiatric Association, 2000). To receive this diagnosis, the person's gender identity must cause "clinically significant distress or impairment in social, occupational, or other important areas of functioning" (Criterion D; American Psychiatric

Association, 2000, p. 576). However, the key characteristic of GID is the experience of *gender dysphoria* or marked distress because the person's birth sex does not match their experienced gender identity.

It is important to understand that neither slight variations in gender role behavior (Bockting & Ehrbar, 2005) nor behaviors that simply conflict with society's gender norms (American Psychiatric Association, 2000, p. xxxi) warrant a diagnosis of GID. Furthermore, people who have been diagnosed with a "physical intersex condition" do not fit within the GID criteria (Criterion C; American Psychiatric Association, 2000, p. 576), though a person with an intersex condition can be diagnosed with GID–Not Otherwise Specified (American Psychiatric Association, 2000, p. 582). The *DSM–IV–TR* criteria, nonetheless, have been criticized for being vague and as being used to diagnosis GID in people who experience no dysphoria (Lev, 2004).

There are several other criticisms regarding GID (Cohen-Kettenis & Pfäfflin, 2010; Meyer-Bahlburg, 2010). First, some have argued that it is society's sanctions regarding gender-atypical behavior that cause gender dysphoria; if society were accepting of individual differences, then people who do not conform to gender norms would suffer no distress (Ault & Brzuzy, 2009). Second, some have suggested that the term "disorder" further stigmatized people who were already ostracized in society (Wilson, 2000; Winters, 2005); thus, a different diagnostic label should be used such as gender dysphoria (Johnson & Wassersug, 2010). Third, GID can be used to deny civil rights including parental rights (Hill et al., 2007; Winters, 2005). Fourth, it has been suggested that requiring transsexuals to engage in psychotherapy to receive transition-related treatment is also stigmatizing and inappropriate (Hale, 2007; Lev, 2009).

On the other hand, there are several reasons why GID can be seen as a justifiable diagnosis. First, it has been argued that even if society were open to all forms of gender expression, transsexuals would still experience marked distress because their anatomy would be incongruent with their gender identity (Bockting & Ehrbar, 2005; Zucker, 2006). Second, the term "disorder" is used for a condition that requires clinical attention and not as a label for a person (American Psychiatric Association, 2000, p. xxxi). Although the term can be replaced, it is likely that any new term would eventually fall out of favor. Third, the diagnosis of a

mental disorder can be used to justify and to facilitate treatment (Bockting & Ehrbar, 2005)—especially when third-party payers are involved—and to challenge legal discrimination (Dasti, 2002; Levi, 2006). Fourth, the necessity to engage in psychotherapy to receive treatment for GID is intended to aid in transition-related issues (e.g., loss of significant relationships, intrapersonal conflicts, and loss of employment) and increase the likelihood of a positive outcome (Meyer et al., 2001). This latter point is especially relevant to secondary transitioners as the few reported regrets in the literature have mainly been expressed by transsexuals in this group (Olsson & Möller, 2006; van Kesteren, Asscheman, Megens, & Gooren, 1997).

It should be noted that the *DSM* is currently under revision and much controversy envelopes the empirical review of GID (Ehrbar, 2010). As of this writing, it appears that GID will be retained as a diagnosable disorder—although there are proposals for changing the name and modifying the criteria (Lawrence, 2010a). However, the diagnostic threshold for GID may become more stringent to decrease the inappropriate use of the diagnosis (Zucker, 2010).

Autogynephilia

As mentioned earlier, there seem to be at least two general groups of MTF transsexuals. Noting this trend, Blanchard (1985) attempted to understand what differentiated those who came out earlier in life and were mainly attracted to men from those who came out later in life and were mainly attracted to women. Of the differences he found, one characteristic was prominent: the latter group more often reported a history of transvestic fetishism or an interest in cross-dressing to express sexual or erotic interests compared to the earlier group (Blanchard, 1989, 1991). Such interest dated to childhood and seemed to go beyond merely cross-dressing to include fantasies of having breasts and a vulva, often accompanied with sexual arousal and masturbation (see Lawrence, 1999a, 1999b). Blanchard (2005) concluded that the motive for many who transitioned later in life was rooted in an extreme paraphilia versus gender dysphoria.

Blanchard termed this phenomenon *autogynephilia* given that the sexual interest was directed at the self as a woman (Blanchard, 2005). As with almost all paraphilias (American Psychiatric Association, 2000), characteristics consistent with autogynephilia have been reported only among men. Although one report claimed to identify autogynephilia among women (i.e., they were sexually aroused about being women), the report was criticized because sexual arousal within a person for features they already possess is markedly different from arousal over physical features that they do not have (Lawrence, 2010b).

Even though Blanchard and others had been studying and publishing reports on autogynephilia for almost two decades, the concept did not receive much public attention until the publication of the book *The Man Who Would Be Queen* (Bailey, 2003), which highlighted Blanchard's theory. Criticisms of the book were intense and multifaceted, and they are too complex to elucidate here. Interested readers can find details in an issue of the *Archives of Sexual Behavior* (2008, volume 37, issue 3) with a comprehensive review by Dreger (2008) and a series of responses.

It should be noted that in the wake of the book controversy, peer-reviewed articles criticizing Blanchard's methodology have begun to emerge (Moser, 2010; Serano, 2010). To date, only one empirical report has offered an alternative explanation for Blanchard's findings. Using a community-based and multiracial/ethnic sample recruited in New York City (versus Blanchard's presumably white [non-Latino] clinical samples), Nuttbrock et al. (2011) found that age and race were significant predictors of characteristics consistent with autogynephilia. They concluded that autogynephilia may be due to a cohort or generational effect and thus will become a "fading phenomenon" (p. 256).

It can be debated whether the intensity of the anger and the *ad hominem* attacks against Blanchard, Bailey, and their supporters were justified. What cannot be debated is the degree to which this controversy strained the relationship between mental health researchers and professionals and the transgender community. We encountered resistance in our own work when we extended our laboratory's research on Disorders of Sex Development and intersex conditions to include the experience of transsexuals. Only through regular engagement with the community and development of relationships with transgender leaders were we able to gain the trust of community members. Even though we were not involved with the work that precipitated the autogynephilia controversy, it is not surprising that we encountered such resistance from a marginalized community whose leaders were angry with researchers who had focused on their lives in a way seen as demeaning.

At the same time, if there are MTF transsexuals motivated to transition because of sexual interests, then it would seem that fully understanding their experiences versus the experiences of those motivated to transition for other reasons would be beneficial (Bailey & Triea, 2007). For instance, are there unique variables that predict a successful transition based on someone's motives? Regardless of how and why people develop a transsexual identity, we believe that transsexuals should have the right to self-determination if there is full consent and if there is evidence that their well-being will likely improve; but we also realize that not everyone holds this position.

Gender Nonconformity in Children

In listening to the life histories of many transsexuals, it is common to hear that the distress over their birth sex began in childhood (e.g., Mason-Schrock, 1996; Morgan & Stevens, 2008). Furthermore, many believe that if they had been allowed to express themselves freely as children and had begun the transition earlier in life, they would have avoided considerable anguish. Consequently, there has been increased interest in determining how best to treat children who express cross-sex interests and behaviors. We briefly review this literature.

Most infants develop a gender identity that is congruent with their birth sex, though the degree to which they adhere to society's norms regarding gender roles may vary. Nevertheless, once a person identifies as male or female, that identity will likely remain constant throughout life (Gouze & Nadelman, 1980; Ruble et al., 2007). This process, however, is not so simple for all children (Zucker, 2005).

A small percentage of children experience significant distress because they express interests and behaviors that are characterized as gender nonconforming (e.g., a girl only playing with boys, which is atypical for young children; or a boy consistently wanting to wear clothing typically worn by girls). Furthermore, some children state that they do not identify with their birth sex. This experience may lead caretakers to seek out professional services (Di Ceglie & Thümmel, 2006; Zucker, 2005). Yet, how best to respond to or treat a child exhibiting marked gender nonconformity is a contentious issue.

On one end of the treatment continuum, professionals have argued that families should support their gender-nonconforming children (e.g., Burke, 1996; Pickstone-Taylor, 2003) and that such children should be allowed to begin the process of transitioning early in life (Johnson, 2008; Spack, 2009). Rather than conducting behavior modification or psychotherapy on the child, it is the family that should receive psychotherapy in order to help them understand and accept their child's gender nonconformity. From this standpoint, those who diagnose children and adolescents with GID and engage in treatments aimed at encouraging gender conformity are engaging in a form of social coercion and control (Hill, Rozanski, Carfagnini, & Willoughby, 2007). Given that there is some evidence that pressuring children to conform to traditional gender roles may cause depressive symptoms (Yunger, Carver, & Perry, 2004), some have claimed that any treatment of children for gender nonconformity will lead to deleterious psychological consequences (Hill et al., 2007).

On the other end of the treatment continuum, professionals have argued that children exhibiting gender nonconformity must be actively treated to make their public appearance and behavior congruent with their birth sex. Although it would be ideal to change society's views on gender nonconformity, for now gender-nonconforming children will likely be subjected to cruel treatment. Thus, the child should learn how to conform while in public to avoid distress (Zucker, 2006). Furthermore, several longitudinal studies (e.g., Drummond, Bradley, Peterson-Badali, & Zucker, 2008; Green, 1987; Wallien & Cohen-Kettenis, 2008) have found that the majority of gender-nonconforming children eventually adopt a gender identity that is congruent with their birth sex—including many who repeatedly voiced wanting to be a member of the opposite sex. Instead of foreshadowing a transsexual identity, childhood gender nonconformity seems more often to predict same-sex attraction in adulthood.

The results of these longitudinal studies should make practitioners cautious about the advice they offer to parents, especially because certain procedures (e.g., providing cross-sex hormones or surgery) may have irreversible and deleterious effects. Unfortunately, there are few if any outcome studies published in peer-reviewed journals (e.g., Cohen-Kettenis, Delemarre-van de Waal, & Gooren, 2008). Because empirically supported treatments

for children and adolescents do not exist, healthcare professionals should proceed with caution.

Transsexualism as an Intersex Condition

Some have argued that transsexuals have an "intersex condition" or that they are biologically between males and females (e.g., Diamond, 2000; Goswami, 2010). Such claims are based on research findings suggesting that transsexuals have anatomical regions that are not as "masculine–feminine" as expected for their birth sex. We reviewed these biological studies in a previous section. In this section, we briefly discuss intersex conditions—now categorized as Disorders of Sex Development (DSD; Houk, Hughes, Ahmed, & Lee, 2006; Vilain et al., 2007)—and argue that transsexualism is not an intersex condition.

Physicians and midwives make the determination of birth sex seem simple: They proclaim "it's a boy" or "it's a girl" by merely looking at a newborn's external genitalia. Typically, this gross determination accurately assesses the characteristics related to biological sex including sex chromosomes, gene expression, sex hormones, and internal reproductive structures (Vilain, 2000). However, in rare instances atypical biological traits may be present (e.g., an XX male or XY female) that fall within the realm of a DSD (Vilain et al., 2007).

DSDs arise from biological anomalies that affect a person's reproductive structures and capabilities. Most people with a DSD are incapable of reproducing. For instance, a developing fetus with two X-chromosomes should develop as a female. However, the accidental presence of male-specific genes will cause the fetus to develop as a male (i.e., with a penis, testis, scrotum, and no female reproductive structures). Yet, there are critical genes on the Y-chromosome necessary to produce spermatozoa; thus, an XX male will be infertile. More information on DSDs can be found in Arboleda and Vilain (2009).

Although not all DSDs result in infertile persons (e.g., women with congenital adrenal hyperplasia are fertile), they all share the characteristic of affecting anatomical and physiological characteristics that play a critical role in reproduction. Yet, the overwhelming majority of transsexuals are fully capable of reproducing in their birth sex. Furthermore, the majority of people with DSDs do not report gender dysphoria (Dreger & Herndon, 2009; Intersex Society of North America, n.d.). Consequently, although anyone may identify as "intersex," transsexualism does not fall under the realm of DSDs or intersex conditions as defined here (Mazur, Colsman, & Sandberg, 2007).

CONCLUSIONS

The transgender community is a highly diverse group of people that is becoming more visible within society. The public emergence of this community has helped reduce the number of people who suffer alone with gender dysphoria. Although many professionals have sought to help transgender people, good intentions do not necessarily translate into good practices. The role of scientific research is critical to the understanding and treatment of transgender people.

As the number of people who openly identify as transgender and who seek mental health services continues to grow, it will be important for psychologists to address the real-life concerns of these individuals. It is essential that there be collaboration between psychological scientists and practitioners to better serve the needs of this community—especially alleviating distress and promoting well-being (Sánchez & Vilain, 2009). Mental health practices for the transgender community cannot depend entirely on anecdotal reports or clinical intuition (Spence, 2001); there must be empirical support for any interventions that are used. Psychological scientists can assess the process and outcome of therapeutic interventions and must translate their findings so that they are relevant to practitioners (Beutler, 2009). Psychological practitioners have the skills to engage directly with transgender people and apply treatment. By working together, psychological scientists and practitioners can focus on important issues to further the scientific base of knowledge and to enhance the quality of life for transgender people.

REFERENCES

American Medical Association. (2008, June). *Resolution 122 on removing financial barriers to care for transgender patients.* Retrieved July 12, 2010 from http://www.ama-assn.org/ama1/pub/upload/mm/16/a08_hod_resolutions.pdf.

American Psychiatric Association. (2000). *Diagnostic and statistical manual of mental disorders* (4th ed., text revision). Washington, DC: Author.

APA Task Force on Gender Identity and Gender Variance. (2008). *Report of the Task Force on Gender Identity and Gender Variance.* Washington, DC: American Psychological Association.

Arboleda, V. A., & Vilain, E. (2009). Disorders of sex development. In J. F. Strauss, III, & R. L. Barbieri (Eds.), *Yen and Jaffe's reproductive endocrinology: Physiology, pathophysiology, and clinical management* (6th ed.). Philadelphia, PA: Saunders Elsevier. doi: 10.1016/B978-1-4160-4907-4.00016-4.

Ault, A., & Brzuzy, S. (2009). Removing Gender Identity Disorder from the *Diagnostic and Statistical Manual of Mental Disorders*: A call for action [Commentary]. *Social Work, 54,* 187–189.

Baba, T., Endo, T., Honnma, H., Kitajima, Y., Hayashi, T., Ikeda, H.,…Saito, T. (2007). Association between polycystic ovary syndrome and female-to-male transsexuality. *Human Reproduction, 22,* 1011–1016. doi: 10.1093/humrep/del474.

Bailey, J. M. (2003). *The man who would be queen.* Washington, DC: Joseph Henry Press.

Bailey, J. M., & Triea, K. (2007). What many transgender activists don't want you to know and why you should know it anyway. *Perspectives in Biology & Medicine, 50,* 521–534.

Bakker, A., van Kesteren, P. J. M., Gooren, L. J. G., & Bezemer, P. D. (1993). The prevalence of transsexualism in the Netherlands. *Acta Psychiatrica Scandinavica, 87,* 237–238. doi: 10.1111/j.1600-0447.1993.tb03364.x.

Ball, J. R. B. (1967). Transsexualism and transvestitism. *Australian & New Zealand Journal of Psychiatry, 1,* 188–195.

Beutler, L. E. (2009). Making science matter in clinical practice: Redefining psychotherapy. *Clinical Psychology: Science & Practice, 16,* 301–317. doi: 10.1111/j.1468-2850.2009.01168.x.

Blanchard, R. (1985). Typology of male-to-female transsexualism. *Archives of Sexual Behavior, 14,* 247–261.

Blanchard, R. (1989). The classification and labeling of nonhomosexual gender dysphoria. *Archives of Sexual Behavior, 18,* 315–334.

Blanchard, R. (1991). Clinical observation and systematic studies of autogynephilia. *Journal of Sex & Marital Therapy, 17,* 235–251.

Blanchard, R. (2005). Early history of the concept of autogynephilia. *Archives of Sexual Behavior, 34,* 439–446. doi: 10.1007/s10508-005-4343-8.

Bockting, W. O. (2008). Psychotherapy and the real-life experience: From gender dichotomy to gender diversity. *Sexologies, 17,* 211–224. doi: 10.1016/j.sexol.2008.08.001.

Bockting, W. O., & Ehrbar, R. (2005). Commentary: Gender variance, dissonance, or disorder? *Journal of Psychology & Human Sexuality, 17,* 125–134.

Brown, G. R., Wise, T. N., Costa, P. T., Herbst, J. H., Fagan, P. J., & Schmidt, C. W. (1996). Personality characteristics and sexual functioning of 188 cross-dressing men. *Journal of Nervous & Mental Disease, 184,* 265–273. doi: 10.1097/00005053-199605000-00001.

Buhrich, N., & McConaghy, N. (1978). Parental relationships during childhood in homosexuality, transvestism, and transsexualism. *Australian & New Zealand Journal of Psychiatry, 12,* 103–108.

Bullough, V. L., Bullough, B., & Smith, R. (1983). A comparative study of male transvestites, male to female transsexuals, and male homosexuals. *Journal of Sex Research, 19,* 238–257.

Burke, P. (1996). *Gender shock.* New York: Anchor.

Burns, A., Farrell, M. L., & Brown, J. C. (1990). Clinical features of patients attending a gender-identity clinic. *British Journal of Psychiatry, 157,* 265–268.

Cohen-Kettenis, P. T., & Arrindell, W. A. (1990). Perceived parental rearing style, parental divorce and transsexualism: A controlled study. *Psychological Medicine, 20,* 613–620.

Cohen-Kettenis, P. T., Delemarre-van de Waal, H. A., & Gooren, L. J. G. (2008). The treatment of adolescent transsexuals: Changing insights. *Journal of Sexual Medicine, 5,* 1892–1897. doi: 10.1111/j.1743–6109.2008.00870.x.

Cohen-Kettenis, P. T., & Pfäfflin, F. (2010). The *DSM* diagnostic criteria for Gender Identity Disorder in adolescents and adults. *Archives of Sexual Behavior, 39,* 499–513. doi: 10.1007/s10508–009–9562-y.

Dasti, J. L. (2002). Advocating a broader understanding of the necessity of sex-reassignment surgery under Medicaid. *New York University Law Review, 77,* 1738–1775.

Davidson, M. (2007). Seeking refuge under the umbrella: Inclusion, exclusion, and organizing within the category transgender. *Sexuality Research & Social Policy, 4*(4), 60–80.

Dessens, A. B., Slijper, F. M. E., & Drop, S. L. S. (2005). Gender dysphoria and gender change in chromosomal females with congenital adrenal hyperplasia. *Archives of Sexual Behavior, 34,* 389–397. doi: 10.1007/s10508–005–4338–5.

Devor, H. (1994). Transsexualism, dissociation, and child abuse: An initial discussion based on nonclinical data. *Journal of Psychology & Human Sexuality, 6,* 49–72. doi: 10.1300/J056v06n03_04.

Devor, A. H., & Matte, N. (2004). ONE Inc. and Reed Erickson: The uneasy collaboration of gay and trans activism. *GLQ: A Journal of Gay and Lesbian Studies, 10,* 179–209.

Di Ceglie, D., & Thümmel, E. C. (2006). An experience of group work with parents of children and adolescents with gender identity disorder. *Clinical Child Psychology & Psychiatry, 11,* 387–396. doi:10.1177/1359104506064983.

Diamond, M. (2000). IV. Sex and gender: Same or different? *Feminism & Psychology, 10,* 46–54. doi: 10.1177/0959353500010001007.

Docter, R. F. (1988). *Transvestites and transsexuals: Toward a theory of cross-gender behavior.* New York: Plenum Press.

Dreger, A. D. (2008). The controversy surrounding *The Man Who Would be Queen*: A case history of the politics of science, identity, and sex in the Internet

age. *Archives of Sexual Behavior, 37,* 366–421. doi: 10.1007/s10508–007–9301–1.

Dreger, A. D., & Herndon, A. M. (2009). Progress and politics in the intersex rights movement: Feminist theory in action. *GLQ: A Journal of Lesbian & Gay Studies, 15,* 199–224. doi: 10.1215/10642684–2008–134.

Drummond, K. D., Bradley, S. J., Peterson-Badali, M., & Zucker, K. J. (2008). A follow-up of girls with gender identity disorder. *Developmental Psychology, 44,* 34–45. doi: 10.1037/0012–1649.44.1.34.

Ehrbar, R. D. (2010). Consensus from differences: Lack of professional consensus on the retention of the gender identity disorder diagnosis. *International Journal of Transgenderism, 12,* 60–74. doi: 10.1080/15532739.2010.513928.

Gehring, D., & Knudson, G. (2005). Prevalence of childhood trauma in a clinical population of transsexual people. *International Journal of Transgenderism, 8,* 23–30. doi: 10.1300/J485v08n01_03.

Goswami, B. A. (2010, March 14). I believe transsexuals are intersexed individuals [Web log post]. Retrieved from http://oiiinternational.com/blog/2544/doctor-milton-diamond-transsexuals-intersexed-individuals/

Gouze, K. R., & Nadelman, L. (1980). Constancy of gender identity for self and others in children between the ages of three and seven. *Child Development, 51,* 275–278.

Green, R. (1971). Diagnosis and treatment of gender identity disorders during childhood. *Archives of Sexual Behavior, 1,* 161–173.

Green, R. (1974). *Sexual identity conflict in children and adults.* London: Gerald Duckworth.

Green, R. (1987). Specific cross-gender behaviour in boyhood and later homosexual orientation. *British Journal of Psychiatry, 151,* 84–88.

Green, R. (2000). Family cooccurence of "gender dysphoria": Ten sibling or parent–child pairs. *Archives of Sexual Behavior, 29,* 499–507.

Grossman, A. H., D'Augelli, A. R., Howell, T. J., & Hubbard, S. (2005). Parents' reactions to transgender youths' gender nonconforming expression and identity. *Journal of Gay & Lesbian Social Services, 18,* 3–16.

Hale, C. J. (2007). Ethical problems with the mental health evaluation standards of care for adult gender variant prospective patients. *Perspective in Biology & Medicine, 50,* 491–505. doi: 10.1353/pbm.2007.0047.

Hare, L., Bernard, P., Sánchez, F. J., Vilain, E., Kennedy, T., & Harley, V. R. (2009). Androgen receptor (*AR*) repeat length polymorphism associated with male-to-female transsexualism. *Biological Psychiatry, 65,* 93–96. doi:10.1016/j.biopsych.2008.08.033.

Henningsson, S., Westberg, L., Nilsson, S., Lundström, B., Ekselius, L., Bodlund, O.,…Landén, M. (2005). Sex steroid-related genes and male-to-female transsexualism. *Psychoneuroendocrinology, 30,* 657–664. doi: 10.1016/j.psyneuen.2005.02.006.

Hill, D. B. (2005). Trans/gender/sexuality: A research agenda. *Journal of Gay & Lesbian Social Services, 18,* 101–109. doi: 10.1300/J041v18n02_06.

Hill, D. B., Rozanski, C., Carfagnini, J., & Willoughby, B. (2007). Gender identity disorders in children and adolescence: A critical inquiry. *International Journal of Sexual Health, 19,* 57–75. doi: 10.1300/J514v19n01_07.

Houk, C. P., Hughes, I. A., Ahmed, F., & Lee, P. A. (2006). Summary of consensus statement on intersex disorders and their management. *Pediatrics, 118,* 753–757. doi: 10.1542/peds.2006–0737.

Hulshoff Pol, H. E., Cohen-Kettenis, P. T., van Haren, N. E. M., Peper, J. S., Brans, R. G. H., Cahn, W., ... Kahn, R. S. (2006). Changing your sex changes your brain: Influences of testosterone and estrogen on adult human brain structure. *European Journal of Endocrinology, 155,* S107–S114. doi: 10.1530/eje.1.02248.

Human Rights Campaign. (2011). *Corporate equality index 2012: Rating American workplaces on lesbian, gay, bisexual, and transgender equality.* Washington, DC: Author. Available at www.hrc.org/cei.

Intersex Society of North America. (n.d.). What's the difference between being transgender or transsexual and having an intersex condition? Retrieved July 14, 2010 from http://www.isna.org/faq/transgender.

Jacob, H. D. (2007). Ethical problems with the mental health evaluation standards of care for adult gender variant prospective patients. *Perspectives in Biology & Medicine, 50,* 491–505. doi: 10.1353/pbm.2007.0047.

Johnson, C. (2008, January 27). Transgender teens: Doctors refine hormone, other therapies. *Foster's Daily Democrat.* Available at http://www.fosters.com/apps/pbcs.dll/article?AID=/20080127/GJNEWS_01/205304745/-1/FOSNEWS.

Johnson, T. W., & Wassersug, R. J. (2010). Gender Identity Disorder outside the binary: When Gender Identity Disorder–Not Otherwise Specified is not good enough [Letter to the Editor]. *Archives of Sexual Behavior, 39,* 597–598. doi: 10.1007/s10508–010–9608–1.

Knowlton, B. (2010, January 6). U.S. job site bans bias over gender identity. *New York Times,* A15.

Koken, J. A., Bimbi, D. S., & Parsons, J. T. (2009). Experiences of familial acceptance-rejection among transwomen of color. *Journal of Family Psychology, 23,* 853–860. doi: 10.1037/a0017198.

Kruijver, F. P. M., Fernández-Guasti, A., Fodor, M., Kraan, E. M., & Swaab, D. F. (2000). Male-to-female transsexuals have female neuron numbers in a limbic nucleus. *Journal of Clinical Endocrinology & Metabolism, 85,* 2034–2041. doi: 10.1210/jc.85.5.2034.

Lane, R. (2008). Truth, lies, and trans science [Commentary]. *Archives of Sexual Behavior, 37,* 453–456. doi: 10.1007/s10508–008–9336–y.

Lawrence, A. A. (1999a). *28 narratives about autogynephilia.* Retrieved July 14, 2010, from http://www.annelawrence.com/agnarratives.html.

Lawrence, A. A. (1999b). *31 new narratives about autogynephilia: Plus five revealing narratives.* Retrieved July 14, 2010, from http://www.annelawrence.com/31narratives.html.

Lawrence, A. A. (2010a). Proposed revisions to the gender identity disorder diagnoses in the DSM-5. *Archives of Sexual Behavior, 39,* 1253–1260. doi: 10.1007/s10508–010–9660–x.

Lawrence, A. A. (2010b). Something resembling autogynephilia in women: Comment on Moser (2009) [Letter to the Editor]. *Journal of Homosexuality, 57,* 1–4. doi: 10.1080/00918360903445749.

Lev, A. I. (2004). *Transgender emergence: Therapeutic guidelines for working with gender variant people and their families.* New York: Haworth Clinical Practice Press.

Lev, A. I. (2009). The ten tasks of the mental health provider: Recommendations for revisions of the World Professional Association for Transgender Health's *Standards of Care. International Journal of Transgenderism, 11,* 74–99. doi: 10.1080/15532730903008032.

Levi, J. L. (2006). Clothes don't make the man (or woman), but gender identity might. *Columbia Journal of Gender & Law, 15,* 90–113.

Lilienfeld, S. O. (2007). Psychological treatments that cause harm. *Perspectives on Psychological Science, 2,* 53–70. doi: 10.1111/j.1745–6916.2007.00029.x.

Luders, E., Sánchez, F. J., Gaser, C., Toga, A., Narr, K. L., Hamilton, L., & Vilain, E. (2009). Regional gray matter variation in male-to-female transsexualism. *NeuroImage, 46,* 904–907. doi:10.1016/j.neuroimage.2009.03.048.

Maguen, S., Shipher, J. C., Harris, H. N., & Welch, L. P. (2007). Prevalence and predictors of disclosure of transgender identity. *International Journal of Sexual Health, 19,* 3–12. doi: 10.1300/J514v19n01_02.

Mason-Schrock, D. (1996). Transsexuals' narrative construction of the "true self." *Social Psychology Quarterly, 59,* 176–192.

Mazur, T., Colsman, M., & Sandberg, D. E. (2007). Intersex: Definition, examples, gender stability, and the case against merging with transsexualism. In R. Ettner, S. Monstrey, & A. E. Eyler (Eds.), *Principles of transgender medicine and surgery* (pp. 235–259). New York: Haworth Press.

McCord, J., McCord, W., & Thurber, E. (1962). Some effects of parental absence on male children. *Journal of Abnormal & Social Psychology, 64,* 361–369.

Meyer, W. III., Bockting, W. O., Cohen-Kettenis, P., Coleman, E., DiCeglie, D., Devore, H., et al. (2001). The Harry Benjamin International Gender Dysphoria Association's Standards of Care for Gender Identity Disorders, sixth version. *Journal of Psychology & Human Sexuality, 13,* 1–30.

Meyer, W. J. III., Webb, A., Stuart, C. A., Finkelstein, J. W., Lawrence, B., & Walker, P. A. (1986). Physical and hormonal evaluation of transsexual patients: A longitudinal study. *Archives of Sexual Behavior, 15,* 121–138.

Meyer-Bahlburg, H. F. L. (2010). From mental disorder to iatrogenic hypogonadism: Dilemmas in conceptualizing gender identity variants as psychiatric conditions. *Archives of Sexual Behavior, 39,* 461–476. doi: 10.1007/s10508–009–9532–4.

Morgan, S. W., & Stevens, P. E. (2008). Transgender identity development as represented by a group of female-to-male transgendered adults. *Issues in Mental Health Nursing, 29,* 585–599. doi: 10.1080/01612840802048782.

Moser, C. (2010). Blanchard's autogynephilia theory: A critique. *Journal of Homosexuality, 57,* 790–809. doi: 10.1080/00918369.2010.486241.

Mueller, A., Gooren, L. J., Naton-Schötz, S., Cupisti, S., Beckman, M. W., & Dittrich, R. (2008). Prevalence of polycystic ovary syndrome and hyperandrogenemia in female-to-male transsexuals. *Journal of Clinical Endocrinology & Metabolism, 93,* 1408–1411. doi: 10.1210/jc.2007–2808.

Newcombe, M. D. (1985). The role of perceived relative parent personality in the development of heterosexuals, homosexuals, and transvestites. *Archives of Sexual Behavior, 14,* 147–164.

Nieder, T. O., Herff, M., Cerwenka, S., Preuss, W., Cohen-Kettenis, P. T., de Cuypere, G.,...Richter-Appelt, H. (2011). Age of onset and sexual orientation in transsexual males and females. *Journal of Sexual Medicine, 8,* 783–791. doi: 10.1111/j.1743–6109.2010.02142.x.

Nuttbrock, L., Bockting, W., Mason, M., Hwahng, S., Rosenblum, A.,...Becker, J. (2011). A further assessment of Blanchard's typology of homosexual versus non-homosexual or autogynephilic gender dysphoria. *Archives of Sexual Behavior, 40,* 247–257. doi: 10.1007/s10508–009–9579–2.

Olsson, S., & Möller, A. (2006). Regret after sex reassignment surgery in male-to-female transsexual: A long-term follow-up. *Archives of Sexual Behavior, 35,* 501–506. doi: 10.1007/s10508–006–9040–8.

Pickstone-Taylor, S. D. (2003). Children with gender nonconformity [Letter to the Editor]. *Journal of the American Academy of Child and Adolescent Psychiatry, 42,* 266. doi: 10.1097/01.CHI.0000037022.34553.9C.

Prince, V., & Bentler, P. M. (1972). A survey of 504 cases of transvestism. *Psychological Reports, 31,* 903–917.

Rametti, G., Carrillo, B., Gómez-Gil, E., Junque, C., Segovia, S., Gomez, A., & Guillamon, A. (2011). White matter microstructure in female to male transsexuals before cross-sex hormonal treatment: A diffusion tensor imaging study. *Journal of Psychiatric Research, 45,* 199–204. doi:10.1016/j.jpsychires.2010.05.006.

Ruble, D. N., Taylor, L. J., Cyphers, L., Greulich, F. K., Lurye, L. E., & Shrout, P. E. (2007). The role of gender constancy in early gender development. *Child Development, 78,* 1121–1136. doi: 10.1111/j.1467–8624.2007.01056.x.

Sánchez, F. J., Bocklandt, S., & Vilain, E. (2009). The biology of sexual orientation and gender identity. In D. W. Pfaff, A. P. Arnold, A. M. Etgen, S. E. Fahrbach, & R. T. Rubin (Eds.), *Hormones, brain and behavior* (Vol. 4, 2nd ed., pp. 1911–1929). San Diego, CA: Academic Press. doi:10.1016/B978–008088783–8.00060–7.

Sánchez, F. J., & Vilain, E. (2009). Collective self-esteem as a coping resource for male-to-female transsexuals. *Journal of Counseling Psychology, 56,* 202–209. doi: 10.1037/a0014573.

Schott, R. L. (1995). The childhood and family dynamics of transvestites. *Archives of Sexual Behavior, 24,* 309–327.

Serano, J. M. (2010). The case against autogynephilia. *International Journal of Transgenderism, 12,* 176–187. doi: 10.1080/15532739.2010.514223.

Shapiro, E. (2003). "Trans"cending barriers: Transgender organizing over the Internet. *Journal of Gay & Lesbian Social Services, 16,* 165–179. doi: 10.1300/J041v16n03_11.

Smith, Y. L. S., van Goozen, S. H. M., Kuiper, A. J., & Cohen-Kettenis, P. T. (2005). Transsexual subtypes: Clinical and theoretical significance. *Psychiatry Research, 137,* 151–160.

Spack, N. P. (2009). An endocrine perspective on the care of transgender adolescents. *Journal of Gay & Lesbian Mental Health, 13,* 309–319. doi: 10.1080/19359700903165381.

Spence, D. P. (2001). Dangers of anecdotal reports. *Journal of Clinical Psychology, 57,* 37–41.

Spijkstra, J. J., Spinder, T., & Gooren, L. J. G. (1988). Short-term patterns of pulsatile luteinizing hormone secretion do not differ between male-to-female transsexuals and heterosexual men. *Psychoneuroendocrinology, 13,* 279–273.

Spiová, L., & Starká, L. (1977). Plasma testosterone values in transsexual women. *Archives of Sexual Behavior, 6,* 477–481.

Starká, L., Spiová, I., & Hynie, J. (1975). Plasma testosterone in male transsexuals and homosexuals. *The Journal of Sex Research, 11,* 134–138.

Stevens, M., Golombok, S., Beveridge, M., & the ALSPAC Study Team. (2002). Does father absence influence children's gender development? Findings from a general population study of preschool children. *Parenting: Science & Practice, 2,* 47–60. doi: 10.1207/S15327922PAR0201_3.

Stoller, R. J. (1968). *Sex and gender: On the development of masculinity and femininity.* New York: Science House.

Stoller, R. J. (1979). Fathers of transsexual children. *Journal of the American Psychoanalytic Association, 27,* 837–866.

Stone, A. L. (2009). More than adding a T: American lesbian and gay activists' attitudes towards transgender inclusion. *Sexualities, 12,* 334–354. doi: 10.1177/1363460709103894.

Stotzer, R. L. (2008). Gender identity and hate crimes: Violence against transgender people in Los Angeles County. *Sexuality Research & Social Policy, 5,* 43–52.

Tsoi, W. F. (1988). The prevalence of transsexualism in Singapore. *Acta Psychiatrica Scandinavica, 78,* 501–504. doi: 10.1111/j.1600–0447.1988.tb06373.x.

van Kesteren, P. J. M., Asscheman, H., Megens, J. A. J., & Gooren, L. J. G. (1997). Mortality and morbidity in transsexual subjects treated with cross-sex hormones. *Clinical Endocrinology, 47,* 337–342. doi: 10.1046/j.1365–2265.1997.2601068.x.

Vasey, P. L., & VanderLaan, D. P. (2010). An adaptive cognitive dissociation between willingness to help kin and nonkin in Samoan *fa'afafine. Psychological Science, 21,* 292–297. doi: 10.1177/0956797609359623.

Vilain, E. (2000). Genetics of sexual development. *Annual Review of Sex Research, 11,* 1–25.

Vilain, E., Achermann, J. C., Eugster, E. A., Harley, V. R., Morel, Y., Wilson, J. D., & Hiort, O. (2007). We used to call them hermaphrodites [Commentary]. *Genetics in Medicine, 9,* 65–66. doi: 10.1097/GIM.0b013e31802cffcf.

Wallien, M. S. C., & Cohen-Kettenis, P. T. (2008). Psychosexual outcome of gender-dysphoric children. *Journal of the American Academy of Child & Adolescent Psychiatry, 47,* 1413–1423. doi: 10.1097/CHI.0b013e31818956b9.

Wilson, K. K. (2000). Gender as illness: Issues of psychiatric classification. In E. L. Paul (Ed.), *Taking sides: Clashing views on controversial issues in sex and gender* (pp. 31–38). Guildford, CT: Dushkin McGraw-Hill.

Winters, K. (2005). Gender dissonance: Diagnostic reform of Gender Identity Disorder for adults. *Journal of Psychology & Human Sexuality, 17,* 71–89.

World Professional Association for Transgender Health. (2011). *Standards of care for the health of transsexual, transgender, and gender nonconforming people* (7th ed.). Minneapolis, MN: Author. Available at www.wpath.org.

Yunger, J. L., Carver, P. R., & Perry, D. G. (2004). Does gender identity influence children's psychological well-being? *Developmental Psychology, 40,* 572–582. doi: 10.1037/0012–1649.40.4.572.

Zhou, J. N., Hofman, M. A., Gooren, L. J., & Swaab, D. F. (1995). A sex difference in the human brain and its relation to transsexuality. *Nature, 378,* 68–70.

Zukcer, K. J. (2005). Gender identity disorder in children and adolescents. *Annual Review of Clinical Psychology, 1,* 467–492. doi: 10.1146/annurev.clinpsy.1.102803.144050.

Zucker, K. J. (2006). Commentary on Langer and Martin's (2004) "how dresses can make you mentally ill: Examining Gender Identity Disorder in children." *Child & Adolescent Social Work Journal, 23,* 533–555.

Zucker, K. J. (2010). The *DSM* diagnostic criteria for Gender Identity Disorder in children. *Archives of Sexual Behavior, 39,* 477–498. doi: 10.1007/s10508–009–9540–4.

5

Biological Foundations of Sexual Orientation

ALEXANDER K. HILL, KHYTAM DAWOOD, AND DAVID A. PUTS

This chapter explores possible causes of sexual orientation. As does any psychological or behavioral trait, sexual orientation has two broad types of causes, proximate and ultimate (Mayr, 1958, 1988). Proximate causes include immediate neurophysiological factors and developmental phenomena, such as early hormone signaling, both of which are influenced by the interaction of genotype with environment. Ultimate causes are evolutionary causes and address the issue of why natural selection favored a particular phenotype or set of phenotypes over the range of alternatives that existed ancestrally.

In recent decades there has been a profusion of research into both proximate and ultimate causes underlying variation in sexual orientation (e.g., Blanchard & Bogaert, 1996; Bailey, Dunne, & Martin, 2000; Vasey & Vanderlaan, 2010). The latter line of inquiry is built upon evidence suggesting that there are genes predisposing individuals to homosexuality, and it seeks to explain how such genes might be maintained despite fitness costs associated with homosexuality in terms of reproductive success. Multiple hypotheses have been proposed, with modest supporting evidence. Research into proximate causation has identified neuroanatomical differences between gay and heterosexual individuals, effects of prenatal hormonal signaling on sexual orientation, and associations between the number of older brothers men have and their sexual orientation. Our goal is to illuminate both proximate factors influencing the spectrum of sexual orientations and ultimate causes maintaining this variation during the evolutionary history of our species.

HOW PREVALENT IS HOMOSEXUALITY?

Sexual orientation, according to LeVay and Baldwin (2009, p. 453), "is the dimension of personality that describes the balance of our sexual attraction to the two sexes." This definition focuses on a psychological construct, attraction to males and females, as opposed to describing sexual behavior or identity, which are correlated with, but not identical to, attraction. Because attraction captures the essence of orientation (i.e., having a particular direction), and is perhaps less likely than behavior or identity to be influenced by cultural and societal norms, most researchers studying the biology of sexual orientation examine sexual attraction.

Historically, the most common method of assessing sexual orientation has been the Kinsey Scale, which ranges from zero (exclusively heterosexual) to six (exclusively homosexual) and can be used to measure four dimensions: attraction, fantasy, behavior, and self-identification (Kinsey, Pomeroy, & Martin, 1948). Studies vary in their statistical treatment of this scale, though a common practice is to create three discrete categories, classifying individuals scoring 0 or 1 as heterosexual, those scoring 2 to 4 as bisexual, and those scoring 5 or 6 as homosexual (Rieger, Chivers, & Bailey, 2005).

Sexual attraction and fantasy are thought to be the most temporally stable of the four dimensions recognized by Kinsey et al. (1948), with self-identification and behavior more susceptible to change throughout the course of life (Klein, Sepekoff, & Wolf, 1985). Because of this, operationalizing sexual orientation as attraction tends to result in more conservative prevalence rates of homosexuality. This method of assessment also shows a sex difference concerning frequency distributions: In females the distribution of sexual attractions appears unimodal and continuous, with the majority of women scoring near the exclusively heterosexual end of the scale and decreasing frequencies as we move toward the exclusively homosexual end (Bailey, Dunne, & Martin, 2000). The distribution of orientation in males, by contrast, appears bimodal, with the majority scoring near the exclusively heterosexual end and another, smaller mode near the exclusively homosexual end, with few in between (Bailey et al., 2000).

Initial research on genital arousal found that men who reported bisexual attraction tended to exhibit greater arousal to one sex, usually men, rather than similar arousal to both sexes (Rieger et al., 2005). However, more recent research (Rosenthal, Sylva, Safron, & Bailey, 2011) has found that men who report both bisexual attraction and past sexual behavior with men and women tend to exhibit similar genital arousal to both male and female sexual stimuli. One explanation is that these men's attraction to both sexes incited them to seek mating opportunities with both men and women. Another, not mutually exclusive, explanation is that their histories of homosexual and heterosexual behavior heightened their attraction and arousal to both sexes. Further research is needed to resolve this (see Janssen, McBride, Yarber, Hill, & Butler, 2008, for further discussion). Other research has shown that women are generally more aroused by images of sexual activity than are men, whose arousal seems more contingent on the sex of the erotic stimulus (Chivers, Seto, & Blanchard, 2007). Lesbians exhibit significantly more genital arousal to sexual stimuli of their preferred sex than do heterosexual women (Chivers, Rieger, Latty, & Bailey, 2004). In terms of the magnitude of the contrast between arousal to preferred versus nonpreferred sex, lesbians are intermediate between men and heterosexual women (Chivers et al., 2004; Rieger et al., 2005).

PROXIMATE CAUSATION

Homosexual attraction seems to exist at similarly low frequencies across human societies (e.g., Dawood, Bailey, & Martin, 2009; Sandfort, 1998, but see Laumann, Gagnon, Michael, & Michaels, 1994). Chandra, Mosher, and Copen (2011) and Gates (Chapter 6, this volume) provide the most recent estimates for the United States. Although variability in frequency estimates may partly be attributed to differences in questions asked, estimates rarely exceed 10% (Diamond, 1993). This cross-cultural consistency suggests that same-sex attraction may not be chiefly the product of learning or socialization (Haider-Markel & Joslyn, 2008). Rather, cross-cultural similarities suggest more intrinsic causes, an idea that has in recent decades directed biological research concerning the causes of sexual orientation. This research has focused on four interrelated areas of study: behavior genetics, prenatal sex hormone exposure, neuroanatomy, and, in males, fraternal birth order. Each of these will be discussed in turn.

Behavior Genetics

Some of the most convincing initial studies of the biological basis of sexual orientation were the product of the emerging field of behavior genetics (Kallmann, 1952). This line of research focusing on homosexuality continued in ensuing decades (e.g., Heston & Shields, 1968; Rainer, Mesnikoff, Kolb, & Carr, 1960), with comparable findings from study to study. For instance, in a review paper, Pillard et al. (1981) found that both lesbians and gay men were more likely than heterosexual men and women to have gay siblings, with monozygotic twins yielding the highest concordance rates in orientation, as would be expected assuming a genetic predisposition to the trait. Shortly thereafter, Pillard et al. (1982), studying a sample of 50 heterosexual and 50 homosexual men, found that roughly 25% of the gay men's brothers were also reported to be gay. Pillard and Weinrich (1986) found gay men reported having roughly four times as many gay brothers as heterosexual men did, suggesting a familial aggregation of genes underlying the trait's variation in men.

Bailey and Benishay (1993) found lesbians had a higher proportion of lesbian sisters and (though nonsignificantly) a higher proportion of gay brothers than heterosexual women. These data suggest that male and female homosexuality may be cofamilial to some degree, a conclusion also suggested by Bailey and Bell (1993). The question of whether this is true to the same degree for males was pursued several years later, with the finding of Bailey et al. (1999) that between 7% and 10% of brothers and 3% and 4% of sisters of gay men were gay themselves. Both of these ranges are higher than expected, suggesting a role for familially aggregated genes. On the other hand, Bailey et al. (1995) found a negative result when exploring whether young men are more likely to be gay if their fathers are: Fewer than 10% of the sons were gay.

The above studies reporting cofamiliality of homosexual orientation suggest a genetic component, but twin studies provide stronger evidence of heritability. For instance, Kendler et al. (2000)

found that monozygotic twins of both sexes were concordant for homosexuality (32%) more often than were dizygotic (13%) or nontwin siblings. In the largest twin study conducted to date, Bailey et al. (2000) used a carefully ascertained twin sample from the Australian Twin Registry to establish heritability estimates for sexual orientation in men and women. This study reported 20% of male MZ twins concordant versus 0% of DZ twins, and 24% of female MZ twins versus 10.5% of DZ twins. In a recent large twin study, Langstrom, Rahman, Carlstrom, and Lichtenstein (2010) estimated a heritability of 0.34 to 0.39 for men and 0.18 to 0.19 for women. In general, although figures may differ slightly from study to study, the trend is clear: as the genetic relatedness of siblings increases, so does their likelihood of concordance for orientation.

Hamer and his colleagues (1993) proposed the first candidate gene for male homosexuality. Hamer's research team found an increased prevalence of homosexuality among male kin on the maternal side, suggesting that male homosexuality may be a sex-linked trait. This led Hamer and his colleagues to examine the X-chromosome and to find that gay brothers share markers at the Xq28 locus much more frequently than would be expected by chance (Hamer et al., 1993). Although Hamer's research team was able to replicate its initial result (Hu et al., 1995), other attempts at replication (Rice, Anderson, Risch, & Ebers, 1999; Sanders et al., 1998) have been unsuccessful. Although Sanders et al. (1998) reported inconclusive evidence of linkage to Xq28, a notable negative finding was that of Rice et al. (1999), who examined four markers on a 12.5-centimorgan region of Xq28 (DXS1113, BGN, Factor 8, and DXS1108) in search of further evidence that male homosexuality is sex-linked. To this end, the researchers used a sample of 52 pairs of siblings, with both members of each pair self-identifying as gay. Because DNA samples from these siblings' mothers were not easily obtainable, the markers genotyped for the siblings were compared with controls from the population. Results indicated that none of the markers in question was shared more often than would be expected from population base rates. The reasons for the discrepancy between this study and the previous studies from Hamer's laboratory are unclear. More recently, Mustanski et al. (2005) also failed to replicate the positive Xq28 finding but reported linkage findings for 7q36, 8p12, and 10q26. However, this study has not been replicated. The first two of these genes have approximately the same maximum likelihood estimation score for maternal and paternal contributions, possible evidence against male homosexuality as a sex-linked trait. Candidate genes continue to be suggested, and the issue is far from resolved.

In addition to the linkage studies described above, two association studies of male sexual orientation have been conducted to date. Unlike linkage studies, which can search the entire genome and examine genetic markers rather than genes, association studies explore the relation between genetic variation at a particular candidate locus and phenotypic variation. Macke et al. (1993) found no significant differences between gay and heterosexual men in the distributions of variants of the androgen receptor gene. Dupree et al. (2004) found no associations between variation in the gene encoding the aromatase enzyme, or differences in its expression, and sexual orientation in men. However, although aromatase is instrumental in masculinizing the brains of some mammals, including laboratory rodents, this may not be the case in humans (Zuloaga, Puts, Jordan, & Breedlove, 2008).

As is evident, behavior genetics has made substantial contributions to the literature on sexual orientation during the past three decades. Most impressive is the repeatedly observed trend of increasing likelihood of concordance for both male and female homosexuality with increasing genetic relatedness between siblings. However, the search for "gay gene(s)" to date has been chiefly an unsuccessful endeavor, lacking replicable results. Future studies are needed to illuminate the genetics of sexual orientation.

Sex Hormones

Like research into the behavior genetics of sexual orientation, studies examining associations between sexual orientation and sex hormone exposure have helped to shed light on its biological components. Early research suggesting links between adult sexual orientation and both prenatal sex hormone signaling (e.g., Ward, 1972; Ellis et al., 1988; Bailey & Pillard, 1991) and gender-related behavior during childhood (Green, 1985) spawned research into possible associations among all three phenomena. Because gender atypicality during childhood may be associated with adult homosexuality, if prenatal hormone exposure affects childhood gender atypicality, this might suggest a link between prenatal sex hormones and adult homosexuality.

Childhood gender nonconformity (CGN) is among the best predictors of adult homosexuality for men, both in retrospective (e.g., Whitam, 1977) and in prospective (e.g., Money & Russo, 1979) studies. For example, Money and Russo (1979) followed 11 gender nonconforming boys in a longitudinal study and obtained much the same findings as had been previously found (e.g., Whitam, 1977). The boys were selected on the basis of (1) "exceptional interest in dressing in girls' clothing," (2) "avoiding play activities typical of boys and preferring those of girls," (3) "walking and talking more like girls than boys," and (4) "stating overtly the wish to be a girl." The boys were prepubertal at the commencement of the study and none exhibited homosexual behavior. In early adulthood all of the boys were found to be gay. Zuger (1984) examined 55 boys with "early effeminate behavior." On follow-up, 64% of the original participants were nonheterosexual, 6% were heterosexual, and in 18% there was either insufficient information from follow-up meetings or too short a follow-up period to warrant categorization of sexual orientation. [See Bailey & Zucker (1995) for a meta-analysis of studies on this topic.]

Further support for the association between CGN and adult homosexuality comes from a study of 44 gender-nonconforming boys and 34 gender-conforming boys (Green, 1985). The boys were matched on "age, gender, and sibling sequence" and the parents on "race, religion, educational level, and marital status." Of the 44 gender-nonconforming boys, 30 were gay or bisexual when scored on the fantasy dimension, and of these, 24 were gay or bisexual in terms of their sexual behavior. Of the boys in the gender-conforming group, all were heterosexual by both measures. More recent research (Lippa, 2008) has found similar results in an ethnically diverse sample of nearly 1000 men from the United States.

Other research has taken a novel route in pursuit of a better understanding of this issue. Rather than relying on self-reports of gender-nonconforming behavior or retrospective accounts of CGN, Rieger et al. (2008) utilized observation of home videos. Gay male, lesbian, and heterosexual adults were shown video footage of both children who grew up to be lesbian or gay or heterosexual. Children who grew up to be lesbian or gay were perceived to be significantly more gender-nonconforming than were other children, and these perceptions

accorded with self-reports of the adults from the videos. Finally, the association between CGN and adult homosexuality has also been observed across cultures. Whitam and Mathy (1991) found results similar to those reported above in Brazil, Peru, the Philippines, and the United States for females.

Results of these studies suggest that CGN and adult homosexuality may be correlated, at least in males. What might be responsible for the association? One answer may involve organizational effects of prenatal or early postnatal exposure to sex hormones on brain regions involved in sexual orientation and other sexually differentiated psychological traits. Research into this possibility employs both "natural experiments" and biomarkers in an effort to establish connections between early sex hormone exposure and sex-atypical behavior and psychology.

Natural experiments. Some males with sex-typical prenatal androgen exposure have undergone gender reassignment shortly after birth due to damage to the penis that required its removal, or to resolve abnormal differentiation of the genitals, as in a condition called cloacal exstrophy. Such males raised as females frequently report sexual attraction to females as adults, with one sample of 35 males all showing adult attraction to females (Mustanski, Chivers, & Bailey, 2002; Reiner & Gearhart, 2004). This suggests that prenatal developmental events, including those dependent on sex hormones or early developmental issues, may have effects on sexual orientation that persist despite discordance with the assigned gender role.

Another condition, congenital adrenal hyperplasia (CAH), is characterized by excess prenatal androgen exposure. Compared to unaffected female controls, females with CAH tend to perform at more male-typical levels on sexually differentiated spatial cognitive tasks (Puts, McDaniel, Jordan, & Breedlove, 2008) and tend to show more male-typical childhood play patterns and adult vocational interests (Berenbaum, 1999; Hines, Brook, & Conway, 2004). CAH women are also more likely than non-CAH women to be lesbian or bisexual (Ehrhardt, Evers, & Money, 1968; Hines et al., 2004; Zucker et al., 1996). For example, Hines et al. (2004) found a statistically significant difference in sexual orientation between CAH and non-CAH women, with 31% of CAH women indicating their sexual behavior during the year preceding the study to be with women or with both men and women.

By contrast, all of the non-CAH women reported their sexual behavior to have been exclusively or mainly with men. Thus, these findings suggest that increased prenatal exposure to androgens masculinizes both gendered behavior and sexual orientation among girls and women; no such effects have been observed among boys or men.

In addition, 46 XY (i.e., chromosomally male) individuals with complete androgen insensitivity syndrome (CAIS) are similar to unaffected female controls in their sexual orientation (Hines, Ahmed, & Hughes, 2003; Money, Schwartz, & Lewis, 1984; Wisniewski et al., 2000). This is remarkable because individuals with CAIS develop testes that remain undescended, and produce normal-to-high male levels of testosterone (Imperato-McGinley et al., 1982). Individuals with CAIS are nonetheless phenotypically female because they lack functional androgen receptors and therefore do not undergo the virilization experienced by non-CAIS individuals (Imperato-McGinley et al., 1982). Their female-typical attraction to men is consistent with the hypothesis that androgen signaling is critical in developing sexual attraction to women. However, this evidence may be confounded by other developmental factors, especially socialization effects. For example, sexual orientation in individuals with CAIS is consistent with gender of rearing. Thus, the rearing environment, rather than the absence of androgen-signaling in the brain, may account for sexual orientation in CAIS women. Such women are socialized as girls and behave in ways culturally appropriate for individuals with a female phenotype. The male-typical gender role behavior of girls with CAH may elicit psychosocial experiences that influence the development of their sexual orientation (but see Pasterski et al., 2005).

Biomarkers. Other research has focused on anatomical differences between males and females that are thought to result from differential exposure to sex hormones during early development. Martin and Nguyen (2004) found that arm, hand, and leg bones that become dimorphic prior to puberty differ not only between males and females but also between androphilic individuals (i.e., heterosexual women and gay men) and gynephilic individuals (i.e., heterosexual men and lesbians). The researchers interpreted this result as reflecting less than typical prepubertal androgen exposure in androphilic men and higher than normal prepubertal androgen exposure in gynephilic women.

Sex hormone exposure may influence not only the development of homosexuality, but also variation in sexual orientation among gays and lesbians. For example, an association has been found between "butch" (masculine-acting) lesbianism and (1) a higher (more male-typical) waist-to-hip ratio (Singh, Vidaurri, Zambarano, & Dabbs, 1999) and (2) increased levels of baseline testosterone within lesbian couples, but not among lesbians generally (Pearcey, Docherty, & Dabbs, 1996).

One of the most heavily researched lines of inquiry into the role of sex hormones on sexual orientation is the association between sexual orientation and the ratio of the second to fourth finger lengths (2D:4D). Because variation in 2D:4D probably results from differences in prenatal sex hormone signaling (Breedlove, 2010; Manning, Scutt, Wilson, & Lewis-Jones, 1998), 2D:4D is frequently used as a proxy for prenatal sex hormone exposure. There has been a recent increase in such research, largely because it is relatively uncomplicated to conduct and is linked in no obvious way to socialization or enculturation, thus decreasing the likelihood that these processes will confound any observed effects. However, the degree to which 2D:4D can elucidate the ontogeny of sexual orientation is unclear. For example, Robinson and Manning (2000) provided evidence that 2D:4D is lower in gay males than it is in heterosexual males, an unexpected pattern given the well-established finding that heterosexual males have lower 2D:4D than heterosexual females (Grimbos, Dawood, Burriss, Zucker, & Puts, 2010; Manning et al., 1998). Manning et al. (2007), however, found *higher* 2D:4D ratios among gay men, whereas Voracek et al. (2005) found *no* difference between gay and heterosexual men.

Among women, lesbians (e.g., Hall & Love, 2003), and specifically "butch" lesbians (Brown, Finn, Cooke, & Breedlove, 2002), have been found to possess a lower (more masculine) 2D:4D ratio than heterosexual women and than "femme" (feminine-acting) lesbians. Although Lippa (2003) found no 2D:4D differences between lesbians and heterosexual women in a large sample, the most recent systematic review of previous research on this topic (Grimbos et al., 2010) concluded that the preponderance of evidence suggests that there is a difference in 2D:4D between lesbians and heterosexual women but not between gay and heterosexual men. This meta-analysis utilized data from 21 studies covering the years 2000 to 2009, including

18 male and 16 female samples comprising 1618 heterosexual men, 1503 gay men, 1693 heterosexual women, and 1014 lesbians. Thus, findings on 2D:4D ratios overall suggest that early androgen signaling is associated with sexual orientation, at least in women.

The ratio of second to fourth finger length is not the only biomarker to display a sexual orientation difference. A meta-analysis (Lalumiere, Blanchard, & Zucker, 2000) found that gay men were 34%, and lesbians 91%, more likely than heterosexual men and women to be left handed or ambidextrous. Because handedness does not appear to be dependent upon socialization and is fixed from an early age, it is thought to be under the control of perinatal neurodevelopmental effects (Hepper, McCartney, & Shannon, 1998; Hepper, Shahidullah, & White, 1991). One hypothesis posits that differential exposure to testosterone prenatally shifts cerebral dominance to the right hemisphere, which could explain why heterosexual males and lesbians are more likely than heterosexual women to be non-right-handed. A related finding is that of more masculine otoacoustic emissions (sound waves emanating from the inner ear) among lesbians, explained by researchers as the product of increased exposure to androgens prenatally (McFadden & Pasanen, 1998, 1999).

Thus, multiple converging lines of evidence provide some support for the hypothesis that variation in prenatal androgen signaling (sensitivity to androgens and/or androgen production) accounts for some variation in sexual orientation among females. The causes of variation in sexual orientation among males are less clear, although evidence strongly suggests the importance of early, probably prenatal or early postnatal, developmental events.

Neurobiology

Sex steroids exert their influence by regulating gene expression in their target tissues (Nelson, 2005). For gene expression changes to influence sexual orientation, the target tissues would presumably be the nervous system, and such changes would affect neural development. In other words, we would expect the neuroanatomy and/or neurophysiology of males and females, as well as that of gay and heterosexual individuals, to differ. An obvious place to look for such differences is the brain.

LeVay (1991) investigated differences in sexual orientation in the interstitial nuclei (i.e., groups of neuronal cell bodies) of the anterior hypothalamus, as there were known human sex differences in the size of these structures, and this brain area relates to sexual behavior in laboratory animals. In a sample of cadavers from 19 gay men, 16 presumably heterosexual men, and six presumably heterosexual women, LeVay found the third nucleus (INAH3) to be roughly twice as large in heterosexual men as in gay men or heterosexual women. He was unable to procure a large enough sample to test for a similar difference in sexual orientation in women. It is possible that LeVay's results were confounded by the fact that all of the gay men, six of the 16 heterosexual men, and one of the six women in his sample had died of AIDS. However, LeVay found that the six heterosexual men who had died of AIDS had an INAH3 that did not differ in size from that of uninfected heterosexual men. This result has been replicated with moderate success, with Byne and colleagues (2001) also reporting a nonsignificant trend toward a smaller INAH3 in gay than in heterosexual men. That said, the neuronal number was about the same in INAH3 between the two groups and AIDS was shown to influence the size of this structure.

Other research on neuroanatomical differences between men and women of different sexual orientations has focused on the hypothalamus. Swaab and Hofman (1990) demonstrated that the suprachiasmatic nucleus (SCN) was 1.7 times as large and contained 2.1 times as many cells in a sample of gay men as in a sample of randomly chosen men. Allen and Gorski (1992) found the anterior commissure to be 34% larger in gay than in heterosexual men.

Although this research suggests differences in sexual orientation in the structure of the hypothalamus, it is impossible to ascertain from these data whether hypothalamic structure influences sexual orientation, sexual behavior influences hypothalamic structure, or whether the two are linked because of a third variable. Even if the first of these possibilities is correct, the overlap between the gay and heterosexual men in the anatomy of these structures suggests that male sexual orientation may not vary as a result of any single neuroanatomical difference.

Research using positron emission tomography (PET) scans indicates that certain aspects of brain functioning differ between gay and heterosexual individuals. For instance, the hypothalamus was activated in gay, but not heterosexual, men after inhalation of putative male pheromones (Savic, Berglund, & Lindstrom, 2005). This trend of sex-atypicality in brain activation after inhalation of pheromones has been shown in lesbians as well (Berglund, Lindstrom, & Savic, 2006). Furthermore, there is evidence that gay men (Hu et al., 2008; Safron et al., 2007) exhibit different brain activation from heterosexual men when exposed to visual sexual stimuli.

Safron et al. (2007) showed gay and heterosexual men male–male and female–female sexual stimuli, as well as images of sexually neutral stimuli. Participants viewed these images while undergoing functional magnetic resonance imaging (fMRI). When viewing sexual images of their preferred sex, men demonstrated increased activity in several brain regions. Hu et al. (2008) obtained similar results, but also showed a difference between the brain regions activated in gay and heterosexual men upon exposure to stimuli of their preferred sex. Of course, the role of past experiences cannot be ruled out as influencing neuroanatomy to the extent that brain regions in gay and heterosexual individuals differ with respect to activation during sexual arousal. Similar research has yet to be done with women.

Other research suggests that, like men, lesbians possess less gray matter (parts of the central nervous system composed largely of neuronal cell bodies) in areas of the perirhinal cortex than do heterosexual women (Ponseti et al., 2007). This finding is important because the perirhinal cortex is located near brain regions (entorhinal cortex, hippocampus, parahippocampal gyrus, and amygdala) involved in olfactory and spatial processing, which have been shown to exhibit differences in sexual orientation such as slower spatial learning and reduced mental rotation ability in gay than in heterosexual men (Rahman & Koerting, 2008; Rahman & Wilson, 2003). Yet other research has shown that the cerebrum of heterosexual men and lesbians (i.e., gynephiles) is asymmetrical in a rightward direction, whereas the cerebrum of gay men and heterosexual women (i.e., androphiles) is not asymmetrical, and that both gay men and lesbians show different amygdala connections than do heterosexual men and women (Savic & Lindstrom, 2008). Of course, it is unclear whether these neuroanatomical phenomena cause variation in sexual orientation, whether some aspect of sexual behavior causes these neuroanatomical differences, or whether these differences are not causally related to sexual orientation at all.

Research on the topic of neuroanatomical differences between lesbian or gay and heterosexual individuals has thus yielded repeated demonstrations of brain differences between the two groups. The differences in brain structure reported have generally indicated that gay men resemble heterosexual women and lesbians resemble heterosexual men.

Fraternal Birth Order

The last of the major lines of research on biological components of sexual orientation concerns a phenomenon that may at first glance seem to have little connection to sexual orientation: birth order. Specifically, a repeated finding has been that the number of a man's (but not a woman's) older brothers increases his likelihood of being gay, each older brother increasing the odds by approximately 33% above the base rate of 2–3% (Blanchard & Bogaert, 1996). This is called the fraternal birth order effect. With a host of studies since the mid-1990s replicating this finding (reviewed in Blanchard, 2008; Bogaert & Skorska, 2011), the fraternal birth order effect is one of the most well-established proximate correlates of sexual orientation.

What is it about the number of older brothers that relates to a man's chances of being gay? One hypothesis is socialization—for instance, that being reared in a home with older brothers in some way "demasculinizes" a boy. This appears not to be the case, as only the number of biological brothers from the same mother predicts a man's likelihood of homosexuality, regardless of the duration of rearing together, or even whether the brothers were reared together at all (Bogaert, 2006). Moreover, no other category of sibling, including older stepbrothers and half-brothers through the father, has an influence or correlation (Bogaert, 2006), nor does spacing of siblings (Blanchard & Bogaert, 1997) or parental age (Blanchard & Sheridan, 1992). Gay men with older brothers have also been shown to have lower birth weights than have heterosexual men with older brothers (Blanchard & Ellis, 2001), and since birth weight is contingent on gestational events, this suggests that whatever phenomenon is responsible for the trend exerts its influence early, during gestation.

Blanchard and Klassen (1997) proposed the maternal immune hypothesis to explain the fraternal birth order effect. According to the hypothesis, when a mother gives birth to a son, maternal and fetal blood mix, and the mother's immune system is exposed to Y-linked (male-specific) antigens. The mother produces antibodies to these male-specific antigens, which can cross the placental barrier in later pregnancies. These antibodies then in some as yet unknown way affect the neural development of every subsequent male fetus (see also Puts, Jordan, & Breedlove, 2006). Because the production of antimale antibodies is bolstered by each subsequent delivery of a son, the mother's immune system can "remember" the number of sons she has previously delivered, increasing the likelihood of later homosexuality by about one-third of the population base rate with each successive son. This theory is admittedly speculative at this point, though it is the only widely accepted explanation of the fraternal birth order effect (Bogaert & Skorska, 2011).

Two recent estimates of the percentage of male homosexuality attributable to the fraternal birth order effect are 15.1% (Cantor, Blanchard, Paterson, & Bogaert, 2002) and 28.6% (Blanchard & Bogaert, 2004). Thus, even among proponents of this theory, most male homosexuality (and all of female homosexuality) is not explained by this phenomenon. Nonetheless, the fraternal birth order effect remains the best-supported of all proximate explanations for the etiology of homosexuality.

ULTIMATE CAUSATION

The discussion thus far has focused on causal agents at the proximate level, including evidence of genes underlying variation in sexual orientation. The prospect of "gay genes" is intriguing from the perspective of evolutionary biology, as lesbians and gay men tend to produce fewer offspring than do heterosexual men and women (Bell & Weinberg, 1978). Even allowing for cultural stigma concerning homosexuality or social pressures to marry and procreate, it is doubtful that lesbians and gay men in any time or place would have equaled the reproductive output of their heterosexual counterparts. Hence the evolutionary conundrum: If there are genes that predispose their bearers to developing a homosexual orientation, and if these genes tend to restrain reproduction, why has natural selection not eliminated them? Several theories have suggested an answer.

Kin Selection

Perhaps the best known of these theories involves kin selection (Hamilton, 1964a, 1964b). E. O. Wilson put the idea this way:

> The homosexual members of primitive societies may have functioned as helpers, either while hunting in company with other men or in more domestic occupations at the dwelling sites. Freed from the special obligations of parental duties, they could have operated with special efficiency in assisting close relatives. Genes favoring homosexuality could then be sustained at a high equilibrium level by kin selection alone. (Wilson, 1975, p. 555)

The assumption is that the "gay genes" reside not only in the lesbians and gay men themselves, but in their close genetic relatives. However, only in certain combinations and/or under particular environmental conditions do these genes increase the probability that an individual will be lesbian or gay, which is why the kin do not possess this trait and the lesbian or gay individuals do. When the kin reproduce (with greater success, aided by their altruistic gay relatives), they replicate copies of the gay genes and thus perpetuate the trait despite its detrimental effect on individual reproductive success. In this way, according to the theory, a lesbian's or gay man's individual reproductive fitness may be decreased, but the reproductive fitness of the gay genes is not.

Research has provided mixed evidence to support this hypothesis. For example, Bobrow and Bailey (2001) tested the theory in an American sample and found no evidence in support of it. They gave gay and heterosexual men questionnaires concerning sentiments and behavior toward kin and found no evidence that gay men behaved more altruistically toward kin than did heterosexual males. In fact, gay men reported giving *less* money than did heterosexual men to oldest and youngest siblings. Similar findings were obtained by Rahman and Hull (2005) in a British sample. These results contradict the central prediction of the kin selection theory. Of course, the United States and Britain are in important respects not representative of the environment in which humans spent the majority of their evolutionary history. Western lesbians and gay men may be more (1) geographically separated and (2) emotionally estranged from kin than are non-Western lesbians and gay men (Bobrow & Bailey, 2001), weakening any tendency they may have to behave more altruistically toward relatives. Because of this, supporting evidence for the kin selection theory, if such evidence exists, may be difficult to find in such a sample.

In light of this, Vasey et al. (2007) conducted a study similar to that of Bobrow and Bailey (2001) in which the researchers examined a culturally recognized category of gender-variant male, the *fa'afafine* of Independent Samoa, who live in conditions that may, in some respects, be more similar to those of our evolutionary past. The researchers found no difference between gynephilic and androphilic males (i.e., heterosexual men and *fa'afafine*) with respect to "overall generosity or financial resources given to kin." However, androphilic males indicated greater levels of "avuncular tendencies" than did gynephilic males. These results prompted Vasey and his colleagues to stress the importance of studying evolutionary predictions in social environments thought to be more similar to those in which our species spent the majority of its evolutionary history. In Independent Samoa, for instance, members of extended families, *aiga*, tend to be geographically clustered near each other, facilitating frequent contact. Furthermore, because the *fa'afafine* have a recognized and unstigmatized place in Samoan culture, they suffer no noticeable estrangement from kin. In Samoa, the researchers note, male androphiles without children of their own have more time and resources to invest in nieces and nephews. To demonstrate that the avuncular tendencies of *fa'afafine* differ from those of heterosexual males, it is necessary to compare childless heterosexual men with childless *fa'afafine*. Vasey and Vanderlaan (2010) found that *fa'afafine* indeed display more altruistic behavior toward nieces and nephews than do childless heterosexual males. Moreover, heterosexual males with and without children did not differ in the extent of their avuncular tendencies, nor was there a negative relationship for heterosexual males between number of children sired and avuncular tendencies. These findings are consistent with the hypothesis that male homosexuality is an adaptation for kin-directed altruism, but they are of course limited to a single cultural group.

However, the kin selection hypothesis for homosexuality may be undermined by the apparent inefficiency of homosexuality for this function. Given androphilic males' investment in pursuing and maintaining homosexual relationships, a lack of sexual motivation, rather than homosexuality, would seem a more efficient means of increasing investment in kin. Moreover, because individuals are twice as genetically related to their own offspring as they are to nieces and nephews, they would have to be exceptionally altruistic for the benefits of investing in nieces and nephews to offset the costs of forgoing reproduction. Finally, perhaps some trait other than homosexuality, for example, traditionally sex-typed "feminine" characteristics such as caring or empathy, causes *fa'afafine* to exhibit more altruism toward kin. Overall, the findings provide limited support for the kin selection hypothesis.

Pleiotropy

Genes may have different effects in different bodies, a phenomenon known as pleiotropy. A gene or collection of genes might propel one individual toward same-sex attraction, whereas the same gene or combination of genes might have a different effect in another individual. If there really are "gay genes," then the effects of such genes in heterosexual individuals may increase reproductive success, offsetting the costs to reproductive fitness incurred when the genes are in gay individuals.

Miller (2000) proposed that women prefer in men typically feminine attributes such as kindness and empathy, which may make men better fathers. According to Miller, men with an intermediate level of behavioral femininity would be desirable as long-term mates, gaining a reproductive advantage over more masculine or more feminine men. Consequently, selection would favor both alleles contributing to behavioral masculinity and alleles contributing to behavioral femininity. The most reproductively successful males might have an intermediate number of each. Due to recombination during sexual reproduction, some males would inherit more alleles contributing to behavioral masculinity, and some would inherit more alleles contributing to behavioral femininity, than is advantageous under natural selection. A small minority of males would inherit an extreme number of alleles contributing to behavioral femininity and would develop a homosexual attraction. Miller points to the correlation between psychological gender-atypicality and sexual orientation (Bailey, Nothnagel, & Wolfe, 1995; Bailey & Zucker, 1995; Green, 1985) in support of this hypothesis. In addition, gay men may have, on average, more feminine fathers than do heterosexual men (Bell, Weinberg, & Hammersmith, 1981).

An advantage of this hypothesis is that it can be applied to both sexes. Regarding lesbians, Miller argues that although men may prefer physically and psychologically feminine women, our female ancestors may also have benefited from some psychological masculinity. For example, psychological masculinity may have helped women procure food and depend less on male support. As with Miller's hypothesis regarding male homosexuality, this hypothesis relies on an association between sexual orientation and gender nonconformity. As noted above, girls with CAH tend to be gender nonconforming in some ways and have a higher-than-base rate chance of being lesbian (Hines et al., 2004). Although consistent with some evidence, this hypothesis has at present little evidence to support it.

Two studies indicate greater reproductive success among the maternal but not paternal kin of gay men compared to heterosexual men (Camperio-Ciani, Corna, & Capiluppi, 2004; Iemmola & Camperio Ciani, 2009), a finding consistent with evidence that a gene contributing to male homosexuality may reside on the X-chromosome. At least one study has found greater reproductive success among both patrilateral and matrilateral kin of gay men (King et al., 2005). Rahman et al. (2008) found increased fecundity among maternal aunts of gay men only among white participants, with non-white heterosexual individuals displaying increased fecundity among most other kin types. In sum, there is some modest evidence (see also Zietsch et al., 2008) that if genes predispose some individuals toward homosexuality, they compensate for the associated decrement in reproduction by increasing the reproductive success of heterosexual individuals in which the same genes reside.

CONCLUSIONS

This chapter has discussed leading avenues of study into biological aspects of sexual orientation at both the proximate and ultimate levels of explanation. At this point in time, relatively little can be stated conclusively. Nevertheless, it is reasonably well-established that (1) both male and female homosexuality are at least partially heritable traits that are (2) sometimes associated with childhood gender nonconformity and (3) are found at similar frequencies across many culturally divergent populations. Early developmental (e.g., prenatal) events may influence within-sex

variation in sexual orientation. Some evidence suggests that early developmental processes influencing female sexual orientation could include androgen signaling. Men's sexual orientation has been found to be associated with fraternal birth order, which could reflect a maternal immune response to male-specific antigens. Less is known at the ultimate level, though it appears that a pleiotropic genetic model is currently the most promising explanatory hypothesis. However, most theories at either level need not be mutually exclusive. Furthermore, the etiology of homosexuality is often studied separately by social and biological scientists, rather than from an interdisciplinary perspective, which may provide additional insights into the proximate and ultimate causes of sexual orientation.

What forms will this research take in the future? Replication of previous results is clearly necessary, and considerable additional research is required to clarify determinants of sexual orientation at the proximate level. Much of the needed research may come from genomics, neuroscience, and related fields. Rigorous exploration of the fraternal birth order effect, and specifically testing of the maternal immune hypothesis, might elucidate the etiology of sexual orientation for some individuals. It may well be the case that convincing tests of ultimate-level explanations for variation in sexual orientation must await a clearer understanding of proximate causes.

REFERENCES

Allen, L. S., & Gorski, R. A. (1992). Sexual orientation and the size of the anterior commissure in the human brain. *Proceedings of the National Academy of Sciences, 89,* 7199–7202.

Bailey, J. M., & Bell, A. P. (1993). Familiality of female and male homosexuality. *Behavior Genetics, 23,* 313–322.

Bailey, J. M., & Benishay, D. S. (1993). Familial aggregation of female sexual orientation. *American Journal of Psychiatry, 150,* 272–277.

Bailey, J. M., Bobrow, D., Wolfe, M., & Mikach, S. (1995). Sexual orientation of adult sons of gay fathers. *Developmental Psychology, 31,* 124–129.

Bailey, J. M., Dunne, M. P., & Martin, N. G. (2000). Genetic and environmental influences on sexual orientation and its correlates in an Australian twin sample. *Journal of Personality and Social Psychology, 78,* 524–536.

Bailey, J. M., Nothnagel, J., & Wolfe, M. (1995). Retrospectively measured individual differences in childhood sex-typed behavior among gay men: Correspondence between self- and maternal reports. *Archives of Sexual Behavior, 24,* 613–622.

Bailey, J. M., & Pillard, R. C. (1991). A genetic study of male sexual orientation. *Archives of General Psychiatry, 48*, 1089–1096.

Bailey, J. M., Pillard, R. C., Dawood, K., Miller, M. B., Farrer, L. A., Trivedi, S., et al. (1999). A family history study of male sexual orientation using three independent samples. *Behavior Genetics, 29*, 79–86.

Bailey, J. M., & Zucker, K. J. (1995). Childhood sex-typed behavior and sexual orientation: A conceptual analysis and quantitative review. *Developmental Psychology, 31*, 43–55.

Bell, A. P., & Weinberg, M. S. (1978). *Homosexualities: A study of diversity among men and women*. New York: Simon & Schuster.

Bell, A. P., Weinberg, M., & Hammersmith, S. (1981). *Sexual preference: Its development in men and women*. Bloomington: Indiana University Press.

Berenbaum, S. A. (1999). Effects of early androgens on sex-typed activities and interests in adolescents with congenital adrenal hyperplasia. *Hormones and Behavior, 35*, 102–110.

Berglund, H., Lindstrom, P., & Savic, I. (2006). Brain response to putative pheromones in lesbian women. *Proceedings of the National Academy of Sciences, 103*, 8269–8274.

Blanchard, R. (2008). Review and theory of handedness, birth order, and homosexuality in men. *Laterality, 13*, 51–70.

Blanchard, R., & Bogaert, A. F. (1996). Homosexuality in men and number of older brothers. *American Journal of Psychiatry, 153*, 27–31.

Blanchard, R., & Bogaert, A. F. (1997). The relation of closed birth intervals to the sex of the preceding child and the sexual orientation of the succeeding child. *Journal of Biosocial Science, 29*, 111–118.

Blanchard, R., & Bogaert, A. F. (2004). Proportion of homosexual men who owe their sexual orientation to fraternal birth order: An estimate based on two national probability samples. *American Journal of Human Biology, 16*, 151–157.

Blanchard, R., & Ellis, L. (2001). Birth weight, sexual orientation and the sex of preceding siblings. *Journal of Biosocial Science, 33*, 451–467.

Blanchard, R., & Klassen, P. (1997). H-Y antigen and homosexuality in men. *Journal of Theoretical Biology, 185*, 373–378.

Blanchard, R., & Sheridan, P. M. (1992). Sibship size, sibling sex ratio, birth order, and parental age in homosexual and nonhomosexual gender dysphorics. *Journal of Nervous and Mental Diseases, 180*, 40–47.

Bobrow, D., & Bailey, J. M. (2001). Is male homosexuality maintained via kin selection? *Evolution and Human Behavior, 22*, 361–368.

Bogaert, A. F. (2006). Biological versus nonbiological older brothers and men's sexual orientation. *Proceedings of the National Academy of Sciences, 103*, 10771–10774.

Bogaert, A. F., & Skorska, M. (2011). Sexual orientation, fraternal birth order, and the maternal immune hypothesis: A review. *Front Neuroendocrinology, 32*, 247–254.

Breedlove, S. M. (2010). Minireview: Organizational hypothesis: Instances of the fingerpost. *Endocrinology, 151*, 4116–4122.

Brown, W. M., Finn, C. J., Cooke, B. M., & Breedlove, S. M. (2002). Differences in finger length ratios between self-identified "butch" and "femme" lesbians. *Archives of Sexual Behavior, 31*, 123–127.

Byne, W., Tobet, S., Mattiace, L. A., Lasco, M. S., Kemether, E., Edgar, M. A.,…Jones, L. B. (2001). The interstitial nuclei of the anterior hypothalamus: An investigation of variation with sex, sexual orientation, and HIV status. *Hormones and Behavior, 40*, 86–92.

Camperio-Ciani, A., Corna, F., & Capiluppi, C. (2004). Evidence for maternally inherited factors favouring male homosexuality and promoting female fecundity. *Proceedings of the Royal Society: Biological Sciences, 271*, 2217–2221.

Cantor, J. M., Blanchard, R., Paterson, A. D., & Bogaert, A. F. (2002). How many gay men owe their sexual orientation to fraternal birth order? *Archives of Sexual Behavior, 31*, 63–71.

Chandra, A., Mosher, W. D., & Copen, C. (2011). *Sexual behavior, sexual attraction, and sexual identity in the United States: Data from the 2006–2008 National Survey of Family Growth*. Washington, DC: U.S. Department of Health and Human Services.

Chivers, M. L., Rieger, G., Latty, E., & Bailey, J. M. (2004). A sex difference in the specificity of sexual arousal. *Psychological Sciences, 15*, 736–744.

Chivers, M. L., Seto, M. C., & Blanchard, R. (2007). Gender and sexual orientation differences in sexual response to sexual activities versus gender of actors in sexual films. *Journal of Personality and Social Psychology, 93*, 1108–1121.

Dawood, K., Bailey, J. M., & Martin, N. G. (2009). Genetic and environmental influences on sexual orientation. In Y.-K. Kim (Ed.), *Handbook of behavior genetics* (pp. 269–279). New York: Springer.

Diamond, M. (1993). Homosexuality and bisexuality in different populations. *Archives of Sexual Behavior, 22*, 291–310.

DuPree, M. G., Mustanski, B. S., Bocklandt, S., Nievergelt, C., & Hamer, D. H. (2004). A candidate gene study of CYP19 (aromatase) and male sexual orientation. *Behavior Genetics, 34*, 243–250.

Ehrhardt, A. A., Evers, K., & Money, J. (1968). Influence of androgen and some aspects of sexually dimorphic behavior in women with the late-treated adrenogenital syndrome. *Johns Hopkins Medical Journal, 123*, 115–122.

Ellis, L., Peckham, W., Ames, M. A., & Burke, D. (1988). Sexual orientation of human offspring may be altered by severe maternal stress during pregnancy. *The Journal of Sex Research, 25*(1), 152–157.

Green, R. (1985). Gender identity in childhood and later sexual orientation: follow-up of 78 males. *American Journal of Psychiatry, 142,* 339–341.

Grimbos, T., Dawood, K., Burriss, R. P., Zucker, K. J., & Puts, D. A. (2010). Sexual orientation and the second to fourth finger length ratio: A meta-analysis in men and women. *Behavioral Neuroscience, 124,* 278–287.

Haider-Markel, D. P., & Joslyn, M. R. (2008). Beliefs about the origins of homosexuality and support for gay rights. *Public Opinion Quarterly, 72,* 291–310.

Hall, L. S., & Love, C. T. (2003). Finger-length ratios in female monozygotic twins discordant for sexual orientation. *Archives of Sexual Behavior, 32,* 23–28.

Hamer, D. H., Hu, S., Magnuson, V. L., Hu, N., & Pattatucci, A. M. (1993). A linkage between DNA markers on the X chromosome and male sexual orientation. *Science, 261,* 321–327.

Hamilton, W. D. (1964a). The genetical evolution of social behaviour. I. *Journal of Theoretical Biology, 7,* 1–16.

Hamilton, W. D. (1964b). The genetical evolution of social behaviour. II. *Journal of Theoretical Biology, 7,* 17–52.

Hepper, P. G., McCartney, G. R., & Shannon, E. A. (1998). Lateralised behaviour in first trimester human foetuses. *Neuropsychologia, 36,* 531–534.

Hepper, P. G., Shahidullah, S., & White, R. (1991). Handedness in the human fetus. *Neuropsychologia, 29,* 1107–1111.

Heston, L. L., & Shields, J. (1968). Homosexuality in twins: A family study and a registry study. *Archives of General Psychiatry, 18,* 149–160.

Hines, M., Ahmed, S. F., & Hughes, I. A. (2003). Psychological outcomes and gender-related development in complete androgen insensitivity syndrome. *Archives of Sexual Behavior, 32,* 93–101.

Hines, M., Brook, C., & Conway, G. S. (2004). Androgen and psychosexual development: Core gender identity, sexual orientation and recalled childhood gender role behavior in women and men with congenital adrenal hyperplasia (CAH). *The Journal of Sex Research, 41,* 75–81.

Hu, S., Pattatucci, A. M. L., Patterson, C., Li, L., Fulker, D. W., Cherny, S. S.,...Hamer, D. H. (1995). Linkage between sexual orientation and chromosome Xq28 in males but not in females. *Nature Genetics, 11,* 248–256.

Hu, S. H., Wei, N., Wang, Q. D., Yan, L. Q., Wei, E. Q., Zhang, M. M., et al. (2008). Patterns of brain activation during visually evoked sexual arousal differ between homosexual and heterosexual men. *AJNR. American Journal of Neuroradiology, 29,* 1890–1896.

Iemmola, F., & Camperio Ciani, A. (2009). New evidence of genetic factors influencing sexual orientation in men: Female fecundity increase in the maternal line. *Archives of Sexual Behavior, 38,* 393–399.

Imperato-McGinley, J., Peterson, R. E., Gautier, T., Cooper, G., Danner, R., Arthur, A., et al. (1982). Hormonal evaluation of a large kindred with complete androgen insensitivity: Evidence for secondary 5 alpha-reductase deficiency. *Journal of Clinical Endocrinology and Metabolism, 54,* 931–941.

Janssen, E., McBride, K. R., Yarber, W., Hill, B. J., & Butler, S. M. (2008). Factors that influence sexual arousal in men: A focus group study. *Archives of Sexual Behavior, 37,* 252–265.

Kallmann, F. J. (1952). Twin and sibship study of overt male homosexuality. *American Journal of Human Genetics, 4,* 136–146.

Kendler, K. S., Thornton, L. M., Gilman, S. E., & Kessler, R. C. (2000). Sexual orientation in a U.S. national sample of twin and nontwin sibling pairs. *American Journal of Psychiatry, 157,* 1843–1846.

King, M., Green, J., Osborn, D. P., Arkell, J., Hetherton, J., & Pereira, E. (2005). Family size in white gay and heterosexual men. *Archives of Sexual Behavior, 34,* 117–122.

Kinsey, A. C., Pomeroy, W. B., & Martin, C. E. (1948). *Sexual behavior in the human male.* Philadelphia: W. B. Saunders.

Klein, F., Sepekoff, B., & Wolf, T. J. (1985). Sexual orientation: A multi-variable dynamic process. *Journal of Homosexuality, 11,* 35–49.

Lalumiere, M. L., Blanchard, R., & Zucker, K. J. (2000). Sexual orientation and handedness in men and women: A meta-analysis. *Psychological Bulletin, 126,* 575–592.

Langstrom, N., Rahman, Q., Carlstrom, E., & Lichtenstein, P. (2010). Genetic and environmental effects on same-sex sexual behavior: A population study of twins in Sweden. *Archives of Sexual Behavior, 39,* 75–80.

Laumann, E. O., Gagnon, J. H., Michael, R. T., & Michaels, S. (1994). *The social organization of sexuality: Sexual practices in the United States.* Chicago: University of Chicago Press.

LeVay, S. (1991). A difference in hypothalamic structure between heterosexual and homosexual men. *Science, 253,* 1034–1037.

LeVay, S., & Baldwin, J. (2009). *Human sexuality* (3rd ed.). Sunderland, MA: Sinauer.

Lippa, R. A. (2003). Are 2D:4D finger-length ratios related to sexual orientation? Yes for men, no for women. *Journal of Personality and Social Psychology, 85,* 179–188.

Lippa, R. A. (2008). The relation between childhood gender nonconformity and adult masculinity-femininity and anxiety in heterosexual and homosexual men and women. *Sex Roles, 59,* 684–693.

Macke, J. P., Hu, N., Hu, S., Bailey, M., King, V. L., Brown, T.,...Nathans, J. (1993). Sequence variation in the androgen receptor gene is not a common determinant of male sexual orientation. *American Journal of Human Genetics, 53,* 844–852.

Manning, J. T., Churchill, A. J., & Peters, M. (2007). The effects of sex, ethnicity, and sexual orientation on self-measured digit ratio (2D:4D). *Archives of Sexual Behavior, 36,* 223–233.

Manning, J. T., Scutt, D., Wilson, J., & Lewis-Jones, D. I. (1998). The ratio of 2nd to 4th digit length: A predictor of sperm numbers and concentrations of testosterone, luteinizing hormone and oestrogen. *Human Reproduction, 13,* 3000–3004.

Martin, J. T., & Nguyen, D. H. (2004). Anthropometric analysis of homosexuals and heterosexuals: Implications for early hormone exposure. *Hormones and Behavior, 45,* 31–39.

Mayr, E. (1988). *Toward a new philosophy of biology: Observations of an evolutionist.* Cambridge, MA: Harvard University Press.

McFadden, D., & Pasanen, E. G. (1998). Comparison of the auditory systems of heterosexuals and homosexuals: Click-evoked otoacoustic emissions. *Proceedings of the National Academy of Sciences, 95,* 2709–2713.

McFadden, D., & Pasanen, E. G. (1999). Spontaneous otoacoustic emissions in heterosexuals, homosexuals, and bisexuals. *Journal of the Acoustical Society of America, 105,* 2403–2413.

Miller, E. M. (2000). Homosexuality, birth order, and evolution: Toward an equilibrium reproductive economics of homosexuality. *Archives of Sexual Behavior, 29,* 1–34.

Money, J., & Russo, A. J. (1979). Homosexual outcome of discordant gender identity/role in childhood: Longitudinal follow-up. *Journal of Pediatric Psychology, 4*(1), 29–41.

Money, J., Schwartz, M., & Lewis, V. G. (1984). Adult erotosexual status and fetal hormonal masculinization and demasculinization: 46,XX congenital virilizing adrenal hyperplasia and 46,XY androgen-insensitivity syndrome compared. *Psychoneuroendocrinology, 9,* 405–414.

Mustanski, B. S., Chivers, M. L., & Bailey, J. M. (2002). A critical review of recent biological research on human sexual orientation. *Annual Review of Sex Research, 12,* 89–140.

Mustanski, B. S., Dupree, M. G., Nievergelt, C. M., Bocklandt, S., Schork, N. J., & Hamer, D. H. (2005). A genomewide scan of male sexual orientation. *Human Genetics, 116,* 272–278.

Nelson, R. J. (2005). *An introduction to behavioral endocrinology* (3rd ed.). Sunderland, MA: Sinauer Associates.

Pasterski, V. L., Geffner, M. E., Brain, C., Hindmarsh, P., Brook, C., & Hines, M. (2005). Prenatal hormones and postnatal socialization by parents as determinants of male-typical toy play in girls with congenital adrenal hyperplasia. *Child Development, 76,* 264–278.

Pearcey, S. M., Docherty, K. J., & Dabbs, J. M., Jr. (1996). Testosterone and sex role identification in lesbian couples. *Physiological Behavior, 60,* 1033–1035.

Pillard, R. C., Poumadere, J., & Carretta, R. A. (1981). Is homosexuality familial? A review, some data, and a suggestion. *Archives of Sexual Behavior, 10,* 465–475.

Pillard, R. C., Poumadere, J., & Carretta, R. A. (1982). A family study of sexual orientation. *Archives of Sexual Behavior, 11,* 511–520.

Pillard, R. C., & Weinrich, J. D. (1986). Evidence of familial nature of male homosexuality. *Archives of General Psychiatry, 43,* 808–812.

Ponseti, J., Siebner, H. R., Kloppel, S., Wolff, S., Granert, O., Jansen, O., et al. (2007). Homosexual women have less grey matter in perirhinal cortex than heterosexual women. *PLoS One, 2,* e762.

Puts, D. A., Jordan, C. L., & Breedlove, S. M. (2006). O brother, where art thou? The fraternal birth-order effect on male sexual orientation. *Proceedings of the National Academy of Sciences, 103,* 10531–10532.

Puts, D. A., McDaniel, M. A., Jordan, C. L., & Breedlove, S. M. (2008). Spatial ability and prenatal androgens: Meta-analyses of congenital adrenal hyperplasia and digit ratio (2D:4D) studies. *Archives of Sexual Behavior, 37,* 100–111.

Rahman, Q., Collins, A., Morrison, M., Orrells, J. C., Cadinouche, K., Greenfield, S., et al. (2008). Maternal inheritance and familial fecundity factors in male homosexuality. *Archives of Sexual Behavior, 37,* 962–969.

Rahman, Q., & Hull, M. S. (2005). An empirical test of the kin selection hypothesis for male homosexuality. *Archives of Sexual Behavior, 34,* 461–467.

Rahman, Q., & Koerting, J. (2008). Sexual orientation-related differences in allocentric spatial memory tasks. *Hippocampus, 18,* 55–63.

Rahman, Q., & Wilson, G. D. (2003). Large sexual-orientation-related differences in performance on mental rotation and judgment of line orientation tasks. *Neuropsychology, 17*(1), 25–31.

Rainer, J. D., Mesnikoff, A., Kolb, L. C., & Carr, A. (1960). Homosexuality and heterosexuality in identical twins. *Psychosomatic Medicine, 22,* 251–258.

Reiner, W. G., & Gearhart, J. P. (2004). Discordant sexual identity in some genetic males with cloacal exstrophy assigned to female sex at birth. *New England Journal of Medicine, 350,* 333–341.

Rice, G., Anderson, C., Risch, N., & Ebers, G. (1999). Male homosexuality: Absence of linkage to microsatellite markers at Xq28. *Science, 284,* 665–667.

Rieger, G., Chivers, M. L., & Bailey, J. M. (2005). Sexual arousal patterns of bisexual men. *Psychological Sciences, 16,* 579–584.

Rieger, G., Linsenmeier, J. A., Gygax, L., & Bailey, J. M. (2008). Sexual orientation and childhood gender nonconformity: Evidence from home videos. *Developmental Psychology, 44,* 46–58.

Robinson, S. J., & Manning, J. T. (2000). The ratio of 2nd to 4th digit length and male homosexuality. *Evolution and Human Behavior, 21,* 333–345.

Rosenthal, A. M., Sylva, D., Safron, A., & Bailey, J. M. (2011). Sexual arousal patterns of bisexual men revisited. *Biological Psychology, 88,* 112–115.

Safron, A., Barch, B., Bailey, J. M., Gitelman, D. R., Parrish, T. B., & Reber, P. J. (2007). Neural correlates of sexual arousal in homosexual and heterosexual men. *Behavioral Neurosciences, 121,* 237–248.

Sanders, A. R., Cao, Q., Zhang, J., Badner, J. A., Goldin, L. R., Guroff, J. J., et al. (1998). *Genetic linkage study of male homosexual orientation.* Paper presented at the 151st annual meeting of the American Psychiatric Association.

Sandfort, T. (1998). Homosexual and bisexual behavior in European countries. In M. Hubert, N. Bajos, & T. Sandfort (Eds.), *Sexual behavior and HIV/AIDS in Europe: Comparisons of national surveys* (pp. 68–105). London: UCL Press.

Savic, I., Berglund, H., & Lindstrom, P. (2005). Brain response to putative pheromones in homosexual men. *Proceedings of the National Academy of Sciences, 102,* 7356–7361.

Savic, I., & Lindstrom, P. (2008). PET and MRI show differences in cerebral asymmetry and functional connectivity between homo- and heterosexual subjects. *Proceedings of the National Academy of Sciences, 105,* 9403–9408.

Singh, D., Vidaurri, M., Zambarano, R. J., & Dabbs, J. M., Jr. (1999). Lesbian erotic role identification: Behavioral, morphological, and hormonal correlates. *Journal of Personality and Social Psychology, 76,* 1035–1049.

Swaab, D. F., & Hofman, M. A. (1990). An enlarged suprachiasmatic nucleus in homosexual men. *Brain Research, 537,* 141–148.

Vasey, P., Pocock, D. S., & VanderLaan, D. P. (2007). Kin selection and male androphilia in Samoan *fa'afafine. Evolution and Human Behavior, 28,* 159–167.

Vasey, P. L., & VanderLaan, D. P. (2010). Avuncular tendencies and the evolution of male androphilia in Samoan fa'afafine. *Archives of Sexual Behavior, 39,* 821–830.

Voracek, M., Manning, J. T., & Ponocny, I. (2005). Digit ratio (2D:4D) in homosexual and heterosexual men from Austria. *Archives of Sexual Behavior, 34,* 335–340.

Ward, I. L. (1972). Prenatal stress feminizes and demasculinizes the behavior of males. *Science, 175*(4017), 82–84.

Whitam, F. L. (1977). Childhood indicators of male homosexuality. *Archives of Sexual Behavior, 6*(2), 89–96.

Whitam, F. L., & Mathy, R. M. (1991). Childhood cross-gender behavior of homosexual females in Brazil, Peru, the Philippines, and the United States. *Archives of Sexual Behavior, 20,* 151–170.

Wilson, E. O. (1975). *Sociobiology: The new synthesis.* Cambridge, MA: Harvard University Press.

Wisniewski, A. B., Migeon, C. J., Meyer-Bahlburg, H. F., Gearhart, J. P., Berkovitz, G. D., Brown, T. R., et al. (2000). Complete androgen insensitivity syndrome: Long-term medical, surgical, and psychosexual outcome. *Journal of Clinical Endocrinology and Metabolism, 85,* 2664–2669.

Zietsch, B. P., Morley, K. I., Shekar, S. N., Verweij, K. J. H., Keller, M. C., Macgregor, S., ... Martin, N. G. (2008). Genetic factors predisposing to homosexuality may increase mating success in heterosexuals. *Evolution and Human Behavior, 29,* 424–433.

Zucker, K. J., Bradley, S. J., Oliver, G., Blake, J., Fleming, S., & Hood, J. (1996). Psychosexual development of women with congenital adrenal hyperplasia. *Hormones and Behavior, 30,* 300–318.

Zuger, B. (1984). Early effeminate behavior in boys. Outcome and significance for homosexuality. *Journal of Nervous and Mental Diseases, 172,* 90–97.

Zuloaga, D. G., Puts, D. A., Jordan, C. L., & Breedlove, S. M. (2008). The role of androgen receptors in the masculinization of brain and behavior: What we've learned from the testicular feminization mutation. *Hormones and Behavior, 53,* 613–626.

6

Demographic Perspectives on Sexual Orientation

GARY J. GATES

Considering sexual orientation as a demographic characteristic is a relatively new practice. Academic scholarship focusing on the distinct demographic, economic, and geographic characteristics of lesbian, gay, and bisexual communities is relatively recent and relies on limited data resources. Unfortunately, no large-scale population-based data sources provide information about the transgender community. As such, this chapter focuses on lesbian, gay, and bisexual people. Because only a few population-based surveys focused on demographic and economic analyses include sexual orientation questions, many demographic studies of lesbian, gay, and bisexual communities use more commonly available data on same-sex cohabiting couples.

This chapter will summarize existing literature that describes the demographic, economic, and geographic characteristics of lesbian, gay, and bisexual populations. It will also present analyses conducted specifically for this chapter using population-based data sources including the U.S. Census Bureau's American Community Survey and the General Social Survey (Smith et al., 2008). The Census Bureau's annual American Community Survey (ACS) surveys approximately two million households each year and is a primary data source for demographic information about the U.S. population. Same-sex couples who identify one partner as either a "husband/wife" or "unmarried partner" can be identified in the ACS. The General Social Survey (GSS) is a biennial national survey of approximately 2000 adults conducted by the National Opinion Research Center at the University of Chicago. The 2008 GSS included questions about both sexual orientation and same-sex sexual behavior.

The chapter begins with a discussion of some of the data and methodological challenges associated with studying sexual orientation as a demographic characteristic. Analyses are then presented to describe estimates of the size of lesbian, gay, and bisexual populations, as well as information about coming out (i.e., disclosure of these identities). The remainder of the chapter considers how lesbian, gay, and bisexual populations compare with the heterosexual population with regard to a variety of demographic characteristics including geographic distribution, age, race/ethnicity, educational attainment, socioeconomic status, family formation, and child-rearing.

DATA RESOURCES AND METHODOLOGICAL CHALLENGES

Outside of surveys primarily designed to assess sexual health and well-being, very few large-scale population-based surveys include questions about sexual orientation. National census surveys constitute the most widely used data to assess population demographic traits. To date, no national census surveys have collected information on sexual orientation. In the United States, none of the widely used surveys designed to assess the demographic and economic characteristics of the population—for example, the American Community Survey, the Current Population Survey, or the Survey of Income and Program Participation—ascertains the sexual orientation of respondents.

As a result of this paucity of data, small sample sizes of people who can be identified as lesbian, gay, or bisexual create a common and often serious methodological problem for demographic analyses. For example, the 2008 General Social Survey included 2023 adult respondents, of whom 1759 responded to the sexual orientation question. From that group, only 60 respondents identified as lesbian, gay, or bisexual and another 16 respondents reported recent same-sex sexual behavior. Although this survey can be used to make relatively precise estimates of the proportion of sexual minorities in the population, that precision is diminished when differences among sexual minorities are assessed based on characteristics such as age, race/ethnicity, or socioeconomic status. The small sample size also precludes assessment of geographic variation within the nonheterosexual sample. Sample size limitations constitute an ongoing challenge in demographic research on lesbian, gay, and bisexual populations.

The data landscape is somewhat better with regard to same-sex couples. It is becoming increasingly common for demographic surveys to include options that allow for the identification of same-sex couples in cohabiting relationships (i.e., couples who live together and who are not simply roommates). In the United States, the 1990 Decennial Census marked the first time that the category of "unmarried partner" was included along with options such as "husband/wife" and "roommate" in what is known as the "relationship to householder" question. The relationship to householder question asks the person filling out the census form (known as the householder) to describe his or her relationship to all other individuals in the household. The "unmarried partner" option was primarily designed to identify unmarried different-sex cohabiters who were not simply roommates. But because the survey collects information about the age and sex of all individuals in the household, researchers could, for the first time, also identify comparable same-sex couples. An increasing number of countries around the world have added similar response items to their national census forms (e.g., Canada, Ireland, the United Kingdom, Australia, and New Zealand).

With increasing legal recognition for same-sex couples (including marriage, civil unions, civil partnerships, and domestic partnerships), demographic surveys have begun to add options to marital and relationship status questions to acquire data on same-sex couples. In the United States, same-sex couples who are in civil unions or registered domestic partnerships cannot be identified on any federal surveys. The U.S. Census Bureau does not collect data to derive accurate estimates of how many legally married same-sex couples live in the United States. However, it does release an estimate of the number of same-sex couples who used the terms "husband/wife" to identify their relationship in the annual American Community Survey. Because the marriages of same-sex couples are not recognized by the U.S. federal government, these couples are not counted as being married in federal statistics.

This policy will be maintained in the release of Census 2010 data (Williams Institute, 2009).

One advantage of data on same-sex couples from national census data collection efforts is that challenges associated with sample size are minimized and consideration of geographic variation and differences across demographic subgroups is feasible. However, these data are not free of methodological challenges. Without a direct sexual orientation question, the identification of same-sex couples often relies on responses to two survey items: relationship to a reference person and the sex of all individuals in the household. Black et al. (2007) and Gates and Steinberger (2011) have documented serious measurement issues that result even if small proportions of different-sex couples inadvertently miscode the sex of one partner and are thus enumerated as a same-sex couple. According to some estimates, between 30% and 50% of couples identified as same-sex in U.S. Census Bureau tabulations may be miscoded different-sex couples. In 2008, the U.S. Census Bureau altered data collection and processing procedures (see O'Connell & Lofquist, 2009) that appear to have substantially reduced the error to an estimated 11% of the same-sex couple sample. Data from either the U.S. Decennial Census or the American Community Survey presented in this chapter follow Gates and Steinberger's (2011) recommendations regarding analytical methods that reduce the impact of the measurement error when analyzing U.S. Census Bureau data.

A final methodological issue common to almost all data on sexual minorities is underreporting. As a stigmatized group without national antidiscrimination protection in employment or public accommodation, sexual minorities may often be reluctant to identify themselves on surveys as lesbian, gay, or bisexual, or as a member of a same-sex couple. In addition to reluctance to identify due to social stigma, the propensity to identify as a member of a sexual minority may also be related to the survey methodology. Surveys that utilize computer technology to decrease human interaction in providing responses increased reporting of a variety of stigmatizing behaviors, including same-sex sexual experiences (Turner et al., 1998).

Although calculating the extent of underreporting of sexual minority status is difficult, evidence of substantial variation across age cohorts in the percent of those who identify as lesbian, gay, or bisexual suggests that underreporting may be decreasing as younger age cohorts feel more comfortable in being open about their sexual orientation identity and same-sex sexual behavior. Findings from the 2008 General Social Survey show that 7.2% of individuals age 18–29 either identified as lesbian, gay, or bisexual; reported same-sex sexual experiences in the past 5 years; or reported that all sexual experiences since age 18 had been with a same-sex partner. This compared to just 3.4% reporting in this way among those aged 30–54, and only 1.4% of those aged 55 and older (Gates, 2010a). With regard to same-sex couples, Gates (2010b) suggested that nearly 10% of same-sex couples self-identified as roommates rather than as either unmarried partners or spouses when they completed their 2010 Census form. This marks an improvement from studies conducted following Census 2000 (Badgett & Rogers, 2003), which suggested that about 20% of same-sex couples designated themselves as roommates. So although underreporting may be declining over time, it remains a factor in interpreting findings from population-based surveys that include lesbian, gay, and bisexual populations.

HOW MANY PEOPLE ARE LESBIAN, GAY, OR BISEXUAL?

Estimates of the size of lesbian, gay, and bisexual populations vary for a variety of reasons. As already discussed, survey methodology can affect the percent of respondents who report stigmatizing identities and behaviors. Whether lesbian, gay, and bisexual sexual orientation is defined strictly by identity or uses definitions that also include sexual behavior or sexual attraction can also create substantial variation in estimates.

Estimates of the percentage of the population who self-identify as lesbian, gay, or bisexual vary between 1% and 4% across the six national surveys shown in Table 6.1. A 2009/2010 Norwegian survey showed the lowest percentage at 1.2%. The U.S. National Survey of Family Growth (2006–2008) reported that 3.7% of respondents identified as lesbian, gay, or bisexual (though this was an age-restricted sample of 18–44 year olds). The most recent survey of all adults in the United States, the 2008 GSS, reported that 2.9% of respondents identified themselves as lesbian, gay, or bisexual. Interestingly, two U.S. surveys that used Internet methodologies reported substantially higher rates of lesbian, gay, and bisexual identity. Indiana University's National Survey of Sexual Health and Behavior, conducted in 2009, found that 5.6% of adults identified as lesbian, gay, or bisexual (Chandra et al., 2011) and Harris Interactive's Online Poll found that 6.8% of respondents identified as nonheterosexual (Harris Interactive & Witeck-Combs, 2010).

TABLE 6.1. PERCENTAGE OF ADULTS WHO SELF-IDENTIFY AS LESBIAN, GAY, OR BISEXUAL IN VARIOUS NATIONAL PROBABILITY SAMPLES

Survey	Country	Year	Age Range	All	Men	Women
Norwegian Living Conditions Survey	Norway	2010	16 and older	1.2% LG: 0.7% B: 0.5%	0.9% LG: 0.6% B: 0.2%	1.5% LG: 0.7% B: 0.8%
Integrated Household Survey	U.K.	2009/2010	16 and older	1.5% LG: 1.0% B: 0.5%	1.6% LG: 1.3% B: 0.3%	1.3% LG: 0.6% B: 0.7%
General Social Survey	United States	2008	18 and older	2.9% LG: 1.7% B: 1.2%	2.2% LG: 1.5% B: 0.7%	3.4% LG: 1.8% B: 1.6%
Canadian Community Health Survey	Canada	2005	18–59	1.9% LG: 1.1% B: 0.8%	2.1% LG: 1.4% B: 0.7%	1.7% LG: 0.8% B: 0.9%
National Survey of Family Growth	United States	2006–2008	18–44	3.7% LG: 2.3% B: 1.4%	2.8% LG: 1.7% B: 1.1%	4.6% LG: 1.1% B: 3.5%
Australian Longitudinal Study of Health and Relationships	Australia	2005	16 and older	2.1% LG: 1.9% B: 0.9%	2.2% LG: 1.0% B: 1.2%	2.0% LG: 0.7% B: 1.3%

The national surveys shown in Table 6.1 show several consistent differences between men and women in sexual identity. Although most surveys show relatively small differences in the overall percentage of men and women who identify as lesbian, gay, or bisexual, women are substantially more likely than men to identify as bisexual. In the Norwegian (Gulløy & Normann, 2010) and United Kingdom (Office of National Statistics, 2010) surveys as in the U.S. General Social Survey (Gates, 2011), women are more than twice as likely as men to identify as bisexual.

Four of the surveys shown in Table 6.1 also posed questions about either sexual behavior or sexual attraction. In all cases, more adults report same-sex attractions and behaviors than self-identify as lesbian, gay, or bisexual. With the exception of the Norwegian survey (Gulløy & Normann, 2010), these differences are substantial. Results from the two U.S. surveys (Gates, 2011; Chandra et al., 2011) and the Australian survey (Ferris, 2005) suggest that adults are two to three times more likely to say that they are (or have been) attracted to individuals of the same sex or have had same-sex sexual experiences than they are to identify themselves as lesbian, gay, or bisexual. With the exception of the U.S. General Social Survey, all of the other surveys also suggest that women are more likely to report same-sex attractions and sexual behaviors than are

men. The data on sexual attractions are presented in Table 6.2.

COMING OUT

Conceptualizing lesbian, gay, and bisexual people as a demographic group requires serious consideration of the notion of "coming out" (i.e., disclosure of a nonheterosexual sexual identity). It is likely that most surveys that ask questions about sexual orientation largely, though evidence suggests not exclusively, capture a relatively "out" lesbian, gay, and bisexual population. Of course, what constitutes being "out" is an open question. Findings from the 2008 General Social Survey (Gates, 2010a) demonstrate that a variety of demographic characteristics are associated with the degree to which individuals are open with others about their sexual orientation and behavior. Also, bisexual men and women report very different experiences of coming out than do lesbians and gay men. Bisexual individuals are less likely to be out and they are more likely to report that their first sense of a same-sex sexual attraction was at an older age than their gay and lesbian counterparts. If being out is correlated with a willingness to identify as a sexual minority on surveys, then statistics on "visible" lesbian, gay, and bisexual populations may be biased by demographic differences that can vary depending on how out or closeted individuals may be.

TABLE 6.2. PERCENTAGE OF ADULTS WHO REPORT SAME-SEX ATTRACTIONS OR BEHAVIORS IN VARIOUS NATIONAL PROBABILITY SAMPLES

Survey	Country	Year	Age Range	Measure	All	Men	Women
Norwegian Living Conditions Survey	Norway	2010	16–59	Any same-sex attraction	1.8%	1.5%	2.2%
General Social Survey	United States	2008	18 and older	Any same-sex sexual experiences since age 18 or lesbian, gay, bisexual identity	8.6%	9.7%	7.5%
National Survey of Family Growth	United States	2006–2008	18–44	Any same-sex attraction	11%	6.5%	16.7%
National Survey of Family Growth	United States	2006–2008	18–44	Men: any anal/oral sex with a man Women: any oral sex or any sexual experience with a woman	8.8%	5.2%	12.5%
Australian Longitudinal Study of Health and Relationships	Australia	2005	16 and older	Any same-sex attraction	6.5%	4.0%	9.1%
Australian Longitudinal Study of Health and Relationships	Australia	2005	16 and older	Any same-sex sexual experience	6.9%	6.4%	7.3%

The 2008 GSS included a module of questions asked to those who identified as lesbian, gay, or bisexual or who reported same-sex sexual experiences (Gates, 2010a). The module included questions about timing of first same-sex attraction, along with timing of coming out to others, and timing of coming out to those in the workplace. In analyses of these data, lesbian, gay, and bisexual individuals are defined as those who self-identified as such, those who have had same-sex sexual experiences in the past 5 years, and those who report exclusively same-sex sexual experiences since they were 18 years of age. Lesbians and gay men are defined as those who identify in this way and also those who report exclusively same-sex sexual experiences either in the past 5 years or since they were 18 years of age. Bisexual individuals are defined as those who identify as bisexual or those who report both same-sex and different-sex sexual partners in the past 5 years. Unfortunately, the sample sizes of lesbian, gay, and bisexual individuals were small; there were only 66 lesbian, gay, or bisexual respondents in all. As such, findings presented from the GSS should be considered more suggestive than conclusive.

Reservations aside, however, the results of the GSS showed that most lesbian, gay, and heterosexual respondents reported being relatively open about their nonheterosexual identities. In all, 87% of lesbian, gay, and bisexual individuals reported having told another person either about their sexual orientation identity or about having had same-sex sexual experiences. Among lesbians and gay men, that figure was more than 95%, whereas it was 75% among bisexual men and women.

More than 75% of lesbian, gay, or bisexual individuals reported that they had their first same-sex sexual attraction before they were 18 years of age. Among lesbians and gay men, that figure was nearly 89%, compared to only 58% among bisexuals. Consistent with this finding, lesbians and gay men were nearly twice as likely as bisexuals to have told another person about their sexual orientation or same-sex sexual behavior before they were 18 years of age (43% vs. 22%, respectively). Bisexual men and women were also less likely than lesbians and gay men to be out in the workplace. In total, approximately two-thirds of lesbian, gay, and bisexual individuals reported having told someone in the workplace about their sexual orientation or same-sex sexual behavior. More than 75% of lesbians and gay

men reported being out to someone at work compared to just over half of bisexuals. Unfortunately, due to the cross-sectional nature of the GSS data, they are not appropriate for studying causes of the differences in coming out behaviors among lesbians, gay men, and bisexuals. Coming out was also treated as a binary construct within the context of a respondent's current identity or behavior and did not capture the full complexity of coming out experiences. A better understanding of how disclosure issues may affect data on lesbian, gay, and bisexual people would take into account complexities of coming out, and would assess possible differences among bisexual, gay, and lesbian identities.

Gates (2010a) also showed that several key demographic characteristics affect the probability of lesbian, gay, and bisexual individuals choosing not to disclose their sexual orientation in the GSS. Age and race/ethnicity were both significant predictors of not being out. Older individuals were more closeted. Relative to those under age 30, adults aged 30–54 were more likely to be closeted and those over age 55 were much more likely than those under 30 years of age to be in the closet. Latinos/as and those in other racial/ethnic categories were much more likely than white individuals to report never having told anyone about their same-sex sexual behavior or nonheterosexual identity.

The GSS data capture closeted individuals who are at least willing to indicate on a survey that they consider themselves to be lesbian, gay, or bisexual, or have had same-sex sexual experiences. It is likely that there are other individuals who would be reluctant to share that information even on an anonymous survey. If that is true, and these individuals share the demographic characteristics that are observed among those who are closeted but willing to report being a sexual minority on surveys, then the visible sexual minority population likely underrepresents bisexuals, older adults, and racial/ethnic minorities. This should be taken into account when interpreting the demographic portrait of the lesbian, gay, and bisexual population presented in the remainder of this chapter.

THE GEOGRAPHIC DISTRIBUTION OF LESBIAN, GAY, AND BISEXUAL COMMUNITIES

Sample size limitations in most surveys that include identification of lesbian, gay, and bisexual people make it difficult to assess how the geographic distribution of nonheterosexual communities might differ from the distribution of the heterosexual population. However, there is substantial evidence that urban areas tend to have high concentrations of lesbian, gay, and heterosexual adults. Furthermore, among nonheterosexual individuals, men appear to be more likely than women to live in urban areas. This finding might stem from the facts that gay men, on average, earn more than lesbians, and that gay men are less likely than lesbians to be rearing children (e.g., Black et al., 2000; Gates & Ost, 2004). Because urban areas tend to be more expensive places to live and are sometimes viewed as less amenable to child-rearing than suburban or rural areas, they may be more attractive to gay men than to lesbians or heterosexual people. Analyses of the 2009 American Community Survey (see Table 6.3) revealed that 23% of the overall U.S. population but only 16% of same-sex couples live in rural areas. Female couples (19%) are more likely than male couples (14%) to live in rural areas. Findings from the United Kingdom's Integrated Household Survey (Office of National Statistics, 2010) also showed that the percentage of adults identifying as lesbian, gay, or bisexual was highest in London and Southwest England (two of the most urban areas of the country) and lowest in Northern Ireland and the East Midlands (which are more rural areas). Andersson et al. (2006) also reported higher proportions of same-sex couples in more urban areas of Norway and Sweden.

Another way to assess geographic distribution is to consider the probability of living in a metropolitan area. As defined by the U.S. Census Bureau, metropolitan areas are usually multicounty regions that constitute the commuting area for large cities. The principal city within a metropolitan area most often constitutes the most urbanized portion of the region, and areas outside of the principal city are generally more suburban. Most areas outside of metropolitan areas are relatively rural, though some metropolitan areas do include areas considered to be rural.

In the U.S. Census data, same-sex couples have been found to be more likely than the rest of the U.S. population to live in the principal city of a metropolitan area. Same-sex couples have also been found to be less likely to live outside the principal city or completely outside a metropolitan area. For instance, 46% of same-sex couples, but only about one-third of the U.S. population has been found to live in the principal city of a metropolitan area. About one in six people in the United States lives outside of a metropolitan area compared to just one in 10 same-sex couples. Similar to the findings regarding urban and rural areas, male same-sex couples are more likely to live in principal cities and less likely to live outside of metropolitan areas than are female same-sex couples.

Although same-sex couples are more likely to live in urban areas than in rural areas, their concentrations are not always highest in highly populated U.S. cities or highly urbanized U.S. states. Table 6.4 shows the top 10 cities (among the 50 largest cities in the United States) ranked by the number of same-sex couples per thousand households (as reported in the 2009 ACS). Three of the top five

TABLE 6.3. GEOGRAPHIC DISTRIBUTION OF THE U.S. POPULATION AND SAME-SEX COUPLES, BY URBAN/RURAL AND METROPOLITAN AREA, 2009 AMERICAN COMMUNITY SURVEY, U.S. CENSUS BUREAU (AUTHOR ANALYSES)

	Population	All Same-Sex Couples	Same-Sex Female Couples	Same-Sex Male Couples
Rural	23%	16%	19%	14%
Urban	77%	84%	81%	86%
Metropolitan area, principal city	33%	46%	41%	51%
Metropolitan area, outside principal city	51%	44%	48%	40%
Not metropolitan area	16%	10%	11%	8%

TABLE 6.4. TOP 10 CITIES (AMONG THE 50 LARGEST U.S. CITIES BY POPULATION) AND STATES RANKED BY SAME-SEX COUPLES PER 1000 HOUSEHOLDS, 2009 AMERICAN COMMUNITY SURVEY, U.S. CENSUS BUREAU (AUTHOR ANALYSES)

Rank	50 Largest U.S. Cities (Population Rank)	Same-Sex Couples per 1000 Households	States	Same-Sex Couples per 1000 Households
1	San Francisco, CA (12)	25.35	District of Columbia	17.97
2	Portland, OR (29)	25.34	Oregon	8.25
3	Atlanta, GA (33)	19.82	Delaware	8.18
4	Seattle, WA (23)	19.18	Massachusetts	8.10
5	Oakland, CA (44)	18.95	Maine	8.02
6	Minneapolis, MN (48)	18.34	Vermont	8.00
7	Washington, DC (27)	17.97	Hawaii	7.86
8	Boston, MA (20)	15.40	California	6.71
9	San Diego, CA (8)	12.50	Colorado	6.57
10	Denver, CO (24)	12.27	Arizona	6.31

cities—Portland, Oregon (2), Atlanta (3), and Oakland (5)—all rank in the lower half of the cities if they were ranked by population size. Conversely, large cities such as New York, Los Angeles, and Chicago all rank in the middle tier when cities are ranked by same-sex couple concentration. Not surprisingly, San Francisco tops the list with a concentration of same-sex couples that exceeds the national average of 5.12 same-sex couples per thousand households by a factor of five. In total, 41 of the 50 largest cities have concentrations of same-sex couples that exceed the national average.

The 10 states with the highest concentration of same-sex couples shown in Table 6.4 are primarily in the Northeast or Western regions of the United States, which are socially liberal sections of the country. The concentration of same-sex couples exceeds the national average in 17 states and the District of Columbia, where the concentration is more than three times the national figure. Not shown in Table 6.4 are the 10 states with the lowest concentrations: Arkansas, Montana, North Dakota, West Virginia, Louisiana, Nebraska, Wyoming, South Dakota, Alabama, and Mississippi. These states are all either in the Great Plains or the South, both socially conservative regions of the country. Although the concentration of same-sex couples tends to be higher in socially liberal parts of the country, Gates (2007) found that conservative areas have generally experienced larger increases in the reported number of same-sex couples in recent years. This finding suggests that as social stigma has declined in the United States, proportionally more couples in conservative areas are willing to identify themselves on government surveys.

DEMOGRAPHIC CHARACTERISTICS: AGE, RACE/ETHNICITY

If being lesbian, gay, or bisexual were a random event in the population, and if sexual orientation development occurred in the absence of homophobic stigma, then we might not expect to see substantial differences in demographic characteristics such as age and race or ethnicity as a function of sexual orientation. As was noted above, however, differences between the characteristics of the "visible" (i.e., those who are willing to self-identify on surveys) and the "invisible" (i.e., those who are not) lesbian, gay, and bisexual populations may in fact mean that there are genuine demographic differences as a function of sexual orientation.

Perhaps because the likelihood of identifying as lesbian, gay, or heterosexual varies substantially by age, nonheterosexual individuals are, on average, younger than heterosexual ones (see Table 6.5). Heterosexual people in the United States have an average age of 45.6 years compared to 36.5 for those who are lesbian, gay, or bisexual. Individuals in same-sex couples are also younger, on average, than their different-sex counterparts (43.5 vs. 48.5, respectively). The age distribution of the full population shows that lesbian, gay, and bisexual people are about as likely as heterosexuals to be middle-aged (30–54) but are twice as likely to be under age 30 and only a third as likely to be over 55 years of age.

TABLE 6.5. AGE AND RACE/ETHNICITY AMONG LESBIAN, GAY, AND BISEXUAL
INDIVIDUALS AND SAME-SEX COUPLES, 2008 AMERICAN COMMUNITY SURVEY, U.S.
CENSUS BUREAU AND 2008 GENERAL SOCIAL SURVEY (AUTHOR ANALYSES)

	Lesbian, Gay, Bisexual (2008 General Social Survey)	Heterosexual (2008 General Social Survey)	Individuals in Same-Sex Couples (2008 American Community Survey)	Individuals in Different-Sex Couples (2008 American Community Survey)
Average age	36.5*	45.6	43.5*	48.5
Age 18–29	42%*	21%	14%*	11%
Age 30–54	48%	49%	68%*	55%
Age 55+	10%*	30%	18%*	34%
White	62%	70%	78%*	75%
African-American	20%	12%	6%*	7%
Latino/a	10%	14%	11%*	12%
Other	8%	4%	5%	6%

*Differences between lesbian/gay/bisexual versus heterosexual or same-sex versus different-sex couples are statistically significant
at $p < 0.05$.

These age differences may be partially a product of cohort differences with regard to willingness to identify as lesbian, gay, or bisexual. It is important to remember also, however, that the HIV epidemic had a devastating effect on what would today be an older cohort of gay and bisexual men, and this may affect the age composition of lesbian, gay, and bisexual communities.

The findings with regard to race and ethnicity do not reveal substantial differences between heterosexual and nonheterosexual individuals. Analyses of the 2008 GSS show that although 62% of lesbian, gay, and bisexual individuals identified as white compared to 70% of heterosexual people, that difference is not statistically significant. Among couples in the 2008 ACS, 78% of individuals in same-sex couples were white, as compared to 75% of individuals in different-sex couples. Although that difference is statistically significant, the broad racial/ethnic distribution does not, as a practical matter, vary much between individuals in same-sex and different-sex couples. Diversity in racial/ethnic characteristics within lesbian, gay, and bisexual communities is particularly important for research. Descriptions of the lesbian, gay, and bisexual population have, in the past, largely been driven by characteristics of the white members of this population, perhaps in part because they are the most numerous. There may, however, be important differences in other demographic characteristics across racial/ethnic groups.

DEMOGRAPHIC CHARACTERISTICS: EDUCATIONAL ATTAINMENT AND SOCIOECONOMIC STATUS

Perhaps one of the most persistent findings in demographic research about lesbian, gay, and bisexual individuals is that they tend to have higher levels of educational attainment than do their heterosexual peers (Black et al., 2000; Romero et al., 2007; Carpenter & Gates, 2008). Higher educational attainment does not, however, necessarily translate into higher earnings for nonheterosexual individuals. Several published studies of gay men have shown that they earn less than similarly skilled heterosexual men (Badgett, 1995; Black et al., 2000, 2003; Allegretto & Arthur, 2001; Carpenter, 2007; Plug & Berkout, 2009; Ahmed & Hammarstedt, 2010), although one study found no earnings differences among men as a function of sexual orientation (Carpenter, 2005). Estimates of the effect of sexual orientation on earnings for females have also been mixed, but many studies have reported that lesbians earn more than other women (Badgett, 1995, Black et al., 2000, 2003; Carpenter, 2007; Plug & Berkout, 2009). Results for women have varied as a function of how sexual orientation is measured and whether bisexual women are included in the studies. Among both men and women, bisexual people have been found to earn less than their gay, lesbian, or heterosexual

TABLE 6.6. EDUCATIONAL ATTAINMENT AND EARNINGS AMONG LESBIAN, GAY, AND BISEXUAL INDIVIDUALS AND SAME-SEX COUPLES, 2008 AMERICAN COMMUNITY SURVEY, U.S. CENSUS BUREAU AND 2008 GENERAL SOCIAL SURVEY (AUTHOR ANALYSES)

	Lesbian, Gay, Bisexual (2008 General Social Survey)		Heterosexual (2008 General Social Survey)	Individuals in Same-Sex Couples (2008 American Community Survey)	Individuals in Different-Sex Couples (2008 American Community Survey)
Less than high school	21.8%		12.7%	5.7%*	11.9%
High school diploma or some college	37.6%*		61.0%	48.4%*	57.2%
College or graduate degree	40.6%*		26.3%	45.9%*	30.8%
Median earnings (men)	$30,000–$39,999		$35,000–$49,999	$46,400	$45,000
	Gay $35,000–$49,999	Bisexual $17,500–$19,999			
Average earnings (men)				$64,440*	$61,585
Median earnings (women)	$15,000–$24,000		$20,000–$24,999	$39,000	$28,000
	Lesbian $20,000–$24,999	Bisexual $7,000–$9,999			
Average earnings (women)				$48,116*	$35,694

*Differences between lesbian, gay, and bisexual versus heterosexual or same-sex versus different-sex couples are statistically significant at $p < 0.05$.

counterparts (Carpenter, 2005). Albelda et al. (2009) also found that greater proportions of bisexual than lesbian or gay people are living below the federal poverty level.

Analyses of the 2008 General Social Survey and the 2008 American Community Survey show results for education that are similar to those observed in other studies (see Table 6.6). Lesbian, gay, and bisexual individuals have been found to be more likely than heterosexuals to have completed a college degree (41% vs. 26%, respectively). Similarly, individuals in same-sex couples are more likely than those in different-sex couples to have completed a college degree (46% vs. 31%).

The reasons for this apparent educational advantage among sexual minorities are not clear. One hypothesis could be based on selection. In this view, younger sexual minority people pursue higher level education as a possible hedge against

anticipated discrimination later in life. Young sexual minority individuals might also see colleges and universities as especially supportive environments, and hence be even more likely than others to view higher education as a more attractive option than the labor force. A different hypothesis would suggest that because colleges and universities are, on average, more supportive than other environments to members of sexual minorities, nonheterosexual individuals are more likely to come out and be open about their sexual orientation in college or university environments. Of course, these two hypotheses are not mutually exclusive. Data that would address these hypotheses are not readily available. It is clear, however, that the apparent educational advantages of nonheterosexual individuals do not translate directly into higher earnings.

The GSS data show that the median earnings of gay and bisexual men ($30,000–$39,999) are lower than the earnings of heterosexual men ($35,000–$49,999). Also consistent with existing research, the median earnings of bisexual men are substantially lower than those of gay men (which are actually the same as the median earnings of heterosexual men). These patterns are not evident in the ACS data in which men in same-sex couples report higher median and average earnings than men in different-sex couples.

In the GSS data, the findings show that lesbians and bisexual women, with median earnings of $15,000–$24,000, earn less than heterosexual women who report median earnings of $20,000–$24,999. This difference is driven entirely by the low earnings of bisexual women (see Table 6.6). The median earnings of lesbians are actually the same as the median earnings of heterosexual women. Women in same-sex couples earn more than women in different-sex couples and the gap between them is substantially larger than the relatively modest gap between men in same-sex couples and men in different-sex couples.

Some research has explored reasons for wage disparities among lesbian, gay, bisexual, and heterosexual individuals. Gates (2009) and Klawitter (2011) both observe that antidiscrimination laws tend to mitigate the wage disadvantage of men in same-sex couples, suggesting that discrimination may be a factor in the earnings disparities of gay and bisexual men. In a study from the Netherlands, Plug and Berkhout (2009) argue that differential selection into lower paying occupations was the driving factor in observed lower wages among gay men. Conversely, Blandford (2003) suggested that earnings advantages among lesbians may at least in part be a result of these women having disproportionately chosen high wage occupations. Blandford (2003) also suggested that selection into lower wage occupations may be a factor that depresses the earnings of gay men. He also theorizes (as do Black et al., 2003) that the relative disadvantage among heterosexual women that comes from lower levels of labor force attachment associated with child-rearing may be a contributor to the observed earnings advantages by lesbians, who are less likely to have children and thus have stronger labor force attachment that yields relatively higher earnings.

FAMILY FORMATION, PARENTHOOD, AND CHILDREN

The prominence of public policy debates regarding relationship recognition and child-rearing for same-sex couples and nonheterosexual individuals has focused significant media, policy, and research attention on lesbian, gay, and bisexual people and their families. Analyses of American television broadcast media by the Gay and Lesbian Alliance Against Defamation (2007) found that lesbian, gay, and bisexual people were most commonly portrayed as both white and male, who were also portrayed as relatively wealthy and living in cities. It is true, as stated above, that many gay men live in cities. Otherwise, however, the contrast of media images with the reality of lesbian, gay, and bisexual communities is quite clear. In fact, a demographic portrait of lesbian, gay, and bisexual individuals and their families reveals substantial racial/ethnic and socioeconomic diversity.

Partnership and Relationship Recognition

Census data from the United States, Canada, Australia, and New Zealand reveal that between 0.6% and 0.7% of all couples in these nations are same-sex couples (Statistics Canada, 2009). Estimates from the 2009 American Community Survey data show that there are 300,890 same-sex female couples and 280,410 same-sex male couples in the United States. Thus, although same-sex couples are a small number of couples overall, over a million lesbian, gay, and bisexual individuals are involved in same-sex couple relationships in the United States alone.

Carpenter and Gates (2008) reported that the percentages of lesbians who cohabit with a female partner are similar to the percentages of heterosexual men and women who cohabit with different-sex partners. Gay men are somewhat less likely than others to cohabit with a same-sex partner. In analyses of data from California, Carpenter and Gates (2008) reported that between 37% and 46% of gay men and between 51% and 62% of lesbians aged 18–59 were in cohabiting unions. This compares to 62% of comparable heterosexuals who were in cohabiting unions. They also noted that female couples were more likely than male couples to be registered as domestic partners. In analyses of administrative data from U.S. states that offer partnership recognition for same-sex couples, Gates et al. (2008) found that women were about twice a likely as men to be in a legally recognized relationship.

In Europe, the pattern has been very different. In analyses of same-sex partnerships in Norway and

Sweden, Andersson et al. (2006) reported that male couples were more likely than their female counterparts to seek legal recognition; that is, 62% of partnerships were male and only 38% were female. Similarly, data from Statistics Canada (2009) showed that 54% of married same-sex couples in 2006 were male. In the United Kingdom, about 51% of civil partnerships were male couples (Office of National Statistics, 2011). Thus, in European countries, gay men have been more likely than lesbians to take advantage of opportunities for legal recognition of their relationships.

Gates and his colleagues (2008) reported that the demand for marriage in the United States has been higher than that for other relationship recognition options, such as civil unions or registered domestic partnerships. In the first year that marriage was offered in Massachusetts, fully 37% of same-sex couples decided to marry. In contrast, when data from the first year that civil unions were available in Vermont, Connecticut, and New Jersey were examined, only 12% of same-sex couples in these states undertook civil unions. In five states that offered registered domestic partnerships, only 10% of same-sex couples registered in the first year (Gates et al., 2008). Thus, the option of marriage, when available, has been pursued by greater proportions of same-sex couples than have other options, such as domestic partnerships or civil unions.

Estimates of the number of same-sex couples who pursue relationship recognition via marriage, civil unions, or registered partnership in the United States are not provided by centralized federal agencies such as the Census Bureau. Data from the 2006 Canadian Census suggest, however, that approximately 2 years after marriage was made widely available to same-sex couples in Canada, more than 16% had married. In the United States, Gates (2010b) estimated that 35% of same-sex couples who live in a state that permits marriage are legally married. Among all same-sex couples in the United States, Gates (2010b) found that 14% reported that they have been legally married; an additional 15% reported being in a civil union or registered domestic partnership. Applied to the ACS estimates, this would imply that there are about 80,000 same-sex couples in the United States who are married, and 85,500 same-sex couples who are in a civil union or registered domestic partnership.

Findings from several studies suggest that couples who have married or pursued some other form of legal recognition for their relationships are more likely to have children. Carpenter and Gates (2008) found that female couples who registered as domestic partners were slightly more likely to be rearing children than those who did not register (34% vs. 29%, respectively). The same pattern was not true for male couples. Among male couples who were not in a registered partnership, 6% had children, but among those in registered partnerships, 2% were rearing children. Among same-sex couples in Canada, those who were married were more than twice as likely as those who were unmarried to be rearing children (16% vs.7.5%, respectively). This pattern was true for both men and women, though female couples were much more likely to be rearing children. Nearly 25% of married female couples had children compared to 15% of unmarried female couples. For men, 9% of married male couples had children, compared to 2% of those in unmarried male couples (Statistics Canada, 2009).

Legal relationship recognition has also been found to be associated with relationships of longer duration. Carpenter and Gates (2008) found that women in registered partnerships reported average relationship durations of nearly 9 years compared to the 8 year average among those who were not registered. Male couples reported longer relationship durations: 11 years, on average, among those who were registered and 8 years, on average, among those who were not registered. These findings are consistent with those of Balsam and her colleagues (2008), who reported that same-sex couples in civil unions were less likely to terminate their relationships than were same-sex couples whose relationships were not legally recognized. The finding of longer average relationship durations among same-sex male as compared to female couples is consistent with findings from a wide range of studies that measured relationship duration among male and female same-sex couples using nonprobabilistic sampling methods (Carpenter & Gates, 2008). Many studies found that lesbians were more likely than gay men to be in a cohabiting relationship, but that the relationships of gay men lasted over longer periods of time. For example, in their study of registered same-sex partners in Norway and Sweden, Andersson et al. (2006) reported that dissolution rates were higher among female same-sex couples than among male same-sex couples.

Evidence is mixed about the overall stability of same-sex and different-sex relationships. Gates and his colleagues (2008) reported that about 2% of same-sex couples in the United States dissolved their relationships each year, or about the same as the percentage of different-sex married couples who divorced each year. Balsam and her colleagues (2008) compared same-sex couples in civil unions to different-sex married couples and also found no difference in dissolution rates. Contrary to these findings, Andersson and his colleagues (2006) found that same-sex couples in registered partnerships had higher rates of dissolution than did different-sex married couples. Assessments of differences in dissolution rates among same-sex and different-sex couples are challenging since the two groups are still, at least in the U.S. context, not subject to the same legal and social conditions as are different-sex couples. Even in states with marriage equality, the lack of federal recognition means that benefits and incentives associated with remaining in a marriage are not the same for same-sex and different-sex couples. Furthermore, legal same-sex relationship forms across the world are still relatively new and a more accurate assessment of relationship duration differences between same-sex and different-sex couples will require more time.

Parenthood and Children

One the most intriguing findings from the 2000 U.S. Decennial Census was that more than one in five same-sex couples were currently rearing children under the age of 18 in their home. This translates into more than 250,000 children being reared by same-sex couples in the United States alone (Gates & Ost, 2004). This was a rather substantial increase over comparable numbers from the 1990 Census. Notably, the proportion of same-sex couples with children was reported to be much higher in the United States than in Canada, where only about one in 10 same-sex couples were rearing children under age 18 in their homes (Statistics Canada, 2009).

Evidence from the 2002 National Survey of Family Growth (NSFG) and the 2008 GSS has revealed that these couples represent only a fraction of all child-rearing among lesbians and gay men. Among lesbians and gay men without children in the NSFG, four in 10 lesbians and fully half of gay men reported wanting to have a child. Furthermore, a third of lesbians and one in six gay men say they already have children, even if they are not presently rearing them in their home (Macomber et al., 2007). Analysis of data from the 2008 GSS revealed that bisexual women were more likely than lesbians to have children. Although 20% of gay men and 46% of lesbians reported that they have had a child, the comparable figures for bisexual men and women were 20% and 66%, respectively.

Thorough reviews of research on lesbian and gay parenting can be found in Biblarz and Stacey (2010), Patterson (1992, 2004, 2006, and Chapter 16, this volume), and Stacey and Biblarz (2001). Perhaps due to the fact that lesbians are more likely than gay men to have children, the majority of this research has focused on lesbian parenting. More research participants in a large portion of the studies also tend to be white and have higher education levels than the general population. Much of the recent literature on lesbian, gay, and bisexual parenting considers intentional parenting among lesbians and gay men, as well as parenting of children born in the context of heterosexual marriages (see Patterson, Chapter 16, this volume).

The characteristics of same-sex couples raising children observed in the 2008 American Community Survey suggest the need for more research that considers parenting among lesbian, gay, and bisexual individuals who are members of racial and ethnic minorities, who are of lower socioeconomic status, and who had children at relatively young ages. Many lesbian, gay, and bisexual parents are nonwhite, many have had relatively little education, and many of their children are apparently from prior different-sex relationships (see Table 6.7).

Among individuals in same-sex couples in the 2008 ACS, rates of child-rearing (of children under age 18 and in the home) were substantially higher among nonwhite than among white individuals (see Table 6.7). African-American women in same-sex couples are nearly twice as likely as their white counterparts to report rearing children (50% vs. 26%, respectively). The 50% of African-American women in same-sex couples with children is only slightly lower than the 52% of African-Americans in different-sex couples who have children. African-American men in same-sex couples are four times more likely than their white counterparts to have children (37% vs. 9%). Latinas and Latinos in same-sex couples also reported high rates of child-rearing (43% and 21%, respectively). In total, 35% of men and women in same-sex couples with children were nonwhite, as compared to 33% of those in comparable different-sex couples.

TABLE 6.7. CHILDREARING AMONG INDIVIDUALS IN
SAME-SEX AND DIFFERENT-SEX COUPLES BY RACE/ETHNICITY,
2008 AMERICAN COMMUNITY SURVEY (AUTHOR ANALYSES)

	Same-Sex Female Partners	Same-Sex Male Partners	Different-Sex Partners
All	30%	13%	45%
White	26%	9%	40%
African-American	50%	37%	52%
Latino/a	43%	21%	67%
American Indian/ Alaska Native	23%	30%	51%
Asian/Pacific Islander	32%	16%	56%
Other (including multiracial)	36%	11%	53%

Nearly half (47%) of women in same-sex couples with children are nonwhite.

Like their parents and caregivers, more children of same-sex couples are nonwhite than those of different-sex couples. More than half (52%) of the children being reared by male same-sex couples and four in 10 (42%) children being reared by same-sex female couples were described as nonwhite, compared to just 38% of children being reared by different-sex couples. Same-sex couples are rearing a racially diverse group of children, and there is as yet limited research on these children.

Childrearing among same-sex couples has also been found to be more common among those with lower levels of education (see Table 6.8). Among individuals in same-sex couples who have less than a high school degree, 50% of women and 46% of men have reported having children, figures that are very comparable to the 49% of those in different-sex couples who have reported having children. Interestingly, although 45% of those in different-sex couples with a graduate degree reported having children, only 24% of comparable women and just 6% of comparable men in same-sex couples reported having children. Again, relatively few studies have assessed the experiences of lesbian, gay, and bisexual parents with relatively little education.

Given the relatively high rates of parenthood reported among less well educated and racial and ethnic minorities within same-sex couples, it is perhaps not surprising that evidence of economic disadvantage among same-sex parents and their children relative to their different-sex counterparts has emerged. In analyses of data from Census 2000, Albelda and colleagues (2009) reported that 20% of children being reared by same-sex couples were living in poverty compared to fewer than 10% of children being reared by different-sex married couples. In the 2008 ACS, same-sex couples with children were more than twice as likely as their different-sex counterparts to report that they received public assistance; only 1% of different-sex couples with children but 2.5% of same-sex couples with children (1.8% of male couples and 2.7% of female couples) reported receiving public assistance.

Although parenting research on intentional parenting among lesbians and gay men is important, the many lesbian, gay, and bisexual individuals who are rearing children from prior heterosexual relationships should not be overlooked. Data from the 2008 ACS offer some information relevant to this topic. In this dataset, children can be identified as a "biological son or daughter," "adopted son or daughter," "stepson or stepdaughter," along with a variety of other relationships including grandchildren, siblings, and cousins. Children can also be designated as a "foster child" or as "unrelated."

Among children under age 18 living with same-sex couples, 68% were identified either as a "biological son or daughter" or a "stepson or stepdaughter" of the reference person in the 2008 ACS. Only 11% were described as adopted and 1.3% as foster children. An additional 6% were described as grandchildren, another 5% as other relatives (e.g.,

TABLE 6.8. CHILDREARING AMONG INDIVIDUALS IN SAME-SEX AND
DIFFERENT-SEX COUPLES BY EDUCATIONAL ATTAINMENT, 2008 AMERICAN
COMMUNITY SURVEY (AUTHOR ANALYSES)

	Individuals in Same-Sex Female Couples	Individuals in Same-Sex Male Couples	Individuals in Different-Sex Couples
Less than high school	50%	46%	49%
High school diploma	37%	24%	41%
Some college	32%	11%	46%
College degree	23%	5%	49%
Graduate degree	24%	6%	45%

siblings and cousins), and 9% were described as "non-relatives" (i.e., in relation to the reference person). A portion of the 68% of children who are a "biological son or daughter" or a "stepson or stepdaughter" may have been conceived via reproductive technologies such as donor insemination. Unfortunately, there is no way to estimate how common this pathway to parenthood may have been in this sample. However, given the expenses associated with these procedures and the evidence regarding economic disadvantage among many same-sex couples, it seems likely that many of these children were not conceived via reproductive technology, but instead came into this world through some type of different-sex relationship. In other words, many of the children may have been conceived in the context of preexisting different-sex relationships (e.g., marriages).

Gates and Romero (2009) reported additional evidence suggesting that many children being reared by same-sex couples may have been conceived in the context of prior relationships with different-sex partners. Using data from Census 2000, they found that men and women in same-sex couples who were previously married were nearly twice as likely as their never-married counterparts to have a child under 18 years of age in the home. Among households in which the reference person was previously married and his or her same-sex partner was not, Gates and Romero (2009) found that nearly 94% of children were designated as "natural born" (fully 10 percentage points higher than in couples in which neither partner was ever married) and 4.5% of children were stepchildren. In the case in which the partner was previously married and the reference person was never married, they reported that nearly 20% of the children are designated as stepchildren. These analyses do not

allow for an explicit determination of the fraction of children being reared by same-sex couples who were conceived within a prior marriage of one of the partners. However, they do offer clear evidence that many same-sex partners with a history of a marital relationship with a different-sex spouse have children. Gates and Romero (2009) also note the relative lack of research on step-parenting in families with same-sex parents (see also, Patterson, Chapter 16, this volume).

Additional evidence of children coming from prior heterosexual relationships of lesbian, gay, and bisexual people comes from the 2008 General Social Survey. Analyses of the GSS revealed that among men who have had children, the average age when they had their first child was nearly 4 years younger among gay and bisexual men than among heterosexual men (25.3 years old vs. 21.6 years old), and this difference was statistically significant. Lesbians and bisexual women also reported having had their first child at slightly younger ages than did their heterosexual counterparts (22.6 years old vs. 23.2 years old), but this difference was not statistically significant. These findings suggest that additional research is needed on lesbian, gay, and bisexual parents who have had children at relatively young ages.

Demographic data on lesbian, gay, and bisexual parents and their children offer a complex portrait of a diverse population with a wide range of family structures. In Census 2000, approximately one in four same-sex couples reported having children under the age of 18 in the home (Gates & Ost, 2004). The proportion of same-sex couples with children has actually declined very slightly since then, and was closer to one in five couples in the 2008 ACS. However, the proportion of same-sex couples with adopted children has increased from

1.8% of all same-sex couples in Census 2000 to nearly 3% in the 2008 ACS. Given the demographic analyses that have been presented, it is likely that declines in social stigma toward same-sex couples and nonheterosexual people more generally have produced two different trends in parenting among lesbian, gay, and bisexual people. On one hand, nonheterosexual individuals are coming out earlier in life and are perhaps becoming less likely to have children with different-sex partners. On the other, increasing numbers of lesbian, gay, and bisexual people are pursuing parenthood after coming out via adoption and using various forms reproductive technology. It appears that among same-sex couples, the declines in the former may be taking place somewhat more rapidly than increases in the latter, and that this has resulted in a somewhat smaller proportion of same-sex couples with children than in previous years.

CONCLUSIONS

Lesbian, gay, and bisexual communities are very diverse. Lesbian, gay, and bisexual individuals and families exist in a variety of forms and circumstances. Unique dynamics of race, ethnicity, socioeconomic status, geography, gender, and sexual orientation all intersect and interact, especially within the realms of parenting and families. Unfortunately, available data for creating a complete demographic portrait of sexual minorities are still quite limited. Notably, almost no population-based data to describe demographic characteristics of the transgender community exist.

Nonetheless, existing research does illuminate the need for lesbian-, gay-, and bisexual-focused research to take diversity into account when describing characteristics, behaviors, and outcomes in this population. To better understand the complexity of lesbian, gay, and bisexual communities, research must take account of more diversity than simply that due to gender and sexual orientation. Very little is known about how racial and ethnic cultural norms intersect with sexual orientation to affect the health and well-being of lesbian, gay, and bisexual people. Results of demographic research on lesbian, gay, and bisexual communities suggest that social scientists must be encouraged to expand the conceptual and theoretical frameworks under which they frame their research so as to consider more of the demographic variation within lesbian, gay, and bisexual communities.

REFERENCES

Ahmed, A. M., & Hammarstedt, M. (2010). Sexual orientation and earnings: A register data-based approach to identify homosexuals. *Journal of Population Economics, 23,* 835–849.

Albelda, R., Badgett, M. V. L., Schneebaum, A., & Gates, G. J. (2009). *Poverty in the lesbian, gay, and bisexual community.* Los Angeles, CA: The Williams Institute, UCLA School of Law.

Allegretto, S., & Arthur, M. (2001). An empirical analysis of homosexual/heterosexual male earnings differentials: Unmarried and unequal? *Industrial and Labor Relations Review, 54,* 631–646.

Andersson, G., Noack, T., Seierstad, A., & Weedon-Fekjaer, H. (2006). The demographics of same-sex marriages in Norway and Sweden. *Demography, 43,* 79–98.

Badgett, M. V. L. (1995). The wage effects of sexual-orientation discrimination. *Industrial and Labor Relations Review, 48,* 726–739.

Badgett, M. V. L., & Rogers, M. A. (2003). *Left out of the count: Missing same-sex couples in Census 2000.* Amherst, MA: Institute for Gay and Lesbian Strategic Studies.

Balsam, K. F., Beauchaine, T. P., Rothblum, E. D., & Solomon, S. E. (2008). Three-year follow-up of same-sex couples who had civil unions in Vermont, same-sex couples not in civil unions, and heterosexual married couples. *Developmental Psychology, 44*(1), 102–116.

Biblarz, T. J., & Stacey, J. (2010). How does the gender of parents matter? *Journal of Marriage and Family, 72,* 3–22.

Black, D., Gates, G. J., Sanders, S. G., & Taylor, L. (2000). Demographics of the gay and lesbian population in the United States: Evidence from available systematic data sources. *Demography, 37,* 139–154.

Black, D., Gates, G. J., Sanders, S. G., & Taylor, L. (2007). *The measurement of same-sex unmarried partner couples in the 2000 U.S. Census.* California Center for Population Research On-line Working Paper Series, CCPR–023–07.

Black, D., Makar, H., Sanders, S. G., & Taylor, L. (2003). The earnings effects of sexual orientation. *Industrial and Labor Relations Review, 56,* 449–469.

Blandford, J. M. (2003). The nexus of sexual orientation and gender in the determination of earnings. *Industrial and Labor Relations Review, 56,* 622–642.

Carpenter, C. S. (2005). Self-reported sexual orientation and earnings: Evidence from California. *Industrial and Labor Relations Review, 58,* 258–273.

Carpenter, C. S. (2007). Revisiting the income penalty for behaviorally gay men: Evidence from NHANES III. *Labour Economics, 14,* 25–34.

Carpenter, C. S., & Gates, G. J. (2008). Gay and lesbian partnership: Evidence from California. *Demography, 45,* 573–590.

Chandra, A., Mosher, W. D., & Copen, C. (2011). National health statistics reports, 36. *Sexual Behavior,*

Sexual Attraction, and Sexual Identity in the United States: Data From the 2006–2008 National Survey of Family Growth. Washington, DC: U.S. Department of Health and Human Services, Centers for Disease Control and Prevention, National Center for Health Statistics.

Ferris, J. (2005). *Australian longitudinal study of health and relationships.* Melbourne, Australia: La Trobe University, Australian Research Centre in Sex, Health and Society.

Gates, G. J. (2007). *Geographic trends among same-sex couples in the US Census and the American Community Survey.* Los Angeles, CA: The Williams Institute, UCLA School of Law.

Gates, G. J. (2009). *The impact of sexual orientation anti-discrimination policies on the wages of lesbians and gay men.* California Center for Population Research On-line Working Paper Series, CCPR–2009–010.

Gates, G. J. (2010a). *Sexual minorities in the 2008 General Social Survey: Coming out and demographic characteristics.* Los Angeles: Williams Institute, UCLA School of Law.

Gates, G. J. (2010b). *Same-sex couples in US Census Bureau data: Who gets counted and why.* Los Angeles: Williams Institute, UCLA School of Law.

Gates, G. J. (2011). *How many people are lesbian, gay, bisexual and transgender?* Los Angeles, CA: The Williams Institute, UCLA School of Law.

Gates, G. J., Badgett, M. V. L., & Ho, D. (2008). *Marriage, registration and dissolution by same-sex couples in the U.S.* Los Angeles, CA: The Williams Institute, UCLA School of Law.

Gates, G. J., & Ost, J. (2004). *The gay & lesbian atlas.* Washington, DC: The Urban Institute Press.

Gates, G. J., & Romero, A. P. (2009). Parenting by gay men and lesbians. In H. E. Peters & C. M. Kamp Dush (Eds.), *Marriage and family: Perspectives and complexities* (pp. 227–243). New York: Columbia University Press.

Gates, G. J., & Steinberger, M. D. (2011). *Same-sex unmarried partner couples in the American Community Survey: The role of misreporting, miscoding, and misallocation.* Working paper presented at UCLA-California Center for Population Research and UC-Berkeley Population Center Miniconference on Census Microdata and Applications, UCLA, 3 June 2011.

Gay and Lesbian Alliance Against Defamation. (2007). *Network responsibility index, primetime programming 2006–2007.* New York: Gay and Lesbian Alliance Against Defamation.

Gulløy, E., & Normann, T. M. (2010). *Sexual identity and living conditions: Evaluation of the relevance of living conditions and data collection.* Oslo–Kongsvinger, Norway: Statistics Norway.

Harris Interactive & Witeck-Combs. (2010). *The lesbian, gay, bisexual, and transgender population at a glance.* Washington, DC: Harris Interactive, Inc.

Klawitter, M. (2011). Multilevel analysis of the effects of antidiscrimination policies on earnings by sexual orientation. *Journal of Policy Analysis and Management, 30*(2), 334–358.

Macomber, J. E., Gates, G. J., Badgett, M. V. L., & Chambers, K. (2007). *Adoption and foster care by gay and lesbian parents in the United States.* Los Angeles, CA: The Williams Institute, UCLA School of Law and Washington, DC: The Urban Institute.

O'Connell, M., & Lofquist, D. (2009). *Changes to the American Community Survey between 2007 and 2008 and their potential effect on the estimates of same-sex couple households.* Washington, DC: U.S. Census Bureau, Housing and Household Economic Statistics Division, Fertility & Family Statistics Branch, September.

Office of National Statistics. (2010). Statistical Bulletin—Integrated Household Survey, *New ONS integrated household survey: Experimental statistics.* Newport, United Kingdom: Office of National Statistics.

Office of National Statistics. (2011). *Civil partnerships: Formation numbers increase.* Newport, United Kingdom: Office of National Statistics.

Patterson, C. J. (1992). Children of lesbian and gay parents. *Child Development, 63,* 1025–1042.

Patterson, C. J. (2004). Family relationships of lesbians and gay men. *Journal of Marriage and Family, 62,* 1052–1069.

Patterson, C. J. (2006). Children of lesbian and gay parents. *Current Directions in Psychological Science, 15,* 241–244.

Plug, E., & Berkout, P. (2009). *Understanding the gay gap: An empirical analysis of sexual orientation, disclosure and earnings.* Bonn, Germany: Institute for the Study of Labor.

Romero, A. P., Baumle, A. K., Badgett, M. V .L., & Gates, G. J. (2007). *Census snapshot: United States.* Los Angeles, CA: The Williams Institute, UCLA School of Law.

Smith, T. W., Marsden, P., Hout, M., & Kim, J. (2008). *General social survey, machine-readable data file.* Chicago: National Opinion Research Center.

Stacey, J., & Biblarz, T. J. (2001). (How) Does the sexual orientation of parents matter? *American Sociological Review, 66,* 159–183.

Statistics Canada. (2009). *2006 Census: Family portrait: Continuity and change in Canadian families and households in 2006: National portrait: Census families.* Ottawa, Canada: Statistics Canada.

Turner, C. F., Ku, L., Rogers, S. M., Lindberg, L. D., Pleck, J. H., & Sonenstein, F. L. (1998). Adolescent sexual behavior, drug use, and violence: Increased reporting with computer survey technology. *Science, 280,* 867–873.

Williams Institute. (2009). *Same-sex couples in the 2008 American Community Survey.* Los Angeles, CA: The Williams Institute, UCLA School of Law.

II

Development over the Life Course

7

The Sexual Identity Development and Health of Lesbian, Gay, and Bisexual Adolescents: An Ecological Perspective

MARGARET ROSARIO AND ERIC W. SCHRIMSHAW

Identity development is the primary developmental task of adolescence (Erikson, 1950/1980). Adolescents are capable of imaging future outcomes, cognitively experimenting with possible future identities, and working toward selected future identities in various domains (e.g., occupational). They also become aware of limitations imposed on future possible identities by themselves, others, and institutions. It is during this developmental period, ranging from puberty to the late teenage years and even spilling into the years of emerging adulthood, that sexual identity generally unfolds (Floyd & Bakeman, 2006; Grov, Bimbi, Nanín, & Parsons, 2006; Savin-Williams & Diamond, 2000).

Sexual identity development proves difficult for all young people, given its corresponding biopsychosocial changes. Nevertheless, it is particularly demanding for youths who discover that the object of their sexual attractions and desires is exclusively or to some extent the same sex. This chapter focuses on the experiences of such lesbian, gay, or bisexual youths, to whom we also refer as sexual minority youths, as compared to peers whose attractions and desires are exclusively focused on the other sex (i.e., heterosexual). Although identity development in general (Kroger, 2007) and sexual identity development in particular (D'Augelli & Grossman, 2001; Parks & Hughes, 2007) are not the exclusive experience of adolescents, nevertheless, both are particularly prevalent in adolescence.

Our aim in this chapter is to understand the experiences and challenges of lesbian, gay, or bisexual youths from two perspectives. First, we begin with a theoretical perspective on sexual identity development to place the development of sexual identity within the larger context of identity development and adaptation. Second, we review what is known about the experiences and challenges of lesbian, gay, or bisexual youths from an ecological perspective that involves the self (including neuroscience), family, peers, and schools. We examine the positive and negative influences of the various experiences on the youths' identity development, health, and well-being. We end by identifying what remains unknown or in need of additional research.

SEXUAL IDENTITY DEVELOPMENT IN THE CONTEXT OF GENERAL IDENTITY DEVELOPMENT THEORY

Sexual identity development, like identity development in general, is a process of formation and commitment/integration (Erikson, 1968). Identity formation is itself a process. It begins with an unfolding inner reality that may raise questions about past identifications and push for a new awareness of possible identities. This, in turn, leads to exploration, in which the individual experiments with the possible identities. Through the process of awareness and exploration, the individual gradually begins to form an identity. Acceptance of and commitment to such an identity and its integration with the sense of self constitute identity integration. Continuity of the identity across time and settings characterizes identity integration, as does the wish and need to be known as such by others. In addition, identity integration lays the foundation for further growth and psychological well-being.

With respect to sexual identity formation, lesbian, gay, or bisexual youths usually become aware of same-sex sexual attractions, then engage in sexual activity with the same sex and perhaps the other sex, and conclude, at some subsequent time, that they are lesbian, gay, or bisexual (e.g., D'Augelli, 2002; Rosario et al., 1996; Savin-Williams & Diamond, 2000). Sexual identity integration also is a multidimensional process: The individual may engage in lesbian-, gay-, or bisexual-related social and recreational activities, work through his or her negative attitudes toward homosexuality (what is often known as "internalized homophobia"), begin to feel more comfortable with the idea that others may know about her or his lesbian, gay, or bisexual identity, and disclose that identity to others (e.g., Rosario, Schrimshaw, & Hunter, 2008b). It should be noted that the order of identity formation and integration may differ with respect to age at developmental initiation, duration of development, and order of developmental events (Floyd & Stein, 2002; Rosario et al., 2008b; Savin-Williams & Diamond, 2000).

Failure to commit and integrate an identity results in identity confusion or diffusion (Erikson, 1956/1980). In addition, a commitment to an identity at odds with the self leads to a "synthetic" identity or a "loss" of identity. Whatever the reason, failure to commit to an identity that is true to the self has negative implications for mental health and for meeting subsequent developmental challenges (Erikson, 1950/1980, 1956/1980). For example, lesbian, gay, or bisexual youths whose sexual identities are less fully developed (e.g., less disclosure, more internalized homophobia) report more psychological distress and lower self-esteem than do their peers whose sexual identity integration is more advanced (Rosario, Schrimshaw, & Hunter, 2011b).

Like any identity, sexual identity development occurs in a social context. The environment, through multiple societal levels (e.g., parents, peers, schools), supports and privileges some identities while discouraging or punishing other identities. Society continues to stigmatize homosexuality, generating multiple challenges that affect all spheres of life for sexual minority individuals (e.g., Herek, 2009; Meyer, 2003; Russell, Franz, & Driscoll, 2001). The challenges are experienced internally and externally. Internal challenges happen when the individual's internalization of society's stigmatization is applied by the individual against the self. The lesbian, gay, or bisexual individual, usually raised by heterosexual parents, is expected by others

and himself or herself to be heterosexual. However, the sexual minority individual's sexual identity development takes a different course, generating a crisis between the self and internalized heterosexual expectations and identifications. External challenges may be experienced as anticipated negative reactions from others in the individual's life (e.g., parents, siblings, friends). In this scenario, others are ignorant of the young person's sexual identity, but she or he is uncertain of or fears the reactions of others if they were to learn about the sexual identity (see D'Augelli, Grossman, & Starks, 2005, Table 4). Finally, the lesbian, gay, or bisexual youth has to deal with the challenges posed by those who suspect or learn of his or her sexual identity. How these individuals may react, whether accepting or rejecting, is never known by the youth until confronted with the reaction. Negative reactions and possible rejection of the youth may have serious implications for the youth's health and adaptation in various life domains (e.g., D'Augelli, 2002; Ryan, Huebner, Diaz, & Sanchez, 2009). Accepting reactions, on the other hand, are welcomed, given their potential implications of support and validation of the youth's developing identity. Moreover, accepting reactions from some individuals may blunt the negative impact of rejecting and negative reactions by other individuals (Rosario, Schrimshaw, & Hunter, 2009).

Nevertheless, accepting reactions accompanied by qualifications may prove stressful. Social constraints, as such phenomena are known, refer to behaviors by the social network, in which an issue of concern to the individual is ignored or misunderstood by a network member, making the individual feel unsupported and alienated (Lepore, Silver, Wortman, & Wayment, 1996). Social constraints were originally proposed and studied in the context of trauma and illness (Badr & Taylor, 2006; Lepore et al., 1996; Ozer & Weinstein, 2004). More recently, they have been extended to include, for example, constraints surrounding discussing gay-related prejudice and discrimination (Lewis, Derlega, Clarke, & Kuang, 2006). Social constraints for lesbian, gay, or bisexual youths might include an understanding imposed by, for example, parents or friends that discussion of the youth's sexual identity, romantic relationships, and other lesbian-, gay-, or bisexual-related experiences are to be kept to a minimum, dispensed with as swiftly as possible, or ignored entirely. The constraints may represent an underlying negative reaction to homosexuality by the other and a desire by the other for the youth to reject the homosexual aspect of the self.

As stressful as the environment may be, it also is the source of potential resources for lesbian, gay, or bisexual individuals. Not all parents, siblings, friends, and others may respond negatively to the youth's sexual identity, as indicated above. Moreover, even those who do respond negatively at first may come to embrace the youth over time (Ben-Ari, 1995; Savin-Williams & Ream, 2003). More importantly, developing friendships with other lesbian, gay, or bisexual individuals provides sources of support and potential romantic relationships (e.g., Ueno, 2005). The network of friendships fosters a sense of community of similar others and creates a communication network of valuable information (e.g., how and where to meet other sexual minority individuals and how to cope with gay-related stressors). Indeed, the direct and indirect links with similar others help forge a social identity and sense of distinctiveness among members of any identity group (Tajfel, 1981; Turner, Hogg, Oakes, Reicher, & Wetherell, 1987). The result is the "lesbian, gay, and bisexual community." Its multiple layers and widespread foci, with a microgroup seeming to exist for every interest and characteristic of its members, constitute one set of people from which lesbian, gay, or bisexual persons expect support and validation.

NEUROCOGNITIVE DEVELOPMENT OF ADOLESCENTS AND ITS COPING IMPLICATIONS FOR LESBIAN, GAY, OR BISEXUAL YOUTHS

The challenges facing lesbian, gay, or bisexual youths are particularly difficult because they pit the newly developing sense of self against an environment that often stigmatizes homosexuality and sexual minority persons. As such, lesbian, gay, or bisexual youths must deal with the challenges with relatively few supports, as will be discussed later, and using their own developmentally limited cognitive capabilities, as will be discussed shortly. Although we are unaware of any neurocognitive research on lesbian, gay, or bisexual youths, there is no reason to believe that sexual minority youths should differ cognitively from heterosexual youths, given a presumably common neurological basis of cognition. As such,

we should be able to gain insights into the cognitive capabilities of lesbian, gay, or bisexual youths from existing neurocognitive research, which has focused on adolescents in general.

Current research suggests that adolescence is a unique developmental period and that the adolescent's evaluations of and responses to challenges involve a complex interplay among brain structures. The prefrontal cortex—the center of all executive functions (e.g., monitoring, strategizing, decision making)—continues to develop throughout adolescence, as evidenced by increasing pruning of synapses and myelination of axons. Adolescents are capable of formal operations, meaning they are able to engage in hypothesis testing and to think about thinking. These capabilities, however, are limited when situations that are being analyzed involve the self as compared to others (Sobesky, 1983), indicating that adolescents' decision-making skills are more problematic when applied to the self. These same skills also function less well when the youth confronts a situation while in the presence of others as compared to being alone (Steinberg, 2005). Overall, the cognitive capabilities of adolescents are on average better than those of children, but less well developed than those of adults in multiple cognitive domains (for details and a review, see Kuhn, 2009).

In addition to its executive functions, the prefrontal cortex is associated with impulse control, as the famous case of Phineas Gage demonstrated (Nolte, 2002).[1] Although development of the prefrontal cortex and that of subcortical limbic regions, such as the nucleus acumbens, are comparable during childhood and adulthood, an inequality occurs in adolescence. During this time, the development of the prefrontal cortex lags behind that of the nucleus acumbens. The functional imbalance means that adolescents are less capable than children or adults of impulse control and, thus, are more likely to engage in risk taking. This model of the adolescent brain (Casey, Getz, & Galvan, 2008) has been confirmed in rodents (Laviola, Adriani, Terranova, & Gerra, 1999) and human imaging studies (e.g., Galvan et al., 2006). Moreover, it has been extended to emotion regulation, given that imaging studies have found that adolescents have greater difficulty than children or adults in regulating amygdala activity (Hare et al., 2008).

Cognitive functioning and impulse control have implications for coping with complex challenges (e.g., sexual identity development). In fact, each of these skills maps onto the two domains of coping proposed by Lazarus and Folkman (1984) for adults and generalized to children and adolescents by others (Compas, Connor-Smith, Saltzman, Harding Thomsen, & Wadsworth, 2001; Grant et al., 2006). Problem-focused coping involves strategies to reduce or eliminate a stressor, in which a stressor is anything that disrupts homeostasis (e.g., Lazarus & Folkman, 1984). Problem-focused coping requires a careful and realistic analysis of the stressor, acquisition of or availability and selection of the appropriate coping strategy from the coping repertoire, and subsequent monitoring and adjustments to changing conditions (e.g., from enlisting additional reinforcements and addressing unintended consequences to desisting once the stressor is adequately addressed). Emotion-focused coping represents the second coping domain. It involves all efforts to regulate emotions, necessary conditions for the cognitive processing required of problem-solving coping. Emotion-focused coping also allows the individual to tolerate a stressor that cannot be reduced.

Given the neurocognitive evidence on the limited cognitive functioning and poor impulse control of adolescents, it is likely that the coping capabilities of adolescents are limited or immature. Furthermore, as per the cognitive neuroscientific research reviewed above, adolescents are likely to be biased toward coping strategies that involve risk taking (e.g., substance use, conduct problems, emotional venting). We suspect that most adolescents are steered away from the poor coping strategies that come naturally to them by the monitoring and guidance provided by, for example, parents, schools, and social policies (e.g., age restrictions on alcohol use). However, lesbian, gay, or bisexual youths often must deal with their sexual identity developmental challenges with few supports. Although this neither means that all sexual minority youths cope poorly nor have parents or others who do not appropriately monitor and guide them, it does suggest that lesbian, gay, or bisexual youths, on average or as a group, may have more difficulty than their heterosexual peers in coping with sexual identity development.

Another set of pertinent but nonneuroscientific observations is relevant: Adolescents have had fewer experiences than adults, which mean adolescents have less experience dealing with or cognitively working through various exigencies. In other words, adolescents' repertoire of potential strategies to address new situations is more restricted than that of adults and strategies shared by both groups are less finely honed or developed in adolescents. Therefore, the coping strategies of adults and adolescents differ qualitatively (e.g., using different strategies) and quantitatively (e.g., using more maladaptive strategies than adults).

For any and all of the above reasons, adolescents (both heterosexual and sexual minority) may have difficulty dealing with complicated and emotionally provocative situations. Undergoing the process of identity formation and integration as lesbian, gay, or bisexual is particularly complicated and emotionally charged. It is a challenge that many lesbian, gay, or bisexual youths face without many of the supports that heterosexual peers possess. Consequently, we would expect health disparities by sexual orientation.

HEALTH DISPARITIES BY SEXUAL ORIENTATION IN YOUTHS

Lesbian, gay, or bisexual youths are at elevated risk for a variety of poor health outcomes relative to heterosexual peers. The health disparities exist regardless of how sexual orientation is defined, be it by sexual attraction, sexual activity or relationship status, or self-identification as lesbian, gay, or bisexual (e.g., see Marshal et al., 2008). In fact, health disparities manifest themselves as soon as there is any awareness that the individual deviates from complete heterosexuality, as found by research on those who identify as "mostly heterosexual" in feelings or desires (Austin et al., 2004; Corliss, Rosario, Wypij, Fisher, & Austin, 2008). Below, we briefly review what is known about health disparities by sexual orientation among young people (for more detailed reviews, see Coker, Austin, & Schuster, 2010; Saewyc, 2011).

Representative samples of the American and other Western populations document elevated psychological morbidity in lesbian, gay, or bisexual youths relative to their heterosexual peers (e.g., Bontempo & D'Augelli, 2002; Eisenberg & Resnick, 2006; Fergusson, Horwood, & Beautrais, 1999; Jorm, Korten, Rodgers, Jacomb, & Christensen, 2002; Russell & Joyner, 2001). For example, lesbian, gay, or bisexual youths are 1.7 to 7.1 times more likely than their heterosexual peers to report attempting suicide (e.g., Eisenberg & Resnick, 2006; Fergusson et al., 1999; Russell & Joyner, 2001; Silenzio, Pena, Duberstein, Cerel, & Knox, 2007; Wichstrøm & Hegna, 2003; see Marshal et al., 2011, for a meta-analysis). Lesbian, gay, or bisexual youths are also much more likely than their heterosexual peers to have a psychiatric diagnosis of major depression, generalized anxiety disorder, or conduct disorder (Fergusson et al., 1999). Moreover, the elevated distress of lesbian, gay, or bisexual youths has been found to persist into adulthood (Fergusson, Horwood, Ridder, & Beautrais, 2005). Thus, the elevated distress found among lesbian, gay, or bisexual adults (e.g., see Meyer, 2003, for a meta-analysis) may be partly attributed to carryover effects of distress that began during youth (see also Meyer and Frost, Chapter 18, this volume).

Use of tobacco, alcohol, and other drugs is elevated among lesbian, gay, or bisexual youths, with prevalence rates at least 50% higher than among heterosexual youths, according to studies of representative samples (Eisenberg & Wechsler, 2003; Russell, Driscoll, & Truong, 2002). A recent meta-analytic study found higher odds of recent substance use among lesbian, gay, or bisexual youths: Sexual minority youths were 1.56 times more likely than heterosexual peers to use marijuana and 3.27 times more likely to use cocaine; in between this range were odds indicating that more lesbian, gay, or bisexual than heterosexual adolescents recently used tobacco, alcohol, and other drugs (Marshal et al., 2008). Diagnosis of nicotine and other substance abuse/dependence is also elevated among lesbian, gay, or bisexual youths (e.g., Fergusson et al., 1999, 2005).

Health disparities exist in sexual risk behaviors for both male and female lesbian, gay, or bisexual youths. Young men who have sex with men (YMSM) are at elevated risk for HIV infection, comprising 84% of all HIV-infected cases among men aged 13–24 years (Centers for Disease Control and Prevention, 2007). Moreover, over the past few years, the numbers of HIV infections among people aged 13–24 years have increased, as have infections among YMSM (Centers for Disease Control and Prevention, 2010). In a representative sample of high school students in Massachusetts, gay and bisexual boys were more likely than other boys to report sex before age 13 years and to have four or more lifetime sexual partners; and gay/bisexual

boys were less likely to use condoms at last sexual intercourse (Goodenow, Netherland, & Szalacha, 2002). Similar results were found among a representative sample of college students across the country (Eisenberg, 2001), in which both male and female lesbian, gay, or bisexual youths as compared with same-sex heterosexual peers reported more than two sexual partners within the past month. Gay and bisexual male youths were less consistent in their condom use, relative to male heterosexual peers, particularly when they reported that they had more than two partners in the past month. In addition, research with a national sample of junior and senior high school students finds that lesbian, gay, or bisexual adolescents were more likely than their heterosexual peers to exchange sex for goods (Udry & Chantala, 2002). Furthermore, in a representative sample of adolescents in British Columbia, Canada, lesbian, gay, or bisexual youths were more likely than their heterosexual peers to have been pregnant or to have impregnated a woman (Saewyc, Poon, Homma, & Skay, 2008). In summary, lesbian, gay, or bisexual youths are more likely than heterosexual youths to report multiple sexual partners, sexual risk behaviors, and potentially negative consequences of those risk behaviors.

Health disparities also are found in eating disorders and related behaviors, although these are underexamined in lesbian, gay, or bisexual youth populations. In a representative sample of Norwegian high school students, gay and bisexual boys were 7–18 times more likely and lesbian and bisexual girls were two to three times more likely to report bulimic symptoms than their same-sex heterosexual peers (Wichstrøm, 2006). Similarly, binge eating and purging were elevated in lesbian, gay, or bisexual youths relative to heterosexual peers in a large study of American youths (Austin et al., 2009).

The elevated poor health of lesbian, gay, or bisexual youths relative to their heterosexual peers may not only be a function of a stigmatized sexual identity, as mentioned above, but may also be a function of various factors occurring across ecological levels involving interpersonal (e.g., family, friends) and community-level (e.g., schools) experiences. Below, we review what is known about the potential negative factors and resiliency resources that may explain the sexual identity development, health, and adaptation of lesbian, gay, or bisexual youths.

PARENTS AND SIBLINGS OF LESBIAN, GAY, AND BISEXUAL YOUTHS

Families play a critical role in the development, health, and well-being of lesbian, gay, or bisexual youths. However, many sexual minority youths are reluctant to disclose their developing sexual orientation to their families for fear of negative reactions, causing difficulties in their relationships, or not being emotionally ready to disclose (D'Augelli, Grossman, & Starks, 2005; Savin-Williams & Ream, 2003). Although parents usually are not the first persons to whom sexual minority youths disclose, many lesbian, gay, or bisexual youths eventually do disclose to their parents, with mothers preceding fathers and mothers being a more common recipient of disclosure than fathers (Beals & Peplau, 2006; D'Augelli, 2002; D'Augelli, Grossman, & Starks, 2008; Rosario et al., 2009; Savin-Williams & Ream, 2003). Likewise, most siblings of lesbian, gay, or bisexual youths are aware of the sexual identities of their brothers and sisters (Beals & Peplau, 2006; D'Augelli et al., 2008; D'Augelli, Hershberger, & Pilkington, 1998; Rosario et al., 2009). Unlike many parents, siblings generally accept their lesbian, gay, or bisexual sisters and brothers (D'Augelli et al., 1998, 2008).

Despite youths' initial fears of negative reactions, parents' reactions to disclosure, among youths who do disclose, are often evenly divided between positive or at least tolerant reactions and somewhat negative or rejecting reactions (D'Augelli, 2002; D'Augelli et al., 1998, 2005; Savin-Williams & Ream, 2003). Consequently, approximately one-third of the lesbian, gay, or bisexual youth population experiences positive reactions and one-third experiences negative reactions, with the remaining one-third of lesbian, gay, or bisexual youths not disclosing to one or both parents even by their late teens and early 20s (D'Augelli, 2002; Rosario et al., 2009; Savin-Williams & Ream, 2003). Negative reactions from parents typically consist of denial, silence, distancing, and avoidance (Savin-Williams & Ream, 2003). Verbal or physical abuse also occurs (D'Augelli et al., 1998; Savin-Williams & Ream, 2003; Valentine, Skelton, & Butler, 2003). Regardless of initial reactions, parents tend to become somewhat more accepting of their child's lesbian, gay, or bisexual identity over time (Beals & Peplau, 2006; Ben-Ari, 1995; Savin-Williams & Ream, 2003; Vincke & Van Heeringen, 2002). Nevertheless, negative initial parental reactions can have profound implications for sexual minority youths' mental health (D'Augelli, 2002; Ryan et al., 2009), substance use (Rosario et al., 2009; Ryan et al., 2009), sexual risk behaviors (Ryan et al., 2009), and self-acceptance (Sheets & Mohr, 2009), even if initial reactions improve over time (Vincke & Van Heeringen, 2002). The poor outcomes are unsurprising considering that the negative parental reactions represent a rejection of the child's sexual identity and, thus, of the child.

Both before and after disclosure to parents, the quality of the relationship between sexual minority youths and their families plays a critical role in the youths' lives, serving as a source of stress or support. Lesbian, gay, or bisexual youths often report less supportive relationships with their parents and less connection or closeness to their parents than do heterosexual youths (Ueno, 2005; Williams, Connolly, Pepler, & Craig, 2005). Moreover, lesbian, gay, or bisexual youths have been found to report less support from their parents than from friends or other adults (Muñoz-Plaza, Quinn, & Rounds, 2002; Nesmith, Burton, & Cosgrove, 1999). The low support from or connection with parents and family is associated with a number of negative outcomes among sexual minority youths, including more depressive symptomatology (Sheets & Mohr, 2009; Rosario, Schrimshaw, & Hunter, 2005; Ueno, 2005), a greater likelihood of suicidality (Eisenberg & Resnick, 2006; D'Augelli, Grossman, Salter et al., 2005), lower life satisfaction (Sheets & Mohr, 2009), lower self-esteem or self-acceptance (Rosario et al., 2008b; Sheets & Mohr, 2009), more school problems (Russell, Seif, & Truong, 2001), and a lower grade-point average (Russell, Seif et al., 2001). In addition, low family support is associated with low levels of sexual identity integration among sexual minority youths, including less disclosure, more internalized homophobia, and lower involvement in lesbian, gay, or bisexual communities (Rosario et al., 2008b).

FRIENDS AND PEERS OF LESBIAN, GAY, AND BISEXUAL YOUTHS

Another critical aspect of the interpersonal lives of lesbian, gay, or bisexual youths is their friends and larger peer networks. Sexual minority youths' relationships with friends and peers can play both beneficial and detrimental roles in the sexual identity development, health, and well-being of lesbian, gay, or bisexual youths. Although sexual minority youths do not differ from heterosexual peers in the number of friends, frequency of contact, or level of emotional closeness with their friends (Diamond & Lucas, 2004; Ueno, 2005; Ueno, Gayman, Wright, & Quantz, 2009; Williams et al., 2005), lesbian, gay, or bisexual youths are more likely than heterosexual youths to report having lost friends and to worry about losing friends (Diamond & Lucas, 2004). The experience of losing friends and the ongoing fear of losing more friends have been associated with psychological distress among lesbian, gay, or bisexual youths (D'Augelli, 2002; Diamond & Lucas, 2004).

Surprisingly, lesbian, gay, or bisexual youths do not report more sexual minority friends than do heterosexual youths (Ueno, 2005). Furthermore, the average quality of sexual minority youths' relationships with their heterosexual and sexual minority friends does not differ (Beals & Peplau, 2006; Ueno et al., 2009). However, lesbian, gay, or bisexual youths may benefit more from having friendships with other sexual minority youths than they do from heterosexual friendships. Specifically, whereas having more friends was beneficial to all youths, having more sexual minority friends was related to less psychological distress among lesbian, gay, or bisexual youths (Ueno, 2005). However, a recent study found that both heterosexual and sexual minority friendships were related to lower distress (Ueno et al., 2009).

Despite fears of losing friends and worries about friends' reactions to disclosure (D'Augelli, 2002; Diamond & Lucas, 2004), the majority of lesbian, gay, or bisexual youths first disclose their sexual orientation to a heterosexual friend and nearly all have told a friend (Beals & Peplau, 2006; D'Augelli et al., 1998; Rosario et al., 2009). Moreover, the quality of youths' relationships with friends appears to be unchanged by the disclosure of sexual orientation (Beals & Peplau, 2006). Indeed, both heterosexual and sexual minority friends are perceived as being more accepting of them than are parents (Beals & Peplau, 2006). In addition, lesbian, gay, or bisexual youths report greater social support for their sexual orientation from friends than they do from their parents (Muñoz-Plaza et al., 2002).

The support and acceptance from friends serve as a protective role for the well-being of lesbian, gay, or bisexual youths. Specifically, more friend support and a high level of sexual identity integration are associated with (Rosario et al., 2008b). Furthermore, more social support from friends is associated with less depressive symptomatology (Rosario et al., 2005; Sheets & Mohr, 2009; Ueno, 2005; Vincke & Van Heeringen, 2002), less suicidality (Rosario et al., 2005), less hopelessness (Vincke & Van Heeringen, 2002), greater self-esteem and self-acceptance (Rosario et al., 2008b; Vincke & Van Heeringen, 2002), greater life satisfaction (Sheets & Mohr, 2009), and fewer school problems (Russell, Seif et al., 2001). In the above noted studies, support from friends was often found to be just as beneficial as support from family, suggesting that both sources of support serve a critical role in the sexual identity development and well-being of lesbian, gay, or bisexual youths (Rosario et al., 2005, 2008b, 2011a; Sheets & Mohr, 2009; Ueno, 2005; Vincke & Van Heeringen, 2002).

LESBIAN, GAY, OR BISEXUAL YOUTHS AND THE SCHOOL SETTING

Sexual minority youths, like their heterosexual peers, spend the majority of their waking time with family, friends, and in school. The school setting has often proven to be problematic for lesbian, gay, or bisexual youths (Kosciw, Greytak, Diaz, & Bartkiewicz, 2010). Many more sexual minority youths than their heterosexual peers report being victimized, teased, or having their personal property damaged or stolen at school (Birkett, Espleage, & Koenig, 2009; Bontempo & D'Augelli, 2002). Given these findings, it is not surprising that lesbian, gay, or bisexual youths report higher rates of school truancy than their heterosexual peers (Birkett et al., 2009; Bontempo & D'Augelli, 2002) and poorer academic performance (Pearson, Muller, & Wilkinson, 2007; Russell, Seif et al., 2001; Szalacha, 2003). As compared to their heterosexual schoolmates, lesbian, gay, or bisexual youths also report poorer health, such as depressive symptoms, suicidality, substance use, and sexual risk behaviors (Birkett et al., 2009; Bontempo & D'Augelli, 2002). Victimization in school has been associated with these negative outcomes (Bontempo & D'Augelli, 2002; Swearer, Turner, Givens, & Pollack, 2008). Although the implications of such victimization for attaining later career potential remain to be examined, developing a career is a developmental task of emerging adulthood (Arnett, 2000). Therefore, abuse in school may have long-term consequences that affect subsequent developmental periods.

Potential reasons for the greater likelihood of abuse experienced by lesbian, gay, or bisexual youths in school include behaving in a gender-nonconforming way (D'Augelli, Pilkington, & Hershberger, 2002; Friedman, Koeske, Silvestre, Korr, & Sites, 2006), disclosing their sexual minority status to others (D'Augelli et al., 2002), or being perceived to be lesbian, gay, or bisexual by others (Swearer et al., 2008). The elevated abuse also varies with intolerance for lesbian, gay, or bisexual individuals in the school setting as indicated, for example, by being in schools in which more students versus fewer students attend religious services, being in schools located in rural/suburban versus urban areas, being in schools that emphasize football, or being in school districts with adults with lower educational achievement (Kosciw, Greyak, & Diaz, 2009; Wilkinson & Pearson, 2009). This set of contextual findings implicates the school climate. As compared with heterosexual peers, lesbian, gay, or bisexual youths find their school climate to be poorer (Birkett et al., 2009; Swearer et al., 2008) and they experience less sense of school belonging (Galliher, Rostosky, & Hughes, 2004; Pearson et al., 2007). These results on the perceived school climate of students in high school have also been found among students in college and graduate school throughout the United States (Rankin, Weber, Blumenfeld, & Frazer, 2010).

However, lesbian, gay, or bisexual youths do well in schools with programs that protect and address their concerns. In such schools, lesbian, gay, or bisexual adolescents experience less harassment and victimization than their peers in schools without supportive programs or materials (Chesir-Teran & Hughes, 2009). Lesbian, gay, or bisexual youths in schools that are sensitive to their needs (by, for example, providing HIV-related instruction) report fewer poor health-related behaviors (e.g., less substance use and fewer sexual risk behaviors) than similar youths in other schools (Blake et al., 2001). In addition, lesbian, gay, or bisexual youths in schools with Gay-Straight Alliances, as compared with peers in schools without such groups, report lower rates of victimization (Chesir-Teran & Hughes, 2009; Goodenow, Szalacha, & Westheimer, 2006), less truancy (Goodenow et al., 2006), less dropping out of school (Walls, Kane, & Wisneski, 2010,) and fewer poor health-related behaviors (Goodenow et al., 2006). As the above makes clear, actual programmatic effort, such as classroom discussion, books in the school library that address homosexuality, and support groups for lesbian, gay, or bisexual youths, proves to be essential (e.g., Chesir-Teran & Hughes, 2009; Goodenow et al., 2006). Merely having anti-discrimination policies that include sexual orientation confers no significant protection (Chesir-Teran & Hughes, 2009), unless, one presumes, such policies are publicized and enforced.

In summary, the school may not be particularly welcoming and nurturing for many sexual minority youths. However, it can become such a setting and, by so doing, ensure the academic progress of lesbian, gay, or bisexual youths, bolster their well-being and health, and allow them the opportunity to develop their sexual identity without diverting psychological resources to coping with anticipated or actual experiences of abuse and other external gay-related stressors.

WHAT WE NEED TO KNOW: THE RESEARCH AGENDA

A discontinuity exists between the theoretical and empirical sections of this chapter that speaks to the gaps in empirical research. Sexual identity development is a complex process that affects subsequent development. Little is known about identity integration among lesbian, gay, or bisexual youths (see Rosario et al., 2008b, for an exception), although data are available on identity formation (e.g., D'Augelli, 2002; Rosario et al., 1996; Savin-Williams & Diamond, 2000) and on changes over time in same-sex attractions or self-identification as lesbian, gay, or bisexual (Diamond, 2008; Ott, Corliss, Wypij, Rosario, & Austin, 2011; Rosario, Schrimshaw, Hunter, & Braun, 2006; Savin-Williams & Ream, 2007). More information is needed about how differences in the process of identity integration may be related to mental health and health-related behaviors (Rosario, Schrimshaw, & Hunter, 2006, 2009, 2011b). We also need to know how changes or consistency in sexual identity may affect subsequent developmental tasks, such as career development or intimate relationships in emerging adulthood. Longitudinal studies are needed that carefully examine these issues, while considering the larger context in which changes take place.

The role of parents and peers and the experience of gay-related stress on sexual identity development and health need to be better understood. In particular, attachment to significant others requires attention because the attachment figures serve as working models (i.e., mental representations) of the self and others, and attachment style affects mental health and future relationships (Bowlby, 1969), including intimate relationships and sexual risk behaviors (Ammaniti, Nicolais, & Speranza, 2007; Mikulincer & Shaver, 2007). Despite its potential explanatory power, we know of only one study in which attachment was examined among lesbian, gay, or bisexual youths (Gwadz, Clatts, Leonard, & Goldsamt, 2004). Romantic relationships are critical for all adolescents and serve as the foundation for intimacy in emerging adulthood. Little is known, however, about the development of romantic relationships among lesbian, gay, or bisexual youths (Elze, 2002; Eyre, Milbrath, & Peacock, 2007) or about the role of such relationships in the youths' development, health, and well-being (Bauermeister et al., 2010; Diamond & Lucas, 2004; Russell & Consolación, 2003). Little also is known about the context beyond family, peers, and school for youths, such as the role of religion, work, or civic engagement in the lives of sexual minority youths.

Despite the growing knowledge about health disparities by sexual orientation and some other experiences of sexual minority youths, we want to emphasize that little is known about how lesbian, gay, or bisexual youths actually cope with the challenges they face, both in terms of sexual identity development and stressors associated with that development. We hypothesize that the coping strategies are still maturing, given the youths' neurocognitive development (e.g., Casey et al., 2008). Indeed, some lesbian, gay, or bisexual youths may use tobacco, alcohol, and other drugs as coping strategies, given the high prevalence of such substance use by lesbian, gay, or bisexual youths (e.g., Marshal et al., 2008). However, such coping strategies are ineffective: Tobacco has been found to amplify rather than attenuate the relation between stress and subsequent psychological distress among sexual minority youths (Rosario, Schrimshaw, & Hunter, 2011a).

Of great importance is the need to identify and understand the psychosocial strengths and resilience of lesbian, gay, or bisexual youths in the face of the enormous challenges they experience. As the health disparities by sexual orientation attest, some sexual minority youths may not cope effectively with these challenges (e.g., Bontempo & D'Augelli, 2002; Marshal et al., 2008, 2011). However, the within-group variability in health found in samples of sexual minority youths suggests that some youths may be doing well despite the challenges they may encounter. We need to understand how the experiences and lives of such youths differ from lesbian, gay, or bisexual peers who may not be functioning as well.

One factor explaining coping variability among sexual minority youths may be development in general. We expect that the challenges of sexual identity development as lesbian, gay, or bisexual should be more difficult for youths undergoing the process at younger as compared to older ages. The reasons have to do with the prefrontal cortex, specifically its continued development during adolescence and its increasing ability to downregulate (e.g., Casey et al., 2008). However, no significant differences in psychological distress have been found in undergoing sexual minority identity formation at early as compared with later ages (D'Augelli, 2002; Floyd & Stein, 2002; Rosario et al., 2011b), perhaps because of the time gap between assessment of distress, which is approximately cotemporaneous with study implementation, and identity formation, which may have occurred years in the past. Increasing time gaps allow intervening processes to unfold and mediate relations. Thus, research is required to examine the intervening process(es) that may not only account for the null findings, but may also resolve the contradiction between the neurocognitve hypothesis and empirical findings. The intervening process, we hypothesize herein, constitutes lesbian, gay, or bisexual identity integration.

Finally, more attention needs to focus on differences (and similarities) in sexual identity development and health by sex, gender atypicality, sexual orientation (e.g., lesbian/gay versus bisexual), ethnicity/race, and the geographic location in which the youth resides (e.g., Grov et al., 2006; Kosciw et al., 2009; Poon & Saewyc, 2009; Rosario, Schrimshaw, & Hunter, 2004). Women in general are hypothesized to be more variable or fluid in their sexual identity than men (e.g., Peplau, 2003) and some have found that more young women than young men identify as bisexual (e.g., Dempsey, Hiller, & Harrison, 2001; Savin-Williams & Diamond, 2000). However, a large national study of Swedish youths found no significant sex differences in bisexual identification (Narring, Stronski Huwiler, & Michaud, 2003) and a large national study of American youths found no significant sex differences in changes over time in the sexual feelings of its sexual minority youths (Ott et al., 2011). The latter study found more change among young women than men, but only among those who described their feelings as "mostly heterosexual." Thus, whatever fluidity exists may not apply to most sexual minority youths. Clearly, more research is needed to clarify these relations. In the process, it should be noted that studies of differences between men and women in sexual identity constitute a research focus distinct from studying change in identity over time in just one sex, such as women (Diamond, 2008).

With respect to health and sex differences, lesbian and bisexual female youths report more substance use than male peers in a representative sample, a pattern similar to heterosexual youths of the other sex (Russell et al., 2002). Gender-atypical patterns relative to heterosexual findings have also been found with internalizing symptoms in another representative sample, in which gay and bisexual male emerging adults were more likely than female peers to meet the criteria for diagnosis of major depression or anxiety disorder, or report suicidal ideation (Fergusson et al., 2005). The findings indicating that lesbian, gay, or bisexual youths report mental health patterns typical of the other sex may be a function of gender atypicality or nonconformity (Rosario, Schrimshaw, & Hunter, 2008a). Research is needed on "butch" and "femme" lesbian and bisexual young women and comparable phenomenon in their male peers. This research should also consider including biological markers of gender atypicality, such as prenatal hormone levels (Brown, Finn, Cooke, & Breedlove, 2002; Ellis & Hellberg, 2005; Martin & Nguyen, 2004).

An important health difference has been found as a function of sexual orientation. Bisexual youths in representative samples report more psychological distress and substance use than lesbian or gay youths (Eisenberg & Wechsler, 2003; Jorm et al., 2002; Russell et al., 2002). Bisexual youths also report more sexual risk behaviors, given that a recent representative sample of New York City high school students (Pathela & Schillinger, 2010) found that more bisexual boys than gay (or heterosexual) male peers reported two or more sexual partners in the past 3 months and five or more sexual partners over the lifetime. In this survey, more bisexual female youths than lesbian (or heterosexual female) peers reported intimate partner violence in the past year and sexual abuse over the lifetime. These and

other representative data (Jorm et al., 2002) suggest that a possible reason for the multiple health disparities by bisexual versus lesbian/gay orientation may be the greater adversity experienced recently and during childhood by bisexuals than by their lesbian/gay peers. However, the nature of the adversity is not well understood and, thus, is in need of investigation.

Hypotheses need to be tested as soon as possible because they may not always be supported. For example, most youths who question their sexual orientation later transition to a heterosexual rather than to a lesbian, gay, or bisexual identity with respect to their feelings (Ott et al., 2011). For another example, the sexual identity development of Latino and black youths is not identical with respect to identity integration, whereas Latino and white youths are rather similar on identity integration (Rosario et al., 2004). These findings are contrary to hypotheses in the literature in which similarity is expected between blacks and Latinos, and the sexual identity development of both groups is expected to be less advanced than that of whites (see Rosario et al., 2004, for details). The findings for questioning youths and youths of various ethnic/racial backgrounds, if replicated, must be understood.

CONCLUSIONS

Much has been learned about lesbian, gay, or bisexual youths in recent years. More still needs to be learned, particularly by using longitudinal designs and samples that attempt both to represent the full range of lesbian, gay, or bisexual youths and to include youths entering puberty when sexual identity development usually begins. If carried out, the research agenda outlined herein should increase our understanding of lesbian, gay, or bisexual youths and sharpen our insights about their development and health as young adults. Accomplishing the research agenda proposed here also should prove invaluable for designing interventions to improve the health and well-being of lesbian, gay, or bisexual youths.

NOTE

[1] Phineas Gage is a landmark case in psychology and medicine. Gage was in charge of blasting rock for a railroad company. As he was preparing a blasting charge, the powder exploded, driving a tamping iron through his lower left eye that exited through the top of the skull. Gage recuperated physically from his injury, a frontal lobotomy; however, his

personality underwent a radical change. The individual who had been a caring, socially skilled, emotionally regulated, and rational man before the accident was transmuted into the opposite. He lost social inhibition and became an impulsive, profane, indulgent, and irrational man. Gage died 12 years after the fateful accident, at the age of 36 years, in 1860.

REFERENCES

Ammaniti, M., Nicolais, G., & Speranza, A. M. (2007). Attachment and sexuality during adolescence: Interaction, integration, or interference. In D. Diamond, S. J. Blatt, & J. D. Lichtenberg (Eds.), *Attachment & sexuality* (pp. 79–105). New York: Analytic Press.

Arnett, J. J. (2000). Emerging adulthood: A theory of development from the late teens through the twenties. *American Psychologist, 55,* 469–480.

Austin, S. B., Ziyadeh, N. J., Corliss, H. L., Rosario, M., Wypij, D., Haines, J., Camargo, C. A., Jr., & Field, A. E. (2009). Sexual orientation disparities in purging and binge eating from early to late adolescence. *Journal of Adolescent Health, 45,* 238–245.

Austin, S. B., Ziyadeh, N. Fisher, L. B., Kahn, J. A., Colditz, G. A., & Frazier, A. L. (2004). Sexual orientation and tobacco use in a cohort study of US adolescent girls and boys. *Archives of Pediatrics and Adolescent Medicine, 158,* 317–322.

Badr, H., & Taylor, C. L. C. (2006). Social constraints and spousal communication in lung cancer. *Psycho-Oncology, 15,* 673–683.

Bauermeister, J. A., Johns, M. M., Sandfort, T. G. M., Eisenberg, A., Grossman, A. H., & D'Augelli, A. R. (2010). Relationship trajectories and psychological well-being among sexual minority youth. *Journal of Youth and Adolescence, 39,* 1148–1163.

Beals, K. P., & Peplau, L. A. (2006). Disclosure patterns within social networks of gay men and lesbians. *Journal of Homosexuality, 51,* 101–120.

Ben-Ari, A. (1995). The discovery that an offspring is gay: Parents', gay men's, and lesbians' perspectives. *Journal of Homosexuality, 30,* 89–112.

Birkett, M., Espelage, D. L., & Koenig, B. (2009). LGB and questioning students in schools: The moderating effects of homophobic bullying and school climate on negative outcomes. *Journal of Youth and Adolescence, 38,* 989–1000.

Blake, S. M., Ledsky, R., Lehamn, T., Goodenow, C., Sawyer, R., & Hack, T. (2001). Preventing sexual risk behaviors among gay, lesbian, and bisexual adolescents: The benefits of gay-sensitive HIV instruction in schools. *American Journal of Public Health, 91,* 940–946.

Bontempo, D. E., & D'Augelli, A. R. (2002). Effects of at-school victimization and sexual orientation on lesbian, gay, or bisexual youths' health risk behavior. *Journal of Adolescent Health, 30,* 364–374.

Bowlby, J. (1969). *Attachment and loss: Volume 1. Attachment.* New York: Basic Books.

Brown, W. M., Finn, C. J., Cooke, B. M., & Breedlove, S. M. (2002). Differences in finger length ratios between self-identified "butch" and "femme" lesbians. *Archives of Sexual Behavior, 31,* 123–127.

Casey, B. J., Getz, S., & Galvan, A. (2008). The adolescent brain. *Developmental Review, 28,* 62–77.

Centers for Disease Control and Prevention. (2007). HIV/AIDS surveillance in adolescents and young adults (through 2007). Slide set, downloaded on July 28, 2010, from www.cdc.gov/hiv/topics/surveillance/resources/slides/adolescents.

Centers for Disease Control and Prevention. (2010). HIV surveillance report, 2008; vol. 20. Downloaded on July 28, 2010, from www.cdc.gov/hiv/topics/surveillance/resources/reports.

Chesir-Teran, D., & Hughes, D. (2009). Heterosexism in high school and victimization among lesbian, gay, bisexual, and questioning students. *Journal of Youth and Adolescence, 38,* 963–975.

Coker, T. R., Austin, S. B., & Schuster, M. A. (2010). The health and health care of lesbian, gay, and bisexual adolescents. *Annual Review of Public Health, 31,* 457–477.

Compas, B. E., Connor-Smith, J. K., Saltzman, H., Harding Thomsen, A., & Wadsworth, M. E. (2001). Coping with stress during childhood and adolescence: Problems, progress, and potential in theory and research. *Psychological Bulletin, 127,* 87–127.

Corliss, H. L., Rosario, M., Wypij, D., Fisher, L. B., & Austin, S. B. (2008). Sexual orientation disparities in longitudinal alcohol use patterns among adolescents: Findings from the Growing Up Today study. *Archives of Pediatric and Adolescent Medicine, 162,* 1071–1078.

D'Augelli, A. R. (2002). Mental health problems among lesbian, gay, and bisexual youths ages 14 to 21. *Clinical Child Psychology and Psychiatry, 7,* 433–456.

D'Augelli, A. R., & Grossman, A. H. (2001). Disclosure of sexual orientation, victimization, and mental health among lesbian, gay, and bisexual older adults. *Journal of Interpersonal Violence, 16,* 1008–1027.

D'Augelli, A. R., Grossman, A. H., Salter, N. P., Vasey, J. J., Starks, M. T., & Sinclair, K. O. (2005). Predicting the suicide attempts of lesbian, gay, and bisexual youth. *Suicide and Life-Threatening Behavior, 35,* 646–660.

D'Augelli, A. R., Grossman, A. H., & Starks, M. T. (2005). Parents' awareness of lesbian, gay, and bisexual youths' sexual orientation. *Journal of Marriage and Family, 67,* 474–482.

D'Augelli, A. R., Grossman, A. H., & Starks, M. T. (2008). Families of gay, lesbian, and bisexual youth: What do parents and siblings know and how do they react? *Journal of GLBT Family Studies, 4,* 95–115.

D'Augelli, A. R., Hershberger, S. L., & Pilkington, N. W. (1998). Lesbian, gay, and bisexual youth and their families: Disclosure of sexual orientation and its consequences. *American Journal of Orthopsychiatry, 68,* 361–371.

D'Augelli, A. R., Pilkington, N. W., & Hershberger, S. L. (2002). Incidence and mental health impact of sexual orientation victimization of lesbian, gay, and bisexual youths in high school. *School Psychology Quarterly, 17,* 148–167.

Dempsey, D., Hillier, L., & Harrison, L. (2001). Gendered (s) explorations among same-sex attracted young people in Australia. *Journal of Adolescence, 24,* 67–81.

Diamond, L. M. (2008). Female bisexuality from adolescence to adulthood: Results from a 10-year longitudinal study. *Developmental Psychology, 44,* 5–14.

Diamond, L. M., & Lucas, S. (2004). Sexual-minority and heterosexual youths' peer relationships: Experiences, expectations, and implications for well-being. *Journal of Research on Adolescence, 14,* 313–340.

Eisenberg, M. (2001). Differences in sexual risk behaviors between college students with same-sex and opposite-sex experiences: Results from a national survey. *Archives of Sexual Behavior, 30,* 575–589.

Eisenberg, M., & Resnick, M. D. (2006). Suicidality among gay, lesbian, and bisexual youth: The role of protective factors. *Journal of Adolescent Health, 39,* 662–668.

Eisenberg, M., & Wechsler, H. (2003). Substance use behaviors among college students with same-sex and opposite-sex experience: Results from a national study. *Addictive Behaviors, 28,* 899–913.

Ellis, L., & Hellberg, J. (2005). Fetal exposure to prescription drugs and adult sexual orientation. *Personality and Individual Differences, 38,* 225–236.

Elze, D. E. (2002). Against all odds: The dating experiences of adolescent lesbian and bisexual women. *Journal of Lesbian Studies, 6,* 17–29.

Erikson, E. (1950/1980). Growth and crises of the healthy personality. In E. Erikson (Ed.), *Identity and the life cycle* (pp. 51–70). New York: Norton.

Erikson, E. (1956/1980). The problem of ego identity. In E. Erikson (Ed.), *Identity and the life cycle* (pp. 107–175). New York: Norton.

Erikson, E. H. (1968). *Identity: Youth and crisis.* New York: Norton.

Eyre, S. L., Milbrath, C., & Peacock, B. (2007). Romantic relationships trajectories of African American gay/bisexual adolescents. *Journal of Adolescent Research, 22,* 107–131.

Fergusson, D. M., Horwood, L. J., & Beautrais, A. L. (1999). Is sexual orientation related to mental health problems and suicidality among young people? *Archives of General Psychiatry, 56,* 876–880.

Fergusson, D. M., Horwood, L. J., & Ridder, E. M., & Beautrais, A. L. (2005). Sexual orientation and mental health in a cohort of young adults. *Psychological Medicine, 35,* 971–981.

Floyd, F. J., & Bakeman, R. (2006). Coming-out across the life course: Implications of age and historical context. *Archives of Sexual Behavior, 35,* 287–296.

Floyd, F. J., & Stein, T. S. (2002). Sexual orientation identity formation among gay, lesbian, and bisexual youths: Multiple patterns of milestone experiences. *Journal of Research on Adolescence, 12,* 167–191.

Friedman, M. S., Koeske, G. F., Silvestre, A. J., Korr, W. S., & Sites, E. W. (2006). The impact of gender-role nonconforming behavior, bully, and social support on sucicidality among gay male youth. *Journal of Adolescent Health, 38,* 621–623.

Galliher, R. V., Rostosky, S. S., & Hughes, H. K. (2004). School belonging, self-esteem, and depressive symptoms in adolescents: An examination of sex, sexual attraction status, and urbanicity. *Journal of Youth and Adolescence, 33,* 235–245.

Galvan, A., Hare, T. A., Parra, C. E., Penn, J., Voss, H., Glover, G., & Casey, B. J. (2006). Earlier development of the accumbens relative to orbitofrontal cortex might underlie risk-taking behavior in adolescents. *Journal of Neuroscience, 26,* 6885–6892.

Goodenow, C., Netherland, J., & Szalacha, L. (2002). AIDS-related risk among adolescent males who have sex with males, females, or both: Evidence from a statewide survey. *American Journal of Public Health, 92,* 203–210.

Goodenow, C., Szalacha, L., & Westheimer, K. (2006). School support groups, other school factors, and the safety of sexual minority adolescents. *Psychology in the Schools, 43,* 573–589.

Grant, K. E., Compas, B. E., Thurm, A. E., McMahon, S. D., Gipson, P. Y., Campbell, A. J., Krochock, K., & Westerholm, R. I. (2006). Stressors and child and adolescent psychopathology: Evidence of moderating and mediating effects. *Clinical Psychology Review, 26,* 257–283.

Grov, C., Bimbi, D. S., Nanín, J. E., & Parsons, J. T. (2006). Race, ethnicity, gender, and generational factors associated with the coming-out process among gay, lesbian, and bisexual individuals. *Journal of Sex Research, 43,* 115–121.

Gwadz, M. V., Clatts, M. C., Leonard, N. R., & Goldsamt, L. (2004). Attachment style, childhood adversity, and behavioral risk among young men who have sex with men. *Journal of Adolescent Health, 34,* 402–413.

Hare, T. A., Tottenham, N., Galvan, A., Voss, H. U., Glover, G. H., & Casey, B. J. (2008). Biological substrates of emotional reactivity and regulation in adolescence during an emotional go-nogo task. *Biological Psychiatry, 63,* 927–934.

Herek, G. M. (2009). Hate crimes and stigma-related experiences among sexual minority adults in the United States: Prevalence estimates from a national probability sample. *Journal of Interpersonal Violence, 24,* 54–74.

Jorm, A. F., Korten, A. E., Rodgers, B., Jacomb, P. A., & Christensen, H. (2002). Sexual orientation and mental health: Results from a community survey of young and middle-aged adults. *British Journal of Psychiatry, 180,* 423–427.

Kosciw, J. G., Greytak, E. A., & Diaz, E. M. (2009). Who, what, where, when, and why: Demographic and ecological factors contributing to hostile school climate for lesbian, gay, bisexual, and transgender youth. *Journal of Youth and Adolescence, 38,* 976–988.

Kosciw, J. G., Greytak, E. A., Diaz, E. M., & Bartkiewicz, M. J. (2010). *The 2009 national school climate survey: The experiences of lesbian, gay, bisexual, and transgender youth in our nation's schools.* New York: Gay, Lesbian, and Straight Education Network (GLSEN).

Kroger, J. (2007). *Identity development: Adolescence through adulthood* (2nd. ed.). Thousand Oaks, CA: Sage.

Kuhn, D. (2009). Adolescent thinking. In R. M. Lerner & L. Steinberg (Eds.), *Handbook of adolescent psychology* (3rd. ed., Vol. 1, pp. 152–186). Hoboken, NJ: Wiley.

Laviola, G., Adriani, W., Terranova, M. L., & Gerra, G. (1999). Psychobiological risk factors for vulnerability to psychostimulants in human adolescents and animal models. *Neuroscience and Biobehavioral Reviews, 23,* 993–1010.

Lazarus, R. S., & Folkman, S. (1984). *Stress, appraisal, and coping.* New York: Springer.

Lepore, S. J., Silver, R. C., Wortman, C. B., & Wayment, H. A. (1996). Social constraints, intrusive thoughts, and depressive symptoms among bereaved mothers. *Journal of Personality and Social Psychology, 70,* 271–282.

Lewis, R. J., Derlega, V. J., Clarke, E. G., & Kuang, J. C. (2006). Stigma consciousness, social constraints, and lesbian well-being. *Journal of Counseling Psychology, 53,* 48–56.

Marshal, M. P., Dietz, L. J., Friedman, M. S., Stall, R., Smith, H., McGinley, J., Thoma, B. C., Murray, P. J., D'Augelli, A. R., & Brent, D. A. (2011). Suicidality and depression disparities between sexual minority and heterosexual youth: A meta-analytic review. *Journal of Adolescent Health, 49,* 115–123.

Marshal, M. P., Friedman, M. S., Stall, R., King, K. M., Miles, J., Gold, M. A., Bukstein, O. G., & Morse, J. Q. (2008). Sexual orientation and adolescent substance use: A meta-analysis and methodological review. *Addiction, 103,* 546–556.

Martin, J. T., & Nguyen, D. H. (2004). Anthropometric analysis of homosexuals and heterosexuals: Implications for early hormone exposure. *Hormones and Behavior, 45,* 31–39.

Meyer, I. H. (2003). Prejudice, social stress, and mental health in lesbian, gay, and bisexual populations: Conceptual issues and research evidence. *Psychological Bulletin, 129,* 674–697.

Mikulincer, M., & Shaver, P. R. (2007). A behavioral systems perspective on the psychodynamics of attachment and sexuality. In D. Diamond, S. J. Blatt, & J. D. Lichtenberg (Eds.), *Attachment & sexuality* (pp. 51–78). New York: Analytic Press.

Mufioz-Plaza, C., Quinn, S. C., & Rounds, K. A. (2002). Lesbian, gay, bisexual and transgender students: Perceived social support in the high school environment. *High School Journal, 85,* 52–63.

Narring, F., Stronski Huwiler, S. M., & Michaud, P-A. (2003). Prevalence and dimensions of sexual orientation in Swiss adolescents: A cross-sectional survey of 16 to 20-year-old students. *Acta Paediatrica, 92,* 233–239.

Nesmith, A. A., Burton, D. L., & Cosgrove, T. J. (1999). Gay, lesbian, and bisexual youth and young adults: Social support in their own words. *Journal of Homosexuality, 37,* 95–108.

Nolte, J. (2002). *The human brain: An introduction to its functional anatomy* (5th ed.). St. Louis, MO: Mosby.

Ott, M. Q., Corliss, H. L., Wypij, D., Rosario, M., & Austin, S. B. (2011). Stability and change in self-reported sexual orientation identity in young people: Application of mobility matrics. *Archives of Sexual Behavior, 40,* 519–532.

Ozer, E. J., & Weinstein, R. S. (2004). Urban adolescents; exposure to community violence: The role of support, school safety, and social constraints in a school-based sample of boys and girls. *Journal of Clinical Child and Adolescent Psychology, 33,* 463–476.

Parks, C. A., & Hughes, T. L. (2007). Age differences in lesbian identity development and drinking. *Substance Use & Misuse, 42,* 361–380.

Pathela, P., & Schillinger, J. A. (2010). Sexual behaviors and sexual violence: Adolescents with opposite-, same-, or both-sex partners. *Pediatrics, 126,* 879–886.

Pearson, J., Muller, C., & Wilkinson, L. (2007). Adolescent same-sex attraction and academic outcomes: The role of school attachment and engagement. *Social Problems, 54,* 523–542.

Peplau, L. A. (2003). Human sexuality: How do men and women differ? *Current Directions in Psychological Science, 12,* 37–40.

Poon, C. S., & Saewyc, E. M. (2009). Out yonder: Sexual-minority adolescents in rural communities in British Columbia. *American Journal of Public Health, 99,* 118–124.

Rankin, S., Weber, G., Blumenfeld, W., & Frazer, S. (2010). *2010 state of higher education for lesbian, gay, bisexual & transgender people.* Charlotte, NC: Campus Pride.

Rosario, M., Meyer-Bahlburg, H. F. L., Hunter, J., Exner, T. M., Gwadz, M., & Keller, A. M. (1996). The psychosexual development of urban lesbian, gay, and bisexual youths. *Journal of Sex Research, 33,* 113–126.

Rosario, M., Schrimshaw, E. W., & Hunter, J. (2004). Ethnic/racial differences in the coming-out process of lesbian, gay, and bisexual youths: A comparison of sexual identity development over time. *Cultural Diversity & Ethnic Minority Psychology, 10,* 215–228.

Rosario, M., Schrimshaw, E. W., & Hunter, J. (2005). Psychological distress following suicidality among gay, lesbian, and bisexual youths: Role of social relationships. *Journal of Youth and Adolescence, 34*, 149–161.

Rosario, M., Schrimshaw, E. W., & Hunter, J. (2006). A model of sexual risk behaviors among young gay and bisexual men: Longitudinal associations of mental health, substance abuse, sexual abuse, and the coming-out process. *AIDS Education and Prevention, 18*, 444–460.

Rosario, M., Schrimshaw, E. W., & Hunter, J. (2008a). Butch/femme differences in substance use and abuse among young lesbian and bisexual women: Examination and potential explanations. *Substance Use & Misuse, 43*, 1002–1015.

Rosario, M., Schrimshaw, E. W., & Hunter, J. (2008b). Predicting different patterns of sexual identity development over time among lesbian, gay, and bisexual youths: A cluster analytic approach. *American Journal of Community Psychology, 42*, 266–282.

Rosario, M., Schrimshaw, E. W., & Hunter, J. (2009). Disclosure of sexual orientation and subsequent substance use and abuse among lesbian, gay, and bisexual youths: Critical role of disclosure reactions. *Psychology of Addictive Behaviors, 23*, 175–184.

Rosario, M., Schrimshaw, E. W., & Hunter, J. (2011a). Cigarette smoking as coping strategy: Negative implications for subsequent psychological distress among lesbian, gay, and bisexual youths. *Journal of Pediatric Psychology, 36*, 731–742.

Rosario, M., Schrimshaw, E. W., & Hunter, J. (2011b). Different patterns of sexual identity development over time: Implications for psychological adjustment of lesbian, gay, and bisexual youths. *Journal of Sex Research, 48*, 3–15.

Rosario, M., Schrimshaw, E. W., Hunter, J., & Braun, L. (2006). Sexual identity development among lesbian, gay, and bisexual youths: Consistency and change over time. *Journal of Sex Research, 43*, 46–58.

Russell, S. T., & Consolación, T. B. (2003). Adolescent romance and emotional health in the United States: Beyond binaries. *Journal of Clinical Child and Adolescent Psychology, 53*, 499–508.

Russell, S. T., Driscoll, A. K., & Truong, N. (2002). Adolescent same-sex romantic attractions and relationships: Implications for substance use and abuse. *American Journal of Public Health, 92*, 198–202.

Russell, S. T., Franz, B. T., & Driscoll, A. K. (2001). Same-sex romantic attraction and experiences of violence in adolescence. *American Journal of Public Health, 91*, 903–906.

Russell, S. T., & Joyner, K. (2001). Adolescent sexual orientation and suicide risk: Evidence from a national study. *American Journal of Public Health, 91*, 1276–1281.

Russell, S. T., Seif, H., & Truong, N. L. (2001). School outcomes of sexual minority youth in the United States: Evidence from a national study. *Journal of Adolescence, 24*, 111–127.

Ryan, C., Huebner, D., Diaz, R. M., & Sanchez, J. (2009). Family rejection as a predictor of negative health outcomes in white and Latino lesbian, gay, and bisexual young adults. *Pediatrics, 123*, 346–352.

Saewyc, E. M. (2011). Research on adolescent sexual orientation: Development, health disparities, stigma, and resilience. *Journal of Research on Adolescence, 21*, 256–272.

Saewyc, E. M., Poon, C. S., Homma, Y., & Skay, C. L. (2008). Stigma management? The links between enacted stigma and teen pregnancy trends among gay, lesbian, and bisexual students in British Columbia. *Canadian Journal of Human Sexuality, 17*, 123–139.

Savin-Williams, R. C., & Diamond, L. M. (2000). Sexual identity trajectories among sexual-minority youths: Gender comparisons. *Archives of Sexual Behavior, 29*, 607–627.

Savin-Williams, R. C., & Ream, G. L. (2003). Sex variations in the disclosure to parents of same-sex attractions. *Journal of Family Psychology, 17*, 429–438.

Savin-Williams, R. C., & Ream, G. L. (2007). Prevalence and stability of sexual orientation components during adolescence and young adulthood. *Archives of Sexual Behavior, 36*, 385–394.

Sheets, R. L., & Mohr, J. J. (2009). Perceived social support from friends and family and psychosocial functioning in bisexual young adult college students. *Journal of Counseling Psychology, 56*, 152–163.

Silenzio, V. M. B., Pena, J. B., Duberstein, P. R., Cerel, J., & Knox, K. L. (2007). Sexual orientation and risk factors for suicidal ideation and suicide attempts among adolescents and young adults. *American Journal of Public Health, 97*, 2017–2019.

Sobesky, W. (1983). The effects of situational factors on moral judgments. *Child Development, 54*, 575–584.

Steinberg, L. (2005). Cognitive and affective development in adolescence. *Trends in Cognitive Sciences, 9*, 69–74.

Swearer, S. M., Turner, R. K., Givens, J. E., & Pollack, W. S. (2008). "You're so gay!": Do different forms of bullying matter for adolescent males. *School Psychology Review, 37*, 160–173.

Szalacha, L. A. (2003). Safer sexual diversity climates: Lessons learned from an evaluation of Massachusetts Safe Schools program for gay and lesbian students. *American Journal of Education, 110*, 58–88.

Tajfel, H. (1981). *Human groups and social categories: Studies in social psychology*. Cambridge, UK: Cambridge University Press.

Turner, J. C., Hogg, M. A., Oakes, P. J., Reicher, S. D., & Wetherell, M. S. (1987). *Rediscovering the social group: A self-categorization theory*. Oxford, UK: Basil Blackwell.

Udry, J. R., & Chantala, K. (2002). Risk assessment of adolescents with same-sex relationships. *Journal of Adolescent Health, 31,* 84–92.

Ueno, K. (2005). Sexual orientation and psychological distress in adolescence: Examining interpersonal stressors and social support processes. *Social Psychology Quarterly, 68,* 258–277.

Ueno, K., Gayman, M. D., Wright, E. R., & Quantz, S. D. (2009). Friends' sexual orientation, relationship quality, and mental health among gay, lesbian, and bisexual youth. *Personal Relationships, 16,* 659–670.

Valentine, G., Skelton, T., & Butler, R. (2003). Coming out and outcomes: Negotiating lesbian and gay identities with, and in, the family. *Environment and Planning D: Society and Space, 21,* 479–499.

Vincke, J., & Van Heeringen, K. (2002). Confidant support and the mental wellbeing of lesbian and gay young adults: A longitudinal analysis. *Journal of Community and Applied Social Psychology, 12,* 181–193.

Walls, N. E., Kane, S. B., & Wisneski, H. (2010). Gay-straight alliances and school experiences of sexual minority youth. *Youth & Society, 41,* 307–332.

Wichstrøm, L. (2006). Sexual orientation as a risk factor for bulimic symptoms. *International Journal of Eating Disorders, 39,* 448–453.

Wichstrøm, L., & Hegna, K. (2003). Sexual orientation and suicide attempt: A longitudinal study of the general Norwegian adolescent population. *Journal of Abnormal Psychology, 112,* 144–151.

Wilkinson, L., & Pearson, J. (2009). School culture and the well-being of same-sex attracted youth. *Gender & Society, 23,* 542–568.

Williams, T., Connolly, J., Pepler, D., & Craig, W. (2005). Peer victimization, social support, and psychosocial adjustment of sexual minority adolescents. *Journal of Youth and Adolescence, 34,* 471–482.

8

Emergent Adulthood in Lesbian and Gay Lives: Individual Development, Life Course, and Social Change

BERTRAM J. COHLER[†] AND STUART MICHAELS

Recent studies of lesbian and gay lives in Western society have focused either on childhood antecedents of a gay identity or on adjustment and developmental tasks that are particularly significant in adolescence or in middle and later adulthood (D'Augelli & Patterson, 1995; Meyer & Northridge, 2007). This chapter uses Arnett's (2000, 2004, 2006a) conception of emergent adulthood as a framework for the study of young adulthood among same-sex-attracted men and women. Social change has fostered a delay for many young adults in making the transition from adolescence to settled adulthood (Cohler & Boxer, 1984). Arnett (2000, 2004, 2006a) has termed this new phase in the course of life "emergent adulthood," a time between adolescence and self-reliant adulthood. Using Arnett's discussion of emergent adulthood, Henig (2010) has portrayed the dilemmas for both young adults and for their families of this developmental stage in a recent cover story in *The New York Times Magazine*. Henig poses the question, "Why are so many people in their 20s taking so long to grow up?"

EMERGENT ADULTHOOD, SAME-SEX ATTRACTION, AND THE LIFE COURSE

Recognizing the importance of studying the impact of social and historical change upon the course of life, developmental science has posed models for this study of the interplay of lives and times (Settersten, 1999). These models are based on the concept of generation or cohort as the vehicle for social change (Baltes, Cornelius, & Nesselroade, 1979; Elder, 1995). Elder and Caspi (1990) have suggested that there is a range of historical events that links lives within a set of adjacent birth years to an historical context, and that these events foster a sense of shared consciousness within a generation (Esler, 1984). However, there is also considerable intracohort variability (Mouw, 2005; Sears, 1991; Settersten, 1999). Factors such as gender (Diamond, 2008) and sexual orientation may lead to considerable variation in this shared understanding of events taking place over the course of life. Sears (1991) has written about the experience of growing up gay and lesbian in the American South during the 1970s and the emergence of the gay rights era that contrasts markedly with the experiences of youth within the same cohort coming of age in large northern cities such as New York and within an earlier generation of lesbian and gay youth (Martin & D'Augelli, 2009). Stein (1997) has shown the changes taking place across cohorts of lesbians over the postwar period.

Life course perspectives are particularly important in the study of lesbian and gay lives. Successive cohorts coming to adulthood over the postwar era have encountered unique historical events and social change that have defined the course of life for a particular cohort (Cohler, 2007; Martin & D'Augelli, 2009). The increased social activism of the 1960s that presaged the emergence of the gay rights era in the 1970s, the emergence of the AIDS pandemic of the 1980s and early 1990s, and the advent of effective antiretroviral treatment for HIV in 1996, together with greater acceptance of diverse sexual orientations and changes in our understanding of

---

[†]Bert Cohler unfortunately passed on May 9, 2012, before this book went to press.

sexuality among men and women since the 1990s, have all been cohort-defining events for both lesbians and gay men (Clendinen & Nagourney, 1999; Diamond, 2008; Stein, 2010). Weststrate and McLean (2009) reported that older generations of lesbians and gay men tended to remember their past in terms of external events such as Stonewall, whereas the present generation in emergent adulthood remembers its past in terms of romance and contacts with other members of the gay and lesbian community. Seidman (2002) suggested that the cohort of lesbian and gay young adults coming of age at the beginning of the twenty-first century has been able to integrate its sexuality into their daily lives with romantic partners, friends, and with their parental family in ways that were more difficult to achieve for earlier cohorts (Martin & D'Augelli, 2009; Savin-Williams, 2005)

Life Course and Emergent Adulthood

In the first half of the twentieth century, the transition from adolescence to settled adulthood was often abrupt; career and marriage followed closely upon completion of formal education. However, social change since World War II has lengthened the time between adolescence and settled adulthood during which more young people have extended their education through college and beyond and have been able to explore a variety of options before deciding on a career and the choice of a life partner or spouse. This search for self-definition was heightened by the Civil Rights movement of the 1960s and the pathos of the Vietnam conflict. Keniston's (1971) concept of *youth* reflected this distinctive time in postwar society when self-reflection and social activism were particularly characteristic of young adults.

The succeeding generation cohort, born during the 1980s, came into its young adult years following this epoch of increased self-exploration and intense search for self-definition (Hunter, 2009). Arnett (1998, 2000, 2001) has maintained that the consequence of this now culturally institutionalized time in the course of life between adolescence and settled adulthood requires a term that is more precise than Keniston's term, proposing *emergent adulthood*. He comments, "There is little doubt that it takes longer to reach full adulthood today than it did in the past...in terms of traditional transitions such as finishing education, becoming financially independent from parents, marriage and parenthood...it

also seems confirmed subjectively by emerging adults' reports that during the 18–25 age period most of them feel not like adolescents and not like adults but somewhere in between, on the way to adulthood but not there yet" (Arnett, 2007, p. 27). Findings reported by Shanahan et al. (2005) and by Osgood, Ruth, Eccles, Jacobs, and Barber (2005) show that "feeling like an adult" is ordinarily associated with marriage, home ownership, and parenthood. Young adults still in school, whether single or living with a partner, were less likely than other young adults to regard themselves as adults. Delayed transition into characteristic adult roles was associated with a pursuit of education that, in the long term, would lead to greater success in the work world (Mitchell, 2007; Osgood et al., 2005). Currently, economic conditions make all of this quite difficult. Furthermore, *The New York Times* (June 13, 2010, p. 20) reports evidence showing that social change has led many young people in emergent adulthood to view marriage and parenthood more as lifestyle choices than as social roles that define adulthood.

Baker (1984) and Horowitz and Bromnick (2007) suggest on the basis of interviews with informants between ages 18 and 25 that emergent adulthood might best be characterized as a time of "contestable adulthood." Collins and van Dulmen's (2006) review of studies of emergent adulthood provides some support for Arnett's emphasis on continued identity exploration (Côté, 2006) but little support for the instability and transitory character of friendships in emergent adulthood. Rather, there appears to be continuity in the nature of relationships with friends in adolescence and emergent adulthood.

Whereas the concept of emergent adulthood highlights social changes in contemporary society, much of the study of emergent adulthood has been based on groups of urban, heterosexual, middle class, and well-educated young adults. There has been much less study of emergent adulthood among same-sex-attracted young adults, or the study of emergent adulthood among young adults of color, those who are socially disadvantaged, or those who are living outside urban areas (Gray, 2009; Sears, 1991). Bynner (2005) and Hendry and Kloep (2007) have observed that Arnett's formulation of emergent adulthood does not take into account social class and gender differences. Galambos, Turner, and Tilton-Weaver (2005) caution further that ethnicity and culture may be associated with differences across societies in understanding the transition from adolescence to adulthood. The study of gay and lesbian emergent adulthood must take into account the very rapid social change that has occurred in the United States in the past few decades. However, it is difficult to find studies providing findings pertinent to the study of emergent adulthood among these most recent cohorts of same-sex-attracted young adults. As Peplau and Fingerhut (2007) have noted in their review of relationships among lesbians and gay men, even studies published in the past few years report findings that have been based on an earlier cohort of lesbians and gay men that may not be relevant to the lives of the present cohort of young adults.

Emergent Adulthood and Same-Sex Attractions

Life course perspectives on the lesbian and gay experience suggest that the cohort of young adults born in the 1980s has encountered a time and social context of living as gay and lesbian that is different from that of prior generations (D'Augelli, 2002; Hershberger & D'Augelli, 1995; Remafedi, 1999, 2002; Rivers & D'Augelli, 2001). Earlier studies emphasized the consequences for young adults struggling with issues of self-esteem during the tumultuous time after Stonewall. The tremendous suffering encountered by previous generations of sexual minority youth coming to adulthood may be contrasted with a somewhat more fortunate experience of many urban-living young adults born in the 1980s. Although many adolescents and young adults continue to define themselves as gay (Russell, Clarke, & Clary, 2009), sexual attraction is no longer the master narrative of becoming gay or lesbian among same-sex-attracted young adults (Cohler,2007; Hammack, Thompson, & Pilecki, 2009; Savin-Williams, 2005). Cohler and Hammack (2007) have described this social change as a shift from narratives of struggle and success to a narrative of emancipation among many same-sex-attracted young adults in the cohort born in the 1980s. Although discrimination on the basis of sexual orientation and antigay prejudice and victimization are still prevalent in many communities (Gray, 2009), they have become somewhat less salient in determining the morale and hopes and fears for the future among lesbians and gay men in the present generation of young adults (Cohler, 2007; Cohler & Hammack, 2007; Hammack et al., 2009; Meyer, 2003; Savin-Williams, 2005a, 2005b; Seidman, 2002).

Although many same-sex-attracted young adults may still accept the identity label as "gay" or "lesbian" (Russell, Clarke, & Clary, 2009), Cohler (2007) and Hammack et al. (2009) showed that many same-sex-attracted young adults in the present cohort also believe that traditional identity labels fail to capture the complex stories of their identity development. Savin-Williams (2005, p. 65) reports that in one recent study 85% of informants had never attended a gay support group. These informants report only positive support from friends and family after announcing their same-sex orientation. The youth in his study regarded themselves as quite ordinary and lead their lives in much the same manner as their peers who do not report same-sex attraction. Consistent with this perspective, Stein (2010, p. 24) has observed that "What we are seeing, quite possibly, is the exhaustion of particular historical construction: a group of individuals who are defined primarily on the basis of their sexual identity." Findings reported by Russell, Clarke, and Clary (2009), however, suggest that awareness of a gay identity for the present cohort of young adults may be more salient than Stein (2010) and Savin-Williams (2005) have claimed. At the same time, the process of developing a gay identity for the present generation of emergent adults may be less difficult than it was for earlier generations (D'Augelli, Rendina, Sinclair, & Grossman 2006/2007; Gray, 2009; Read, 2001; Seidman, 2002).

EMERGENT ADULTHOOD AND THE LIFE COURSE AMONG SAME-SEX-ATTRACTED MEN AND WOMEN

There has been little consideration of the specific dimensions of emergent adulthood among same-sex-attracted women and men (Arnett, 2006b; Friedman & Morgan, 2009; Lefkowitz & Gillen, 2006; Mitchell, 2007). Arnett (2006b, p. 318) has commented that "among persons who are lesbian, gay, bisexual or transgendered, coming out tends to occur right around the time emerging adulthood begins." However, within the present generation of lesbian and gay men, the process of coming out more often occurs in mid-adolescence so that many lesbians and gay men have already realized a gay identity prior to emergent adulthood (Cohler & Galatzer-Levy, 2000; D'Augelli et al, 2006/2007). Although recognizing both the relative paucity of study of same-sex-attracted men and women in emergent adulthood, and also the impact of social change upon the experience of same-sex attraction for the present cohort, it is important to consider what is known about the manner in which this cohort has negotiated the developmental tasks of work, intimate relationships and friendships, and the anticipation of parenthood. Much of the evidence for this study is based on narratives of same-sex-attracted, well-educated, young adult men and women. Systematic study of emergent adulthood for same-sex-attracted women and men similar to that among heterosexual men and women (Arnett & Tanner, 2006) is an important next step in the study of the life course of same-sex-attracted men and women.

Emergent Adulthood, Same-Sex Attraction, and Careers

Reviewing the implications of emergent adulthood for beginning a career, Hamilton and Hamilton (2006) observe that younger workers are more often concentrated in low-salary jobs, frequently change jobs, and often experience periods of unemployment when they may be forced to return home for financial and social support. In addition, college graduates often leave college with the burden of debt that financed their education. Ever greater periods of postsecondary education mean delayed entrance into the adult roles of work, committed relationships, and the assumption of parenthood but also reflects recognition of a labor market that increasingly rewards higher education (Sandefur, Eggerling-Boeck, & Park, 2005). Young adulthood is a time of questioning, including the search for the best match between interests and talents. Young adults may change jobs several times across the first decade of their employment as they search for a match between talents and skills and the demands of their jobs (Arnett, 2004, 2006b). Shanahan, Porfeli, Mortimer, and Erickson (2005) report that finding a promising career appears less salient in the subjective sense of being an adult than other transitions such as having an intimate partner, having your own residence, and becoming a parent.

Within earlier cohorts of same-sex-attracted men and women, it was common to select careers such as accountant or librarian in which work did not lead to situations in which it became important to disclose your gay or lesbian identity or to find those few "gay-friendly" careers that supported diverse sexualities. As contrasted with past times in which self-identified lesbians and gay men

entering the work world were concerned with the implications of antigay prejudice for keeping their job or realizing promotions, much of this bias in the workplace has been reduced over the past two decades (Griffith & Hebl, 2002). Undergraduates planning to attend professional school now learn from peers that sexual orientation plays little role in admission or in placement following graduation. Same-sex-attracted men and women in law, medicine, or business school have an opportunity to serve as interns in settings with mentors who are comfortably "out" at work and who may have same-sex domestic partners or spouses.

Although, as Griffith and Hebl (2002) note, there may be subtle discrimination in the workplace, many firms include antidiscrimination training in issues such as sexual orientation and gender expression for all new employees. Griffith and Hebl (2002) report that about 75% of all adults favor laws against discrimination in the workplace. Badgett (1996) and Griffith and Hebl (2002) observe that career planning for same-sex-attracted young adults often includes evaluation of the diversity policy of particular employment sectors and firms. In this regard, the transition from college or professional/graduate school to the work world involves a consideration for same-sex-attracted graduates that is somewhat different from their heterosexual peers. Findings regarding workplace satisfaction among same-sex-identified men and women suggest that those who feel safe in disclosing their sexual orientation at work also report increased morale and satisfaction with their work (Rostosky & Riggle, 2002). Although earlier generations often struggled with disclosure of their sexual orientation until they had realized some job security, the present generation that is often "out" before finding a job is much more comfortable in disclosing their sexuality at the beginning of their job.

A particularly detailed account of emergent adulthood and issues associated with beginning careers among lesbians and gay men as contrasted with their heterosexual counterparts in an earlier cohort of same-sex-attracted men and women has been provided by Friskopp and Silverstein (1995) in their account of lesbians and gay men enrolled at the Harvard Business School (HBS) in the late 1980s and 1990s. This is one of the few studies to consider the career paths of lesbians and gay men as contrasted with their heterosexual counterparts. In their interviews with earlier cohorts of HBS graduates, Friskopp and Silverstein report that many of these graduates were reluctant to disclose their sexual orientation while they were at the HBS, but have since become much more open. This is an example of reverse socialization or cross-identification in which members of the most recent cohorts of HBS who have experienced few of the social tensions of preceding generations have encouraged these older cohorts through alumni activities to rethink their own ways of coping with their sexuality. Furthermore, anticipating increased social support in the workplace and the community and less concern with family rejection than in earlier generations, the manner in which these young adults negotiate the transition to work has implications for the manner in which they manage subsequent life course transitions such as intimate relationships and anticipation of parenthood (Elder, 1995).

In their report of their survey of the lives of earlier cohorts of HBS students and in their interviews with the cohort of HBS students at the time of their study, Friskopp and Silverstein (1995) reported on the activism of this earlier cohort of HBS students who challenge their heterosexual fellow students and faculty when encountering antigay prejudice, and who educate their fellow students and faculty through signed columns in the HBS newspaper and inclusion of support for lesbian, gay, bisexual, and transgender students in admissions material. It is important to note that Friskopp and Silverstein's report focuses on an elite group of men and women with unusual social and cultural capital. Findings from their survey lead Friskopp and Silverstein to conclude (1995, p. 211) that most gay professionals come out at work and a majority comfortably discuss their social life and family at work and in their class reunion books. One student (Friskopp & Silverstein, 1995, p. 62) observed that the more open nonheterosexual people are, the greater the respect that they earn from fellow students and faculty.

Friskopp and Silverstein's (1995) findings are more promising for the future success of lesbians and gay men in corporate life than the earlier report of Woods and Lucas (1993) on gay men in the corporate world. Woods and Lucas report that many gay men in corporate settings emulate their heterosexual co-workers and avoid disclosing their sexuality. Woods and Lucas survey all levels of corporate life and show the tactics that gay men at work use to avoid disclosing their sexual orientation. It may be that the situation for lesbians and gay men at higher management with the elitism of one of the most prestigious business schools in the world is quite different from that of lesbians and gay men lacking in this privileged education and working in traditional firms. However, the findings reviewed in this chapter suggest that the report of Woods and Lucas (1993) is less relevant for the present generations of lesbians and gay men beginning their careers.

Vignettes of the management of their sexual orientation among the HBS students within the corporate world include that of Ann Bilyew (Friskopp & Silverstein, 1995, p. 257), who is in her 20s has held several jobs prior to her enrollment at the HBS, and has been out since high school. She has listed her co-presidency of the HBS gay and lesbian association on her résumé and has arranged for her partner to have privileges at the HBS fitness center. In her placement at a prestigious consulting firm in the summer between her first and second year at the HBS, she talked about her partner at work and received complete acceptance from her managing partner and from senior management. Other vignettes report similar stories of HBS students who are out at work. One student reported that he had written to consulting firms interviewing HBS students regarding possible problems in recruiting him as an out gay graduate of the HBS. Consulting firms responded that what he did or who he was in his time away from work was not their concern; their only concern was his skill in solving clients' problems.

The concept of emerging adulthood emphasizes the importance of family support in the struggle to finally realize self-reliance and to achieve financial independence from parents (Aquilino, 2006; Mitchell, 2007). The recent changes enacted in health insurance regulations that permit parents to keep their young adult offspring on their family policy to age 26 reflect the importance of continuing family support during the time of emergent adulthood. Previous study of the relationship between self and family among same-sex-attracted youth and their families had identified a period of conflict before parents became reconciled to their young adult offspring's sexual orientation (Cohler, 2004; Savin-Williams, 2001). Arnett (2006b) suggests that lesbians and gay men coming out to disapproving families may have greater difficulty than their heterosexual counterparts in being able to obtain assistance and support during the time of emergent adulthood. These gay and lesbian young adults had to learn to make their life on their own without counting on their parents and may have been motivated to build lesbian, gay, and bisexual social networks. However, Friedman and Morgan (2009) report that the lesbian college students in their study were comfortable in turning to both friends and family for support; women who were "out" to their family and friends also felt comfortable discussing their sexuality with their parents.

The social change that is characteristic of the present cohort of lesbians and gay men may be reflected in some easing of tensions between parents and their young adult children who are out to their families. Friskopp and Silverstein (1995) observe that HBS students and alumni in their survey reported little conflict with their family regarding their sexuality. They also report that senior management in the firms in which they have interned or worked have even less difficulty than parents regarding their sexuality. Osgood et al. (2005) noted that the pursuit of higher education is associated with delayed entrance into adulthood. Receiving assistance from your parents is important while attending college or graduate school. It is likely that with reduced conflict between generations in the family regarding the sexual orientation of offspring, more gay young adults than in earlier cohorts will be able to continue living at home while pursuing graduate studies or internships, and may be little different from their heterosexual peers in realizing continuing parental financial and emotional support.

Emergent Adulthood, Same-Sex Attraction, and Intimate Relationships

Collins and Sroufe (1999) have observed that romantic relationships are a reflection of the basic motive to create and to maintain close relationships. Closeness refers to the extent to which persons affect and are affected by others over some time, and is marked by interdependence, intimacy, and trust (Collins & van Dulmen, 2006). Intimate relationships are generally both voluntary and symmetrical, and are marked by love, passion, and, most often, by sexual intimacy. Although experience with dating and sexual intimacy is characteristic of adolescence for both same-sex-attracted boys and girls, as well as their heterosexual peers, it is during the time of emergent adulthood that there is increased concern with intimacy, companionship, and most often the search for another man or woman with whom to spend their life in a committed relationship (Erikson, 1997).

Intimacy and partnership in emergent gay and lesbian adulthood. Although there has been much study of relationships among lesbians and gay men, little of this study has focused on the time of emergent adulthood (Carrington, 1999; Fingerhut & Peplau, Chapter 12, this volume; Goldberg, 2010; James & Murphy, 1998; Kurdek, 2005; Peplau & Cochran, 1990; Peplau & Fingerhut, 2007). Patterson (2000) reports that 40–60% of gay men and 45–80% of lesbians are involved in romantic relationships. Fingerhut and Peplau (Chapter 12, this volume) report that 41% of gay men and 60% of lesbians are currently living with a same-sex partner. Harry and DeVall (1978) and Nardi (1999) both reported that gay men view their relationships with their romantic partners as that of a "best friend," although with the possibility of gay marriage, this view of the partner may change. Nardi (1999) and Peplau and Fingerhut (2007) observe that the boundaries between friendship and romantic relationships may be complex. Young adult women experience greater fluidity than men in the gender of the person with whom they enjoy an intimate relationship (Diamond, 2008).

In a classic study reported over 25 years ago contrasting gay, lesbian, and heterosexual couples, Blumstein and Schwartz (1983) reported little difference in the rate of dissolution of relationships between heterosexual and same-sex-attracted couples. It should be noted that this study reports on earlier cohorts of same-sex-attracted and heterosexual couples when higher levels of stigma and social disapproval may have additionally burdened these relationships. Kurdek (2005) reports that both in the United States and in Scandinavia, the rate of dissolution among gay and lesbian couples is significantly greater than that among heterosexual couples. Lesbian couples have a somewhat shorter duration of a romantic relationship than gay men. It has been suggested (Kurdek, 2004, 2005; Peplau & Fingerhut; 2007; Patterson, 2009) that the somewhat greater rate of dissolution of gay and lesbian relationships compared to those among heterosexual married couples may be accounted for by the lack of formal marriage that makes dissolution of the marital relationship a complex legal issue. Without the legal sanctions of marriage or the bonds of parenthood, there are fewer constraints for dissolving relationships among gay and lesbian couples than among heterosexual couples (Badgett, 2009; Peplau & Fingerhut, 2007; see also Fingerhut and Peplau,

Chapter 12, this volume). An unhappy heterosexual marriage may endure over longer periods of time than an unhappy intimate same-sex relationship. In addition, both discrimination against gay and lesbian couples seeking to marry and legal barriers to parenthood among lesbian and gay couples further discourage the long-term stability of these relationships (Patterson, 2009). Realization of parenthood ensures greater stability of the marital relationship. Comparison of gay and lesbian couples with children and their heterosexual peers shows that breakup rates are comparable (Fingerhut and Peplau, Chapter 12, this volume).

Overall, gay, lesbian, and heterosexual couples report similar levels of satisfaction in their relationships (Kurdek, 2005; Patterson, 2000). Kurdek (2004) reports that gay and lesbian couples report receiving less social support than their heterosexual couples yet do not show more problems in their relationship than heterosexual couples. However, these studies do not focus explicitly on emergent adulthood. Cohler and Galatzer-Levy (2000), Fingerhut and Peplau (Chapter 12, this volume), Patterson (2000), and Peplau and Cochran (1988, 1990) all report that gay men are less likely than their lesbian counterparts or, presumably, heterosexual couples, to believe in monogamy in their relationships. However, the meaning of monogamy may be somewhat different within gay, lesbian, and heterosexual intimate relationships.

Once again, there may be cohort differences in this concern with monogamy. D'Augelli et al. (2006/2007) reported findings based on a group of gay and lesbian adolescents of diverse ethnic groups on the cusp of emergent adulthood. Nearly two-thirds of the males and four-fifths of the females planned to seek monogamy in future relationships, although males were less certain than females of the importance of long-term relationships. As contrasted with two-third of the females, a third of the males expected to marry a same-sex partner. Lesbian couples are somewhat more likely than gay couples to remain monogamous and are less focused on the sexual aspects of the relationship (Goldberg, 2010), but are also somewhat less likely than gay couples or cohabiting heterosexual couples to remain together over long periods of time (Fingerhut and Peplau, Chapter 12, this volume). A critical factor preserving relationships is the advent of parenthood: Couples with children are much less likely to break up than childless

couples for both same-sex-attracted and heterosexual couples (see Fingerhut and Peplau, Chapter 12, this volume). Study is needed regarding the reasons why relationships among gay men persist longer than those among lesbians. Part of the reason may be that lesbians may become disappointed that emotional needs are not being fulfilled in the relationship (Peplau & Cochran, 1990) whereas this is somewhat less of a concern for gay men.

One of the characteristics of emergent adulthood is the search for and the beginning of a long-term committed intimate relationship. The same social changes that have led to increased visibility of gay and lesbian life in contemporary society (Fee, 1996) have also led many same-sex-attracted young adults to anticipate permanency of their committed intimate relationships. This belief is strengthened by increasing legal recognition of same-sex marriage in at least some states in the United States, Canada, South Africa, and a number of countries in Europe. Badgett (2009) has documented the recent historical move extending marriage to same-sex-attracted couples that reflects the increasing visibility of lesbian, gay, bisexual, and transgender communities. As Badgett noted, one particular advantage of same-sex marriage is that it eliminates the gender-based subordination of the wife to her husband that historically existed in heterosexual marriage.

The increasing visibility of gay marriage also fosters social activism more generally on behalf of lesbian, gay, bisexual, and transgender communities (Taylor, Kimport, Van Dyke, & Anderson, 2009). The account of the marriage of one gay couple during the time of emergent adulthood (Whyte, Merling, & Merling, 2000) illustrates the significance of gay marriage in the transition from emergent to settled adulthood. Andy Merling, a graduate psychology student, and his partner Doug, a beginning television producer, decided to take advantage of Canada's gay marriage law to marry in Toronto where Andy grew up in a conservative Toronto Jewish neighborhood. The couple overcame the initial resistance of both the synagogue congregation and also Andy's parents, and were able to arrange all the details of a traditional Jewish marriage. Consistent with Badgett's (2009) discussion, Andy and Doug were able to bring social change into a conservative religious community and showed both the advantages of gay marriage and also the importance of marriage itself for both the couple and the community.

Emergent adulthood and friendships among gay and lesbian young adults. Evidence concerning the long-term stability of relationships in gay and lesbian emergent adulthood is shown in the study of friendships among same-sex-attracted men and women with each other and with their heterosexual peers (Nardi, 1999; Weinstock, 1998). This study includes both those friendships among same-sex-attracted men and women and also relationships between gay men and women and their heterosexual peers. Fee (1996) has observed that modern friendships are voluntary, reflect personal desires, are informal, and are based on interpersonal equality. Although not explicitly focusing on friendships within the time of emergent adulthood, Weinstock (1998) has provided a careful review of studies concerning the relationships of lesbians and gay men and their heterosexual peers. Weinstock notes that there has been very little systematic study of friendships among young adult lesbians and gay men.

Weinstock (1998) observes that studies of relationships among lesbians and gay men and their heterosexual peers have been particularly overlooked. Quenqua (2009) has addressed this issue of friendships between gay and heterosexual men and women during the time of emergent adulthood. According to his account, more than 40% of heterosexual young adults have a gay best friend. These friendships may be somewhat gender atypical: Gay and heterosexual male friends share more emotional relationships than among heterosexual male friends more generally, whereas lesbians support enhanced instrumental activities with their heterosexual woman friends. Among gay men, long-lasting friendship with heterosexual peers is both valued and prized for the combination of both normative masculine interests and also the ability to talk about more intimate issues. Nardi (1999) noted the more typical "feminine" concerns with emotionality that gay men bring to their friendships with men.

There is a danger in viewing friendships among heterosexual young adult men as stereotypically and conventionally masculine. A number of factors have led both gay and heterosexual young adult men to seek enhanced intimacy, trust, and emotionality in ways that were less characteristic of earlier cohorts (Connell, 2005; Green, 2002). Green (2002) reported that gay young adults report greater closeness with heterosexual peers than in past cohorts, and greater comfort than gay men in earlier cohorts about their own place in the community. Nardi (1999) and Connell (2005) observed that close friendships within the present cohort of young adult men represent a new way of understanding masculinity itself. Homosociality and homoeroticism appear less stigmatized in same-sex friendship relations among young adults in recent than in earlier cohorts. Heterosexual men report awareness of their sexual attraction to their gay best friends but this awareness of their attraction does not ordinarily make them uncomfortable (Fee, 1996; Green, 2002; Nardi, 1999; Tillmann-Healy, 2001).

Gay men in Fee's (1996) study of young adults report that their friendships with other gay men are characterized by a closeness based on their common experience of being gay and that this is missing in their friendships with their heterosexual friends. Gay men also foster a more relaxed view of what masculinity means with their heterosexual friends as a consequence of their friendship. Fee (1996) and Connell (2005) suggest that for both gay and heterosexual men, same-sex attraction challenges their sense of themselves as masculine. Nardi (1999) and Connell (2005) maintain that although the friendship among gay men and heterosexual men reproduces core elements of a traditional masculinity, these relationships also challenge this traditional masculinity in which emotional closeness is viewed as a challenge to being a man. The openness that characterizes the lives of gay men in contemporary society has the effect of changing the manner in which in this generation of both young adult gay and heterosexual men understand friendships between men.

Fee (1996) reports on the experience for young gay men of "coming out" to their heterosexual friends who, in turn, "come over" to this friendship with their gay friends, and thereupon begin to learn the culture of the gay community. Price (1999) and Tillmann-Healy (2001) have reported on young adult relationships among gay and heterosexual friends. Much of this discussion focuses on friendships among gay and heterosexual young adult men for whom the potentially erotic quality of the friendship is more problematic than among lesbian and heterosexual women friends. Reports of friendships between young adult gay and heterosexual friends reported by Nardi (1999) and Weinstock

(1998) suggest that boundaries between gay and heterosexual men are not as rigid as in the past.

Much of the change in friendships among gay and heterosexual men in the present generation in emergent adulthood is reflected in a recent personal account by Tillmann-Healy (2001). Lisa Tillmann-Healy was a graduate student in anthropology studying qualitative ethnography. Her husband Doug was a recent graduate and was an intern in pharmacy when they met David, her husband's gay pharmacy supervisor. David and his partner were part of a gay softball team and invited Doug to play on their team. Lisa provides a detailed account of their friendship with the gay men on the baseball team. There is much good natured banter and sexual innuendos that Lisa Tillmann-Healy suggests reflect prevailing concepts of masculinity in contemporary society. Lisa reports on Doug's experiences with his gay friends, including gatherings at gay bars after the game, and Doug's initial embarrassment when his teammates make it clear to their gay friends that Doug is heterosexual. Doug reports occasional sexual approaches by gay men in the bar and he acknowledges that he is aware of his own attraction toward his gay friends, and enjoys a fantasy of "hooking up" with them. However, he is not uncomfortable with this awareness nor does he feel that his masculinity is challenged.

More to the point of the present discussion regarding friendships in emergent adulthood, their young adult gay friends have mostly known each other since childhood, and the gay baseball team has remarkable longevity. David and his partner break-up during the course of this narrative but remain good friends and each continues to play on the team. Tensions do sometimes arise among the gay men in this circle of friends when a couple breaks up or when a friendship includes sexual intimacy that is later regretted. However, these tensions are resolved as this long time circle of friends continues to play on their softball team, and all the members of the team, together with Doug and Lisa, continue to socialize after the game at a local gay bar. Few of the men move away during the course of her narrative; consistent with Collins and von Dulmen's (2006) review of friendships during emergent adulthood, there is little geographic mobility within this group of friends. This narrative again shows social change in the relationships between same-sex-attracted men and their heterosexual peers.

Gay and Lesbian Emergent Adulthood and the Transition to Parenthood

One of the traditional signs of the transition from emergent to settled adulthood (Cohler & Boxer, 1984) is the anticipation of parenthood. In their discussion of subjective age identity in the United States, Shanahan, Porfeli, Mortimer, and Erickson (2005) report that becoming a parent is strongly associated with feeling like an adult. The transition to parenthood among both heterosexual and lesbian and gay couples has been studied, although generally without a specific focus on the anticipation of parenthood in emergent adulthood (Cohler, 2005; Cowan & Cowan, 1992; Galatzer-Levy & Cohler, 1993; Goldberg, 2010; Patterson, 2002). Adopting a family systems perspective, including the family's relationships with both other kin and the larger community, the Cowans have highlighted the problems posed for the transition from couplehood to parenthood. Satisfaction with their marriage, work, and ties with their own parental families have much to do with the ability of the couple to make this transition to parenthood.

Lesbian and gay young adults during the time of emergent adulthood anticipate not only a long-term committed relationship or marriage but also often preparation for parenthood (Berkowitz & Marsiglio, 2007; Patterson & Riskind, 2010). Reviews of the transition to gay and lesbian parenthood by Goldberg (2010), Patterson (2000, 2002), Patterson and Riskind, (2010), and Riskind and Patterson (2010) suggest that many lesbians and gay men look forward to parenthood. D'Augelli at al. (2006/2007) report that more than 80% of gay young men and nearly all lesbians in their study looked forward to having their own children. Peplau and Fingerhut (2007) have reported that 50% of gay men and lesbians who are not parents would like to become parents. Patterson and Riskind (2010) and Riskind and Patterson (2010) reported similar findings showing that over 50% of gay men and 75% of lesbians expressed a desire to become parents. Although a somewhat smaller proportion of gay men than their heterosexual young adult peers expressed parenting intentions, lesbians were just as likely as their heterosexual counterparts to plan to have children. Younger lesbian women were particularly likely to look forward to becoming parents. This finding shows that the present lesbian emergent adult cohort has a particularly favorable view of parenthood (D'Augelli et al., 2006/2007;

Patterson & Riskind, 2010). Problems in realizing the transition to parenthood may arise when same-sex-attracted young adult men and women harbor deep-seated ambivalence about their sexuality, when they believe that being gay and being a parent are inconsistent, when their partner does not share the desire to become parents, or where the local lesbian and gay communities do not support lesbian and gay parenthood (Black, Gates, Sanders, & Taylor, 2002; Patterson, 2009; see also, Patterson, Chapter 16, this volume).

Johnson and O'Connor (2002) and Patterson (1998, 2009) have described the several pathways into parenthood among same-sex couples. Perhaps because of the myriad obstacles to becoming parents, same-sex couples are highly motivated and make particularly good parents (Patterson, 2000, 2002). Much of the discussion of the transition to parenthood among lesbian and gay couples has been focused on the problems of arranging to become parents and surmounting the legal obstacles such as adoption by both parents whose relationship may not be legally recognized as marriage (Allen & Demo, 1995; Green, 2002; Patterson, 2009; Patterson & Riskind, 2010). Gay men generally adopt in order to become parents unless one or the other partner already has a child from a previous heterosexual marriage. Often, these couples are presented with the challenge that many of the children who are available for adoption are those with special needs (Green, 1999). Although surrogacy may be a route to parenthood among gay men (Bergman et al., 2010; Patterson & Riskind, 2010), it is often prohibitively expensive. Lesbian couples may take advantage of new reproductive technologies in participating together in becoming parents (Chan, Raboy, & Patterson, 1998). The expense and legal problems pose a challenge for some gay and lesbian couples seeking this route to parenthood.

Patterson and Riskind (2010) have shown that, overall, fewer lesbian and gay adults than their heterosexual counterparts have become parents, although they express the desire to become parents. However, as the possibility of assuming parenthood becomes a reality for the present cohort of lesbian and gay young adults, this social change may be reflected in increased realization of parenthood among same-sex-attracted couples. Using 2000 census data, Peplau and Fingerhut (2007) have estimated that more than a third of lesbian couples

and a fifth of gay men in relationships are raising children. Goldberg (2010) has reviewed findings from published studies that show that about a third of all lesbian households include children. Of these families, 20% include a child from a previous heterosexual marriage of one or both partners so that the primary obstacle is often that of arranging for adoption by the other partner.

With increasing social acceptance of families headed by same-sex couples, and the increasing visibility of these families in the community, anticipatory socialization may facilitate the transition to parenthood among young adult same-sex couples in the present cohort to an extent that was less possible in earlier cohorts of gay and lesbian young adults. Young adult same-sex couples are more likely than those in earlier cohorts to meet other same-sex couples with children in their community and to learn how they too might become parents. Both gay and lesbian and heterosexual parents spend increasing amounts of time with other parents rather than with their single friends; the significance of same-sex couplehood recedes and is replaced by identification with parenthood as same-sex couples meet other parents on the neighborhood playground, in their children's' school, and in the community (Patterson & Riskind, 2010; Patterson, Chapter 16, this volume).

Among the Populace: Emergent Adulthood in the Life of Bryan

One particularly rich account of emergent adulthood among same-sex-attracted young adults in the most recent cohort coming to adulthood over the past decade has been narrated by Bryan, a graduate student in English and Computer Science at the University of Missouri. In a blog of more than 600 pages (amongthepopulace.com) portraying his life in college and in his postcollege career that he has since removed from the Internet, Bryan has described his life, his work, his university studies, and his relationship with his partner Matt and their life with their many gay and heterosexual friends. Cohler (2007) has written in greater detail of Bryan's life with his partner Matt and their friends in his discussion of the life of same-sex-attracted men who were born in the 1980s. Bryan's blog reflects a sense of being between adolescence and settled adulthood and still financially dependent upon his family that Arnett has described as characteristic in emergent adulthood.

Bryan reports being aware of his same-sex attractions while in high school in his intimate relationship with Kyle, a fellow member of his high school tennis team. Bryan met Matt at college and the two soon became lovers and then became life partners. Bryan observes about Matt that "There are times when I feel that there is absolutely no way I can function without Matt. It's almost as if he completes my being…I hate it when he is gone. It's as if a part of me is missing." Bryan and Matt are both runners and typically begin the day by a long run together, followed by a shower and a time for intimacy before beginning the day. When Matt is away visiting his father, Bryan wears Matt's tee-shirt for his daily run.

Both Bryan and Matt's parents are divorced; the two fathers are very supportive of their gay sons and have themselves become good friends. Bryan's father owns a cabin at a nearby lake and has made Bryan and Matt co-owners. An accountant, Bryan's father has created a limited partnership for the men in the lake property and Bryan writes that he and Matt have become legal partners in spite of Missouri laws against domestic partnership and gay marriage. Matt's father, who is a lawyer, has a spare bedroom that has become Matt and Bryan's bedroom when they stay over for the weekend. When Matt's father and girlfriend go skiing at Vail, they often invite Bryan and Matt along to enjoy their ski vacation with them. When Bryan turned 21, his father gave him the gift of a weekend with Matt at an elegant hotel, and Matt's father arranged a dinner for the couple at one of the best restaurants in Kansas City.

Bryan observes: "what's the big deal about being gay…it is only one facet of my life and there are many things in my life that are important." In one posting Bryan observes that "We have a very good group of friends that we hang out with. They are both gay and straight…If somebody wants to know that I'm gay, fine I will tell them." In another posting he observes that "It's not that Matt and I 'choose' not to be involved with the gay community; we choose to be members of a much larger community…our idea…is to be members of a huge community sharing, experiencing, and learning about all the differences and similarities between individuals. Rather than flying a rainbow flag that says, 'Hey, I'm gay,' I would rather fly a flag that says 'Hey, I'm me and I'm part of it all!' And on that flag, a smaller rainbow patch is more than

welcome." Finally, Bryan observes that "being gay is only a part of my life. The gay factor is only a part of who a person is and it shouldn't be the dominating factor in a person's life. Does my being gay have anything to do with my progressing through college and graduate school? NO…I'm a person, a student, young, career minded, relationship oriented, a nervous wreck getting good grades, a Thunderbird enthusiast, a wannabe runner…and I just happen to be a gay individual who is in a relationship with another guy who feels the same way." Bryan is much more concerned with his work and studies and his relationship with Matt and their friends than he is with the struggle to construct a gay identity. Although acknowledging his identity as a gay man, it is not a master narrative of his identity but only one element of his identity as a young adult.

At college, his first roommate, Tyler, was a heterosexual man and a student athlete. Bryan and Tyler have remained best friends and each included the other in their circle of friends. Bryan's relationship with Tyler is consistent with Fee's (1996) description of a heterosexual man "coming over" to join his gay friend. Tyler joined a fraternity and moved out of the dormitory. Tyler and his fraternity brothers welcome Bryan and Matt whenever the couple drops by the fraternity house. Bryan, Matt, Tyler, Tyler's girlfriend Kristi, and Jeff, another fraternity brother, and Jeff's current girl friend all meet in the evenings and on the weekend at a local sports bar. The interpersonal relations within this gay and heterosexual friendship group parallel the description provided by Tillmann-Healy (2001) regarding her husband's experiences as a member of a gay baseball team and the heterosexual couple's close ties with their gay friends on the team. On one occasion, Bryan and Matt took Tyler and Jeff to a gay bar where the two heterosexual boys were pestered by some obnoxious gay patrons. Although they were bemused by the attention they were receiving, Tyler and Jeff reported that they were not annoyed by this unwanted attention. They did not feel threatened that their masculinity was compromised or that they needed to respond to this annoying situation.

Sometimes Bryan, Matt, and their group headed out to the lake for the weekend. Bryan and his father had added extra space to their cabin to accommodate Bryan's friends. Bryan met Lee, a shy, closeted East Asian student when they both worked as computer consultants for the University.

Bryan often invited Lee along to the cabin and Lee became friends with Bryan's group, who had no trouble including their newest member. There were often good natured jokes about everyone's sexuality, as when Tyler commented at breakfast about the strange noises coming from the several bedrooms at night.

Bryan and Matt decided to rent an apartment and invited Tyler and Kristi to join them. The two couples lived in rather close quarters and enjoyed sharing their meals together, renting movies, and inviting their friends over. As everyone graduated from college, Tyler and Kristi became engaged and eventually moved out to their own apartment. Matt graduated from law school and joined his father's law firm. Bryan continued in his graduate English program working on Faulkner. Bryan and Matt still hang out with now married Tyler and Kristi (Jeff and his girl friend have in the meantime broken off their relationship). Both Bryan and Matt continue their friendships with both their gay and heterosexual friends whom they have known since high school. The couple dreams of having a home of their own in one of the newly renovated and trendy inner city neighborhoods, and perhaps beginning a family as well. Bryan's blog reflects a view of gay lives in emergent adulthood as typically "normal." His blog illustrates the process of being gay during the time of emergent adulthood where he negotiates the tasks of identity as a gay man, his career, relations with his family, realizing committed intimacy, and his relationships with his gay and heterosexual friends, and looks forward to the advent of parenthood. His blog also shows the social change that has facilitated the realization of his goal to simply be another person "among the populace" and not unique simply because he is gay.

CONCLUSIONS

Bryan's journal during the time of his emergent adulthood reflects the social change taking place in the acceptance of same-sex attraction within his cohort in contemporary middle-class urban society (Seidman, 2002). Life course perspectives (Elder, 1995; Elder & Caspi, 1990) offer an important means for understanding changes in the role of self and changes in social roles over the course of a lifetime, and in the context of social change across generation cohorts in society for same-sex-attracted men and women. The cohort of same-sex-attracted men and women born in the 1980s and coming to

adulthood at the millennium has made the transition from adolescence to young adulthood at a time in which the increased social activism central to the concerns of previous postwar generations had led to decreasing antigay prejudice and stereotyping (Meyer, 2003). The struggle for visibility has succeeded in removing at least some of the stigma from the awareness of same-sex attraction (Cohler & Hammack, 2007; Hammack, Thompson, & Pilecki, 2009; Seidman, 2002).

The question we have addressed in the present chapter concerns the impact of this social change upon the lives of same-sex-attracted young adult men and women in this most recent generation cohort making the transition from adolescence to young adulthood. Arnett (2001, 2004, 2006a) views emergent adulthood as the realization of increased self-reliance following a time of continuing dependence upon family resources, together with the struggle to realize career aspirations and committed intimate relationships. Consistent with Arnett's description of emergent adulthood, Shanahan et al. (2005) observe that "Young people who have cohabited or married, had at least one child, and have owned their home or rented their own apartment are significantly more likely to report feeling like an adult" (p. 243).

Although there has been increasing study of emergent adulthood among heterosexual young adults (Arnett, 2004; Arnett & Tanner, 2006), there has been little study of emergent adulthood among lesbians and gay men (Friedman & Morgan, 2009; Hammack, Thompson, & Pilecki, 2009). Reviewing those roles most central in emergent adulthood, work, intimate relationships, friendships, and family ties, together with the anticipation of parenthood, we have shown that social change has had a significant impact upon the manner in which same-sex-attracted young adults negotiate the developmental tasks and role transitions accompanying emergent adulthood in contemporary urban society. There is increased visibility of the lesbian and gay lifeway in contemporary urban society. This visibility has been fostered by generally positive descriptions of lesbians and gay men in the media. As a result, lesbians and gay men in this generation in emergent adulthood encounter somewhat less stereotyping and antigay prejudice than earlier generations of same-sex-attracted men and women. However, these findings are based primarily on the study of advantaged same-sex-attracted young adults. Much less is known about emergent adulthood among disadvantaged groups in which racial and ethnic stereotyping may add to the impact of antigay prejudice.

Lesbians and gay men are able to relate to the workplace with increased comfort and with decreased concern that as a sexual minority their road to advancement would be compromised. Increased acceptance of gay and lesbian alternatives to heterosexuality has also led to increased closeness among same-sex-attracted offspring and their family. Same-sex-attracted young adults in the present cohort may be more comfortable than young adults in earlier cohorts in returning home while pursuing college or graduate education to families that are more accepting of their sexuality than was possible among same-sex-attracted offspring and their parents in previous cohorts (Cohler, 2004). They join the 40% of their generation of heterosexual young adults who also return home for some time while searching for work or while completing their education (Mitchell, 2007).

Although same-sex-attracted young adults in the present cohort may feel "in between" adolescence and settled adulthood, there is little evidence of particular concern with issues of identity and their place in society that are believed to be a central concern in emergent adulthood (Arnett, 2004; Collins & van Dulmen, 2006; Côté, 2006). Indeed, as Bryan's blog so well shows, many same-sex-attracted young adults seem remarkably self-directed, unconcerned with their identity, and little concerned with their sexuality beyond acknowledging that being lesbian or gay is one facet of who they are. One possibility is that lesbians and gay men in emergent adulthood have already had to struggle with issues of identity, including sexual identity, beginning with early adolescence and the challenge of "coming out," and have developed a certain "crisis competence" as a result of their effort to come to terms with their sexuality in contemporary society (Cohler & Galatzer-Levy, 2000; Kimmel, 1993). Their heterosexual peers may not have been confronted with issues of identity until the time of emergent adulthood. It should also be noted that the experience of emergent adulthood as formulated by Arnett focuses on middle-class young adult men and women in the context of urban life. It is important to consider urban–rural differences in the experience of emergent adulthood among same-sex-attracted men and women (Gray, 2009),

as well as among young adults from other ethnic groups and young adults from disadvantaged backgrounds (Hendry & Kloep, 2007a).

REFERENCES

Allen, K. R., & Demo, D. H. (1995). The families of lesbians and gay men: A new frontier in family research. *Journal of Marriage and the Family, 57*, 111–127.

Aquilino, W. S. (2006). Family relationships and support systems in emerging adulthood. In J. J. Arnett & J. L. Tanner (Eds.), *Emerging adults in America: Coming of age in the 21st century* (pp. 193–217). Washington, DC: American Psychological Association.

Arnett, J. J. (1998). Learning to stand alone: The contemporary American transition to adulthood in cultural and historical context. *Human Development, 41*, 295–315.

Arnett, J. J. (2000). Emerging adulthood: A theory of development from the late teens through the twenties. *American Psychologist, 55*, 469–480.

Arnett, J. J. (2001). Conceptions of the transition to adulthood: Perspectives from adolescence through midlife. *Journal of Adult Development, 8*, 133–143.

Arnett, J. J. (2004). *Emerging adulthood: The winding road from the late teens through the twenties*. New York: Oxford University Press.

Arnett, J. J. (2006a). Emerging adulthood: Understanding the new way of coming of age. In J. J. Arnett & J. L. Tanner (Eds.), *Emerging adults in America: Coming of age in the 21st century* (pp. 3–19). Washington, DC: American Psychological Association.

Arnett, J. J. (2006b). The psychology of emerging adulthood: What is known, and what remains to be known? In J. J. Arnett & J. L. Tanner (Eds.), *Emerging adults in America: Coming of age in the 21st century* (pp. 303–330). Washington, DC: American Psychological Association.

Arnett, J. J. (2007). Suffering, selfish, slackers? Myths and reality about emerging adults. *Journal of Youth and Adolescence, 36*, 23–29.

Arnett, J. J., & Tanner, J. L. (2006) (Eds.), *Emerging adults in America: Coming of age in the 21st century*. Washington, DC: American Psychological Association.

Badgett, M. V. L. (1996). Employment and sexual orientation: Disclosure and discrimination in the workplace. *Journal of Gay and Lesbian Social Services, 4*, 29–52.

Badgett, M. V. L. (2009). *When gay people get married: What happens when societies legalize same-sex marriage*. New York: New York University Press.

Baker, C. D. (1984). The "search for adultness": Membership work in adolescent adult talk. *Human Studies, 7*, 301–323.

Baltes, P., Cornelius, S., & Nesselroade, J. (1979). Cohort effects in developmental psychology. In J. R. Nesselroade & P. B. Baltes (Eds.), *Longitudinal research in the study of behavior and development* (pp. 61–87). New York: Academic Press.

Bergman, K., Jay-Green, R., Padrón, E., & Rubino, R. R. (2010). Gay men who become fathers via surrogacy: The transition to parenthood. *Journal of GLBT family Studies, 6*, 111–141.

Berkowitz, D., & Marsiglio, W. (2007). Gay men: Negotiating procreative, father and family identities. *Journal of Marriage and Family, 69*, 366–381.

Black, D., Gates, G., Sanders, S., & Taylor, L. (2002). Why do gay men live in San Francisco? *Journal of Urban Economics, 51*, 54–76.

Blumstein, P., & Schwartz, P. (1983). *American couples: Money, work, sex.* New York: William Morrow.

Bynner, J. (2005). Rethinking the youth phase of the life-course: The case for emerging adulthood? *Journal of Youth Studies, 8*, 367–384.

Carrington, C. (1999). *No place like home: Relationships and family life among lesbians and gay men.* Chicago: The University of Chicago Press.

Chan, R., Raboy, B., & Patterson, C. (1998). Psychosocial adjustment among children conceived via donor insemination by lesbian and heterosexual mothers. *Child Development, 69*, 443–457.

Clendinen, D., & Nagourney, A. (1999). *Out for good: The struggle to build a gay rights movement in America.* New York: Simon & Schuster.

Cohler, B. J. (2004). The experience of ambivalence within the family: Young adults "coming out" gay or lesbian and their parents. In K. Pillemer & K. Lüscher (Eds.), *Intergenerational ambivalence: New perspectives on parent-child relations in later life* (pp. 255–284). Boston: Elsevier.

Cohler, B. J. (2005). Life course social science perspectives on the GLBT family. *Journal of LGBT family Studies, 1*, 69–95.

Cohler, B. J. (2007). *Writing desire: Sixty years of gay auto-biography.* Madison, WI: The University of Wisconsin Press.

Cohler, B. J., & Boxer, A. M. (1984). Middle adulthood: Settling into the world—person, time, and context. In D. Offer & M. Sabshin (Eds.), *Normality and the life-cycle* (pp. 145–204). New York: Basic Books.

Cohler, B. J., & Galatzer-Levy, R. M. (2000). *The course of gay and lesbian lives: Social and psychoanalytic perspectives.* Chicago: The University of Chicago Press.

Cohler, B. J., & Hammack, P. L. (2007). The psychological world of the gay teenager: Social change, narrative, and "normality." *Journal of Youth and Adolescence, 36*, 47–59.

Collins, W. A., & Sroufe, L. A. (1999). Capacity for intimate relationships: A developmental construction. In W. Furman, B. B. Brown, & C. Feiring (Eds.), *The development of romantic relationships in adolescence* (pp. 125–147). New York: Cambridge University Press.

Collins, W. A., & van Dulmen, M. (2006). Friendships and romance in emerging adulthood: Assessing distinctiveness in close relationships. In J. J. Barnett & J. L. Tanner (Eds.), *Emerging adults in America: Coming of age in the 21st century* (pp. 219–234). Washington, DC: The American Psychological Association.

Connell, R. W. (2005). *Masculinities* (2nd ed.). Berkeley: University of California Press.

Côté, J. E. (2006). Emerging adulthood as an institutionalized moratorium: Risks and benefits to identity formation. In. J. J. Arnett & J. L. Tanner (Eds.), *Emerging adults in America: Coming of age in the 21st century* (pp. 85–116). Washington, DC: American Psychological Association.

Cowan, C. P., & Cowan, P. A. (1992). *When partners become parents: The big life change for couples.* New York: Basic Books.

D'Augelli, A. R. (2002). Mental health problems among lesbian, gay, and bisexual youths ages 14 to 21. *Clinical Child Psychology and Psychiatry, 7*, 433–456.

D'Augelli, A. R., & Patterson, C. J. (Eds.). (1995). *Lesbian, gay, and bisexual identities over the lifespan: Psychological perspectives.* New York: Oxford University Press.

D'Augelli, A. R., Rendina, H. J., Sinclair, K. O., & Grossman, A. H. (2006/2007). Lesbian and gay youth's aspirations for marriage and raising children. *Journal of LGBT Issues in Counseling, 1*(4), 77–98.

Diamond, L. M. (2008). *Sexual fluidity: Understanding women's love and desire.* Cambridge, MA: Harvard University Press.

Elder, G. (1995). The life-course paradigm: Social change and individual development. In P. Moen, G. H. Elder, Jr., & K. Lüscher (Eds.), *Examining lives in context: Perspectives on the ecology of human development* (pp. 101–139). Washington, DC: American Psychological Association.

Elder, G. H., & Caspi, A. (1990). Studying lives in a changing society: Sociological and personological explorations. In A. I. Rabin, R. A. Zucker, R. A. Emmons, & S. Frank (Eds.), *Studying persona and lives* (pp. 201–247). New York: Springer Publishing.

Erikson, E. H. (1997). *The life cycle completed.* New York: Norton.

Esler, A. (1984). "The truest community:" Social generations as collective mentalities. *Journal of Political and Military Sociology, 12*, 99–112.

Fee, D. H. (1996). *Coming over: Friendship between straight and gay men.* Unpublished dissertation: The University of California at Santa Barbara (UMI/ProQuest AAT 9704291).

Friedman, C., & Morgan, E. M. (2009). Comparing sexual-minority and heterosexual young women's friends and parents as sources of support for sexual issues. *Journal of Youth and Adolescence, 38*, 920–936.

Friskopp, A., & Silverstein, S. (1995). *Straight jobs, gay lives: Gay and lesbian professionals, the Harvard Business School and the American workplace.* New York: Simon & Schuster/Touchstone Books.

Galambos, N. L., Turner, P. K., & Tilton-Weaver, L. C. (2005). Chronological and subjective age in emerging adulthood: The crossover effect. *Journal of Adolescent Research, 20,* 538–556.

Galatzer-Levy, R. L., & Cohler, B. J. (1993). *The essential other: A developmental psychology of the self.* New York: Basic Books.

Goldberg, A. E. (2010). *Lesbian and gay parents and their children: Research on the family life cycle.* Washington, DC: American Psychological Association.

Gray, M. (2009). *Out in the country: Youth, media and queer visibility in America.* New York: New York University Press.

Green, J. (1999). *The velveteen father: An unexpected journey to parenthood.* New York: Ballentine Books.

Green, A. I. (2002). *Sexual orientation and social structure: A comparative study of urban heterosexual and homosexual careers.* Unpublished doctoral dissertation, New York University (UMI Dissertation Unit Number 3062813).

Griffith, K. H., & Hebl, M. R. (2002). The disclosure dilemma for gay men and lesbians: "Coming out" at work. *Journal of Applied Psychology, 87,* 1191–1199.

Hamilton, S. F., & Hamilton, M. A. (2006). School, work and emerging adulthood. In J. J. Arnett & J. L. Tanner (Eds.), *Emerging adults in America: Coming of age in the 21st century* (pp. 257–278). Washington, DC: American Psychological Association.

Hammack, P., Thompson, E. M., & Pilecki, A. (2009). Configurations of identity among sexual minority youth: Context, desire, and narrative. *Journal of Youth and Adolescence, 38,* 867–883.

Harry, J., & DeVall, W. B. (1978). *The social organization of gay couples.* New York: Praeger.

Hendry, L. B., & Kloep, M. (2007a). Conceptualizing emerging adulthood: Inspecting the emperor's new clothes? *Child Development Perspectives, 1,* 74–79.

Hendry, L. B., & Kloep, M. (2007b). Redressing the emperor! A rejoinder to Arnett. *Child Development Perspectives, 1,* 83–85.

Henig, R. M. (2010). What is it about 2-somethings? *New York Times Magazine,* August 22, 2010, pp. 28–37, 46–49.

Hershberger, S. L., & D'Augelli, A. R. (1995). The impact of victimization on the mental health and suicidality of lesbian, gay, and bisexual youth. *Developmental Psychology, 31,* 65–74.

Horowitz, A. D., & Bromnick, R. D. (2007). "Contestable adulthood:" Variability and disparity in markers for negotiating the transition to adulthood. *Youth and Society, 39,* 209–231.

Hunter, J. D. (2009). Wither adulthood? *The Hedgehog Review, 11,* 7–17.

James, S. E., & Murphy, B. C. (1998). Gay and lesbian relationships in a changing social context. In C. J. Patterson & A. R. D'Augelli (Eds.), *Lesbian, gay, and bisexual identities in families: Psychological perspectives* (pp. 99–121). New York: Oxford University Press.

Johnson, S. M., & O'Connor, E. (2002). *The gay baby boom: The psychology of gay parenthood.* New York: New York University Press.

Keniston, K. (1971). *Youth and dissent: The rise of a new opposition.* New York: Harcourt, Brace Jovanovich.

Kimmel, D. (1993). Adult development and aging: A gay perspective. In L. Garnets & D. Kimmel (Eds.), *Psychological perspectives on lesbian and gay male experiences* (pp. 517–534). New York: Columbia University Press.

Kurdek, L. A. (2004). Are gay and lesbian cohabiting couples *really* different from heterosexual married couples? *Journal of Marriage and the Family, 66,* 880–900.

Kurdek, L. A. (2005). What do we know about gay and lesbian couples? *Psychological Science, 14,* 251–254.

Lefkowitz, E. S., & Gillen, M. M. (2006). "Sex is just a normal part of life:" Sexuality in emerging adulthood. In J. J. Arnett & J. L. Tanner (Eds.), *Emerging adults in America: Coming of age in the 21st century* (pp. 235–256). Washington, DC: American Psychological Association.

Martin, J. I., & D'Augelli, A. R. (2009). Timed lives: Cohort and period effects in research on sexual orientation and gender identity. In W. Meezan & J. I. Martin (Eds.), *Handbook of research with lesbian, gay, bisexual, and transgendered populations* (pp. 191–209). New York: Routledge.

Meyer, I. H. (2003). Prejudice, social stress, and mental health in lesbian, gay, and bisexual populations: Conceptual issues and research evidence. *Psychological Bulletin, 129,* 674–697.

Meyer, I. H., & Northridge, M. E. (Eds.). (2007). *The health of sexual minorities: Public health perspectives on lesbian, gay, bisexual and transgendered populations.* New York: Springer.

Mitchell, B. A. (2007). *The boomerang age: Transitions to adulthood in families.* New Brunswick, NJ: Aldine Transaction Books.

Mouw, T. (2005). Sequences of early adult transitions: A look at variability and consequences. In R. A. Settersten, F. F. Furstenberg, & R. G. Rumbaut (Eds.), *On the frontier of adulthood: Theory, research, and public policy* (pp. 256–291). Chicago: The University of Chicago Press.

Nardi, P. (1999). *Gay men's friendships: Invincible communities.* Chicago: The University of Chicago Press.

Osgood, D. W., Ruth, G., Eccles, J. S., Jacobs, J. E., & Barber, B. L. (2005). Six paths to adulthood: Fast starters, parents without careers, educated partners, educated singles, working singles, and slow starters. In R. A. Settersten, Jr., F. F. Furstenberg, & R. G. Rumbaut (Eds.), *On the frontier of adulthood: Theory, research, and public policy* (pp. 225–255). Chicago: The University of Chicago Press.

Patterson, C. J. (2000). Family relationships of lesbians and gay men. *Journal of Marriage and the Family, 62*, 1052–1069.

Patterson, C. J. (2002). Lesbian and gay parenthood. In M. Bornstein (Ed.), *Handbook of parenting* (Vol. 3, pp. 317–338). Mahwah, NJ: Erlbaum.

Patterson, C. J. (2009). Children of lesbian and gay parents: Psychology, law, and policy. *American Psychologist, 64*, 727–736.

Patterson, C. J., & Riskind, R. G. (2010). To be a parent: Issues in family formation among gay and lesbian adults. *Journal of GLBT Family Studies, 6*, 326–340.

Peplau, L. A., & Cochran, S. D. (1988). Value orientations in the intimate relationships of gay males. In J. DeCecco (Ed.), *Gay relationships* (pp. 195–216). New York: Harrington Park Press.

Peplau, L. A., & Cochran, S. (1990). A relationship perspective on homosexuality. In D. McWhirter, S. A. Sanders, & J. M. Reinisch (Eds.), *Homosexuality/heterosexuality: Concepts of sexual orientation* (pp. 321–349). New York: Oxford University Press.

Peplau, L. A., & Fingerhut, A. W. (2007). The close relationships of lesbians and gay men. *Annual Review of Psychology, 58*, 405–424.

Price, J. (1999). *Navigating differences: Friendships between gay and straight men*. New York: Haworth Press.

Quenqua, D. "I love you, man (as a friend)." *The New York Times*, June 26, 2009.

Read, K. (2001). *How I learned to snap: A small town coming-out and coming of age story*. Athens, GA: Hill Street Press.

Remafedi, G. (1999). Suicide and sexual orientation: Nearing the end of the controversy? *Archives of General Psychiatry, 56*, 885–886.

Remafedi, G. (2002). Suicidality in a venue-based sample of young men who have sex with men. *Journal of Adolescent Health, 31*, 305–310.

Riskind, R. G., & Patterson, C. J. (2010). Parenting intentions and desires among childless lesbian, gay, and heterosexual individuals. *Journal of Family Psychology, 24*, 78–81.

Rivers, I., & D'Augelli, A. R. (2001). The victimization of lesbian, gay, and bisexual youths in university communities. In A. R. D'Augelli & C. J. Patterson (Eds.), *Lesbian, gay, and bisexual identities in youth: Psychological perspectives* (pp. 199–223). New York: Oxford University Press.

Rostosky, S. S., & Riggle, E. D. B. (2002). "Out" at work: The relation of actor and partner workplace policy and internalized homophobia to disclosure status. *Journal of Counseling Psychology, 49*, 411–419.

Russell, S. T., Clarke, T. J., & Clary, J. (2009). Are teens "post-gay"? Contemporary adolescents' sexual identity labels. *Journal of Youth and Adolescence, 38*, 884–890.

Sandefur, G. D., Eggerling-Boeck, J., & Park, H. (2005). Off to a good start: Postsecondary education and early adult life. In R. A. Settersten, F. F. Furstenberg, & R. G. Rumbaut (Eds.), *On the frontier of adulthood: Theory, research, and public policy* (pp. 292–319). Chicago: The University of Chicago Press.

Savin-Williams, R. C. (2001). *"Mom, Dad, I'm gay:" How families negotiate coming out*. Washington, DC: American Psychological Association.

Savin-Williams, R. C. (2006). Who's gay? Does it matter? *Current Directions in Psychological Science, 15*, 40–44.

Sears, J. (1991). *Growing up gay in the south: Race, gender, and journeys of the spirit*. New York: Harrington Park Press.

Seidman, S. (2002). *Beyond the closet: The transformation of gay and lesbian life*. New York: Routledge.

Settersten, R. A. (1999). *Lives in time and place: The problems and promises of developmental science*. Amityville, NY: Baywood Publishing Company.

Shanahan, M. R., Porfeli, E. S., Mortimer, J. S., & Erickson, L. M. (2005). Subjective age identity and the transition to adulthood. In R. A. Settersten, F. F. Furstenberg, & R. G. Rumbaut (Eds.), *On the frontier of adulthood: Theory, research, and public policy* (pp. 225–255). Chicago: The University of Chicago Press.

Stein, A. (1997). *Sex and sensibility: Stories of a lesbian generation*. Berkeley: University of California Press.

Stein, A. (2010). The incredible shrinking lesbian world and other queer conundra. *Sexualities, 13*, 21–32.

Tanner, J. L. (2006). Recentering during emerging adulthood: A critical turning point in human development. In J. J. Arnett & J. L.Tanner (Eds.), *Emerging adults in America: Coming of age in the 21st century* (pp. 21–56). Washington, DC: American Psychological Association.

Taylor, V., Kimport, K.,Van Dyke, N., & Anderson, E. A. (2009). Culture and mobilization: Tactical repertoires, same-sex weddings, and the impact on gay activism. *American Sociological Review, 74*, 865–890.

Tillmann-Healy, L. M. (2001). *Between gay and straight: Understanding friendship across sexual orientation*. Lanham, MD. AltaMira Press/Rowman & Littlefield Publishers.

Weinstock, J. S. (1998). Lesbian, gay, bisexual and transgender friendships in adulthood. In C. J. Patterson & A. R. D'Augelli (Eds.), *Lesbian, gay, and bisexual identities in families* (pp. 122–153). New York: Oxford University Press.

Weststrate, N. M., & McLean, K. C. (2009). The rise and fall of gay: A cultural-historical approach to gay identity development. *Memory, 18*, 225–240.

Whyte, D., Merling, A., Merling, R., & Merling, S. (2000). *The wedding: A family's coming out story*. New York: Avon Books.

Woods, J. D., & Lucas, J. H. (1993). *The corporate closet: The professional lives of gay men in America*. New York: The Free Press.

9

Sexual Orientation, Middle Adulthood, and Narratives of Transition and Change

ANDREW J. HOSTETLER

Along with adolescence, middle adulthood has long been portrayed as a time of potentially dramatic or disruptive change (e.g., Jaques, 1965; Levinson, 1978, 1996; Sheehy, 1976). Evidence from nonclinical samples indicates that the experience of a "midlife crisis" is not the norm, and life-course transitions are often more predictable and orderly than once believed (Wethington, 2000). Nevertheless, the midlife crisis continues to be a popular narrative device for describing a wide range of experiences across adulthood (Wethington, 2000), and the persistent idea that middle age can be a time of change or renewal challenges assumptions about developmental continuity across the lifespan. Although the stereotypical crisis is associated with (heterosexual, white) men, middle adulthood as a time of transition is also a recurrent theme in the life stories of women (Moen & Wethington, 1999) and sexual minorities. For lesbian, gay, bisexual, and transgender persons, in particular, the nature of these transitions has changed dramatically over the past few decades.

For many lesbians and gay men of the Baby Boom and earlier cohorts, middle adulthood (ages approximately 40 to 60) was a time for coming out, for overcoming "developmental delay," and for catching up with heterosexual peers, and/or—for many men with HIV/AIDS—preparing for a long illness and perhaps premature death. In the 1980s and 1990s, the eventual emergence of a normative gay and lesbian life course, parallel to heterosexual life in many ways, seemed likely. Indeed, many currently middle-aged men and women confront similar developmental tasks, irrespective of sexual orientation. At the same time, increasingly diverse manifestations of gender and sexual identity have challenged essentialist narratives about sexual orientation and simple, linear models of the life course. Research on cross-cultural differences, sexual fluidity, multidimensionality of sexual orientation, and the experience of transgender individuals has uncovered new stories of transition. In addition, the growing visibility of age-stratified sexual identities (e.g., bears, leather folk) and a growing divide between lesbian, gay, and bisexual singles and those choosing marriage and children (Hostetler, 2004, 2009c) have refocused attention on age and developmental "stage" as central themes of "sexual stories" (Plummer, 1995). In this chapter, I explore shifting narratives of midlife within lesbian, gay, bisexual, and transgender communities, and the general role of sexuality in middle adulthood in creating the kinds of stories that inspire social change.

GENERAL THEORETICAL APPROACH

The present chapter is theoretically grounded in the idea that narrative provides an essential tool for rendering change and unanticipated experiences meaningful (e.g., midlife crisis, coming out). This is in keeping not only with the narrative perspective in psychology (Bruner, 1990; Cohler, 1982; Edwards & Potter, 1992; Sarbin, 1986), but also with ecological and life course approaches (Bronfenbrenner, 1979; Elder, 1998). Specifically, narratives of the life course represent important cultural or macrosystemic influences on human development. Such narratives provide a shared framework for understanding both the expected flow of experience (i.e., continuity) and eruptive change (i.e., discontinuity) (King, Burton, & Geise, 2009; McAdams, 1993), and are shaped by historical events and circumstances within a given society. In turn, these narratives contribute to distinctive identities tied to generation or birth cohort—concepts key to the life course perspective (Clausen, 1993; Elder, 1998).

These concepts are particularly crucial to the study of lesbian, gay, bisexual, and transgender lives (Herdt & Boxer, 1996; Kertzner, 2001b; Kimmel, 1993). Whereas "cohort" refers to a band of birth years, "generation" more commonly indexes both age (though sometimes indeterminately) and an ethos or shared consciousness specific to an age group (Gilleard & Higgs, 2007; Mannheim, 1928). However, as employed by life course scholars (e.g., Elder, 1998), cohort analysis is grounded in the idea that human development is shaped by socio-historical processes. Thus, I use the two terms interchangeably. Whereas Herdt and Boxer (1996) and Kimmel (1993) offer detailed analysis of cohort membership as it impacts lesbian, gay, bisexual, and transgender development, I adopt a somewhat narrower approach, while also acknowledging the difficulty of precise cohort classification and the reality of intracohort variability. This chapter focuses on the Baby Boom (born ~1946–1964) and subsequent generations, with some reference to the earlier "Silent Generation" (born ~1925–1945), for two primary reasons. First, Baby Boomers and "Generation X" (born ~1965–1980) are the two cohorts currently in midlife. Second, Boomers have played a crucial role with respect to how gay midlife and middle adulthood in general are currently understood and experienced.

Given increasing longevity, as well as delayed marriage and parenting, ideas about the timing and focus of middle adulthood have shifted significantly over time. The modern psychological study of midlife began with Erikson (1963), who did not give this period special treatment, and for whom the midlife generativity crisis was about moving beyond the self to embrace broader social concerns such as the welfare of future generations. In the hands of the next generation of writers (e.g., Jaques, 1965; Levinson, 1978, 1996; Sheehy, 1976), the midlife crisis became at least as much about self-exploration and the pursuit of deferred dreams and new freedoms (following or even during active parenting). The view of middle adulthood as a time of new possibilities emerged as part of broader generational discourses about self-discovery, self-improvement, and empowerment in the late-1960s and the 1970s. These discourses were originally tied to political movements, including Feminism and Gay Liberation, but the personal

largely supplanted the political as Baby Boomers aged beyond young adulthood and cultivated the idea that middle age could be a "rejuvenating experience" (Gilleard & Higgs, 2007, p. 18). More than just straightforward resistance to age-related decline (e.g., Cardona, 2008), the Boomer midlife experience reflects a complicated mix of identification with younger generations and new ideas [the opposite of what Neugarten (1968) found for earlier cohorts of middle-aged adults] and active efforts to forge a mature identity (Biggs, Phillipson, Leach, & Money, 2007).

That a mature midlife identity could be considered compatible with being openly gay is also largely an achievement of the Baby Boom generation (though the "homophile" movement of the 1950s and early 1960s undeniably set the stage). Specifically, the lesbian and gay Boomers who participated in and/or were influenced by the Gay Liberation movement helped to redefine what it meant to be lesbian or gay, creating new stories about lesbian and gay life, including midlife. But although Boomer ideas and experiences have significantly contributed to current understandings of this developmental period, subsequent cohorts will likely reshape middle adulthood in their own ways. Generational change is particularly central to the experiences of lesbian, gay, and bisexual individuals, for whom relatively rapid gains in social acceptance and institutional recognition and especially impactful historical events (e.g., the AIDS epidemic, the passage of same-sex marriage laws) have led to pronounced cohort differences (Herdt & Boxer, 1996; Hostetler & Herdt, 1998). At the same time, experiences of discontinuity may be characteristic of midlife—as the point of entry into the second half of life—somewhat irrespective of cohort. Similarly, sexuality is rarely completely static across the lifespan, but cultural resources are not always available to make sense of change. Accordingly, middle adulthood and sexual development may be uniquely linked to the kind of meaning-making efforts that can be catalysts not only for individual development, but also for social and cultural change.

MIDLIFE COMING OUT STORIES, "OFF-TIME" AND NORMLESS DEVELOPMENT

Whether or not they were directly involved in the Gay Liberation Movement, many lesbian and gay Boomers came out while still young adults; the oldest Boomers were 23 at the time of the 1969 Stonewall Riots and 27 was the average coming out age for some samples of gay men and women then in their 60s (D'Augelli & Grossman, 2001). Their coming out stories were important engines of both personal and social change. However, early-adult coming out experiences were more common among white, middle-class individuals living in large urban areas than among other groups. For many same-sex attracted men and women, from both the Boomer and older cohorts, the signature personal and political act of coming out did not happen until middle adulthood. Even among those who came out earlier, many experienced midlife developmental disruptions and/or struggled in the absence of established developmental norms.

Although perhaps not the most common pathway for lesbian, gay, and bisexual Boomers (or for younger cohorts), midlife transitions to a gay or lesbian identity could be considered exemplars of late-twentieth-century cultural narratives of personal development, given Boomer discourses about liberation/empowerment and about new possibilities for middle age. Coming out stories, along with addiction recovery and sexual abuse survival stories, have been described as paradigmatic Western narratives of "suffering, surviving, and surpassing" (Plummer, 1995). Specifically, Plummer argued that characteristic modernist ideas about human nature are revealed by these narratives of early trauma or perceived difference, subsequent denial or concealment of this core aspect of self, and its eventual integration into one's identity with the support of fellow travelers. Accordingly, *midlife* coming out stories bring together several related, Boomer-inspired ideas about liberation/rejuvenation/rebirth of the self.

What it means to "surpass," beyond living a happy and fulfilling life, is not entirely clear, though it is a question to which I will return. And although midlife coming out experiences have been portrayed primarily in terms of personal growth, they also reflect "off-time" development (Neugarten, 1964) that can interfere with other expected developmental processes and transitions (Hostetler, 2009a; Kertzner, 2001a, 2001b; Kimmel & Sang, 1995; Siegel & Lowe, 1994). Many newly "out" middle-aged men and women (and even those who came out in their 30s) experienced a second or "delayed" adolescence (Siegel & Lowe, 1994), reflecting a general developmental delay of intimacy,

generativity, and other postadolescent developmental concerns. For example, many gay men from the Boomer and older cohorts who came out in middle adulthood struggled to find appropriate venues and opportunities (i.e., beyond the bar scene) for realizing long-term intimacy (Hostetler, 2009c). At the same time, spending time in bars, nightclubs, and other youth-oriented venues may have contributed to a sense of "accelerated aging," or of feeling older than your chronological age, among many men (Bennett & Thompson, 1990; Friend, 1980, 1987; Kelly, 1977). For many Boomer women, on the other hand, motherhood in the context of heterosexual marriage delayed the adoption of a lesbian identity and related milestones (Institute of Medicine, 2011), reversing the normative developmental sequence.

Above and beyond disruptions in the timing and sequence of development, the course of lesbian and gay life—and particularly the second half of life—has been characterized as underdetermined relative to heterosexual life, as perhaps best illustrated by the concept of "uncharted lives" (Siegel & Lowe, 1994). For example, Kimmel and Sang (1995, p. 192) argued that in the absence of established life patterns, "creating self-relevant norms and expectations" for development is a major task for lesbians and gay men in middle adulthood. Both off-time and "uncharted" development pose not only challenges to, but also additional opportunities for, personal growth and agency, and these first generations of openly gay middle-aged and older adults have been seen as pioneers, blazing the trail for future cohorts.

Indeed, these developmental storylines are narratives not only of individual developmental but also of historical change. The theme of historical progress is integral to many midlife coming out stories, if only as an unacknowledged backdrop, including the story of Howard, who was a 74-year-old, white World War II veteran when I interviewed him in the late 1990s (see Hostetler, 2009c). In response to a question about how an earlier recognition of same-sex marriage might have affected him, he said:

> My whole life would have been different. I wouldn't have been so homophobic early on in my life. I would have been establishing relationships much earlier. Your question is tied to an entire climate of what gay was like in the

1940's, the War years and '50s...As much as I lament all that I've lost in my generation, I'm so much better off than the generation that preceded me.

This and similar stories portray the present as more hospitable to gay people than the past and also anticipate a more enlightened time to come. However, the presumption of inevitable progress and an easier path for future generations of lesbians and gay men was severely challenged by the intrusion of another historical event—the emergence of AIDS in the early 1980s. In fact, the AIDS epidemic was perhaps the most cohort-defining episode of the late twentieth century, and its impact on Boomer (and Silent Generation) gay and bisexual men (and, to a lesser extent, women) provides compelling evidence for the life course theory principle that historical time and place profoundly shape individual development (Elder, 1998).

Most of the consequences of the epidemic were obviously very negative. For Boomer gay men (the oldest of whom turned 40 in 1986), HIV/AIDS not only shaped their experience of sexuality, but also decimated their social networks, generating rapid losses uncharacteristic of modern middle age, and further disrupted developmental timetables (Hostetler, 2009a; Kertzner, 2001b). These losses affected more than just gay men, of course, and many lesbians were among the dedicated caregivers (Fredriksen-Goldsen, 2005). HIV-positive men also faced the likelihood, if not certainty, of a premature death. This led to a sense of developmental "telescoping" for many men forced to confront a wide range of developmental tasks at once (Bennett & Thompson, 1990; Borden, 1989; Cohler, Hostetler, & Boxer, 1998). The emergence of more effective treatments in the mid-1990s extended lives and removed the threat of imminent death. However, many of those spared struggled with "survivor guilt," and not all have experienced the prospect of additional, sometimes unplanned-for years as an unmitigated blessing (Cohler et al., 1998). Moreover, early drug treatments [e.g., zidovudine (AZT)] had serious and sometimes fatal side effects. Even for many survivors, then, their midlife experience has been dominated by a chronic medical condition directly linked to their sexuality. And as the epidemic has largely faded from the public eye, even in lesbian and gay communities (despite relatively high new infection rates), many survivors may feel disconnected from younger cohorts who did not experience the AIDS era. With respect to positive impact, the AIDS crisis brought the lesbian and gay male communities closer together, provided valuable and rewarding caregiving experiences, forced many HIV-positive men to come out to their families (alienating some family members but leading to closer relationships with others), and transformed and energized gay activism.

It is also arguably true that although AIDS temporarily slowed the slow march toward equality, it also increased the visibility of gay and lesbian people and issues, facilitating the progress achieved over the past 15 years or so (e.g., legal recognition for marriages of same-sex couples). Although gay Boomers, the youngest of whom are currently in their late-40s, have certainly benefited from these changes, the course of their middle (and late) adulthood has been shaped in indelible ways by the events and developmental complications described above. At the same time, the smoother, more continuous path envisioned for future generations clearly seems overly simplistic, and a poor fit for the actual experiences of the gay and lesbian Gen-Xers now in middle adulthood.

FRACTURED AND FLUID IDENTITIES AND THE PERSISTENCE OF DISCONTINUITY

The themes reflected in Boomer and pre-Boomer narratives of middle adulthood gesture toward a future in which nonheterosexual identities and life course development will proceed "on time" and with more cultural guideposts. Of course, the idea of a normative lesbian and gay life course is not endorsed by all, including queer theorists and activists who have celebrated the freedom of life on the margins, and constructivist social scientists who have argued that sexuality is fluid, malleable, and shaped in meaningful ways by the sociocultural context (Herdt, 1997; Warner, 1999; Weeks, 1985). With the oldest lesbian and gay Gen-Xers now in their mid-40s, it is clear that diversity, discontinuity, and even fragmentation continue to characterize gay and lesbian developmental pathways through middle adulthood.

First, although midlife coming out transitions have become less common, they have not entirely become a thing of the past. In many communities and parts of the country, experiences of nondisclosure continue to dominate the early adult years of many who will eventually embrace a lesbian, gay, bisexual, or transgender identity. For example, although some evidence suggests that African-American and Latina lesbians become aware of their same-sex attractions relatively early, lesbian and gay people of color, in general, tend to disclose their sexual identities to others later than Anglo-American counterparts, largely out of fear of alienating themselves from the communities that have sustained them (Institute of Medicine, 2011). Even for those who come out in their late 20s or 30s, developmental delay can follow them into midlife.

Above and beyond differences in the timing of identity formation, the experiences of many men and women do not always fit neatly into predominantly white, middle-class categories and storylines. For example, research on the "down low" (DL) phenomenon within the African-American community (but practiced by men of various racial/ethnic backgrounds) suggests that "gay," "homosexual," or even "bisexual" may not be appropriate labels for these men (Phillips, 2005). DL men value their heterosexual roles and relationships, sometimes including heterosexual marriage and children, while also enjoying extramarital same-sex encounters and relationships. Adopting a gay identity or even long-term same-sex relationship may not appeal to these men. In other words, the different dimensions of their sexual identity—sexual, affectional, relational, and social—do not line up in a conventional way. Importantly, this fragmentation does not necessarily pose problems for well-being or for experiencing a coherent sense of self. Unfortunately, little is known about how the DL identity plays out over time; some of these men may develop an openly gay identity at some point in their lives.

In general, the idea of a life course pathway organized around same-sex attractions and relationships is historically recent and relatively rare in the anthropological record (Herdt, 1997; Hostetler, 2009b). And although this has become the standard for many same-sex attracted men and women in a growing number of cultures around the world, their lived experiences are often more complicated. Many men and particularly women experience their sexuality as fluid across the course of adult life (Kaminski, 2000; Rose & Zand, 2000). Recent longitudinal data suggest that many women shift between same- and cross-sex relationships over the course of adulthood, though same-sex experiences may be more common in early adulthood (Diamond, 2008). Although there may be a biological basis for the apparently higher rates of bisexuality among women (e.g., Lippa, 2006), the experience of sexual fluidity appears to be as much a function of women's biographies, which may be especially likely to shift course in middle adulthood, when many women experience a greater sense of freedom compared to earlier periods in their lives (Moen & Wethington, 1999). For example, in their study of women who identified as lesbians after identifying as heterosexual for at least 10 years, Kitzinger and Wilkinson (1995) asserted that these transitions should not be characterized simply as late coming out experiences, but rather as discursive acts involving redefinition of the word "lesbian" in a way that accorded with who these women already were.

Over the past two decades or so, bisexual and transgender identities have also become more visible. Whereas the former have further undermined "either/or" assumptions about sexuality and linear models of life course development, the latter have inspired a fundamental reexamination of the nature of gender, sexuality, and the relationship between the two. The category of "bisexual" covers a wide range of experiences: predominantly heteroerotic, predominantly homoerotic, sequentially monogamous (with one or both genders), "polyamorous," and so forth (Rust, 2002). At the same time, it should not be assumed that shifting between same-sex and cross-sex partners is subjectively experienced as a significant transition. And, for most bisexuals, "same-sex and other-sex activities…are harmonious, rather than conflicting, forms of sexual expression" (Rust, 2002, p. 212). At the same time, we know relatively little about the experiences of bisexual individuals in middle or late adulthood (but see Dworkin, Chapter 3, this volume).

For transgender individuals, gender transitions/transgender identification increasingly seems to occur in adolescence and early adulthood. However, transgender men and women come out and/or transition later, on average, than gay men and lesbians (Institute of Medicine, 2011), and such transitions are usually gradual (as reflected in the designations of "pre-op" and "post-op," referring to whether or not an individual has undergone surgery), and can begin or extend into middle adulthood (Whitten, 2003). Midlife transitions, though challenging for all involved, can be particularly difficult for partners/spouses and children, for whom the first part of the adjustment process can be like mourning a death (Joslin-Roher & Wheeler, 2009). Both male-to-female (MTF) and female-to-male (FTM) transitions are sometimes accompanied by shifts in sexual object choice (e.g., Daskalos, 1998), further challenging existing classificatory systems and beliefs about the continuity of sexual identity.

Even among those whose sexual identities remain stable from young adulthood, many encounter difficulty integrating their identities across the different spheres of their lives, thereby experiencing synchronous (as opposed to diachronous) discontinuity. Most obviously, many middle-aged gay men and women remain somewhat hidden or closeted within their families of origin, even as they lead otherwise open lives. Many others are unable to be open in the workplace, silenced by the threat of anti-gay discrimination, harassment, or even violence. Across studies, between 13% and 62% of lesbian, gay, bisexual, and transgender employees report discrimination (Badgett, 1996). There is also evidence of an earnings-related "sexual orientation premium" in addition to the more well-established marriage premium, meaning that gay men may earn less, on average, than their married heterosexual counterparts (Allegretto & Arthur, 2001; Badgett, 1995, 1997). And, at a time when their careers should be peaking, many middle-aged lesbian and gay employees may encounter glass ceilings (Bradford & Ryan, 1991; Kimmel & Sang, 1995). According to the limited research on the topic, transgender men and women may encounter the most serious employment-related difficulties, as they have relatively lower educational attainment, higher unemployment rates, lower wages, and are overrepresented in low-paying jobs (Whitten, 2003).

Workplace disclosure of sexual orientation is influenced by many factors, including race, gender, occupation, and income. Lesbians and gay men of color have been described as less likely to disclose sexual identities in the workplace than are their white counterparts, and also less able to select occupations that match their disclosure preferences (Badgett, 1996). The association between disclosure and income appears to be U-shaped, with individuals on both the lower and higher ends of the income distribution less likely to disclose their sexual orientation in the workplace. The interactive effects of gender and sexual orientation in the workplace also appear to be complicated. First, there is

some evidence that "single" women make more than married counterparts (Badgett, 1996). And despite the potential for homophobia and heterosexism within the workplace, lesbians who are not parents otherwise enjoy greater career continuity, and some may even experience less discrimination, compared to heterosexual women who interrupt their careers to raise children (Kimmel & Sang, 1995; Moen & Wethington, 1999).

More commonly, however, lesbian and gay adults are at risk for discrimination, harassment, and violence in multiple contexts, and such encounters can obviously directly impact physical and psychological well-being, and also force some victims to revisit sexual identity issues that had previously been resolved (Patterson, 2008). According to Herek and Garnets (2007), the pervasive effects of heterosexism—in the workplace, the legal system, and in religious/spiritual communities—can undermine happiness and well-being. In light of the ongoing challenges of integrating an openly lesbian or gay identity across the full range of life domains, Rust (1993) has recommended that coming out be conceptualized as a lifelong developmental process of describing "one's social location within a changing social context" (quoted in Kaminski, 2000, p. 91).

Above and beyond these examples of fluidity, discontinuity, and fragmentation, there are other reasons to believe that middle adulthood can offer a unique context and catalyst for transformations of "sexual stories." The emergence of the gay "bear" sexual identity and community provides a particularly intriguing case in point. Although there are variations and subidentities, bears are generally stocky, unapologetically hairy (face and body), and relatively unconcerned with the latest fashion trends (pursuing a more "natural" masculine look), and they seek similar sexual partners (Hennen, 2005). The bear world appeals to and welcomes men of all ages, but middle-aged and older men seem to be overrepresented among men claiming this identity, and available roles are at least somewhat stratified by age (e.g., bears and bear cubs). The evolution of the bear community is a least partially a response to unforgiving standards of appearance and beauty that many men encounter in the broader gay community, standards that are also ageist. The bear community provides opportunities for sex, love, and validation that many middle-aged and older men struggle to find in the bars, clubs, and other venues that cater primarily to young men.

In conjunction with the apparently greater sexual fluidity among women, the emergence of this and similar gay male sexual identities (e.g., leather men) would seem to support McIntosh's (1992) claim that "women seem to broaden their experiences as they get older, whereas men become narrower and more specialized" (quoted in Kitzinger & Wilkinson, 1995, p. 95).

In addition to the experiences of fluidity and other transitions already addressed, entering middle adulthood can also provoke substantial reflection related to sexuality among lesbians. According to Fullmer, Shenk, and Eastland (1999), many mature lesbians find themselves caught between two contradictory cultural constructions that make it difficult to maintain a coherent sense of identity: Whereas lesbians are defined by their sexuality, older women are stereotypically defined by a lack of sexual appeal and therefore by asexuality. For lesbians whose midlife roles are defined by motherhood, on the other hand, discontinuity may take the form of being "thrown into the mainstream" for the first time in their adult lives, with their daily routines and concerns more closely resembling those of their heterosexual peers (Donaldson, 2000, p. 132).

For many others, living life outside traditional norms and expectations seems to foster an unusual amount of reflection about and self-conscious engagement in their development. And middle adulthood, as the point of entry into a second half of life that is increasingly long and undefined, provides a particularly rich context for developmental innovation. Whether or not gay men actually become narrower in their sexual interests as they age, the life stories and lived experiences of lesbian, gay, bisexual, and transgender people at midlife (i.e., the intersection of sexual minority identities and middle adulthood) could ultimately expand understandings and conceptualizations of the life course and serve as an engine for developmental and social change. I consider this possibility in the next section.

NARRATIVES OF INTIMACY, FAMILY, AND GENERATIVITY AT MIDLIFE AND BEYOND

In many ways, the brighter future envisioned in midlife narratives of lesbians and gay men from the Baby Boom and earlier generations has been realized. Lesbian and gay individuals may be coming out at earlier ages, sometimes as early as the preteen years (Savin-Williams, 2005), and generally face fewer educational or career barriers and less social rejection. Accordingly, their development is largely "on-time." As more gay men and lesbians seek and obtain career positions commensurate with their credentials, marry, become parents, and so forth, nonheterosexual orientation per se may cease to be a major source of the kind of the discontinuity and keenly experienced difference that drives narrative, meaning-making processes (King et al., 2009; McAdams, 1993). But as demonstrated in the previous section, the easy integration of sexual identity into an otherwise normative life course may be more characteristic of the most privileged lesbians and gay men, and, even for this group, experiences of homophobia and heterosexism can disrupt an otherwise smooth passage through the adult years. Whether lesbian and gay midlife narratives are beginning to reflect a more normative course of development may not be the most relevant question given longer, healthier lifespans (at least in wealthy nations) and an increasingly undefined second half of life (Rubinstein, 2002). As current and future generations of gay men and lesbians fashion the stories of their mature years, their efforts and innovations could inform broader developmental, moral, and existential debates.

Lesbian and gay innovation has long been recognized in the area of families of choice, or quasikinship relationships based on voluntary, as opposed to biological, bonds (Weston, 1991). Although same-sex marriage will likely be legally recognized in most of the United States within a generation, this possibility was almost unfathomable when Boomers came of age, and gay and lesbian family life continues to be characterized by diversity and a high degree of creativity. According to Kimmel's (1992) research, gay men and lesbians tend to occupy three family-related roles: partners/spouses, caregivers/providers for families of origin, and members of close friendship networks (i.e., chosen families). The creation of "substitute" families of friends appears to have been more common among older cohorts, but it may also be somewhat developmentally specific and more typical of the early adult years (Weinstock, 2000).

Regardless, the existence of such relationships has challenged heteronormative assumptions about family and elevated the life course profile of friendship. Specific innovations/differences that have been observed include the greater tendency, particularly among lesbians, to remain friends with former lovers, the greater exchange of caregiving support among friends, and unusual levels of intimacy between gay male friends compared to their heterosexual counterparts (Nardi, 1999; Tully, 1989; Weinstock, 2000). Although friends may play a somewhat limited role in the lives of many middle-class, heterosexual couples at midlife, some research suggests that lesbians have a renewed sense of appreciation for their friends at this time (Rothblum et al., 1995). Others define their friends as extended family or even as in-laws (in the case of friendships that predate a romantic relationship) as a strategy to maintain longtime friendships and integrate them into a family that may now include a partner and children (Rose, 1996; Weinstock, 2000). Some lesbians have even carved out new roles as "grandmothers of choice," serving as substitute or "surplus" grandparents for the grandchildren of close friends (Mitchell, 2000). And single gay men and lesbians have been at the vanguard in creating rewarding single lifestyles, creating narratives of "voluntary singlehood" that promote well-being in mid- and later-life (Hostetler, 2009c, 2012).

But increasingly the political and cultural focus within lesbian and gay communities has shifted to marriage, partnership, and more traditional manifestations of family. Although the number of legally recognized marriages of same-sex couples is still relatively small, it is estimated that 30–50% of all same-sex couples will eventually get married or register their partnerships (Ash & Badgett, 2006). Thus far, lesbians have also been more likely to get married than gay men (Belluck, 2008). Whether in an officially recognized relationship or not, approximately 50% of gay men and up to 75% of lesbians are partnered at any time (Ash & Badgett, 2006; Herek, 2006; Hostetler, 2009c; Kurdek, 1995), and important differences in experiences have been observed based on relationship status and couple type. For example, a recent longitudinal study found that being in a civil union was associated with greater relationship stability than being in a partnership without having undertaken a civil union (Balsam, Beauchaine, Rothblum, & Solomon, 2008). Cohabitation and registration of a domestic partnership appear to be more common among highly educated, middle- and upper-middle-class white couples (Ash & Badgett, 2006). Unmarried partners are more likely to be uninsured compared to married partners, and single

lesbians and particularly gay men tend to fare poorly compared to coupled counterparts, with lower levels of happiness and well-being and greater risk for job loss and serious illness (Ash & Badgett, 2006; King & Smith, 2004; Wayment & Peplau, 1995). These disparities emphasize the importance of marriage/partnership benefits and rights, but will hopefully also inspire efforts by researchers, policy makers, and service providers to promote the well-being and cultural inclusion of individuals irrespective of relationship status.

Even as same-sex relationships have seemingly become more conventional, lesbian and gay couples have expanded the range of possible and workable roles and relationship patterns. Whereas lesbian couples may be the most monogamous of all couple types, gay male couples are the least, but sexual nonexclusivity does not necessarily threaten the stability or quality of gay male relationships (Herek, 2006; Kurdek, 1995). Lesbian and gay couples may also enjoy greater freedom with respect to gender roles, and evidence indicates that gay and particularly lesbian couples may be more egalitarian than cross-sex couples (Kimmel, 1979; Kurdek, 2004; Patterson, 2000, Chapter 16, this volume; however, for criticism of this view, see Carrington, 1999).

Despite having significantly less external support than the average heterosexual couple, many same-sex couples nevertheless enjoy relationships of comparable quality and duration, and rear children who are equally well adjusted (Herek, 2006; Kurdek, 2004; Patterson, 2000, Chapter 16, this volume). Although, according to an analysis based on 2000 Census date, only 27% of same-sex couples have children under 18 living at home, compared to 43% of opposite-sex couples (Patterson & Riskind, 2010), these parents may have spent more time weighing the decision to become a parent and may have invested considerably more time in achieving this goal. This reflects the obvious difficulties entailed in becoming a gay parent, as well as the greater planning required to protect children from stigma and discrimination (deBoer, 2009; Patterson, 2000). Aspiring gay and lesbian parents with the requisite resources may also be more likely to adopt infants or children across racial lines (Farr & Patterson, 2009). Finally, with respect to extended family relationships, lesbian couples may be more integrated into the families of their spouses/partners at midlife compared to their heterosexual counterparts (Weinstock, 2000).

In addition to the challenges and rewards of relationships, family, and work life, middle adulthood provides opportunities for psychological and spiritual growth and maturation, for heterosexual and nonheterosexual persons alike (Kertzner, 2001a, 2001b; Kimmel & Sang, 1995). For many lesbians and gay men, middle adulthood is a time for moving beyond the sexual identity concerns of early adulthood and "integrating...sexual orientation into broader developmental themes" (Kimmel & Sang, 1995, p. 192). As is also the case for heterosexuals, middle adulthood can bring greater self-acceptance, appreciation for diversity, perspective, wisdom, relational skill, and cognitive flexibility (Hall & Gregory, 1991; Kertzner, 2001a, 2001b; Kimmel & Sang, 1995; Sang, 1993). At the same time, the experiences described above—navigating roles and relationships in the absence of well-defined norms, figuring out how to protect your child from homophobic bullying, and coping with the potential for and reality of prejudice—may present both formidable barriers and unique opportunities for psychological growth.

The simultaneous challenges and opportunities confronted by middle-aged lesbians and gay men are perhaps best illustrated by their experiences of generativity—the traditional Eriksonian midlife task. For lesbian, gay, and heterosexual parents, alike, generativity needs are at least partially fulfilled in the context of the parental role. For gay men and lesbian women who encounter "developmental delay," who do not parent, and/or who have limited access to mentoring roles, the achievement of generativity is not so straightforward (Cohler et al., 1998; Cornett & Hudson, 1987; Hostetler, 2009a). But even for gay and lesbian parents, their life histories and specific parental experiences of social injustice may make them ponder, more than the average white, middle-class, heterosexual parent, if true generativity demands something more. Indeed, the most important questions about sexual identity and middle adulthood may have to do with the "legacy of individual lives for future generations and the role of the self in the world" (Kertzner, 2001b, p. 88).

On this point, King and colleagues (2009) identified an important gay and lesbian contribution in their exploration of gay maturity and the meaning of the "good life." They claimed that coming out represents a rare intersection of *hedonic* and *eudaimonic* aspects of well-being (e.g., happiness

and authenticity/realization of potential) (Ryan & Deci, 2001). Certainly, being true to oneself and leading an authentic life can provide a positive example for others. However, generativity—which many would argue is an essential ingredient of the good life—requires broader forms of social engagement. Unfortunately, current visions of the "good life" do not necessarily inspire thought or action beyond self-interest. Even scholarship on the so-called "third age" of the healthy postretirement years reflects a growing emphasis on individual lifestyles and leisure pursuits (i.e., consumption) and other activities that are meaningful to the individual without necessarily being socially beneficial (e.g., Rubinstein, 2002). Lesbian and particularly gay male communities have not been immune to these trends, which threaten to produce more self-absorption and less compassion, undermining a sense of collective purpose (Hostetler, 2009a).

At the same time, the distinctive lived experiences and life stories of lesbian and gay people could inspire new narratives of middle adulthood at a time when the second half of life is undergoing major transformations. To begin with, lesbian, gay, bisexual, and transgender identities overlap with the full range of cultural, ethnic, and other identities. The sociopolitical commitments of lesbians and gay men, many of whom grew up as outsiders even in their own families, have made important contributions to a moral discourse of diversity and mutual acceptance in an increasingly global society (e.g., Adelman, 2000). Although early developmental challenges complicate the course of lesbian and gay development in many ways, some evidence suggests that successfully confronting these challenges can pay dividends starting in middle adulthood. For example, the increased autonomy and assertiveness observed among recent cohorts of heterosexual women at midlife may not be characteristic of middle-aged lesbians, who may embrace a broader understanding of gender roles at an earlier age (Adelman, 2000; Sang, 1990). Similarly, some evidence indicates that middle-aged gay men and lesbians are more securely attached in their relationships, on average, than heterosexual male counterparts—a potential benefit of the coming out process (Roisman, Clausell, Holland, Fortuna, & Elieff, 2008). Accordingly, gay men and women, or at least those who have consolidated their identities, could actually be somewhat more likely than heterosexual counterparts to explore broad moral and existential concerns in middle adulthood. In the final section, I explore the possibilities for new, hopefully more generative narratives—stories of "surpassing" (Plummer, 1995) in a broader sense—in middle adulthood and beyond.

CONCLUSIONS

The present chapter has focused on the diverse, shifting stories that provide a sense of meaning and purpose to middle-aged lesbian, gay, bisexual, and transgender adults. I have drawn particular attention to the unexpected or eruptive life experiences that are major catalysts for adults' meaning-making efforts, while also acknowledging that even expectable transitions and changes are culturally "underscripted," particularly in mid- and later-life. The idea that gay and lesbian lives are relatively uncharted presumes that heterosexual lives are fully scripted. However, the continuing popularity of the midlife crisis narrative should dispel any notion that the search for meaning or the need for storytelling in middle adulthood is unique to sexual minority individuals.

In their classic ethnography of lesbian, gay, and bisexual youth in Chicago, Herdt and Boxer (1996) found that nonheterosexual adolescents were not able to project themselves as far into the future as were their heterosexual peers. This finding would seem to support the "uncharted" theory until we consider that heterosexual adolescents were able to project themselves only to an average age of 55, with the advent of grandparenthood; the full list of developmental events was relatively sparse even in the accounts of heterosexual youth. Moreover, despite the lack of universal same-sex marriage rights, sexual-minority individuals are not alone in their struggles to construct narratives of intimacy beyond "happily ever after" (Berlant, 2008). Indeed, given that maturational and cultural milestones in adulthood are few and far between, development is widely understood to be meaning-focused following adolescence, particularly in the second half of life. Combined with shifting time perspectives and changing experiences of the body as we age into our 30s and 40s, it seems pretty clear that the transition to middle adulthood may be unique in its potential to stimulate self-reflection and revision of life narratives.

Moreover, the barriers to a more generative future addressed above do not, of course, just affect members of sexual minorities. Indeed, the many global problems we are confronting—climate change, the undue influence of multinational corporations, continuing famine, disease, conflict, and oppression—essentially amount to a collective crisis of generativity. Can we find the will, as a global community, to combat social injustice and achieve a better, more sustainable way of life for future generations? This is precisely the kind of question that is supposed to propel development in middle adulthood. Unfortunately, dominant cultural narratives about life in middle and late adulthood increasingly seem to emphasize consumption, individual lifestyle choices, and the preservation of youthfulness (Biggs et al., 2007; Cardona, 2008; Gilleard & Higgs, 2007). These stories, which shape self-understandings regardless of sexual orientation, do not seem to provide a solid basis for either human growth or cultural progress. Fortunately, other stories are also emerging, stories that will hopefully be embraced by both current and future generations of middle-aged adults.

New narratives about the life course emerge when lived realities do not match expectations and when experience literally does not make sense. These new narratives open up new options and ways of being in the world. For lesbian, gay, bisexual, and transgender people, stories have been engines of change. After all, coming out narratives made Gay Liberation possible (and vice versa). Similarly, "queer" stories about diversity, discontinuity, and the perils of sexual categorization have contributed significantly to our understanding of how cultures and individuals shape each other, even if these stories are not always clear about how and to what end cultures should be transformed.

As lesbians and gay men are integrated in the fabric of life in the modern Western world (and beyond), their voices are contributing to an emerging discourse of global social justice and mutual care. Lesbian, gay, bisexual, and transgender people have acquired valuable skills for building families and communities in the absence of biological kinship and across multiple forms of difference, and for providing care to individuals (e.g., persons with HIV/AIDS) who might otherwise be neglected (e.g., Fredriksen-Goldsen, 2005). Although the second half of life remains relatively unscripted, lesbian, gay, bisexual, and transgender people—by virtue of their experiences of living, growing, and thriving somewhat outside the flow of normative developmental time—can play an important role in the creation of new cultural scripts. Hopefully, these will be stories of compassion, community, and cross-cultural and intergenerational solidarity.

REFERENCES

Adelman, M. R. (2000). Preface. In M. R. Adelman (Ed.), *Midlife lesbian relationships: Friends, lovers, children, and parents* (pp. xiii–xvii). Binghamton, NY: Harrington Park Press.

Allegretto, S. A., & Arthur, M. M. (2001). An empirical analysis of heterosexual/homosexual male earnings differentials: Unmarried and unequal? *Industrial and Labor Relations Review*, 54, 631–646.

Ash, M. A., & Badgett, M. V. L. (2006). Separate and unequal: The effect of unequal access to employment. *Contemporary Economic Policy*, 24, 582–599.

Badgett, M. V. L. (1995). The wage effects of sexual orientation discrimination. *Industrial and Labor Relations Review*, 48, 726–739.

Badgett, M. V. L. (1996). Employment and sexual orientation: Disclosure and discrimination in the workplace. *Journal of Gay & Lesbian Social Services*, 4(4), 29–52

Badgett, M. V. L. (1997) Review: The corporate closet: The professional lives of gay men in America. *Feminist Studies*, 23(3), 607–632.

Balsam, K., Beauchaine, T., Rothblum, E., & Solomon, S. (2008). Three-year follow-up of same-sex couples who had civil unions in Vermont, same-sex couples not in civil unions, and heterosexual married couples. *Developmental Psychology*, 44, 102–116.

Belluck, P. (2008). Gay couples find marriage is a mixed bag. *New York Times* (6/15/08).

Bennett, K. C., & Thompson, N. L. (1990). Accelerated aging and male homosexuality: Australian evidence in a continuing debate. *Journal of Homosexuality*, 20, 65–75.

Berlant, L. (2008). *The female complaint: The unfinished business of sentimentality in American culture*. Durham, NC: Duke University Press.

Biggs, S., Phillipson, C., Leach, R., & Money, A.-M. (2007). The mature imagination and consumption strategies. *International Journal of Ageing and Later Life*, 2, 31–59.

Borden, W. (1989). Life review as a therapeutic frame in the treatment of young adults with AIDS. *Health and Social Work*, 14, 253–259.

Bradford, J., & Ryan, C. (1991). Who we are: Health concerns of middle-age lesbians. In B. Sang, J. Warshow, & A. Smith (Eds.), *Lesbians at midlife: The creative transition* (pp. 147–163). San Francisco: Spinsters Ink.

Bronfenbrenner, U. (1979). *The ecology of human development: Experiments by nature and design*. Cambridge, MA: Harvard University Press.

Bruner, J. (1990). *Acts of meaning*. Cambridge, MA: Harvard University Press.

Cardona, B. (2008). "Health ageing" policies and anti-ageing ideologies and practices: On the exercise of responsibility. *Medicine, Health Care, and Philosophy*, 11, 475–483.

Carrington, C. (1999). *No place like home: Relationships and family among lesbians and gay men*. Chicago: University of Chicago Press.

Clausen, J. (1993). *American lives: Looking back at the children of the Great Depression*. New York: Free Press.

Cohler, B. J. (1982). Personal narrative and life course. In P. Baltes & O. G. Brim, Jr. (Eds.), *Life-span development and behavior* (Vol. 4, pp. 205–241). New York: Academic Press.

Cohler, B. J., Hostetler, A. J., & Boxer, A. (1998). Generativity, social context, and lived experience: Narratives of gay men in middle adulthood. In D. McAdams & E. de St. Aubin (Eds.), *Generativity and adult development: How and why we care for the next generation* (pp. 265–309). Washington, DC: American Psychological Association Press.

Cornett, C. W., & Hudson, R. A. (1987). Middle adulthood and the theories of Erikson, Gould, and Vaillant: Where does the gay man fit? *Journal of Gerontological Social Work*, 10, 61–73.

D'Augelli, A. R., & Grossman, A. H. (2001). Disclosure of sexual orientation, victimization, and mental health among lesbian, gay, and bisexual older adults. *Journal of Interpersonal Violence*, 16, 1008–1027.

Daskalos, C. (1998). Changes in the sexual orientation of six heterosexual male-to-female transsexuals. *Archives of Sexual Behavior*, 27, 605–614.

deBoer, D. (2009). Focus on the family: The psychosocial context of gay men choosing fatherhood. In P. Hammack & B. J. Cohler (Eds.), *The story of sexual identity: Narrative perspectives on the gay and lesbian life course* (pp. 327–346). New York: Oxford University Press.

Diamond, L. M. (2008). Female bisexuality from adolescence to adulthood: Results from a 10-year longitudinal study. *Developmental Psychology*, 44, 5–14.

Donaldson, C. (2000). Midlife lesbian parenting. In M. R. Adelman (Ed.), *Midlife lesbian relationships: Friends, lovers, children, and parents* (pp. 119–138). Binghamton, NY: Harrington Park Press.

Edwards, D., & Potter, J. (1992). *Discursive psychology*. Newbury Park, CA: Sage.

Elder, G. H., Jr. (1998). The life course as developmental theory. *Child Development*, 69, 1–12.

Erikson, E. H. (1963). *Childhood and society* (revised edition). New York: Norton.

Farr, R. H., & Patterson, C. J. (2009). Transracial adoption by lesbian, gay, and heterosexual couples: Who completes transracial adoptions, and with what results? *Adoption Quarterly*, 12, 187–204.

Fredriksen-Goldsen, K. I. (2005). HIV/AIDS caregiving: Predictors of well-being and distress. *Journal of Gay & Lesbian Social Services, 18*, 53–73. doi:10.1300/J041v18n03–04.

Friend, R. A. (1980). GAYging: Adjustment and the older gay male. *Alternative Lifestyles, 3*, 213–248.

Friend, R. A. (1987). The individual and the social psychology of aging: Clinical implications for lesbians and gay men. *Journal of Homosexuality, 14*(1/2), 307–331.

Fullmer, E. M., Shenk, D., & Eastland, L. J. (1999). Negating identity: A feminist analysis of the social invisibility of older lesbians. *Journal of Women & Aging, 11*, 131–148.

Gilleard, C., & Higgs, P. (2007). The third age and the baby boomers: Two approaches to the social structuring of late life. *International Journal of Ageing and Later Life, 2*, 13–30.

Hall, M., & Gregory, A. (1991). Subtle balances: Love and work in lesbian relationships. In B. Sang, J. Warshow, & A. Smith (Eds.), *Lesbians at midlife: The creative transition* (pp. 122–133). San Francisco: Spinsters Ink.

Hennen, P. (2005). Bear bodies, bear masculinity: Recuperation, resistance, or retreat? *Gender & Society, 19*, 25–43.

Herdt, G. (1997). *Same sex, different cultures: Exploring gay and lesbian lives.* Boulder, CO: Westview Press.

Herdt, G., & Boxer, A. (1996). *Children of Horizons: How gay and lesbian teens are leading a new way out of the closet* (revised edition). Boston: Beacon Press.

Herek, G. M. (2006). Legal recognition of same-sex relationships: A social science perspective. *American Psychologist, 61*, 607–621.

Herek, G. M., & Garnetts, L. D. (2007). Sexual orientation and mental health. *Annual Review of Clinical Psychology, 3*, 353–375.

Hostetler, A. J. (2004). Old, gay and alone? The ecology of well-being among middle-aged and older single gay men. In G. Herdt & B. deVries (Eds.), *Gay and lesbian aging: A research agenda for the 21st Century* (pp. 143–176). New York: Springer.

Hostetler, A. J. (2009a). Generativity and time in gay men's life stories. In P. Hammack & B. J. Cohler (Eds.), *The story of sexual identity: Narrative perspectives on the gay and lesbian life course* (pp. 397–424). New York: Oxford University Press.

Hostetler, A. J. (2009b). Homosexuality and bisexuality: Cultural and historical perspectives. In R. A. Shweder, T. R. Bidell, A. C. Dailey, S. D. Dixon, P. J. Miller, & J. Modell (Eds.), *The child: An encyclopedic companion* (pp. 460–462). Chicago: University of Chicago Press.

Hostetler, A. J. (2009c). Single by choice? Assessing and understanding voluntary singlehood among mature gay men. *Journal of Homosexuality, 56*, 499–531.

Hostetler, A. J. (2012). Singlehood and subjective well-being among mature gay men: The impact of family, friends, and of being "single by choice." *Journal of GLBT Family Studies, 8*(4) (in press).

Hostetler, A. J., & Herdt, G. (1998). Culture, sexual lifeways and developmental subjectivities: Rethinking sexual taxonomies. *Social Research, 65*, 249–290.

Institute of Medicine. (2011). *The health of lesbian, gay, bisexual, and transgender people: Building a foundation for better understanding.* Washington, DC: The National Academies Press.

Jaques, E. (1965). Death and the mid-life crisis. *International Journal of Psychoanalysis, 46*, 502–514.

Joslin-Roher, E., & Wheeler, D. (2009). Partners in transition: The transition experience of lesbian, bisexual, and queer identified partners of transgender men. *Journal of Gay & Lesbian Social Services, 21*, 30–48.

Kaminski, E. (2000). Lesbian health: Social context, sexual identity, and well-being. *Journal of Lesbian Studies, 4*, 87–101.

Kelly, J. J. (1977). The aging male homosexual: Myth & reality. *The Gerontologist, 17*, 328–332.

Kertzner, R. M. (2001a). The adult life course and homosexual identity in midlife gay men. *Annual Review of Sex Research, 12*, 75–92.

Kertzner, R. M. (2001b). Book review: *Golden men: The power of gay midlife* (H. Kooden & C. Flowers). *Journal of Gay & Lesbian Psychotherapy, 5*, 99–102.

Kimmel, D. C. (1979). Life history interviews of aging gay men. *International Journal of Aging and Human Development, 10*, 239–248.

Kimmel, D. C. (1992). The families of older gay men and lesbians. *Generations, 17*, 37–38.

Kimmel, D. C. (1993). Adult development and aging: A gay perspective. In L. D. Garnets & D. C. Kimmel (Eds.), *Psychological perspectives on lesbian and gay male experiences* (pp. 517–534). New York: Columbia University Press.

Kimmel, D. C., & Sang, B. E. (1995). Lesbians and gay men in midlife. In A. R. D'Augelli & C. J. Patterson (Eds.), *Lesbian, gay, and bisexual identities over the lifespan* (pp. 190–214). New York: Oxford University Press.

King, L. A., Burton, C. M., & Geise, A. C. (2009). The good (gay) life: The search for signs of maturity in the narratives of gay adults. In P. Hammack & B. J. Cohler (Eds.), *The story of sexual identity: Narrative perspectives on the gay and lesbian life course* (pp. 375–396). New York: Oxford University Press.

King, L. A., & Smith, N. G. (2004). Gay and straight possible selves: Goals, identity, subjective well-being, and personality development. *Journal of Personality, 72*, 967–994.

Kitzinger, C., & Wilkinson, S. (1995). Transitions from heterosexuality to lesbianism: The discursive production of lesbian identities. *Developmental Psychology, 31*, 95–104.

Kurdek, L. A. (1995). Lesbian and gay couples. In. A. R. D'Augelli & C. J. Patterson (Eds.), *Lesbian, gay and* bisexual identities over the lifespan: Psychological perspectives (pp. 243–261). New York: Oxford University Press.

Kurdek, L. A. (2004). Are gay and lesbian cohabiting couples really different from heterosexual couples? Journal of Marriage and Family, 66, 880–900.

Levinson, D. J. (1978). The seasons of a man's life. New York: Alfred Knopf.

Levinson, D. J. (1996). The seasons of a woman's life. New York: Alfred Knopf.

Lippa, R. A. (2006). Is high sex drive associated with increased sexual attraction to both sexes? It depends on whether you are male or female. Psychological Science, 17, 46–52.

Mannheim, K. (1928). The problem of generations. In K. Mannheim (Ed.), Essays on the sociology of knowledge (pp. 276–322). London: Routledge & Kegan Paul.

McAdams, D. (1993). The stories we live by: Personal myths and the making of the self. New York: W. Morrow.

Mitchell, V. (2000). The bloom is on the rose: The impact of midlife on the lesbian couple. In M. R. Adelman (Ed.), Midlife lesbian relationships: Friends, lovers, children, and parents (pp. 33–48). Binghamton, NY: Harrington Park Press.

Moen, P., & Wethington, E. (1999). Midlife development in a life course context. In S. L. Willis & J. D. Reid (Eds.), Life in the middle: Psychological and social development in middle age (pp. 3–23). San Diego: Academic Press.

Nardi, P. M. (1999). Gay men's friendships: Invincible communities. Chicago: University of Chicago Press.

Neugarten, B. L. (1964). Summary and implications. In B. L. Neugarten (Ed.), Personality in middle and later life: Empirical studies (pp. 188–200). New York: Atherton.

Neugarten, B. (1968). The awareness of middle age. In B. Neugarten (Ed.), Middle age and aging (pp. 93–98). Chicago: University of Chicago Press.

Patterson, C. J. (2000). Family relationships of lesbians and gay men. Journal of Marriage & the Family, 62, 1052–1069.

Patterson, C. J. (2008). Sexual orientation across the life span: Introduction to the special section. Developmental Psychology, 44, 1–4.

Patterson, C. J., & Riskind, R. G. (2010). To be a parent: Issues in family formation among gay and lesbian adults. Journal of GLBT Family Studies, 6, 326–340. doi:10.1080/1550428X.2010.490902.

Phillips, L. (2005). Deconstructing "down low" discourse: The politics of sexuality, gender, race, AIDS, and anxiety. Journal of African American Studies, 9, 3–15.

Plummer, K. (1995). Telling sexual stories: Power, change and social worlds. New York: Routledge.

Roisman, G. I., Clausell, E., Holland, A., Fortuna, K., & Elieff, C. (2008). Adult romantic relationships as contexts of human development: A multimethod comparison of same-sex couples with opposite-sex dating, engaged, and married dyads. Developmental Psychology, 44, 91–101. doi:10.1037/0012–1649.44.1.91.

Rose, S. (1996). Lesbian and gay love scripts. In E. D. Rothblum & L. A. Bond (Eds.), Preventing heterosexism and homophobia (pp. 151–173). Thousand Oaks, CA: Sage.

Rose, S., & Zand, D. (2000). Lesbian dating and courtship from young adulthood to midlife. In M. R. Adelman (Ed.), Midlife lesbian relationships: Friends, lovers, children, and parents (pp. 77–104). Binghamton, NY: Harrington Park Press.

Rothblum, E. D., Mintz, B., Cowan, D. B., & Haller, C. (1995). Lesbian baby boomers at midlife. In K. Jay (Ed.), Dyke life: From growing up to growing old, a celebration of the lesbian experience (pp. 61–76). New York: Basic Books.

Rubinstein, R. L. (2002). The third age. In R. S. Weiss & S. A. Bass (Eds.), Challenges of the third age: Meaning and purpose in later life (pp. 29–40). New York: Oxford University Press.

Rust, P. C. R. (2002). Bisexuality: The state of the union. Annual Review of Sex Research, 13, 180–240.

Ryan, R. M., & Deci, E. I. (2001). On happiness and human potentials: A review of research on hedonic and eudaimonic well-being. Annual Review of Psychology, 52, 141–166.

Sang, B. E. (1990). Reflections of midlife lesbians on their adolescence. Journal of Women & Aging, 2, 111–117.

Sang, B. E. (1993). Existential issues of midlife lesbians. In L. D. Garnets & D. C. Kimmel (Eds.), Psychological perspectives on lesbian and gay male experiences (pp. 500–516). New York: Columbia University Press.

Sarbin, T. (Ed.) (1986). Narrative psychology: The storied nature of human conduct. New York: Praeger and Greenwood Press.

Savin-Williams, R. C. (2005). The new gay teenager. Cambridge, MA: Harvard University Press.

Sheehy, G. (1976). Passages: Predictable crises of adult life. New York: Dutton.

Siegel, S., & Lowe, E. (1994). Uncharted lives: Understanding the life passages of gay men. New York: Dutton.

Tully, C. (1989). Caregiving: What do midlife lesbians view as important? Journal of Gay & Lesbian Psychotherapy, 1, 87–103.

Warner, M. (1999). The trouble with normal: Sex, politics, and the ethics of queer life. Cambridge, MA: Harvard University Press.

Wayment, H., & Peplau, L. A. (1995). Social support and well-being among lesbian and heterosexual women: A structural modeling approach. Personality and Social Psychology Bulletin, 21, 1189–1199.

Weeks, J. (1985). Sexuality and its discontents: Meanings, myths, and modern sexualities. Boston: Routledge & Kegan Paul.

Weinstock, J. S. (2000). Lesbian friendships at midlife: Patterns and possibilities for the 21st Century. In M. R. Adelman (Ed.), *Midlife lesbian relationships: Friends, lovers, children, and parents* (pp. 1–32). Binghamton, NY: Harrington Park Press.

Weston, K. (1991). *Families we choose: Lesbians, gays, kinship*. New York: Columbia University Press.

Wethington, E. (2000). Expecting stress: Americans and the "midlife crisis." *Motivation and Emotion, 24*, 85–103.

Whitten, T. M. (2003). Life course analysis—the courage to search for something more: Middle adulthood issues in the transgender and intersex community. *Journal of Human Behavior in the Social Environment, 8*, 189–224.

10

Sexual Orientation and Aging in Western Society

ARNOLD H. GROSSMAN, JOHN A. FRANK, AND
MICHAEL J. MCCUTCHEON

Human development among all people is plastic, multidimensional, and reflects their specific cultural contexts (Bronfenbrenner, 1979; Lerner, 1984); this is most evident among lesbian, gay, and bisexual (LGB) older adults who have witnessed the meaning of homosexuality and the stigma toward sexual orientation (i.e., same-sex attraction, identity, and behavior) change during their lifetimes. For example, LGB older adults have experienced major changes such as the removal of the diagnosis "homosexuality" from the psychiatric nomenclature so that it is no longer considered a "mental disorder" (Bayer, 1981), the legalization of same-sex marriage in six states and the District of Columbia in the United States and in 10 countries worldwide (CNS News, 2011; The Task Force; 2011), and the 2003 U.S. Supreme Court decision (*Lawrence* et al. v. *Texas*) that rendered consensual same-sex behavior no longer illegal in the United States (Barsky, 2009). Consequently, in examining the lives of LGB older adults, it is imperative to consider "cohort effects," i.e., those individuals born in the same time interval and aging together, having unique experiences during their youth when basic values, societal attitudes, and beliefs are established (Alwin, 2002; Ryder, 1965), as well as "period effects," such as shifts in attitudes of society across cohorts (Cherlin, 1992), which affect the individual. Martin and D'Augelli (2009) concluded that "cohort and period effects on changing attitudes, behaviors, or identities among LGBT people have hardly been examined in quantitative research" (p. 196); this observation is particularly accurate for research focusing on lesbian, gay, bisexual, and transgender (LGBT) older adults. Therefore, it is important to be aware that much research on the psychology of sexual orientation and LGB aging adults may have falsely homogenized participants'

life trajectories. Within this framework, the purpose of this chapter is to inform readers of the developmental issues related to the psychology of sexual orientation and aging in Western society. Although it is important to recognize the diversity of LGB experiences with regard to ethnicity, race, religion, and socioeconomic status, it is also vital to understand the developmental experiences across diversity groupings that are shared by members of minority groups based on their sexual minority status.

Among the individual characteristics valued in Western society are those of being young, attractive, and heterosexual (Grossman, 2000); therefore, being an LGB older adult means that you are a member of at least two minority groups. Being a member of any minority group frequently leads to marginalization, isolation, and discrimination. Having the combined minority group status of being both a sexual minority and an older adult communicates to aging LGB people that they are not a part of mainstream society. As a result of these societal messages, LGB elders experience oppression and disempowerment that threatens their physical and mental health and social well-being (DiPlacido, 1998). Furthermore, the minority statuses impose enormous adaptive tasks on developmental trajectories (Mallon, 1999). Although sexual minority stigma had been the focus of attention for most of their lives, that stigma is now combined with the stigma associated with aging. These two statuses tend to overshadow their other social identities such as being professionals, spouses/partners, parents/grandparents, extended family members, and friends (Grossman, 2000).

Although not all researchers discuss the contextual frameworks in which the LGB older participants lived when the studies were conducted, it should be recognized that most (if not all) of the research participants lived their early developmental years (approximately 40 years) at a time when "homosexuality" was classified as a mental illness and when same-sex sexual behavior was unlawful in all 50 of the United States. Therefore, when today's LGB older adults living in the United States discovered their same-sex attractions, they also realized that their identities were considered pathological and their behaviors illegal; these were the realities for approximately the first 30 years of their lives (assuming their same-sex attractions occurred during their adolescent years). They grew up with strong admonishments that being LGB was undesirable and immoral (Grossman, 2000). These views remained largely unchallenged until the 1969 Stonewall Riots (i.e., street demonstrations that occurred after police raided the Stonewall Inn, a gay bar in New York City's Greenwich Village), which marked the beginning of the modern LGBT civil rights movement (Harris, 1981). This event occurred when today's LGB older adults were approximately 35 years of age or older.

Findings from research have indicated that many LGB people experienced cognitive dissonance when they realized they were nonheterosexual and that recognition led to their experiencing "minority stress" (DiPlacido, 1998; Meyer, 1995). Studies have linked minority stress to mental health problems, emotional distress, and depressive mood symptoms among gay and bisexual men, and excessive cigarette smoking, heavy alcohol consumption, excessive weight, and high-risk sexual behaviors among lesbian and bisexual women. However, there is also evidence indicating that some LGB individuals cope successfully with minority stress (DiPlacido, 1998; Meyer, 1995). Social support and personality characteristics such as hardiness and high self-esteem have been found to moderate the negative effects of stress (DiPlacido, 1998; Grossman, D'Augelli, & Hershberger, 2000). Witten and Eyler (2012) reminded us that many in the current cohort of LGBT older adults overcame the difficulties of invalidating, threatening, and persecuting social environments; they achieved the wisdom that accompanies trials successfully faced and challenges mastered to live their final years with dignity and grace.

In summary, a major cultural shift in Western society occurred during the lives of today's LGB older adults as same-sex sexual identities have become more accepted. For example, the results of a Gallup poll conducted in the United States in May 2007 (Saad, 2007) indicated that less than half (49%) of the respondents thought that homosexual behavior was morally wrong, whereas more than half (57%) thought that homosexuality was an acceptable lifestyle—with smaller percentages of older people, 45% (55+ years), than younger people, 75% (18–34 years), agreeing. Therefore, today's younger people reported being more accepting of sexual minority lifestyles than their older counterparts.

Although there has been a cultural shift, including decreased stigma associated with being LGB, many LGB older adults still do not disclose their sexual orientation. Some of the invisibility results from societal ageism and concurrent stereotypes of older people that exist in many LGB communities; however, its main outcome results from a decision made by many LGB people to cope with societal stigma by remaining out of sight. They managed the stigmas associated with their sexual orientations by choosing to reside, work, and play in subcultures that provided them with support and protected them from the negative stereotypes (Barret, 1998). Although the strategy may have succeeded in protecting them from experiencing verbal and physical victimization, it also enhanced their invisibility. As a consequence, many mental health and other service providers and researchers do not realize that older LGB persons exist. When older people identify themselves as LGB, they are either regarded as people whose existences are atypical or their identities tend to be ignored. Among those who recognize LGB older adults, is that they are asexual and not interested in dating or romantic partners (Greene, 2000). Overall, the scenarios of invisibility and of misconceptions about LGB older adults lead to significant outcomes, including myths about them, inadequate services for them, and insufficient inclusion in studies by gerontologists. Consequentially, early studies were designed to address these shortcomings.

EARLY STUDIES, PRE-2000

Early studies of LGB older adults were motivated to generate data that would examine the myths about them as being lonely, unhappy, and "inverted" (Jacobson & Grossman, 1996; Wright & Canetto, 2009). However, they were limited by small, homogeneous samples. As the LGB older adult community was a hidden population, the participants in early studies were those who were most visible or who came forward as research participants for personal and social reasons. Using Friend's (1989, 1990) identity continuum as a reference, most of what we know about LGB older people describes those in the "Affirmative" group (i.e., men and women who challenged heterosexist ideology and reconstructed positive images and identities), but we know almost nothing about individuals on the continuum labeled "Passing" (i.e., accepted heterosexist discourse and being conditionally comfortable with their gay or lesbian identities) or "Stereotypic" (i.e., embraced and conformed to the traditional, negative myths commonly used in heterosexual society to describe older lesbians and gay men). Another limitation of these initial studies was that the findings frequently did not systematically include bisexual participants, who were small in number and most often were categorized with the male and female homosexual groups (Grossman, 2008).

Among the first studies was one conducted by Kelly (1977). The study included 261 gay men aged 16 to 79, 30 of whom were between the ages of 65 and 75. The men reported maintaining a satisfactory sex life and did not consider themselves as effeminate older people. The salient problems reported by the older men were similar to those of most older adults, i.e., stigmatization related to age, fear of institutionalization, and loss of people who were emotionally supportive as they aged. The data also revealed problems unique to older gay men, the most important of which were experiencing rules, laws, attitudes, and practices that were discriminatory because they were gay, as well as the lack of economic assistance and physical security, the absence of children to provide emotional support, and the inability of being visited by partners in hospitals and nursing homes. Additionally, discriminatory laws prevented them from their rightful inheritance of a life partner's assets and property.

One of the best known early studies was conducted by Berger (1982). A major limitation of the study is that it included any individual who self-identified as gay and was 40 years or older. Berger argued that there was "universal agreement" that a gay person of this age was no longer considered to be young. The age range of the 112 participants was 40 to 72; only 30% of the 112 people were over 60. Although the study did not include many older gay men, it aimed to refute assumed

psychological aspects of their lives, i.e., most men in the study did not feel lonely, unwanted, or isolated. They maintained their earlier level of sexual activity, but had fewer partners. They reported their self-acceptance was hard won and they had to be very self-reliant all of their lives; however, age brought them new freedom. Most of their friends were their own age; and about half of the participants believed that younger gay men were indifferent or hostile to them, but those who socialized with younger gay men had a better adjustment.

Vacha (1985), in his interviews of 17 gay men, also aimed to contradict the stereotype of sad and lonely older gay men; however, with the emphasis on youth in gay male culture, he also wondered how older gay men coped with aging. The main themes of his findings were (1) the importance of sex in all stages of a gay man's life, (2) the need to deny their homosexuality in their early lives, (3) the importance of required military service in either hastening or retarding the development of a healthy gay identity, (4) the frequent use of drugs and alcohol, (5) the difficulty in achieving a long-term relationship, and (6) harassment by their families and the police. In writing about this study, Cruikshank (1990) noted that Vacha did not comment about the high degree of internalized homophobia that was evident in the interviews as well as the unusually high incidence of physical illness. She also observed that the men lived in a world of "psychological danger" due to their emotional/sexual identities, including being rejected by their families and dismissed from their jobs, receiving dishonorable discharges from the military, and experiencing physical danger from random beatings and police brutality as well as assaults by the men brought home as casual sex partners.

In a study of older lesbians, Kehoe (1988) surveyed 100 women between the ages of 60 and 86 living in the United States. The women self-identified as lesbians and most of their friends were often younger lesbians; they met them at social gatherings or through other friends. Only 5% participated in a senior center program or used its services; and the majority expressed a preference for exclusively lesbian or lesbian/gay-only retirement communities, nursing homes, and/or social organizations. The majority reported being free of serious psychological problems, but loneliness was the one most often mentioned. More friends than family members were aware of their lesbianism. The majority of the women (58%) were never married to a man and 73% were childless. Forty-two percent were in a relationship with a woman; however, more than half (53%) had no physical/sexual encounters within the past year. Seventy-two percent reported good or excellent physical health and 82% reported good or excellent emotional health. The majority (60%) said they had a partner or friend who would take care of them if they were physically ill, and they would visit a mental health professional or physician for help with emotional problems. Seventy-five percent indicated that they did not drink alcohol, two-thirds did not smoke, and the majority exercised daily. Eighty-four percent felt positive about being lesbians, and approximately half felt the same about aging. However, 34% reported experiencing age discrimination, most often in social situations with younger people.

Adleman (1991) reported that psychological adjustment to aging in a sample of 25 lesbians (mean age 64) and 27 gay men (mean age 65) was related to achieving a positive gay identity in the face of homophobia and discrimination. However, Adleman (1991) also noted the damaging effects of the negative attitudes on older lesbians who were forced to live with fear of disclosure and discovery from co-workers and family for extended periods of time. The data supported a prescribed sequence of developing a positive gay identity among the sample: i.e., awareness of same-sex attractions, sexual experimentation with members of the same sex, and self-identification as lesbian or gay. Additionally, Adleman (1991) found that high life-satisfaction was associated with having both gay/lesbian and heterosexual friendships.

Quam and Whitford (1992) reported on the adaptation and age-related expectations of 80 gay and lesbian adults (41 men and 39 women) over the age of 50. Being active in the gay and lesbian community and describing their sexual identity were identified as assets in accepting their own aging and in developing positive coping skills. Approximately two-thirds of the participants (64%) reported that they attended or participated in gay/lesbian social groups; but only 8.8% reported going to a general senior club or center. Over 50% of the women reported that their closest friends were lesbians, whereas approximately 25% of the men reported that most of their friends were gay men.

A study that included homosexual participants was reported by Dorfman and her colleagues (1995). The sample consisted of 108 people (55 women and 53 men) between the ages of 60 and 93 years (mean = 69.3), of whom 56 were homosexual (23 women and 33 men) and 52 were heterosexual (32 women and 20 men). The researchers found no significant differences regarding depression and social support between the homosexual and heterosexual participants, and lower depression was associated with larger social networks. The homosexual people reported significantly more support from friends, whereas heterosexual people derived more social support from families of origin.

Similar findings were reported by Beeler, Rawls, Herdt, and Cohler (1999). They found that a large percentage (89%) of the 160 participants (i.e., 49 gay men and 51 lesbians, 45–90 years) indicated that they could turn to at least three friends for advice and emotional support if they were facing "a serious problem," and 60% indicated that they had six or more such friends. Approximately two-thirds of the participants (68%) identified a "family of choice" with whom they socialized on holidays. Beeler et al. (1999) derived three primary implications regarding planning and providing services for older gay men and lesbians. First, they indicated that there was a need to recognize diversity among the gay and lesbian population, e.g., people who were single, partnered, with children, and who were transitioning from a heterosexual lifestyle into the gay and lesbian community. Second, it was important to consider the social context in which services were provided, e.g., community organizations catering to young white gay men will have difficulty in recruiting older lesbians and people of color. Third, a community organizing approach offered more promise in meeting the needs of the older gay men and lesbians than one providing specific services, as it will involve older gay men and lesbians to identify, plan, and implement services that most meet their needs.

The results of a study of 71 participants (54 men and 17 women), ages 50–80 years (mean = 60.8), who self-identified as gay men, lesbians, and bisexuals, were reported by Jacobs, Rasmussen, and Hohman (1999). The authors concluded that social support services for the LGB older populations are optimally provided in LGB environments. Among their pertinent findings were that the LGB participants used social and support groups in the LGB community and that LGB community services were rated significantly more adequate in meeting their needs in times of emotional crises than non-LGB services. Additionally, it was found that both men and women were interested in participating in social groups that were segregated by gender.

The early studies tended to focus on the positive psychosexual adjustment of LGB older adults, on the social contexts of the lives, and on combating stereotypes. They focused on examining sources of social support, friendship families, LGB social groups, and LGB communities. Later studies, reported on in the next section, tend to focus on the mental health of LGB older adults, the effects of their disclosing their sexual orientation and becoming more visible, and their joining as couples, as well as reports of their support networks, their life trajectories, and the effects of victimization.

GROSSMAN, D'AUGELLI, AND O'CONNELL'S 2000–2001 STUDY

One of the recent research studies focused specifically on LGB older adults (ages 60 and older) was conducted by Grossman, D'Augelli, and O'Connell (2001). They surveyed 416 LGB older adults at 19 sites in North America, aged 60 to 91, about their physical and mental health as well as other aspects of their individual and social contexts. (For descriptions of sites, assessments, and procedures see D'Augelli, Grossman, Hershberger, & O'Connell, 2001; Grossman, D'Augelli, & O'Connell, 2001; and Grossman, D'Augelli, & Hershberger, 2000.) Of the 416 participants, 297 (71%) identified as male and 119 (29%) as female, and a large majority identified as lesbian or gay (92%) and 8% as bisexual (25 males and 9 females). One-third (32%) of the participants were parents. One-half of the participants (47% of the males and 50% females) had a current same-sex partner (no opposite sex partners were reported), with relationships averaging 15.5 years (with no significant differences between male and female relationships with respect to longevity). Not all of those with partners resided with them; 63% reported living alone and 29% lived with a partner. Seventy-four percent of the participants were retired, 18% were working, 3% were receiving disability payments, and 5% were continuing to work despite being retired from other work. It is important to note that 59% of the participants had yearly incomes that were less than $35,000.

Seventy-five percent of the participants in the study by Grossman et al. (2001) described their

physical health as good to excellent, 21% said fair, and only 4% reported their physical health status to be poor or very poor. There was no apparent difference in physical health between men and women or between gay men/lesbians and bisexuals. However, individuals living with a partner reported significantly better physical health than those living alone; physical health was also related to household income, with those reporting better physical health having higher incomes. Additionally, individuals who experienced less lifetime victimization and identified more people in their social networks were found to report better physical health. Sixty percent of the older adults indicated that their physical health never or seldom stood in the way of doing the things they wanted to do, and 57% regularly participated in exercise activities (e.g., walking, hiking, jogging, biking, or swimming). As to their abilities to perform physical activities, 55% said that their ability had not changed in the past 5 years; however, 37% said it was somewhat or much worse and 8% said it was somewhat or much better. Thirty-six percent of the participants reported having a physical disability or handicap, and 16% of those indicated that they required an assistive device, e.g., cane.

Eighty-four percent of the participants indicated that their ability to think clearly and their concentration were good or excellent, and 68% said their cognitive functioning had not changed in the past 5 years. However, 20% indicated that their cognitive functioning had become worse, and 12% reported that their ability to think clearly had improved. Concurrent with their ability to think clearly and concentrate, 73% reported that their memory was good or excellent, but 29% indicated that their memory had become worse in the past 5 years. However, almost two-thirds (65%) said their memory had stayed the same in the previous 5-year period (D'Augelli, Grossman, Hershberger, & O'Connell, 2001).

Eighty-four percent of the participants in the Grossman et al. (2001) study reported that their mental health was good or excellent, whereas 14% said fair and 2% said poor. No differences were found between men and women or between gay men/lesbians and bisexuals; however, older adults living with a partner rated their mental health significantly more positively than those who lived alone. Eighty percent of the participants reported that they were "glad to be lesbian, gay, or bisexual,"

8% reported being depressed about their sexual orientation, and 9% said they had received counseling to stop their same-sex feelings at some point in their lives. Surprisingly, 17% said they wished they were heterosexual. Ten percent of the sample had sometimes or often considered suicide, and 4% had considered committing suicide in the past year. No differences were found in suicidal thoughts between those who currently lived alone and those who currently lived with a partner or between gay men/lesbians and bisexual people; in addition, of those who ever had thought of suicide, 29% said those thoughts were related to their sexual orientation, with men reporting significantly more suicidality related to their sexual orientation than women. Reporting on changes in their mental health status over the past 5 years, 33% reported that their mental health was currently better than it was 5 years ago, 54% said it had stayed the same, and 13% indicated that it had become worse. Eleven percent of the older adults described themselves as having a mental disability or illness, and mental health was significantly and positively related to household income, with those older adults reporting higher income having better mental health. However, a significant negative relationship was found between victimization and mental health, indicating that those older adults reporting more victimization also reported lower levels of mental health.

Grossman et al. (2001) reported that loneliness (UCLA Loneliness Scale; Hays & DiMatteo, 1987) was experienced by some LGB older adults. Feelings of isolation were reported by 13% of the participants, and 27% reported that they felt a lack of companionship. The participants who had higher incomes and more people in their social networks were found to be less lonely. No significant differences in loneliness were found either between men and women or between gay men/lesbians and bisexuals; in addition, those living with partners reported significantly less loneliness than those living alone. Most of the older LGB adults reported fairly high levels of self-esteem (Rosenberg Self-Esteem Scale; Rosenberg, 1965) and low levels of internalized homophobia (Revised Homosexuality Attitude Inventory; Shidlo, 1994), with men reporting significantly more negative attitudes toward homosexuality than women. Those living alone reported more internalized homophobia than those living with a partner. There was no difference in internalized homophobia between gay men/lesbians and bisexuals; however, those people with higher household incomes, more people in their support networks, and greater involvement in LGB organizations reported less internalized homophobia.

As reported on the Alcohol Use Disorders Identification Test (AUDIT) (Bohn, Babor, & Kranzler, 1995), only 38 (9%) of the participants in the study by Grossman et al. (2001) were classified as "problem drinkers." Men reported significantly more alcohol use than women, and more men could be classified as "problem drinkers." No significant involvement with drugs [i.e., drug use over the past 12 months (Drug Abuse Screening Test-DAST-10; Skinner, 1982)] was reported by any of the participants, with 83% of the older adults reporting no past evidence of drug use.

Analyses were conducted to compare the 260 older LGBT adults who lived alone (63% of the sample) with the 122 (29%) who lived with a partner on major study variables. Not surprising, those who lived with partners fared much better. They reported they were significantly less lonely and in significantly better physical and mental health. Partnered older LGB adults also reported more people in their support networks and proportionately more people in those networks who were aware of their sexual orientation; in addition, they were more satisfied with the support their networks provided (Grossman et al., 2000).

One of the important contributions of the Grossman et al. (2000) study was its investigation of the support networks of the participants. The networks of the 416 older adults were composed of 2612 individuals; the average network had 6.3 people. Close friends were the most frequently listed network members—with 90% of the participants listing at least one. Other significant categories of network members were partners (44%), other relatives (39%), siblings (33%), and social acquaintances (32%). Only 15% listed co-workers, 4% parents, and 3% husbands/wives (from previous heterosexual marriages). Network members' ages ranged from 15 to 94 (average age = 58); half (49%) were under 60 years; however, the participants were significantly older than their network members by an average of 10 years with no significant difference between men and women. Men's networks consisted of more gay/bisexual males (54%) than women's networks (10%), and women's networks consisted of more women (75%) than men (26%). Bisexual women's and men's networks contained significantly more heterosexual people when compared to those of lesbian and gay participants. Finally, women (lesbian and bisexual) listed significantly more people in their networks than did men. An average of six people in the networks "definitely knew" of the participants' sexual orientation, an average of two people "definitely or probably suspected," and an average of 2.5 people "did not know or suspect." The participants were more satisfied with the support they received from those who definitely knew of their sexual orientation than from those who suspected or were unaware of it. Also, they were "most" satisfied with the support given by their lovers/partners and "very" satisfied with the support from close friends or co-workers. Contrary to expectations, they were not significantly more satisfied with the support they received from people who were of the same sexual orientation or from people who were close to their ages. Also, the more satisfied the older LGB adults felt with the support they received, the less lonely they felt. Examining the types of support the LGB older adults received revealed that almost three-fourths (72%) reported general social support, almost two-thirds (62%) reported emotional support, and more than half (54%) reported practical support. Other types of support received were advice and guidance (41%), and financial help (13%) (Grossman, D'Augelli, & Hershberger, 2000).

The limitations of the study by Grossman et al. (2000, 2001) should be noted. Although it had a more heterogeneous sample than other studies of this population, its sample was not a random one. There was more variability in income and educational level of the participants in this study than in previous studies; also, most of the participants were predominately well-educated, racially white or of European descent, and middle class.

In the years following the study by Grossman et al. (2001), research has continued to progress and build on the existing findings about the LGB older adult population. The findings from the studies described above have been supported, expanded, and, in some cases, challenged. The following section on recent studies presents findings on the perceptions of aging among LGB individuals, the societal attitudes about older LGB people, the experiences with caregivers, financial resources, and the mental and physical health of this population.

RECENT STUDIES

In an effort to assess perceptions of aging among gay and lesbian individuals, Schope (2005) surveyed 74 gay men and 109 lesbians (average ages 34.4 and 39.9, respectively). Some of the major findings are as follows: *Gay and lesbian perceptions of aging*: (1) gay men felt gay society viewed growing older more negatively than lesbian society; among the gay men, almost 84% indicated that gay men view growing older negatively; (2) gay men were found to be significantly more negative than lesbians in their attitudes about growing older; approximately one-third of the gay men perceived their own aging in negative terms; and (3) gay male respondents believed that they turn old at a much earlier age (i.e., 38.8 years) than lesbian respondents (i.e., 48.4 years). *Ageism among gay and lesbian individuals*: (1) gay men are more ageist than lesbians and (2) both gay men and lesbians were fearful of aging. *Fear of negative evaluation*: (1) gay men were more fearful of negative evaluations of other gay men than lesbians were of other lesbians and (2) both younger gay men and lesbians tended to be more concerned with how society perceived them than were older gay men and lesbians.

"Still Out, Still Aging: The MetLife study of Lesbian, Gay, Bisexual, and Transgender Baby Boomers" (2010) provided findings from a survey of 1201 LGBT individuals aged 45–64. Half of the respondents had families that were supportive of their sexual orientations and 29% reported that they were not guarded about their sexual orientation with anyone. Although 74% acknowledged that being LGBT would prepare them in certain ways for aging (e.g., be more accepting of others, greater inner strength, greater self-reliance), 54% believed that their sexual orientation would also add to the challenges of growing old. "Still Out, Still Aging" (2010) also found that visibility among lesbian and gay elders may be increasing, but visibility among bisexual elders remains relatively low. Seventy-four percent of gay men and 76% of lesbians were "out," but only 16% of bisexual participants were.

Floyd and Bakeman (2006) explored the implications of age and the historical context in which LGB people were raised on their decision to disclose their sexual minority status and other "coming out" milestones. They recruited 767 participants aged 18–74 years old. Participants who self-identified as LGB during adolescence, as opposed to those who did not self-identify until adulthood, were more likely to report that self-identification preceded a first same-sex sexual encounter, whereas adult self-identifiers reported a same-sex sexual experience prior to self-identifying as LGB. More than 60% of those who self-identified during adolescence were from recent cohorts; they also reported younger ages of disclosure to parents and to someone other than a parent. Floyd and Bakeman (2006) argued that because of the abounding negative social attitudes many elderly LGB people experienced while growing up, their comfort with coming out and advocating for themselves and their specific needs was often mitigated. The current context of increasingly tolerant attitudes toward an LGB identity promotes experiencing of the "coming out" milestones at increasingly younger ages.

Although societal attitudes toward young people disclosing nonheterosexual identities may be shifting, the stereotypes of older lesbians and gay men appear to be relatively stable. A study of 394 college undergraduates (aged 18–28, mean age 18.71) compared stereotypes of older adult gay men and lesbians with stereotypes of older adult heterosexuals (Wright & Canetto, 2009). The respondents, nearly 98% of whom identified as heterosexual, overwhelmingly characterized older people, regardless of sexual orientation, as being "frail" and more "judicious" than younger people. They also attributed traditionally masculine traits and characteristics to older lesbians and feminine traits and characteristics to older gay men conforming to prevalent stereotypes. These findings suggest that young adults may be more understanding and tolerant of the LGB people in their same age cohort, but not necessarily of aging LGB persons.

Working to abate the invisibility of aging lesbians, Jones and Nystrom (2002) interviewed 62 lesbians (aged 55–95) about their life course experiences. The majority of women described coming out as a long process, reflecting the sociopolitical attitudes of the times in which they were coming of age. Overall, participants expressed great satisfaction with regard to their current daily lives and many reported having been associated with LGB community events or organizations. However, they also believed that the Gay Rights Movement, though a positive influence on the lives of gay men and younger lesbians, had little positive impact on the life experiences or general well-being of people their age. The women saw housing, financial security, and the potential loss of support of partners

and friends via death as the primary concerns at this stage in their lives. They also reported that the ability to maintain independent lives and control over their housing was paramount. Although the women reported experiencing discrimination based on sexual orientation, gender, or age, they believed that the adversity served to make them stronger and more self-sufficient individuals.

Because of the negative attitudes and societal climates that exist for some LGB older adults, they experience unique needs in terms of healthcare, finances, and social support. The Chicago Task Force on LGBT Aging (Wiggins, 2003) conducted a community survey of 280 older adults (94% identified as LGB) and found a need for access to preventive healthcare services, advocacy from healthcare professionals, a senior center for social and intellectual stimulation, and the education of healthcare providers about sexual orientation/gender identity and the sexual health needs of LGB older adults. These results were supported in a related study by Brotman, Ryan, and Cormier (2003) of 32 people in focus groups of older gay men and lesbians and their families. These findings reaffirmed the impact of discrimination on the health and access to health services among these populations, issues relating to invisibility, and historic and current barriers to healthcare.

In a nationwide study of the Women's Health Initiative (Valanis, Bowen, Bassford, Whitlock, Charney, & Carter, 2000), 93,311 women over the age of 50 were questioned to examine differences between heterosexuals and nonheterosexuals with regard to health characteristics, risk factors, and practices. Findings suggested that lesbian and bisexual women reported higher socioeconomic status (SES) than their heterosexual counterparts, and that they reported using alcohol and cigarettes more often. Additionally, nonheterosexual women in this study scored lower than heterosexuals on social support and mental health measures. Nonheterosexuals also reported lower rates of health screenings and higher rates of obesity. The authors asserted that these health disparities call for more attention and interventions by healthcare workers and their nonheterosexual female patients with regard to their healthcare.

A key issue in the lack of senior support in the LGB community has been the inability of organizations to overcome the problem of LGB elder invisibility and to develop appropriate senior services.

Organizations have often failed to locate and entice older community members to participate in their events. The fear of being discriminated against in mainstream systems has often resulted in LGB elders avoiding services and putting their health and safety at risk. Heaphy, Yip, and Thompson (2003) reported findings from a study of 266 older LGB individuals living in England. Utilizing a mixed methods design of surveying all participants and interviewing 20, the authors found that only 35% of the sample perceived healthcare service providers as having positive attitudes toward LGB clients. Only 16% of participants reported feeling as if their healthcare service provider had any knowledge about LGB lifestyles and specific needs. A desire for health providers and care facilities to overtly indicate LGB friendliness was shared by 77% of the sample. Not surprisingly, when Johnson and colleagues (2005) surveyed 127 LGBT people of all ages regarding their plans for the future, they found that 73% believed discrimination against LGBT people existed in retirement/care facilities and 34% reported they would hide their sexual orientation in a retirement/care facility.

In a survey of 317 individuals (ages 15–90), Jackson and colleagues (2008) explored the perceptions of discrimination against the LGB elder community in healthcare settings. Most respondents, regardless of orientation or gender identity, believed that both employees and residents of care facilities treat nonheterosexual residents worse. However, heterosexual and LGBT respondents differed when asked about social and health service accessibility; 61% of heterosexual respondents reported that they believed nonheterosexuals have equal access to services, whereas only 40% of LGBT respondents believed this to be true. With regard to sexual orientation disclosure, 66% of LGBT respondents who claimed they suspected discrimination in healthcare settings reported they would refuse to hide their sexual orientation if they eventually decided to live in a long-term care facility. Additionally, after interviewing 36 chronically ill LGB adults over 50 years old, Fredriksen-Goldsen and colleagues (2009) found that 50% of the LGB elders receiving care experienced discrimination from their caregivers based on sexual orientation, 47% based on age, and 58% on disability status.

Focus group and survey data on the health and housing needs of 257 aging lesbians in Toronto (Ross, Scott, & Wexler, 2003) demonstrated that there was both a need for health and mental healthcare providers to be educated about the needs of older lesbians and a need for lesbian communities to respond to lesbian health needs. Group discussions focused on the need to establish communities to promote reciprocity and decreased isolation among younger and older lesbians, i.e., with older lesbians sharing wisdom and experience and younger lesbians taking on physical tasks. One participant commented, "We aren't out as much as gay men; therefore, people don't really know our needs" (p.24), highlighting the invisibility of this community and the need for more knowledge among people providing services.

To better understand the attitudes of care providers toward "out" LGB elders, Brotman and colleagues (2007) interviewed informal, unpaid caregivers who had a personal relationship with the LGB person for whom they provided care. Participants reported that actual and anticipated discrimination often mediated their willingness to obtain necessary resources. Historically, some gay and lesbian couples have attempted to avoid discrimination by claiming to be "friends" or "roommates" (Brotman et al., 2003). The 2007 study found that doing so made the showing of affection in times of illness or distress particularly difficult for partners who are also caregivers and advocates.

In addition to perceptions of bias, securing financial resources is also an obstacle to care in old age for LGB individuals. In an exploratory study of 59 LGBT people, McFarland and Sanders (2003) reported on the social networks and preparedness for old age of LGBT people aged 49–86 (mean age 59) from Metropolitan Community Churches (MCC). They found that 51% of respondents reported that they lacked sufficient support for the physical and psychological challenges associated with aging, 70% believed that they were financially unprepared for the aging process, and a majority indicated that they were not considering utilizing an assisted living facility (54%), adult day care (78%), a nursing home (81%), a care manager, or any type of care management service (88%) in old age. The primary reason given for not considering these options was a belief about the lack of LGBT competency among staff members. These findings were echoed in a study of 25 lesbians aged 55 to 73 (median age 64) conducted by Richard and Brown (2006); they found that older lesbians hesitated to use social service agencies due to a fear of bias. In a study conducted on the training and experience of 1071 nursing home social service directors from across the country, Bell and colleagues (2010) found that 76% of respondents had not received any training on homophobia in the past 5 years.

In a study of 26 LGB elders aged 65–84 who participated in group discussions, Orel (2004) found findings similar to those of McFarland and Sanders (2003) with several notable exceptions. Orel found that all of the female participants in the focus groups experienced financial constraints when seeking healthcare as a result of relying solely on government-sponsored programs. Most male participants had supplemental insurance that covered their expenses and reported less concern over healthcare. Additionally, in their qualitative study of 25 older lesbians, Richard and Brown (2006) found that older lesbians' financial concerns were "compounded by their histories of choosing non-traditional employment" (p. 54). Reporting on the discrimination experienced by participants from healthcare providers, Orel (2004) noted that participants who "came out" to healthcare providers experienced less discrimination and were kept from their partners in hospitals less often than participants who did not disclose their sexual orientation to their healthcare providers.

Claassen (2005) reported findings divergent from those listed above in an ethnographic study of 44 older lesbians aged 62 to 82. The majority of the women were white, wealthy, and/or retired. Claassen focused on finances and wealth and on how these women achieved economic autonomy at a time when many older women faced economic hardship. In comparing the sample to the U.S. population aged 55 and over, Claassen found that those in the sample were more than twice as likely to have a private pension, own stocks, or receive rental or trust income. Although almost all of the women were homeowners, they were less likely than the general population aged 55 and over to be engaged in paid labor. At a time when women were routinely considered poor credit risks, the women's successes in obtaining mortgages and/or buying investment properties, as early as the 1940s, are noteworthy. Contrary to a mid-twentieth century prediction that being lesbian would lead to unhappiness and loneliness in old age, the women in Classen's study lived satisfying lives with much social activity.

Heaphy and colleagues (2004) focused on how LGB elders planned for late-in-life care and how they perceived nursing homes and residential care facilities; they also asked the elders who they would turn to for support in times of crisis. About one-third (31%) reported making plans for care for future serious illness and only 17% reported making plans for care in old age. Of the respondents who had children, very few thought that they should or could depend on their children as they age. The most common reason individuals gave for delaying future planning was fear. This fear of planning and lack of motivation to prepare for the future were echoed in the study's findings about LGB elders' perceptions of residential care and nursing homes. Many of the women (77%) and men (63%) reported feeling that living in such facilities was undesirable. When asked who they would turn to first for emotional support in a crisis, 59% reported friends, 34% reported partners, and only 9% reported members of their family origin. In an effort to better understand the social networks of the aging LGB population, Shippy, Cantor, and Brennan (2004) surveyed 223 gay men (age 50–82). On average, participants had five friends in their social networks. In addition, 36% of participants had partners in their networks, 32% had at least one parent, 15% had at least one child, 75% had at least one sibling, 61% had at least one other relative, and 93% had at least one friend. When in need of assistance, most men with partners sought out their partners for help, and men without partners primarily went to their friends. In spite of available social networks for most of the participants, 26% believed that instrument support and 20% believed that emotional support was either only occasionally available or not available at all.

Considering the increase in homosexual parenting in recent years (Patterson, 1994), it is important to examine the ways in which grandparents navigate the task of coming out to their grandchildren. A qualitative study of 11 grandfathers (Fruhauf, Orel, & Jenkins, 2009) found that coming out to a grandchild was, in fact, easier than coming out to your own children. Participants cited their adult children as instrumental assets in discussing the topic with their grandchildren; however, some grandfathers reported having little or no role with regard to how or when the information was relayed to their grandchildren because the adult parents chose to have the conversation with their children privately. Investigating the impact of growing supportive communities, Brown and colleagues (2001) reported on 69 gay men sampled in previous studies who were adjusting well to old age with the help of their social networks. The majority reported spending 50% or more of their time with gay friends in their same age cohorts. Contrary to the stereotype of gay men experiencing strained familial bonds, the majority of the respondents were in regular contact with family members and also had disclosed their orientation to their families. The men rated deaths of friends, physical decline, and loneliness as the most troubling aspects of aging. Participants noted that gaining wisdom, having fewer financial pressures, and experiencing long-term family and friend relationships were among the best aspects of growing old.

In addition to the findings listed above on the social networks of LGB elders, Masini and Barrett (2008) conducted an online survey of the social networks of 220 LGB older adults over age 50 (mean age 57). They found that "close friends and partners were more likely than family members to provide emotional, practical, advice, and socializing support" (p. 104). Participants who reported receiving more support from friends also reported a higher quality of life, lower depression, lower anxiety, and less internalized homophobia. In the study described earlier, Heaphy (2009) found that most participants found it more difficult to meet a partner as their age increased. Many of the men in the study voiced difficulties in meeting partners in gay locales because they were often perceived as being ageist. Older lesbians in the sample reported the problem of small, invisible, seemingly nonexistent lesbian locales and community spaces. However, lesbians reported feeling as though ageism was less prevalent in lesbian communities, compared with gay male and heterosexual communities. The study also provided findings on the social networks of LGB older people with regard to families and friends. Thirty-four percent of the women and 22% of the men said that their sexual orientation had been a catalyst for distancing them from their families of origin. Nearly all of the women (96%) and men (94%) rated friendships as either "important" or "very important." And with regard to aging, 76% of women and 84% of men reported feeling that their friendships had become increasingly important as they became older. Measuring depression among 2881 men who have sex with men surveyed in the Urban Men's Health Study, Mills and colleagues (2004)

found that 17% of gay men between the ages of 50 and 69 and 5% of gay men over 70 years old suffered from depression. Using the same sample from the Urban Men's Health Study, Paul and colleagues (2002) found that 12% of men over 55 had attempted suicide and 20% had a plan for suicide at one point in their lives. Chernin and Johnson (2003) note that when separated from their partners or friends through death or due to institutional barriers, such as homophobia, LGB older people experience isolation, depression, and other affective disorders. To help them face issues that come with aging, e.g., developing pride and a sense of integrity associated with their life's accomplishments and navigating end-stage decisions, Chernin and Johnson (2003) described the need for additional counseling as they get older. Others may need financial consultation, medical referrals, and counseling to cope with day-to-day issues or distressing thoughts.

David and Knight (2008) studied the differences in levels of stress among different age and ethnic groups of gay men. The sample consisted of 383 gay males, 51% white and 49% black. White participants generally reported higher levels of sexual orientation disclosure than black participants, and black participants were prone to report higher levels of homonegativity than white participants. Additionally, "Older" black men reported higher levels of perceived racism than both "Younger" and "Middle"-aged blacks, as well as higher levels of perceived ageism compared to "Older" white participants. In a case study of two older gay men in Australia, Porter, Russell, and Sullivan (2004) focused on the special needs of old and poor gay men. Their study illustrated the dire situation of growing old in poverty, remaining single, and not having any connections to the gay community. Because these men relied on the social and health services of a system that did not recognize nonheterosexual people, their health and well-being were further jeopardized. The presence (or absence) of caring relationships is a significant contributor to their well-being and a primary factor in the construction of identity of these men. Therefore, in response to the stories of the older, poor gay men in the study, the authors argued that addressing social isolation becomes an important issue that requires the attention not only of the mainstream care and support services for older adults, but also of the gay community.

DISCUSSION

Our current knowledge about sexual orientation and aging is based on a relatively limited number of qualitative and quantitative studies about LGB older adults. There has been a lack of population-based studies on aging that incorporate measures of sexual orientation. In a recently published 25-year review of the literature, Fredriksen-Goldsen and Muraco (2010) found only 58 articles published between 1984 and 2008 on LGB adults over the age of 50. The resulting analyses updated previous reviews of research on sexual orientation and aging (Jacobson & Grossman, 1996; Kimmel, Rose, & David 2006; Reid, 1995). Other factors that have limited our knowledge of sexual orientation and aging are ambiguities of defining sexual orientation, the reluctance of individuals to disclose their sexual minority identities (Fredriksen-Goldsen & Muraco, 2010), and the unclear definition of what constitutes being an older adult in diverse lesbian, gay, and bisexual communities.

Using a life course approach, Fredriksen-Goldsen and Muraco (2010) examined social interaction and context to demonstrate how LGB aging has been influenced by time and period, and how cohort effects age-related processes. The two primary research domains of LGB older adults identified were (1) the interplay of lives and historical times and (2) linked and interdependent lives. The first domain focused on development in the context of negative stereotypes about the mental health statuses of LGB older adults, e.g., being depressed, sexually undesirable, and maladjusted to aging. Another major factor identified in early studies was LGB older adults experiencing their early developmental years in a context dominated by hate, intolerance, and discrimination of LGB people (Reid, 1995). Contrary to these experiences, studies have found that the majority of LGB older adults reported positive psychosocial functioning, favorable feelings about sexuality and aging, being no more depressed than their heterosexual counterparts, and good or excellent mental health. Among the predictors of positive psychosocial adjustment were accepting, disclosing, and managing a lesbian or gay identity, which was found to be associated with higher levels of life satisfaction and self-esteem, satisfaction with social support, and positive adjustment to aging (Fredriksen-Goldsen and Muraco, 2010). As was the case for their heterosexual counterparts, LGB older adults of higher SES reported larger social

networks; being partnered also indicated good or excellent mental and physical health, lower internalized homophobia, less loneliness, less victimization based on sexual orientation, and higher self-esteem (D'Augelli, Grossman, Hershberger, & O'Connell, 2001).

With regard to the integrity of lives and historical times, two other major cumulative effects of the social location of LGB older adults in society that have been found to be similar to their heterosexual counterparts are gender and race. Older lesbians tend to report lower incomes compared to older gay men (Grossman et al., 2000; Quam & Whitford, 1992), and African-American older gay men experience significantly higher levels of racism than both younger white and African-American men (David & Knight, 2008). Similarly, ageism affects LGB older adults, as well as their heterosexual counterparts.

The second domain, linked and interdependent lives, focused on social relationships across the lifespan. As many self-identified LGB older adults had limited relationships with their families of origin as a result of coming out and rejection, the prevailing stereotype was that they were isolated, lonely, and lacked social support (Fredriksen-Goldsen & Muraco, 2010; Reid, 1995). However, research studies showed that, overall, many LGB older adults have relationships with some family members, have committed same-sex and other-sex partners, and have friends and co-workers. Along with "chosen families," they have created substantial support networks with individuals providing emotional, social, community, and other types of support (Grossman et al., 2000, 2001; Orel, 2004; Weston, 1991). Some older lesbians and gay men have children living in their homes, as a result of a previous heterosexual union, foster parenting, adoption, surrogacy, or donor insemination (Black, Gates, Sanders, & Taylor, 2000), and some are grandparents (Orel & Fruhauf, 2006). However, not all LGB older adults who would benefit from social support have access to it; for example, Hostetler (2004) found that single elder gay men in his sample suffered from isolation.

A third domain affecting the lives of many of today's LGB people as they become older adults, i.e., the Baby Boomers who are joining the age category "young old," is the changing institutional acceptance of lesbians and gays in society. For example, more than a dozen Western countries permit same-sex marriage or civil unions (Truthful Politics, 2011); in addition, a recent Pew Research Center (2011) study indicated that the majority of Americans (58%) state that homosexuality should be accepted rather than discouraged by society. Nearly two-thirds (63%) of those younger than 50 years of age and 52% of those 50 and older favor societal acceptance of homosexuality. Consequently, not only have professional mental health associations dropped homosexuality as a pathology, they and the public are now favoring the acceptance versus the discouragement of homosexuality. Furthermore, 45% of Americans currently favor allowing lesbians and gays to marry legally, whereas 46% are opposed. In 2009, only 35% supported same-sex marriage, and 54% were opposed. The impact of these societal changes on the lives of LGB older adults is yet to be determined; however, the mitigation of hate, intolerance, and discrimination cannot be denied.

A fourth domain having an impact on the lives of many of today's LGB older adults focuses on barriers to equitable health services and healthcare, the competence of providers to offer services to LGB persons, and health disparities between LGB and their heterosexual counterparts, e.g., breast cancer, obesity, and alcohol consumption among some lesbian and bisexual women and HIV/AIDS and prostate cancer among some gay and bisexual men (Blank, Asencio, Descartes, & Griggs, 2009; Institute of Medicine, 2011). Other factors specific to LGB older adults and their health relate to their degree of "outness" and their sexual behavior patterns, as well as their experiences of watershed events such as the Stonewall Riots and the HIV/AIDS crisis (Blank et al., 2009). A major concern of LGB older adults is being cared for as they become older, as elder care is usually provided by family members, and many LGB older adults are not related to each other by blood or legal ties and they may have weak ties to their families of origin. Also, obtaining care from mainstream resources may not be acceptable to many LGB older adults due to fears of bias in the provision of care (Grossman, D'Augelli, & Dragowski, 2007). As indicated previously, Jacobs et al. (1999) found that LGB older adults rated services in the LGB community to be significantly more adequate in meeting their needs in times of crises than non-LGB services. Therefore, some in the LGB community have organized informal groups to meet their needs. Hash and Netting

(2009) described two case examples of older lesbians meeting their social and care needs as well as those of their communities. The lesbians created and/or sustained support systems including a unique system of community care based on the assumptions about mutual aid and assistance. In one community, the members also networked in finding supportive healthcare providers.

RECOMMENDATIONS FOR FUTURE RESEARCH

This chapter examines the more than 30 years of research about LGB older adults. Although it provides a significant portrait of the lives of groups of LGB older adults, it also demonstrates the substantial gaps in our knowledge. Many of the studies address areas of concern related to cohort and period effects, however, none of them directly assesses how the feelings, thoughts, and behaviors of LGB older adults are directly affected by the historical changes that have occurred, such as the depathologizing of homosexuality, the decriminalizing of sexual behaviors, the ability to obtain a civil union in some locales, the availability of same-sex marriage, and the existence of several retirement communities for nonheterosexual people. These and similar topics need to be addressed in future research. Outcomes of these changes also need to be examined with regard to the experience of aging singly and as a couple; the experiences of living as a "widow" or "widower," with its attendant needs for services; being a married or divorced bisexual person in a same-sex or other-sex marriage; being "single" or living alone in a community of LGB older adults; and the differences between having and not having adult children to provide needed assistance in old age.

Another recommendation for future research is the systematic collection of information about developmental trajectories across the lifespans of LGB people. This will not only clarify how early developmental experiences have an impact on aging, but will also highlight the importance of social structures (e.g., retirement communities and assisted living facilities) and life experiences (e.g., stigma and discrimination) on cohorts of young–old, old, and old–old LGB adults. Furthermore, it will elucidate whether living the life of "other" has cumulative negative psychosocial or other health effects on the lives of LGB older adults. These studies should recognize the multidimensional aspects of aging, including contextual factors such as race, ethnicity, SES, levels of community engagement, and geographic locations. We also suggest that future developmental studies examine the role of gender.

Future research should examine within-group differences of aging between the three groups of sexual minority older adults. The impact of the differences in society's attitudes toward those aging as gay men, as lesbians, or as bisexual men or women is not known. It is also necessary to determine how the age at which people become aware that they are LGB, self-label as LGB, and disclose that they are LGB influence the aging process and to determine if psychological and social differences that exist by gender are important. Little is known about what impact changing their LGB identity-based category over the course of their lives has on aging among nonheterosexual people, or if other factors, such as relationships based on intimacy and care over time, have a greater impact over time on people's well-being. Furthermore, comparing the psychological and social adjustment of LGB older adults who can pass as heterosexual with those who cannot, in various social and cultural contexts, will provide vital information for educational, social, counseling, and other mental health service providers.

Finally, future research studies should address methodological issues that limited the generalizability of findings as well as the scope and diversity of existing studies. For example, diverse sampling techniques need to be used so as to reach previously underrepresented populations. Using methods such as respondent-driven and target sampling to supplement population-based and random sampling techniques will assist in studying a range of LGB older adults, including those who are not living openly as LGB and those of various races and ethnicities. The other major methodological issue relates to measuring sexual orientation. Measuring aspects of same- and other-sex romantic and sexual attractions, same-sex behaviors, and identities at various developmental transitions (e.g., puberty, adolescence, young adulthood, middle-age, young–old, and old–old) is recommended. Optimal development later in life will challenge researchers to design studies that will depict the psychological and social development and the adjustment outcomes of LGB older adults living in changing and variable cultural contexts.

THE IMMEDIATE FUTURE LOOKS BRIGHTER

Three signs of progress for LGBT communities occurred in the past 2 years. In February 2010, the U.S. Department of Health and Human Services (HHS) awarded a grant to establish the first and only technical assistance resource center aimed at improving the quality of service and supports offered LGBT older adults. Awarded to Services and Advocacy for GLBT Elders (SAGE) in partnership with 10 leading organizations nationwide, the $900,000 3-year grant is working to ensure that LGBT older adults have necessary and culturally appropriate supports to age successfully by providing training to aging service providers and LGBT agencies nationwide. It is also offering educational tools to LGBT older people (National Resource Center on LGBT Aging, 2010). On March 1, 2012 SAGE opened the first full-time senior center in the United Sates focused on providing services to LGBT older adults in New York City. Not only does the SAGE Center serve LGBT older people citywide, but it also provides a model for those senior groups, who are members of the SAGE-Net, in communities across the United States.

The Affordable Care Act provides HHS with the opportunity to collect demographic data to further improve the understanding of healthcare disparities. Using data on the current knowledge of the health status of LGBT populations provided by the Institute of Medicine (2011), HHS will follow the recommendations, including the collection of data on sexual orientation and gender identity in health surveys administered by HHS and other relevant surveys. Consistent methods for collecting and reporting health data will help in better understanding the risk and protective factors of health in LGBT communities, including those among LGB older adults (HealthCare.gov, 2011). These three significant actions will begin a new phases of assistance for researchers and providers in learning about and addressing the needs of LGB older adults, including filling in the gaps created by the lack of data.

REFERENCES

Adleman, M. (1991). Stigma, gay lifestyles, and adjustment to aging: A study of later-life gay men and lesbians. In J. A. Lee (Ed.), *Gay midlife and maturity* (pp. 7–32). New York: Haworth Press.

Alwin, D. F. (2002). Taking time seriously: Studying social change, social structure, and human lives.

In P. Moen, G. H. Elder, Jr., & K. Luscher (Eds.), *Examining lives in context: Perspectives on the ecology of human development* (pp. 211–262). Washington, DC: American Psychological Association.

Barret, B. (1998). Gay and lesbian activism: A frontier in social advocacy. In C. C. Lee & G. R. Walz (Eds.), *Social action: A mandate for counselors* (pp. 83–98). Alexandria, VA: American Counseling Association.

Barsky, A. E. (2009). Social work research and the law: How LGBT research can be structured and used to affect judicial decisions. In W. Meezan & J. I. Martin (Eds.), *Handbook of research with lesbian, gay, bisexual, and transgender populations* (pp. 190–207). New York: Routledge.

Bayer, R. (1981). *Homosexuality and American psychiatry: The politics of diagnosis.* New York: Basic Books.

Beeler, J. A., Rawls, T. D., Herdt, G., & Cohler, B. J. (1999). The needs of older lesbians and gay men in Chicago. *Journal of Gay and Lesbian Social Services, 9*(1), 31–49.

Bell, S. A., Bern-Klug, M., Kramer, K. W. O., & Saunders, J. B. (2010). Most nursing home social service directors lack training in working with lesbian, gay and bisexual residents. *Social Work in Health Care, 49*(9), 814–831.

Berger, R. (1982). *Gay and gray.* Chicago: University of Chicago Press.

Black, D., Gates, G., Sanders, S., & Taylor, L. (2000). Demographics of the gay and lesbian population in the United States: Evidence from available systematic data sources. *Demography, 37*(2), 139–154.

Blank, T. O., Asencio, M., Descartes, L., & Griggs, J. (2009). Intersection of older GLBT health issues: AGING, HEALTH, and GLBTQ family and community life. *Journal of GLBT Family Studies, 5*(1), 9–34.

Bohn, M. J., Babor, T. F., & Kranzler, H. R. (1995). The Alcohol Use Disorders Identification Test (AUDIT): Validation of a screening instrument for use in medical settings. *Journal of Studies in Alcohol, 56*(4), 423–432.

Bronfenbrenner, U. (1979). *The ecology of human development.* Cambridge, MA: Harvard University Press.

Brotman, S., Ryan, B., Collins, S., Chamberland, L., Cormier, R., Julien, D., Meyer, E., Peterkin, A., & Richard, B. (2007). Coming out to care: Caregivers of gay and lesbian seniors in Canada. *The Gerontologist, 47*(4), 490–503.

Brotman, S., Ryan, B., & Cormier, R. (2003). The health and social service needs of gay and lesbian elders and their families in Canada. *The Gerontologist, 43*(2), 192–202.

Brown, L. B., Alley, G. R., Sarosy, S., Quarto, G., & Cook, T. (2001). Gay men: Aging well! *Journal of Gay & Lesbian Social Services, 13*(4), 41–54.

Cherlin, A. J. (1992). *Marriage, divorce, and remarriage* (rev. ed.). Cambridge, MA: Harvard University Press.

Chernin, J. N., & Johnson, M. R. (2003). *Affirmative psychotherapy and counseling for lesbians and gay men.* Thousand Oaks, CA: Sage.

Claassen, C. (2005). *Whistling women: A study of the lives of older lesbians.* Binghamton, NY: Haworth Press.

CNS News. (2011). Retrieved May 28, 2011, from http://www.cnsnews.com/news/article/10-countries-now-allow-same-sex-marriage

Cruikshank, M. (1990). Lavender and gray: A brief survey of lesbian and gay aging studies. *Journal of Homosexuality, 20*(3/4), 77–87.

D'Augelli, A. R., Grossman, A. H., Hershberger, S. L., & O'Connell, T. S. (2001). Aspects of mental health among older lesbian, gay, and bisexual adults. *Aging & Mental Health, 5*(2), 149–158.

David, S., & Knight, B. G. (2008). Stress and coping among gay men: Age and ethnic differences. *Psychology and Aging, 23*(1), 62–69.

DiPlacido, J. (1998). Minority stress among lesbians, gay men, and bisexuals: A consequence of heterosexism, homophobia, and stigmatization. In G. M. Herek (Ed.), *Stigma and sexual orientation: Understanding prejudice against lesbians, gay men, and bisexuals* (pp. 138–159). Thousand Oaks, CA: Sage.

Dorfman, R., Walters K., Burke P., Hardin L., Karanik T., Raphael S., et al. (1995). Old, sad and alone: The myths of the aging homosexual. *Journal of Gerontological Social Work, 24*(1/2), 29–44.

Floyd, F. J., & Bakeman, R. (2006). Coming-out across the life course: Implications of age and historical context. *Archives of Sexual Behavior, 35*(3), 287–297.

Fredriksen-Goldsen, K. I., Kim, H. J., Muraco, A., & Mincer, S. (2009). Chronically ill midlife and older lesbians, gay men, and bisexuals and their informal caregivers: The impact of the social context. *Sexuality Research & Social Policy: A Journal of the NSRC, 6*(4), 52–64.

Fredriksen-Goldsen, K., & Muraco, A. (2010). Sexual orientation and aging: A review of the literature (1980–2008). *Research on Aging, 32*(3), 372–413.

Friend, R. A. (1989). Older lesbian and gay people: Responding to homophobia. *Journal of Homosexuality, 14*(3/4), 241–263.

Friend, R. A. (1990). Older lesbian and gay people: A theory of successful aging. *Journal of Homosexuality, 20*(3/4), 99–118.

Fruhauf, C. A., Orel, N. A., & Jenkins, D. A. (2009). The coming-out process of gay grandfathers: Perceptions of their adult children's influence. *Journal of GLBT Family Studies, 5*(1/2), 99–118.

Greene, B. (2000). Beyond heterosexism and across the cultural divide: Developing an inclusive lesbian, gay and bisexual psychology. A look to the future. In B. Greene & G. L. Croom (Eds.), *Education, research and practice in lesbian, gay, bisexual and transgender psychology: A resource manual* (pp. 1–45). Thousand Oaks, CA: Sage.

Grossman, A. (2000). Homophobia and its effects on the inequitable provision of health and leisure services for older gay men and lesbians. In C. Brackenridge, D. Howe, & F. Jordan (Eds.), *JUST leisure: Equity, social exclusion, and identity* (pp. 105–118). Eastbourne, UK: LSA Publications.

Grossman, A. (2008).The unique experiences of older gay and bisexual men: Associations with health and well-being. In R. J. Wolitski, R. Stall, & R. O. Valdiserri (Eds.), *Unequal opportunity: Health disparities affecting gay and bisexual men in the United Sates* (pp. 303–326). New York: Oxford University Press.

Grossman, A. H., D'Augelli, A. R., & Dragowski, E. A., (2007). Caregiving and care receiving among older lesbian, gay, and bisexual adults. *Journal of Gay & Lesbian Social Services, 18*(3/4), 15–38.

Grossman, A. H., D'Augelli, A. R., & Hershberger, S. L. (2000). Social support networks of lesbian, gay, and bisexual adults 60 years of age and older. *Journal of Gerontology: Psychological Sciences, 55B*(3), P171–P179.

Grossman, A. H., D'Augelli, A. R., & O'Connell, T. S. (2001). Being lesbian, gay, bisexual, and 60 or older in North America. *Journal of Gay and Lesbian Social Services, 13*(4), 23–40.

Harris, M. (1981). Why the gays came out of the closet. In M. Harris (Ed.), *America now: The anthropology of a changing culture* (pp. 98–115). New York: Simon & Schuster.

Hash, K. M., & Netting, F. E. (2009). It takes a community: Older lesbians meeting social and care needs. *Journal of Gay & Lesbian Social Services, 21*(4), 326–342.

Hays, R. D., & DiMatteo, M. R. (1987). A short-form measure of loneliness. *Journal of Personality Assessment, 51*(1), 69–81.

HealthCare.gov (2011). http://www.healthcare.gov/news/factsheets/2011/06/lgbt06292011a.html.

Heaphy, B. (2009). Choice and its limits in older lesbian and gay narratives of relational life. *Journal of GLBT Family Studies, 5*(1/2), 119–138.

Heaphy, B., Yip A. K. T., & Thompson, D. (2003). *Lesbian, gay and bisexual lives over 50.* Nottingham: York House.

Heaphy, B., Yip, A. K. T., & Thompson, D. (2004). Ageing in a non-heterosexual context. *Ageing & Society, 24*(6), 881–902.

Hostetler, A. J. (2004). Old, gay, and alone? The ecology of well-being among middle aged and older single gay men. In G. Herdt & B. DeVries (Eds.), *Gay and lesbian aging: Research and future directions* (pp. 143–176). New York: Springer.

Institute of Medicine. (2011). *The health of lesbian, gay, bisexual, and transgender people: Building a foundation for better understanding.* Washington, DC: The National Academies Press.

Jackson, N. C., Johnson, M. J., & Roberts, R. (2008). The potential impact of discrimination fears of older gays, lesbians, bisexuals, and transgender individuals living in small-to moderate-sized cities on long-term health care. *Journal of Homosexuality, 54*(3), 325–339.

Jacobs, R., Rasmussen, L., & Hohman, M. (1999). The social support needs of older lesbians, gay men, and bisexuals. *Journal of Gay and Lesbian Social Services, 9*(1), 1–30.

Jacobson, S., & Grossman, A. H. (1996). Older lesbians and gay men: Old myths, new images, and future directions. In R. C. Savin-Williams & K. M. Cohen (Eds.), *The lives of lesbians, gays, and bisexuals: Children to adults* (pp. 345–373). Fort Worth, TX: Harcourt Brace College Publishers.

Johnson, M. J., Jackson, N. C., Arnette, J. K., & Koffman, S. D. (2005). Gay and lesbian perceptions of discrimination in retirement care facilities. *Journal of Homosexuality, 49*(2), 83–102.

Jones, T. C., & Nystrom, N. M. (2002). Looking back…looking forward: Addressing the lives of lesbians 55 and older. *Journal of Women and Aging, 14*(3/4), 59–76.

Kehoe, M. (1988). Lesbians over 60 speak for themselves. *Journal of Homosexuality, 16*(3/4), 1–111.

Kelly, J. (1977). The aging male homosexual: Myth and reality. *The Gerontologist, 17*(4), 328–332.

Kimmel, D., Rose, T., & David, S. (2006). *Lesbian, gay, bisexual, and transgender aging: Research and clinical perspectives.* New York: Columbia University Press.

Lerner, R. M. (1984). *On the nature of human plasticity.* Cambridge: Cambridge University Press.

Mallon, G. P. (1999). Knowledge for practice with transgendered persons. In G. P. Mallon (Ed.), *Social services width transgendered youth* (pp. 1–18). New York: Haworth Press.

Martin, J. I., & D'Augelli, A. R. (2009). Timed lives: Cohort and period effects in research on sexual orientations and gender identity. In W. Meezan & J. I. Martin (Eds.), *Handbook of research with lesbian, gay, bisexual, and transgender populations* (pp. 190–207). New York: Routledge.

Masini, B. E., & Barrett, H. A. (2008) Social support as a predictor of psychological and physical well-being and lifestyle in lesbian, gay and bisexual adults aged 50 and over. *Journal of Gay and Lesbian Social Services, 20*(1/2), 91–110.

McFarland, P. L., & Sanders, S. (2003). A pilot study about the needs of older gays and lesbians: What social workers need to know. *Journal of Gerontological Social Work, 40*(3), 67–80.

MetLife. (2010). *Still out, still aging: The MetLife study of lesbian, gay, bisexual, and transgender baby boomers.* Westport, CT: MetLife Mature Market Insurance.

Meyer, I. H. (1995). Minority stress and mental health in gay men. *Journal of Health and Social Behavior, 36,* 38–56.

Mills, T. C., Paul, J., Stall, R., Pollack, L., Canchola, J., Chang, Y. J., Moskowitz, T., & Catania, J. A. (2004). Distress and depression in men who have sex with men: The urban men's health study. *American Journal of Psychiatry, 161*(2), 278–285.

National Resource Center on LGBT Aging. (2010). Retrieved from http://www.lgbtagingcenter.org/about/background.cfm.

Orel, N. A. (2004). Gay, lesbian, and bisexual elders: Expressed needs and concerns across focus groups. *Journal of Gerontological Social Work, 43*(2/3), 57–77.

Orel, N. A., & Fruhauf, C. A. (2006). Lesbian and bisexual grandmothers' perceptions of the grandparent-grandchild relationship. *Journal of GLBT Family Studies, 2*(1), 43–70.

Patterson, C. J. (1994). Lesbian and gay couples considering parenthood: An agenda for research, services, and advocacy. *Journal of Gay and Lesbian Social Services, 1*, 33–55.

Paul, J., Catania, J., Pollack, L., Moskowitz, J., Canchola, J., Mills, T., Binson, D., & Stall, R. (2002). Suicide attempts among gay and bisexual men: Lifetime prevalence and antecedents. *American Journal of Public Health, 92*(8), 1338–1345.

Pew Research Center. (2011). "Most Say Homosexuality Should Be Accepted by Society." Retrieved from www.people-press.org/category/publications/2011.

Porter, M., Russell, C., & Sullivan, G. (2004). Gay, old, and poor: Service delivery to aging gay men in inner city Sydney, Australia. *Journal of Gay & Lesbian Social Services, 16*(2), 43–57.

Quam, J. K., & Whitford, G. S. (1992). Adaptation and age-related expectations of older gay and lesbian adults. *The Gerontologist, 32*(2), 367–374.

Reid, J. D. (1995). Development in late life: Older lesbian and gay lives. In A. R. D'Augelli & C. J. Patterson (Eds.), *Lesbian, gay, and bisexual identities over the lifespan: Psychological perspectives* (pp. 215–240). New York: Oxford University Press.

Richard, C. A., & Brown, A. H. (2006). Configurations of informal social support among older lesbians. *Journal of Women and Aging, 18*(4), 49–64.

Rosenberg, M. (1965). *Society and the adolescent self-image.* Princeton, NJ: Princeton University Press.

Ross, E., Scott, M., & Wexler, E. (2003). *Environmental scan on the health and housing needs of aging lesbians.* Toronto: OLIVE and Sherbourne Health Centre.

Ryder, N. B. (1965). The cohort as a concept in the study of social change. *American Sociological Review, 30*(6), 843–861.

Saad, L. (2007). Tolerance for gay rights at high water mark. Retrieved from http://www.gallup.com/poll/27694/tolerance-gay-rights-highwater-mark-aspx

Schope, R. D. (2005). Who's afraid of growing old? Gay and lesbian perceptions of aging. *Journal of Gerontological Social Work, 45*(4), 23–39.

Shidlo, A. (1994). Internalized homophobia: Conceptual and empirical issues in measurement. In B. Greene & G. Herek (Eds.), *Lesbian and gay psychology: Theory, research, and clinical applications* (pp. 176–205). Thousand Oaks, CA: Sage

Shippy, R. A., Cantor, M. H., & Brennan, M. (2004). Social networks of aging gay men. *The Journal of Men's Studies, 13*(1), 107–120.

Skinner, H. (1982). *The Drug Abuse Screening Test (DAST): Guidelines for administration and scoring.* Toronto: Addiction Research Foundation.

The Task Force. (2011). Retrieved from http://www.thetasktorce.org/reports_and_research/relationship_recognition.

Truthful Politics. (2011). Retrieved from www.truthfulpolitics.com/issues/gay-marriage/.

Vacha, K. (1985). *Quiet fire: Memoirs of older gay men.* Trumansburg, NY: The Crossing Press.

Valanis, B. G., Bowen, D. J., Bassford, T., Whitlock, E., Charney, P., & Carter, R. A. (2000). Sexual orientation and health. *Archives of Family Medicine, 9*, 843–853.

Weston, K. (1991). *Families we choose: Lesbians, gays, kinship.* New York: Columbia University Press.

Wiggins, P. (Ed.) (2003). *LGBT persons in Chicago: Growing older—A survey of needs and perceptions.* Chicago: Chicago Task Force on LGBT Aging.

Witten, T.M., & Eyle, A. E.V. (Eds.) (2012). *Gay, lesbian, bisexual and transgender aging: Challenges in research, practice and policy.* Baltimore: Johns Hopkins University Press.

Wright, S., & Canetto, S. (2009). Stereotypes of older lesbians and gay men. *Educational Gerontology, 35*(5), 424–452.

III

Domains of Experience

11

Work, Career, and Sexual Orientation

JONATHAN J. MOHR AND RUTH E. FASSINGER

Sigmund Freud (1930) once famously opined that the communal life of human beings rests on a two-fold foundation of love and work. Because sexual orientation as a status variable is defined by the sex of a person and her or his intimate partner choices, and because stigmatization of sexual orientation is directed at "deviant" sexual partner choices, it is understandable that writing on the psychology of sexual orientation has focused on the love aspect of Freud's pairing. That is, scholarly interest primarily has focused on relationships and how sexual minority people come to understand, accept, embrace, and live out their same-sex relationship choices.

However, the work aspect of Freud's pairing is equally important. Indeed, the majority of adults spend the bulk of their waking hours engaged in work, and, if the educational arena is included as the locus of vocational preparation for children and adolescents, then it is safe to assert that most people spend most of their lives preparing for or engaging in work. Blustein (2008) has pointed to work as a source of identity, a means of fulfillment for those lucky enough to find work that is desirable and rewarding, and a primary contribution that many people make to society. The workplace also is the center of interaction between people and the world around them, and it therefore also functions as the nexus of discrimination and marginalization for those subject to oppression in society, including lesbian, gay, and bisexual people.

Thus, love and work are inextricably linked in the lives of sexual minority people, and the study of sexual orientation in relation to work and career is critically important. The inclusion of work issues not only contributes to a more comprehensive psychology of sexual orientation, but the inclusion of sexual minority issues in considerations of work creates a more fully fleshed out psychology of work

and career—relevant to vocational, industrial/ organizational, occupational health, community, and consulting psychologists, as well as those who engage in counseling and clinical interventions with individuals, groups, and families.

The purpose of this chapter is to explore the link between sexual orientation and issues of work and career. Our organization of the chapter reflects the multilevel nature of career and work issues. Although human experience generally is influenced by factors at multiple levels, this fact is particularly apparent when examining the workplace. Workers' experiences are influenced by the units and organizations in which they work, which, in turn, are influenced by regulatory mechanisms established by cities, states, and nations. Thus, we begin in the first section by outlining broad contextual issues (societal and organizational) that provide the backdrop for more specific workplace factors (discrimination and support, identity disclosure and concealment), which we then discuss in the second section. In the third section, we explore how these workplace factors filter down into lesbian, gay, and bisexual individuals' experiences of work and career, including the special task of leadership. We then briefly note some positive aspects of lesbian, gay, and bisexual career development and work behavior, and we conclude with a call for more integrative approaches to understanding lesbian, gay, and bisexual vocational issues.

Our review covers literatures from subspecialties as diverse as industrial/organizational psychology, higher education, community psychology, and counseling psychology. Our discussion is limited by the general focus on white, "out" gay male, upper/ middle class, temporarily able-bodied, working populations; knowledge about other groups is growing very slowly (Croteau et al., 2008). Also, the current literature is an amalgam of theoretical speculation with more limited empirical study, which is reflected in our review. We offer observations and suggestions regarding needed research throughout the chapter, but space constraints preclude recommendations for practice. Finally, although we regard education and work as one continuum of vocational behavior, due to limited space, we focus here on adults in the workplace.

CONTEXTUAL FACTORS IN WORK AND CAREER

We begin with a discussion of societal and organizational issues—i.e., macrolevel factors—because they are critical to understanding the work issues of sexual minorities. Macrolevel factors do not need to be recognized to affect the experiences of lesbian, gay, and bisexual workers. For example, a job applicant may not realize that she or he was passed over for a position because of a company's preference for hiring employees who appear to be heterosexual, and may attribute the failure to lack of personal competence; this is a distal minority stressor (Meyer, 2003) because it can contribute to stress in minority people without being noticed. Lesbian-, gay-, and bisexual-affirming practices can be viewed as distal minority supports because they may indirectly have a positive influence on the experiences of nonheterosexual employees, for example, by attracting socially progressive workers who are more likely than others to contribute to a positive work environment for nonheterosexual colleagues.

On the other hand, awareness of macrolevel factors related to sexual orientation may also directly influence lesbian, gay, and bisexual workers' appraisals and coping strategies regarding safety and job security. For example, at present, the attorney general of Virginia had advised public universities in that state to remove sexual orientation from employment nondiscrimination policies because the state legislature had not included sexual orientation as a protected class, despite widespread support within universities for continuing the protection (Helderman, 2010). The well-publicized events related to this advice likely heightened university employees' awareness of their protected status, as well as their recognition that protection could be removed by elected state officials. For some lesbian, gay, and bisexual workers, the knowledge that an attempt might be made to remove sexual orientation from university nondiscrimination policies may have decreased perceived job security

and increased attempts to conceal their sexual orientation; such stigma-related perceptions and coping responses can be viewed as proximal minority stressors (Meyer, 2003) because they contribute to stress in minority people through the subjective experience of stigma. Conversely, the perception of situations as lesbian-, gay-, and bisexual-affirming can be viewed as proximal minority supports, as some lesbian, gay, and bisexual Virginians' heightened awareness of their protected status may have increased their sense of job security and decreased their need to conceal their nonheterosexual status. Thus, whether experienced distally and indirectly, or proximally and consciously, macrolevel factors are a critical backdrop to the work lives of sexual minority people.

Societal Context

For lesbian, gay, and bisexual individuals, societal norms related to gender and sexual orientation exert powerful influences on educational and career trajectories. Moradi, Mohr, Worthington, and Fassinger (2009) highlighted ways in which lesbian, gay, bisexual, and transgender individuals participate in a common experience of gender transgression, i.e., defying societal norms for gender-"acceptable" behavior (e.g., self-presentation, physical characteristics, intimate partner gender). Also, sexual minorities share similar experiences of stigmatization of these gender-transgressive choices. Because gender and sexual orientation are often confounded in the public eye (e.g., viewing desire for same-sex partners as a wish to be the other sex; viewing gender-nonconforming behavior as a sign of homosexuality), norms for both gender and sexual orientation contribute to the stigmatization and marginalization of sexual minority people.

The U.S. educational system is widely considered to be a primary agent of gender socialization, a staunch guardian of gender norms, and a stern enforcer of conformity regarding gender and sexuality (Chesir-Teran, 2003). Such strongly embedded heterosexism in schools affects nonheterosexual students' mental health and academic success (see Sears, 2005). Perhaps it is not surprising that gender stereotypes and gender-related constraints on behavior and success in education follow both males and females into adulthood and are manifested in the workplace (Fassinger, 2005, 2008). A discussion of gender-related workplace issues is beyond the scope of this chapter, but it bears noting as a context for lesbian, gay, and bisexual workers that the literature suggests a much narrower band of acceptability and effectiveness of stereotypically feminine than masculine behaviors in work contexts, coupled with a persistent lack of acceptance of gender-atypical behavior or presentation (see Fassinger, Shullman, & Stevenson, 2010, for application of this literature to lesbian and gay leadership). Such norms present a classic double-bind for women and an even more complicated conundrum for lesbian, gay, and bisexual people. That is, if stereotypically masculine behavior is viewed as effective, successful, and more appropriate for men than women, then women are caught in the bind of needing to display masculine behaviors to be viewed as successful but feminine behaviors to have credibility as women. When well-documented stereotypes of gay men as feminine and lesbians as masculine are overlaid upon these basic gendered assumptions, it becomes clear that lesbian, gay, and bisexual workers are in a precarious position regarding the display of "acceptable" workplace behaviors (Fassinger et al., 2010).

Moreover, societal stereotypes regarding sexual orientation are not merely neutral but are stigmatizing. There is robust documentation of sexual stigma, and Herek's comprehensive work (e.g., 2007, 2009; Herek, Gillis, & Cogan, 2009) presents a cogent explanation of the effects of sexual stigma in both institutions (as heterosexism) and individuals (as enacted, felt, and internalized stigma). Stigma specific to education and work arenas is well-documented, and, as discussed below, is linked to a host of negative outcomes related to work experiences and personal adjustment (Fassinger, 2008). A striking example of the societal acceptance of heterosexism is found in federal law. At present, the U.S. federal law continues to permit employment discrimination based on worker sexual orientation and gender identity, despite the presence of legal protections for other sociodemographic categories (King & Cortina, 2010).

Organizational Context
Employers, like the jurisdictions in which they reside, express values related to sexual orientation through their policies and practices. Organizational positions on lesbian, gay, and bisexual issues can be characterized on a continuum ranging from a hostile and heterosexist stance to a neutral stance of compliance with regulations to an affirming stance of inclusion and advocacy (Rocco, Landorf, & Delgado, 2009). Organizations can express these perspectives in a variety of domains, including recruitment, hiring, promotion, and firing; employee training experiences; strategic planning; public statements and philanthropy in support of nonheterosexual people; affinity groups; and employee benefits. In this section, we briefly discuss each of these domains.

High stakes decisions such as hiring, firing, and promotion are often included in discussions of lesbian, gay, and bisexual organizational issues due to the lack of legal protection from discrimination on the basis of sexual orientation in many jurisdictions. Although organization-wide policies of discrimination against lesbian, gay, and bisexual employees are relatively rare, there are some examples of this in both the private and public sectors. In 1991, the food store and restaurant chain Cracker Barrel implemented a policy requiring the termination of employees "whose sexual preferences failed to demonstrate normal heterosexual values" (Allen, 2005, p. 20). This decision was justified with both a moral rationale (i.e., compatibility of lesbian, gay, and bisexual employees with the company's philosophy) and a business rationale (i.e., compatibility of nonheterosexual employees with the company's customer base). Pressure from consumer groups ultimately led the chain's parent group to include sexual orientation in its nondiscrimination policy (Allen, 2005).

Of course, the absence of discriminatory policies does not guarantee lesbian, gay, and bisexual applicants and workers fair treatment or an affirming work environment. Individual acts of bias and harassment can occur toward people perceived as being lesbian, gay, or bisexual, even if no organizational policy sanctions discrimination. Moreover, a lack of hostile policies offers no assurance the organization will address practices that—intentionally or not—marginalize nonheterosexual applicants and workers (e.g., offering health benefits only to families defined by heterosexual marriage). When organizations do not anticipate and address equity issues associated with sexual orientation, a "null environment" is created that supports business as usual from the perspective of heterosexual norms (Fassinger, 1995). In such environments, some nonheterosexual applicants and workers will choose to minimize the possibility of bias and harassment by hiding their sexual orientation (Ragins, 2004)—a burden that their heterosexual counterparts do not have to bear.

For these reasons, employers adopting an inclusive perspective have identified and implemented a number of lesbian-, gay-, and bisexual-affirming practices and policies (Day & Greene, 2008; Rocco, Landorf, & Delgado, 2009). One of the most common recommendations is inclusion of sexual orientation as a protected class in all nondiscrimination statements. As Day and Greene (2008) noted, the commitment to nondiscrimination and inclusiveness should be clearly communicated to all employees and should include follow-up on allegations of bias. Inclusiveness can be reflected in recruitment procedures, such as using inclusive language in advertisements and application forms; placing advertisements in lesbian, gay, and bisexual professional venues; using lesbian, gay, and bisexual recruiters; and using interviewers who are comfortable using inclusive language. Other examples of affirming practices include parity in employee benefits and the processes needed to access those benefits, discussion of sexual orientation in training experiences (e.g., new employee orientation, diversity trainings), creation of affinity groups for nonheterosexual and heterosexual ally employees, visible advocacy for lesbian, gay, and bisexual causes outside of the organization, and organization-wide dissemination of legislative changes that may affect lesbian, gay, and bisexual employees. Parity in work-life benefits and policies is particularly important because it both contributes to a lesbian-, gay-, and bisexual-affirming climate and helps to correct significant economic disparities based on sexual orientation (Hornsby & Munn, 2009).

Employers are increasingly adopting such inclusive practices. For example, the percentage of Fortune 500 companies with sexual orientation nondiscrimination policies increased from 51% in 2000 to 85% in 2008 (Human Rights Campaign, 2009). Moreover, 57% of Fortune 500 companies offered domestic partner benefits in 2008. Considerable diversity in practices was found in Button's (2001) survey of 38 companies with lesbian, gay, and bisexual contacts listed through the National Gay and Lesbian Task Force. Of nine affirming practices studied, organizations had adopted anywhere from one to eight practices. The least common practices were diversity trainings devoted exclusively to lesbian, gay, and bisexual issues (8%) and benefits that included health insurance for domestic partners (40%). The most frequently adopted practices were diversity trainings that included discussion of lesbian, gay, and bisexual issues (79%) and written nondiscrimination statements (95%).

Social and Organizational Influences on Workers' Experiences

This discussion has made clear that jurisdictions and organizations differ widely in the degree to which sexual orientation disparities are recognized and corrected. Such macrolevel differences may give rise to shared experiences among job seekers and workers in relation to jurisdictions and organizations. This possibility raises interesting and practically important questions about the degree to which such shared experiences exist, as well as whether there are macrolevel antecedents and consequences of differences in laws, policies, and practices. However, very little research has been conducted on the effects of macrolevel variables on workers' experiences at the jurisdiction and organization levels. One of the few such studies is Button's (2001) organization-level analysis of data from lesbian, gay, and bisexual workers in 38 companies. Results indicated that there was substantial agreement among workers within the same organization regarding levels of institutional discrimination toward lesbian, gay, and bisexual employees. Also, the number of lesbian-, gay-, and bisexual-affirming policies and practices within companies was negatively associated with workers' shared perceptions regarding discrimination. Another study focused on the degree to which state-level protections for nonheterosexual people—including employment nondiscrimination—mitigate the negative effects of sexual prejudice on mental health (Hatzenbuehler, Keyes, & Hasin, 2009). The disparity between heterosexual and nonheterosexual people in the prevalence of psychiatric disorders was greatest in states without formal protections for lesbian and gay people. In short, a small but emerging body of research suggests that macrolevel factors such as organizational policies and state laws may influence, in aggregate, the experiences of lesbian, gay, and bisexual people within organizations and jurisdictions.

Despite the challenges of conducting this type of research, we believe it represents a critical part of efforts to understand the effects of laws, regulations, policies, and practices on workers. Fascinating and important questions remain unexplored. Do organizations differ in the degree to which sexual orientation disparities exist in job commitment, job satisfaction, opportunities for advancement, and productivity? If so, then—as hypothesized by Day and Greene (2008)—might these differences be accounted for by the degree to which organizations have adopted lesbian-, gay-, and bisexual-affirming policies and practices? Moreover, could an economic case be made for adoption of such affirming policies, as suggested by King and Cortina (2010)?

Macrolevel research on sexual orientation and work issues also provides opportunities to learn more about processes through which organizations change or stay the same. For example, it would be valuable to investigate the success of different organizational change strategies in creating an affirming environment for employees of all sexual orientations while minimizing backlash. One particularly important question to address is how change efforts can be designed so as not to antagonize employees whose religious beliefs include the view of homosexuality as immoral (Kaplan, 2006). Also, organizational theories may prove useful in studying the role that employees play in maintaining the organizational climate for sexual diversity. For example, the Attraction-Selection-Attrition Theory highlights ways in which the homogeneity of workers' values may be maintained within an organization through processes related to the applicant pool, hiring and firing decisions, and worker turnover (Schneider, Goldstein, & Smith, 1995).

In this section we have emphasized the perspective that jurisdictions and organizations can influence heterosexual and nonheterosexual workers' experiences through laws, policies, and practices related to sexual orientation. However, it is important to note that people can influence the organizations in which they work and the jurisdictions in which they live. Such *bottom-up effects* have been discussed extensively in the organizational literature (Kozlowski & Klein, 2000). As noted above, in some cases people may contribute to the maintenance of organizational practices through individual decisions. However, people can also contribute to change by challenging policies, practices, and laws. For example, Githens and Aragon (2009) offered a case study of a company in which an informal group of employees organized an effort to ask upper-level management to implement several lesbian-, gay-, and bisexual-affirming practices.

INDIVIDUAL EXPERIENCES RELATED TO WORK AND CAREER

Individual experiences in educational and workplace environments depend upon a complex interaction of the broadly contextual and more specific workplace factors discussed above and "person" factors, including attributes such as personality, abilities, talents, cognitive styles, needs, values, self-confidence, and expectations. Central to development for nonheterosexual individuals is their coming to terms with a stigmatized identity and their decisions about how to live that identity in a context of societal prejudice and marginalization. "Coming out" to self and others requires awareness of external and internalized stigma, both of which are so deeply culturally conditioned that the process of replacing negative self-perceptions and beliefs with self-acceptance and self-confidence is a lifelong task for many nonheterosexual individuals. The existence of stigma creates normative challenges for lesbian, gay, and bisexual people, such as bias and rejection in relationships (e.g., with family of origin, peers, and healthcare professionals); lack of supportive role models and communities; and unique barriers in common life tasks (e.g., developing romantic relationships, rearing children, retiring) (see Meyer and Frost, Chapter 18, this volume).

How are these normative experiences expressed in the workplace? A steadily growing body of research has begun to document the challenges—and, to a lesser extent, the positive experiences—lesbian, gay, and bisexual people face in their work and careers. We begin this section by reviewing this research. We then describe major theories of vocational behavior, and highlight applications of these theories to lesbian, gay, and heterosexual people. The chapter ends with sections on the intersection of leadership and sexual orientation issues at work, and positive facets of work and career for nonheterosexual people.

Discrimination and Social Support

To what extent do lesbian, gay, and bisexual workers encounter heterosexist and discriminatory behavior? In one survey of 534 lesbian, gay, or bisexual members of national gay rights organizations, 33.9% of respondents reported having faced such discrimination, 22.4% reported verbal harassment related to sexual orientation, 10.5% reported actual or threatened physical harassment related to sexual orientation, 13.3% resigned from a job because of discrimination related to sexual orientation, and 6.1% reported having been fired from a job because of their sexual orientation (Ragins, Singh, & Cornwell, 2007). Most estimates of perceived discrimination have been based on convenience samples. However, two surveys of national probability samples yielded similar findings. Estimates of formal discrimination related to hiring, firing, and promotion decisions were 10.2% in one survey (Herek, 2009) and 18.0% in the other (Henry J. Kaiser Family Foundation, 2001).

One disadvantage of survey studies is that it is difficult to determine whether a behavior occurred and, if so, whether it was motivated by heterosexism. In fact, lesbian, gay, and bisexual workers themselves are not always sure whether behaviors reflect discrimination, as evidenced by the considerable number of "unsure" responses to perceived discrimination questions in a survey of lesbian, gay, and bisexual workers (Ragins et al., 2007). Several studies have addressed this concern by using experimental methods to test for the differential treatment of workers or job applicants based on their sexual orientation. For example, Weichselbaumer (2003) found that fictitious female applicants were less likely to be invited for job interviews when their résumés reflected managerial experience in a lesbian, gay, or bisexual organization. In another field experiment, Hebl, Foster, Mannix, and Dovidio (2002) recruited university students to pose as job applicants for positions in a variety of retail stores. Store representatives were terser and more negative with confederates when their baseball caps sported the words "Gay and Proud" than when the caps sported the words "Texan and Proud." No evidence of formal discrimination was found, however.

When are lesbian, gay, and bisexual workers most likely to report discrimination? Research on demographic variables suggests that these workers' perception of workplace heterosexism is unrelated to gender or race (Ragins, Cornwell, & Miller, 2003). In contrast, discrimination among lesbian, gay, and bisexual workers has been found to be lower in work environments with a higher proportion of female and nonheterosexual co-workers (Ragins et al., 2003; Waldo, 1999). This finding probably reflects the greater-than-average levels of lesbian-, gay-, and bisexual-affirming attitudes among women and among nonheterosexual people.

Ragins et al. (2003) also found that lesbian, gay, and bisexual workers reported less discrimination when their work group was racially heterogeneous. The authors speculated that racially diverse groups may increase the awareness of diversity in a way that supports intolerance of any discrimination.

Although it is generally believed that lesbian-, gay-, and bisexual-affirming organizational policies will reduce the prevalence of discriminatory and heterosexist behavior, support for this view has been mixed. A negative association between such affirming organizational policies and perceived discrimination was observed in some studies (Button, 2001; Ragins & Cornwell, 2001) but not in others (Waldo, 1999). Despite mixed findings, studies have consistently found a positive association between protective policies and job satisfaction (e.g., Button, 2001; Ellis & Riggle, 1995; Ragins & Cornwell, 2001). It is worth noting that most studies examining policies have relied on participant self-report data. Thus, the policy variables created in these studies confound the actual presence or absence of policies with participants' knowledge of organizational policies.

The main potential consequences of perceived discrimination and heterosexism that have been investigated are negative health outcomes, work attitudes (e.g., job dissatisfaction, intention to quit, disengagement), and work outcomes (e.g., lack of promotion opportunities, lower wages). The rationale underlying this research is that discrimination and heterosexism contribute to a stressful and inhospitable work environment, which, in turn, can increase health problems and job dissatisfaction. Although perceived work discrimination appears to be only weakly associated with physical health problems, it is clearly linked to psychological distress (Smith & Ingram, 2004; Waldo, 1999) and negative work attitudes (Button, 2001; Ragins & Cornwell, 2001; Smith & Ingram, 2004; Waldo, 1999). Such findings provide a compelling monetary rationale for organizational intolerance of discrimination since organizations that reduce heterosexism may be more likely than others to retain lesbian, gay, and bisexual employees.

In contrast to the growing literature on perceived discrimination, relatively little research has explored lesbian or gay workers' positive workplace experiences or sources of resilience in coping with prejudice, bias, and fear of rejection. Social support is the facet of positive experience that researchers have most often studied with respect to lesbian, gay, and bisexual workers. The gay men interviewed for one study revealed that some of their most significant emotional support came from heterosexual female peers (Rumens, 2010). Many participants reported receiving support in coping with heterosexism. Perceived acceptance from work friends often provided a foundation for emotional support related to other facets of life (e.g., death of a parent, child care). Perceived support predicted both work and life satisfaction in another sample of nonheterosexual workers (Huffman et al., 2008). Research is needed to examine the development of workplace friendships, including the role of both general support and lesbian-, gay-, and bisexual-related support in the well-being of nonheterosexual workers.

Identity Disclosure and Concealment

Unlike visible characteristics that can determine a person's risk of prejudice (e.g., gender, race, pregnancy status), sexual orientation can be concealed. This attribute of sexual orientation is a double-edged sword: Although it provides lesbian, gay, and bisexual workers with the opportunity to evade stigmatization through concealment, it requires workers to make ongoing decisions about whether to "display or not to display; to tell or not to tell; to let on or not to let on; to lie or not to lie; and in each case, to whom, how, when, and where" (Goffman, 1963, p. 42)—a process often referred to as identity management. Identity management decisions can require workers to use cognitive and affective resources that might otherwise be available for work-related tasks (Ragins, 2004). Moreover, even when lesbian, gay, and bisexual workers adopt a relatively consistent identity management strategy across situations, workers must contend with possible negative consequences of those strategies. For example, the decision to conceal one's sexual orientation at work may hamper development of support networks and reduce one's sense of authenticity; likewise, the decision to disclose one's sexual orientation openly at work may increase the chances of being the target of formal or interpersonal discrimination.

Perhaps the most basic question of all is "How 'out' are lesbian, gay, and bisexual workers?" Surveys conducted in the United States have generally found that most workers disclose their orientation to some but not all co-workers. In one population-based sample, 55% of nonheterosexual

participants reported being out to their boss and 72% reported being out to co-workers (Henry J. Kaiser Family Foundation, 2001). Workers in another probability sample indicated that 51% were out to their boss and other supervisors and 58% were out to co-workers (Herek, Norton, Allen, & Sims, 2010). These statistics obscure striking within-group differences. Herek et al. (2010) found the highest disclosure rates among lesbian and gay male workers (ranging from 70% to 80% depending on group and disclosure target) and the lowest among bisexual men (ranging from 14% to 18% depending on the disclosure target). Such marked discrepancies point to the importance of not viewing nonheterosexual people as a monolithic sexual minority group (Moradi, Mohr, Worthington, & Fassinger, 2009).

Empirical work on lesbian, gay, and bisexual identity management at work has addressed the fact that workers use different strategies to conceal or reveal their sexual orientation. For example, Griffin (1992) described four identity management strategies used by participants in her study of lesbian and gay teachers. *Passing* involves actively cultivating a façade of heterosexuality, and *covering* involves concealing information that either directly or indirectly provides clues about one's sexual orientation. Being *implicitly out* involves sharing information that may lead others to guess one's orientation without actually disclosing one's sexual orientation identity, whereas being *explicitly out* involves clear communication of one's nonheterosexual identity.

Not surprisingly, disclosure levels have been found to be higher to the degree that lesbian, gay, and bisexual workers perceive their work climate as affirming; conversely, disclosure levels are lower when perceived heterosexism is high (e.g., Button, 2001; Brenner, Lyons, & Fassinger, 2010; Chrobot-Mason, Button, & DiClementi, 2001; Ragins & Cornwell, 2001; Smith & Ingram, 2004; Waldo, 1999). Research has also indicated that people who affirm their own nonheterosexual orientation are more likely than others to disclose their identity at work and less likely to use concealing strategies (Button, 2001; Chrobot-Mason et al., 2001). What are the consequences of the use of identity management strategy in the workplace? The degree to which workers use concealing or revealing strategies does not appear to have a strong influence on overall work attitudes and distress level; however, workers' disclosure-related fears (e.g., fear of being shunned or fired) robustly predicted work attitudes and distress in one study (Ragins, Singh, & Cornwell, 2007). Moreover, results from a recent study suggest that daily mood may shift substantially in response to use of these identity management strategies (Mohr et al., 2010). For example, on days in which concealing strategies were used, workers evidenced increases in negative affect and decreases in positive affect (Mohr et al., 2010). Such findings highlight the potential importance of investigating within-person variability in identity management use. Finally, identity concealment has been linked to reduced task efficiency (Barreto, Ellemers, & Banal, 2006) and decreased work group functioning (Chrobot-Mason et al., 2001).

A number of intriguing new directions in disclosure research have emerged in recent years. One line of work has focused on the reciprocal and interactive relations between experiences at work and experiences outside of work. Ragins (2004) described several examples of interplay between these different spheres of life, including one she has labeled *disclosure disconnects*: differences in disclosure levels at work and outside of work. Lesbian, gay, and bisexual workers may be more open about their sexual identity in their home life than at work; conversely, they may be relatively open at work but not yet out in other life spheres (e.g., family of origin, neighborhood). Ragins (2004) noted that such disconnects may lead to loss of control in identity management and lack of psychological congruence in identity, both of which may increase levels of perceived stress in lesbian, gay, and bisexual workers. Day and Schoenrade (2000) provided some indirect support for these propositions in their finding that outness at work was associated with less home–work conflict. Ragins (2004) also discussed ways that social support experienced in a person's life outside of work may influence the disclosure process at work. For example, lesbian, gay, and bisexual adults who receive strong support for their sexual identity from family and friends may feel more able to cope with potentially negative co-worker reactions to identity disclosure, and thus may be more likely than others to disclose their identity at work. Ragins (2004) noted that this dynamic may also work in the opposite direction (i.e., work support may bolster a person's ability to cope with disclosure at home) but that the positive effects are more likely in the home-to-work direction.

Another important direction for disclosure research is the experiences of heterosexual workers. For example, King, Reilly, and Hebl (2008) studied heterosexuals' reactions to disclosure by nonheterosexual co-workers and found support for the notion that reactions were most positive when the disclosure had occurred in the context of a well-established relationship. Also, Ragins (2004) discussed ways in which heterosexuals' experiences with nonheterosexual colleagues may be influenced by courtesy stigma (i.e., stigma by association). Ragins reviewed evidence from social psychological research that heterosexuals' social status may suffer when they are viewed as being friends with lesbian, gay, and bisexual people, and suggested that some heterosexuals may try to avoid this outcome by distancing themselves from nonheterosexual workers whose sexual identities are well known.

Research on identity management and disclosure has provided critical data on the experiences of lesbian, gay, and bisexual workers; however, advances are needed to address typical limitations of this research. For example, most studies have used cross-sectional data and relied on retrospective memory for events that may have occurred weeks or months in the past. Moreover, although identity management is typically described in terms of behavior in specific situations, research in this area has focused on what workers view as their typical use of identity management strategies. These limitations may be addressed through longitudinal designs, as well as ecological assessment methods that permit researchers to study situations as they occur in the workplace.

Theories of Vocational Behavior and Nonheterosexual Individuals

Vocational psychologists (both researchers and interventionists) tend to rely on three broad approaches to understanding vocational or career behavior: developmental theories, person–environment (P-E) fit theories, and theories that address social and cognitive decision-making processes. Each of these classes of theories offers a means of conceptualizing ways in which vocational development intersects with sexual identities, and each provides directions for research.

Developmental approaches. Vocational development theory, based largely on the classic work of Super (1957), focuses on age-appropriate developmental tasks, negotiated in a predictable sequence, that lead to the implementation of the self-concept in fulfilling life and career choices. There is an emphasis on readiness and possessing adequate skills for negotiating each new task in the individual's trajectory, and the thwarting of developmental progress can occur when tasks cannot be negotiated successfully. This theoretical approach suggests several potential developmental impediments to vocational progress for nonheterosexual people.

For example, if successful career development depends on a strong and healthy self-concept, then self-stigmatization (with all of the attendant confusion, lack of self-confidence, anxiety, and negative social comparison) clearly can compromise progress, and it is reasonable to assume that sexual identity issues may need some resolution before vocational progress can occur. Indeed, research indicates that career development trajectories are delayed or otherwise compromised for many individuals, with diversions of developmental energy into dealing with discrimination and the coming out process before career considerations can be faced (Schmidt & Nilsson, 2006).

In addition, familial lack of support or ostracism may remove the only source of stability and financial means of pursuing an education, and the literature on lesbian, gay, and bisexual adolescents documents clearly the downward trajectory of individuals who run away from or are banned from their homes (Ryan & Futterman, 1998). Finally, it is worth noting that many nonheterosexual individuals come out and experience significant life changes when already well into adulthood. When this happens, it may result in vocational displacement and the need for movement into a different occupation or career based on perceived and/or actual barriers. For example, a Catholic priest who came out as gay in midlife might find it necessary to leave the priesthood and find another occupation. Such processes beg empirical attention.

P-E fit approaches. A second class of career approaches, person–environment fit theories (also called P-E fit theories), is exemplified by John Holland's (1997) hexagonal model of career behavior and by work adjustment theory (Lofquist & Dawis, 1984). Holland's theory is widely used by career centers in secondary and postsecondary educational institutions in the United States, which often are organized according to its structure. Such theories assume that a match between the individual (whose personality is expressed through interests, abilities, needs, and values) and the work environment (which also exhibits a personality based on its particular demands and rewards) will produce the most appropriate and satisfying vocational choices. As might be expected in a theoretical approach reliant on accurate assessment, P-E fit theories have led to the creation of a wide range of individual and environmental assessments, particularly interest and skill inventories.

If successful vocational choice, entry, adjustment, and success rely upon a match between the individual and the environment, it seems clear that pervasive sexual stigma in educational institutions and workplaces exerts profound disruptive influences on the capacity of the individual to find a good fit in such contexts. Obviously, overt educational and workplace discrimination (as noted above and including widely documented problems such as wage inequities, lack of legal protection, discriminatory performance evaluations, discrimination in hiring and promotion, peer ostracism, and harassment; Ragins, 2004) constitutes the most serious impediment to vocational processes from a fit perspective. However, even environments that do not exhibit overt discrimination may represent unwelcoming, unsupportive workplaces that (as noted above) force difficult decisions about identity management and lead to bifurcated public–private identities for many lesbian, gay, and bisexual individuals.

In addition to environmental barriers, P-E fit assumptions also raise questions about the accuracy and validity of the measures used to assess individual and organizational characteristics. Pope (1992) has written about bias in testing with lesbian, gay, and bisexual people, and Chung (2003) has written about the specific issues related to career assessment with these populations. Issues include flat profiles in interest inventories that can characterize individuals struggling with depression or occupational stereotypes that inhibit the expression of their true interests. In addition, there is the issue of lack of validation studies in lesbian, gay, and bisexual populations of theoretical assumptions or the measures that tap those tenets; Chung and Harmon (1994), for example, found that the Holland code classifications of career aspirations of gay men were less gender-traditional than those of heterosexual men. Croteau and his colleagues (2008) called for increased empirical attention to assessment of career-related variables for nonheterosexual people.

Social and cognitive approaches. The third major class of theoretical approaches to understanding career behavior includes theories focused on cognitive and social processes in career decision making, the most widely used being the social learning theory of Krumboltz (1994) and the social-cognitive career theory of Lent, Brown, and Hackett (2006). With an emphasis on cognitions and socially learned beliefs about self and careers, these theories posit that impediments to optimal vocational behavior are found in factors that function to limit choices, distort outcome expectations, or otherwise obfuscate clarity in decision making.

Occupational stereotyping is one example of such impediments, as it sets up a cognitive block against considering the full range of possible vocational choices because of perceptions of certain careers as inappropriate for or inhospitable to sexual minority people. To the extent that other minority statuses (e.g., race, gender, disability) interact with sexual identity, the constriction in opportunities can be daunting; indeed, Adams, Cahill, and Ackerling (2004) found a complex array of constraints in the career decision making and expectations of Latino lesbian and gay students. Another impediment is the lack of "out" sexual minority role models in many occupations, which interacts with occupational stereotyping to maintain perceptions of some occupations as inappropriate for nonheterosexual individuals. Moreover, research suggests that even when role models are present, lesbian, gay, and bisexual individuals may experience less direct support and guidance in their career decision making than do their heterosexual peers, perhaps because models are more distant or individuals' own levels of self-disclosure prevent full consideration of their sexual stigmatization in making career-related choices (Nauta, Saucier, & Woodard, 2001).

Identity disclosure is also an important factor in this class of theories, as it affects many aspects of career decision making, from how to represent gay-related leadership activities on a résumé to how to deal with dual-career issues in negotiating a job search for one or both members of a same-sex couple. Limited self-disclosure almost guarantees that many vocational decisions will be made in isolation, without feedback or accurate knowledge, and in the absence of assistance, and little is known at present about the precise effects of hidden identities in career decision making. Moreover, even those empowered to aid people in career planning, such as guidance or career counselors, may harbor attitudinal biases against sexual minorities or a lack of awareness of issues related to sexual orientation (Croteau et al., 2008), which renders their "help" compromised at best and harmful at worst. It thus may be difficult for lesbian, gay, and bisexual individuals to make decisions in anything other than an atmosphere of secrecy, ignorance, confusion, and constricted "choices."

Lesbian, Gay, and Bisexual Leadership

Barriers and difficulties notwithstanding, many lesbian, gay, and bisexual workers rise to positions of leadership in their organizations. Although research on lesbian, gay, and bisexual leadership is scant, Fassinger and her colleagues (2010) developed what is thought to be the first model of lesbian, gay, and bisexual leadership, examining leadership enactment along three dimensions: (1) sexual orientation, particularly regarding identity disclosure; (2) gender orientation, including leader gender; and (3) situation, conceptualized in their model as the composition of the group being "led." Fassinger et al. (2010) noted that the context of stigma and marginalization likely influences all levels of leadership development. Lesbian, gay, and bisexual individuals may lack confidence in their capacity to assume leadership roles, they may be prevented from assuming such roles in particular occupations or organizations, they may be compromised in their effectiveness and success as leaders, and they may be regarded negatively even if they are successful. Moreover, for nonheterosexual individuals who hold multiple minority statuses (e.g., ethnicity, disability), the effects of marginalization likely are compounded in their leadership enactment.

In terms of the sexual orientation dimension, the extant literature suggests complex and interesting effects on leadership of lesbian, gay, and bisexual individuals. These include perceptions by nonheterosexual leaders of positive effects of their sexual minority identity in fostering behaviors such as challenging the organizational status quo, exhibiting flexibility, valuing inclusion, and maintaining a nonjudgmental stance toward others (see Coon, 2001; Snyder, 2006; Shallenberger, 1994). More negative outcomes reported include constraints in their capacity to advance to leadership as "out" sexual minorities (e.g., Coon, 2001) and the pernicious presence of intolerance toward nonheterosexual individuals even in those exposed to diversity training (Horne, Rice, & Israel, 2004). Relatively neutral effects include leaders reporting having worked to achieve high competence as a buffer against discrimination based on their sexual orientation (Coon, 2001; Snyder, 2006).

Self-disclosure of sexual orientation is a central issue for many lesbian, gay, and bisexual leaders. Although self-disclosure at any level of the organization presents a conundrum, for leaders, whose task is one of influencing groups of others to move toward some defined goal, the attitudes of the group being led come into play. Avolio (2007) noted that followers' willingness to follow leaders likely depends in part on perceptions of their similarity of values, and sexual minority status may represent a perceived difference in values that seems unbridgeable for some. For nonheterosexual leaders in groups with low or varying levels of tolerance of sexual minority status, leadership challenges are likely very different from those of a leader in a gay-affirmative group. Followers and leaders bring with them lifetimes of experiences, beliefs, and demographic and identity locations, which shape their work together in unique leader-by-situation interactions, the variability of which will arise from the salience of those dimensions at any given time (Fassinger et al., 2010). Such complexities in lesbian, gay, and bisexual leadership and the dearth of literature suggest numerous possibilities for future research, including determination of (1) when and how the sexual identity of the leader matters, (2) which characteristics of lesbian, gay, and bisexual leaders interact with the situation to shape outcomes, (3) what differentiates effective and poor lesbian, gay, and bisexual leadership (including the possible role of identity), and (4) how lesbian, gay, and bisexual leadership mentoring might be achieved (Fassinger et al., 2010).

Positive Aspects of Lesbian, Gay, and Bisexual Career Development and Work Behavior

Despite the difficulties encountered by many nonheterosexual individuals in trying to negotiate vocational decisions, there are many positive aspects of the intersection of sexual identity and career development. For example, a stable identity in one area may provide reassurances of stability in the face of dramatic shifts in the other; indeed, a career client of one of us once stated that she was much more terrified of telling her parents that she was quitting

her engineering major than she had been in revealing to them that she was lesbian. A second benefit is the development of "crisis competence" (Friend, 1990), the development of skills and strengths in the coming out process that equip a person for challenges such as experiencing rejection, finding socially supportive networks, becoming independent in thought and action, and other qualities that aid in career planning. Similarly, the clarity regarding people's values, beliefs, needs, and desires developed in the coming out process may strengthen their self-concept in a way that enables vocational development, although this conjecture begs empirical exploration.

There is also considerable evidence that sexual minority individuals exhibit less rigid gender roles and are more open to considering careers that are nontraditional for their gender, which opens up a wider range of occupational possibilities; particularly for women, such options often offer higher status, better compensation, and increased opportunities for advancement (Fassinger, 2005). Similarly, evidence suggests that same-sex couples are more egalitarian in their relationships and less tied to traditional family structures than their heterosexual peers; again, especially for women, this opens up more possibilities for the equal valuing of both people's careers and equitable division of household labor and childcare that make the home–work interface more manageable for women (Fassinger, 2008). In addition, the ties that many lesbian, gay, and bisexual individuals form to their communities can buffer the stress encountered in the workplace and can provide an outlet for social and political action that allows for a proactive approach to managing their identity in a culture of sexual stigma.

CONCLUSIONS

In many ways, lesbian, gay, and bisexual workers are probably not very different from heterosexual workers. Lesbian, gay, and bisexual workers bring diverse interests, aspirations, talents, resources, skills, life experiences, and foibles to the workplace. However, the societal stigmatization and marginalization of nonheterosexuality, combined with the concealability of sexual orientation, have created critical differences in the career and work experiences of heterosexual and nonheterosexual workers— differences that have implications for vocational decision making, work attitudes, individual economic prosperity, opportunities for advancement, and even life outside of work. In this chapter, we have reviewed research and theory on manifestations of these differences.

In the past several decades there has been an impressive surge in writing on the work lives of lesbian, gay, and bisexual people (Croteau et al., 2008). Scholarship in this area increasingly reflects the multilevel nature of work and career, and we believe that research on work- and career-related issues for lesbian, gay, and bisexual people will profit from the growing interest in reflecting this complexity. A related welcome development is the increasing degree of permeability across disciplines, both inside and outside of psychology. Diverse literatures have emerged in this research area, and we believe the quality of work will benefit from greater interaction between industrial/organizational psychologists, vocational counseling psychologists, community psychologists, educators, economists, policy analysts, and others whose expertise can inform this complex area of study.

REFERENCES

Adams, E. M., Cahill, B. J., & Ackerling, S. J. (2004). A qualitative study of Latino lesbian and gay youths' experiences with discrimination and the career development process. *Journal of Vocational Behavior, 66,* 199–218.

Allen, R. L. (2005, April 18). Industry comes out of closet, debuts hiring, promotion programs for gays and lesbians. *Nation's Restaurant News, 39,* 20.

Avolio, B. J. (2007). Promoting more integrative strategies for leadership theory-building. *American Psychologist, 62,* 25–33.

Barreto, M., Ellemers, N., & Banal, S. (2006). Working under cover: Performance-related self-confidence among members of contextually devalued groups who try to pass. *European Journal of Social Psychology, 36,* 337–352.

Blustein, D. L. (2008). The role of work in psychological health and well-being. *American Psychologist, 63,* 228–240.

Brenner, B. R., Lyons, H. Z., & Fassinger, R. E. (2010). Can heterosexism harm organizations? Predicting the perceived organizational citizenship behaviors of gay and lesbian employees. *Career Development Quarterly, 58,* 321–335.

Button, S. B. (2001). Organizational efforts to affirm sexual diversity: A cross-level examination. *Journal of Applied Psychology, 86,* 17–28.

Chesir-Teran, D. (2003). Conceptualizing and assessing heterosexism in high schools: A setting-level approach. *American Journal of Community Psychology, 31,* 267–279.

Chrobot-Mason, D., Button, S. B., & DiClementi, J. D. (2001). Sexual identity management strategies: An exploration of antecedents and consequences. *Sex Roles, 45,* 321–336.

Chung, Y. B. (2003). Ethical and professional issues in career assessment with lesbian, gay, and bisexual persons. *Journal of Career Assessment, 11,* 96–112.

Chung, Y. B., & Harmon, L. W. (1994). The career interests and aspirations of gay men: How sex-role orientation is related. *Journal of Vocational Behavior, 45,* 223–239.

Coon, D. W. (2001). *A study of gay and lesbian leaders.* Publication # AAT 3032549. Washington: Seattle University.

Croteau, J. M., Bieschke, K. J., Fassinger, R. E., & Manning, J. L. (2008). Counseling psychology and sexual orientation: History, selective trends, and future directions. In S. D. Brown & R.W. Lent (Eds.), *Handbook of counseling psychology* (4th ed., pp. 194–211). New York: Wiley & Sons.

Day, N. E., & Greene, P. G. (2008). A case for sexual orientation diversity management in small and large organizations. *Human Resource Management, 47,* 637–654.

Day, N. E., & Schoenrade, P. (2000). The relationships among reported disclosure of sexual orientation, anti-discrimination policies, top management support, and work attitudes of gay and lesbian employees. *Personnel Review, 29,* 346–366.

Ellis, A. L., & Riggle, E. D. B. (1995). The relation of job satisfaction and degree of openness about one's sexual orientation for lesbians and gay men. *Journal of Homosexuality, 30,* 75–85.

Fassinger, R. E. (1995). From invisibility to integration: Lesbian identity in the workplace. *The Career Development Quarterly, 44,* 148–167.

Fassinger, R. E. (2005). Theoretical issues in the study of women's career development: Building bridges in a brave new world. In W. B. Walsh & M. L. Savickas (Eds.), *Handbook of vocational psychology* (3rd ed., pp. 85–124). Mahwah, NJ: Erlbaum.

Fassinger, R. E. (2008). Workplace diversity and public policy. *American Psychologist, 63,* 252–268.

Fassinger, R. E., Shullman, S. L., & Stevenson, M. R. (2010). Toward an affirmative lesbian, gay, bisexual, and transgender leadership paradigm. *American Psychologist, 65,* 201–215.

Freud, S. (1957). Civilization and its discontents. In J. Strachey (Ed. and Trans.), *The standard edition of the complete psychological works of Sigmund Freud* (Vol. 21, pp. 64–148). London: Hogarth Press. (Original work published in 1930.)

Friend, R. A. (1990). Older lesbian and gay people: A theory of successful aging. *Journal of Homosexuality, 20,* 99–118.

Githens, R. P., & Aragon, S. R. (2009). LGBT employee groups: Goals and organizational structures. *Advances in Developing Human Resources, 11,* 121–135.

Goffman, E. (1963). *Stigma: Notes on the management of spoiled identity*. New York: Simon & Schuster.

Griffin, P. (1992). From hiding out to coming out: Empowering lesbian and gay educators. In K. M. Harbeck (Ed.), *Coming out of the classroom closet* (pp. 167–196). Binghamton, NY: Harrington Park Press.

Hatzenbuehler, M. L., Keyes, K. M., & Hasin, D. S. (2009). State-level policies and psychiatric morbidity in lesbian, gay, and bisexual populations. *American Journal of Public Health, 99,* 2275–2281.

Hebl, M. R., Foster, J. B., Mannix, L. M., & Dovidio, J. F. (2002). Formal and interpersonal discrimination: A field study of bias toward homosexual applicants. *Personality and Social Psychology Bulletin, 28,* 815–825.

Helderman, R. S. (2010, March 6). Virginia attorney general to colleges: End gay protections. *The Washington Post*. Retrieved from http://www.washingtonpost.com

Henry J. Kaiser Family Foundation. (2001). Inside-OUT: A report on the experiences of lesbians, gays and bisexuals in America and the public's views on issues and policies related to sexual orientation. Menlo Park: The Henry J. Kaiser Family Foundation. http://www.kff.org/kaiserpolls/3193-index.cfm (accessed June 2010).

Herek, G. M. (2007). Confronting sexual stigma and prejudice: Theory and practice. *Journal of Social Issues, 63,* 905–925.

Herek, G. M. (2009). Hate crimes and stigma-related experiences among sexual minority adults in the United States: Prevalence estimates from a national probability sample. *Journal of Interpersonal Violence, 24,* 54–74.

Herek, G. M., Gillis, R., & Cogan, J. C. (2009). Internalized stigma among sexual minority adults: Insights from a social psychological perspective. *Journal of Counseling Psychology, 56,* 32–43.

Herek, G. M., Norton, A. T., Allen, T. J., & Sims, C. L. (2010). Demographic, psychological, and social characteristics of self-identified lesbian, gay, and bisexual adults in a U.S. probability sample. *Sexuality Research and Social Policy, 7,* 176–200.

Holland, J. L. (1997). *Making vocational choices: A theory of vocational personalities and work environments*. Odessa, FL: Psychological Assessment Resources.

Horne, S., Rice, N. D., & Israel, T. (2004). Heterosexual student leader attitudes regarding lesbian, gay, and bisexual students. *NASPA Journal, 41,* 760–772.

Hornsby, E. E., & Munn, S. L. (2009). University work life benefits and same-sex couples. *Advances in Developing Human Resources, 11,* 67–81.

Huffman, A., Watrous, K., & King, E. B. (2008). Diversity in the workplace: Support for lesbian, gay, and bisexual workers. *Human Resource Management, 47,* 237–253.

Human Rights Campaign. (2009). *The state of the workplace for lesbian, gay, bisexual and transgender Americans 2007–2008*. Retrieved from http://www.hrc.org/documents/HRC_Foundation_State_of_the_Workplace_2007–2008.pdf on April 14, 2010.

Kaplan, D. M. (2006). Can diversity training discriminate? Backlash to lesbian, gay, and bisexual diversity initiatives. *Employee Responsibilities and Rights Journal, 18,* 61–72.

King, E. B., & Cortina, J. (2010). The social and economic imperative of LGBT-supportive organizations. *Industrial-Organizational Psychology: Perspectives of Science and Practice, 3,* 69–78.

King, E. B., Reilly, C., & Hebl, M. R. (2008). The best and worst of times: Dual perspectives of coming out in the workplace. *Group and Organization Management, 33,* 566–601.

Kozlowski, S. W. J., & Klein, K. J. (2000). A multilevel approach to theory and research in organizations: Contextual, temporal, and emergent processes. In K. J. Klein & S. W. J. Kozlowski (Eds.), *Multilevel theory, research, and methods in organizations: Foundations, extensions, and new directions* (pp. 3–90). San Francisco: Jossey-Bass.

Krumboltz, J. D. (1994). Improving career development theory from a social learning perspective. In M. Savickas & R. Lent (Eds.), *Convergence in career development theories* (pp. 9–31). Palo Alto, CA: Consulting Psychologist Press.

Lent, R. W., Brown, S. D., & Hackett, G. (2006). Social cognitive career theory. In D. Brown (Ed.), *Career choice and development* (pp. 255–311). San Francisco: Jossey-Bass.

Lofquist, L. H., & Dawis, R. V. (1984). Research on work adjustment and satisfaction: Implications for career counseling. In S. Brown & R. Lent (Eds.), *Handbook of counseling psychology* (pp. 216–237). New York: Wiley.

Meyer, I. H. (2003). Prejudice, social stress, and mental health in lesbian, gay, and bisexual populations: Conceptual issues and research evidence. *Psychological Bulletin, 129,* 674–697.

Mohr, J. J., King, E. B., Peddie, C., Kendra, M. S., Jones, K., & McShea, H. (2010, August). Everyday identity management experiences of lesbian, gay, and bisexual workers. In Jonathan J. Mohr & Eden B. King (Chairs), Advances in Sexual Minority Research on Career and the Workplace. Symposium conducted at the annual meeting of the American Psychological Association, San Diego, CA.

Moradi, B., Mohr, J. J., Worthington, R. L., & Fassinger, R. E. (2009). Counseling psychology research on sexual (orientation) minority issues: Conceptual and methodological challenges and opportunities. *Journal of Counseling Psychology, 56,* 5–22.

Nauta, M. M., Saucier, A. M., & Woodard, L. E. (2001). Interpersonal influences on students' academic and career decisions: The impact of sexual orientation. *Career Development Quarterly, 49,* 352–362.

Pope, M. (1992). Bias in the interpretation of psychological tests. In S. Dworkin & F. Guiterrez (Eds.),

Counseling gay men and lesbians: Journey to the end of the rainbow (pp. 277–292). Alexandria, VA: American Counseling Association.

Ragins, B. R. (2004). Sexual orientation in the workplace: The unique work and career experiences of gay, lesbian, and bisexual workers. *Research in Personnel and Human Resources Management, 23,* 37–112

Ragins, B. R., & Cornwell, J. M. (2001). Pink triangles: Antecedents and consequences of perceived workplace discrimination against gay and lesbian employees. *Journal of Applied Psychology, 86,* 1244–1261.

Ragins, B. R., Cornwell, J. M., & Miller, J. S. (2003). Heterosexism in the workplace: Do race and gender matter? *Group & Organization Management, 28,* 45–74.

Ragins, B. R., Singh, R., & Cornwell, J. M. (2007). Making the invisible visible: Fear and disclosure of sexual orientation at work. *Journal of Applied Psychology, 92,* 1103–1118.

Rocco, T. S., Landorf, H., & Delgado, A. (2009). Framing the issue/framing the question: A proposed framework for organizational perspectives on sexual minorities. *Advances in Developing Human Resources, 11,* 7–23.

Rumens, N. (2010). Firm friends: Exploring the supportive components in gay men's workplace friendships. *The Sociological Review, 58,* 135–155.

Ryan, C., & Futterman, D. (1998). *Lesbian and gay youth: Care and counseling.* New York: Columbia University Press.

Schmidt, C. K., & Nilsson, J. E. (2006). The effects of simultaneous developmental processes: Factors relating to the career development of lesbian, gay, and bisexual youth. *Career Development Quarterly, 55,* 22–37.

Schneider, B., Goldstein, H. W., & Smith, D. B. (1995). The attraction-selection-attrition framework: An update. *Personnel Psychology, 48,* 747–773.

Sears, J. T. (2005). *Gay, lesbian, and transgender issues in education: Programs policies, and practices.* New York: Haworth Press.

Shallenberger, D. (1994). Professional and openly gay: A narrative study of the experience. *Journal of Management Inquiry, 3,* 119–142.

Smith, N. G., & Ingram, K. M. (2004). Workplace heterosexism and adjustment among lesbian, gay, and bisexual individuals: The role of unsupportive social interactions. *Journal of Counseling Psychology, 51,* 57–67.

Snyder, K. (2006). *The G quotient: Why gay executives are excelling as leaders...and what every manager needs to know.* San Francisco: Jossey-Bass.

Super, D. E. (1957). *The psychology of careers.* New York: Harper & Row.

Waldo, C. R. (1999). Working in a majority context: A structural model of heterosexism as a minority stress in the workplace. *Journal of Counseling Psychology, 46,* 218–232.

Weichselbaumer, D. (2003). Sexual orientation discrimination in hiring. *Labour Economics, 10,* 629–642.

12

Same-Sex Romantic Relationships

ADAM W. FINGERHUT AND LETITIA ANNE PEPLAU

Same-sex couples are increasingly visible in American society, with sympathetic portrayals in popular films, television shows, and magazines. At the same time, there has been a heated public debate in the United States about legalizing marriage for same-sex couples. A few states now permit legal marriage for same-sex couples but most states and the federal government (through the Defense of Marriage Act) have laws defining marriage as exclusively between a man and a woman.

Researchers studying same-sex couples have become part of the ongoing public conversation about marriage equality. Two broad research topics have been center stage. First, policy makers and attorneys have turned to social science research to answer basic questions about the lives of lesbians and gay men. In particular, are the relationships of same-sex couples fundamentally similar to those of heterosexual men and women and are same-sex relationships influenced by the same dynamic processes as heterosexual couples? Second, what is the social and psychological impact of legalizing same-sex relationships and of the divisive public debates on this topic? In the sections that follow, we review empirical research addressing these two broad topics. (For other reviews of research on same-sex relationships, see Biblarz & Savci, 2010; Kurdek, 2005; Patterson, 2000; and Peplau & Fingerhut, 2007.)

CHARACTERISTICS OF SAME-SEX ROMANTIC RELATIONSHIPS

Those in favor of marriage for same-sex couples emphasize that same-sex and heterosexual couples are very similar, and thus allowing same-sex couples to marry will not change the institution of marriage in any meaningful way. In contrast, those who oppose marriage equality suggest that same-sex couples are fundamentally different from heterosexual couples and that they should be excluded from the institution of marriage. We review empirical findings on core aspects of same-sex couple relationships, highlighting many consistent similarities and the few areas of difference among these couple types.

It should be noted that studies of same-sex relationships may include individuals who identify as bisexual. A common practice among researchers is to focus on the gender of partners in couples and not necessarily on their sexual identities. Thus, although researchers often refer to "lesbian" and "gay male" couples (as we too will do in this chapter), these labels may obscure variations in the sexual identities of partners. This is, of course, also true of studies of "heterosexual couples." As a result, little is known about the experiences in committed relationships of individuals who identify as bisexual.

Relationship Formation

Establishing a satisfying, committed intimate relationship is an important life goal for most people, and many are successful in doing so. In a large Internet survey, 60% of lesbians and 41% of gay men reported being in a serious relationship or marriage, as did 64% of heterosexual women and 58% of heterosexual men (Lippa, 2007). In analyses of representative surveys from California, Carpenter and Gates (2008) estimated rates of cohabitation by lesbians and gay men aged 18–59. Depending on the survey, 37–46% of gay men and 51–62% of lesbians reported being in a same-sex cohabiting relationship. The comparable statistic for heterosexual individuals who were married or cohabiting was 62%.

Researchers have also investigated the qualities that lesbians and gay men look for in a romantic partner (reviewed by Peplau & Spalding, 2000).

Like their heterosexual counterparts, lesbians and gay men tend to emphasize affection, dependability, and similarity of interests and values. Gender differences have also been reported, with men, both gay and heterosexual, more likely to emphasize a partner's physical attractiveness and with lesbian and heterosexual women giving more importance to personality characteristics. In a recent Internet survey, men were significantly more likely than women to value good looks and less likely to emphasize honesty, humor, kindness, and dependability (Lippa, 2007). Small differences based on sexual orientation were also found. In particular, lesbians and gay men tended to rank religion and parenting ability lower in importance for a romantic partner than did heterosexual men and women.

Relationship Quality

Stereotypes have often characterized same-sex relationships as unhappy and maladjusted. In an illustrative study, heterosexual college students described gay and lesbian relationships as "less in love," less satisfying, and more prone to discord than heterosexual relationships (Testa, Kinder, & Ironson, 1987). More recent research suggests that these stereotypes may be changing. Skinner and Goodfriend (2009) asked college students to evaluate an excerpt from a fictional couple's initial counseling session. Participants read one of three versions, which differed only in the names associated with the couple (e.g., Jennifer and David, Jennifer and Amy). The researchers predicted that the same-sex couples would be rated more negatively than the heterosexual couple. In fact, no significant differences were found in students' ratings of satisfaction, closeness, commitment, or investment in the relationship among the three vignettes. Ratings of the vignettes were also made by 96 professional counselors. Counter to prediction, counselors actually gave significantly higher ratings for satisfaction and investment to the same-sex couples than to the heterosexual couple. Counselors' ratings of commitment and closeness did not vary by couple type.

Across many studies using diverse methods, research has consistently found similarities in the quality of committed same-sex and heterosexual relationships (Balsam, Beauchaine, Rothblum, & Solomon, 2008; Kurdek, 2005; Peplau & Fingerhut, 2007). Of course, both same-sex and heterosexual couples run the gamut from exceptionally happy to miserable and conflict-ridden, but on average sexual orientation is not predictive of relationship quality. On average, same-sex and heterosexual couples do not differ on standardized measures of love, trust, or relationship satisfaction (e.g., Holmberg, Blair, & Phillips, 2010).

In the most comprehensive longitudinal study of same-sex couples currently available, Kurdek (1998, 2008) followed both partners in cohabiting same-sex and heterosexual married couples over the first 10 years of cohabitation. None of the same-sex couples were rearing children. All comparisons controlled for age, education, income, and years of cohabitation. At initial testing, the lesbian, gay male, and heterosexual couples did not differ in relationship satisfaction as assessed by the Dyadic Adjustment Scale. Over time, partners in same-sex couples who stayed together showed consistent levels of relationship quality with no reliable temporal decline over time. In contrast, heterosexual married couples who stayed together did decline in average relationship quality over time, with the largest decrease occurring for married couples with children. This finding is consistent with the broader literature showing declines in marital quality associated with parenthood (Bradbury & Karney, 2010).

Researchers have also investigated factors that enhance or detract from relationship quality. Do the same processes affect relationship quality in both same-sex and heterosexual couples? In an illustrative study of same-sex cohabiting and heterosexual married couples, Kurdek (2004) demonstrated that in all types of couples, relationship quality was higher when partners were less neurotic, adopted a pattern of greater equality in their relationship, handled conflict more effectively, and perceived greater social support for their relationship.

Research testing other predictors of relationship quality has also shown similarities between heterosexual and same-sex couples. For example, consistent with predictions based on social exchange theory, an individual's relationship satisfaction tends to be high when he or she perceives many rewards and few costs from the relationship (e.g., Beals, Impett, & Peplau, 2002; Duffy & Rusbult, 1986). In a comparison of same-sex and heterosexual couples, Conley, Roesch, Peplau, and Gold (2009) found support for the "positive illusions" hypothesis—the idea that people in romantic relationships are more satisfied when they view their partner more favorably than the partner sees himself or herself. Finally, gay, lesbian, and heterosexual couples report greater relationship satisfaction when partners are similar in background and attitudes (Kurdek & Schmitt, 1987; Mohr & Fassinger, 2006).

To examine relationship processes, relationship researchers commonly bring heterosexual couples into laboratory settings and observe how the partners behave while interacting during standard, structured discussion tasks. These methods have been extended to same-sex couples (e.g., Gottman et al., 2003). Roisman, Clausell, Holland, Fortuna, & Elief (2008) observed and coded the conversations of committed same-sex couples and engaged/married heterosexual couples as they discussed and tried to resolve a problem in their relationship. Controlling for demographic factors, lesbian and gay male couples were generally indistinguishable from their committed heterosexual counterparts. All types of couples had similar positive views of their relationships and interacted in similar ways during the discussion aimed at resolving a relationship conflict. In another study, Julien and colleagues (2003) observed same-sex and heterosexual couples as they engaged in both a conflict (problem-solving) and a social support discussion. Results showed that couples who scored higher on relationship quality expressed less negativity during the conflict interaction and more positivity in both the conflict and support interactions. No significant differences were found among couple types in the level of positive or negative behaviors or in the association of these behaviors with overall relationship quality.

A third observational study by Baucom, McFarland, and Christensen (2010) examined the "demand–withdraw" interaction pattern. Demand–withdraw behavior occurs when one partner makes a complaint or request for a change and the other partner avoids the request or withdraws from the discussion. The extent to which partners demand and withdraw can be reliably coded when partners are observed during a structured problem-solving discussion. Results were similar for gay, lesbian, dating heterosexual, and married heterosexual couples. Individuals demanded more when discussing a problem they had identified, and withdrew more when discussing their partner's issue. Regardless of sexual orientation, women demanded at a higher level than men, and men withdrew at higher levels than women. Finally, greater levels of demand and withdraw behavior during interaction were associated with lower levels of relationship satisfaction for all couples.

Taken together, the research on relationship quality consistently demonstrates that many lesbians and gay men establish satisfying intimate relationships, that the average level of reported relationship quality in same-sex and heterosexual couples is comparable, and that the same processes contribute to relationship quality among all types of couples.

Sexuality

Researchers have studied a range of topics concerning sexuality in same-sex couples (reviewed by Peplau, Fingerhut, & Beals, 2004). Several consistent findings have emerged. Same-sex couples vary widely in the frequency of sexual behavior in their relationships, with a general tendency for sexual frequency to decline over time in long-term couples. This mirrors the pattern generally found for heterosexual couples (Christopher & Sprecher, 2000). Additionally, studies have consistently documented high average levels of sexual satisfaction in same-sex couples that are comparable to those reported by heterosexual couples. For example, Kurdek (1991) found no significant differences in sexual satisfaction among gay, lesbian, and heterosexual couples.

Researchers have begun to investigate factors that are associated with sexual satisfaction in same-sex couples. Not surprisingly, sexual satisfaction and sexual frequency are linked. In the American Couples Study (Blumstein & Schwartz, 1983), for example, the correlation between sexual frequency and sexual satisfaction was almost identical for lesbians, gay men, and heterosexual husbands and wives, ranging from $r = 0.46$ to 0.50 (controlling for age and duration of relationship). Research also shows that in all types of couples, greater sexual satisfaction is also correlated with greater overall relationship satisfaction (see also Blumstein & Schwartz, 1983; Holmberg et al., 2010; Peplau, Cochran, & Mays, 1997). A new research direction has been to examine how individuals' motives for engaging in sex affect their evaluation of sexual experiences. In a study of women in same-sex and heterosexual relationships, Sanchez and colleagues (2011) assessed how often women in same-sex and in heterosexual relationships had sex with their partner for approval motives (e.g., "for fear your partner won't love you anymore if you don't") and for intimacy motives (e.g., "to make an emotional connection with your partner"). Results demonstrated that among both lesbian and heterosexual women, having sex to enhance intimacy with a partner was associated with greater sexual satisfaction whereas having sex to earn a partner's approval was associated with sexual dissatisfaction.

One aspect of sexuality in which differences have been found among gay, lesbian, and heterosexual couples concerns sexual exclusivity in committed relationships. On average, gay men are less likely to endorse sexual exclusivity than are lesbians or heterosexuals. For example, in the American Couples Study (Blumstein & Schwartz, 1983), only 36% of gay men indicated that it was important to be sexually monogamous, compared to 75% of husbands, 84% of wives, and 71% of lesbians. Reports of actual behavior mirror beliefs about exclusivity. In the American Couples Study, 82% of gay men reported having engaged in extradyadic sex, compared to only 26% of husbands, 21% of wives, and 28% of lesbians. More recent data are provided by a survey of highly committed same-sex couples who obtained civil unions in Vermont (Solomon, Rothblum, & Balsam, 2005). Among lesbians, 86% said they had agreed to be monogamous, only 9% said they had ever had sex with another person since the current relationship began, and only 5% said they had ever had a "meaningful love affair." Among gay men, 50% said they had agreed to be monogamous, 58% said they had ever had sex with someone else since the current relationship began, but only 6% said they had ever had a meaningful affair. Interestingly, attitudes regarding monogamy, particularly among gay men, may be changing and may be subject to cohort effects. As evidence of this, D'Augelli, Rendina, Grossman, and Sinclair (2008) showed that in a sample of lesbian, gay, and bisexual adolescents age 16–22, 92% of female and 82% of male participants believed they would be in a monogamous relationship after the age of 30.

Though popular opinion suggests that extradyadic sex is always detrimental to relationships, this has not been found in empirical research. Kurdek (1991) found that sexual fidelity was positively related to relationship satisfaction for lesbian and heterosexual couples, but not for gay male couples. The impact of extradyadic sex on a committed relationship may depend on the partners' expectations or explicit agreements about sexual openness. As Blumstein and Schwartz (1983, p. 282) noted, "All non-monogamy is not the same. Some is 'cheating,' and some occurs in an 'open relationship.'" In the

American Couples Study, 65% of gay couples agreed that nonmonogamy was permissible under some circumstances, compared to only 29% of lesbian couples and 15% of married couples (Blumstein & Schwartz, 1983, footnote 27, p. 585). In the study of same-sex civil unions in Vermont, only 50% of gay men had an agreement with their partner to be monogamous compared to 86% of lesbians (Solomon et al., 2005). Researchers have investigated factors that affect gay men's decisions about sexual exclusivity versus openness. For example, in a large Internet study, Wheldon and Pathak (2010) found that 49% of gay men in a primary romantic relationship had explicit agreements to be monogamous. Nonmonogamy agreements were associated with being older, being in a longer lasting relationship, and endorsing traditional views of masculinity (e.g., that men should be independent, aggressive, and emotionally restrained). The association with traditional masculinity remained even after controlling for demographic characteristics and relationship length.

In summary, research consistently documents many similarities in the sexual experiences of lesbians and gay men in relationships and in factors that affect their sexual satisfaction. The one area of difference is the pattern of less sexual exclusivity among gay male couples.

Division of Household Labor

Most coupled gay men and lesbians are in dual-earner relationships, so neither partner is the exclusive breadwinner and each partner has some measure of economic independence (Blumstein & Schwartz, 1983; Herek, Norton, Allen, & Sims, 2010). Studies of the division of household tasks rely on partners' self-reports. Comparative research among cohabiting couples has found that lesbians and gay men generally report dividing housework more equitably than do heterosexual couples. For example, Kurdek (1993) compared the division of housework (e.g., cleaning, cooking, shopping) among cohabiting same-sex couples and married heterosexual couples, none of whom had children. Among heterosexual couples, wives typically did most of the housework. In contrast, lesbian and gay couples divided household tasks more equally. Lesbian partners tended to report that the same tasks were done equally often by each partner; gay male partners were more likely to have each partner specialize in certain tasks. In research comparing same-sex couples in civil unions in Vermont to heterosexual couples, Solomon, Rothblum, and Balsam (2005) also documented greater sharing of household tasks by same-sex couples. The presence of children typically increases the gendered divisions in heterosexual marriages, with wives largely responsible for childcare. In contrast, lesbian couples who are raising children together generally report a pattern of sharing (Patterson, Sutfin, & Fulcher, 2004), although there may be variations associated with race, social class, and biological relatedness (Biblarz & Savci, 2010). Comparable studies for gay fathers are not currently available.

Qualitative research can provide insights into the lives of couples not available through self-reports. In an illustrative study, Carrington (1999) conducted in-depth interviews with 52 mostly middle class same-sex couples and families from the San Francisco area. He also conducted weeklong observations of eight of these family households. Carrington (1999) suggested that same-sex couples' reports of equal sharing of household activities reflect their ideals but often mask substantial observable differences between partners' actual contributions. He suggested that equal sharing of domestic activities was far from universal and was most common among affluent couples who relied on paid help or when both partners had less demanding jobs with more flexible schedules.

In summary, when it comes to household tasks, same-sex couples do not adopt "husband" and "wife" roles. Although the allocation of housework may not be perfectly equal in same-sex couples, it is typically more balanced than in heterosexual couples.

Relationship Stability

Many adults want an intimate relationship that is not only close and satisfying, but that also endures over time. Relationship researchers have investigated factors that contribute to partners' sense of psychological commitment and to the longevity of their relationship. The most widely used analysis of commitment is Rusbult's (1983) investment model. This model proposes that commitment is based on three general factors that increase dependence on the relationship. These are positive attractions, such as love and satisfaction, that increase each partner's desire to stay together; the availability of desirable alternatives to the current relationship; and barriers to leaving a relationship, including investments that increase the emotional, psychological, or financial

costs of ending a relationship, as well as feelings of moral or religious obligation. In turn, psychological commitment predicts relationship stability.

Research has consistently shown that this model applies not only to heterosexual couples but also to same-sex couples. For example, in an analysis of data from lesbian couples in the American Couples Study, Beals et al. (2002) showed that relationship satisfaction, the quality of alternatives, and investments each predicted psychological commitment, which in turn predicted relationship stability. In a study of 304 gay and lesbian couples, Kurdek (2008) demonstrated that satisfaction, alternatives, and investments each predicted commitment. Comparative studies including both same-sex and heterosexual couples also find strong support for the investment model (Duffy & Rusbult, 1986). In sum, research clearly documents that the same general processes appear to affect relationship commitment in same-sex and heterosexual couples.

Two important differences in the commitment experiences of same-sex and heterosexual couples have emerged in the research literature. First, studies show that, on average, gay and lesbian couples perceive fewer barriers to ending a relationship than do married heterosexuals (e.g., Kurdek, 1998). This is not surprising given that same-sex couples are less likely to have children together and are denied access to legal marriage in most states. As Kurdek (2005, p. 253) noted, what is impressive about gay and lesbian couples is that "they manage to endure without the benefits of institutional supports."

Second, the social climate of prejudice and discrimination against lesbians and gay men can take a toll on relationships. All relationships can be challenged by environmental stresses, whether the loss of a job, a car accident, or a health crisis. In addition, as noted by Meyer and Frost (Chapter 18, this volume), lesbians and gay men are also subject to minority stress based on their stigmatized status in society. Studies have begun to demonstrate that aspects of minority stress (internalized homophobia, or negative feelings about being gay/lesbian, concerns about social stigma, and experiences of prejudice and discrimination) are associated with lower relationship quality and commitment. In a study of same-sex couples, Mohr and Fassinger (2006) showed that internalized homonegativity and stigma sensitivity were each significantly and negatively correlated with relationship quality, including satisfaction and commitment. Individuals who felt better about being gay or lesbian and worried less about being rejected because of their sexual orientation rated their relationships as higher in quality. Lehmiller and Agnew (2006) found that a measure of "marginalization"—the extent of perceived disapproval of your relationship by society, family, and friends—was a significant predictor of commitment in romantic relationships, even after controlling for satisfaction, alternatives, and investments. Gay men and lesbians who experienced more social disapproval reported less commitment. Of note is a recent study by Fingerhut and Maisel (2010) that demonstrated that relationship formalization can buffer individuals against the potential negative effects of minority stress on relationship well-being. More specifically, higher levels of internalized gay-related stress (i.e., internalized homophobia) were associated with lower relationship satisfaction among those who had not formalized their relationship via a ceremony, but not for those who had formalized their relationship in this way.

Given the challenges of antigay prejudice and discrimination, we might anticipate that there would be fewer long-term relationships among lesbians and gay men than among heterosexuals. However, beginning in the 1980s, studies have documented the existence of very long-lasting same-sex relationships (e.g., Johnson, 1990; McWhirter & Mattison, 1984). Carpenter and Gates (2008) analyzed data from large population-based surveys of gay men and lesbians in California. The relationships of lesbians and gay men were relatively long-lasting, and were longer for those who had registered as domestic partners (8.9 years for lesbians and 12.3 years for gay men) than for those who lived together without registering (7.8 for lesbians and 9.6 for gay men). Given that the mean age in the sample was about 40, the data indicated that many lesbians and gay men had spent a substantial part of their adult life with the same partner.

In longitudinal research, Kurdek (2004) compared the relationship dissolution rates over 11–12 years for same-sex and heterosexual couples. For heterosexuals, the breakup rate was 3% for parent couples and 19% for nonparent couples. None of the same-sex couples had children. The breakup rate was 19% for gay couples and 24% for lesbian couples. These data show that dissolution was primarily related to parenthood, not to sexual orientation. In a 3-year follow-up of same-sex couples in civil unions

in Vermont, Balsam et al. (2008) reported that 4% of the civil union couples had broken up compared to 9% of same-sex couples not in civil unions and 3% of married heterosexuals. In a more recent investigation of states that offer some form of legal recognition to same-sex couples, Badgett and Herman (2011) found that same-sex couples who had a legally recognized union were less likely to end their relationship than different-sex couples who did not have a legally recognized union. More specifically, an average of 1.1% of same-sex couples ended their legal relationship in comparsison to approximately 2% of married different-sex couples. In the future, government statistics on the dissolution of same-sex marriage and civil unions/registered partnerships will provide more definitive information about the relationship stability of same-sex couples.

In summary, research has provided a consistent body of empirical evidence about the nature of same-sex couples and the processes that affect couple relationships. Many similarities and a few differences have been found between same-sex and heterosexual couples. This research has helped to inform legal decision making and has provided a basis for public policy. In 2004, the Council of Representatives of the American Psychological Association (APA) adopted a policy statement on Sexual Orientation and Marriage (Paige, 2005). They noted that "psychological research on relationships and couples provides no evidence to justify discrimination against same-sex couples," and resolved that "APA believes that it is unfair and discriminatory to deny same-sex couples legal access to civil marriage." Additionally, in 2011, the APA issued a resolution supporting marriage for same-sex couples stating that the APA "supports full marriage equality for same-sex couples" (American Psychological Association, 2011).

THE DEBATE ABOUT SAME-SEX MARRIAGE IN THE UNITED STATES

In this section, we turn to recent research investigating the attitudes of lesbians and gay men toward marriage, comparing the experiences of same-sex couples whose relationships are legally recognized or not, and exploring the potential impact of the marriage controversy itself. These are new research topics but ones that are critical to understanding the lives of lesbians and gay men and the relationships of same-sex couples in the United States today.

Attitudes about Legal Recognition

The heterosexual majority in the United States is divided in their views on extending marriage rights to same-sex couples, though opinions appear to be ever-changing. In a 2010 poll, 53% of adults said that marriage between same-sex couples should not be recognized by law, 44% supported marriage for same-sex couples, and only 3% were unsure (Saad, 2010). A year later, in a 2011 poll, these numbers appear to have reversed: 45% of adults said that marriage between same-sex couples should not be recognized by law, 53% supported marriage for same-sex couples, and only 3% were unsure (Gallup Poll, 2011). Attitudes are more supportive of legally recognized civil unions. In a nationwide poll taken in 2010, 66% of adults responded that gay and lesbian couples should be allowed to form civil unions (ABC News/Washington Post Poll, 2010). For some Americans, opposition to marriage for same-sex couples is based on religious convictions. In a national poll, 48% of adults said they view "homosexual relationships between consenting adults" as morally wrong, and 50% said this is not a moral issue (CNN/Opinion Research Corporation Poll, 2010). Similarly, 2012 Gallup Poll data show that almost half of Americans see gay/lesbian relationships as morally unacceptable (Saad, 2012). This deep division in public opinion sets the stage for heated debates about legalizing same-sex relationships.

In contrast to heterosexual men and women, an overwhelming majority of lesbian, gay, and bisexual individuals support marriage equality for same-sex couples. In a national probability sample of 662 lesbian, gay, and bisexual individuals, 78% agreed with the statement "The law should allow two people of the same sex to marry" (Herek et al., 2010). Furthermore, a majority of lesbian, gay, and bisexual individuals report that they would like to get married if given the opportunity. In a national survey of lesbian, gay, and bisexual individuals (Kaiser Family Foundation, 2001), 74% of respondents stated that they would like to marry someone of the same sex someday, if given the opportunity. In a large international study of more than 1200 lesbian, gay, and bisexual individuals (of which the majority were in a same-sex relationship) (Harding & Peel, 2006), 74% of lesbians, 63% of gay men, and 61% of bisexuals indicated that they would like to get married someday. Finally, in a study of lesbian and gay youth age 16–22 years old

(D'Augelli, Rendina, Grossman, & Sinclair, 2008), 78% of females and 61% of males said that if it were legal to marry a same-sex partner, it was very likely or extremely likely that they would do so.

The evidence also indicates that same-sex couples prefer marriage to civil unions. Analyses by Gates, Badgett, and Ho (2008) estimated that in the first year that various states adopted civil unions/registered partnerships, only 12% of eligible same-sex couples chose this option. In contrast, in the first year that Massachusetts permitted same-sex couples to marry, 37% of eligible couples did so.

Although most lesbians and gay men recognize the tangible benefits of legal relationship recognition and believe that same-sex couples should have the right to marry, some have expressed concerns about possible negative consequences. Lannutti (2005) noted a set of tensions that arises from discussions of same-sex marriage within the lesbian and gay community. For example, there is disagreement as to whether legal recognition will strengthen or weaken same-sex relationships. In Lannutti's (2005, 2007) interviews with lesbian and gay people, many suggested that legal recognition would help solidify a couple's relationship by making a formal commitment and by validating a relationship in the eyes of others. In contrast, some expressed concern that legal recognition would lead lesbian and gay individuals to marry for the wrong reasons, either because it is a fad or expected or to make a political statement. Ultimately this might have negative effects on relationships. In interviews with same-sex couples in the United Kingdom (Clarke, Burgoyne, & Burns, 2007), similar concerns were expressed. For example, one gay man worried that a legal contract would turn his commitment into "a duty rather than a desire" and that "it could detract from the relationship" (p. 187).

Concerns also exist about the effects of legalization of same-sex marriage on broader lesbian, gay, and bisexual communities. One concern is that marriage might create division within communities, for example, by fostering a new social hierarchy in which couples who marry would be favored and couples who choose not to marry would be marginalized from the only community they have (Lannutti, 2005). Yep, Lovaas, and Elia (2003) expressed concerns about the changing fabric of lesbian, gay, and bisexual communities in their contrast between two positions on same-sex marriage. The assimilationist or liberal position is that lesbian, gay, and bisexual individuals deserve full equality, that same-sex marriage will promote relationship stability, and that same-sex marriage will indicate that nonheterosexual individuals have gained an equal footing with their heterosexual counterparts. In contrast, the separatist position suggests that same-sex marriage entrenches lesbian, gay, and bisexual individuals and communities in a patriarchal and oppressive institution and fails to liberate or bring equality to nonheterosexual people. Finally, Polikoff (2008), in her book *Beyond (Straight and Gay) Marriage,* suggested that gay rights advocates are thinking too narrowly in pushing for marriage rights. Rather than focus on marriage, she suggested that there needs to be a push for laws that value all families and that allow adult individuals to define what relationships are meaningful to them. In summary, although concerns have been voiced about possible problems that marriage might create, a large majority of lesbians, gay men, and bisexuals endorse marriage equality.

The Impact of Legal Recognition

In 2004, Massachusetts became the first U.S. state to permit same-sex couples to marry. At present, Connecticut, Iowa, New Hampshire, New York, Vermont, and Washington, DC have also legalized marriage for same-sex couples.[1] Many more states and municipalities provide legal alternatives through civil unions or registered domestic partnerships. The experiences of the pioneering couples who have made use of these options provide evidence about the impact of legal recognition on individuals and couples.

Data from married same-sex couples suggest positive benefits from legal recognition. Ramos, Goldberg, and Badgett (2009) analyzed survey data from approximately 550 individuals who married a same-sex partner in Massachusetts during the first 5 years in which such marriages were legal. Seventy-two percent of the respondents reported that marriage made them feel closer to their partner, and 69% reported feeling more accepted in the community. In addition, almost half (48%) reported that they were less concerned about legal problems following the marriage. Of the participants with children (28% of the sample), almost all agreed or somewhat agreed that marriage benefited the children and that the children were happier as a result of this formalized commitment. For example, in open-ended responses, parents reported that their children felt more protected, secure, and stable and

that they believed that marriage legitimated their families. Most respondents reported many and various benefits from their marriage.

Qualitative data corroborate the benefits of marriage for individuals and same-sex couples. Schecter, Tracy, Page, and Luong (2008) interviewed both partners in 50 married and unmarried same-sex couples in Massachusetts. Those who married reported that legal marriage changed the way they and others viewed their relationship. Married individuals reported greater commitment to their partner and felt more accepted in society. Some noted that the legitimacy of legal marriage reduced their personal feelings of marginalization and internalized homophobia.

Because the availability of civil marriage for same-sex couples in the United States has been so limited, researchers have investigated the potential effects of other forms of relationship recognition. In 2000, Vermont was the first state to legalize civil unions that provide same-sex couples with rights and responsibilities equivalent to marriage, at least at the state level. Solomon, Rothblum, and Balsam (2004) compared same-sex couples who obtained a civil union with same-sex couples who did not. They found relatively few differences between these two types of couples. Though individuals in different couple types did not differ on measures of relationship satisfaction or functioning, men and women in civil unions were more likely to consider themselves "married." Women in civil unions were more open about their sexual orientation with family and peers. Men in civil unions reported significantly more commitment to their relationship, were less likely to have considered dissolution, and were more likely to have joint bank accounts. As noted earlier, in a 3-year follow-up, same-sex couples in civil unions were significantly less likely to have ended their relationship than same-sex couples not in civil unions (Balsam et al., 2008). In a study by Riggle, Rostosky, and Horne (2010), lesbian, gay, and bisexual individuals in committed relationships ($n = 1353$) were compared with those in legally recognized relationships (including marriage, but also domestic partnerships and civil unions; $n = 406$). Controlling for a variety of factors including education and relationship length, individuals in legal unions reported less internalized homophobia, less depression, less stress and more life meaning than those who were in committed relationships that were not legally recognized.

Additional evidence for the psychological and social benefits of legalizing same-sex relationships comes from research conducted outside of the United States (e.g., Eskridge & Spedale, 2006). Alderson (2004) interviewed 43 individuals (from 22 couples) who were in legally recognized same-sex marriages; the overwhelming majority married either in Canada or the Netherlands. Many spoke very clearly of the benefits that marriage had had on their relationship. For example, one woman stated that "being married is a lot about being 100% in this relationship and not 99.9% or 98% or just really, you know, standing in it and saying, 'This is it. We'll give it everything we have'" (p. 118). Others spoke of the social acceptance and social understanding that marriage provided for their relationship. Another woman noted: "People understand the word 'marriage'…'This is my wife' and they know what you mean" (p. 119). In interviews with 19 couples in the Netherlands, Badgett (2009) reported very similar results. Importantly, participants reported that access to marriage removed a stressor from their lives and made them feel more included in society.

Taken together, these studies strongly suggest that legal recognition can provide benefits for same-sex couples. A goal for future research will be to assess the extent to which these positive outcomes are attributable to legal recognition, and are not merely selection effects attributable to different characteristics of same-sex couples who do and do not seek legal recognition for their relationships.

Marriage Amendments and Lesbian, Gay, and Bisexual Individuals

The controversy about legal recognition for the marriages for same-sex couples has been very public and often vitriolic. The heated public discourse in media ads, radio and television news and talk shows, rallies, and personal conversations has highlighted for many lesbian, gay, and bisexual individuals that their relationships are not equal to those of heterosexuals. Majority votes to amend state constitutions in order to ban legal recognition of marriages of same-sex couples may have further increased feelings of stigma. Though both sides of the debate have at times resorted to extreme rhetoric, the consequences of such actions are likely to inflict greater harm on nonheterosexual than on heterosexual individuals (Riggle, Thomas, & Rostosky, 2005). First, the rights of heterosexual individuals are not at issue in these debates. Because heterosexual people are in the majority and have higher status in the social hierarchy, they are less vulnerable. Furthermore, the marriage debate itself may be a stressor for lesbian, gay, and bisexual individuals in same-sex relationships as their relationships are being called into question.

Researchers began to investigate the impact of public controversies surrounding marriage equality after the November 2006 election, in which seven U.S. states passed constitutional amendments limiting marriage to heterosexual couples. Following the election, researchers collected data from lesbian, gay, and bisexual individuals across the country to assess the impact of the election on social and psychological well-being (Riggle, Rostosky, & Horne, 2009; Rostosky, Riggle, Horne, & Miller, 2009). The researchers found several significant differences between lesbian, gay, and bisexual individuals in one of the seven states in which an amendment had recently passed and lesbian, gay, and bisexual individuals living in states in which same-sex marriage was not up for debate or in which an amendment had passed in a previous election. Individuals in the seven amendments states reported being exposed to more negative messages about lesbians and gay men in various media outlets and in personal conversations. They also reported significantly more depressive symptoms, stress, and negative affect, and significantly less positive affect. At the same time, these individuals also reported significantly more exposure to positive messages about gay men and lesbians. Furthermore, many lesbian, gay, and bisexual individuals in amendment states reported receiving substantial amounts of support from friends, families, and colleagues.

In in-depth interviews with 57 same-sex couples living in one of the states that passed an amendment in 2006, Lannutti (2010) explored participants' experiences in discussing the amendment with members of their extended social network. Individuals described mixed experiences. Almost 50% received social support including expressions of sympathy or the sense that network members really listened to their concerns. More than 25% of the respondents felt a sense of solidarity with their extended social network—that other people shared their views or would take action to help. At the same time, some participants had negative experiences, with 11% reporting being avoided or condemned by a network member. Although it might be expected that lesbian, gay, and bisexual individuals would experience predominantly negative social and psychological outcomes in the face of marriage amendments, the research findings suggest otherwise. Overall, research results showed that lesbian, gay, and bisexual individuals experienced marriage initiatives as stressful but that they were simultaneously able to make meaning out of the experience and to derive some benefit.

Most studies of the effects of ballot initatives to prevent same-sex marriage have been retrospective. This raises the possibility that responses were affected not only by the debate before the election but also by the outcome. To distinguish the potential effects of electoral campaigns from the outcomes of those campaigns, Maisel and Fingerhut (2011) collected data regarding California's Proposition 8 campaign in the days preceding the November 2008 election. Lesbian, gay, and bisexual Californians completed an online survey that contained both quantitative and qualitative measures to assess how the campaign had affected respondents and their close relationships with friends, family, colleagues, and significant others. Roughly 75% of participants indicated that they thought about Proposition 8 "a great deal." Using an adjective checklist to indicate the extent to which they had experienced a variety of emotions, participants reported experiencing both positive emotions (e.g., pride, interest) and negative emotions (e.g., anger, upset). Importantly, however, on average participants reported higher levels of negative than positive emotions.

In open-ended responses, participants reported both benefits and negative consequences of the Proposition 8 campaign on their social relations. In terms of their intimate relationships, some participants reported that the campaign had brought them closer to their partner, as they worked together to stand up for the legal recognition of their relationship. Others described increased conflict in their intimate relationship either because of different opinions about how involved to be in the campaign or because of a general increase in stress and unease that spilled over into the relationship. Participants also reported that the campaign affected their relationships with family, friends, and co-workers. Some discussed being surprised by the level of support they received from members of their social network. Others said the campaign increased tension in some of their relationships or led to the ending of an important relationship.

As the controversy over same-sex marriage continues, more research is needed to better understand the impact of such debates on the lives of lesbian, gay, and bisexual individuals and on same-sex couples. For example, although we have evidence that exposure to stressors increased during these campaigns, we know very little about strategies that may protect lesbian, gay, and bisexual individuals from harmful consequences of these stressors. Research on racial and ethnic minorities (e.g., Padilla, 2008) has suggested that political activism may be an important coping strategy in the face of discrimination. Similarly, researchers have found that political activism is a coping strategy often used by gay and lesbian youth to help them through the process of coming out (Pendragon, 2010). Research on activism and other potential mechanisms that help lesbian, gay, and bisexual individuals and same-sex couples to cope successfully with stressful situations would be valuable.

DIRECTIONS FOR FUTURE RESEARCH

The research presented in this chapter clearly shows that many same-sex couples succeed in creating satisfying and long-lasting relationships despite the continuing challenges of social stigma. Evidence demonstrates that, in general, same-sex couples are comparable to heterosexual couples both in the quality of their relationships and in the processes that affect relationship functioning. These data provide no scientific basis for denying same-sex couples access to civil marriage. At the same time, research shows that the continuing controversy about marriage equality can be a significant stressor for lesbian, gay, and bisexual individuals and same-sex couples. The limited evidence currently available suggests that for those same-sex couples who choose to marry, civil marriage can provide both personal and relationship benefits.

Many important questions remain about the experiences of same-sex couples. Studies of both same-sex and heterosexual couples often recruit nonrepresentative samples of adults who are typically white and middle class. We know less about low-income couples and about ethnic minority couples. Studies of same-sex relationships, especially those that ask couples to take part in person rather than through anonymous questionnaires or online surveys, may disproportionately include couples who are generally comfortable in disclosing their sexual orientation. The tendency to recruit participants from more politically liberal and urban settings is a further limitation.

As noted earlier, we know very little about the experiences of bisexual individuals in couple relationships. Neither research on same-sex couples nor research on heterosexual couples has typically reported the sexual identity of participants. Consequently, studies of "lesbian," "gay male," and "heterosexual" couples include some individuals who undoubtedly identify as bisexual. A recent U.S. national probability survey of self-identified lesbian, gay, and bisexual individuals found that most bisexuals who were currently in a committed relationship had a different-sex partner (Herek et al., 2010). Whereas all coupled lesbians and almost all coupled gay men had a same-sex partner, the majority of coupled bisexual men (88%) and women (90%) had a partner of the other sex. In other words, self-identified bisexuals are much more likely to be found in "heterosexual" couples than in same-sex couples. To advance our understanding of the experiences of bisexuals in intimate relationships, an important step would be for researchers to systematically report the sexual identity of participants and, when the size of a sample permits, to investigate the experiences of couples in which one or both partners identify as bisexual.

Research has provided beginning insights about unique stressors affecting same-sex couples, but more research is needed. For many same-sex couples, experiences of stigma, prejudice, and discrimination create added stress in daily life. Research analyzing the sources of minority stress has been valuable. However, at this point, we need to know more about how these stressors affect couple relationships, how couples cope with different types of stressors, and what factors enable some couples to be resilient in the face of these challenges. For some couples, the epidemic of HIV/AIDS has been an important stressor, both through the potential threats to their own health and through the loss of friends and loved ones to AIDS. We know surprisingly little about the impact of HIV/AIDS on same-sex couples (for exceptions, see Hoff et al., 2009; Paul, Hays, & Coates, 1995; Remien, Wagner, Dolezal, & Carballo-Dieguez, 2001) or possible ways in which life-extending treatments for HIV/AIDS are affecting couples today (see Herrick, Friedman, and Stall, Chapter 14, this volume).

The legalization of same-sex relationships through domestic partnerships, civil unions, and marriage will provide new opportunities for researchers. Increasingly, investigators will be able to use government records to identify representative samples of same-sex couples, as has been done for heterosexual couples through marriage records. Government records about the dissolution of same-sex relationships through separation or divorce will make it possible to chart more systematically patterns of relationship stability over time. In the future, as same-sex couples obtain legal rights and responsibilities more comparable to those of heterosexuals and as the stigma of being in a same-sex couple diminishes, researchers will be able to provide a more comprehensive analysis of the impact of equality on individuals and couples.

NOTES

1. In addition to these states in the United States, the following countries also permit marriage for same-sex couples: Argentina, Belgium, Canada, Denmark, Iceland, Netherlands, Norway, Portugal, South Africa, Spain, and Sweden.

REFERENCES

ABC News/Washington Post Poll, February 4–8, 2010. Poll retrieved July 21, 2010 from http://www.washingtonpost.com/wp-srv/politics/polls/postpoll_021010.html.

Alderson, K. G. (2004). A phenomenological investigation of same-sex marriage. *The Canadian Journal of Human Sexuality, 13,* 107–122.

American Psychological Association. (2011). *Resolution on marriage equality for same-sex couples.* Washington, DC: Author.

Badgett, M. V. L. & Herman, J. L. (2011). *Patterns of relationship recognition by same-sex couples in the United States.* Retrieved from the Williams Institute http://williamsinstitute.law.ucla.edu/wp-content/uploads/Badgett-Herman-Marriage-Dissolution-Nov-2011.pdf.

Badgett, M. V. L. (2009). *When gay people get married: What happens when societies legalize same-sex marriage.* New York: New York University Press.

Balsam, K. F., Beauchaine, T. P., Rothblum, E. D., & Solomon, S. E. (2008). Three-year follow up of same-sex couples who had civil unions in Vermont, same-sex couples not in civil unions, and heterosexual married couples. *Developmental Psychology, 44,* 102–116.

Baucom, B. R., McFarland, P. T., & Christensen, A. (2010). Gender, topic, and time in observed demand-withdraw interaction in cross- and same-sex couples. *Journal of Family Psychology, 24,* 233–242.

Beals, K., Impett, E., & Peplau, L. A. (2002). Lesbians in love: Why some relationships endure and others end. *Journal of Lesbian Studies, 6*(1), 53–64.

Biblarz, T. J., & Savci, E. (2010). Lesbian, gay, bisexual, and transgender families. *Journal of Marriage and Family, 72,* 480–497.

Blumstein, P., & Schwartz, P. (1983). *American couples.* New York: Pocket Books.

Bradbury, T. N., & Karney, B. R. (2010). *Intimate relationships.* New York: Norton.

Carpenter, C., & Gates, G. J. (2008). Gay and lesbian partnership: Evidence from California. *Demography, 45,* 573–590.

Carrington, C. (1999). *No place like home: Relationships and family life among lesbians and gay men.* Chicago: University of Chicago Press.

Christopher, F. S., & Sprecher, S. (2000). Sexuality in marriage, dating, and other relationships: A decade review. *Journal of Marriage and the Family, 62,* 999–1017.

Clarke, V., Burgoyne, C., & Burns, M. (2007). Romance, rights, recognition, responsibilities and radicalism: Same-sex couples' views on civil partnership and marriage. In V. Clarke & E. Peel (Eds.), *Out in psychology: Lesbian, gay, bisexual, trans and queer perspectives* (pp. 173–193). New York: John Wiley & Sons Ltd.

CNN/Opinion Research Corporation Poll, May 21–23, 2010. Poll retrieved July 20, 2010 from http://www.pollingreport.com/civil.htm.

Conley, T. D., Roesch, S. C., Peplau, L. A., & Gold, M. S. (2009). A test of positive illusions versus shared reality models of relationship satisfaction among gay, lesbian and heterosexual couples. *Journal of Applied Social Psychology, 39,* 1417–1431.

D'Augelli, A. R., Rendina, H. J., Grossman, A. H., & Sinclair, K. O. (2008). Lesbian and gay youths' aspirations for marriage and raising children. *Journal of LGBT Issues in Counseling, 1,* 77–98.

Duffy, S., & Rusbult, C. E. (1986). Satisfaction and commitment in homosexual and heterosexual relationships. *Journal of Homosexuality, 12,* 1–23.

Eskridge, W. N., Jr., & Spedale, D. R. (2006). *Gay marriage: For better or for worse? What we've learned from the evidence.* New York: Oxford University Press.

Fingerhut, A. W., & Maisel, N. C. (2010). Relationship formalization and individual and relationship well-being among same-sex couples. *Journal of Social and Personal Relationships, 27,* 956–969.

Gallup Poll, May 5–8, 2011. Poll retrieved May 14, 2012 from http://www.gallup.com/ poll/117328/ Marriage.aspx?utm_source=email-a-friend&utm_medium=email&utm_campaign=sharing&utm_content=morelink.

Gates, G. J., Badgett M. V. L., & Ho, D. (2008). *Marriage, registration, and dissolution by same-sex couples in the U.S.* Retrieved from the Williams Institute http://williamsinstitute.law.ucla.edu/wp-content/uploads/Gates-Badgett-Ho-Couples-Marr-Regis-Dissolution-Jul-2008.pdf.

Gottman, J. M., Levenson, R. W., Gross, J., Frederickson, B. L., McCoy, K., Rosenthal, L., Ruef, A., & Yoshimoto, D. (2003). Correlates of gay and lesbian couples' relationship satisfaction and relationship dissolution. *Journal of Homosexuality, 45,* 23–43.

Harding, R., & Peel, E. (2006). "We Do"? International perspectives on equality, legality and same-sex relationships. *Lesbian & Gay Psychology Review, 7,* 123–140.

Herek, G. M., Norton, A. T., Allen, T. J., & Sims, C. L. (2010). Demographic, psychological, and social characteristics of self-identified lesbian, gay, and bisexual adults in a U.S. probability sample. *Sexuality Research & Social Policy, 7,* 176–200.

Hoff, C. C., Chakravarty, D., Beougher, S. C., Darbes, L. A., Dadasovich, R., & Neilands, T. B. (2009). Serostatus differences and agreements about sex with outside partners among gay male couples. *AIDS Education and Prevention, 21,* 25–38.

Holmberg, D., Blair, K. L., & Phillips, M. (2010). Women's sexual satisfaction as a predictor of well-being in same-sex versus mixed-sex relationships. *Journal of Sex Research, 47,* 1–11.

Johnson, S. (1990). *Staying power: Long-term lesbian couples.* Tallahassee, FL: Naiad Press.

Julien, D., Chartrand, E., Simard, M-C., Bouthillier, D., & Begin, J. (2003). Conflict, social support, and relationship quality: An observational study of heterosexual, gay male, and lesbian couples' communication. *Journal of Family Psychology, 17,* 419–428.

Kaiser Family Foundation. (2001). *Inside-OUT: A report on the experiences of lesbians, gays and bisexuals in America and the public's views on issues and policies related to sexual orientation.* Menlo Park, CA: Author.

Kurdek, L. A. (1991). Correlates of relationship satisfaction in cohabiting gay and lesbian couples: Integration of contextual, investment, and problem-solving models. *Journal of Personality and Social Psychology, 61,* 910–922.

Kurdek, L. A. (1993). The allocation of household labor in gay, lesbian, and heterosexual married couples. *Journal of Social Issues, 49,* 127–139.

Kurdek, L. A. (1998). Relationship outcomes and their predictors: Longitudinal evidence from heterosexual married, gay cohabiting, and lesbian cohabiting couples. *Journal of Marriage and the Family, 60,* 553–568.

Kurdek, L. A. (2004). Are gay and lesbian cohabiting couples really different from heterosexual married couples? *Journal of Marriage and Family, 66,* 888–900.

Kurdek, L. A. (2005). What do we know about gay and lesbian couples? *Current Directions in Psychological Science, 14,* 251–254.

Kurdek, L. A. (2008). Change in relationship quality for partners from lesbian, gay male, and heterosexual couples. *Journal of Family Psychology, 22,* 701–711.

Kurdek, L. A., & Schmitt, J. P. (1987). Partner homogamy in married, heterosexual cohabiting, gay, and lesbian couples. *Journal of Sex Research, 23,* 212–232.

Lannutti, P. J. (2005). For better or worse: Exploring the meanings of same-sex marriage within the lesbian, gay, bisexual and transgendered community. *Journal of Social and Personal Relationships, 22, 1,* 5–18.

Lannutti, P. J. (2007). The influence of same-sex marriage on the understanding of same-sex relationships. *Journal of Homosexuality, 53,* 135–151.

Lannutti, P. J. (2010). *Examining communication about marriage amendments: Same-sex couples and their extended social networks.* Unpublished manuscript.

Lehmiller, J. L., & Agnew, C. R. (2006). Marginalized relationships: The impact of social disapproval on romantic relationship commitment. *Personality and Social Psychology Bulletin, 32,* 40–51.

Lippa, R. A. (2007). The preferred traits of mates in a cross-national study of heterosexual and homosexual men and women: An examination of biological and cultural influences. *Archives of Sexual Behavior, 36,* 193–208.

Maisel, N. C., & Fingerhut, A. W. (2011). *California's ban on same-sex marriage: The campaign and its effects on gay, lesbian, and bisexual individuals.* Unpublished manuscript, Department of Psychology, Loyola Marymount University.

McWhirter, D. P., & Mattison, A. M. (1984). *The male couple: How relationships develop.* Englewood Cliffs, NJ: Prentice-Hall.

Mohr, J. J., & Fassinger, R. E. (2006). Sexual orientation identity and romantic relationship quality in same-sex couples. *Personality and Social Psychology Bulletin, 32,* 1085–1099.

Padilla, A. M. (2008). Social cognition, ethnic identity, and ethnic specific strategies for coping with threat due to prejudice and discrimination. *Nebraska Symposium on Motivation, 53,* 7–42.

Paige, R. U. (2005). Proceedings of the American Psychological Association, Incorporated, for the legislative year 2004. *American Psychologist, 60,* 436–511.

Patterson, C. J. (2000). Family relationships of lesbians and gay men. *Journal of Marriage and the Family, 62,* 1052–1069.

Patterson, C. J., Sutfin, E. L., & Fulcher, M. (2004). Division of labor among lesbian and heterosexual parenting couples. *Journal of Adult Development, 11,* 179–89.

Paul, J. P., Hays, R. B., & Coates, T. J. (1995). The impact of the HIV epidemic on U.S. gay male communities. In A. R. D'Augelli & C. J. Patterson (Eds.), *Lesbian, gay, and bisexual identities over the lifespan: Psychological perspectives* (pp. 345–397). New York: Oxford University Press.

Pendragon, D. K. (2010). Coping behaviors among sexual minority female youth. *Journal of Lesbian Studies, 14,* 5–15.

Peplau, L. A., Cochran, S. D., & Mays, V. M. (1997). A national survey of the intimate relationships of African-American lesbians and gay men: A look at commitment, satisfaction, sexual behavior and HIV disease. In B. Greene (Ed.), *Ethnic and cultural diversity among lesbians and gay men* (pp. 11–38). Newbury Park, CA: Sage Publications.

Peplau, L. A., & Fingerhut, A. W. (2007). The close relationships of lesbians and gay men. *Annual Review of Psychology, 58,* 10.1–10.20.

Peplau, L. A., Fingerhut, A., & Beals, K. P. (2004). Sexuality in the relationships of lesbians and gay men. In J. Harvey, A. Wenzel, & S. Sprecher (Eds.), *Handbook of sexuality in close relationships* (pp. 350–369). Mahwah, NJ: Erlbaum.

Peplau, L. A., & Spalding, L. R. (2000). The close relationships of lesbians, gay men and bisexuals. In C. Hendrick & S. S. Hendrick (Eds.), *Close relationships: A sourcebook* (pp. 111–124). Thousand Oaks, CA: Sage Publications.

Polikoff, N. D. (2008). *Beyond (straight and gay) marriage: Valuing all families under the law.* Boston, MA: Beacon Press.

Ramos, C., Goldberg, N. G., & Badgett, M. V. L. (2009). *The effects of marriage equality in Massachusetts: A survey of the experiences and impact of marriage on same-sex couples.* Retrieved from the Williams Institute at http://escholarship.org/uc/item/9dx6v3kj.

Remien, R. H., Wagner, G., Dolezal, C., & Carballo-Diéguez, A. (2001). Factors associated with HIV sexual risk behavior in male couples of mixed HIV status. *Journal of Psychology & Human Sexuality, 13,* 31–48.

Riggle, E. D. B., Rostosky, S. S., & Horne, S. G. (2009). Marriage amendments and lesbian, gay, and bisexual individuals in the 2006 election. *Sexuality Research and Social Policy: Journal of NSRC, 6,* 80–89.

Riggle, E. D. B., Rostosky, S. S., & Horne, S. G. (2010). Psychological distress, well-being, and legal recognition in same-sex couple relationships. *Journal of Family Psychology, 24,* 82–86.

Riggle, E. D. B., Thomas, J. D., & Rostosky, S. S. (2005). The marriage debate and minority stress. *PS: Political Science & Politics, 38,* 221–224.

Roisman, G. I., Clausell, E., Holland, A., Fortuna, K., & Elief, C. (2008). Adult romantic relationships as contexts for human development: A multimethod comparison of same-sex couples with opposite-sex dating, engaged and married dyads. *Developmental Psychology, 44,* 91–101.

Rostosky, S. S., Riggle, E. D., Horne, S. G., & Miller, A. D. (2009). Marriage amendments and psychological distress in lesbian, gay, and bisexual (LGB) adults. *Journal of Counseling Psychology, 56,* 56–66.

Rusbult, C. E. (1983). A longitudinal test of the investment model: The development (and deterioration) of satisfaction and commitment in heterosexual involvements. *Journal of Personality and Social Psychology, 45,* 101–117.

Saad, L. (2010). *Americans' acceptance of gay relations crosses 50% threshold.* Retrieved July 21, 2010 from Gallup at http://www.gallup.com/poll/135764/americans-acceptance-gay-relations-crosses-threshold.aspx.

Saad, L. (2012). *U.S. acceptance of gay/lesbian relations is the new normal.* Retreived May 14, 2012 from Gallup at http://www.gallup.com/poll/154634/Acceptance-Gay-Lesbian-Relations-New-Normal.aspx.

Sanchez, D. T., Moss-Racusin, C. A., Phelan, J. E., & Crocker, J. (2011). Relationship contingency and sexual motivation in women. *Archives of Sexual Behavior, 40,* 99–110.

Schecter, E., Tracy, A. J., Page, K. V., & Luong, G. (2008). Shall we marry? Legal marriage as a commitment event in same-sex relationships. *Journal of Homosexuality, 54,* 400–422.

Skinner, M. D., & Goodfriend, W. (2009). Perceptions of positive relationship traits in gay and lesbian couples. *Journal of Homosexuality, 56,* 319–335.

Solomon, S. E., Rothblum, E. D., & Balsam, K. F. (2004). Pioneers in partnership: Lesbian and gay male couples in civil unions compared with those not in civil unions and married heterosexual siblings. *Journal of Family Psychology, 18,* 275–286.

Solomon, S. E., Rothblum, E. D., & Balsam, K. F. (2005). Money, housework, sex, and conflict: Same-sex couples in civil unions, those not in civil unions, and heterosexual married siblings. *Sex Roles, 52,* 561–575

Testa, R. J., Kinder, B. N., & Ironson, G. (1987). Heterosexual bias in the perception of loving relationships of gay males and lesbians. *Journal of Sex Research, 23,* 163–172.

Wheldon, C. W., & Pathak, E. B. (2010). Masculinity and relationship agreements among male same-sex couples. *Journal of Sex Research, 47,* 460–470.

Yep, G. A., Lovaas, K. E., & Elia, J. P. (2003). A critical appraisal of assimilationist and radical ideologies underlying same-sex marriage in LGBT communities in the United States. *Journal of Homosexuality, 45,* 45–64.

13

Lesbian and Bisexual Women's Physical Health

JANE M. SIMONI, LARAMIE SMITH, KEREN LEHAVOT, KAREN FREDRIKSEN-GOLDSEN, AND KARINA L. WALTERS

Researchers have documented alarming health disparities between people of color and white individuals in the United States (Adler & Rehkopf, 2008), but only recently have they begun to examine potential disparities based on sexual orientation—especially for sexual minority women. The U.S. Department of Health and Human Services (HHS, 2010) characterized health disparities as differences in health impacting groups of people who have systematically encountered obstacles to healthcare as a result of social, economic, and environmental disadvantage. In fact, the U.S. Centers for Disease Control and Prevention (CDC) (2011) identified health disparities related to sexual orientation as one of the main gaps in current health disparities research. This research is important in determining whether sexual minority women as a group are at risk for adverse health outcomes and, if so, what preventive measures or other interventions are needed to address the disparities. To date, we know little about the health needs of sexual minority women, hindering the development of relevant public policies and programs (Krehely, 2009).

The limited data on the health of lesbians, gay men, bisexuals, and transgender individuals were evident in Boehmer's (2002) analysis of 3.8 million citations of articles published between 1980 and 1999. She found only 3800 (0.1%) related to lesbian, gay, bisexual, and transgender issues; a recent review is consistent (Snyder, 2011). The dearth of relevant data on sexual minority women specifically led the U.S. Institute of Medicine in 1991 to commission a report on lesbian health, highlighting the need for population-based research on the prevalence and incidence of clinical problems in lesbians (Solarz, 1999), and again in 2010 to commission a report on lesbian, gay, bisexual, and transgender health (Institute of Medicine, 2011).

To date, most of the research on health disparities among sexual minorities has focused not on physical health but on mental health outcomes, including alcohol and substance use (e.g., Cochran, Sullivan, & Mays, 2003); see Cochran and Mays, Chapter 15, this volume. Fewer studies have focused specifically on physical health outcomes among lesbian and bisexual women, whose situations and concerns appear to be largely different from those of gay men (Conron, Mimiaga, & Landers, 2010).

In this chapter, we consider the challenges of conducting research to examine health disparities based on sexual orientation, particularly for sexual minority women, and describe some of the major studies in this area. We briefly review the evidence for disparities in cardiovascular disease and cancer as well as sexually transmitted infections, asthma, and diabetes. Disparities in risk factors (e.g., obesity, smoking) for adverse health outcomes are also presented. We consider the factors and mechanisms that might place sexual minority women at greater risk for compromised health and conclude with directions for future research.

METHODOLOGICAL CHALLENGES IN HEALTH RESEARCH ON SEXUAL MINORITY WOMEN

Several methodological factors render research on physical health disparities among sexual minority women especially challenging. First, there is no clear consensus for defining sexual minority status. Basing it on same-sex behavior (ever, within a definitive time frame, or ongoing), relationship status, attraction and desire, or self-identity each leads to the identification of different target populations. Even if a consensus could be reached regarding defining characteristics, there is no clear sampling frame from which to randomly select a sample. Even with a clear sampling frame, some sexual minority women might be reluctant to participate in research given the stigma related to minority sexual orientation and, for some, given the cultural irrelevance of the lesbian, gay, bisexual, and transgender nomenclature to capture same-sex romantic relationships or identities. Any particular sample, therefore, may suffer from a lack of generalizability to the population overall.

Given these barriers, most research on physical health disparities among sexual minority women relies on one of two methodological approaches. In the first approach, some measure of sexual orientation is included in a large population-based health survey. The major advantages to this approach are that a population-based sample of sexual minority women can be included (or at least invited to participate) and identical outcomes can be assessed among both sexual minority women and other women. If the overall response rate is high, it may be possible to generalize findings from this sample to the overall population. One drawback is that a certain percentage of participants in such surveys consistently fails to provide data on their sexual orientation and those that do may not always feel comfortable providing accurate information on other variables. The small subgroup sizes reduce the statistical power to detect differences and limit opportunities to explore within-group differences among sexual minority women that might be related to protective or risk-enhancing factors. Finally, although this approach yields provide some initial descriptive and comparative data, it often fails to allow for the exploration of explanatory or theoretical pathways because some important factors may not be included or are not measurable across groups (e.g., coming out experiences and other sexual orientation-specific stressors).

A second methodological approach is to target sexual minority women specifically, ideally in a population-based fashion, and collect extensive data on their health outcomes and risk factors. This approach can result in a rich data set developed from a large sample of sexual minority women and can provide an opportunity to explore within-group differences—identifying potential pathways for risk and resiliency. On the other hand, no clear comparison group exists for the purpose of identifying disparities. Dibble, Roberts, and Nussey (2004) overcame this limitation by recruiting a sample of lesbians and their heterosexual sisters as a comparison group. In another innovative approach, Aaron et al. (2001) collected data from sexual minority women with measures similar to those used in a prior population-based study of women so that they could compare their sample with that in the original study. Of course, the different sampling strategies in each limit the validity of the comparisons.

MAJOR HEALTH STUDIES AMONG SEXUAL MINORITY WOMEN

We identified eight large population-based health studies in which sexual orientation was assessed, and three large health studies specifically targeting sexual minority women (see Table 13.1). The studies summarized in Table 13.1, along with other smaller studies, have explored a range of outcomes with the aim of examining health disparities among sexual minority women. The variables of interest can be grouped as (1) major health conditions such as cardiovascular disease and cancer and, to a lesser extent, sexually transmitted illnesses, diabetes, and asthma and (2) risk factors for adverse health outcomes such as obesity and smoking.

DISPARITIES IN MAJOR HEALTH CONDITIONS

Cardiovascular Disease

Cardiovascular disease (CVD) affects the heart or blood vessels and includes arteriosclerosis, coronary artery disease, and hypertension. Leading to heart attacks and strokes, CVD is one of the primary causes of death in the United States, accounting for nearly 50% of all deaths among women each year (Roberts, Dibble, Nussey, & Casey, 2003). Three studies have demonstrated that sexual minority women report higher levels of CVD-related conditions. First, in the Massachusetts Behavioral Risk Factor Surveillance Study (BRFSS) (Conron et al., 2010), compared to the referent group of heterosexual women (1.3%), bisexual women (3.3%) and lesbians (1.8%) were more likely to report that they suffered from heart disease. Similar results were found for risk of cardiovascular disease: compared to the reference group of heterosexual women (27.3%), both bisexual women (41.0%) and lesbians (34.0%) were more likely to report risk. All analyses were adjusted for age, gender, and education attainment. The second study, the Washington State BRFSS study (Dilley, Simmons, Boysun, Pizacani, & Stark,

TABLE 13.1. MAJOR STUDIES EXAMINING PHYSICAL HEALTH DISPARITIES AMONG WOMEN ACCORDING TO SEXUAL ORIENTATION

Population-Based Surveys Comparing Women Based on Sexual Orientation

Study and Reference	Sampling Procedures and Sexual Minority Selection Criteria	Total Sample of Sexual Minority Women (N) (n, % total sample)
California Women's Health Survey (Burgard et al., 2005)	**Sampling Procedures:** Cross-sectional random digit-dial survey of women (≥18 years) residing in California (1998–2000). **Selection Criteria:** Sexually active female respondents self-reporting the gender of their sexual partners. Proportions of sexual minority women shown had reported any same-gender sexual partners in the previous 5 years (1998 survey) or in their lifetime (1999–2000 surveys).	N = 11,204 Any reported female sexual partners = 350 (3.12%)
Nurses' Health Study II (Case et al., 2004)	**Sampling Procedure:** Biennial mail survey, starting in 1989, of all registered nurses (RNs), 25–43 years, residing in 14 U.S. states. **Selection Criteria:** Female RNs who self-reported a sexual orientation identity on a single item added to the survey in 1995.	N = 90,823 Bisexual = 317 (0.3%) Lesbian = 694 (0.8%)
California Quality of Life Survey (Cochran & Mays, 2007)	**Sampling Procedures:** Follow-back to the 2003 California Health Interview Survey (CHIS), a stratified multistate random-digit telephone interview of adults assessing gender of sexual partners in the past year and sexual orientation identity. **Selection Criteria:** A probability subsample (18–70 years during CHIS) of those who were willing to be recontacted and originally responded in English or Spanish. Overselected for sexual minorities.	N = 1,172 Lesbian = 48 (4.09%) Bisexual = 38 (3.24%) Homosexually experienced heterosexual = 28 (2.39%)
Massachusetts Behavioral Risk Factor Surveillance Surveys (2001–2008) (Conron et al., 2010)	**Sampling Procedures:** Annual geographically stratified random-digit dial telephone survey of one adult (≥18 years) per participating household in Massachusetts in English, Spanish, or Portuguese. **Selection Criteria:** Aggregate data from 2001–2008 on female respondents (18–64 years) who self-reported sexual orientation identity.	N = 40,852 Lesbian = 719 (1.76%) Bisexual = 432 (1.06%)
Los Angeles County Health Survey (Diamant & Wold, 2003)	**Sampling Procedures:** Cross-sectional population-based random-digit dial telephone survey of one adult (≥18 years) per participating household in Los Angeles County (September–December 1999) in English, Spanish, Cantonese, Mandarin, Korean, or Vietnamese. **Selection Criteria:** Female respondents (18–64 years) who self-reported a sexual orientation identity.	N = 4,135 Lesbian = 43 (1.04%) Bisexual = 69 (1.7%)
2000 National Alcohol Survey (Drabble & Trocki, 2005)	**Sampling Procedures:** Cross-sectional (November 1999–June 2000) household computer-assisted telephone survey of adults (≥18 years) in 50 U.S. states in English and Spanish. **Selection Criteria:** Females who self-reported the sexual orientation identity or gender of their sexual partners over the previous 5 years.	N = 3,880 Lesbian = 36 (0.9%) Bisexual = 50 (1.3%) Homosexually experienced heterosexual = 71 (1.8%)
No Study Name Reported (Gruskin et al., 2001)	**Sampling Procedures:** Stratified random mail survey of adult (≥20 years) members of the Kaiser Permanente Medical Care Program in Northern California in 1996. **Selection Criteria:** Females who self-reported their sexual orientation identity as either lesbian/bisexual or heterosexual.	N = 8,113 Lesbian/Bisexual = 120 (1.5%)

(continued)

TABLE 13.1. (CONTINUED)

Population-Based Surveys Comparing Women Based on Sexual Orientation

Study and Reference	Sampling Procedures and Sexual Minority Selection Criteria	Total Sample of Sexual Minority Women (N) (n, % total sample)
No Study Name Reported (Gruskin & Gordon, 2006)	**Sampling Procedures:** Two independent cross-sectional mail surveys (1999, 2002) of a stratified random sample of English-speaking adult (≥20 years) members of the Kaiser Permanente Medical Care Program in Northern California. **Selection Criteria:** Females (20–64 years) who self-reported their sexual orientation identify as lesbian or heterosexual (bisexual identity was not equivalently assessed across both surveys).	N = 12,398 Lesbian = 210 (1.72%)
Washington State Behavioral Risk Factor Surveillance System (Fredriksen-Goldsen et al., 2010; Dilley et al., 2010)	**Sampling Procedures:** Annual population-based random-digit dial telephone survey of one noninstitutionalized adult (≥18 years) per participating Washington State household in English or Spanish. **Selection Criteria:** Aggregate data from 2003–2007 on female respondents (18–50+ years) who self-reported their sexual orientation identity.	N = 67, 821[*] Bisexual = 717 (1.1%) Lesbian = 779 (1.4%)
Women's Health Initiative (Valanis et al., 2000)	**Sampling Procedures:** A representative sample of postmenopausal women (50–79 years) at 40 U.S. clinical centers recruited using a variety of methods (e.g., postal mailings, public notices, electronic media, community and medical sources) to participate in an observational study or one of three trials. **Selection Criteria:** Women self-reporting the gender of their sexual partners in their "adult lifetime" (lifetime lesbian) regardless of current sexual activity or "after age 45" (adult lesbian) if sexually active since age 45 and completing a baseline assessment by February 28, 1997.	N = 93,311 No adult sex = 1420 (1.5%) Bisexual = 740 (0.8%) Lifetime lesbian = 264 (0.3%) Adult lesbian = 309 (0.33%)

Large Surveys Targeting Sexual Minority Women

The Epidemiologic Study of Health Risk in Lesbians (Aaron et al., 2001)	**Sampling Procedures:** Cross-sectional, community-based survey in the greater Pittsburg, PA area (1998). Nonprobability sample of self-identified sexual minority women recruited through specific local lesbian and gay mailing lists, social organizations, community-wide events, and volunteer snowball sampling. **Selection Criteria:** Women (≥18 years) self-reported a lesbian sexual orientation identity. The current analysis did not include nonlesbian-identified respondents or lesbians <18 years.	Lesbian = 1010
National Lesbian Healthcare Survey (Bradford, Ryan, & Rothblum, 1994)	**Sampling Procedures:** Cross-sectional survey of self-identified lesbians (1984–1985) recruited in 50 U.S. states through GLB-specific mental health organizations, practitioners, professional organizations, and newspapers as well as volunteer social networks. Broader (non GLB-specific) strategies included distribution by local and state agencies and outreach efforts of bookstores, women's organizations, and prisons. **Selection Criteria:** Results reflect the response of 1917 self-identified lesbians out of a total 1925 respondents to the *National Lesbian Health Care Survey*. Selection criteria of the lesbian sample were not specified.	Lesbian = 1917
(No Study Name Reported) (Diamant et al., 2000)	**Sampling Procedures:** Health survey printed in a major gay and lesbian biweekly magazine (March 21, 1995 issue of *The Advocate*). **Selection Criteria:** Female respondents self-reporting a lesbian sexual orientation identity. The current analysis did not include international, bisexual, or "unsure" respondents.	Lesbian = 6935

Responses are based on Fredriksen-Goldsen et al. (2010) and Dilley et al. (2010) sampled from 2003–2006 Behavioral Risk Factor Surveillance Study (BRFSS) data.

[*]Responses are based on Fredriksen-Goldsen et al. (2010) and Dilley et al. (2010) sampled from 2003–2006 Behavioral Risk Factor Surveillance Study (BRFSS) data.

2010), indicated an increased risk for heart disease among bisexual women but not lesbians. Third, in the Nurses' Health Study II (Case et al., 2004), bisexual (but not lesbian) women were about 50% more likely than heterosexual women to report ever having a nonpregnancy-related high blood pressure reading.

Three other studies show no difference in CVD-related disease according to sexual orientation, or that sexual minority women were at *less* risk. First, the Women's Health Initiative (WHI) (Valanis et al., 2000) compared age-standardized prevalence of various heart health conditions (e.g., myocardial infarctions, angina, hypertension, and stroke). The study differentiated between women who had regarded themselves as lesbian for their entire lives ("lifetime lesbians") and those who had come out in adult life ("adult lesbians"). "Adult lesbian" women (4.3%) and "lifetime lesbian" women (3.1%) reported higher levels of myocardial infarctions than bisexual (1.2%) and heterosexual women (2.0%) but a slightly lower respective prevalence of stroke (0.5% and 1.0%) and hypertension (30.0% and 30.3%) compared to bisexual (1.8% stroke; 32.1% hypertension) and heterosexual (1.2% stroke; 31.6% hypertension) women. In adjusted analyses, however, there were no statistically significant differences according to sexual orientation. Second, the Cochran and Mays' (2007) study, based on the California Quality of Life Survey, also indicated nonsignificant findings in CVD-related disease by sexual orientation in analyses adjusting for age, educational attainment, race/ethnicity, relationship status, U.S. nativity, and family income. Heterosexual women reported similar if not slightly elevated levels of heart disease (weighted prevalence, 3.2%) and hypertension (14.9%) compared to lesbian (2.6%, 12.6%) and bisexual (0.7%, 7.4%) women. As the sample included only 48 lesbian and 38 bisexual women, the results should be interpreted with caution. Third, in the Los Angeles County Health Survey by Diamant and colleagues (2000), 5% of heterosexual women self-reported heart disease compared to 4% of lesbians and no bisexual women; these differences were nonsignificant in unadjusted bivariate analyses. With respect to hypertension, however, unadjusted analyses indicated the prevalence was higher among heterosexual women (17%) than among lesbians (8%) or bisexual women (6%, *p* < 0.01). These findings also should be interpreted with caution because of the small sample sizes of lesbians (*n* = 51) and bisexual women (*n* = 36).

Overall, the data are mixed. The findings of higher prevalence of CVD-related outcomes in sexual minority women, particularly bisexual women, were inconsistent with null findings or findings of lower risk for sexual minority women (although two of the studies in this latter group used small samples of sexual minority women). Most analyses adjusted for age and education, but only two controlled for race/ethnicity. This is important because women of color, who might be less likely to identify as sexual minority, are more at risk for heart disease. Many of the studies on CVD include respondents who are fairly young (less than 45 years old) and primarily white. As CVD is more prevalent among women of color and women over the age of 55, these studies probably yield an undercount of diagnosable CVD conditions, thereby limiting statistical power and potentially underestimating disparities.

Cancer

Cancer is second only to heart disease as the most prevalent cause of death in the general United States population (American Cancer Society, 2008). However, the prevalence and mortality of cancer among sexual minority women are unclear. As a reportable disease, cancer is carefully tracked at the federal and state levels of government, but data are not collected on the sexual orientation of individuals diagnosed with cancer. Given methodological limitations, most research to date has examined differences in the prevalence of risk factors associated with various cancers (e.g., breast, cervical, lung) and on rates of cancer screening among sexual minority women compared to heterosexual women (Brown & Tracy, 2008; Rankow, 1995). The few studies examining the actual prevalence of cancer typically rely on self-reported diagnosis and relatively few employ large population-based samples (Bowen, Boehmer, & Russo, 2007).

Larger studies examining self-reported disease or evaluating the relative risk of cancer in sexual minority women have yielded mixed evidence for disparities based on sexual orientation (Cochran et al., 2001; Frisch, Smith, Grulich, & Johansen, 2003; Kavanaugh-Lynch, White, Daling, & Bowen, 2002; Valanis et al., 2000). For example, age-adjusted analyses from the WHI (Valanis et al., 2000) indicated that a higher percentage of bisexual women (17.6%) and lesbians (14%) than heterosexual women (11.9%) reported having received a cancer diagnosis from a physician. This was true for both breast and cervical cancer.

However, in a study of aggregated data from seven independent survey samples of 11,876 sexual minority women and a nationally representative sample of U.S. women, an age-adjusted analysis comparing self-reported breast cancer rates revealed no disparities (Cochran et al., 2001). Thus, questions about disparities with regard to cancer rates as a function of sexual orientation remain open.

Other Health Outcomes

Data with respect to other health outcomes are even rarer, but we located some studies addressing disparities in sexually transmitted illnesses, diabetes, and asthma.

Attempts to estimate disparities in sexually transmitted infections (STI) between sexual minority women and other women are made more challenging because national and local STI surveillance data have either excluded same-gender sex among women as a risk factor or subsumed it under a hierarchy of other behaviors viewed as higher risk in risk classification schemes (Marrazzo, 2004). Thus, available data are usually derived from small studies that directly measure the prevalence of common STIs, usually among clinic attendees, and from surveys that query sexual minority women about their STI history. Transmission of human papillomavirus (HPV) requires only skin-to-skin or mucosa contact, which can easily occur in the context of female-to-female sex (Marrazzo, 2004). Although prevalence rates have not been extensively studied, HPV was present in 19% of lesbians who reported no previous sex with men in one study (Marrazzo et al., 1998) and 13% of sexual minority women in another (Eaton et al., 2008).

Beyond female-to-female sex, sexual minority women may be at risk for STIs, including HIV, through several other means, including consensual sex with men, intravenous drug use (IDU), and sexual abuse. For example, in a study of 498 lesbians and bisexual women living in California, 40% reported unprotected vaginal or anal sex with men during the past 3 years, including unprotected sex with gay and bisexual men or with male injection drug users; 10% reported injecting drugs; and 1.2% reported an HIV-positive diagnosis (Lemp et al., 1995). Despite these risks, the CDC does not include female-to-female HIV transmission as an exposure category, and the prevalence of HIV infection

among sexual minority women is not specifically tracked (Aaron et al., 2001; Cochran & Mays, 2007; Marrazzo et al., 1998; Simoni et al., 2010).

The few relevant studies on asthma and diabetes that we could locate pointed to disparities in asthma but not diabetes. Specifically, analyses from the 2003–2006 Washington State BRFSS (controlling for age and education) indicated that compared to heterosexual women (11.2%), lesbian (17.7%) and bisexual women (21.0%) were more likely to have asthma. Compared to heterosexual women (6.3%), neither bisexuals (5.8%) nor lesbians (5.1%) were more likely to have diabetes (Dilley et al., 2010). Based on analyses adjusting for age, race/ethnicity, educational attainment, relationship status, nativity, and family income, Cochran and Mays (2007) reported that lesbian (13.1%), bisexual (13.1%), and homosexually experienced heterosexual (24.5%) women were more likely than exclusively heterosexual women (8.6%) to report asthma; they noted no group differences in diabetes (2.2%, 1.3%, 0.0% versus 6.9%, respectively; all prevalence data are weighted). Based on analyses of data from the Massachusetts BRFSS (adjusting for age and education), lesbians were more likely than heterosexual women to report that a health provider had told them they had asthma but were not more likely to report this about diabetes (Conron et al., 2010).

DISPARITIES IN RISK FACTORS FOR DISEASE

In the absence of solid data on the incidence and prevalence of disease among sexual minority women, which limits the extent to which disparities with heterosexual women can be identified, researchers have looked to data on risk factors as "proxy indicators" for an at-risk population (Dibble et al., 2004). Next, we consider the major risk factors that have been studied: obesity, smoking, diet and exercise, as well as other cancer-specific risk factors.

Obesity

Obesity is pandemic in the United States, with 66% of adults considered overweight (defined as having a body mass index or BMI > 25) and 31% obese (BMI > 30; National Institute of Diabetes and Digestive Kidney Disease, 2006). Obesity is related to hypertension, diabetes, hyperlipidemia, CVD, joint disease, thromboembolic disorders, multiple cancers, and higher all-cause mortality (National Institutes of Health, 1998).

A greater prevalence of obesity among sexual minority women compared to heterosexual women is one of the most consistent findings of health disparities between these groups. A review of 19 articles that included measures of obesity and sexual orientation concluded that a higher percentage of sexual minority than heterosexual women are obese (Bowen, Balsam, & Ender, 2008). Results from three large population-based studies are consistent with this conclusion (Boehmer, Bowen, & Bauer, 2007; Case et al., 2004; Valanis et al., 2000). For example, in the Nurses' Health Study II, lesbians had a 20% greater prevalence of being overweight and a 50% (40% for bisexuals) greater prevalence of obesity compared to heterosexual women. Importantly, it appears that disparities in weight status among sexual minority women begin as early as adolescence. In a prospective study of youth who provided self-reported information from six waves of data, sexual minority female adolescents reported consistently elevated BMI relative to their heterosexual peers (Austin et al., 2009). Evidence suggests the greater BMI is not due to greater muscle density or lean body mass rather than fat (Roberts et al., 2003).

Smoking

Almost half a million people die prematurely from smoking or exposure to secondhand smoke in the United States each year, and another 8.6 million have a serious illness caused by smoking (Centers for Disease Control and Prevention, 2010). Despite the risks, over 46 million people, 20.6% of all adults age 18 and older (23.1% of men and 18.3% women), are current smokers (American Lung Association, 2010).

The literature on tobacco use and sexual orientation demonstrates clear and consistent disparities. Several studies, including those based on data from the large population-based surveys, have demonstrated higher rates of smoking among sexual minority women compared to heterosexual women, with rates among adult sexual minority women ranging from 11% to 50% compared to 28% in general adult samples (Ryan, Wortley, Easton, Pederson, & Greenwood, 2001). In a review article, Hughes and Jacobson (2003) identified 16 studies of lesbian and bisexual women, nine of which had comparison groups. On average, lesbians reported rates of smoking rates that were 1.5 to 2 times higher than rates among heterosexual women (Lee, Griffin, & Melvin, 2009). As is the case with obesity, smoking disparities in sexual minority women appear to begin before adulthood.

Diet and Exercise

Evidence for disparities in diet and exercise between sexual minority women and heterosexual women is mixed. Several studies have found no disparities. Specifically, Valanis et al. (2000) and Case et al. (2004) reported lesbians and heterosexual women exercise similarly, and Dilley et al. (2010) found no differences among lesbian, bisexual, and heterosexual women in sufficiency of physical activity or in consumption of fruit and vegetables.

Some studies have found that sexual minority women were more likely than other women to report risk factors relating to diet and exercise, whereas others found the reverse. For example, Aaron et al. (2001) reported that although there was little difference based on sexual orientation in the reporting of any physical activity in the past month, a higher percentage of lesbians reported engaging in vigorous activity compared with the general population of women. In their study of lesbians and their sisters, Roberts et al. (2003) found that lesbians were less likely to have eaten red meat in the past year but did not differ from their sisters on other nutritional variables. With regard to exercise, the lesbians were significantly more likely to exercise at least weekly yet did not differ in the number of times per week they exercised, the length of the exercise session, or the exercise vigor (Roberts et al., 2003).

Cancer-Specific Risk Factors

Although cancer etiologies vary, some risk factors have been identified as more or less strongly associated with cancer. Most theorized risks do not differ by sexual orientation, but some of the weakly associated risks are related (Henderson, 2009; Koh, 2010). Factors more prevalent among lesbians and their relative risk of association with cancer include nulliparity, delay of childbearing until after the age of 30 years (versus before age 20), daily consumption of two to five alcoholic drinks (versus no alcohol), and urban residence (Case et al., 2004; Koh, 2010). Sexual minority women also have fewer of the protective factors for cancer, including a history of lactation and lower postmenopausal BMI. However, lesbians are less likely to report hormone replacement therapy, which is a risk factor for cancer.

In a comprehensive review of 51 studies from 1981 to 2007 examining cancer disparities among lesbians, Brown and Tracy (2008) found most of the studies focused on issues related to screening and prevention in cervical and breast cancers. These studies consistently reported higher rates of risk factors, fewer reproductive-related protective factors, and less frequent routine screenings, which can lead to earlier detection and treatment in samples of sexual minority women. In comparison, ovarian, colorectal, and lung cancer among sexual minority women have received limited attention.

FACTORS TO EXPLAIN DISPARITIES BASED ON SEXUAL ORIENTATION

Disparities in health outcomes between sexual minority women and heterosexual women are likely determined by greater exposure to adversity and unequal access to health-promoting resources. Most of the factors involved may be rooted in the pervasive social stigma that affects sexual minority women at multiple levels (Krehely, 2009; Meyer, 2003).

The most widely cited reasons for sexual minority women's health disparities is lack of routine screening and preventive care and delayed treatment (Koh, 2010). Indeed, several studies have shown that despite evidence that sexual transmission of HPV between women occurs, sexual minority women (including young lesbians) undergo routine Pap smear screening less often than national guidelines advise and less often than do heterosexual women (Aaron et al., 2001; Cochran et al., 2001; Diamant & Wold, 2003; Marrazzo, Koutsky, Kiviat, Kuypers, & Stine, 2001).

There are, however, some exceptions. In a community-based survey of 1010 self-identified lesbians, Aaron et al. (2001) reported that compared to women in a comparison sample drawn from the general population, lesbians were more likely to report ever having had a mammogram. Aaron et al. (2001) and Conron et al. (2010) found that for women at least 40 years old, there were no statistically significant sexual orientation differences in lifetime mammography or receipt of a Pap test within the prior 3 years. Moreover, lesbians were 1.8 times more likely than heterosexual women to have had an HIV test.

Although the exact reasons for suboptimal screening and preventive care among lesbians are unclear (Marrazzo et al., 2001), the main barriers likely relate to sexual minority women's reduced access to insurance, which in turn results from lack of financial resources (i.e., greater poverty) and inequities in the structure of employment-sponsored programs. Lack of data limit our ability to determine the full impact of financial barriers, but inequities in insurance coverage are well documented (Diamant et al., 2000; Dilley et al., 2010, Valanis et al., 2000), with potentially even less coverage for bisexual than lesbian women (Conron et al., 2010).

Even if they have insurance, sexual minority women might not seek services because they do not perceive the medical necessity. In one study of over 1000 sexual minority women, fewer than half of those with a clear risk factor for HIV perceived themselves to be at risk (Einhorn & Polgar, 1994). In another study, many lesbians were found to mistakenly believe that they did not need to have Pap smears because they were not sexually active with men (Marrazzo et al., 2001).

Beyond lack of access and misconceptions about appropriate screening, another major barrier for sexual minority women is fear of discriminatory or inappropriate treatment once they do enter care. Indeed, overt homophobia and lack of culturally competent care for sexual minority women in the healthcare system have been documented (O'Hanlan, 2007). This may be due in part to the lack of instruction at most medical schools on the health needs of nonheterosexual people (Makadon, 2006; Tesar & Rovi, 1998), leaving few providers trained in how to offer competent care. Not surprisingly, many sexual minority women decline to disclose their sexual orientation to healthcare providers, which only further diminishes the chances that their physicians can provide optimal care or educate them about specific risk behaviors and other health concerns.

Comorbidity with documented disparities in mental health issues, sexual abuse, and victimization also might contribute to worse health outcomes among sexual minority women. Specifically, there are consistent reports of mental health disparities among sexual minority compared to heterosexual individuals (see Cochran and Mays, Chapter 15, this volume), and mental health is associated with physical health outcomes. Based on data from the California Quality of Life Survey ($N = 2272$ adults), Cochran and Mays (2007) found that lesbian, bisexual, and homosexually experienced heterosexual women reported a greater variety of health conditions and limitations compared with exclusively heterosexual women; however, these differences mostly disappeared when mental distress levels were taken into account.

Sexual minority women appear to be at elevated risk for sexual abuse, compared to heterosexual women (see Balsam and Hughes, Chapter 19, this volume). Sexual abuse is associated with adverse mental and physical health outcomes (Lehavot, Walters, & Simoni, 2010; Midei, Matthews, & Bromberger, 2010). Reports from population-based studies of adolescents suggest that disparities in unwanted sexual contact begin early in life (Saewyc et al., 2006). These have been linked empirically with obesity and other negative outcomes among adult sexual minority women (Aaron & Hughes, 2007; Midei et al., 2010).

FUTURE DIRECTIONS

The literature on physical health disparities among sexual minority versus heterosexual women is characterized by a dearth of population-based epidemiological data and by a reliance on self-report assessments. Consequently, much of the work on disparities is based on conclusions derived from differential risk factors rather than clear indicators of differences in health outcomes. Some clarity is beginning to emerge from the few studies that do provide empirical data, however. Specifically, there seems to be consistent support for the finding that sexual minority women are more likely than their heterosexual peers to smoke, be overweight, and have asthma. Data on cardiovascular disease are limited and fail to indicate clear differences between lesbians and heterosexual women; however, there are consistent findings for the increased risk among bisexual women. The findings for diet and exercise are mixed. Few cancer studies have documented disparities based on sexual orientation, but there seem to be clear differences in some risks for cancer.

This review suggests multiple avenues for future research. Clearly, more research is needed on physical health outcomes and chronic conditions based on representative samples of sexual minority women and comparable groups of heterosexual women. The recent decision to incorporate items on sexual orientation into many U.S. national surveys is a substantial step in this direction (http://www.hhs.gov/news/press/2011pres/06/20110629a.html). Future research should not continue to rely on samples composed disproportionately of white, middle-class women, but should include sexual minority women in all their diversity. Data on low-income women, women of color, adolescents, and older adults are needed to represent the diversity of sexual minority communities. In addition, research that samples sexual minority women across age and ethnicity could yield important information on potential pathways to health inequities. Such studies could also highlight protective factors that may buffer the impact of traumatic stressors on physical and mental health outcomes. Important subgroup differences (Fredriksen-Goldsen, Kim, Barkan, Balsam, & Mincer, 2010) and distinctions among women who identify as lesbian, as bisexual, or as heterosexual but have a history of same-sex sexual partners, need to be considered more closely, given reports of disproportionate health burdens among the last two groups (Cochran & Mays, 2007; Conron et al., 2010).

Research on transgender individuals is desperately needed (Lawrence, 2007). Despite the unique health concerns of transgender people, very few studies of this population have been reported (for more information, see Sánchez and Vilain, Chapter 4, this volume). Also, almost all of the research in this field has been conducted in the United States. Studies of transgender individuals in other countries are needed to understand the health concerns of women in diverse political, economic, and cultural environments. The results of such studies might also provide a better context for interpreting studies based in the United States.

Methodologically sound studies based on clear conceptual frameworks that consider both mental and physical health outcomes as well as mechanisms underlying potential disparities would be helpful in illuminating not only disparities but also underlying determinants. Researchers in this area need to expand theoretical frameworks to understand how social inequities can become embodied as poor health among sexual minority women. Studying the embodiment of trauma and associated stressors (e.g., stigma, discrimination, and hate crimes) and corresponding health consequences could assist in identifying the forces driving intergenerational patterns of health and disease among sexual minority women (Krieger, 1999). In addition, resistance, positive coping, and resiliency can be studied by utilizing a stress-and-coping framework (e.g., Walters & Simoni, 2002) to delineate not only how stressful events have direct effects but also how protective factors can buffer the impact of these events on health and wellness.

Research requires support from funding agencies, yet historically, lesbian, gay, bisexual, and transgender health issues, especially those of sexual minority women, have been marginalized compared to those of the general population (Boehmer, 2002; Institute of Medicine, 2011). Furthermore, lesbian, gay, bisexual, and transgender people have historically not been regarded by U.S. federal agencies as a "minority" population for the purpose of research on health disparities. To overcome the lack of data and to provide a more accurate assessment of lesbian, gay, bisexual, and transgender health outcomes and concerns, advocates have called for the creation of a dedicated U.S. Office of Lesbian, Gay, Bisexual, and Transgender Health (Krehely, 2009).

It is not premature to consider intervening to promote sexual minority women's health, especially in areas in which there is clear evidence of disparities, such as with smoking, obesity, and asthma. Intervention is needed at multiple levels and should involve the evaluation and dissemination of the most effective strategies. Interventions should specially target sexual minority women, as they are unlikely to engage in health promotion activities geared to gay men or to heterosexual women, at least according to research in the area of safer sex (Power, McNair, & Carr, 2009). Interventions should be firmly grounded in relevant theory and empirical research. For example, recent work offers suggestions for heightening lesbians' perceptions of vulnerability to STI acquisition that might guide intervention development (Eaton et al., 2008).

Health promotion interventions for sexual minority women might address any of the factors implicated in their health disparities. For example, media campaigns to destigmatize sexual minority status, with accompanying changes in the legal system, might decrease underlying minority stress. Moreover, capitalizing on lesbian social networks would facilitate creative strategies for diffusion of innovative prevention campaigns. Key opinion leaders at the community level could lead health intervention campaigns utilizing natural support systems (Morris, Zavisca, & Dean, 1995). Reducing financial barriers and expanding insurance coverage might also improve access to care among sexual minority women. In the meantime, prioritizing cultural competency training among providers could reduce provider ignorance and bias; Krehely (2009) suggests that federally funded programs might be required to incorporate such training in their curricula.

In conclusion, the literature on sexual orientation and health disparities among women is limited, although it is increasing rapidly in both quality and scope. Compared to other women, sexual minority women seem to shoulder an additional burden of minority stress, and they are often at an economic disadvantage as well; as a result of these and related processes, the health of sexual minority women suffers. Although more definitive findings are needed in some areas, there is already sufficient evidence to justify address. Ignoring the health concerns of sexual minority women in national health care priorities was never acceptable and can no longer be tolerated.

REFERENCES

Aaron, D. J., & Hughes, T. L. (2007). Association of childhood sexual abuse with obesity in a community sample of lesbians. *Obesity, 15,* 1023–1028.

Aaron, D. J., Markovic, N., Danielson, M. E., Honnold, J. A., Janosky, J. E., & Schmidt, N. J. (2001). Behavioral risk factors for disease and preventive health practices among lesbians *American Journal of Public Health, 91,* 972–975.

Adler, N. E., & Rehkopf, D. H. (2008). US disparities in health: Descriptions, causes, and mechanisms. *Public Health, 29,* 235.

American Cancer Society (ACS). (2008). Cancer facts and figures 2008.

American Lung Association. (2010). *Smoking out a deadly threat: Tobacco use in the LGBT community.* American Lung Association.

Austin, S. B., Ziyadeh, N. J., Corliss, H. L., Haines, J., Rockett, H., Wypij, D., et al. (2009). Sexual orientation disparities in weight status in adolescence: Findings from a prospective study. *Obesity, 17,* 1776.

Boehmer, U. (2002). Twenty years of public health research: Inclusion of lesbian, gay, bisexual, and transgender populations. *American Journal of Public Health, 92,* 1125.

Boehmer, U., Bowen, D. J., & Bauer, G. R. (2007). Overweight and obesity in sexual-minority women: Evidence from population-based data. *American Journal of Public Health, 97,* 1134.

Bowen, D. J., Balsam, K. F., & Ender, S. R. (2008). A review of obesity issues in sexual minority women. *Obesity, 16,* 221–228.

Bowen, D. J., Boehmer, U., & Russo, M. (2007). Cancer and sexual minority women. In I. H. Meyer & M. E. Northridge (Eds.), *The health of sexual minorities: Public health perspectives on lesbian, gay, bisexual, and transgender populations* (pp. 523–538). New York: Springer.

Bradford, J., Ryan, C., & Rothblum, E. D. (1994). National Lesbian Health Care Survey: Implications for mental health care. *Journal of Consulting and Clinical Psychology, 62,* 228–242.

Brown, J. P., & Tracy, J. K. (2008). Lesbians and cancer: An overlooked health disparity. *Cancer Causes and Control, 19,* 1009–1020.

Burgard, S. A., Cochran, S. D., & Mays, V. M. (2005). Alcohol and tobacco use patterns among heterosexually and homosexually experienced California women. *Drug and Alcohol Dependence, 77*, 61–70.

Case, P., Bryn Austin, S., Hunter, D. J., Manson, J. E., Malspeis, S., Willett, W. C., et al. (2004). Sexual orientation, health risk factors, and physical functioning in the nurses' health study II. *Journal of Women's Health, 13*, 1033–1047.

Centers for Disease Control and Prevention (CDC). (2011). CDC health disparities and inequalities report—United States, 2011. *MMWR 2011, 60*(Suppl), 1–116.

Centers for Disease Control and Prevention (CDC). (2010). *Tobacco use: Targeting the nation's leading killer.* Atlanta: Department of Health and Human Services.

Cochran, S. D., & Mays, V. M. (2007). Physical health complaints among lesbians, gay men, and bisexual and homosexually experienced heterosexual individuals: Results from the California Quality of Life Survey. *American Journal of Public Health, 97*, 2048.

Cochran, S. D., Mays, V. M., Bowen, D., Gage, S., Bybee, D., Roberts, S. J., et al. (2001). Cancer-related risk indicators and preventive screening behaviors among lesbians and bisexual women. *American Journal of Public Health, 91*, 591–597.

Cochran, S. D., Sullivan, J. G., & Mays, V. M. (2003). Prevalence of mental disorders, psychological distress, and mental health services use among lesbian, gay, and bisexual adults in the United States. *Journal of Consulting and Clinical Psychology, 71*, 53–61.

Conron, K. J., Mimiaga, M. J., & Landers, S. J. (2010). A population-based study of sexual orientation identity and gender differences in adult health. *American Journal of Public Health, 100*, 1953–1960.

Diamant, A. L., & Wold, C. (2003). Sexual orientation and variation in physical and mental health status among women. *Journal of Women's Health, 12*, 41–49.

Diamant, A. L., Wold, C., Spritzer, K., & Gelberg, L. (2000). Health behaviors, health status, and access to and use of health care: A population-based study of lesbian, bisexual, and heterosexual women. *Archives of Family Medicine, 9*, 1043.

Dibble, S. L., Roberts, S. A., & Nussey, B. (2004). Comparing breast cancer risk between lesbians and their heterosexual sisters. *Women's Health Issues, 14*, 60–68.

Dilley, J. A., Simmons, K. W., Boysun, M. J., Pizacani, B. A., & Stark, M. J. (2010). Demonstrating the importance and feasibility of including sexual orientation in public health surveys: Health disparities in the Pacific Northwest. *American Journal of Public Health, 100*, 460–467.

Drabble, L., & Trocki, K. (2005). Alcohol consumption, alcohol-related problems, and other substance use among lesbian and bisexual women. *Journal of Lesbian Studies, 9*, 19–30.

Eaton, L., Kalichman, S., Cain, D., Cherry, C., Pope, H., Fuhrel, A., et al. (2008). Perceived prevalence and risks for human papillomavirus (HPV) infection among women who have sex with women. *Journal of Women's Health, 17*, 75–84.

Einhorn, L., & Polgar, M. (1994). HIV-risk behavior among lesbians and bisexual women. *AIDS Education and Prevention, 6*, 514–523.

Fredriksen-Goldsen, K. I., Kim, H. J., Barkan, S. E., Balsam, K. F., & Mincer, S. L. (2010). Disparities in health-related quality of life: A comparison of lesbians and bisexual women. *American Journal of Public Health, 100*, 2255–2261.

Frisch, M., Smith, E., Grulich, A., & Johansen, C. (2003). Cancer in a population-based cohort of men and women in registered homosexual partnerships. *American Journal of Epidemiology, 157*, 966.

Gruskin, E. P., & Gordon, N. (2006). Gay/lesbian sexual orientation increases risk for cigarette smoking and heavy drinking among members of a large northern California health plan. *BMC Public Health, 6*, 241.

Gruskin, E. P., Hart, S., Gordon, N., & Ackerson, L. (2001). Patterns of cigarette smoking and alcohol use among lesbians and bisexual women enrolled in a large health maintenance organization. *American Journal of Public Health, 91*, 976.

Henderson, H. J. (2009). Why lesbians should be encouraged to have regular cervical screening. *Journal of Family Planning and Reproductive Health Care, 35*, 49–52.

Hughes, T. L., & Jacobson, K. (2003). Sexual orientation and smoking. *Current Women's Health Reports, 3*, 254–261.

Institute of Medicine. (2011). *Lesbian, gay, bisexual and transgender health issues and research gaps and opportunities.* Retrieved January 29, 2011, from http://www.iom.edu/activities/SelectPops/LGBTHealthIssues.aspx.

Kavanaugh-Lynch, M. H. E., White, E., Daling, J. R., & Bowen, D. J. (2002). Correlates of lesbian sexual orientation and the risk of breast cancer. *Journal of the Gay and Lesbian Medical Association, 6*, 91–95.

Koh, A. S. (2010). "But I'm not sick. Why should I get a check-up?" Health screening for lesbians. In S. L. Dibble & P. A. Robertson (Eds.), *Lesbian health 101: A clinician's guide* (pp. 1–22). San Francisco: UCSF Nursing Press.

Krehely, J. (2009). How to close the LGBT health disparities gap. *Center for American Progress*, 1–9.

Krieger, N. (1999). Embodying inequality: A review of concepts, measures, and methods for studying health consequences of discrimination. *International Journal of Health Services, 29*, 295–352.

Lawrence, A. A. (2007). Transgender health concerns. In I. H. Meyer & M. E. Northridge (Eds.), *The health of sexual minorities: Public health perspectives on lesbian, gay, bisexual, and transgender populations* (pp. 473–505). New York: Springer.

Lee, J. G., Griffin, G. K., & Melvin, C. L. (2009). Tobacco use among sexual minorities in the USA, 1987 to May 2007: A systematic review. *Tobacco Control, 18,* 275.

Lehavot, K., Walters, K. L., & Simoni, J. M. (2010). Abuse, mastery, and health among lesbian, bisexual, and two-spirit American Indian and Alaska Native women. *Psychology of Violence, 1,* 53–67.

Lemp, G. F., Jones, M., Kellogg, T. A., Nieri, G. N., Anderson, L., Withum, D., et al. (1995). HIV seroprevalence and risk behaviors among lesbians and bisexual women in San Francisco and Berkeley, California. *American Journal of Public Health, 85,* 1549.

Makadon, H. J. (2006). Improving health care for the lesbian and gay communities. *New England Journal of Medicine, 354,* 895–897.

Marrazzo, J. M. (2004). Barriers to infectious disease care among lesbians. *Emerging Infectious Diseases, 10,* 1974–1978.

Marrazzo, J. M., Koutsky, L. A., Kiviat, N. B., Kuypers, J. M., & Stine, K. (2001). Papanicolaou test screening and prevalence of genital human papillomavirus among women who have sex with women. *American Journal of Public Health, 91,* 947–952.

Marrazzo, J. M., Koutsky, L. A., Stine, K. L., Kuypers, J. M., Grubert, T. A., Galloway, D. A., et al. (1998). Genital human papillomavirus infection in women who have sex with women. *The Journal of Infectious Diseases, 178,* 1604–1609.

Meyer, I. H. (2003). Prejudice, social stress, and mental health in lesbian, gay, and bisexual populations: Conceptual issues and research evidence. *Psychological Bulletin, 129,* 674.

Midei, A. J., Matthews, K. A., & Bromberger, J. T. (2010). Childhood abuse is associated with adiposity in midlife women: Possible pathways through trait anger and reproductive hormones. *Psychosomatic Medicine, 72,* 215.

Morris, M., Zavisca, J., & Dean, L. (1995). Social and sexual networks: Their role in the spread of HIV/AIDS among young gay men. *AIDS Education and Prevention, 7,* 24–35.

National Institute of Diabetes and Digestive and Kidney Disease. (2006). *Statistics related to overweight and obesity.* Washington, DC: U.S. Department of Health and Human Services.

National Institutes of Health (US), National Heart, Lung, and Blood Institute, North American Association for the Study of Obesity, & Panel, N. O. E. I. E. (1998). *Clinical guidelines on the identification, evaluation, and treatment of overweight and obesity in adults: The evidence report.* North American Association for the Study of Obesity.

O'Hanlan, K. A. (2007). Health care of lesbian and bisexual women. In I. H. Meyer & M. E. Northridge (Eds.), *The health of sexual minorities: Public health perspectives on lesbian, gay, bisexual, and transgender populations* (pp. 506–522). New York: Springer.

Power, J., McNair, R., & Carr, S. (2009). Absent sexual scripts: Lesbian and bisexual women's knowledge, attitudes and action regarding safer sex and sexual health information. *Culture, Health & Sexuality, 11,* 67–81.

Rankow, E. J. (1995). Breast and cervical cancer among lesbians. *Women's Health Issues, 5,* 123–129.

Roberts, S. A., Dibble, S. L., Nussey, B., & Casey, K. (2003). Cardiovascular disease risk in lesbian women. *Women's Health Issues, 13,* 167–174.

Ryan, H., Wortley, P. M., Easton, A., Pederson, L., & Greenwood, G. (2001). Smoking among lesbians, gays, and bisexuals: A review of the literature. *American Journal of Preventive Medicine, 21,* 142–149.

Saewyc, E. M., Skay, C. L., Pettingell, S. L., Reis, E. A., Bearinger, L., Resnick, M., et al. (2006). Hazards of stigma: The sexual and physical abuse of gay, lesbian, and bisexual adolescents in the United States and Canada. *Child Welfare, 85,* 19.

Simoni, J. M., Evans-Campbell, T., Andrasik, M. P., Lehavot, K., Valencia-Garcia, D., & Walters, K. L. (2010). HIV/AIDS among women of color and sexual minority women. In N. F. Russo (Ed.), *Handbook of diversity in feminist psychology* (pp. 335–365). New York: Springer Publishing Co.

Snyder, J. E. (2011). Trend analysis of medical publications about LGBT persons: 1950–2007. *Journal of Homosexuality, 58,* 164–188.

Solarz, A. L. (Ed.). (1999). *Lesbian health: Current assessment and directions for the future.* Washington, DC: National Academies Press.

Tesar, C. M., & Rovi, S. L. D. (1998). Survey of curriculum on homosexuality/bisexuality in departments of family medicine. *Family Medicine, 30,* 283–287.

U.S. Department of Health and Human Services (2010). The Secretary's Advisory Committee on National Health Promotion and Disease Prevention Objectives for 2020. Phase I report: Recommendations for the framework and format of Healthy People 2020. Section IV. Advisory Committee findings and recommendations. Retrieved January 2010 from http://www.healthypeople.gov/hp2020/advisory/PhaseI/sec4.htm#_Toc211942917.

Valanis, B. G., Bowen, D. J., Bassford, T., Whitlock, E., Charney, P., & Carter, R. A. (2000). Sexual orientation and health: Comparisons in the Women's Health Initiative sample. *Archives of Family Medicine, 9,* 843.

Walters, K. L., & Simoni, J. M. (2002). Reconceptualizing Native women's health: An "indigenist" stress-coping model. *American Journal of Public Health, 92,* 520.

14

Gay Men's Health and the Theory of Cultural Resilience

AMY L. HERRICK, MARK S. FRIEDMAN, AND RON STALL

According to the United States Department of Health and Human Services, health disparities are population-specific differences in the presence of disease, health outcomes, or access to healthcare (Health Resources and Services Administration, 2000). One population that experiences immense health disparities is men who have sex with men. This chapter explores health disparities among men who identify as gay, bisexual, queer, same gender loving, or some other sexual minority term, as well as men who engage in same-sex sexual behavior. Sexual orientation is a complex multidimensional construct and we do not intend to minimize the diversity inherent in this group, yet for the sake of simplicity, we will collectively refer to these individuals as men who have sex with men. In this chapter we will discuss why health disparities exist and offer a framework to address them. We suggest that current prevention and health promotion efforts could be greatly improved by expanding the current public health paradigm to include a focus on resilience.

HEALTH DISPARITIES AMONG MEN WHO HAVE SEX WITH MEN

The information we have about health disparities among gay men or men who have sex with men (MSM) is limited. Most information available about health inequalities experienced by MSM concerns sexual health (Wolitski, Stall, & Valdiserri, 2008). This is not necessarily because this is the area of greatest disparity, but, as a result of the HIV/AIDS epidemic, because this is where the greatest amount of research has been done. As more research is conducted that examines the association between same-sex sexual orientation and/ or behavior and other health outcomes, evidence of

health disparities in other areas of health is likely to emerge. For instance, many studies have shown that MSM smoke cigarettes at greater rates than heterosexual men (Greenwood et al., 2005; Ryan, Wortley, Easton, Pederson, & Greenwood, 2001; Tang et al., 2004. However, to our knowledge there is no evidence of disparities in rates of lung cancer. This is not necessarily because disparities do not exist; it may be because the research has not yet been done.

Another limiting factor in our understanding of health disparities among gay men is the homogeneity in the samples in most research studies. Historically, most sexual minority health research has been conducted with samples that are disproportionately white. A survey of MSM health research may give the impression that MSM are mainly white, middle class, and highly educated, obviously an inaccurate portrayal of the great diversity of MSM individuals and communities. Non-MSM health research has demonstrated immense disparities based on race/ethnicity, with African-Americans and Latinos faring much worse than whites on many health indicators (Arias, 2007; Hummer, 1996; Orsi, Margellos-Anast, & Whitman, 2010). The limited research that has been conducted with MSM of color suggests that these race/ethnicity-based health disparities also exist among MSM (Diaz, Peterson, & Choi, 2007; Harawa et al., 2004). However, more research is needed to understand the context and the extent of health disparities among MSM of color.

Another issue that limits a full understanding of health disparities among gay men is inconsistencies in the assessment of sexual orientation. Studies typically use identity, behavior, attraction, *or* a combination of these constructs to categorize an individual as gay. These methods all have limitations.

For instance, terms used for self-identification as gay are not necessarily consistent across different gay men's communities. Whereas "queer" or "yag" (gay spelled backward) are terms often used by young gay men, these terms are less frequently used, or may even be perceived as offensive, by older gay men. Similarly inconsistent patterns of identification appear across racial/ethnic groups with some African-American gay men more likely to prefer the term "same gender loving" to the more commonly used "gay" or "homosexual." Different methods for collecting sexual orientation data are often unavoidable as each research question and health topic requires a tailored approach. For a study of sexually transmitted diseases, it is best to classify individuals based on same-sex sexual behaviors, whereas a study of adolescent suicide risk might more effectively use measures of sexual attraction or sexual identity. Inconsistencies in what is defined as sexual minority limit the generalizations that can be made about health disparities in the gay male population.

Perhaps the greatest limiting factor in our understanding of health disparities among MSM is the exclusion of sexual orientation information in population-based studies and in clinical trials. Few large-scale studies currently include questions about same-sex sexual behavior, sexual identity, or sexual attraction, making it impossible to draw conclusions about how the prevalence of conditions such as cancer, diabetes, or heart disease may vary between MSM and non-MSM populations. The large-scale studies that do include sexual orientation questions, such as the National Longitudinal Study of Adolescent Health (in its latest wave of data collection), the National Health and Nutrition Examination Survey, and the Youth Risk Behavior Survey (in this survey, questions about sexual orientation are voluntary and are added by individual states), have contributed greatly to our understanding of gay men's health (Galliher, Rostosky, & Hughes, 2004; Garofalo, Wolf, Kessel, Palfrey, & DuRant, 1998; Marshal, Friedman, Stall, & Thompson, 2009; Saewyc et al., 2006). Many sexual minority health researchers have urged the routine inclusion of questions about sexual orientation in population-based questionnaires. Until a sexual orientation assessment, preferably including items concerning attraction, behavior, and self-identification, is added to such data collection tools, our depth and breadth of understanding about MSM health disparities will be limited.

Despite these limitations, there is still quite a bit of information about health disparities among MSM. A complete synthesis all of the literature documenting disparate negative health outcomes among gay men is beyond the scope of this chapter. For a comprehensive recent review, the reader is referred to Wolitski et al. (2008). Instead, the chapter focuses on HIV for two main reasons. First, HIV represents perhaps the greatest health disparity faced by gay men and has been the most critical health concern for gay and sexual men since the first cases of AIDS were reported in 1981. Second, the HIV epidemic can provide a framework for examining the etiology of health disparities. We will also focus broadly on the mechanisms by which gay men and MSM have developed other health disparities as a result of social marginalization and homophobia.

HIV AMONG MEN WHO HAVE SEX WITH MEN

According to a 2010 surveillance report released by the Centers for Disease Control and Prevention (CDC) regarding HIV prevalence rates in the United States, males who reported having sex with other men accounted for 73% of all new HIV infections and 75% of all people living with HIV. Even though gay men make up only a small minority of the U.S. population, the majority (53%) of all new infections are attributed to male-to-male sexual contact (Centers for Disease Control and Prevention, July 2010). Subpopulation estimates from the same year suggested that 72% of new HIV infections among males were in MSM (Centers for Disease Control and Prevention, 2008b). Epidemiological data indicate that not only are the rates of HIV infection high among MSM, but the trends in infection are alarming. From 2004 to 2007, there was an estimated 26% annual increase in HIV/AIDS diagnoses among MSM (Centers for Disease Control and Prevention, 2009b).

Nearly 30 years into the epidemic, the human immunodeficiency virus (HIV) has become a disease of adolescents and young adults. It is estimated that 50% of all new HIV infections in the United States occur among individuals under the age of 25 (Centers for Disease Control and Prevention, 2005b). Similar to subpopulation disparities among adults, the burden of HIV disease among youth is also being shouldered by MSM. Surveillance data indicate that 76% of new youth HIV infections occur among MSM (Wolitski, Valdiserri, Denning, & Levine, 2001). The magnitude of this disparity in infection rates is further demonstrated by the fact that only 5–7% of the U.S. male population reports having had sex with other men, yet MSM make up over two-thirds of all persons currently infected with HIV (Centers for Disease Control and Prevention, 2007). A study of high-risk young persons who visited sexually transmitted disease (STD) clinics found seroprevalence rates among young heterosexual men to be less than 3% compared to 21% for young MSM (Centers for Disease Control and Prevention, 2001b).

Within the MSM population the burden of HIV infection is also unequally distributed. In particular, racial and ethnic minorities are more likely to be infected with HIV than white MSM, with African-Americans experiencing the highest rates of infection (Centers for Disease Control and Prevention, 2000, 2001a; Easterbrook et al., 1993; Lemp et al., 1994; Valleroy et al., 2000). Half (49%) of all new HIV infections in 2005 occurred in African-Americans, despite the fact that African-Americans make up an estimated 13% of the U.S. population (Centers for Disease Control and Prevention, 2006). Among these individuals, male-to-male sexual contact accounted for 63% of the new infections (Centers for Disease Control and Prevention, 2008a). In a study of MSM in five major U.S. cities, 46% of African-American MSM were HIV positive (Centers for Disease Control and Prevention, 2005a). The racial disparity in rates of HIV is even more pronounced among young MSM (YMSM). CDC surveillance data have shown that adult African-American MSM are five times more likely to be infected with HIV than white MSM. In comparison, African-American YMSM ages 13 to 19 have a rate of infection 19 times higher than of white YMSM (Hall, Byers, Ling, & Espinoza, 2007). The majority (76%) of HIV-seropositive youth (Rangel, Gavin, Reed, Fowler, & Lee, 2006), regardless of race/ethnicity or sexual minority identity, were infected through unprotected anal intercourse (Kingsley et al., 1987; Vittinghoff et al., 1999). Latino men also experience higher rates of HIV compared to white men. In 2006, the rate of new HIV infections among Latino men was 2.5 times that of white men. In the same year, HIV/AIDS was the fourth leading cause of death among Latino men aged 35–44 (Centers for Disease Control and Prevention, August 2009).

As with white and African-American men, the leading pathway to HIV infection among Latino men is sexual contact with other men (Centers for Disease Control and Prevention, 2009a).

Despite over two decades of prevention efforts aimed at MSM, rates of HIV infection remain high. A 2008 report released by the CDC showed that MSM accounted for 46% of all new HIV/AIDS infections and HIV infection rates among young MSM increased at a rate of approximately 12% each year between 2001 and 2006 (Centers for Disease Control and Prevention, 2008c). During the same 6-year time period, the number of HIV/AIDS cases among African-Americans increased regardless of age, but the number of new HIV/AIDS cases among African-American MSM aged 13 to 24 increased by an astounding 93% (Centers for Disease Control and Prevention, 2008c). This report further noted that MSM were the only risk group that experienced an increase in infection rates during this time.

It must be noted that CDC incidence and prevalence estimates—including the estimates presented here—are typically made available 2–3 years after the data are collected. It is therefore possible that the HIV risk that MSM are currently facing is worse than the data suggest. In fact, according to analysis conducted by Stall and colleagues, even if the incidence of HIV among MSM remains at the current level, by the time a cohort of young MSM who are currently 18 years olds reaches the age of 40, 41% of them will be HIV positive (Stall et al., 2009). Thus, the trends that have been seen in rates of HIV among MSM are alarming.

UNDERSTANDING HEALTH DISPARITIES AMONG MSM

MSM also experience disparities in rates of other psychosocial health outcomes, such as illicit drug use, alcohol misuse/abuse, and depression. Marshal et al. (2008) conducted a meta-analysis study focusing on the relationship between sexual orientation and substance use. Using 18 studies and 125 independent effect size estimates, the researchers found that the odds of substance use among sexual minority youth was significantly higher than among heterosexual youth. This pattern of increased rates of substance use has long been shown to exist among adult MSM as well (Chesney, Barrett, & Stall, 1998; McCabe, Hughes, Bostwick, West, &

Boyd, 2009; Woody et al., 2001). In a recent study of over 1000 high school youth in Massachusetts, sexual minority male youth were found to have significantly higher depressive symptomotology scores than heterosexual youth (Almeida, Johnson, Corliss, Molnar, & Azrael, 2009). The results of a meta-analysis on the relationship between mental health outcomes and sexual orientation conducted by King et al. (2008) found that MSM were more than twice as likely as heterosexual men to experience both lifetime depression and depression in the past year. These studies demonstrate that disparities in psychosocial health outcomes are present in MSM at a young age and suggest that they continue into adulthood.

Syndemic Processes

These negative psychosocial health outcomes are thought to interact to form a syndemic, a set of cooccurring health conditions that together can lower overall health and increase susceptibility to disease. According to the CDC, a syndemic two or more afflictions, interacting synergistically, contributing to excess burden of disease in a population" (Centers for Disease Control and Prevention, 2011). For example, psychosocial health problems such as substance use, depression, and intimate partner violence have been found to interact so that their impact on the overall health of the individual is greater than would be expected from an additive effect (Stall et al., 2003). Although many studies involving MSM have shown interconnections among health problems, such as substance use and high-risk sex (Hirshfield, Remien, Humberstone, Walavalkar, & Chiasson, 2004; Stall et al., 2001), two studies have focused on the syndemic condition in samples of adult gay men (Stall et al., 2003) and young gay men (Mustanski, Garofalo, Herrick, & Donenberg, 2007). Using a probability sample of MSM in four major U.S. cities, Stall and colleagues (2003) found that the more psychosocial health problems an individual reported, the greater their risk for both participation in sexual risk behaviors and HIV infection. Mustanski and colleagues (2007) found similar results in a sample of young MSM; the experience of each additional psychosocial health problem significantly increased the odds of unprotected anal intercourse, having multiple sex partners, and HIV seroprevalence. These two studies demonstrated that as the number of psychosocial conditions experienced by an individual

increased, the individual's likelihood of engaging in HIV sexual risk behaviors increased, as did their likelihood of HIV infection. It has been suggested that this set of cooccurring health problems may be driving the HIV epidemic among MSM and may reinforce other health disparities among MSM as well (Stall et al., 2003).

Theoretical Explanations of Syndemic Processes

To fully understand syndemic processes we must determine the causes of the disparities in psychosocial health outcomes that make up the syndemic condition. Several theories have been posited to explain these disparities by focusing on the associations between adversity and health outcomes. One such theory is the Minority Stress Theory (see Meyer and Frost, Chapter 18, this volume). This theory suggests that experiences of social discrimination based on sexual orientation lower the overall health of sexual minority individuals (Diaz, 1998; Meyer, 1995, 2003). This process happens over time as minority individuals are exposed to both explicit and implicit discrimination and social marginalization. These experiences cause stress, have a negative impact on an individual's self-esteem, increase emotional distress, and render the individual more vulnerable to health problems, such as depression and substance use. Meyer (1995) originally conceived of minority stress as stemming from three sources: internalized homophobia, perceived stigma, and prejudice (violence and/or discrimination). Using a sample of 741 gay men recruited from New York City, Meyer (1995) found that these three forms of minority stress, when taken together, significantly predicted five psychological distress outcomes— demoralization, guilt, suicide, AIDS-related traumatic stress response, and sexual problems. These findings support Meyer's hypothesis that experiences of minority stress contribute to poor health among gay men.

In their study on the effects of minority stress in the lives of Latino MSM, Diaz, Ayala, Bein, Henne, and Marin (2001) found that the most men had been exposed to negative views about homosexuality while growing up. Of the sample, 91% reported hearing that gay people were not normal, 71% heard that gay people grow up to be alone, and 70% were told that their homosexuality would damage their family relationships. These experiences of social discrimination were associated with low self-esteem and social isolation, which in turn were correlated with more psychological distress. This study, along with others (Meyer, 1995; Stall, Friedman, & Catania, 2007), suggests that social marginalization experienced during development has effects on health outcomes in adulthood.

Another theory that recognizes the importance of life circumstances on the health status of minority populations is the Theory of Syndemic Production (Stall et al., 2007). Similar to Minority Stress Theory, the Theory of Syndemic Production posits that cultural and social marginalization experienced by MSM puts them at risk for long-term negative health outcomes. Syndemic Production differs from Minority Stress in that it focuses on the impact of early life events and the collective effect of marginalization throughout the life course. In other words, the adversity that a young gay man experiences during boyhood and adolescence contributes to the development of the negative psychosocial health conditions across the life course and into adulthood.

Both Minority Stress Theory and the Theory of Syndemic Production focus on the long-term negative health effects of living in a world that not supportive or is outwardly hostile toward sexual minority group members. The social response to an individual's minority sexual identity (or non-traditional gender presentation) negatively impacts long-term health outcomes, rather than the identity or presentation itself. Studies have found that YMSM who reported serious childhood adversity were significantly less likely to exhibit positive outcomes when compared to their peers (Gwadz et al., 2006 Koblin et al., 2006; Safren & Heimberg, 1999; Savin-Williams, 1994). The correlation between experiences of adversity and negative health outcomes is particularly problematic given the prevalence of adversity within this highly stigmatized population. It is estimated that sexual minority youth hear homophobic slurs such as "faggot" or "sissy" approximately 26 times during a typical school day (Bart, 1998) and that 31% of sexual minority youth report having been threatened or injured at school in the past year (Chase, 2001). In summarizing the results of studies using national probability samples of lesbian, gay, and bisexual individuals, Herek and Sims (2008) found that as many as 32% reported having experienced a hate crime based on their sexual orientation at some point in their lives. Perhaps even more detrimental are the pervasive forms of adversity such as institutionalized homophobia and heterosexism. For example, looking at data from a national probability sample, Hatzenbuehler, McLaughlin, Keyes, and Hasin (2010) found that among lesbian and gay individuals living in states that instituted same-sex marriage bans during the 2004/2005 elections, psychiatric disorders increased significantly from before to after the ban. No such increases in psychiatric disorders were observed among heterosexual men and women in these states, or among lesbian and gay individuals in states that did not enact such bans. MSM of color, compared to white MSM, may experience even more adversity based on sexual orientation due to cultural norms that consider heterosexuality the only acceptable sexual identity (Ernst, Francis, Nevels, & Lemeh, 1991; Harper, 2007; Stokes & Peterson, 1998).

UNDERSTANDING RESILIENCE

Overcoming Adversity: Evidence for Strengths and Protective Factors

In the lives of gay men, adversity and marginalization are pervasive. Many gay men grew up being told that they were abnormal or immoral. As adults, gay men living in the United States are denied equal rights. However, negative health outcomes that result from living in hostile environments are not universal. Although many have experienced some form of adversity, the majority have not experienced the deleterious effects of those experiences in terms of cooccurring psychosocial health problems or HIV infection. Rather, most gay men cope with adversity and are somehow protected from the potential negative consequences of negative experiences. This capacity for an individual to cope successfully with adversity is called "resilience." Resilience necessitates two components: (1) exposure to adversity and (2) achievement of positive situational adaptation in the face of this exposure (Luthar, Cicchetti, & Becker, 2000). The difference between those who survive or thrive and those who do not may be in part explained by the existence of protective factors. That is, some individuals may have strengths and resources (skills, social support, personality traits, etc.) that buffer the effects of adverse experiences, thereby preventing the development of health problems. These protective factors moderate the association between adversity and risk by providing resources that facilitate coping (Rew & Horner, 2003). The Search Institute, a youth advocacy organization, developed an index of 40 protective factors that predict resilience among youth at risk (Roehlkepartain, Benson, & Sesma, 2003). They have found that there is an inverse relationship between the number of assets and the likelihood of youth participating in risky behaviors. Resilience is a characteristic of an individual, but it results from the interplay of individual and environmental factors (Garmezy, 1991; Olsson, Bond, Burns, Vella-Brodrick, & Sawyer, 2003). When individuals have access to sufficient protective resources, they can recover from adverse circumstances. This ability to recover does not render a person invincible; at increased levels of adversity, factors that were previously protective may no longer function in this way (Garmezy, 1991).

Protective factors are the building blocks of resilience. Not unlike risk factors, protective factors exist on multiple levels of influence with reciprocal associations among these levels (Luthar et al., 2000). In some cases, protective factors may be the obverse of risk factors (and vice versa). For instance, high levels of self-esteem might protect against engagement in health risk behaviors such as unprotected anal intercourse, whereas low levels of self-esteem might be associated with this behavior. However, in some cases risk factors and protective factors are not the obverse of each other. For example, gay men who report high levels of openness about their sexual orientation may be at risk for HIV-related conditions including victimization (Chesir-Teran & Hughes, 2009). Yet the obverse of being out (i.e., remaining in the closet) is also a risk factor rather than a protective factor (Hays et al., 1997; Waldo, McFarland, Katz, MacKellar, & Valleroy, 2000). In some cases, factors may only be protective and have little or nothing to do with risk. For example, participating in community events may be protective against health risks, but it is highly unlikely that not participating in these activities would constitute risk (yet to our knowledge neither of these relationships has been evaluated among gay men). Protective factors are not the same for all people, nor are they necessarily stable across the life course. Many variables, including developmental stage, age, and individual personality, may cause protective factors to be more or less effective across individuals or over

time. Furthermore, protective factors may interact with other factors.

Few studies have investigated resilience in MSM communities. There has, however, been some investigation of specific protective factors that contribute to resilience. Studies focusing on sexual minority youth, for example, have found that condom self-efficacy, perceived susceptibility to HIV infection, positive attitudes toward practicing safe sex, and perceived self-control are associated with consistent safer sex (Rotheram-Borus, Rosario, Reid, & Koopman, 1995; Waldo et al., 2000). Self-acceptance, when combined with family support, has been found to buffer effects of victimization on mental health outcomes, but neither factor was protective when measured alone (Hershberger & D'Augelli, 1995). In fact, self-acceptance (defined as a positive view of your sexual orientation) was much more highly associated with mental health than was victimization. Being more educated and more gay identified (on the Kinsey Scale) predicted safer anal sex (Ross, Henry, Freeman, Caughy, & Dawson, 2004). High self-esteem has also been found to be correlated with low levels of emotional distress (Resnick et al., 1997).

Some of the strongest factors protective against risk-taking behaviors among young MSM can be found on the interpersonal level. Close and warm parental relationships appear to be quite influential in protecting against HIV risk. Parental/family connectedness was protective against emotional distress, experienced violence, substance use, and risky sexual activity in populations of youth (Resnick et al., 1997). Studies have found similar patterns of protection among young MSM populations (Jaccard, Dittus, & Gordon, 1996; Voisin, 2002); however, sexual minority youth report less parental/family connectedness than their peers (Williams, Connolly, Pepler, & Craig, 2005). Qualitative studies of parental relationships have found that these relationships were perceived to be important protective factors even when coming out was not well received (Warwick, Douglas, Aggleton, & Boyce, 2003) and that most parents came to accept their children's sexuality and were generally concerned about their health (LaSala, 2007). LaSala (2007) found that most youth reported that their relationship with parents influenced their decision to engage in safer sex, regardless of how accepting their parents were of their sexuality. Thus, parents may not need to be accepting of their child's sexual orientation to provide the general support that fosters resilience (Fenaughty & Harre, 2003).

Peer relationships also play an important role in protecting against HIV risk, although this association does not appear to be as straightforward for sexual minorities as it is for heterosexual people. For instance, peer support for condom use is associated with abstinence, safer sex behaviors, and health-promoting behaviors (e.g., smoking cessation) in heterosexual populations (Diclemente, 1991; DiIorio et al., 2001; Maxwell, 2002), but this same association has not been found among sexual minorities (Hays, Kegeles, & Coates, 1990; Rotheram-Borus et al., 1995). This may be due in part to the heteronormative pressures and victimization sexual minorities experience at the hands of their peers. Likewise, Williams and colleagues found that sexual minority youth reported less companionship with their best friends than did heterosexual youth (Williams et al., 2005). However, peer relationships with other sexual minority youth may provide some protection against risk (Ueno, 2005).

In general, the social support provided by the daily presence of close personal relationships appears to be very important. When these relationships have been evaluated, they have been shown to be strong moderators of risk for young MSM. Perceived social support is associated with a reduced likelihood of depression and suicidality, increased self-esteem, and less sexual risk behaviors (Anderson, 1998; Williams et al., 2005). Research on the interpersonal relationships of young MSM has barely begun and much more work is needed to understand how these relations function and how they can be promoted.

Though religious affiliation and high values placed on religiosity have shown some protective effects (Resnick et al., 1997; Rostosky, Danner, & Riggle, 2007), the organizational/community level factor that appears to be most important in the development of resilience among youth is the school community. School connectedness has been shown to be associated with emotional health of youth, as measured by emotional distress, violence, and suicidality (Resnick et al., 1997). However, very little is known about how school environments—and other organizational/community level environments—influence the healthy development of sexual minority youth.

THE THEORY OF CULTURAL RESILIENCE

Because gay men are stigmatized in our culture, many have experienced a significant amount of adversity in their lives. As previously noted, these experiences of adversity can contribute significantly to risk behaviors and contribute to the negative health outcomes among MSM. However, lesbian and gay communities and individuals resist cultural attack and turn marginalization into pride. Such an occurrence is an example of "cultural resilience." MSM and other sexual minorities have developed a culture in which pride is a central tenet. This culture of pride may well increase the resilience of MSM and MSM communities, buffering individuals from negative messages that are abundant in the dominant culture. In addition, protective factors that may be present in the lives of young gay men can become stronger across the life course as they become more involved with their communities.

Cultural Resilience Theory (see Figure 14.1) is an attempt to explain the process of overcoming adversity specifically as it relates to gay men and other sexual minority communities and individuals. Strengths and protective factors can break down the syndemic process thereby preventing adversity from resulting in negative health outcomes. Until such a time that adversity experienced by MSM through homophobia and cultural marginalization is eliminated, ways to prevent the harmful effects of this adversity will be needed. Understanding and capitalizing on Cultural Resilience will likely increase the effectiveness of existing prevention programs, and in this way also improve the health of gay men and other MSM.

IMPLICATIONS FOR PREVENTION

In a meta-analysis of the efficacy of HIV prevention interventions targeted at MSM, Herbst and colleagues (2005) found that these interventions resulted in a 23% reduction in the odds of engaging in unprotected anal intercourse and a 61% increase in the odds of condom use during anal sex. This suggests that current prevention paradigms are functioning effectively to some degree. Nonetheless, there is no evidence that overall health disparities between MSM and non-MSM are diminishing. To minimize or eliminate health disparities, prevention efforts will need to be increased. Cultural Resilience Theory can be useful in guiding such efforts.

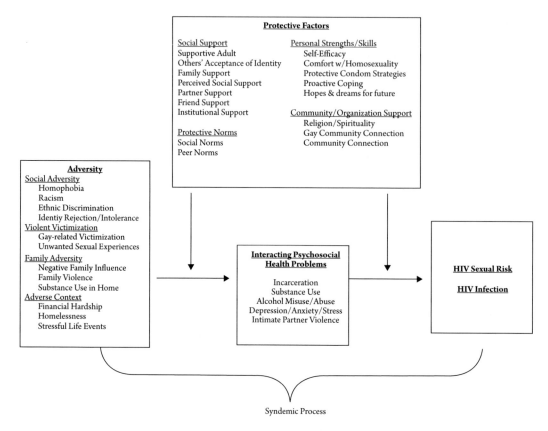

FIGURE 14.1. Model of Cultural Resilience Theory.

Cultural Resilience Theory suggests that experiences of sexuality related adversity lead to increased participation in risky behaviors and to the development of cooccurring psychosocial health conditions. These syndemic conditions in turn contribute to health disparities. Both steps in this process could be moderated by protective factors. The predominant public health approach is to attempt to eliminate health disparities by eliminating adversity, eliminating risk factors, or eliminating psychosocial health problems. As demonstrated by Herbst et al. (2005), this approach has had some success. However, interventions and health promotion efforts could be improved by addressing protective factors that moderate these processes.

The content and impact of positive youth development programs support our contention that health promotion may be as important as risk reduction in the elimination of health disparities. Positive youth development programs are driven by the philosophy that resilience and competency building are critical in supporting healthy development among youth

(Roth & Brooks-Gunn, 2003). Positive youth development programs promote bonding, build competencies, enhance belief in the future, and enhance self-efficacy, positive identity, prosocial norms, spirituality, and self-determination (Catalano, Berglund, Ryan, Lonczak, & Hawkins, 2004). Such programs often attempt to strengthen familial, educational, and community systems (Gavin, Catalano, David-Ferdon, Gloppen, & Markham, 2010). A comprehensive review found that at least some positive youth development programs improve interpersonal skills, strengthen relationships with peers and adults, and increase self-control, self-efficacy, academic achievement, problem-solving, and other competencies. Some of these programs may also decrease drug and alcohol use, aggressive behavior, violence, and high-risk sexual behavior (Catalano et al., 2004). Other reviews have found that positive youth development programs are effective in promoting adolescent sexual and reproductive health and that their effects are sustained over time (Gavin et al., 2010; Kirby, 2001; Solomon & Card, 2004). Gavin et al.

(2010) suggest that positive youth development programs target a different and complementary set of factors compared to traditional health education programs, and that although traditional programs provide youth with knowledge and skills to reduce risk, positive youth development programs provide motivation to use the skills. Together, the findings suggest that health disparities among gay and bisexual men could be reduced by promoting healthy development through a focus on protective factors and resilience.

CONCLUSIONS

It has been 30 years since HIV began to decimate the MSM population in the United States and health disparities among MSM were forced into the forefront of consciousness for lesbian and gay communities. Since that time, much important prevention work has been done to address these disparities. Nonetheless, health disparities still exist among MSM.

Future studies are needed to expand our knowledge of the ecological context of health risk among MSM. To accomplish this, it will be important to expand the scope of prevention research to focus on protective factors as well as risk factors. There is as much to be learned from those who have faced adversity and thrived as there is from those who have experienced negative outcomes. There is also a need to examine protective factors beyond those at the individual level. Community and interpersonal protective factors may facilitate individual efforts to develop resilience. To the extent that this view is correct, a narrow focus on individual level risk and protective factors will not be likely to eliminate health disparities. There also needs to be a focus on identifying modifiable protective factors that will have direct applicability to prevention and health promotion programs. Many MSM health studies have demonstrated an association between health risk behaviors and individual personality characteristics such as sensation seeking (Adam, Teva, & de Wit, 2008; Newcomb, Clerkin, & Mustanski, 2010) or impulsivity (Patterson, Semple, Zians, & Strathdee, 2005; Semple, Zians, Grant, & Patterson, 2006). Although knowledge of these factors is necessary for our understanding of prevention, personality characteristics are difficult to change. It is more feasible to change interpersonal or community contexts by developing a mentor program or setting up community centers, or by making policy level changes such as the adoption of antibullying legislation.

It has long been acknowledged that sexual minorities face health disparities, not because of who they are, but because of the environments in which they live. Even so, prevention efforts have a tendency to focus on changing the individual with messages about more condom use, less substance use, and so forth. Although data show that MSM exhibit considerable strengths in reducing or avoiding health-related risks, these strengths have been underemphasized in public health prevention work. Cultural Resilience Theory and other strength-based approaches provide powerful frameworks that can serve to advance prevention and health promotion by identifying new variables and new mechanisms that will increase the effectiveness of current public health interventions and improve the health of men who have sex with men.

REFERENCES

Adam, P. C., Teva, I., & de Wit, J. B. (2008). Balancing risk and pleasure: sexual self-control as a moderator of the influence of sexual desires on sexual risk-taking in men who have sex with men. *Sexually Transmitted Infections, 84*(6), 463–467.

Almeida, J., Johnson, R. M., Corliss, H. L., Molnar, B. E., & Azrael, D. (2009). Emotional distress among LGBT youth: The influence of perceived discrimination based on sexual orientation. *Journal of Youth and Adolescence, 38*(7), 1001–1014.

Anderson, A. (1998). Strengths of gay male youth: An untold story. *Child and Adolescent Social Work Journal, 15*(1), 55–71.

Arias, E. (Ed.) (2007). *National vital statistics reports* (Vol. 56). Hyattsville, MD: National Center for Health Statistics.

Bart, M. (1998). Creating a safer school for gay students. *Counseling Today*, September.

Catalano, R., Berglund, M., Ryan, J., Lonczak, H., & Hawkins, J. (2004). Positive youth development in the United States: Research findings on evaluations of positive youth development programs. *Annals of the American Academy of Political and Social Science, 591*, 98.

Centers for Disease Control and Prevention. (2000). HIV/AIDS among racial/ethnic minority men who have sex with men—United States, 1989–1998. *MMWR, 49*, 4–11.

Centers for Disease Control and Prevention. (2001a). HIV incidence among young men who have sex with men—seven U.S. cities, 1994–2000. *MMWR, 50*, 440–444.

Centers for Disease Control and Prevention. (2001b). *HIV prevalence trends in selected populations in the*

United States: Results from national serosurveillance, 1993–1997. Atlanta, GA: Centers for Disease Control and Prevention.

Centers for Disease Control and Prevention. (2005a). HIV prevalence, unrecognized infection, and HIV testing among men who have sex with men—five U.S. cities, June 2004–April 2005. *MMWR, 54,* 597–601.

Centers for Disease Control and Prevention. (2005b). *HIV/AIDS among youth.* Atlanta, GA: Centers for Disease Control and Prevention.

Centers for Disease Control and Prevention. (2006). Racial/ethnic disparities in diagnoses of HIV/AIDS— 33 states, 2001–2004. *MMWR, 55,* 121–125.

Centers for Disease Control and Prevention. (2007). *HIV/AIDS surveillance report, 2005.* Atlanta, GA: Centers for Disease Control and Prevention.

Centers for Disease Control and Prevention. (2008a). *HIV prevalence estimates—United States, 2006.* Atlanta, GA: Centers for Disease Control and Prevention.

Centers for Disease Control and Prevention. (2008b). *Subpopulation estimates from the HIV incidence surveillance system—United States, 2006.* Atlanta, GA: Centers for Disease Control and Prevention.

Centers for Disease Control and Prevention. (2008c). Trends in HIV/AIDS diagnoses among men who have sex with men—33 states, 2001–2006. *MMWR, 57,* 681–686.

Centers for Disease Control and Prevention. (August 2009). *HIV/AIDS facts: HIV/AIDS among Hispanics/ Latinos.* Atlanta, GA: Centers for Disease Control and Prevention.

Centers for Disease Control and Prevention. (2009a). *HIV/AIDS surveillance report, 2007.* Atlanta, GA: Centers for Disease Control and Prevention.

Centers for Disease Control and Prevention. (2009b). *HIV/AIDS surveillance report, 2007.* Atlanta, GA: Centers for Disease Control and Prevention.

Centers for Disease Control and Prevention. (July 2010). *HIV in the United States.* Atlanta, GA: Centers for Disease Control and Prevention.

Centers for Disease Control and Prevention. (2011). Spotlight on syndemics. Retrieved October 27, 2011, http://www.cdc.gov/syndemics/.

Chase, A. (2001). Violent reaction: What do teen killers have in common. *In These Times, 25*(16), 1.

Chesir-Teran, D., & Hughes, D. (2009). Heterosexism in high school and victimization among lesbian, gay, bisexual, and questioning students. *Journal of Youth and Adolescence, 38,* 963–975.

Chesney, M. A., Barrett, D. C., & Stall, R. (1998). Histories of substance use and risk behavior: precursors to HIV seroconversion in homosexual men. *American Journal of Public Health, 88,* 113–116.

Diaz, R. M. (1998). *Latino gay men and HIV: Culture, sexuality, and risk behavior.* New York: Routledge.

Diaz, R. M., Ayala, G., Bein, E., Henne, J., & Marin, B. V. (2001). The impact of homophobia, poverty, and racism on the mental health of gay and bisexual Latino men: Findings from 3 US cities. *American Journal of Public Health, 91,* 927–932.

Diaz, R., Peterson, J., & Choi, K. (2007). Social discrimination and health outcomes in African American, Latino, and Asian/Pacific Islander gay men. *Unequal Opportunity, 1,* 327–355.

Diclemente, R. J. (1991). Predictors of HIV-preventive sexual behavior in a high-risk adolescent population: The influence of perceived peer norms and sexual communication on incarcerated adolescents' consistent use of condoms. *Journal of Adolescent Health, 12,* 385–390.

DiIorio, C., Dudley, W. N., Kelly, M., Soet, J. E., Mbwara, J., & Sharpe Potter, J. (2001). Social cognitive correlates of sexual experience and condom use among 13- through 15-year-old adolescents. *Journal of Adolescent Health, 29,* 208–216.

Easterbrook, P. J., Chmiel, J. S., Hoover, D. R., Saah, A. J., Kaslow, R. A., Kingsley, L. A., et al. (1993). Racial and ethnic differences in human immunodeficiency virus type 1 (HIV-1) seroprevalence among homosexual and bisexual men. The Multicenter AIDS Cohort Study. *American Journal of Epidemiology, 138,* 415–429.

Ernst, F. A., Francis, R. A., Nevels, H., & Lemeh, C. A. (1991). Condemnation of homosexuality in the Black community: A gender-specific phenomenon? *Archives of Sexual Behavior, 20,* 579–585.

Fenaughty, J., & Harre, N. (2003). Life on the seesaw: A qualitative study of suicide resiliency factors for young gay men. *Journal of Homosexuality, 45,* 1–22.

Galliher, R. V., Rostosky, S. S., & Hughes, H. K. (2004). School belonging, self-esteem, and depressive symptoms in adolescents: An examination of sex, sexual attraction status, and urbanicity. *Journal of Youth and Adolescence, 33,* 235–245.

Garmezy, N. (1991). Resilience in children's adaptation to negative life events and stressed environments. *Pediatric Annals, 20,* 459–460, 463–456.

Garofalo, R., Wolf, R. C., Kessel, S., Palfrey, S. J., & DuRant, R. H. (1998). The association between health risk behaviors and sexual orientation among a school-based sample of adolescents. *Pediatrics, 101,* 895–902.

Gavin, L., Catalano, R. F., David-Ferdon, C., Gloppen, K., & Markham, C. (2010). A review of positive youth development programs that promote adolescent and reproductive health. *Journal of Adolescent Health, 46,* S75–S91.

Greenwood, G. L., Paul, J. P., Pollack, L. M., Binson, D., Catania, J. A., Chang, J., et al. (2005). Tobacco use and cessation among a household-based sample of US urban men who have sex with men. *American Journal of Public Health, 95,* 145–151.

Gwadz, M. V., Clatts, M. C., Yi, H., Leonard, N. R., Goldsamt, L., & Lankenau, S. (2006). Resilience among young men who have sex with men in New York City. *Sexuality Research and Social Policy, 3*, 13–21.

Hall, H. I., Byers, R. H., Ling, Q., & Espinoza, L. (2007). Racial/ethnic and age disparities in HIV prevalence and disease progression among men who have sex with men in the United States. *American Journal of Public Health, 97*, 1060–1066.

Harawa, N. T., Greenland, S., Bingham, T. A., Johnson, D. F., Cochran, S. D., Cunningham, W. E., et al. (2004). Associations of race/ethnicity with HIV prevalence and HIV-related behaviors among young men who have sex with men in 7 urban centers in the United States. *Journal of Acquired Immune Deficiency Syndromes, 35*, 526–536.

Harper, G. W. (2007). Sex isn't that simple: culture and context in HIV prevention interventions for gay and bisexual male adolescents. *American Psychologist, 62*, 803–819.

Hatzenbuehler, M. L., McLaughlin, K. A., Keyes, K. M., & Hasin, D. S. (2010). The impact of institutional discrimination on psychiatric disorders in lesbian, gay, and bisexual populations: a prospective study. *American Journal of Public Health, 100*, 452–459.

Hays, R. B., Kegeles, S. M., & Coates, T. J. (1990). High HIV risk-taking among young gay men. *AIDS, 4*, 901–907.

Hays, R. B., Paul, J., Ekstrand, M., Kegeles, S. M., Stall, R., & Coates, T. J. (1997). Actual versus perceived HIV status, sexual behaviors and predictors of unprotected sex among young gay and bisexual men who identify as HIV-negative, HIV-positive and untested. *AIDS, 11*, 1495–1502.

Health Resources & Services Administration. (2000). *Eliminating health disparities in the United States.* Washington, DC: Author.

Herbst, J. H., Sherba, R. T., Crepaz, N., Deluca, J. B., Zohrabyan, L., Stall, R. D., et al. (2005). A meta-analytic review of HIV behavioral interventions for reducing sexual risk behavior of men who have sex with men. *Journal of Acquired Immune Deficiency Syndrome, 39*, 228–241.

Herek, G. M., & Sims, C. (2008). Sexual orientation and violent victimization: Hate crimes and intimate partner violence among gay and bisexual males in the United States. In R. J. Wolitski, R. Stall, & R. O. Valdiserri (Eds.) (2008). *Unequal opportunity: Health disparities affecting gay and bisexual men in the United States* (pp. 35–71). New York: Oxford University Press. http://www.cdc.gov/syndemics/ (2009). Retrieved July, 2009, from http://www.cdc.gov/syndemics/.

Hershberger, S. L., & D'Augelli, A. R. (1995). The impact of victimization on the mental health and suicidality of lesbian, gay and bisexual youth. *Developmental Psychology, 31*, 65–74.

Hirshfield, S., Remien, R. H., Humberstone, M., Walavalkar, I., & Chiasson, M. A. (2004). Substance use and high-risk sex among men who have sex with men: A national online study in the USA. *AIDS Care, 16*, 1036–1047.

Hummer, R. A. (1996). Black-white differences in health and mortality. *Sociological Quarterly, 37*, 105–125.

Jaccard, J., Dittus, P. J., & Gordon, V. V. (1996). Maternal correlates of adolescent sexual and contraceptive behavior. *Family Planning Perspectives, 28*, 159–165, 185.

King, M., Semlyen, J., Tai, S. S., Killaspy, H., Osborn, D., Popelyuk, D., et al. (2008). A systematic review of mental disorder, suicide, and deliberate self harm in lesbian, gay and bisexual people. *BMC Psychiatry, 8*, 70.

Kingsley, L. A., Detels, R., Kaslow, R., Polk, B. F., Rinaldo, C. R., Jr., Chmiel, J., et al. (1987). Risk factors for seroconversion to human immunodeficiency virus among male homosexuals. Results from the Multicenter AIDS Cohort Study. *Lancet, 1*(8529), 345–349.

Kirby, D. (2001). *Emerging answers: Research findings on programs to reduce teen pregnancy.* Washington, DC: The National Campaign to Prevent Teen Pregnancy.

Koblin, B. A., Torian, L., Xu, G., Guilin, V., Makki, H., Mackellar, D., et al. (2006). Violence and HIV-related risk among young men who have sex with men. *AIDS Care, 18*, 961–967.

LaSala, M. C. (2007). Parental influence, gay youths, and safer sex. *Health and Social Work, 32*, 49–55.

Lemp, G. F., Hirozawa, A. M., Givertz, D., Nieri, G. N., Anderson, L., Lindegren, M. L., et al. (1994). Seroprevalence of HIV and risk behaviors among young homosexual and bisexual men. The San Francisco/Berkeley Young Men's Survey. *Journal of the American Medical Association, 272*, 449–454.

Luthar, S. S., Cicchetti, D., & Becker, B. (2000). The construct of resilience: a critical evaluation and guidelines for future work. *Child Development, 71*, 543–562.

Marshal, M. P., Friedman, M. S., Stall, R., King, K. M., Miles, J., Gold, M. A., et al. (2008). Sexual orientation and adolescent substance use: A meta-analysis and methodological review. *Addiction, 103*, 546–556.

Marshal, M. P., Friedman, M. S., Stall, R., & Thompson, A. L. (2009). Individual trajectories of substance use in lesbian, gay and bisexual youth and heterosexual youth. *Addiction, 104*, 974–981.

Maxwell, K. A. (2002). Friends: The role of peer influence across adolescent risk behaviors. *Journal of Youth and Adolescence, 31*, 267–277.

McCabe, S. E., Hughes, T. L., Bostwick, W. B., West, B. T., & Boyd, C. J. (2009). Sexual orientation, substance use behaviors and substance dependence in the United States. *Addiction, 104*, 1333–1345.

Meyer, I. H. (1995). Minority stress and mental health in gay men. *Journal of Health and Social Behavior, 36*, 38–56.

Meyer, I. H. (2003). Prejudice, social stress, and mental health in lesbian, gay, and bisexual populations: Conceptual issues and research evidence. *Psychological Bulletin, 129*, 674–697.

Mustanski, B., Garofalo, R., Herrick, A., & Donenberg, G. (2007). Psychosocial health problems increase risk for HIV among urban young men who have sex with men: Preliminary evidence of a syndemic in need of attention. *Annals of Behavioral Medicine, 34*, 37–45.

Newcomb, M., Clerkin, E., & Mustanski, B. (2010). Sensation seeking moderates the effects of alcohol and drug use prior to sex on sexual risk in young men who have sex with men. *AIDS and Behavior, 15*, 565–575.

Olsson, C. A., Bond, L., Burns, J. M., Vella-Brodrick, D. A., & Sawyer, S. M. (2003). Adolescent resilience: A concept analysis. *Journal of Adolescence, 26*, 1–11.

Orsi, J. M., Margellos-Anast, H., & Whitman, S. (2010). Black-white health disparities in the United States and Chicago: A 15-year progress analysis. *American Journal of Public Health, 100*, 349–356.

Patterson, T., Semple, S., Zians, J., & Strathdee, S. (2005). Methamphetamine-using HIV-positive men who have sex with men: correlates of polydrug use. *Journal of Urban Health, 82*, 120–126.

Rangel, M. C., Gavin, L., Reed, C., Fowler, M. G., & Lee, L. M. (2006). Epidemiology of HIV and AIDS among adolescents and young adults in the United States. *Journal of Adolescent Health, 39*, 156–163.

Resnick, M. D., Bearman, P. S., Blum, R. W., Bauman, K. E., Harris, K. M., Jones, J., et al. (1997). Protecting adolescents from harm: Findings from the National Longitudinal Study on Adolescent Health. *Journal of the American Medical Association, 278*, 823–832.

Rew, L., & Horner, S. D. (2003). Youth Resilience Framework for reducing health-risk behaviors in adolescents. *Journal of Pediatric Nursing, 18*, 379–388.

Roehlkepartain, E. C., Benson, P. L., & Sesma, A. (2003). *Signs of progress in putting children first: Developmental assets among youth in St. Louis Park, 1997–2001.* Minneapolis, MN: The Search Institute.

Ross, M. W., Henry, D., Freeman, A., Caughy, M., & Dawson, A. G., Jr. (2004). Environmental influences on safer sex in young gay men: A situational presentation approach to measuring influences on sexual health. *Archives of Sexual Behavior, 33*, 249–257.

Rostosky, S. S., Danner, F., & Riggle, E. D. (2007). Is religiosity a protective factor against substance use in young adulthood? Only if you're straight! *Journal of Adolescent Health, 40*, 440–447.

Roth, J., & Brooks-Gunn, J. (2003). What exactly is a youth development program? Answers from research and practice. *Applied Developmental Science, 7*, 94–111.

Rotheram-Borus, M. J., Rosario, M., Reid, H., & Koopman, C. (1995). Predicting patterns of sexual acts among homosexual and bisexual youths. *American Journal of Psychiatry, 152*, 588–595.

Ryan, H., Wortley, P. M., Easton, A., Pederson, L., & Greenwood, G. (2001). Smoking among lesbians, gays, and bisexuals: A review of the literature. *American Journal of Preventive Medicine, 21*, 142–149.

Saewyc, E. M., Skay, C. L., Pettingell, S. L., Reis, E. A., Bearinger, L., Resnick, M., et al. (2006). Hazards of stigma: The sexual and physical abuse of gay, lesbian, and bisexual adolescents in the United States and Canada. *Child Welfare, 85*, 195–213.

Safren, S. A., & Heimberg, R. G. (1999). Depression, hopelessness, suicidality, and related factors in sexual minority and heterosexual adolescents. *Journal of Consulting and Clinical Psychology, 67*, 859–866.

Savin-Williams, R. C. (1994). Verbal and physical abuse as stressors in the lives of lesbian, gay male, and bisexual youths: associations with school problems, running away, substance abuse, prostitution, and suicide. *Journal of Consulting and Clinical Psychology, 62*, 261–269.

Semple, S. J., Zians, J., Grant, I., & Patterson, T. L. (2006). Methamphetamine use, impulsivity, and sexual risk behavior among HIV-positive men who have sex with men. *Journal of Addictive Diseases, 25*, 105–114.

Solomon, J., & Card, J. (2004). *Making the list: Understanding, selecting, and replicating effective teen pregnancy prevention programs.* Washington, DC: National Campaign to Prevent Teen Pregnancy.

Stall, R., Duran, L., Wisniewski, S. R., Friedman, M. S., Marshal, M. P., McFarland, W., et al. (2009). Running in place: Implications of HIV incidence estimates among urban men who have sex with men in the United States and other industrialized countries. *AIDS and Behavior, 13*, 615–629.

Stall, R., Friedman, M., & Catania, J. (2007). Interacting epidemics and gay men's health: A theory of syndemic production among urban gay men. In R. J. Wolitski, R. Stall, & R. O. Valdiserri (Eds.), *Unequal opportunity: Health disparities affecting gay and bisexual men in the United States* (pp. 251–274). New York: Oxford University Press.

Stall, R., Mills, T. C., Williamson, J., Hart, T., Greenwood, G., Paul, J., et al. (2003). Association of co-occurring psychosocial health problems and increased vulnerability to HIV/AIDS among urban men who have sex with men. *American Journal of Public Health, 93*, 939–942.

Stall, R., Paul, J. P., Greenwood, G., Pollack, L. M., Bein, E., Crosby, G. M., et al. (2001). Alcohol use, drug use and alcohol-related problems among men who have sex with men: The Urban Men's Health Study. *Addiction, 96*, 1589–1601.

Stokes, J. P., & Peterson, J. L. (1998). Homophobia, self-esteem, and risk for HIV among African American men who have sex with men. *AIDS Education and Prevention, 10*, 278–292.

Tang, H., Greenwood, G. L., Cowling, D. W., Lloyd, J. C., Roeseler, A. G., & Bal, D. G. (2004). Cigarette smoking among lesbians, gays, and bisexuals: How serious a problem? *Cancer Causes Control, 15*, 797–803.

Ueno, K. (2005). Sexual orientation and psychological distress in adolescence: Examining interpersonal stressors and social support processes. *Social Psychology Quarterly, 68,* 258–277.

Valleroy, L. A., MacKellar, D. A., Karon, J. M., Rosen, D. H., McFarland, W., Shehan, D. A., et al. (2000). HIV prevalence and associated risks in young men who have sex with men. Young Men's Survey Study Group. *Journal of the American Medical Association, 284,* 198–204.

Vittinghoff, E., Douglas, J., Judson, F., McKirnan, D., MacQueen, K., & Buchbinder, S. P. (1999). Per-contact risk of human immunodeficiency virus transmission between male sexual partners. *American Journal of Epidemiology, 150,* 306–311.

Voisin, D. R. (2002). Family ecology and HIV sexual risk behaviors among African American and Puerto Rican adolescent males. *American Journal of Orthopsychiatry, 72,* 294–302.

Waldo, C. R., McFarland, W., Katz, M. H., MacKellar, D., & Valleroy, L. A. (2000). Very young gay and bisexual men are at risk for HIV infection: The San Francisco Bay Area Young Men's Survey II. *Journal of Acquired Immune Deficiency Syndromes, 24,* 168–174.

Warwick, I., Douglas, N., Aggleton, P., & Boyce, P. (2003). Young gay men and HIV/AIDS: Towards a contextual understanding of sexual risk. *Sex Education, 3,* 215–229.

Williams, T., Connolly, J., Pepler, D., & Craig, W. (2005). Peer victimization, social support, and psychosocial adjustment of sexual minority adolescents. *Journal of Youth and Adolescence, 34,* 471–482.

Wolitski, R. J., Stall, R., & Valdiserri, R. O. (Eds.). (2008). *Unequal opportunity: Health disparities affecting gay and bisexual men in the United States.* New York: Oxford University Press.

Wolitski, R. J., Valdiserri, R. O., Denning, P. H., & Levine, W. C. (2001). Are we headed for a resurgence of the HIV epidemic among men who have sex with men? *American Journal of Public Health, 91,* 883–888.

Woody, G. E., VanEtten-Lee, M. L., McKirnan, D., Donnell, D., Metzger, D., Seage, G., et al. (2001). Substance use among men who have sex with men: Comparison with a national household survey. *Journal of Acquired Immune Deficiency Syndromes, 27,* 86–90.

15

Sexual Orientation and Mental Health

SUSAN D. COCHRAN AND VICKIE M. MAYS

Mental health is shaped by the complementary forces of nature and nurture (Rutter, 2002). Although genes may create liabilities, or vulnerabilities, for the onset and course of psychiatric disorders, the environment, including the social environment, also exerts powerful influences on individuals' mental health. These social environmental effects accrue in a variety of ways: through developmental experiences such as possible exposure to childhood maltreatment (Briere & Jordan, 2009), through social advantages or disadvantages conferred by individual characteristics such as age, gender or race/ethnicity (Kessler et al., 2005; Mays, Cochran, Barnes, & Woods, 2007), in the harmful effects of social rejection such as actual or anticipated experiences with discrimination (Kessler, Mickelson, & Williams, 1999), and in the ways in which life experiences create and support resiliency in the face of adversity (Rutter, 2002).

In this mix, sexual orientation emerges as a potentially relevant individual characteristic that may affect both the risk for psychological morbidity and the effectiveness of intervention approaches. Having said that, we recognize that the topic of sexual orientation and mental health is inherently controversial and risks stigmatizing an already much maligned population (Herek, 2009b; Herek & Garnets, 2007; Rothblum, 1994). Indeed, despite the removal of homosexuality as a medical diagnosis in 1973 (Drescher, 2010), 25 years later, nearly a third of Americans erroneously believed that homosexuality per se is a mental illness (Kaiser Family Foundation, 1999). Even today, although this question is no longer asked in public opinion polls, 43% of Americans report that homosexual behavior is "morally wrong" (Pew Research Center, 2010). But just as empirical findings from years of research on women's health helped to "depathologize" being

female by contextualizing women's experiences in the world (Rothblum, 1994), our goal here is to present some of the recent empirical findings related to sexual orientation and mental health in the hopes of inviting informed discourse. The findings suggest that sexual orientation is strongly related to several environmental exposures that are harmful to mental health (Kessler et al., 1999; Kilpatrick & Acierno, 2003; Mays et al., 2007) including victimization (Herek, 2009b) and discrimination (Hatzenbuehler, Nolen-Hoeksema, & Dovidio, 2009; Mays & Cochran, 2001; Meyer, 2003; Meyer & Dean, 1995). An emerging series of published papers, both in the United States and elsewhere, also repeatedly document that individuals with minority sexual orientation experience somewhat elevated risk for some forms of psychiatric morbidity (Cochran, 2001; King et al., 2008; Meyer, 2003), presumably as a consequence of these higher levels of social adversity. Taken together, the work suggests that sexual orientation is associated with alterable mental health disparities at the population level.

In this chapter, we focus on four key topics related to sexual orientation and mental health. First, we begin by highlighting several methodological issues that are relevant to understanding research on the associations between sexual orientation and mental health morbidity and its treatment. However, we touch on only those factors that are particularly important in the field of population-based survey research targeting sexual orientation issues. Second, we review findings from primarily population-based or systematically sampled surveys for evidence of sexual orientation-related disparities in mental health morbidity. Our emphasis will be on those studies that either included heterosexual comparison groups or used sophisticated research designs to minimize uncontrolled selection bias. Although problematic, alcohol and drug use reflect important mental health issues for the sexual minority community in their own right; two other chapters in this book (see Simoni et al., Chapter 13, and Herrick et al., Chapter 14, this volume) cover these particular topics in greater detail. Consequently, our coverage will be limited to those instances in which dysfunctional drug and alcohol use rises to level of diagnosable disorders. Third, we present preliminary findings from several population-based studies investigating sexual orientation-related differences in patterns of mental health services use. Although much has been written in the practice literature on model interventions for the sexual minority community (Bieschke, Perez, & DeBord, 2007; Herek & Garnets, 2007), our focus will be restricted to the ways in which sexual orientation might influence access to and utilization of mental health services in general. Finally, we close with some discussion of important future directions for research on sexual orientation and mental health, particularly in the context of large-scale population-based surveys. Because the majority of empirical work to date has not specifically addressed either transgender or gender identity concerns, we further limit our review primarily to lesbian, gay, and/or bisexual sexual orientations.

METHODOLOGICAL ADVANCES IN THE STUDY OF SEXUAL ORIENTATION AND MENTAL HEALTH

Research on sexual orientation and mental health has undergone a number of methodological transitions over the years in tandem with changes in scholarly views of homosexuality (Cochran, 2001). Early "illness models" construed homosexuality as inherently pathological (Gonsiorek, 1996); hence, a reliance on clinical case studies to describe the ways in which homosexuality led to pathological adjustment appeared to be a reasonable research methodology (Cochran, 2001; Drescher, 2010). The fatal flaw evident in this approach was exposed when Evelyn Hooker (Hooker, 1957) chose a new methodological design, sampling two similar groups of men from *nonclinical settings* who varied in their sexual orientation. Contrary to prevalent expectations, Hooker found few differences in psychiatric morbidity associated with homosexuality. That

is, when gay men were sampled outside of clinical settings and compared to comparable heterosexual men, they did not evidence higher rates of psychopathology. Her research findings, the growing voice of an emerging gay and lesbian civil rights movement, and accumulating research findings from similarly drawn nonclinical samples in other studies led the American Psychiatric Association in 1973 to remove homosexuality as a psychiatric diagnosis from the authoritative psychiatric *Diagnostic and Statistical Manual* (Drescher, 2010; Herek & Garnets, 2007). Following this event, empirical research on mental health concerns among sexual orientation minorities waned somewhat (Cochran, 2001), although researchers continued to pursue other topics related to the ways in which minority sexual orientation might shape life experiences (Rothblum, 1994).

In the mid-1980s, a third methodological transition occurred quite unexpectedly with the onset of the AIDS epidemic (Cochran, 2001). Given how many deaths had occurred, HIV researchers became increasingly concerned about the mental health impact of the AIDS epidemic on gay and bisexual men. At the same time, survey researchers, seeking new ways to track HIV-related risk behaviors in the general population, began to include questions related to sexual behavior, and occasionally sexual orientation identity, in large population-based health surveys. Mental health researchers interested in research questions broader than HIV-related risk taking soon began to use these data sets to investigate possible disparities that might be associated with sexual orientation. Strong evidence emerged that sexual minority youth were at elevated risk for suicide attempts when compared to their heterosexual peers (Faulkner & Cranston, 1998; Fergusson, Horwood, & Beautrais, 1999; Garofalo, Wolf, Kessel, Palfrey, & DuRant, 1998; Garofalo, Wolf, Wissow, Woods, & Goodman, 1999; Remafedi, French, Story, Resnick, & Blum, 1998; Saewyc, Bearinger, Heinz, Blum, & Resnick, 1998). This work treated sexual orientation as similar to other well-documented individual risk indicators (e.g., age, gender, race, ethnicity, educational background) known to be correlated with mental health (Kessler et al., 2005; Mays et al., 2007).

As a consequence of the inclusion of these variables within standard population-based surveys, researchers for the first time could confidently conduct comparative studies (e.g., lesbian/

gay/bisexual versus heterosexual) with samples that were representative of the general population, including the general nonheterosexual population (Corliss, Cochran, & Mays, 2008). Three major methodological improvements associated with this survey approach were key to moving the field forward. First, respondents were selected using highly articulated sampling frames that minimized selection bias. Questions related to sexual orientation were asked during the course of interviews, typically during assessments of HIV-related risk behaviors or reproductive histories in which such questions were contextualized as health assessments. Involvement with gay communities and public identification as lesbian, gay, or bisexual were not relevant to study participation. That is, not only were sexual orientation minorities selected from nonclinical settings, but they were also selected from *non-lesbian/gay/bisexual settings,* permitting for the first time generalization of findings to nonheterosexual persons in general. Also, equivalent heterosexual comparison groups were often built into the sampling design allowing valid tests of possible sexual orientation differences while controlling for the influence of extraneous variables. Second, because population-based surveys are generally large, expensive survey operations, often conducted by agencies within the federal government, the quality of the data sets collected was high. The measures used sometimes included standardized screening instruments or, for psychiatric epidemiology studies conducted by academic researchers, mental health diagnostic schedules. This created an opportunity for researchers to investigate sexual orientation-related hypotheses using assessments that were well respected in the social sciences and in the field of public health. Third, many of these data sets are readily available to researchers with the requisite skills to use them (Sell, 2010) permitting many researchers to conduct high-quality studies for relatively low cost. Individual scientists interested in sexual orientation topics could readily graft their studies onto existing data sets using secondary data analysis techniques. An emerging consequence of the success of this work is that research on sexual orientation is increasingly being mainstreamed into the survey research literature. Today, many large mental health and substance use surveys routinely and successfully include assessments of respondents' sexual orientation identity and/or sexual histories (Sell, 2010).

Despite these strengths, there are several methodological issues that have relevance both for interpreting the findings we report below and also for the future of survey research studies on sexual orientation. One concern is how sexual orientation is defined and measured in these studies (Cochran, 2001). Sexual orientation is a multidimensional concept (Weinrich et al., 1993) that, for some people, may change over the life course, particularly during adolescence and young adulthood (see Diamond, 2003, and Chapter 1, this volume). The majority of studies using the new methodology are, however, cross-sectional in design. Furthermore, most employ limited assessments of sexual orientation reflecting the general limitations of survey research (i.e., where multiple topics must be covered during interviews that are always constrained by time limits). The earliest data sets generally included only one measure of sexual orientation (either gender of sexual partners or sexual orientation identity), but later data sets often measured multiple dimensions of sexual orientation (e.g., attraction, behavior, identity) as researchers became more confident in both the methodology of ascertaining sexual orientation in general population health surveys and the scientific value of the information obtained.

Comparative studies also demand that discrete groups of individuals varying in sexual orientation be formed. As with all measures of individual characteristics (Mays, Ponce, Washington, & Cochran, 2003), this can be complicated. For example, if the gender of sexual partners is the only measure available in a survey data set, its use to classify for sexual orientation can generate several potential problems. In adults, one estimate from an earlier national household survey (Laumann, Gagnon, Michael, & Michaels, 1994) is that only 42% of those who report any same-sex sexual partners in adulthood also self-identify as gay, homosexual, or bisexual. In adolescents, sexual experience can be confounded with timing of sexual debut. Furthermore, classification for bisexuality is confounded with higher rates of partner change if the time frame on which people are reporting is relatively short. Classification by sexual history alone would also tend to bias upward the prevalence of disorders associated with sexual impulsivity (Bailey, 1999), especially among those individuals labeled as bisexual. Also, respondents who are not engaging in sexual experiences during the time frame for assessments are often discarded, and this may be upward of 20% of any particular sample (Cochran & Mays, 2000b).

Because of limitations such as these, many recent data sets now measure both sexual behavior and identity, but much of the work reported below uses one or the other depending on what is available in the existing data set. Even if identity is measured, some surveys offer respondents the optional categories of "unsure" or "questioning." Research literature on sexual minority youth has explored these concepts among adolescents (Russell, Clarke, & Clary, 2009) and sometimes adults (Bostwick, Boyd, Hughes, & McCabe, 2010). In surveys of the general adult population, however, individuals who chose these responses often appear, for the most part, to be indicating that they do not fully understand the sexual orientation question in the first place. That is, they are "unsure" about how to answer the question, not necessarily "unsure" about what their sexual orientation is. Haunting all of this is the chance that rare miscodes of gender (via accidents of data input) may swamp the number of truly coded sexual minorities due to the relatively low base rate of minority sexual orientation in general population surveys.

Measurement of gender identity or transgender identity has rarely been done in general population surveys. A variety of conceptual complexities and methodological barriers to such a practice exist at the moment, including a lack of experience with questions that work well in general population surveys (for transgender issues more generally, see Sánchez and Vilain, Chapter 4, this volume). Thus, findings at this point generally do not include transgender respondents.

A third methodological issue concerns how respondents are sampled in any particular study. The relatively low prevalence of sexual minorities in the overall population [generally thought to be 2–4% in an unselected general population sample (Cochran, 2001)] presents several analytic challenges for general population surveys. Survey samples need to be quite large to have enough representation of nonheterosexual persons to detect statistically significant differences. Many studies are forced to create a single group of individuals with minority sexual orientation, despite expected heterogeneity of mental health burden within lesbian, gay, and bisexual populations (Cochran & Mays, 2009). Furthermore, findings across studies are not always consistent, reflecting the fact that many of these studies have been somewhat underpowered.

These challenges have pushed researchers to adopt increasingly creative sampling methods. For example, the Urban Men's Health Survey (Catania et al., 2001) used U.S. census data to map households with two same-gender male adults in order to identify high gay density neighborhoods. Catania and his colleagues (2001) then drew a sample of homosexually experienced men from four of these urban settings to examine HIV risk behaviors among men who have sex with men. Other researchers have adopted venue-based time-space sampling in gay male neighborhoods or socializing locations (Binson, Woods, Pollack, & Sheon, 2005). Some have used a yoked-sampling approach in which lesbian and gay couples identifiable from administrative data (such as marriage certificates or registered domestic partner registries) are systematically sampled and then asked to recruit friends and siblings who can serve as a heterosexual comparison group (Balsam, Beauchaine, Rothblum, & Solomon, 2008). The California Quality of Life Surveys (Cochran & Mays, 2009) and the California Health Interview Survey MSM Follow-up Study (Xia et al., 2006) used double sampling techniques taking advantage of an existing population-based survey sample, the California Health Interview Survey, which routinely measures sexual orientation in its biennial administration. Double sampling allowed a cost-efficient approach to oversampling persons with minority sexual orientation so as to increase statistical power. And finally, another emerging technique is to double sample from Internet pools of previously screened research volunteers with known sexual orientation, to create samples with a diversity of sexual orientation for web-based surveys (Herek, 2009a). What is common to all of these systematic sampling methods is an emphasis on sampling lesbian, gay, and bisexual individuals (and heterosexual comparison groups) with techniques that minimize selection bias and generally create opportunities for comparative studies (Corliss et al., 2008).

Selection bias, however, is not the only concern to be considered in evaluating research on sexual orientation and mental health. There are also issues related to potential response bias as well as the problem of confounded hypotheses. For example, some lesbian, gay, and bisexual persons may be reluctant to disclose either a minority identity or positive histories of a same-gender sexual partner during the course of study interviews. If the threshold for disclosure of this sensitive information also affects the likelihood of disclosure of psychological symptoms then estimates drawn from self-disclosing sexual minority respondents may be biased upward (Cochran, 2001). Confounded findings can occur when two concepts are assessed with a single survey item and sexual minority individuals differ from heterosexual people on one but perhaps not both of the concepts. For example, some of the research we review below indicates that lesbian, gay, and bisexual people are more likely than heterosexual individuals to seek mental health services or healthcare for emotional concerns. If a survey question asks respondents a confounded question (e.g., "Has a doctor ever diagnosed you with depression"), those individuals who have sought mental healthcare from a doctor may be more likely to answer affirmatively than those who have not seen a doctor (but may also have had depression). In this instance, the prevalence of depression among sexual minorities might be biased upward and the findings would be misleading.

Finally, although the majority of the work to date postulates that associations between homosexuality and mental illness are generated by a third causal factor, such as minority stress (Meyer, 2003), harmful childhood experiences arising from familial and social marginalization (D'Augelli, Grossman, & Starks, 2006), discrimination (Mays & Cochran, 2001), or possibly differences in social demography (Burgard, Cochran, & Mays, 2005), many of the systematically sampled data sets that have been used to investigate sexual orientation-related differences in either risk factors for psychological morbidity or prevalence of disorders were not designed to test these hypotheses. With a few notable exceptions, sexual orientation-related topics that might be of causal relevance, such as disclosure of your homosexuality to others (Balsam & Mohr, 2007) or childhood gender atypicality (D'Augelli et al., 2006), are not generally measured in the available data sets in which surveys are targeted at the general population. Nevertheless, the emerging literature on sexual orientation and mental health offers a new look at the ways in which social adversity may exert its effects on psychological wellbeing (Cochran & Mays, 2009). Researchers are also increasingly finding creative ways, using existing data sets, to examine links between potential causal factors and mental health disparities linked to sexual orientation.

DISPARITIES IN MENTAL HEALTH MORBIDITY

The earliest evidence of possible sexual orientation-related differences in mental health from this third methodological wave of studies focused on reports of suicide attempts, particularly among adolescents (Balsam, Beauchaine, Mickey, & Rothblum, 2005; Barney, 2003; Botnick et al., 2002; Cochran & Mays, 2000a; Consolacion, Russell, Sue, Russell, & Joyner, 2004; DiStefano, 2008; Faulkner & Cranston, 1998; Fergusson et al., 1999; Fergusson, Horwood, Ridder, & Beautrais, 2005; Garofalo et al., 1999; Gilman et al., 2001; Herrell et al., 1999; Hershberger, Pilkington, & D'Augelli, 1997; Huebner, Rebchook, & Kegeles, 2004; Jiang, Perry, & Hesser, 2010; Jorm, Korten, Rodgers, Jacomb, & Christensen, 2002; Noell & Ochs, 2001; Paul et al., 2002; Ploderl, Kralovec, & Fartacek, 2010; Remafedi et al., 1998; Russell & Joyner, 2001; Saewyc et al., 1998; Skegg, Nada-Raja, Dickson, Paul, & Williams, 2003; Zhao, Montoro, Igartua, & Thombs, 2010). Across studies, individuals classified as sexual orientation minorities reported rates of suicide attempts approximately 2.6 times greater than those classified as heterosexual (King et al., 2008). Over the past decade, these findings have been remarkably robust despite different types of study designs, different definitions of sexual orientation minority status, varying time frames for measuring suicide attempts (e.g., lifetime versus. prior 12 months), various age groups of study interest (e.g., adolescents versus adults), and wide geographic locations including studies from Australasia, Europe, and North America (King et al., 2008). Indeed, the 2001 Surgeon General's Report on Suicide identified youth with minority sexual orientation as a vulnerable population (Surgeon General, 2001).

Whether this finding is paralleled by higher rates of suicide-related mortality is, however, unclear. Many of these suicide attempts are serious enough to require medical treatment (Nasuti, Cochran, & Mays, 2010). For example, one study of high school students in Rhode Island (Jiang et al., 2010) found that about 10% of adolescents with minority sexual orientation reported receiving medical attention for a suicide attempt in the 12 months prior to their interview. This compares to 3.1% of heterosexual youth in the same survey. But tracking sexual orientation differences in deaths due to intentional injury or suicide is methodologically difficult at the moment. Mortality statistics are generally derived from death certificates, which do not typically include any information pertaining to an individual's sexual orientation.

However, there are some emerging opportunities that do allow for investigation of this concern. For example, in Denmark, same gender couples have had an opportunity to acquire registered (same-sex) domestic partner (RDP) status since 1990. Because RDP status is recorded on death certificates, it is possible to use this information to classify at least those sexual minorities who are in legally registered relationships. Two studies (Mathy, Cochran, Olsen, & Mays, 2009; Qin, Agerbo, & Mortensen, 2003) used this information to investigate sexual orientation differences in suicide mortality. Both found a higher completed suicide rate among those in RDPs compared to heterosexually married individuals, with the effect achieving statistical significance only among men. Indeed, men with current or former RDP status had a 6-fold increase in age-adjusted risk for suicide mortality compared to married or formerly married men (Mathy et al., 2009).

In the United States, markers of sexual orientation have been measured long enough in some national surveys that routine tracking of mortality information on respondents is beginning to appear in data archives. In contrast to the findings from Denmark, the one U.S. study, using up to 18 years of mortality follow-up for men first interviewed in the National Health and Nutrition Examination Survey III (NHANES III), found no evidence of sexual orientation-related differences in suicide mortality (Cochran & Mays, 2011). This was so, even though there were sexual orientation-related differences observed among these men in their lifetime reports of suicide attempts when they were first interviewed in 1988–1994 (Cochran & Mays, 2000a). In the earlier study, those men who reported any male sexual partners were more likely than men reporting only female sexual partners to have attempted suicide. Given the small numbers of homosexually classified men in the NHANES III ($n = 85$), and the relative rarity of suicide-related mortality, these findings are clearly in need of replication. At this point, however, it appears that the robust evidence for sexual orientation differences in suicide attempts has not been matched by similar robust evidence for sexual orientation differences in suicide-related mortality.

Rapidly following the emergence of findings concerning suicide attempts, studies using the new methodological approach began to appear in the research literature, documenting similar sexual orientation-related differences in the prevalence of some mental disorders. Using data from both cross-sectional general population-based surveys (Cochran & Mays, 2000a, 2000b, 2009; Cochran, Mays, Alegria, Ortega, & Takeuchi, 2007; Cochran, Mays, & Sullivan, 2003; Dilley, Simmons, Boysun, Pizacani, & Stark, 2010; Gilman et al., 2001; Hatzenbuehler, Keyes, & Hasin, 2009; Hatzenbuehler, McLaughlin, Keyes, & Hasin, 2010; McCabe, Hughes, Bostwick, West, & Boyd, 2009; Midanik, Drabble, Trocki, & Sell, 2007; Sandfort, Bakker, Schellevis, & Vanwesenbeeck, 2006; Sandfort, de Graaf, & Bijl, 2003; Sandfort, de Graaf, Bijl, & Schnabel, 2001) and longitudinal cohort studies (Fergusson et al., 1999, 2005), researchers observed, with few exceptions (Balsam et al., 2005), somewhat higher levels of depressive distress, major depression, generalized anxiety disorder, panic attacks, alcohol dependency, and drug dependency among individuals with minority sexual orientation as compared to heterosexual individuals.

In Table 15.1, we summarize findings from several of these studies. These particular studies were selected because all of them included heterosexual comparison groups, used systematic sampling methods from the general population, administered similar standardized screening or diagnostic instruments, and the papers presented sufficient detail on 1 year prevalence of a common set of measured disorders to allow for pooling of estimates. However, these studies all used somewhat different methods to classify for sexual orientation, depending on what was available in the existing data set. Some used reports of the genders of sexual partners, and others utilized self-classification into various sexual orientation identity statuses. Across these studies, however, sexual minority men evidenced a somewhat higher prevalence of major depression, generalized anxiety disorder, panic, alcohol dependency, and drug dependency than did heterosexual men. Sexual minority women displayed a higher prevalence of recent major depression, generalized anxiety disorder, and alcohol dependency than did heterosexual women.

This greater level of risk is not consistent with earlier "illness" models of homosexuality in which the expectation would be that nearly all sexual minorities would meet criteria for diagnosable

TABLE 15.1. ONE-YEAR PREVALENCE ESTIMATES, ADJUSTED ODDS RATIOS OF PSYCHIATRIC DISORDERS, AND POOLED ESTIMATES OF SEXUAL ORIENTATION DIFFERENCES BY GENDER DERIVED FROM SEVERAL POPULATION-BASED SURVEYS

Psychiatric Disorder	Study Survey	Men				Women			
		Prevalence (%)		Adj. OR	(95% CI)	Prevalence (%)		Adj. OR	(95% CI)
		Sexual Minority	Heterosexual			Sexual Minority	Heterosexual		
Major Depression									
	1996 National Survey on Drug Abuse (NSDA)[1]	13.3	5.1	2.94	(1.38–6.28)*	15.0	8.4	1.79	(0.74–4.32)
	National Comorbidity Survey (NCS)[2]	10.3	7.2	1.56	(0.81–2.31)	34.5	12.9	3.69	(3.10–4.28)*
	Netherlands Mental Health Survey (NEMESIS)[3]	9.8	3.9	1.96	(0.88–4.37)	11.6	7.3	1.03	(0.38–2.80)
	Midlife Survey of Adult Development (MIDUS)[4]	31.0	10.2	3.57	(1.71–7.43)*	33.5	16.8	1.88	(0.71–4.98)
	National Latino and Asian American Survey (NLAAS)[5]	8.1	6.0	1.11	(0.31–4.02)	16.0	9.2	1.94	(1.17–3.21)*
	California Quality of Life Survey (Cal-QOL)[6]	21.8	8.7	2.57	(1.65–4.17)*	26.8	14.4	1.66	(1.16–2.51)*
	Pooled estimates of effects	15.7	6.9	2.33	(1.64–3.32)*	22.9	11.5	1.88	(1.33–2.65)*
Generalized Anxiety Disorder									
	1996 NSDA	3.1	1.6	2.32	(0.55–9.70)	3.5	2.6	1.54	(0.49–4.86)
	NCS	0.9	1.9	0.70	(0.00–2.69)	13.5	4.0	3.82	(3.00–4.64)*
	MIDUS	2.9	1.8	1.35	(0.19–9.34)	14.7	3.8	3.88	(1.18–12.77)*
	NEMESIS	1.2	0.8	1.43	(0.18–11.55)	1.4	0.0	—[9]	
	NLAAS	10.9	6.8	1.53	(0.77–3.01)	11.3	10.3	1.16	(0.60–2.26)
	Cal-QOL	15.5	5.9	2.55	(1.54–4.42)*	13.9	7.6	1.59	(1.14–2.26)*
	Pooled estimates of effects	5.8	3.1	1.69	(1.05–2.73)*	9.7	4.7	1.89	(1.20–2.97)*
Panic									
	1996 NSDA	6.4	2.0	4.30	(1.53–12.13)*	7.2	3.8	1.78	(0.40–8.33)
	NCS	1.0	1.4	0.98	(0.00–2.98)	5.9	3.0	2.03	(0.84–3.22)
	MIDUS	17.9	3.8	5.09	(2.00–12.99)*	17.1	8.6	2.05	(0.72–5.82)
	NEMESIS	3.7	0.9	2.70	(0.73–9.91)	2.3	3.2	0.65	(0.09–4.90)
	Cal-QOL	7.2	3.0	2.31	(1.66–4.71)*	14.0	7.1	1.71	(1.02–2.96)*
	Pooled estimates of effects	7.2	2.2	3.01	(1.92–4.72)*	9.3	5.1	1.35	(0.77–2.36)
Alcohol Dependency									
	1996 NSDA	10.6	7.6	1.33	(0.55–3.22)	7.0	2.2	2.85	(1.16–6.98)*
	NCS	12.1	11.6	1.05	(0.34–1.76)	15.3	4.1	4.37	(3.59–5.15)*

MIDUS	8.9	5.6	1.30	(0.40–4.23)	11.8	3.4	2.51	(0.60–10.48)
NEMESIS	11.0	5.5	1.41	(0.67–3.01)	7.0	1.0	3.72	(0.98–14.05)
NLAAS	0.6	3.0	0.19	(0.03–1.05)	1.0	0.9	1.00	(0.12–8.13)
National Alcohol Survey—gay/lesbian identity[7]	10.4	5.8	—[9]		11.5	2.3	5.6	(1.4–22.5)*
National Alcohol Survey—bisexual identity	5.5	5.8	—[9]		16.7	2.3	5.8	(1.8–18.7)*
NESARC—gay/lesbian identity[8]	16.8	6.1	2.9	(1.7–5.1)*	13.3	2.5	3.6	(1.8–7.3)*
NESARC—bisexual identity	19.5	6.1	4.2	(2.2–8.2)*	15.6	2.5	2.9	(1.6–5.5)*
Cal-QOL—gay/lesbian identity	8.9	6.3	1.76	(0.88–3.71)	4.7	2.8	1.73	(0.64–4.85)
Cal-QOL—bisexual identity	13.0	6.3	1.96	(0.72–6.20)	12.8	2.8	3.02	(1.38–6.60)*
Pooled estimates of effects	10.7	6.3	1.50	(1.12–1.99)*	10.6	2.4	3.35	(2.36–4.75)*
Drug Dependency								
1996 NSDA	5.7	2.8	2.05	(0.86–4.93)	5.0	1.3	3.27	(1.23–8.70)*
NCS	9.2	4.0	2.52	(1.71–3.32)*	4.1	2.1	1.90	(0.46–3.34)
MIDUS	9.2	2.7	2.46	(0.55–11.07)	6.5	1.5	3.45	(0.39–30.64)
NEMESIS	0.0	0.9	—[9]		2.3	0.4	4.44	(0.50–39.60)
NLAAS	0.5	1.3	0.34	(0.04–2.72)	2.9	0.2	12.05	(1.10–132.08)*
NESARC—gay/lesbian identity	3.2	0.5	4.2	(1.3–14.1)*	5.7	0.4	12.4	(2.9–54.1)*
NESARC—bisexual identity	5.1	0.5	6.3	(1.5–26.8)*	3.0	0.4	2.1	(0.4–12.1)
Cal-QOL—gay/lesbian identity	4.1	2.8	1.96	(0.70–5.81)	0.3	1.9	0.18	(0.03–1.00)
Cal-QOL—bisexual identity	5.6	2.8	1.67	(0.38–8.22)	7.5	1.9	2.43	(0.84–7.50)
Pooled estimates of effects	4.7	2.0	2.04	(1.3–3.20)*	4.1	1.1	2.16	(0.51–9.17)

Notes: The surveys selected utilized common methods of sample selection including heterosexual control groups and investigated a common set of psychiatric disorders using diagnostic or screening instruments. Odds ratios are adjusted (Adj. OR) for confounders at the study level. Pooled estimates were derived assuming a random study effect; all surveys that reported adjusted odds ratios are used to calculate the pooled odds ratio. Where study odds ratios are missing, the pooled odds ratio is biased somewhat upward.

[1] From Cochran and Mays (2000). Sexual orientation classification used the gender of sexual partners in 12 months prior to the interview; psychiatric diagnoses were made by Composite International Diagnostic Interview—Short Form (CIDI-SF) assessment.

[2] From Gilman et al. (2001). Sexual orientation classification used the gender of sexual partners in 5 years prior to the interview; psychiatric diagnoses were made by Composite International Diagnostic Interview (CIDI) assessment.

[3] From Sandfort et al. (2001). Sexual orientation classification used the gender of sexual partners in 12 months prior to the interview; psychiatric diagnoses were made by CIDI assessment.

[4] From Cochran et al. (2003). Sexual orientation classification used the sexual orientation identity; psychiatric diagnoses were made by CIDI-SF assessment.

[5] From Cochran et al. (2009). Sexual orientation classification used the sexual orientation identity and genders of sexual partners in 12 months prior to the interview; psychiatric diagnoses were made by CIDI assessment; major depression was estimated by "Any depressive disorder," GAD was estimated by "Any anxiety disorder," and both alcohol and drug dependency include diagnoses of abuse.

[6] From Cochran and Mays (2009). Sexual orientation classification used the sexual orientation identity and genders of sexual partners, lifetime; psychiatric diagnoses were made by CIDI-SF assessment.

[7] From Midanik et al. (2007). Sexual orientation classification used the sexual orientation identity; *DSM-IV* diagnoses were made by reporting three or more core symptoms of alcohol dependency.

[8] From McCabe et al. (2009). Sexual orientation classification used the sexual orientation identity; psychiatric diagnoses were made by the Alcohol Use Disorder and Associated Disabilities Interview Schedule *DSM-IV* version IV (AUDADIS-IV) assessment.

[9] Not reported.

*p < 0.05.

disorders of one type or another. Instead, the elevated risk is on the order of the size of differences seen commonly between men and women, between individuals of varying racial/ethnic background, or among people reporting different income levels (Cochran & Mays, 2009). Hence, sexual orientation appears to function like other major social characteristics in shaping individuals' risk for mental health morbidity. At the same time, across the majority of these studies most individuals with minority sexual orientation, like most heterosexual individuals, did not evidence recent psychological morbidity of clinical concern.

Major depression is the most common disorder experienced by individuals with minority sexual orientation. Approximately 20% of lesbian, gay, and bisexual persons report experiencing major depression on an annual basis. Among sexual minority men, the second most common disorder is alcohol dependency. For sexual minority women, alcohol dependency, which is relatively rare among heterosexual women, is as common as it is among sexual minority men.

Information on possible sexual orientation-related differences in less commonly measured disorders is less often reported in the research literature, but it too suggests small elevations in risk associated with minority sexual orientation. For example, in a Dutch study (Sandfort et al., 2001) a higher 1-year prevalence of agoraphobia, obsessive–compulsive disorder, and bipolar disorder was reported among Dutch men who reported any male sexual partners in the year prior to the interview as compared to Dutch men who reported only female sexual partners. In the United States, Hatzenbuehler and his colleagues (Hatzenbuehler, Keyes, et al., 2009), using information available in the National Epidemiologic Survey on Alcohol and Related Conditions (NESARC), observed greater 1-year prevalence rates of social anxiety, phobia, and posttraumatic stress disorder among lesbian, gay, and bisexual individuals than among heterosexual persons.

SEXUAL ORIENTATION-RELATED DISPARITIES IN EXPOSURE TO MENTAL HEALTH MORBIDITY RISK FACTORS

Although the reasons for these differences in psychological morbidity are not fully understood, research is also increasingly documenting the ways

in which sexual orientation influences a person's experiences in the world, including its influence on exposures to events that are known to be harmful for mental health (Cochran & Mays, 1994, 2009; Mays, Cochran, & Rhue, 1993; Mays, Cochran, & Roeder, 2004). One of the most frequently proffered theoretical models for conceptualizing sexual orientation-related vulnerabilities for mental health morbidity is the minority stress model (Meyer, 2003) and its emerging variants (Hatzenbuehler, Nolen-Hoeksema et al., 2009). At its core, this model posits that widespread, negative views of homosexuality generate greater exposure to negative events among sexual orientation minorities. This, in turn, leads to self-perceptions of possessing a stigmatized identity and higher expectations of social rejection. Eventually the elevated level of social adversity generates higher rates of mental health morbidity.

That sexual minorities report more frequent experiences with everyday discrimination than heterosexual persons do is now well documented across a number of studies using varied designs, measures, and source populations (Almeida, Johnson, Corliss, Molnar, & Azrael, 2009; Burgess, Tran, Lee, & van Ryn, 2007; Gordon & Meyer, 2007; Hatzenbuehler, Nolen-Hoeksema, & Erickson, 2008; Herek, 2009a; Krieger & Sidney, 1997; Mays & Cochran, 2001; McCabe, Bostwick, Hughes, West, & Boyd, 2010; Raymond, Chen, Stall, & McFarland, 2010; Sandfort et al., 2003). Furthermore, several studies have also shown that perceptions of discrimination are strongly and positively associated with mental health morbidity among lesbian, gay, and bisexual persons (Almeida et al., 2009; Burgess et al., 2007; Cochran & Mays, 2007; Mays & Cochran, 2001). Most recently, research has also documented that simply living in a state with fewer rights for members of sexual minorities is associated with higher rates of mental health morbidity among lesbian, gay, and bisexual individuals (Hatzenbuehler, Keyes, et al., 2009; Hatzenbuehler et al., 2010).

Thus, one of the hallmarks of antigay stigma is that it may inflict harm on individuals at a number of different levels, including the macro or social level, the interpersonal level, and the intrapsychic level (Ross, Dobinson, & Eady, 2010). These effects may also be chronic in nature. During childhood and adolescence, both gender nonconformity and emerging attractions to others of the same sex can be early risk factors for maltreatment from families and peers, including childhood sexual abuse (Almeida et al., 2009; Corliss, Cochran, & Mays, 2002; D'Augelli et al., 2006; Fergusson et al., 2005; Paul, Catania, Pollack, & Stall, 2001; Savin-Williams & Dube, 1998). Exposure to childhood maltreatment is associated with both early initiation of drug use (Relf, Huang, Campbell, & Catania, 2004) and later increased risk for adult psychopathology (Briere & Jordan, 2009; Fergusson et al., 2005; Sandfort et al., 2003). Social adversity linked to antigay stigma continues in adulthood where individuals with minority sexual orientation face a higher risk than do heterosexuals for exposure to hate crimes and violence (Herek, 2009a; Mills et al., 2004). Even in advancing age, sexual minority individuals confront issues that vary somewhat from their heterosexual peers, including concerns about personal safety, as the need for assistance from others increases (D'Augelli, Grossman, Hershberger, & O'Connell, 2001).

There can be little doubt that antigay discrimination is harmful for the mental health of individuals with a minority sexual orientation. In addition to social adversity, there are also other factors that may contribute to the mental health disparities being documented in recent studies. Many of these are simply a consequence of the ways in which sexual orientation interacts with the life course. For example, the family structures of nonheterosexual persons are often different from those of heterosexual women and men (Carpenter & Gates, 2008), including lower rates of marriage or cohabitation with relationship partners and less likelihood of parenting, both of which are associated with substance use and mental health morbidity (Office of Applied Studies-SAMHSA, 2010). Levels of education appear to be somewhat higher among lesbian and gay persons than among heterosexuals (Carpenter & Gates, 2008). All of this may lead to different career paths, as well as financial resources, and structures of social networks (Badgett & Frank, 2007; Mays, Chatters, Cochran, & Mackness, 1998). The cumulative effect of these differences over time may influence risks for psychiatric disorders as well.

VARIABILITY OF RISK WITHIN THE SEXUAL MINORITY POPULATION

Although the accumulating evidence has convincingly shown that mental health disparities are linked to sexual orientation, there is also an emerging recognition that the sexual orientation minority population itself is diverse, both in terms of life experiences and the burden of mental health morbidity. One source of diversity in risk is gender. Gender, like sexual orientation, is a key social status that has been linked repeatedly to differential risk for psychiatric disorders. In general, women, as a group, are somewhat more at risk than men are for mood and anxiety disorders (Kessler et al., 2005) but men are more likely than women to be at risk for alcohol and drug use disorders (Compton, Thomas, Stinson, & Grant, 2007; Hanna & Grant, 1997).

Among sexual minority individuals, the expected gender differences appear to be present for some disorders but not for others. For example, mood and anxiety disorders have been found to be more prevalent among women with minority sexual orientation, but alcohol and, possibly, drug use disorders do not appear to be more common among men with minority sexual orientation as compared to women (see Table 15.1). Why lesbians and bisexual women experience greater than expected risk, based on their gender, for alcohol and drug use disorders is not fully understood, but may reflect more tolerant norms in the gay community for alcohol and drug use by women (Cochran, 2001). A second gender difference that is an important risk factor for psychological morbidity is living with HIV infection (Cochran & Mays, 2007). Studies examining associations between HIV risk and gay men in the United States have repeatedly shown the negative psychological effects of the epidemic among both infected and uninfected men, including some evidence for higher rates of diagnosable disorders among HIV infected gay and bisexual men when compared to men who are not (Berg, Mimiaga, & Safren, 2004; Cochran & Mays, 2009). With current estimates suggesting that perhaps 16% of gay men in the United States are living with an HIV infection (Xu, Sternberg, & Markowitz, 2010), HIV represents a widespread risk factor for mental health morbidity among men with minority sexual orientation.

A second source of diversity that has received attention in recent years is the potential impact of multiply stigmatized social statuses on mental health morbidity. For example, members of ethnic/racial minorities, who are also members of sexual minorities, may experience discrimination both in their own racial/ethnic communities for not being heterosexual and in the visible (and predominantly white) gay community for being an ethnic/racial minority (Harper, Jernewall, & Zea, 2004; Mays et al., 1993, 1998). Although there has been concern that dual sources of stigma may lead to an even greater mental health morbidity burden among ethnic/racial minorities (Yoshikawa, Wilson, Chae, & Cheng, 2004), findings to date suggest that this is not necessarily the case (Cochran & Mays, 2009; Consolacion et al., 2004; Kertzner, Meyer, Frost, & Stirratt, 2009; Meyer, Dietrich, & Schwartz, 2008). Instead, current evidence suggests that individual risk is an additive function of both ethnic/racial background and sexual orientation status. For example, although Asian-American and Latino sexual minority individuals interviewed in the National Latino and Asian American Survey evidenced somewhat higher rates of some disorders than heterosexual respondents also interviewed in that study, their observed rates of psychological morbidity were generally lower than published studies of sexual orientation minorities, most of whom have been white. These findings presumably reflect the well-known protective properties of Asian-American and Hispanic ethnic/racial status in the United States observed in several psychiatric epidemiological surveys (Cochran et al., 2007).

Finally, a third source of heterogeneity of risk among sexual minorities is sexual orientation status itself. In the earliest general population studies, methodological limitations precluded investigation of relative differences in risk among individuals classified as lesbian or gay, bisexual, or homosexually experienced but heterosexually identifying. Increasingly, though, improvements in research design and the quality of data sets have permitted researchers to examine patterns of mental health and substance use morbidity as a function of differences in self-identification (e.g., lesbian, gay, or bisexual), sexual attractions (e.g., primarily or exclusively the same or other gender), and sexual behavior histories. This work is rapidly demonstrating that mental health disparities are heterogeneously distributed among sexual orientation minorities (Austin, Roberts, Corliss, & Molnar, 2008; Bostwick et al., 2010; Burgard et al., 2005; Cochran & Mays, 2009; Drabble, Midanik, & Trocki, 2005; Kertzner et al., 2009; Meyer et al., 2008; Midanik et al., 2007; Trocki, Drabble, & Midanik, 2009).

The patterns of heterogeneity emerging from these later studies are also inconsistent with historical views of homosexuality as being, in and of itself, pathological (Terry, 1999). "Illness" models of homosexuality imply that greater degrees of homosexuality should result in greater risk for psychological morbidity. Instead, these recent studies suggest that among sexual minority women, bisexual women are particularly at risk for suicide attempts, misuse of alcohol (Burgard et al., 2005), and mood and anxiety disorders (Kertzner et al., 2009), but, with the exception of mood disorders, self-identified lesbians often show prevalences of disorders equal to those of heterosexual women (Bostwick et al., 2010; Cochran & Mays, 2009). Among men, heterosexually identified men reporting lifetime histories of sex with other men appear to be at greatest risk for psychological morbidity when compared to exclusively heterosexual men (Cochran & Mays, 2009).

In sum, population-based and longitudinal cohort studies have revealed that sexual orientation is a core social status characteristic that, like race and gender, can at times be linked to mood, anxiety, and substance use disorders. Overall, the incremental risk associated with minority sexual orientation is approximately 1.5 to 2 times the risk experienced by heterosexual individuals (Cochran & Mays, 2009) and similar in size to the associations documented between gender and mental health disorders (Kessler et al., 2005). At the same time, most lesbian, gay, and bisexual individuals, like most heterosexual women and men, *do not* meet criteria for a mental disorder at any given point in time. Furthermore, sexual orientation-related disparities are not evidenced equally among sexual minority individuals who vary in their attractions, sexual behaviors, and self-professed identities. This fact suggests that differences in life experiences provide differential sources of both risk and protection for mental health morbidity in this population. In particular, findings from recent studies of social and interpersonal stressors that are more commonly experienced by members of sexual minorities suggest that social adversity plays an important role in creating the sexual orientation-related mental health disparities identified over the past decade.

SEXUAL ORIENTATION DIFFERENCES IN ACCESS TO AND USE OF MENTAL HEALTH SERVICES

Although much has been written on appropriate and inappropriate approaches to working with lesbian, gay, and bisexual clients (Davison, 2001; Division 44/CLGBC Joint Task Force, 2000; Rothblum, 1994), empirical research on the ways in which this population uses mental health services is still in its infancy (Bieschke, McClanahan, Tozer, Grzegorek, & Park, 2000). Nevertheless there is some tentative evidence that lesbians and gay men, as compared to heterosexual individuals, have higher levels of perceived need for mental health services (Burgess et al., 2007; Cochran et al., 2003), are more likely to use mental health services (Bakker, Sandfort, Vanwesenbeeck, van Lindert, & Westert, 2006; Balsam et al., 2005; Cochran & Mays, 2000b; Cochran et al., 2003; Grella, Greenwell, Mays, & Cochran, 2009; Tjepkema, 2008), begin doing so at earlier ages (Jones & Gabriel, 1999), have more episodes of treatment (Liddle, 1997), and remain in treatment longer (Liddle, 1997). In Table 15.2, we present summarized findings from several population-based studies in which sexual orientation-related differences in the use of mental health services in the previous 12 months were assessed. Because each of the surveys defined mental health services quite differently, resulting in large variations in prevalence of use, a summary estimate of the prevalence across these studies makes little sense. However, the "sexual orientation effect" can be summarized across studies and clearly reveals that lesbian, gay, and bisexual persons were more likely to use mental health services, however defined, than were matched groups of heterosexual women and men.

Sexual orientation may affect receipt of mental health services in a number of relevant ways. One concern is potential problems in accessing mental health services. For example, there is some reason to believe that lesbians and gay men may experience different structural barriers than heterosexual people do when seeking mental health services. This may happen through differential levels of health insurance coverage among individuals with minority sexual orientation (Ponce, Cochran, Pizer, & Mays, 2010). Furthermore, insurance-based healthcare delivery systems may limit the ability of those with minority sexual orientation to access providers who possess characteristics that matter to them, such as being knowledgeable about sexual minority issues. Other problems can occur in seeking care including restrictions on therapist choice, lack of information about provider's interest in or competence with respect to sexual minority issues, and

loss of confidentiality for those individuals who are more reticent to disclose their sexual orientation to gatekeepers in services delivery. How such issues might affect access to care is as yet unknown.

A second issue has to do with the quality of services actually received. In contrast to the views of many sexual minority individuals, some mental health providers may view treatment needs for sexual minority patients as not requiring a special set of skills, an opinion that is in stark contrast to the views of lesbian, gay, and bisexual persons (Garnets, Hancock, Cochran, Goodchilds, & Peplau, 1991; Herek & Garnets, 2007). In addition, providing appropriate mental health services for lesbian, gay, and bisexual individuals can be complicated by negative stereotypes of homosexuality and gender identity that are widely held (Herek, 2009b), even among some service providers. Furthermore, the continuing polarized debate (Haldeman, 1994; Spitzer, 2003) within the psychotherapy profession over the feasibility and ethics of so-called "conversion therapies" (in which the goal of therapy is to achieve heterosexual functioning) suggests that some providers may inappropriately act to treat sexual orientation rather than patients' presenting complaints (Bartlett, Smith, & King, 2009). To what extent these issues affect day-to-day experiences of persons with minority sexual orientation who are seeking mental health services awaits further study.

FUTURE DIRECTIONS

The ambivalence surrounding minority sexual orientation has occupied a particularly problematic space for psychology and the other mental health professions over the years (Drescher, 2010; Terry, 1999). In the past decade or so, however, the measurement of sexual orientation in general population research has provided a rich, new database of answers to questions about mental health disparities associated with sexual orientation. Indeed, the number and complexity of new questions emerging in the published literature are a result of the historical change in availability of high-quality data.

Looking ahead, we anticipate that the field will identify answers to many of the questions that have been raised in this review. For example, having demonstrated the existence of disparities, it is critical that research now aggressively pursue the "why" questions. What lies at the heart of these increased risks? Why is it that sexual minority youth are

TABLE 15.2. ONE-YEAR PREVALENCE OF MENTAL HEALTH SERVICES USE (VARIOUSLY DEFINED), ADJUSTED STUDY ODDS RATIOS, AND POOLED ESTIMATES OF SEXUAL ORIENTATION DIFFERENCES BY GENDER AND SEXUAL ORIENTATION DERIVED FROM SEVERAL POPULATION-BASED SURVEYS

	Men				Women			
	Prevalence (%)				Prevalence (%)			
Study Survey	Sexual Minority	Heterosexual	Adj. OR	(95% CI)	Sexual Minority	Heterosexual	Adj. OR	(95% CI)
1996 National Survey on Drug Abuse (NSDA)[1]	16.1	5.9	3.10	(1.52–6.31)*	15.1	6.3	2.90	(1.26–6.70)*
Midlife Survey of Adult Development (MIDUS)[2]	56.7	24.9	3.78	(1.90–7.51)*	66.0	35.8	3.37	(1.39–8.19)*
Canadian Community Health Survey (CCHS)—gay/lesbian identity[3]	7.7	2.5	2.13	(1.46–3.11)*	10.0	4.0	2.09	(1.32–3.31)*
Canadian Community Health Survey (CCHS)—bisexual identity	5.8	2.5	1.49	(0.88–2.51)	10.7	4.0	1.57	(1.05–2.35)*
Dutch National Survey of General Practice (DNSGP-2)—gay/lesbian classification[4]	15.6	4.5	1.60	(0.70–3.63)	19.0	7.5	2.06	(1.07–3.98)*
Dutch National Survey of General Practice (DNSGP-2)—bisexual classification	4.0	4.5	1.10	(0.14–8.94)	16.9	7.5	2.32	(1.07–5.05)*
California Quality of Life Survey (Cal-QOL)[5]	42.5	17.1	2.76	(1.79–4.36)*	55.3	27.1	2.08	(1.25–3.47)*
Pooled estimates of effects			1.81	(1.30–2.53)			1.92	(1.38–2.68)

Notes: The surveys selected utilized common methods of sample selection including heterosexual control groups and reported gender-based mental healthcare use in the past year. Odds ratios are adjusted (Adj. OR) for confounders at the study level. Pooled estimates are derived assuming a random study effect.

[1]From Cochran and Mays (2000). Sexual orientation classification used the gender of sexual partners in the 12 months prior the to interview; mental health services were defined as receiving any treatment or counseling for drug or alcohol use and/or inpatient or outpatient services for psychological or emotional reasons.

[2]From Cochran et al. (2003). Sexual orientation classification used the sexual orientation identity; mental health services were defined as any care from a mental health specialist or from a general practitioner for emotional concern, attending a self-help group, or taking psychiatric medication.

[3]From Tjepkema (2008). Sexual orientation classification used the sexual orientation identity; mental health services were defined as treatment by a psychologist.

[4]From Bakker et al. (2006). Sexual orientation classification used the gender of sexual attractions; mental health services were defined as consulting a mental healthcare professional (including a psychiatrist).

[5]From Grella et al. (2009). Sexual orientation classification used the sexual orientation identity; mental health services were defined as accessing any mental health or substance use treatment (inpatient, outpatient, from a general practitioner as well as a mental healthcare specialist) or the use of psychiatric medication.

*$p < 0.05$.

targeted for maltreatment in the first place (Roberts, Austin, Corliss, Vandermorris, & Koenen, 2010)? Conversely, why is it that most lesbian, gay, and bisexual persons live fulfilling lives despite the high levels of social adversity with which many of them must contend (Nellos, Cochran, & Mays, 2002)? Indeed, although an increased risk for common mental health disorders has been observed repeatedly in recent studies, it is still generally true that the majority of lesbian, gay, and bisexual individuals show no evidence of mental health morbidity.

A major topic that is not addressed above is the way in which gender variance may also affect risk for psychiatric morbidity. Gender variance, like minority sexual orientation, increases the risk for both exposure to violence and to the harmful effects of social stigmatization (Bith-Melander et al., 2010; Corliss, Belzer, Forbes, & Wilson, 2007; Nuttbrock et al., 2010; Sanchez & Vilain, 2009). At present, however, the measurement of gender atypicality or transgender identity in general population surveys is in its infancy (Almeida et al., 2009). As survey research on sexual orientation-related topics matures, and with the growing sense that gender atypicality is a critical source of maltreatment for some lesbian, gay, and bisexual individuals (Corliss et al., 2002; D'Augelli et al., 2006; Rosario, 2008), we anticipate greater efforts to include questions pertaining to gender variance and transgender concerns in population-based surveys of the future. Population-based studies of transgender and gender variance concerns are likely to provide important new insights into day-to-day experiences, health concerns, and mental health burdens among gender-variant and transgender people.

Finally, as our review of treatment access and utilization revealed, there is a pressing need for health services research addressing the needs and concerns of lesbian, gay, and bisexual individuals. Clinical trials assessing the effectiveness of gay affirmative therapy (Bieschke et al., 2000; Bieschke et al., 2007) are also needed (Cochran, 2001), especially given the movement in psychology toward evidence-based practice (McHugh & Barlow, 2010). It would also be useful to identify effective training approaches for clinicians who are likely to work with lesbian, gay, and bisexual clients, especially given the evidence that many clinicians lack specific training to do so (Rock, Carlson, & McGeorge, 2010) and that some approach their work with harmful stereotypes about the nature of sexual orientation (Bartlett et al., 2009; Garnets et al., 1991).

REFERENCES

Almeida, J., Johnson, R. M., Corliss, H. L., Molnar, B. E., & Azrael, D. (2009). Emotional distress among LGBT youth: The influence of perceived discrimination based on sexual orientation. *Journal of Youth and Adolescence, 38*(7), 1001–1014.

Austin, S. B., Roberts, A. L., Corliss, H. L., & Molnar, B. E. (2008). Sexual violence victimization history and sexual risk indicators in a community-based urban cohort of "mostly heterosexual" and heterosexual young women. *American Journal of Public Health, 98*(6), 1015–1020.

Badgett, M., & Frank, J. (Eds.). (2007). *Sexual orientation discrimination: An international perspective* New York: Routledge.

Bailey, J. M. (1999). Homosexuality and mental illness. *Archives of General Psychiatry, 56*, 883–884.

Bakker, F. C., Sandfort, T. G., Vanwesenbeeck, I., van Lindert, H., & Westert, G. P. (2006). Do homosexual persons use health care services more frequently than heterosexual persons: Findings from a Dutch population survey. *Social Science and Medicine, 63*(8), 2022–2030.

Balsam, K. F., Beauchaine, T. P., Mickey, R. M., & Rothblum, E. D. (2005). Mental health of lesbian, gay, bisexual, and heterosexual siblings: Effects of gender, sexual orientation, and family. *Journal of Abnormal Psychology, 114*(3), 471–476.

Balsam, K. F., Beauchaine, T. P., Rothblum, E. D., & Solomon, S. E. (2008). Three-year follow-up of same-sex couples who had civil unions in Vermont, same-sex couples not in civil unions, and heterosexual married couples. *Developmental Psychology, 44*(1), 102–116.

Balsam, K. F., & Mohr, J. J. (2007). Adaptation to sexual orientation stigma: A comparison of bisexual and lesbian/gay adults. *Journal of Counseling Psychology, 54*(3), 306–319.

Barney, D. D. (2003). Health risk-factors for gay American Indian and Alaska Native adolescent males. *Journal of Homosexuality, 46*(1–2), 137–157.

Bartlett, A., Smith, G., & King, M. (2009). The response of mental health professionals to clients seeking help to change or redirect same-sex sexual orientation. *BMC Psychiatry, 9*, 11.

Berg, M. B., Mimiaga, M. J., & Safren, S. A. (2004). Mental health concerns of HIV-infected gay and bisexual men seeking mental health services: An observational study. *AIDS Patient Care STDS, 18*(11), 635–643.

Bieschke, K. J., McClanahan, M., Tozer, E., Grzegorek, J. L., & Park, J. (2000). Programmatic research on the treatment of lesbian, gay, and bisexual clients: The past, the present, and the course for the future. In R. M. Perez, K. A. DeBord, & K. J. Bieschke (Eds.), *Handbook of counseling and psychotherapy with lesbian, gay, and bisexual clients* (pp. 309–336). Washington, DC: American Psychological Association.

Bieschke, K. J., Perez, R. M., & DeBord, K. A. (Eds.), (2007). *Handbook of counseling and psychotherapy with lesbian, gay, bisexual, and transgender clients* (2nd ed.). Washington, DC: American Psychological Association.

Binson, D., Woods, W. J., Pollack, L., & Sheon, N. (2005). Bringing HIV/STI testing programmes to high-risk men. *International Journal of Sexually Transmitted Disease and AIDS, 16*(9), 600–604.

Bith-Melander, P., Sheoran, B., Sheth, L., Bermudez, C., Drone, J., Wood, W., et al. (2010). Understanding sociocultural and psychological factors affecting transgender people of color in San Francisco. *Journal of the Association of Nurses in AIDS Care, 21*(3), 207–220.

Bostwick, W. B., Boyd, C. J., Hughes, T. L., & McCabe, S. E. (2010). Dimensions of sexual orientation and the prevalence of mood and anxiety disorders in the United States. *American Journal of Public Health, 100*(3), 468–475.

Botnick, M. R., Heath, K. V., Cornelisse, P. G., Strathdee, S. A., Martindale, S. L., & Hogg, R. S. (2002). Correlates of suicide attempts in an open cohort of young men who have sex with men. *Canadian Journal of Public Health, 93*(1), 59–62.

Briere, J., & Jordan, C. E. (2009). Childhood maltreatment, intervening variables, and adult psychological difficulties in women: An overview. *Trauma Violence Abuse, 10*(4), 375–388.

Burgard, S. A., Cochran, S. D., & Mays, V. M. (2005). Alcohol and tobacco use patterns among heterosexually and homosexually experienced California women. *Drug & Alcohol Dependence, 77*(1), 61–70.

Burgess, D., Tran, A., Lee, R., & van Ryn, M. (2007). Effects of perceived discrimination on mental health and mental health services utilization among gay, lesbian, bisexual and transgender persons. *Journal of LGBT Health Research, 3*(4), 1–14.

Carpenter, C., & Gates, G. J. (2008). Gay and lesbian partnership: Evidence from California. *Demography, 45*(3), 573–590.

Catania, J. A., Osmond, D., Stall, R. D., Pollack, L., Paul, J. P., Blower, S., et al. (2001). The continuing HIV epidemic among men who have sex with men. *American Journal of Public Health, 91*(6), 907–914.

Cochran, S. D. (2001). Emerging issues in research on lesbians' and gay men's mental health: Does sexual orientation really matter? *American Psychologist, 56*(11), 931–947.

Cochran, S. D., & Mays, V. M. (1994). Depressive distress among homosexually active African American men and women. *American Journal of Psychiatry, 151*(4), 524–529.

Cochran, S. D., & Mays, V. M. (2000a). Lifetime prevalence of suicide symptoms and affective disorders among men reporting same-sex sexual partners: Results from NHANES III. *American Journal of Public Health, 90*(4), 573–578.

Cochran, S. D., & Mays, V. M. (2000b). Relation between psychiatric syndromes and behaviorally defined sexual orientation in a sample of the US population. *American Journal of Epidemiology, 151*(5), 516–523.

Cochran, S. D., & Mays, V. M. (2007). Physical health complaints among lesbians, gay men, and bisexual and homosexually experienced heterosexual individuals: Results from the California Quality of Life Survey. *American Journal of Public Health, 97*(11), 2048–2055.

Cochran, S. D., & Mays, V. M. (2009). Burden of psychiatric morbidity among lesbian, gay, and bisexual individuals in the California Quality of Life Survey. *Journal of Abnormal Psychology, 118*(3), 647–658.

Cochran, S. D., & Mays, V. M. (2011). Sexual orientation and mortality among U.S. men, age 17 to 59 years: Results from the NHANES III. *American Journal of Public Health, 101*(6), 1133–1138.

Cochran, S. D., Mays, V. M., Alegria, M., Ortega, A. N., & Takeuchi, D. (2007). Mental health and substance use disorders among Latino and Asian American lesbian, gay, and bisexual adults. *Journal of Consulting and Clinical Psychology, 75*(5), 785–794.

Cochran, S. D., Mays, V. M., & Sullivan, J. G. (2003). Prevalence of mental disorders, psychological distress, and mental health services use among lesbian, gay, and bisexual adults in the United States. *Journal of Consulting and Clinical Psychology, 71*(1), 53–61.

Compton, W. M., Thomas, Y. F., Stinson, F. S., & Grant, B. F. (2007). Prevalence, correlates, disability, and comorbidity of DSM-IV drug abuse and dependence in the United States: Results from the national epidemiologic survey on alcohol and related conditions. *Archives of General Psychiatry, 64*(5), 566–576.

Consolacion, T. B., Russell, S. T., Sue, S., Russell, S. T., & Joyner, K. (2004). Sex, race/ethnicity, and romantic attractions: Multiple minority status adolescents and mental health. *Cultural Diversity and Ethnic Minority Psychology, 10*(3), 200–214.

Corliss, H. L., Belzer, M., Forbes, C., & Wilson, E. C. (2007). An evaluation of service utilization among male to female transgender youth: Qualitative study of a clinic-based sample. *Journal of LGBT Health Research, 3*(2), 49–61.

Corliss, H. L., Cochran, S. D., & Mays, V. M. (2002). Reports of parental maltreatment during childhood in a United States population-based survey of homosexual, bisexual, and heterosexual adults. *Child Abuse and Neglect, 26*(11), 1165–1178.

Corliss, H., Cochran, S., & Mays, V. (2008). Sampling approaches to studying mental health concerns in the lesbian, gay, and bisexual community. In J. Martin & W. Meezan (Eds.), *Handbook of research methods with gay, lesbian, bisexual, and transgender populations* (pp. 131–158). New York: Harrington Park Press.

D'Augelli, A. R., Grossman, A. H., Hershberger, S. L., & O'Connell, T. S. (2001). Aspects of mental health among older lesbian, gay, and bisexual adults. *Aging and Mental Health, 5*(2), 149–158.

D'Augelli, A. R., Grossman, A. H., & Starks, M. T. (2006). Childhood gender atypicality, victimization, and PTSD among lesbian, gay, and bisexual youth. *Journal of Interpersonal Violence, 21*(11), 1462–1482.

Davison, G. C. (2001). Conceptual and ethical issues in therapy for the psychological problems of gay men, lesbians, and bisexuals. *Journal of Clinical Psychology, 57*(5), 695–704.

Diamond, L. M. (2003). New paradigms for research on heterosexual and sexual-minority development. *Journal of Clinical and Child Adolescent Psychology, 32*(4), 490–498.

Dilley, J. A., Simmons, K. W., Boysun, M. J., Pizacani, B. A., & Stark, M. J. (2010). Demonstrating the importance and feasibility of including sexual orientation in public health surveys: Health disparities in the Pacific Northwest. *American Journal of Public Health, 100*(3), 460–467.

DiStefano, A. S. (2008). Suicidality and self-harm among sexual minorities in Japan. *Quality of Health Research, 18*(10), 1429–1441.

Division 44/CLGBC Joint Task Force. (2000). Guidelines for psychotherapy with lesbian, gay, and bisexual clients. *American Psychologist, 55*(12), 1440–1451.

Drabble, L., Midanik, L. T., & Trocki, K. (2005). Reports of alcohol consumption and alcohol-related problems among homosexual, bisexual and heterosexual respondents: Results from the 2000 National Alcohol Survey. *Journal of Studies on Alcohol, 66*(1), 111–120.

Drescher, J. (2010). Queer diagnoses: Parallels and contrasts in the history of homosexuality, gender variance, and the diagnostic and statistical manual. *Archives of Sexual Behavior, 39*(2), 427–460.

Faulkner, A. H., & Cranston, K. (1998). Correlates of same-sex sexual behavior in a random sample of Massachusetts high school students. *American Journal of Public Health, 88*(2), 262–266.

Fergusson, D. M., Horwood, L. J., & Beautrais, A. L. (1999). Is sexual orientation related to mental health problems and suicidality in young people? *Archives of General Psychiatry, 56*(10), 876–880.

Fergusson, D. M., Horwood, L. J., Ridder, E. M., & Beautrais, A. L. (2005). Suicidal behaviour in adolescence and subsequent mental health outcomes in young adulthood. *Psychological Medicine, 35*(7), 983–993.

Garnets, L., Hancock, K. A., Cochran, S. D., Goodchilds, J., & Peplau, L. A. (1991). Issues in psychotherapy with lesbians and gay men. A survey of psychologists. *American Psychologist, 46*(9), 964–972.

Garofalo, R., Wolf, R. C., Kessel, S., Palfrey, S. J., & DuRant, R. H. (1998). The association between health risk behaviors and sexual orientation among a school-based sample of adolescents. *Pediatrics, 101*(5), 895–902.

Garofalo, R., Wolf, R. C., Wissow, L. S., Woods, E. R., & Goodman, E. (1999). Sexual orientation and risk of suicide attempts among a representative sample of youth. *Archives of Pediatrics and Adolescent Medicine, 153*(5), 487–493.

Gilman, S. E., Cochran, S. D., Mays, V. M., Hughes, M., Ostrow, D., & Kessler, R. C. (2001). Risk of psychiatric disorders among individuals reporting same-sex sexual partners in the National Comorbidity Survey. *American Journal of Public Health, 91*(6), 933–939.

Gonsiorek, J. C. (1996). Mental health and sexual orientation. In R. C. Savin-Williams & K. M. Cohen (Eds.), *The lives of lesbians, gays, and bisexuals: Children to adults* (pp. 462–478). Fort Worth, TX: Harcourt Brace College Publishers.

Gordon, A. R., & Meyer, I. H. (2007). Gender nonconformity as a target of prejudice, discrimination, and violence against LGB individuals. *Journal of LGBT Health Research, 3*(3), 55–71.

Grella, C. E., Greenwell, L., Mays, V. M., & Cochran, S. D. (2009). Influence of gender, sexual orientation, and need on treatment utilization for substance use and mental disorders: Findings from the California Quality of Life Survey. *BMC Psychiatry, 9,* 52.

Haldeman, D. C. (1994). The practice and ethics of sexual orientation conversion therapy. *Journal of Consulting and Clinical Psychology, 62*(2), 221–227.

Hanna, E. Z., & Grant, B. F. (1997). Gender differences in DSM-IV alcohol use disorders and major depression as distributed in the general population: Clinical implications. *Comprehensive Psychiatry, 38*(4), 202–212.

Harper, G. W., Jernewall, N., & Zea, M. C. (2004). Giving voice to emerging science and theory for lesbian, gay, and bisexual people of color. *Cultural Diversity and Ethnic Minority Psychology, 10*(3), 187–199.

Hatzenbuehler, M. L., Keyes, K. M., & Hasin, D. S. (2009). State-level policies and psychiatric morbidity in lesbian, gay, and bisexual populations. *American Journal of Public Health, 99*(12), 2275–2281.

Hatzenbuehler, M. L., McLaughlin, K. A., Keyes, K. M., & Hasin, D. S. (2010). The impact of institutional discrimination on psychiatric disorders in lesbian, gay, and bisexual populations: A prospective study. *American Journal of Public Health, 100*(3), 452–459.

Hatzenbuehler, M. L., Nolen-Hoeksema, S., & Dovidio, J. (2009). How does stigma "get under the skin"?: The mediating role of emotion regulation. *Psychological Science, 20*(10), 1282–1289.

Hatzenbuehler, M. L., Nolen-Hoeksema, S., & Erickson, S. J. (2008). Minority stress predictors of HIV risk behavior, substance use, and depressive symptoms:

Results from a prospective study of bereaved gay men. *Health Psychology, 27*(4), 455–462.

Herek, G. M. (2009a). Hate crimes and stigma-related experiences among sexual minority adults in the United States: Prevalence estimates from a national probability sample. *Journal of Interpersonal Violence, 24*(1), 54–74.

Herek, G. M. (2009b). Sexual stigma and sexual prejudice in the United States: A conceptual framework. *Nebraska Symposium on Motivation, 54*, 65–111.

Herek, G. M., & Garnets, L. D. (2007). Sexual orientation and mental health. *Annual Review of Clinical Psychology, 3*, 353–375.

Herrell, R., Goldberg, J., True, W. R., Ramakrishnan, V., Lyons, M., Eisen, S., et al. (1999). Sexual orientation and suicidality: A co-twin control study in adult men. *Archives of General Psychiatry, 56*(10), 867–874.

Hershberger, S. L., Pilkington, N. W., & D'Augelli, A. R. (1997). Predictors of suicide attempts among gay, lesbian, and bisexual youth. *Journal of Adolescent Research, 12*(4), 477–497.

Hooker, E. (1957). The adjustment of the male overt homosexual. *Journal of Projective Techniques, 21*, 17–31.

Huebner, D. M., Rebchook, G. M., & Kegeles, S. M. (2004). Experiences of harassment, discrimination, and physical violence among young gay and bisexual men. *American Journal of Public Health, 94*(7), 1200–1203.

Jiang, Y., Perry, D. K., & Hesser, J. E. (2010). Adolescent suicide and health risk behaviors: Rhode Island's 2007 Youth Risk Behavior Survey. *American Journal of Preventive Medicine, 38*(5), 551–555.

Jones, M. A., & Gabriel, M. A. (1999). Utilization of psychotherapy by lesbians, gay men, and bisexuals: Findings from a nationwide survey. *American Journal of Orthopsychiatry, 69*(2), 209–219.

Jorm, A. F., Korten, A. E., Rodgers, B., Jacomb, P. A., & Christensen, H. (2002). Sexual orientation and mental health: Results from a community survey of young and middle-aged adults. *British Journal of Psychiatry, 180*, 423–427.

Kaiser Family Foundation. (1999). *Americans on Values Follow-Up Survey, 1998.* Retrieved 05/07, 2010, from http://www.kff.org/kaiserpolls/1441-index.cfm.

Kertzner, R. M., Meyer, I. H., Frost, D. M., & Stirratt, M. J. (2009). Social and psychological well-being in lesbians, gay men, and bisexuals: The effects of race, gender, age, and sexual identity. *American Journal of Orthopsychiatry, 79*(4), 500–510.

Kessler, R. C., Berglund, P., Demler, O., Jin, R., Merikangas, K. R., & Walters, E. E. (2005). Lifetime prevalence and age-of-onset distributions of DSM-IV disorders in the National Comorbidity Survey Replication. *Archives of General Psychiatry, 62*(6), 593–602.

Kessler, R. C., Mickelson, K. D., & Williams, D. R. (1999). The prevalence, distribution, and mental health correlates of perceived discrimination in the United States. *Journal of Health and Social Behavior, 40*(3), 208–230.

Kilpatrick, D. G., & Acierno, R. (2003). Mental health needs of crime victims: Epidemiology and outcomes. *Journal of Traumatic Stress, 16*(2), 119–132.

King, M., Semlyen, J., Tai, S. S., Killaspy, H., Osborn, D., Popelyuk, D., et al. (2008). A systematic review of mental disorder, suicide, and deliberate self harm in lesbian, gay and bisexual people. *BMC Psychiatry, 8*, 70.

Krieger, N., & Sidney, S. (1997). Prevalence and health implications of anti-gay discrimination: A study of black and white women and men in the CARDIA cohort. *International Journal of Health Services, 27*(1), 157–176.

Laumann, E. O., Gagnon, J. H., Michael, R. T., & Michaels, S. (1994). *The social organization of sexuality: Sexual practices in the United States.* Chicago, IL: University of Chicago Press.

Liddle, B. J. (1997). Gay and lesbian clients' selection of therapists and utilization of therapy. *Psychotherapy: Theory, Research, Practice and Training, 34*(1), 11–18.

Mathy, R. M., Cochran, S. D., Olsen, J., & Mays, V. M. (2009). The association between relationship markers of sexual orientation and suicide: Denmark, 1990–2001. *Social Psychiatry and Psychiatric Epidemiology, 46*(2), 111–117.

Mays, V. M., Chatters, L. M., Cochran, S. D., & Mackness, J. (1998). African American families in diversity: Gay men and lesbians as participants in family networks. *Journal of Comparative Family Studies, 29*, 73–88.

Mays, V. M., & Cochran, S. D. (2001). Mental health correlates of perceived discrimination among lesbian, gay, and bisexual adults in the United States. *American Journal of Public Health, 91*(11), 1869–1876.

Mays, V. M., Cochran, S. D., Barnes, N., & Woods, J. (2007). Race, racism and discrimination in the physical health outcomes of African Americans. *Annual Review of Psychology, 58*, 201–225.

Mays, V. M., Cochran, S. D., & Rhue, S. (1993). The impact of perceived discrimination on the intimate relationships of black lesbians. *Journal of Homosexuality, 25*(4), 1–14.

Mays, V. M., Cochran, S. D., & Roeder, M. R. (2004). Depressive distress and prevalence of common problems among homosexually active African American women in the United States. *Journal of Psychology and Human Sexuality, 12*(2/3), 27–46.

Mays, V. M., Ponce, N. A., Washington, D. L., & Cochran, S. D. (2003). Classification of race and ethnicity: Implications for public health. *Annual Review of Public Health, 24*, 83–110.

McCabe, S. E., Bostwick, W. B., Hughes, T. L., West, B. T., & Boyd, C. J. (2010). The relationship between discrimination and substance use disorders among lesbian, gay, and bisexual adults in the United States. *American Journal of Public Health, 100*(10), 1946–1952.

McCabe, S. E., Hughes, T. L., Bostwick, W. B., West, B. T., & Boyd, C. J. (2009). Sexual orientation, substance use behaviors and substance dependence in the United States. *Addiction, 104*(8), 1333–1345.

McHugh, R. K., & Barlow, D. H. (2010). The dissemination and implementation of evidence-based psychological treatments. A review of current efforts. *American Psychologist, 65*(2), 73–84.

Meyer, I. H. (2003). Prejudice, social stress, and mental health in lesbian, gay, and bisexual populations: Conceptual issues and research evidence. *Psychological Bulletin, 129*(5), 674–697.

Meyer, I. H., & Dean, L. (1995). Patterns of sexual behavior and risk taking among young New York City gay men. *AIDS Education and Prevention, 7*(5), 13–23.

Meyer, I. H., Dietrich, J., & Schwartz, S. (2008). Lifetime prevalence of mental disorders and suicide attempts in diverse lesbian, gay, and bisexual populations. *American Journal of Public Health, 98*(6), 1004–1006.

Midanik, L. T., Drabble, L., Trocki, K., & Sell, R. L. (2007). Sexual orientation and alcohol use: Identity versus behavior measures. *Journal of LGBT Health Research, 3*(1), 25–35.

Mills, T. C., Paul, J., Stall, R., Pollack, L., Canchola, J., Chang, Y. J., et al. (2004). Distress and depression in men who have sex with men: The Urban Men's Health Study. *American Journal of Psychiatry, 161*(2), 278–285.

Nasuti, L., Cochran, S. D., & Mays, V. M. (2010). Sexual orientation and suicide attempts: Results from the California Quality of Life Survey II. Paper presented at the American Public Health Association meetings, November 1010, Denver CO. Abstract available at https://apha.confex.com/apha/138am/webprogram/Paper219260.html.

Nellos, C., Cochran, S. D., & Mays, V. M. (2002). *Trends in life satisfaction among individuals reporting same-gender sexual behavior in the 1988–2000 General Social Survey.* Paper presented at the American Public Health Association Meetings, Philadelphia, PA.

Noell, J. W., & Ochs, L. M. (2001). Relationship of sexual orientation to substance use, suicidal ideation, suicide attempts, and other factors in a population of homeless adolescents. *Journal of Adolescent Health, 29*(1), 31–36.

Nuttbrock, L., Hwahng, S., Bockting, W., Rosenblum, A., Mason, M., Macri, M., et al. (2010). Psychiatric impact of gender-related abuse across the life course of male-to-female transgender persons. *Journal of Sex Research, 47*(1), 12–23.

Office of Applied Studies–SAMHSA. (2010). *National Household Survey on Drug Abuse: Population estimates, 2009, Office of Applied Studies, SAMHSA.* Rockville, MD: U.S. Department of Health and Human Services.

Paul, J. P., Catania, J., Pollack, L., Moskowitz, J., Canchola, J., Mills, T., et al. (2002). Suicide attempts among gay and bisexual men: Lifetime prevalence and antecedents. *American Journal of Public Health, 92*(8), 1338–1345.

Paul, J. P., Catania, J., Pollack, L., & Stall, R. (2001). Understanding childhood sexual abuse as a predictor of sexual risk-taking among men who have sex with men: The Urban Men's Health Study. *Child Abuse & Neglect, 25*(4), 557–584.

Pew Research Center. (2010). *Americans' Acceptance of Gay Relations Crosses 50% Threshold.* From http://pewforum.org/Gay-Marriage-and-Homosexuality/Majority-Continues-To-Support-Civil-Unions.aspx.

Ploderl, M., Kralovec, K., & Fartacek, R. (2010). The relation between sexual orientation and suicide attempts in Austria. *Archives of Sexual Behavior, 39*(6), 1403–1414.

Ponce, N., Cochran, S., Pizer, J., & Mays, V. M. (2010). Unequal access to health insurance for same sex couples: A California analysis. *Health Affairs, 29*(8), 1539–1548.

Qin, P., Agerbo, E., & Mortensen, P. B. (2003). Suicide risk in relation to socioeconomic, demographic, psychiatric, and familial factors: A national register-based study of all suicides in Denmark, 1981–1997. *American Journal of Psychiatry, 160*(4), 765–772.

Raymond, H., Chen, Y. H., Stall, R. D., & McFarland, W. (2010). Adolescent experiences of discrimination, harassment, connectedness to community and comfort with sexual orientation reported by adult men who have sex with men as a predictor of adult HIV status. *AIDS and Behavior, 23*(1), 23–28.

Relf, M. V., Huang, B., Campbell, J., & Catania, J. (2004). Gay identity, interpersonal violence, and HIV risk behaviors: An empirical test of theoretical relationships among a probability-based sample of urban men who have sex with men. *Journal of the Association of Nurses in AIDS Care, 15*(2), 14–26.

Remafedi, G., French, S., Story, M., Resnick, M. D., & Blum, R. (1998). The relationship between suicide risk and sexual orientation: Results of a population-based study. *American Journal of Public Health, 88*(1), 57–60.

Roberts, A. L., Austin, S. B., Corliss, H. L., Vandermorris, A. K., & Koenen, K. C. (2010). Pervasive trauma exposure among U.S. sexual orientation minority adults and risk of posttraumatic stress disorder. *American Journal of Public Health, 100*(12), 2433–2441.

Rock, M., Carlson, T. S., & McGeorge, C. R. (2010). Does affirmative training matter? Assessing CFT students' beliefs about sexual orientation and their level of affirmative training. *Journal of Marital and Family Therapy, 36*(2), 171–184.

Rosario, M. (2008). Elevated substance use among lesbian and bisexual women: Possible explanations and intervention implications for an urgent public health concern. *Substance Use and Misuse, 43*(8–9), 1268–1270.

Ross, L. E., Dobinson, C., & Eady, A. (2010). Perceived determinants of mental health for bisexual people:

A qualitative examination. *American Journal of Public Health, 100*(3), 496–502.

Rothblum, E. D. (1994). "I only read about myself on bathroom walls": The need for research on the mental health of lesbians and gay men. *Journal of Consulting and Clinical Psychology, 62*(2), 213–220.

Russell, S. T., Clarke, T. J., & Clary, J. (2009). Are teens "post-gay"? Contemporary adolescents' sexual identity labels. *Journal of Youth and Adolescence, 38*(7), 884–890.

Russell, S. T., & Joyner, K. (2001). Adolescent sexual orientation and suicide risk: Evidence from a national study. *American Journal of Public Health, 91*(8), 1276–1281.

Rutter, M. (2002). The interplay of nature, nurture, and developmental influences: The challenge ahead for mental health. *Archives of General Psychiatry, 59*(11), 996–1000.

Saewyc, E. M., Bearinger, L. H., Heinz, P. A., Blum, R. W., & Resnick, M. D. (1998). Gender differences in health and risk behaviors among bisexual and homosexual adolescents. *Journal of Adolescent Health, 23*(3), 181–188.

Sanchez, F. J., & Vilain, E. (2009). Collective self-esteem as a coping resource for male-to-female transsexuals. *Journal of Counseling Psychology, 56*(1), 202–209.

Sandfort, T. G., Bakker, F., Schellevis, F. G., & Vanwesenbeeck, I. (2006). Sexual orientation and mental and physical health status: Findings from a Dutch population survey. *American Journal of Public Health, 96*(6), 1119–1125.

Sandfort, T. G., de Graaf, R., & Bijl, R. V. (2003). Same-sex sexuality and quality of life: Findings from the Netherlands Mental Health Survey and Incidence Study. *Archives of Sexual Behavior, 32*(1), 15–22.

Sandfort, T. G., de Graaf, R., Bijl, R. V., & Schnabel, P. (2001). Same-sex sexual behavior and psychiatric disorders: Findings from the Netherlands Mental Health Survey and Incidence Study (NEMESIS). *Archives of General Psychiatry, 58*(1), 85–91.

Savin-Williams, R. C., & Dube, E. M. (1998). Parental reactions to their child's disclosure of a gay/lesbian identity. *Family Relations: Interdisciplinary Journal of Applied Family Studies, 47*(1), 7–13.

Sell, R. (2010). *Gaydata.org.* Retrieved 05/05, 2010, from http://www.gaydata.org/.

Skegg, K., Nada-Raja, S., Dickson, N., Paul, C., & Williams, S. (2003). Sexual orientation and self-harm in men and women. *American Journal of Psychiatry, 160*(3), 541–546.

Spitzer, R. L. (2003). Can some gay men and lesbians change their sexual orientation? 200 participants reporting a change from homosexual to heterosexual orientation. *Archives of Sexual Behavior, 32*(5), 403–417.

Surgeon General. (2001). *National strategy for suicide prevention: Goals and objectives for action.* Washington, DC: DHHS.

Terry, J. (1999). *An American obsession: Science, medicine, and homosexuality in modern society.* Chicago: University of Chicago Press.

Tjepkema, M. (2008). Health care use among gay, lesbian and bisexual Canadians. *Health Reports, 19*(1), 53–64.

Trocki, K. F., Drabble, L. A., & Midanik, L. T. (2009). Tobacco, marijuana, and sensation seeking: Comparisons across gay, lesbian, bisexual, and heterosexual groups. *Psychology of Addictive Behavior, 23*(4), 620–631.

Weinrich, J. D., Snyder, P. J., Pillard, R. C., Grant, I., Jacobson, D. L., Robinson, S. R., et al. (1993). A factor analysis of the Klein Sexual Orientation Grid in two disparate samples. *Archives of Sexual Behavior, 22*(2), 157–168.

Xia, Q., Molitor, F., Osmond, D. H., Tholandi, M., Pollack, L. M., Ruiz, J. D., et al. (2006). Knowledge of sexual partner's HIV serostatus and serosorting practices in a California population-based sample of men who have sex with men. *AIDS, 20*(16), 2081–2089.

Xu, F., Sternberg, M. R., & Markowitz, L. E. (2010). Men who have sex with men in the United States: Demographic and behavioral characteristics and prevalence of HIV and HSV-2 infection: results from National Health and Nutrition Examination Survey 2001–2006. *Sexually Transmitted Disease, 37*(6), 399–405.

Yoshikawa, H., Wilson, P. A., Chae, D. H., & Cheng, J. F. (2004). Do family and friendship networks protect against the influence of discrimination on mental health and HIV risk among Asian and Pacific Islander gay men? *AIDS Education and Prevention, 16*(1), 84–100.

Zhao, Y., Montoro, R., Igartua, K., & Thombs, B. D. (2010). Suicidal ideation and attempt among adolescents reporting "unsure" sexual identity or heterosexual identity plus same-sex attraction or behavior: Forgotten groups? *Journal of the American Academy of Child and Adolescent Psychiatry, 49*(2), 104–113.

16

Sexual Orientation and Family Lives

CHARLOTTE J. PATTERSON

In the lives of most people, family relationships are central. Like others around them, lesbian, gay, and bisexual people are born into families, sustain lifelong relationships with members of their birth families, and create new families of their own. For the heterosexual majority, laws and customs have been built up over time to recognize and protect important family relationships. In some jurisdictions, however, some or all of the family ties of nonheterosexual people are not recognized by law or custom, creating many challenges for them and for their family members. In the contemporary world, the family lives of lesbian, gay, and bisexual people are contested terrain, and family ties of non-heterosexual people are often subject to a variety of special stressors.

Controversy about the family lives of lesbian, gay, and bisexual people takes many forms. Media portrayals of sexual minority individuals vary across an enormous range. Political, cultural, and religious leaders may support or oppose legal recognition for same-sex couple relationships. Controversy has also surrounded parenting by lesbian, gay, and bisexual adults, with some observers expressing fear about the impact of lesbian or gay parents on children, and others suggesting that nonheterosexual people may bring many special strengths to parenthood. Almost nothing about lesbian, gay, and bisexual individuals' family lives has gone uncontested.

Some aspects of the family relationships of non-heterosexual people have, however, been more subject to challenge than others. Public controversies have often focused on family formation within the context of nonheterosexual identities. It is generally understood that lesbian and gay adults have mothers, fathers, siblings, and other relatives in their families of origin. It is not, however, as widely presumed that nonheterosexual individuals might form long-term partnerships and/or marry same-sex partners, and have children. Members of a same-sex couple and their children generally have no trouble identifying themselves as each other's family members, but this attitude may not be shared by public authorities such as legislatures and courts. In short, the legitimacy of family ties in nonheterosexual peoples' families of origin is rarely challenged from the outside, but the legitimacy of ties within their families of creation is more often the subject of public controversy.

Thus, when a youth reveals a nonheterosexual identity to his or her parents, this revelation very rarely causes any public controversy. Private questions about family ties do, however, sometimes arise. Some parents find it difficult or impossible to accept that a family member could identify as nonheterosexual, and may therefore deny any connection with gay sons or lesbian daughters by "disowning" them and/or by banishing them from the family home. Lesbian, gay, and bisexual youth and young adults put connections within their families of origin at risk when they acknowledge minority identities and "come out" to parents. The risk is, however, private in nature; it does not involve the law. Challenges to lesbian, gay, and bisexual individuals' ties within the family of origin are most often private in nature, and they most often occur within the family itself.

Challenges to relationships within families of creation for nonheterosexual people, in contrast, are most often public. Thus, the family ties of lesbian, gay, and bisexual people within families of origin usually go without public controversy and those within families of creation most often go without private challenge. This asymmetrical nature of debate relevant to the family lives of non-heterosexual individuals shapes the character of the research literatures in the two areas. Research on families of origin generally has focused on private relationships—e.g., on how antigay prejudice may affect family interactions, relationships, and overall family climate. Research on families of creation has more often focused on the interface of families with institutions and contexts external to them—e.g., the impact of barriers to family formation that have been erected in law and policy. Of course, these are matters of emphasis; parent–adolescent relationships do not occur in a legal vacuum, nor do legal challenges to same-sex marriage occur without relation to families of origin. Overall, however, the research literature on these two topics are quite different in character.

In what follows, psychological research and theory about families of origin are reviewed first. Based on a life course perspective, research on adolescents and young adults is reviewed first, followed by that on middle adulthood, and then by research on relationships with families of origin in later adulthood. An overview of research and theory on families of creation is presented next, focusing on the formation and maintenance of same-sex couple relationships as well as on issues related to parenthood. A third section presents a summary of research on children and other relatives of nonheterosexual individuals. In a final section, conclusions and suggestions for further research are offered.

FAMILIES OF ORIGIN

In this section, research and theory on nonheterosexual individuals' relationships within families of origin are presented first. Research about adolescents and young adults is reviewed next, followed by that on middle adulthood, and then the literature on later adulthood. Issues within the family are the primary focus.

Adolescents and Young Adults

For young lesbian, gay, and bisexual young people, relationships with their parents are an issue of great concern (see also Rosario and Schrimshaw, Chapter 7, this volume). Some youngsters may begin to recognize same-sex attractions and desires as early as 8 or 9 years of age, but few disclose these to parents at this time. Some may disclose nonheterosexual identities to parents while in middle school or high school (Herdt & Boxer, 1996), but others wait until the end of adolescence or even until early adulthood (Savin-Williams, 1998; Savin-Williams & Diamond, 2000). Thus, many nonheterosexual youth spend large portions of their adolescence attempting to keep their sexual desires and attractions secret from parents (Savin-Williams & Diamond, 2000).

As social climates have been changing over recent years, some lesbian and gay youth seem to be coming out earlier (Herdt & Boxer, 1996; Savin-Williams, 2005). For example, Floyd and Bakeman (2006) surveyed 767 adults about their coming out experiences. They found that most participants reported being aware of same-sex attractions in early adolescence, but most did not recall disclosing lesbian or gay identities to anyone until they were in their 20s. Interestingly, younger adults recalled having come out to parents and others sooner than did older adults. This result suggests the importance of historical change in making possible greater openness about sexual identities (Floyd & Bakeman, 2006). On the other hand, more recent evidence suggests that even among older lesbian and gay adults, many remember coming out at early ages (Calzo, Antonucci, Mays, & Cochran, 2011). Thus, questions about historical change in age at coming out are not yet settled.

When youth do want to talk about their sexual minority identities, they are likely to worry about parental reactions (D'Augelli, Grossman, Starks, & Sinclair, 2010; D'Augelli, Hershberger, & Pilkington, 1998). Most youth report telling a friend before telling parents, and most report that they told their mothers before they told their fathers (Rosario, Schrimshaw, & Hunter, 2009). Some parents may respond in neutral or positive ways to this kind of news about their offspring, but initial responses from parents have generally been described as more negative (Savin-Williams, 2001). As parents adjust over time to the reality that their son or daughter may not be heterosexual, parental reactions often grow more accepting, but complete acceptance upon first disclosure is apparently not yet commonplace.

The extremity of parental negative responses to a youth's disclosure of nonheterosexual identity may vary across a wide range. Some parents may offer support or mild disapproval, but others may be much more rejecting. In a review of seven population-based high school health surveys conducted in the United States and Canada, the prevalence of physical abuse by family members was greater for sexual minority youth than for their heterosexual peers (Saewyc et al., 2006). The risk of homelessness is also greater among nonheterosexual than among heterosexual youth (Cochran,

Stewart, Ginzler, & Cauce, 2002; Corliss, Cochran, Mays, Greenland, & Seeman, 2009) It is not clear whether the elevated risk of homelessness occurs because some maltreated youth leave home, because some parents have ejected nonheterosexual youth from their homes, or for some other reason. It is clear, however, that parental reactions to sons' and daughters' disclosure of nonheterosexual identities can span a wide range of emotions, with varying consequences for youth.

Reactions of family members to learning of youth nonheterosexuality are associated with many important outcomes among adolescents and young adults. Many investigators have reported strong correlations between youth reports about parental behavior and youth symptoms. For example, working with data from the National Longitudinal Study of Adolescent Health, Needham and Austin (2010) found that nonheterosexual young adults who saw their parents as supportive reported less drug use, fewer depressive symptoms, and less suicidal ideation. Similar findings have been reported by others (Ryan, Huebner, Diaz, & Sanchez, 2009; Rosario, Schrimshaw, & Hunter, 2009). Working with a community sample of lesbian, gay, and bisexual adolescents, Ryan, Russell, Huebner, Diaz, and Sanchez (2010) found that supportive parental behavior was associated with greater self-esteem, more perceived social support, and better overall physical health among these youth.

Thus, relationships with parents are a crucial context for development of nonheterosexual adolescents and young adults. Rejection of youth by parents and other family members can prove difficult or even devastating for youth development during the transition to adulthood. Acceptance and support, on the other hand, are associated with positive outcomes.

Middle and Later Adulthood

The role of the family of origin in the lives of nonheterosexual adults is as yet little understood. One important issue is the extent to which a lesbian, gay, or bisexual adult has disclosed a nonheterosexual identity to parents and siblings. As discussed above, many adolescents and young adults disclose lesbian, gay, or bisexual identities to parents. On the other hand, some middle aged and older adults report that they have never disclosed nonheterosexuality to parents or siblings. For example, in one study of 416 nonheterosexual adults over 60 years

of age, parents and siblings were among the most likely members of social networks to be described as not knowing or suspecting a participants' lesbian, gay, or bisexual identity (Grossman, D'Augelli, & Hershberger, 2000). In the Metlife Study of lesbian, gay, bisexual, and transgender adults, 45 to 64 years of age, most participants described members of their families of origin as aware of and supportive of their sexual identities, but 20% of lesbians and gay men reported being guarded about their nonheterosexual identities with parents and siblings (Metlife, 2010). Thus, many lesbian and gay adults appear to enjoy warm and close relationships with parents and siblings, but others have experienced distance and rejection.

Research has also consistently found that lesbian and gay adults report receiving less social support from members of their families of origin, but more from friends, than do their heterosexual counterparts (Kurdek, 2005). In a study of a community sample of lesbian, gay, and heterosexual people over 60 years of age, Dorfman and her colleagues (1995) found that although lesbians and gay men received more support from friends, and heterosexual adults received more support from family members, the overall levels of support were the same for both groups. Because some lesbians and gay men have suffered intolerance and rejection at the hands of parents and siblings, the overall level of contact and support that adults receive from members of their families of origin seems to vary as a function of sexual orientation.

Rejection and distance can be emotional, but they can also be behavioral in nature. Perhaps as a result of rejection by family members, or for other reasons, lesbian and gay adults may choose to live at greater distances from their parents than do their heterosexual siblings. For example, Rothblum and Factor (2001) reported that lesbians lived further away from their parents than did their heterosexual sisters. Working with data from the 1990 and 2000 United States Census, Rosenfeld (2007) also found that same-sex couples were more likely than heterosexual couples to live in a different state than the one in which they had been born. When families of origin are not supportive, lesbian and gay adults may seek to distance themselves both emotionally and geographically from them.

Despite whatever distancing of lesbian and gay adults from their families of origin may be taking place, nonheterosexual adults are still among the most likely caregivers for their own aging parents. Among 45- to 64-year-old adults in the Metlife Study who said they were providing care for another person, parents and partners/spouses were the two most frequent categories for lesbian and gay as well as for heterosexual adults (Metlife, 2010). At the same time, lesbian and gay adults were far more likely than heterosexual adults to be providing care for a friend, perhaps because of the prominence of friends in the social networks of lesbian and gay adults (Metlife, 2010). In fact, the place played by families of origin in the lives of heterosexual adults may be taken for many lesbians and gay men by networks of close friends in what have been termed "chosen families," which are discussed below (see also, Grossman, Frank, and McCutcheon, Chapter 10, this volume).

FAMILIES OF CREATION

In this section, research on the formation and maintenance of same-sex couple relationships is considered. Because this topic has been treated at length elsewhere in this volume (see Fingerhut and Peplau, Chapter 12, this volume), only a very abbreviated overview is offered here. This is followed by a review of issues related to parenthood and chosen families.

Same-Sex Couple Relationships

The formation, maintenance, and dissolution of same-sex couple relationships have all been the topics of considerable research. Recent public controversies over legal recognition of the relationships of same-sex couples have formed an important aspect of the background against which studies in this area have been conducted in recent years (Badgett, 2009). Legal and policy climates in which lesbian and gay individuals negotiate their relationships have changed more rapidly in some jurisdictions than in others, with the result that from a global perspective, legal environments for same-sex couples are now extremely diverse. In some jurisdictions (e.g., in Canada and in some parts of Europe and the United States), legal recognition for same-sex couples is now commonplace, whereas in others (e.g., in African and Asian nations, as well as in most of the United States), such recognition is forbidden by law (Patterson, Riskind, & Tornello, in press).

This state of affairs has had several implications for members of sexual minorities. Levels of minority stress (see Meyer and Frost, Chapter 18, this volume) experienced by same-sex couples vary dramatically across contexts, and significant associations between legal recognition for same-sex couple relationships and mental health of same-sex couples have been reported (Hatzenbuehler, Keyes, & Hasin, 2009; Riggle, Rostosky, & Horne, 2010). Moreover, aspects of the debates over such policies themselves have proven to be stressful for lesbian and gay adults (Riggle, Rostosky & Horne, 2009; Rostosky, Riggle, Horne, & Miller, 2009). On the other hand, research has also revealed that those who have achieved legal recognition for their same-sex couple relationships are less likely to experience the dissolution of those relationships than are those who did not receive legal recognition (Balsam, Beauchaine, Rothblum, & Solomon, 2008). Thus, many aspects of same-sex couple relationships are affected by the nature of legal and policy climates in which they take place. For a further discussion of same-sex couple relationships, see Fingerhut and Peplau (Chapter 12, this volume).

Pathways to Parenthood

Parenthood is one of the world's most universal desires. According to data from the 2002 National Survey of Family Growth (NSFG), more than 90% of American women either have children or expect to do so in the future; only 6% are voluntarily childless (Chandra, Martinez, Mosher, Abma, & Jones, 2005). Moreover, parenthood is even more valued by adults living outside the United States; a Gallup Poll found that the majority of adults in 14 of 16 countries considered parenthood to be necessary for personal fulfillment (Patterson & Riskind, 2010).

Despite the cultural value placed on parenthood, lesbian and gay adults are less likely than heterosexual adults to become parents. In the 2002 NSFG, 35% of lesbians aged 15 to 44 reported having given birth to at least one child, compared to 65% of same-aged heterosexual women. For men, the comparable figures were 16% of gay men compared to 48% of heterosexual men (Gates, Badgett, Macomber, & Chambers, 2007).

Despite the reduced probability of parenthood among lesbian and gay adults, some nonheterosexual men and women are parents. Especially among older cohorts, many of these individuals had children in the context of heterosexual marriages that dissolved when one or both members of the couple came out as lesbian or gay. Thus, many lesbian and gay adults are parenting children who were born or adopted in the context of previous heterosexual relationships. In an Internet study of gay fathers, Tornello and Patterson (2011) reported that a great majority of those over 50 years of age had children from previous marriages, whereas fewer than half of those under 50 reported having had children in this way. Moreover, they also found this pattern to be characteristic of gay fathers from Canada, the United Kingdom, Australia, and New Zealand (Patterson & Tornello, 2010). Some evidence suggests the existence of a similar pattern of behavior among older and younger lesbian women (Morris, Balsam, & Rothblum, 2002).

Thus, although some nonheterosexual adults married opposite-sex partners, had children, and later came out as gay or lesbian, other pathways to parenthood are becoming available to at least some lesbian and gay adults today (Goldberg, 2010; Golombok & Tasker, 2010; Mallon, 2004; Riskind & Patterson, 2010). In particular, lesbians are conceiving children via donor insemination and gay men are conceiving children via in vitro fertilization and surrogacy. Both coupled lesbians and gay men are also becoming adoptive and foster parents (Brodzinsky & Pertman, 2012).

With an increase in the number of different pathways to parenthood for nonheterosexual adults has come an increase also in the diversity of families formed in these ways. For instance, transracial adoptions seem to be more common among same-sex than opposite-sex couples (Farr & Patterson, 2009). Likewise, given that many nonheterosexual individuals use various forms of assisted reproductive technology in their efforts to have children, social and biological (e.g., genetic) parenting roles may often be filled by different people. For instance, social parents may live with their children but not have any genetic links with them, or sperm donors may be genetically linked with children they do not know. In other cases, gay men and lesbian women may join together to bear and rear children; they may live in a single home or they may maintain multiple households (Telingator & Patterson, 2008). Many new contexts for child rearing are emerging in lesbian and gay communities.

Despite the existence of lesbian mothers and gay fathers who are rearing children today, many fewer lesbian or gay than heterosexual adults express a desire for parenthood. For example, data from the 2002 NSFG revealed that of childless participants who were 15 to 44 years of age, 67% of heterosexual men but only 52% of gay men expressed a desire to become parents; for women, the comparable figures were 53% of heterosexual women but only 41% of lesbian women (Gates et al., 2007). Moreover, among men who expressed an interest in becoming fathers, many fewer gay than heterosexual men said that they intended to do so (Riskind & Patterson, 2010). More recent Internet surveys reported that the gap between parenting desires and parenting intentions was significant for both gay men and lesbian women, relative to their heterosexual peers (Riskind, Nosek, & Patterson, 2011). Thus, like heterosexual individuals who experience infertility or other forms of involuntary childlessness, nonheterosexual adults who do not realize their hopes of having children may be at risk for considerable emotional pain.

Transitions to Parenthood

Regardless of parental sexual orientation, the transition to parenthood is a time of upheaval that involves substantial changes in parents' pre-existing relationships and routines. As families adjust to caring for a newborn infant or newly adopted child, they make changes in their ways of managing daily life; inevitably, new tasks are added, and familiar ones are transformed. New parents find themselves with more work and less free time than they had before becoming parents. These changes in turn may influence overall parental well-being and adjustment. How this process unfolds in heterosexual families has been the subject of considerable research (e.g., Cowan & Cowan, 1988), but it is only beginning to be studied among families headed by lesbian and gay parents (Goldberg, 2010).

With respect to perinatal issues, such as pregnancy loss, infant mortality, and postpartum depression, relatively little is yet known (Ross, 2005). Due to contextual factors such as the availability of social support, as well as to the added investment that many lesbians have made to become pregnant, there is some suggestion that the pain of pregnancy loss may be amplified for them, relative to that among heterosexual women (Peel, 2010). Lesbian women may also be at heightened risk for postpartum depression compared to heterosexual women (e.g., Ross, 2005; Ross, Steele, Goldfinger, & Strike, 2007; Trettin, Moses-Kolko, & Wisner, 2006). Almost nothing is known about other perinatal issues for lesbians or bisexual women, or about the experiences of gay or bisexual men in this regard.

Some information is available about the transformation of lesbian and gay parents' social relationships after the birth or adoption of a child. Like other new parents, lesbian and gay parents are very likely to report decreases in sexual activity during the transition to parenthood (Gartrell et al., 2000; Goldberg & Sayer, 2006; Mallon, 2004). Overall satisfaction with couple relationships seems to fall during this period (Goldberg & Sayer, 2006). Also like other new parents, however, many first-time lesbian mothers and gay fathers remark on how the new member of the family has drawn other family members closer together. Even family members whose initial reactions may have been icy have been described as warming up after the arrival of an infant or child (Goldberg, 2006; Patterson, 1998). Thus, some lesbian mothers may have experiences of greater social support from their own parents than do lesbian women who remain childless (DeMino, Appleby, & Fisk, 2007). Consistent with this view, Gartrell and her colleagues (2000, 2006) reported that in their longitudinal study of lesbian mothers and their children, grandparents were increasingly open in their social networks about daughters' lesbian identities.

Lesbian mothers and gay fathers also report that their social support networks shift in such a way as to allow more contact with other parents over time (Goldberg, 2010). Because fewer lesbian and gay than heterosexual adults have children, this shift may, however, have different results for nonheterosexual than for heterosexual parents. Whereas heterosexual parents are likely to find this shift results in them feeling more embedded in a unified parenting community, some lesbian and gay parents may experience it as more of a splintering of their social lives into time with childless lesbian and gay friends, on the one hand, or with heterosexual parents, on the other. The greater numbers of childless adults in lesbian and gay as compared to heterosexual communities can also cut both ways; it can make parenting somewhat less normative for lesbian and gay adults, but it can also mean greater availability of willing courtesy "aunts" and "uncles" for some families (Patterson, 1998).

As enormous an adjustment as the transition to parenthood is for lesbian and gay adults, it appears that, similar to heterosexual adults, most navigate it with success. Lesbian and gay parents of young children rate their own parental competence as being high (Farr, Forssell, & Patterson, 2010). A substantial research literature has found that mental health is relatively high among lesbian and gay parents (Goldberg, 2010; Golombok & Tasker, 2010; Patterson, 2011, in press), as well as among their children (Biblarz & Stacey, 2010; Patterson, 2009). Thus, despite some special issues, the transition to parenthood appears to leave most lesbian and gay parents in a position to be successful in their roles as parents.

The Social Worlds of Parents and Children

Lesbian and gay parents have been found to maintain generally supportive relationships both with their children and their teenaged offspring (Brewaeys et al., 1997; Golombok et al., 1983; Wainright, Russell, & Patterson, 2004). Most studies have focused on lesbian mothers and have highlighted the greater involvement of co-mothers than of fathers or stepfathers in heterosexual parent families (Tasker & Golombok, 1997). Research is beginning to explore these issues among gay fathers as well as among lesbian mothers and the results thus far have been consistent with findings for lesbian mothers (e.g., Farr & Patterson, 2011; Golombok & Tasker, 2010).

One aspect of parenting that has received considerable research attention is the division of labor among same-sex versus opposite-sex parenting couples. Focusing on childcare, many investigators have found that lesbian couples report that they divide labor more evenly than do heterosexual couples (Chan, Brooks, Raboy, & Patterson, 1998; Ciano-Boyce & Shelley-Sirici, 2002; Patterson, Sutfin, & Fulcher, 2004; Tasker & Golombok, 1998; Vanfraussen, Ponjaert-Kristoffersen, & Brewaeys, 2003). Others have reported that a relatively even division of childcare is also more characteristic of gay male couples than it is of heterosexual couples (Farr & Patterson, 2011). Still others have, however, found that biological lesbian mothers report doing more childcare than do nonbiological mothers (Bos, van Balen, & van den Boom, 2007; Goldberg, Downing, & Sauck, 2008; Johnson & O'Connor, 2002; Patterson, 1995). Despite considerable research, many questions remain to be addressed in this area.

Research has also focused on children's contacts with members of their extended families, especially grandparents. Patterson and her colleagues found that most children of lesbian mothers were described by their mothers as being in regular contact with grandparents (Fulcher, Chan, Raboy, & Patterson, 2002; Patterson, Hurt, & Mason, 1998). In one study that included both children of lesbian and heterosexual parents, there were no differences in frequency of contact with grandparents as a function of sexual orientation (Fulcher et al., 2002). Gartrell and her colleagues (2000) have also reported that most grandparents acknowledged the children of lesbian mother families as grandchildren. Thus, although the meager available evidence suggests that intergenerational relationships are generally satisfactory in lesbian mother families, no data have been reported about gay father families in this regard, and much remains to be learned about the qualities of intergenerational relationships in lesbian mother and gay father families.

Children's contacts with adult friends of their lesbian mothers have also been assessed in a handful of studies (Fulcher et al., 2002; Golombok et al., 1983; Patterson et al., 1998). In all of these studies, children were described as having contact with adult friends of their mothers, and most lesbian mothers reported that their friends were a mixture of lesbian, gay, and heterosexual individuals. Children in lesbian mother homes were as likely to have contact with adult males as were other children. Thus, findings to date suggest that children of lesbian mothers have positive contacts with a wide range of adults in the context of their daily lives.

Issues may emerge for some parents as they decide whether to disclose their nonheterosexual identities in contexts such as schools, churches, and hospitals, in which heterosexuality is often assumed. Some lesbian mothers report withholding information about their sexual identities in healthcare settings, especially when they perceive situations to be unsafe (Perlesz, Brown, McNair, Lindsay, Pitts, & de Vaus, 2006). Some lesbian and gay parents also report selective disclosure at their children's schools, based on their evaluations of individual attitudes and school climate (Casper & Schulz, 1999; Perlesz et al., 2006). Most lesbian and gay parents express desire for as much openness as possible in the context of maintaining a safe and welcoming environment for themselves and for their children (Tasker & Patterson, 2007). The perceived need for nondisclosure is a form of minority stress that can be extremely difficult for lesbian and gay parents to handle (Casper & Shulz, 1999).

Grandparents

In studies of lesbian and gay elders, one finding that emerges very clearly is that fewer lesbian and gay than same-aged heterosexual older people have children. For example, in Adelman and her colleagues' study of older sexual minority adults, only 28% of gay men and 57% of lesbian women over 65 years of age reported having had children (Adelman, Gurevitch, de Vries, & Blando, 2006); similar findings have also been reported by others (Grant, 2009). Because lesbian and gay elders are less likely than their heterosexual peers to have had children, they are also less likely to be grandparents. A further discussion of these issues can be found in Grossman, Frank, and McCutcheon (Chapter 10, this volume).

Even though grandparents may be uncommon among lesbian and gay populations, it is nevertheless true that some lesbians and gay men have become grandparents. Research on this population is still quite new, but a qualitative study of 16 lesbian or bisexual grandmothers living in the United States revealed how central sexual identities were to the women's experience of grandmother roles (Orel & Fruhauf, 2006). A similar study of 11 gay grandfathers, also living in the United States, was conducted by Fruhauf, Orel, and Jenkins (2009). Both studies emphasized the importance of what has been called the "lineal bridge"—i.e., the role of grandparents' relationships with adult children in mediating grandparent–grandchild relationships. The important role of parents in blocking or facilitating contact between grandparents and grandchildren has often been emphasized in the literature on aging, but due to the existence of antigay attitudes and stereotypes, it may be especially important in the context of gay and lesbian grandparenthood.

Overall, little is known about grandparenting experiences of older members of sexual minorities. Some scholars have suggested that other family relationships, such as those with siblings, may increase in importance with age, especially for lesbian, gay, and bisexual individuals who have fewer links to family members (Beeler, Rawls, Herdt, & Cohler, 1999). Much remains to be learned about grandparenting and other family relationships among older lesbian, gay, and bisexual individuals.

Chosen Families

A number of scholars have emphasized the importance for sexual minority individuals of "chosen families" that many lesbians and gay men have created (Weston, 1991). "Chosen families" are defined as networks of people to whom one feels emotionally close despite the lack of genetic or legal ties. In the recent Metlife Study (Metlife, 2010), a majority of 45- to 64-year-old nonheterosexual respondents agreed that they have a "chosen family," made up of close friends who are considered to be family members. In the same study, lesbian and gay adults also described themselves as more likely than their heterosexual counterparts to turn to close friends for advice, support, and help in an emergency (Metlife, 2010). In view of the alienation of some lesbian and gay adults from their families of origin, and in view of their reduced likelihood of parenthood and grandparenthood relative to their heterosexual peers, many lesbian and gay adults place special weight on close friendships (DeVries & Hoctel, 2006).

CHILDREN OF LESBIAN AND GAY PARENTS

In this section, research on children of lesbian and gay parents is presented first. Research on offspring of lesbian and gay parents during infancy and childhood, then during adolescence and young adulthood is considered. Important distinctions exist between children born in the context of preexisting heterosexual marriages and children born in the context of parents' already-established nonheterosexual identities. This brief presentation is not, however, organized around this distinction; instead, these differences are simply noted where they emerge in the context of research findings. More extensive reviews of this material can be found in Biblarz and Stacey (2010), Goldberg (2010), Patterson (2000, 2009a,b, in press), and Stacey & Biblarz (2001).

Infancy and Childhood

Research on children with lesbian and gay parents began with studies that were focused on families in which children had been born in the context of heterosexual marriages (Patterson, 1992). After parental separation and divorce, children in these families were usually living with their divorced lesbian mothers. To address legal questions that emerged in the context of child custody disputes, researchers compared development among children of divorced lesbian mothers to that among children of divorced heterosexual mothers. Few significant differences were reported in these studies (Patterson, 1992, 1997; Stacey & Biblarz, 2001).

One of the most important of these early studies was conducted by Golombok and her colleagues in the United Kingdom (Golombok, Spencer, & Rutter, 1983). Studying a group of 10-year-old children reared by divorced lesbian mothers, and comparing them to a matched group reared by heterosexual mothers, Golombok and her colleagues assessed many aspects of the children's development and adjustment. Their findings revealed that across teacher-report as well as parent-report assessments, there were no differences as a function of sexual orientation in children's behavior or relationships. In other words, they found that children of divorced lesbian mothers were developing in positive ways, and in ways that were extremely similar to children of divorced heterosexual mothers. Results such as these were cited in legislatures and courtrooms throughout the United States and also in Europe, as lesbian mothers sought custody of their children (Patterson, 2009; Richman, 2009).

The early studies were based on convenience samples, but these gave way over time to studies based on rational or, in some cases, representative sampling frames. For instance, Golombok and her colleagues compared the development of 7-year-old children with lesbian mothers to that among same-aged children with single heterosexual mothers and to that among same-aged children living with heterosexual mothers and fathers, all drawn from the Avon Longitudinal Study of Parents and Children, a population-based study of parents and children in the United Kingdom (Golombok et al., 2003). Consistent with earlier findings, their results showed that children of lesbian mothers were, on average, well adjusted and had positive relationships with their parents. Similar results with a diverse array of lesbian mother families were reported by Chan, Raboy, and Patterson (1998) in the United States and by Bos, van Balen, and van den Boom (2007) in the Netherlands. Longitudinal studies of children born to lesbian mothers also reported positive outcomes among the children (Gartrell, Deck, Rodas, Peyser, & Banks, 2005).

In addition to comparing the development of children of lesbian or gay parents with those of heterosexual parents, researchers have also studied diversity among children of nonheterosexual parents (Goldberg, 2010; Patterson, 1992). There is considerable diversity in pathways to family formation among lesbian and gay adults, and research has focused on outcomes for children in different types of families. Thus, research on children in adoptive families (e.g., Farr, Forssell, & Patterson, 2010), on children conceived using various forms of assisted reproductive technology (e.g., Bos & van Balen, 2008), and on children of gay fathers as well as lesbian mothers (Farr et al., 2010) has confirmed that, on average, children of nonheterosexual parents develop in positive ways. In all these family configurations, children whose relationships with their parents are warm and supportive fare better than do others with less positive relationships with parents (Patterson, 2009).

Another aspect of diversity that has received some study is the extent to which children and their parents live in social environments that are supportive of their families. Evidence has emerged that support from family members, co-workers, and others is related to psychological well-being among lesbian mothers (Goldberg & Smith, 2011) and that those who live in places in which the laws are more supportive of lesbian and gay parenting feel less stress in their daily lives (Goldberg & Smith, 2011; Shapiro, Peterson, & Stewart, 2009). The impact of law and policy on parents may well come ultimately to affect children as well, but this possibility has not yet received systematic study.

Thus, a considerable body of research on children of nonheterosexual parents has revealed that development and adjustment among them is similar to that among children of heterosexual parents. There has been more cross-sectional than longitudinal research, and more research on children with lesbian mothers than on those with gay fathers. Overall, however, the body of research is substantial and its results are clear.

Adolescence and Young Adulthood

Although a substantial body of research on children exists, many fewer studies have focused on adolescents or young adults with lesbian or gay parents. Early studies (e.g., Huggins, 1989) reported results that were consistent with findings on children, but were based on small nonrepresentative samples. A follow-up of the children in the Golombok et al. (1983) study in early adulthood also reported healthy outcomes (Tasker & Golombok, 1997). For example, young adult offspring of divorced lesbian mothers were no more likely than those of divorced heterosexual mothers to experience depression or anxiety; they were also no more likely than others to have sought professional help for psychiatric problems.

In one series of studies, adolescent offspring of same-sex couples, drawn from a national sample, were compared with a matched group of adolescent offspring of opposite-sex couples (Wainright & Patterson, 2006, 2008; Wainright, Russell, & Patterson, 2004). These authors reported no significant differences between adolescents living with same- and opposite-sex parents on self-reported assessments of psychological well-being, such as self-esteem and anxiety; measures of school outcomes, such as grades and trouble in school; or measures of family relationships, such as parental warmth and care from adults and peers (Wainright et al., 2004). Adolescents in the two groups were as likely to say that they had been involved in a romantic relationship in the past 18 months, and they were equally likely to report having engaged in sexual intercourse. There were also no significant differences in self-reported substance use, delinquency, or peer victimization between those reared by same- or opposite-sex couples (Wainright & Patterson, 2006). Moreover, across many different measures, peer relations (e.g., popularity) were similar in the two groups (Wainright & Patterson, 2008). Thus, the findings were consistent with those from research with children.

Also consistent with earlier research findings on children were the results relevant to diversity within this national sample (Wainright et al., 2004). Although the gender of a parent's partner was not an important predictor of adolescent well-being, other aspects of family relationships were significantly associated with adolescent adjustment. Parents who reported having close relationships with their offspring had adolescents who reported more favorable adjustment (Wainright et al., 2004). Thus, consistent with the findings of research with children, those from research with adolescents suggested the importance of the qualities of parent–child relationships in predicting outcomes.

Other investigators have studied the special issues of adolescents and young adults with lesbian and gay parents without comparing them to others. For example, Goldberg (2007a) interviewed a group of adults, 19 to 50 years of age (average age = 30 years), who had at least one nonheterosexual parent.

She found that these individuals often reported that having had nonheterosexual parents made them more tolerant and flexible in their attitudes toward gender and sexuality (Goldberg, 2007a). In a related study with the same group of participants, Goldberg also reported that there was considerable variability in how these individuals navigated issues of disclosure; some were quite open about their parent's nonheterosexual identity, but others did not disclose this to anyone (Goldberg, 2007b). Gartrell and Bos (2010) have also reported on the variety of experiences described by their participants as adolescents.

In summary, extensive research on both children and adolescents has come to similar conclusions. Overall, parental sexual orientation has not emerged as a strong predictor of child or adolescent developmental outcomes. In contrast, the qualities of relationships with parents have emerged as critical predictors of both child and adolescent outcomes. These results have implications for theories of child and adolescent development, and they are relevant to many public policy debates that involve child adoption, child custody, and legal recognition of same-sex marriages.

SUMMARY, DISCUSSION, AND CONCLUSIONS

Research on lesbian and gay family lives has expanded greatly in recent years. Beyond simply bearing witness to the very existence of lesbian and gay family lives, the results of existing studies, taken together, paint a remarkable picture of resilience, despite discrimination and stigma. Indeed, the evidence suggests that despite obstacles, lesbian and gay couples have often been able to create supportive relationships and social networks. The evidence also suggests that home environments provided by lesbian and gay parents have been as likely as those provided by heterosexual parents to enable psychosocial growth among family members. Lesbian and gay youth struggle against antigay prejudice in many areas of their lives; the evidence shows that with family support, they do so with greater success. Overall, research is beginning to provide glimpses of conditions under which lesbian and gay family lives go well.

Much research on lesbian and gay parenting has focused primarily on comparisons between lesbian and gay parent families, on the one hand, and heterosexual parent families, on the other. At least to some extent, this approach reflects the concern of researchers to address prejudices and negative stereotypes that have often been influential in legal decision making relevant to lesbian and gay couples, parents, and their children in the United States (Patterson, 2009). Now that results of research have begun to converge on answers to questions posed in this way, it will also be important for research to address a broader range of issues in this area.

Important research questions arise from a focus on the interests of lesbian and gay parented families themselves. For instance, many lesbian and gay couples with children are interested in distinctions between the experiences of biological and nonbiological parents (Patterson, 1998). How important are biological linkages in influencing experiences of parenthood? Similarly, both lesbian and gay parented families are concerned about the qualities of their children's experiences at school, and significant research in this area has been reported. It would seem likely that, in the future, scholarship will increasingly concern itself with the study of sources of strength and resilience in lesbian and gay couples as well as among lesbian and gay parents and their children.

In the meantime, however, the central results of research to date have important implications. If psychosocial development among children born to lesbian mothers and gay fathers is, as research suggests, essentially normal, then developmental theories about the importance of parental heterosexuality might need to be reconsidered. Although many possible approaches to such a task are possible (Patterson, 1992), one promising approach is to focus on the significance of family process rather than structure. Thus, structural variables such as parental sexual orientation may ultimately be seen as less important in mediating children's developmental outcomes than qualities of family interactions, relationships, and processes. By including variables of both types, future research will facilitate comparisons between them.

Results of research with lesbian and gay parents and their children also have implications for family law and policy (Patterson, 2009). If, as would appear to be the case, neither parents nor children in lesbian and gay families run any special risk of maladjustment or other psychosocial problems, then it becomes more and more difficult to justify prejudice and discrimination against them. Without such justification, many legal precedents and public policies relevant to lesbian and gay parent families require reconsideration. Ultimately, lesbian and gay couples and parents may come to be viewed as couples and parents like others, whose unique qualities are unrelated to family law. Policies might be designed to protect their legitimate interests, as well as those of their family members (Patterson, 2009). Considerable progress has been made in this area over the years (Richman, 2009), but much remains to be done.

A number of issues have gone all but unstudied to date in the research literature on lesbian and gay family lives. For instance, with notable exceptions, little attention has been devoted to the specifics of assessment of sexual orientation or to possible changes in sexual orientation over time. Similarly, bisexuality has received relatively little study. With some exceptions (e.g., Moore, 2008; Rosario et al., 2004, 2009) the ethnic, racial, and socioeconomic diversity of lesbian and gay family lives have yet to be systematically explored. Challenges emerging from queer theory have not yet been met by social science research (Gamson & Moon, 2004). These and other issues all provide important research opportunities for the future.

From a methodological perspective, it would be useful to have more studies that follow couples or parents and their children over time. Some valuable efforts have been made in this regard (Goldberg & Sayer, 2006; Tasker & Golombok, 1997). Longitudinal studies of the relationships between lesbians, gay men, and members of their families of origin could also be helpful in describing predictable sequences of reactions to distinctive life events (e.g., coming out to parents, marriage of same-sex partners). To avoid the difficulties associated with retrospective reporting, these studies should utilize prospective longitudinal designs.

Another methodological issue in the literature to date is the relative dearth of observational data. Observational studies of couples, parents, and children, as well as of lesbian and gay adults with members of their families of origin could provide rich information about the family lives of lesbian, gay, and heterosexual youth and adults. Such observational data could be collected from dyads or triads or larger family groups, at home or in the laboratory, in a single visit or in repeated sessions over time; this could add tremendously to our knowledge about parenting and relationships among lesbians and gay men. Some observational data are

beginning to emerge (e.g., Farr & Patterson, 2011) but more such efforts are needed.

Overall, the study of lesbian and gay parent family lives can be seen as a context in which to explore the limits of existing theoretical perspectives, and also to develop the uses of new ones. The study of lesbian and gay family lives can also inform discussions of public policy, especially in areas such as the legal recognition of the marriages of same-sex couples. Future work in this area has the potential to improve our understanding of lesbian and gay family lives, broaden existing theoretical notions about family structure and process, and inform legal decision making relevant to lesbian and gay parent family lives. The rapid changes in attitudes, social climates, and legal rulings relevant to lesbian and gay people during recent years have transformed daily lives for many lesbians and gay men. The experiences associated with family lives of nonheterosexual people will no doubt also be affected by future events. Another role for research in the years ahead, then, is to document the ways in which changes over time in attitudes, behaviors, and public policies both influence, and are influenced by, lesbians, gay men, and their families.

REFERENCES

Adelman, M., Gurevitch, J., de Vries, B., & Blando, J. A. (2006). Openhouse: Community building in the LGBT aging population. In D. Kimmel, T. Rose, & S. David (Eds.), *Lesbian, gay, bisexual, and transgender aging: Research and clinical perspectives* (pp. 247–264). New York: Columbia University Press.

Badgett, M. V. Lee (2009). *When gay people get married: What happens when societies legalize same-sex marriage.* New York: NYU Press.

Balsam, K. F., Beauchaine, T. P., Rothblum, E. D., & Solomon, S. E. (2008). Three-year follow-up of same-sex couples who had civil unions in Vermont, same-sex couples not in civil unions, and heterosexual married couples. *Developmental Psychology, 44,* 102–116.

Beeler, J. A., Rawls, I. W., Herdt, G., & Cohler, B. J. (1999). The needs of older lesbians and gay men in Chicago. *Journal of Gay and Lesbian Social Services, 9,* 31–49.

Biblarz, T. J., & Stacey, J. (2010). How does the gender of parents matter? *Journal of Marriage and Family, 72,* 3–22.

Bos, H. M. W., van Balen, F., & van den Boom, D. C. (2007). Child adjustment and parenting in planned lesbian-parent families. *American Journal of Orthopsychiatry, 77,* 38–48.

Brewaeys, A., Ponjaert, I., Van Hall, E. V., & Golombok, S. (1997). Donor insemination: Child development and family functioning in lesbian mother families. *Human Reproduction, 12,* 1349–1359.

Brodzinsky, D. M., & Pertman A. (2012). *Adoptions by lesbians and gay men: A new direction in family diversity.* New York: Oxford University Press.

Calzo, J. P., Antonucci, T. C., Mays, V. M., & Cochran, S. D. (2011). Retrospective recall of sexual orientation identity development among gay, lesbian, and heterosexual adults. *Developmental Psychology, 47,* 1658–1673.

Casper, V., & Schultz, S. (1999). *Gay parents, straight schools: Building communication and trust.* New York: Teachers College Press.

Chan, R. W., Brooks, R. C., Raboy, B., & Patterson, C. J. (1998). Division of labor among lesbian and heterosexual parents: Associations with children's adjustment. *Journal of Family Psychology, 12,* 402–419.

Chan, R. W., Raboy, B., & Patterson, C. J. (1998). Psychosocial adjustment among children conceived via donor insemination by lesbian and heterosexual mothers. *Child Development, 69,* 443–457.

Chandra, A., Martinez, G. M., Mosher, W. D., Abma, J. C., & Jones, J. (2005). *Fertility, family planning, and reproductive health of U. S. women: Data from the 2002 National Survey of Family Growth.* Hyattsville, MD: National Center for Health Statistics.

Ciano-Boyce, C., & Shelley-Sireci, L (2002). Who is mommy tonight? Lesbian parenting issues. *Journal of Homosexuality, 43,* 1–13.

Cochran, B. N., Stewart, A. J., Ginzler, J. A., & Cauce, A. M. (2002). Challenges faced by homeless sexual minorities: Comparison of gay, lesbian, bisexual, and transgender homeless adolescents with their heterosexual counterparts. *American Journal of Public Health, 92,* 773–777.

Corliss, H. L., Cochran, S. D., Mays, V. M., Greenland, S., & Seeman, T. E. (2009). Age of minority sexual orientation development and risk of childhood maltreatment and suicide attempts in women. *American Journal of Orthopsychiatry, 79,* 511–521.

D'Augelli, A. R., Grossman, A. H., Starks, M. T., & Sinclair, K. O. (2010). Factors associated with parents' knowledge of gay, lesbian, and bisexual youths' sexual orientation. *Journal of GLBT Studies, 6,* 178–198.

D'Augelli, A. R., Hershberger, S. L., & Pilkington, N. W. (1998). Lesbian, gay and bisexual youths and their families: Disclosure of sexual orientation and its consequences. *American Journal of Orthopsychiatry, 68,* 361–371.

DeMino, K. A., Appleby, G., & Fisk, D. (2007). Lesbian mothers with planned families: A comparative study of internalized homophobia and social support. *American Journal of Orthopsychiatry, 77,* 165–173.

De Vries, B., & Hoctel, P. (2006). The family-friends of older gay men and lesbians. In N. Teunis & G. Herdt (Eds.), *Sexual inequalities and social justice* (pp. 213–232). Berkeley: University of California Press.

Dorfman, R., Walters, K., Burke, P., Hardin, L., et al. (1995). Old, sad, and alone: The myth of the aging homosexual. *Journal of Gerontological Social Work, 24,* 29–44.

Farr, R. H., Forssell, S. L., & Patterson, C. J. (2010). Gay, lesbian, and heterosexual adoptive parents: Couple and relationship issues. *Journal of GLBT Family Studies, 6,* 199–213.

Farr, R. H., & Patterson, C. J. (2009). Transracial adoption by lesbian, gay, and heterosexual couples: Who completes transracial adoptions and with what results? *Adoption Quarterly, 12,* 187–204.

Farr, R. H., & Patterson, C. J. (2011). *Coparenting and division of labor among lesbian, gay, and heterosexual couples: Associations with adopted children's outcomes.* Unpublished Manuscript, Department of Psychology, University of Virginia.

Floyd, F. J., & Bakeman, R. (2006). Coming-out across the life course: Implications of age and historical context. *Archives of Sexual Behavior, 35,* 287–296.

Fruhauf, C. A., Orel, N. A., & Jenkins, D. A. (2009). The coming-out process of gay grandfathers: Perceptions of their adult children's influences. *Journal of GLBT Family Studies, 5,* 99–108.

Fulcher, M., Chan, R. W., Raboy, B., & Patterson, C. J. (2002). Contact with grandparents among children conceived via donor insemination by lesbian and heterosexual mothers. *Parenting: Science and Practice, 2,* 61–76.

Gartrell, N., Banks, A., Reed, N., Hamilton, J., Rodas, C., & Deck, A. (2000). The national Lesbian Family Study: 3. Interviews with mothers of five-year-olds. *American Journal of Orthopsychiatry, 70,* 542–548.

Gartrell, N., & Bos, H. (2010). US National Longitudinal Lesbian Family Study: Psychological adjustment of 17-year-old adolescents. *Pediatrics, 126,* 28–36.

Gartrell, N., Deck, A., Rodas, C., Peyser, H., & Banks, A. (2005). The National Lesbian Family Study: 4. Interviews with the 10-year-old children. *American Journal of Orthopsychiatry, 75,* 518–524.

Gartrell, N., Deck, A., Rodas, C., Peyser, H., & Banks, A. (2006). The National Lesbian Family Study: Interviews with mothers of 10-year-olds. *Feminism and Psychology, 16,* 175–192.

Gates, G. J., Badgett, M. V. L., Macomber, J. E., & Chambers, K. (2007). *Adoption and foster care by gay and lesbian parents in the United States.* Los Angeles, CA: The Williams Institute, UCLA Law School.

Goldberg, A. (2006). The transition to parenthood for lesbian couples. *Journal of GLBT Family Studies, 2,* 13–42.

Goldberg, A. (2007a). (How) does it make a difference? Perspectives of adults with lesbian, gay, and bisexual parents. *American Journal of Orthopsychiatry, 77,* 55–62.

Goldberg, A. (2007b). Talking about family: Disclosure practices of adults raised by lesbian, gay and bisexual parents. *Journal of Family Issues, 28,* 100–131.

Goldberg, A. (2010). *Lesbian and gay parents and their children.* Washington, DC: APA.

Goldberg, A., Downing, J., & Sauck, C. (2008). Perceptions of children's parental preferences in lesbian two-mother households. *Journal of Marriage and Family, 70,* 419–434.

Goldberg, A. E., & Sayer, A. (2006). Lesbian couples' relationship quality across the transition to parenthood. *Journal of Marriage and Family, 68,* 87–100.

Goldberg, A. E., & Smith, J. Z. (2011). Stigma, social context, and mental health: Lesbian and gay couples across the transition to adoptive parenthood. *Journal of Counseling Psychology, 58,* 139–150.

Golombok, S., Perry, B., Burston, A., Murray, C., Mooney-Somers, J., Stevens, M., & Golding, J. (2003). Children with lesbian parents: A community study. *Developmental Psychology, 39,* 20–33.

Golombok, S., Spencer, A., & Rutter, M. (1983). Children in lesbian and single-parent households: Psychosexual and psychiatric appraisal. *Journal of Child Psychology and Psychiatry, 24,* 551–572.

Golombok, S., & Tasker, F. (2010). Gay fathers. In M. E. Lamb (Ed.), *The role of the father in child development* (5th ed., pp. 319–340). New York: Wiley.

Grant, J. M. (2009). *Outing age—public policy issues affecting lesbian, gay, bisexual, and transgender elders.* Washington, DC: National Gay and Lesbian Task Force.

Grossman, A. H., D'Augelli, A. R., & Hershberger, S. L. (2000). Social support networks of lesbian, gay, and bisexual adults 60 years of age and older. *Journal of Gerontology, 55B,* P171–P179.

Hatzenbuehler, M. L., Keyes, K. M., & Hasin, D S. (2009). State-level policies and psychiatric morbidity in lesbian, gay, and bisexual populations. *American Journal of Public Health, 99,* 2275–2281.

Herdt, G., & Boxer, A. (1996). *Children of Horizons: How gay and lesbian teens are leading a new way out of the closet.* Boston: Beacon.

Huggins, S. L. (1989). A comparative study of self-esteem of adolescent children of divorced lesbian mothers and divorced heterosexual mothers. In F. W. Bozett (Ed.), *Homosexuality and the family* (pp. 123–135). New York: Harrington Park Press.

Johnson, S., & O'Connor, E. (2002). *The gay baby boom: The psychology of gay parenthood.* New York: New York University Press.

Kurdek, L. A. (2005). What do we know about gay and lesbian couples? *Current Directions in Psychological Science, 14,* 251–254.

Mallon, G. P. (2004). *Gay men choosing parenthood.* New York: Columbia University Press.

Metlife. (2010). *Still out, still aging: The Metlife study of lesbian, gay, bisexual, and transgender baby boomers.* New York: Metlife.

Morris, J., Balsam, K., & Rothblum, E. (2002). Lesbian and bisexual mothers and non-mothers Demographics and the coming-out process. *Journal of Family Psychology, 16,* 144–156.

Needham, B. L., & Austin, E. L. (2010). Sexual orientation, parental support, and health during the transition to young adulthood. *Journal of Youth and Adolescence, 39,* 1189–1198.

Orel, N. A., & Fruhauf, C. A. (2006). Lesbian and bisexual grandmothers' perceptions of the grandparent-grandchild relationship. *Journal of GLBT Family Studies, 2,* 43–70.

Patterson, C. J. (1992). Children of lesbian and gay parents. *Child Development, 63,* 1025–1042.

Patterson, C. J. (1995). Families of the lesbian baby boom: Parents' division of labor and children's adjustment. *Developmental Psychology, 31,* 115–123.

Patterson, C. J. (1998). Family lives of children with lesbian mothers. In C. J. Patterson & A. R. D'Augelli (Eds.), *Lesbian, gay, and bisexual identities in families: Psychological perspectives* (pp. 154–176). New York: Oxford University Press.

Patterson, C. J. (2000). Sexual orientation and family life: A decade review. *Journal of Marriage and the Family, 62,* 1052–1069.

Patterson, C. J. (2009). Children of lesbian and gay parents: Psychology, law, and policy. *American Psychologist, 64,* 727–736.

Patterson, C. J. (In press). Family lives of lesbian and gay adults. In G. W. Peterson & K. R. Bush (Eds.), *Handbook of marriage and the family.* New York: Springer.

Patterson, C. J., Hurt, S., & Mason, C. (1998). Families of the lesbian baby boom: Children's contacts with grandparents and other adults. *American Journal of Orthopsychiatry, 68,* 390–399.

Patterson, C. J., & Riskind, R. G. (2010). To be a parent: Issues in family formation among gay and lesbian adults. *Journal of GLBT Family Studies, 6,* 326–340.

Patterson, C. J., Riskind, R. G., & Tornello, S. L. (In press). Sexual orientation, marriage, and parenthood in global perspective. In A. Abela & J. Walker (Eds.), *Contemporary issues in family studies: Global perspectives on partnerships, parenting and support in a changing world.* New York: Wiley Blackwell.

Patterson, C. J., Sutfin, E. L., & Fulcher, M. (2004). Division of labor among lesbian and heterosexual parenting couples: Correlates of specialized versus shared patterns. *Journal of Adult Development, 11,* 179–189.

Patterson, C. J., & Tornello, S. L. (2010). Gay fathers' pathways to parenthood: International perspectives. *Zeitschrift fur Familienforschung (Journal of Family Psychology), 5,* 103–114.

Peel, E. (2010). Pregnancy loss in lesbian and bisexual women: An online survey of experiences. *Human Reproduction, 25,* 721–727.

Perlesz, A., Brown, R., McNair, R., Lindsay, J., Pitts, M., & de Vaus, D. (2006). Lesbian family disclosure: Authenticity and safety within private and public domains. *Lesbian and Gay Psychology Review, 7,* 53–64.

Richman, K. D. (2009). *Courting change: Queer parents, judges, and the transformation of American law.* New York: NYU Press.

Riggle, E., Rostosky, S., & Horne, S. (2010). Psychological distress, well-being, and legal recognition in same-sex couple relationships. *Journal of Family Psychology, 24,* 82–86.

Riskind, R. G., & Patterson, C. J. (2010). Parenting intentions and desires among childless gay, lesbian, and heterosexual individuals. *Journal of Family Psychology, 24,* 78–81.

Riskind, R. G., Nosek, B., & Patterson, C. J. (2011). *Differences in parenting intentions and desires as a function of sexual orientation:* Unpublished Manuscript, Department of Psychology, University of Virginia.

Rosario, M., Schrimshaw, E. W., & Hunter, J. (2009). Disclosure of sexual orientation and subsequent substance use and abuse among lesbian, gay, and bisexual youths: Critical role of disclosure reactions. *Psychology of Addictive Behaviors, 23,* 175–184.

Rosenfeld, M. J. (2007). *The age of independence.* Cambridge, MA: Harvard University Press.

Ross, L. E. (2005). Perinatal mental health in lesbian mothers: A review of potential risk and protective factors. *Women's Health, 41,* 113–128.

Ross, L. E., Steele, L. S., Goldfinger, C., & Strike, C. (2007). Perinatal depressive symptomatology among lesbian and bisexual women. *Archives of Women's Mental Health, 10,* 53–59.

Rostosky, S. S., Riggle, E. D. B., Horne, S. G., & Miller, A. D. (2009). Marriage amendments and psychological distress in lesbian, gay, and bisexual (LGB) adults. *Journal of Consulting Psychology, 58,* 56–66.

Rothblum, E. D., & Factor, R. (2001). Lesbians and their sisters as a control group: Demographic and mental health factors. *Psychological Science, 12,* 63–69.

Ryan, C., Huebner, D., Diaz, R. M., & Sanchez, J. (2009). Family rejection as a predictor of negative health outcomes in white and Latino lesbian, gay, and bisexual young adults. *Pediatrics, 123,* 346–352.

Ryan, C., Russell, S. T., Huebner, D., Diaz, R. M., & Sanchez, J. (2010). Family acceptance in adolescence and the health of LGBT young adults. *Journal of Child and Adolescent Psychiatric Nursing, 23,* 205 213.

Saewyc, E. M., Skay, C. L., Pettingell, S. L., Reis, E. A., Bearinger, L., Resnick, M., Murphy, A., & Combs, L. (2006). Hazards of stigma: The sexual and physical abuse of gay, lesbian, and bisexual adolescents in the United States and Canada. *Child Welfare, 85,* 195–213.

Savin-Williams, R. C. (1998). Lesbian, gay and bisexual youths' relationships with their parents. In C. J. Patterson & A. R. D'Augelli (Eds.), *Lesbian, gay and bisexual identities in families: Psychological perspectives* (pp. 75–98). New York: Oxford University Press.

Savin-Williams, R. C. (2001). *Mom, Dad, I'm gay.* Washington, DC: APA.

Savin-Williams, R. C. (2005). *The new gay teenager.* Cambridge, MA: Harvard University Press.

Savin-Williams, R. C., & Diamond, L. M. (2000). Sexual identity trajectories among sexual-minority youths: Gender comparisons. *Archives of Sexual Behavior, 29,* 607–627.

Shapiro, D. N., Peterson, C., & Stewart, A. J. (2009). Legal and social contexts and mental health among lesbian and heterosexual mothers. *Journal of Family Psychology, 23,* 255–262.

Stacey, J., & Biblarz, T. J. (2001). (How) Does sexual orientation of parents matter? *American Sociological Review, 65,* 159–183.

Tasker, F. L., & Golombok, S. (1997). *Growing up in a lesbian family: Effects on child development.* New York: Guilford Press.

Tasker, F. L., & Golombok, S. (1998). The role of co-mothers in planned lesbian-led families. In G. A. Dunne (Ed.), *Living difference: Lesbian perspectives on\work and family life* (pp. 49–68). New York: Harrington Park Press.

Tasker, F., and Patterson, C. J. (2007). Research on gay and lesbian parenting: Retrospect and prospect. *Journal of GLBT Family Studies, 3,* 9–34.

Telingator, C., & Patterson, C. J. (2008). Children and adolescents of lesbian and gay parents. *Journal of the American Academy of Child and Adolescent Psychiatry, 47,* 1364–1368.

Tornello, S. L., & Patterson, C. J. (2011). *Age, life pathways, and experiences of gay fathers: A life course perspective.* Unpublished Manuscript, Department of Psychology, University of Virginia.

Trettin, S., Moses-Kolko, E. L., & Wisner, K. L. (2006). Lesbian perinatal depression and the heterosexism that affects knowledge about this minority population. *Archives of Women's Mental Health, 9,* 67–73.

Vanfraussen, K., Ponjaert-Kristoffersen, I., & Brewaeys, A. (2003). Family functioning in lesbian families created by donor insemination. *American Journal of Orthopsychiatry, 73,* 78–90.

Wainright, J. L., & Patterson, C. J. (2006). Delinquency, victimization, and substance use among adolescents with female same-sex parents. *Journal of Family Psychology, 20,* 526–530.

Wainright, J. L., & Patterson, C. J. (2008). Peer relations among adolescents with female same-sex parents. *Developmental Psychology, 44,* 117–126.

Wainright, J. L., Russell, S. T., & Patterson, C. J. (2004). Psychosocial adjustment and school outcomes of adolescents with same-sex parents. *Child Development, 75,* 1886–1898.

Weston, K. (1991). *Families we choose: Lesbians, gays, kinship.* New York: Columbia University Press.

IV

Communities and Contextual Issues

17

Attitudes about Sexual Orientation

STACEY S. HORN

In the past decade, major changes have occurred in the United States and elsewhere regarding sexual orientation and the legal and civil liberties afforded to lesbian and gay people. Since 2000, six U.S. States[1] and the District of Columbia and 11 countries around the world[2] have passed legislation regarding the rights of same-sex couples to legally marry (CBS News online, 2010; National Gay and Lesbian Taskforce, 2010). Additionally, in the United States, the Texas sodomy law was repealed (2003) and hate crimes legislation including hate crimes based on sexual orientation has been passed (2009). At the same time, however, in more than 70 countries across the globe, homosexuality continues to be illegal and carries sentences from imprisonment to death. In much of the world, lesbian and gay people face discrimination and serious threats to their overall rights (Meldrom, 2010). Sexual orientation has become a central lever in political and culture wars being waged across the United States and the globe. Issues related to sexual orientation, such as same-sex marriage, same-sex adoption, and safe schooling for lesbian, gay, bisexual, and transgender students have been polarizing forces not only in elections, but also for communities.

The example of Proposition 8 in California is a case in point. After the Supreme Court of California in 2008 voted that banning same-sex marriage was unconstitutional and made marriage legal for lesbian and gay couples in California with all of the same rights and privileges accorded to opposite sex couples, Proposition 8 was introduced with the intention of putting the Supreme Courts' decision to a vote of the California people to amend their constitution to define legitimate marriage as between opposite-sex couples only. Individuals and groups contributed hundreds of thousands of dollars to campaigns either for or against Proposition 8. In fact, the campaign quickly moved beyond California with the Church of the Latter Day Saints (the Mormon Church) becoming one of the major contributors actively working to pass Proposition 8. In an official press release from the Mormon Church, the Church leaders state:

> The focus of the Church's involvement is specifically same-sex marriage and its consequences. The Church does not object to rights (already established in California) regarding hospitalization and medical care, fair housing and employment rights, or probate rights …
>
> The Church has a single, undeviating standard of sexual morality: intimate relations are proper only between a husband and a wife united in the bonds of matrimony.
>
> The Church's opposition to same-sex marriage neither constitutes nor condones any kind of hostility towards homosexual men and women. Protecting marriage between a man and a woman does not affect Church members' Christian obligations of love, kindness and humanity toward all people. (The Church of Jesus Christ of the Latter-Day Saints, 2008)

The preceding issues provide an illustration of the range of contemporary attitudes about sexual orientation and highlight the complexity of these attitudes. On the one hand, the Mormon Church clearly states that same-sex sexuality is wrong and falls outside the boundaries of sexual morality. On the other hand, the Church supports the fair treatment of lesbian and gay people in matters related to hospitalization and medical care, housing, and employment but not marriage. Furthermore, the Church clearly states that their position on marriage should not be equated with condoning "hostility" toward lesbian and gay people, suggesting that their members are obligated to treat lesbian and gay individuals with "love, kindness, and humanity."

The purpose of this chapter is to shed some light on this complexity by reviewing the psychological literature on attitudes about homosexuality. First, I will provide a brief overview of the ways that attitudes about sexual orientation have been studied historically. Then, I will review current trends in research on attitudes about sexual orientation. Finally, I will provide a framework for understanding the complexities of contemporary attitudes about sexual orientation and how this framework might help continue to shape research in this area.

HISTORICAL OVERVIEW OF RESEARCH ON ATTITUDES ABOUT SEXUAL ORIENTATION

Due to the history of homophobia and heterosexism in our culture, it is only in the past 20–25 years that a systematic body of research on this type of prejudice has emerged. In fact, prior to the removal of homosexuality from the *Diagnostic and Statistical Manual (DSM)* in 1973 by the American Psychiatric Association (APA), what little research there was on gay and lesbian people focused almost exclusively on homosexuality as a disorder and was conducted from a clinical or epidemiological frame (Herek, 1994). The removal of homosexuality from the *DSM* prompted a considerable change in the public discourse around issues of homosexuality. Moreover, just prior to the APA's historic action, the concept of homophobia—the irrational fear or contempt of gay and lesbian individuals—was introduced into the psychological literature (Weinberg, 1972). Homophobia then became of phenomenon of increased interest to psychologists.

Even though this area of research is relatively young, particularly compared to the long history of research on other forms of prejudice and discrimination, this research has documented the prevalence of sexual prejudice[3] (particularly in the United States) and has delineated a number of correlates of this type of prejudice (for reviews see Herek, 1994, 2000a). Numerous studies provide evidence that sexual prejudice is related to demographic, psychological, and social factors (Herek, 1994; 2000a; Kite & Whitley, 1998). Studies have repeatedly shown that males, older individuals, those with lower levels of educational attainment, and those living in the South or Midwest score higher on measures

of sexual prejudice (for reviews see Herek, 1994, 2000a). Additionally, authoritarianism (Haddock & Zanna, 1998), traditional attitudes about gender roles (Kite & Whitley, 1998), conservative political ideologies (Strand, 1998), and adherence to fundamentalist religious beliefs (Herek, 1994) have also been found to be correlated with higher levels of sexual prejudice. Studies have also documented that a lack of interpersonal contact and having negative experiences with gay and lesbian individuals are associated with higher levels of sexual prejudice (Herek & Glunt, 1993).

One feature of this earlier research regarding attitudes about sexual orientation is that most of the research utilized measures of explicit attitudes that resulted in unidimensional scores that could range from extremely negative attitudes to positive attitudes regarding sexual orientation. Van de Ven, Bornholt, and Bailey (1996), Horn (2006, 2008), and others have argued that utilizing a single attitudinal measure that combines participants' responses regarding their beliefs about homosexuality or homosexual behavior (e.g., it is a sin, it is unnatural), their attitudes toward or stereotypes of gay and lesbian people (e.g., gay men caused HIV/AIDS to exist), and their judgments about the civil rights and liberties extended toward the gay and lesbian community (e.g., same-sex marriage should not be made legal) into a single score of sexual prejudice masks its multifaceted nature. Furthermore, this research provides evidence that individuals' beliefs, attitudes, and behaviors toward gay and lesbian people are related but independent dimensions of sexual prejudice (Haddock & Zanna, 1998; Van de Ven et al., 1996).

For example, in national polls conducted in the 1990s and early 2000s regarding attitudes about sexual orientation, half of the respondents reported that homosexual behavior was always wrong, evaluated homosexuality as unnatural, and viewed lesbians and gay men as "disgusting" (Herek, 1994; Polling Data, 2010). Contrary to these negative views, however, a majority of individuals did not endorse employment discrimination or denial of other types of civil liberties because of sexual orientation (Polling Data, 2010). These results provide evidence for the heterogeneity of individuals' attitudes and beliefs about homosexuality in that individuals can hold very negative stereotypes about gay and lesbian people but also believe that they deserve the same rights and protections as anyone else (Haddock & Zanna, 1998; Herek, 2000b; Kite & Whitley, 1994; Van de Ven et al., 1996).

Furthermore, in the past 10 years, criticism has been directed toward the initial measures of attitudes developed in the 1980s and 1990s. Morrison and colleagues argue, for example, that these measures tend to focus on more overt and explicit measures of prejudice. They contend that modern prejudice is more covert and implicit (Morrison & Morrison, 2002; Steffens, 2005). Research on implicit attitudes (defined as relatively nonconscious and noncontrollable attitudinal biases regarding different groups; Nosek, 2007) has found that even individuals who express fairly positive explicit attitudes toward lesbians and gay men exhibit strong negative implicit biases toward them (Dasgupta & Rivera, 2008; Steffens, 2005). This research also provides evidence that implicit attitudes may be more variable and more sensitive to situational context than explicit attitudes (Dasgupta & Rivera, 2008; Steffens & Buchner, 2003). Taken together, this research provides additional evidence for the complexity of attitudes about sexual orientation.

CONTEMPORARY ATTITUDES ABOUT SEXUAL ORIENTATION

In the past 10 years there has been a proliferation of research on attitudes about sexual orientation. A PsychInfo search utilizing the keywords of "gay" and "attitudes" found 1803 peer-reviewed journal articles published between 2000 and 2010. This is more than double the number of peer-reviewed articles published between 1990 and 1999 ($n = 711$) and exponentially more than the number of articles published between 1980 and 1989 ($n = 214$). Much of the research published in the past decade continues to investigate the correlates of attitudes about sexual orientation utilizing single multiitem measures of attitudes, most frequently the Attitudes Towards Gays and Lesbians Scale (ATGL); however, more research is being conducted utilizing multidimensional constructs and investigating correlates of attitudes toward lesbian and gay rights.

In general, research conducted within the past 10 years provides evidence that the correlates of sexual prejudice identified in past research continue to be important and are relevant for both explicit and implicit or covert attitudes (e.g., gender, race/ethnicity, income level, political affiliation; Brown & Henriquez, 2008; Negy & Eisenman, 2005;

Olson, Cadge, & Harrison, 2006; Steffens, 2005). In addition to investigating demographic characteristics, researchers have also continued to investigate personality attributes that may explain additional variation in attitudes, as well as begun to investigate factors that help to explain some of the demographic differences in attitudes related to gender, race, and religion (e.g., social dominance, authoritarianism, gender-role attitudes, intergroup contact; Brown & Henriquez, 2008; Lemelle & Battle, 2004; Olson, Cadge, & Harrison, 2006). In studies that test multiple predictors of sexual prejudice, gender role attitudes and knowing a gay or lesbian person have most consistently explained variance in attitudes toward lesbian and gay people.

One limitation within the literature on attitudes about sexual orientation is that most studies continue to draw participants from college classes in the United States, Canada, and the United Kingdom. Interestingly, these samples usually include more female than male participants and also tend to include more European-American/white participants than participants from other ethnic groups. So, although there is a small and growing body of research on attitudes among younger and older participants, much of what has been published is about sexual prejudice in individuals in their early 20s, in North American and the United Kingdom.

In addition, as stated above, much of the research on correlates of sexual prejudice still utilizes unidimensional measures of explicit attitudes and also conflates attitudes toward lesbians with attitudes toward gay men. More and more research, however, has begun to assess attitudes toward lesbian and gay men separately (Herek, 2000a) and is separating out different dimensions of attitudes, such as attitudes toward individuals compared to attitudes about civil liberties and rights (Morrison & Morrison, 2002; Horn, 2006) as well as investigating implicit attitudes (Dasgupta & Rivera, 2008; Steffens, 2005). In addition, a growing body of research on attitudes toward bisexual women and men has emerged (Eliason, 2001), and a few studies have begun to address attitudes toward sexual orientation as distinct from attitudes toward gender conformity (e.g., Blashill & Powlishta, 2009; Schope & Eliason, 2004). In the next section, I will review the research from the past 10 years on attitudes about sexual orientation with a particular focus on issues that extend previous research, as well as on areas that have been the focus of considerable research attention.

I will begin by reviewing research that has specifically investigated ethnic, racial, and cultural variation in attitudes about sexual orientation. Second, I will address how age is related to individuals' attitudes about sexual orientation and review studies that have included non-college-aged participants. Next, I will examine how attitudes vary in relation to the identity of the person (e.g., gay, lesbian, gender nonconforming) being presented. This research will cover differential attitudes about lesbians, gay men, bisexual women, bisexual men, as well as research on how gender conformity/nonconformity is related to individuals' attitudes. I will then examine four areas within the literature that have received considerable attention in the past 10 years: traditional beliefs about gender roles and sexism, beliefs about the determinants of homosexuality, intergroup contact, and religion.

Ethnic, Racial, and Cultural Variation

Although a majority of the research on attitudes about sexual orientation includes primarily European-American and U.S. participants, a small but growing body of research has begun to focus on attitudes within other populations. Within the United States, researchers have begun to specifically investigate attitudes about sexual orientation among African-American and Latino populations. The general trend in research comparing African-American and Latino participants' attitudes about sexual orientation to European-American participants' attitudes, particularly using unidimensional measures of attitudes, is that European-Americans hold more favorable attitudes toward sexual orientation than do either African-Americans or Latinos (Herek, 2000b; Nierman, Thompson, Bryan, & Mahafley, 2007).

The growing body of literature, particularly on African-Americans' attitudes, however, presents a more complex picture than this. In a study using public opinion polls, Lewis (2003) found that although African-Americans disapproved of homosexuality at higher levels than did European-Americans, there were no racial differences in attitudes regarding sodomy laws, civil liberties, and employment discrimination. In fact, African-Americans were more likely than European-Americans to support laws prohibiting discrimination based on sexual orientation, even after controlling for religion and education. Furthermore, African-Americans' attitudes were less affected by religious attendance, fundamentalism, education, and age—all significant predictors of attitudes among European-Americans. These results provide some evidence that African-Americans distinguish between attitudes about the acceptability of homosexuality and the equitable treatment of lesbian and gay people.

Studies that investigated both ethnicity and religion provide some evidence that African-American and European-American differences in attitudes (utilizing a unidimensional measure) may be the result of differences in religious affiliation rather than race (Negy & Eisenman, 2005; Schulte & Battle, 2004). That is, when religion is accounted for in these studies, race becomes nonsignificant, suggesting that religiosity is a critical component of African-Americans' sexual prejudice (Negy & Eisenman, 2005).

Little research has been conducted on Latino attitudes about sexual orientation. Herek and Gonzalez-Rivera (2006) investigated Mexican born and Mexican-Americans' attitudes about sexual orientation and found that although men held more negative attitudes than women about gay men, there were no gender differences in attitudes toward lesbians. This was because women held more negative attitudes toward lesbians than gay men, whereas men held equally negative attitudes toward both lesbians and gay men. In addition, Herek and Gonzalez-Rivera (2006) found that individuals who identified as Mexican, rather than as Mexican-American, held more negative attitudes about lesbians, but no differences on attitudes about gay men were obtained. In general, this study provides evidence of similar patterns of correlates (e.g., conservative Christian religion; conservative political ideology) for attitudes toward lesbians and gay men, except that women in this sample held much more negative attitudes toward lesbians than in other studies. Much of the research on populations outside of North America and the United Kingdom also utilizes unidimensional measures of explicit attitudes and investigates how a number of predictors relate to those attitudes. In general, across countries (e.g., Chile, Germany, Turkey, United Kingdom), the correlates/predictors of negative attitudes seem to be similar to those in the United States. Being male, socially conservative, more religious, having less education, less income, and less contact with a lesbian or gay person predict more negative attitudes (Cardenas & Barrientos,

2008; Cirakoglu, 2006; Gelbal & Dunyan, 2006; Nierman, Thompson, Boyan, & Mahaffley, 2007). These studies also investigated factors that may be particularly salient in the country of interest. For example, in Chile, Nierman and colleagues found that gender role attitudes mediated the relationship between gender and attitudes toward lesbians and partially mediated the relationship between gender and attitudes toward gay men. In Turkey, Gelbal and Dunyan (2006) found that having had sex education in school and more liberal attitudes about sex predicted more positive attitudes toward lesbians and gays among college students.

These results suggest that although certain correlates of attitudes about sexual orientation may be common across all social and cultural contexts (such as gender), the social and cultural context plays a critical role in shaping attitudes about sexual orientation. Macrolevel differences between countries such as their laws and policies about sexual orientation, the legal protections and rights they afford lesbian and gay people, the degree of religiosity within a country, and the social and cultural norms regarding gender are likely to be related to individuals' attitudes about sexual orientation. In particular, these factors may be associated with implicit attitudes as these types of attitudes are more sensitive to situational variation and context (Dasgupta & Rivera, 2008). An interesting area for future research will be to investigate individuals' attitudes across countries that differ along the dimensions listed above to determine the extent to which and how these macrolevel factors relate to individuals' explicit and implicit attitudes about sexual orientation.

Age Differences

In studies investigating attitudes about sexual orientation within the general population, age is often included as a factor. In general, these studies suggest that negative attitudes about sexual orientation are more prevalent among older adults than younger adults (Hicks & Lee, 2006; Olson et al., 2006). Although few studies have investigated attitudes about sexual orientation across the lifespan, there is a growing developmental literature that investigates adolescents' attitudes and beliefs about sexual orientation and sexual prejudice.

The literature on adolescents' attitudes about sexual orientation suggests that age may be related to some aspects of individuals' attitudes about sexual orientation, but not others. In a study investigating adolescents' attitudes and beliefs, Horn (2006) found that that older adolescents and young adults were more comfortable interacting with gay and lesbian peers at school, less likely to endorse stereotypes regarding homosexuality, and less likely to view exclusion and teasing of a gay or lesbian peer as acceptable than younger adolescents. Interestingly, however, there were no age-related differences in beliefs about whether homosexuality was right or wrong. Research also provides evidence that as young people advance through high school, they are increasingly likely to have a lesbian or gay friend (Heinze & Horn, 2009) and more likely to hold biological/genetic beliefs about the origins of homosexuality (Horn & Heinze, 2011). Both intergroup friendship and biological/genetic beliefs about the origins of homosexuality were related to more positive attitudes about sexual orientation, suggesting that age-related differences in adolescents' attitudes may have more to do with these factors than adolescents simply becoming more tolerant as they grow older. Horn (2006, 2008) argues, however, that developmental factors related to identity, puberty, and social cognition may also be related to the age-related differences in adolescents' attitudes. Studies show that middle adolescence, a time when identity and pubertal development are occurring for most young people and when issues related to social norms, social hierarchies, and social conventions are particularly salient, is a time in which individuals tend to hold the most negative views toward sexual orientation (Horn, 2006, 2008), providing some support for this claim.

As stated above, the large majority of studies investigating attitudes toward sexual orientation utilize college-aged samples. In the past 10 years a few studies have begun to investigate attitudes in either younger or older individuals. Given that adolescents and young adults perpetrate the majority of hate crimes against lesbians and gay people (Franklin, 2000), research on attitudes about sexual orientation in adolescence and the developmental factors related to these attitudes is quite important.

Issues Related to the Identity of the Target

Another criticism of research on attitudes about sexual orientation has been that research has often assessed attitudes about a generic gay target or about gay men only. Recent research provides evidence, however, that individuals' attitudes differ depending on the gender, sexual orientation, and gender identity/conformity of the target (Fingerhut & Peplau, 2006).

In terms of sexual orientation, research provides consistent evidence that individuals hold more negative attitudes about gay men than lesbians, both in regard to explicit and implicit attitudes (Cardenas & Barrientos, 2008; Herek, 2002; Steffens, 2005). In investigating these differences more closely, however, Herek (2000b) found that most of the difference between attitudes about lesbians and gay men had to do with male participants' extremely negative attitudes toward gay men. These patterns may differ as a function of cultural contexts, as Herek and Gonzalez-Rivera (2006) found that among Latino/as, women expressed more negative attitudes toward lesbians than gay men, whereas men's attitudes toward gay men and lesbians did not differ.

Most of the research to date on attitudes about sexual orientation has investigated attitudes about same-sex sexual orientations. Very few studies have investigated attitudes about bisexual sexual orientations. The few studies that have been conducted find similar correlates of negative attitudes about bisexuality as those found regarding lesbians and gay men such as age, religious and political conservatism, traditional gender role attitudes, and contact with lesbian and gay people (Eliason, 2001; Herek, 2002; Israel & Mohr, 2004). Interestingly, studies that have investigated attitudes about both bisexuality and same-sex sexuality find that individuals hold more negative attitudes about bisexuals than about gay men or lesbians (Eliason, 2001; Herek, 2002; Israel & Mohr, 2004). Similar to its role in research on same-sex sexuality, however, the gender of participant made a difference. Herek (2000b, 2002) suggests that males' attitudes related more to the gender of the target, regardless of sexual orientation. That is, males held more negative attitudes toward gay and bisexual men than toward lesbians and bisexual women. Female participants' attitudes, however, related more to the sexual orientation of the target. Females held more negative attitudes toward bisexuals—men and women—than toward gay men or lesbians. These results emphasize the complexity of attitudes about sexual orientation and demonstrate that for different individuals attitudes may be related to different underlying cognitive and affective structures.

Research on attitudes about sexual orientation compared to gender conformity provides further evidence for the complexity of these attitudes. One argument against utilizing a monolithic gay target is that it is difficult to determine whether individuals' responses reflect their attitudes about sexual orientation per se or whether their responses reflect attitudes about conformity to perceived gender norms or gender roles (Horn, 2007). In fact, past research provides evidence that individuals perceive "the typical gay man" to be more feminine and less masculine than their heterosexual counterparts (Fingerhut & Peplau, 2006). Thus, some of the previous research on attitudes about sexual orientation may be conflating attitudes about sexual orientation with attitudes about gender conformity, especially for males.

Recent research investigating these issues provides evidence that both sexual orientation and gender conformity/normativity affect individuals' attitudes, particularly for male targets. In a study investigating males' attitudes about male targets, Blashill and Powlishta (2009) found that gender-nonconforming males were rated more negatively on a number of measures than gender-conforming males and that gay men were rated more negatively than heterosexual men. Interestingly, no interactions between sexual orientation and gender conformity were obtained. In a study of adolescents' judgments about the acceptability of lesbian, gay, and gender nonconforming targets, Horn (2007), however, did find evidence of an interaction between sexual orientation and gender conformity. Horn found that males judged the heterosexual target who was gender nonconforming in appearance and mannerisms as less acceptable than a gay target who was gender conforming or who participated in a gender atypical activity. Female participants, however, rated all of the lesbian targets as less acceptable than all of the heterosexual targets, regardless of gender conformity. These results suggest that for males, assumptions about masculinity and male gender roles may be salient in relation to their attitudes about sexual orientation.

Taken together, the results of studies on the importance of target provide compelling evidence that attitudes about sexual orientation are strongly linked with individuals' assumptions about gender roles and gender normativity and that these associations may play out differently for men and women. Given the narrow notions of masculinity and what it means to be an "acceptable" man in North American culture, it is not surprising that attitudes about sexual orientation are entangled with attitudes and beliefs about gender roles and gender expression.

Gender Roles and Sexism

Another way that research has investigated the relationship between gender role attitudes and attitudes about sexual orientation has been to assess gender role attitudes of participants. In general, studies investigating adherence to traditional gender roles of participants have focused primarily on attitudes about gay men and have typically included only men as participants. Overwhelmingly, however, results of these studies provide evidence that individuals who adhere more strongly to traditional gender roles exhibit more negative attitudes about gay men, engage in more discriminatory behaviors toward gay men, and are less comfortable with gay men (Davies, 2004; Goodman & Moradi, 2008; Parrott, 2009). Davies (2004), however, found that adherence to traditional gender roles did not predict negative attitudes about civil rights for gay men, suggesting that beliefs about gender roles may be more important regarding attitudes about people and behaviors, rather than attitudes about civil liberties and rights. Although the assumption is that gender role attitudes will be more predictive of males' attitudes toward gay men, Goodman and Moradi (2008) found no differences related to either the gender of the participant or the gender or the target (Goodman & Moradi, 2008). In addition, the one study that investigated women's beliefs about gender roles and their attitudes toward lesbians also found that holding socially conservative attitudes about feminine roles predicted antilesbian attitudes among college-aged females (Wilkinson, 2006).

Beliefs about the Origins of Homosexuality

There is considerable consistency in the results of studies investigating the relationships between beliefs about the origins of homosexuality and individuals' attitudes about lesbian and gay people. This research provides clear evidence that individuals who believe homosexuality is biological or genetic, and therefore presumed to be immutable, hold more favorable attitudes about lesbian and gay people (Haslam & Levy, 2006; Hegarty, 2002; Hegarty & Pratto, 2001; Horn & Heinze, 2011). Furthermore, research by Horn and Heinze (2011) also provides evidence that individuals

with biological beliefs about homosexuality are more comfortable interacting with lesbian and gay peers, are more likely to evaluate exclusion and teasing of lesbian and gay peers as wrong, and are more likely to use moral reasoning in justifying their judgments.

Conversely, individuals who believe homosexuality is a "lifestyle choice" or learned, and therefore to some degree mutable, hold more negative attitudes about lesbian and gay people (Haslam & Levy, 2006; Hegarty, 2002; Hegarty & Pratto, 2001; Horn & Heinze, 2011). In particular, those who believe sexuality results from socialization (e.g., parenting) hold the most negative beliefs, are least comfortable interacting with lesbian and gay peers, are less likely to evaluate exclusion and teasing of a lesbian or gay peer as wrong, and use more stereotypes, religious opposition, and normative assumptions in their reasoning (Horn & Heinze, 2011).

Very few of these studies, however, measure beliefs in the same way. Despite this diversity in measures, however, most studies utilize theoretically determined items regarding beliefs (based on attribution theory or essentialism) and tend to compare beliefs related to the immutability of sexual orientation (e.g., sexual orientation is not something that can change, it is biological or genetic) to beliefs related to sexual orientation as a "lifestyle choice" (e.g., sexual orientation can be controlled or changed). In a qualitative study investigating individuals' lay theories about the origins of sexual orientation, however, Sheldon and colleagues (2007) found that individuals held a diversity of beliefs about the origins of sexual orientation, such as genetics, upbringing, trauma or abuse, influence of other lesbian and gay people, and choice. This research suggests that individuals' theories about the origins of homosexuality are more multifaceted than the biological/choice continuum and that these beliefs may be differentially related to individuals' attitudes about lesbian and gay people.

In support of the idea that individuals' beliefs about homosexuality are multifaceted, Horn and Heinze (2011), utilizing latent class analysis, found four different profiles regarding individuals' beliefs about the origin of homosexuality. Individuals were somewhat equally divided in their beliefs that homosexuality resulted from early sexual trauma and choice (27% of cases), choice alone (25.0%), genetics or biology (24%), and various socialization practices such as parenting or socializing with lesbian and gay people (24.0%). Furthermore, they found that most of the differences on measures of sexual prejudice occurred between those who believed in biological origins and those who believed that sexual orientation is a matter of socialization (e.g., parenting). Individuals who believed that sexual orientation was a choice often fell between these two groups on measures of sexual prejudice suggesting that the two-dimensional framework of biology versus choice oversimplifies individuals' beliefs about the origins of homosexuality, especially in relation to how these beliefs are associated with attitudes about lesbian and gay people.

Intergroup Contact

Similar to other work on prejudice and intergroup relations, a significant amount of research on attitudes about sexual orientation has investigated the "contact hypothesis." The "contact hypothesis," first proposed by Allport (1979), suggests that intergroup contact between individuals will decrease group-based prejudices. In research on sexual prejudice, intergroup contact has emerged as one of the most salient predictors of decreased negative explicit and implicit attitudes toward lesbian and gay individuals (Anderssen, 2002; Heinze & Horn, 2009; Dasgupta & Rivera, 2008; Lemm, 2006; Vonofakou, Hewstone, & Voci, 2007). These studies have found that the type of contact is central to increased positive attitudes. In some studies, although acquaintance with someone who is lesbian or gay related to decreased prejudice (Anderssen, 2002), in other studies this was not the case (Heinze & Horn, 2009). Studies converge, however, on the effects of high-quality, intimate, and/or personally satisfying contact on individuals' attitudes. Across numerous studies, individuals who reported that they had a high-quality relationship with a lesbian or gay person, in most cases a friendship, also reported more positive explicit and implicit attitudes toward lesbian and gay people, more comfort interacting with lesbian and gay people, evaluated homosexuality as less wrong than did individuals reporting no contact (or minimal contact) with lesbian and gay people, and were more likely to view the negative treatment of lesbian and gay peers in terms of fairness and harm rather than stereotypes and normative assumptions (Dasgupta & Rivera, 2008; Heinze & Horn, 2009; Lemm, 2006; Vonofakou, et al., 2007). Interestingly, Dasgupta and Rivera

found that short-term exposure to admired lesbian and gay people (reading about lesbian and gay actors, athletes, politicians, and other public figures) had a positive effect on individuals' implicit attitudes toward lesbian and gay people, suggesting that who the contact is with may also be an important factor in understanding the relationship between intergroup contact and attitudes.

Religion and Religiosity

In the past ten years, considerable research attention has focused on the role of religion as related to sexual prejudice. Although there is evidence that religious beliefs are related to levels of sexual prejudice, the picture is much more complex than initially hypothesized and is contingent upon how both religion and attitudes are measured (Wilkinson, 2004). In a meta-analysis of the role of religion in attitudes toward lesbian and gay people, Whitley (2009) found that fundamentalism, religious orthodoxy, intrinsic religious orientation, and religious attendance all related to higher levels of sexual prejudice.

Although attendance at religious services is associated with negative attitudes toward lesbian and gay people, religious denomination does not seem to be as salient a factor in sexual prejudice as is religious fundamentalism. Religious fundamentalism is defined as "the belief that there is one set of religious teachings that clearly contain the ... essential inerrant truth about humanity and the deity" (Altemeyer & Hunsberger, 1992, p. 118). Even studies in which denomination predicts variation in individuals' attitudes (Newman, 2002), the denominations most related to negative attitudes are those that typically ascribe to more fundamentalist beliefs, such as conservative or evangelical Protestants. Across denominations, then, fundamentalism, rather than denomination, emerges as the strongest predictor of negative attitudes, even controlling for other factors such as religious orthodoxy and authoritarianism (Whitley, 2009).

In addition to religious fundamentalism, having an intrinsic religious orientation is also associated with negative attitudes toward lesbian and gay people. An intrinsic religious orientation refers to the extent that individuals truly believe the teachings of their religion and work to incorporate these beliefs into how they live their daily lives (Whitley, 2009). This is in contrast to individuals whose religious motivation comes from a "desire to obtain social rewards from being religious" (Kirkpatrick, 1989, p. 13) or for whom religion provides a source of "personal relief, comfort, and protection" from the challenges of life (Kirpatrick, 1989, p. 13). Although both of these orientations are extrinsic in nature, the first one is referred to as a social extrinsic orientation whereas the second one is referred to as a personal extrinsic orientation (Kirkpatrick, 1989). Interestingly, in relation to attitudes about sexual orientation, people high on intrinsic religious orientation hold more negative attitudes than people low on intrinsic religious orientation, whereas level of extrinsic orientation does not differentiate people in terms of their attitudes about sexual orientation (Whitley, 2009).

An emerging trend in research on the relationship between religion and sexual prejudice in the past 10 years has been to differentiate between attitudes toward same-sex sexual behavior and attitudes toward lesbian and gay people. Although some of these studies provide evidence that religious individuals differentiate between behavior and people in their judgments and attitudes (Bassett, Kirnan, Hill, & Schultz, 2005; Mak & Tsang, 2008; Rosik, Griffith, & Cruz, 2007), other studies have reported more mixed results (Bassett et al., 2001). These studies provide evidence to suggest that individuals who are high on intrinsic religious orientation make the distinction between behavior and people in their judgments about sexual orientation, whereas individuals with other religious orientations do not. Mak and Tsang (2008) suggest that religious individuals, rather than being prejudiced per se, have antipathy toward behaviors that violate religious values (e.g., premarital sex). To support their position, they assessed attitudes toward gay and heterosexual individuals described as celibate or sexually active outside of marriage. They found that individuals were more likely to help an individual who was celibate, regardless of sexual orientation, than an individual who was sexually active. Rosik et al., (2007) provide similar results and suggest that measures of sexual prejudice that are not sensitive to the complexity of attitudes among religiously identified individuals fail to appreciate differences between religiously formed judgments and prejudice against lesbian and gay people and that this serves to inhibit efforts to "reduce homophobia within conservative religious communities" (p. 10). Given the complexity of relationships between different facets of religion and religious

identity and attitudes about sexual orientation, more research in this area is warranted.

ATTITUDES ABOUT SEXUAL ORIENTATION: A MULTIDIMENSIONAL FRAMEWORK

Although concordance across studies and across time regarding the correlates of attitudes about sexual orientation exists (e.g., gender, gender role attitudes, authoritarianism, religious fundamentalism, and intergroup contact), contemporary attitudes about sexual orientation are complex and multifaceted. In the final section of this chapter, I will present a framework for the analysis of attitudes about sexual orientation, provide a synthesis of the research presented above, as well as present some recommendations for future research in this area.

Based on the review of the literature, it appears that attitudes about sexual orientation vary based on four major factors (see Figure 17.1): (1) the demographic and situational characteristics of study participants (e.g., gender, age, contact with nonheterosexual people), (2) the personality attributes of study participants (e.g., authoritarianism, gender role attitudes), (3) the characteristics of the perceived target (e.g., gender, sexual orientation, gender conformity), and (4) the specific issue being addressed (e.g., acceptability of homosexuality, general attitudes about lesbian and gay people, civil rights). Additionally, a fifth dimension that has not been the focus of systematic study, but that also may have a significant effect on attitudes about sexual orientation, is the larger context in which people live and interact. These dimensions are depicted in Figure 17.1.

These dimensions independently relate to attitudes about sexual orientation, and they are also linked with one another in interesting and important ways. For example, although demographic factors have been some of the most studied and salient correlates of attitudes about sexual orientation, these factors may be less important after accounting for other factors such as personality variables. Gender differences in attitudes about sexual orientation may have more to do with individuals' beliefs about gender roles and sexism than about gender itself. Thus, one fruitful avenue for future research on sexual orientation would be to investigate patterns of relationships across the five dimensions

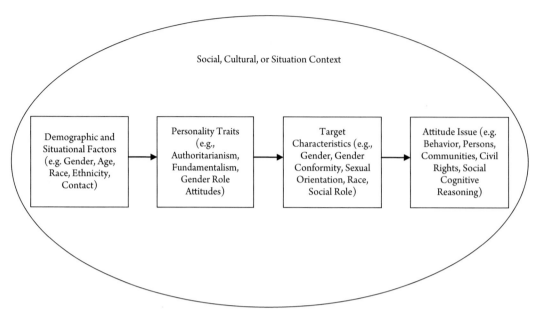

Social, Cultural, or Situation Context

| Demographic and Situational Factors (e.g. Gender, Age, Race, Ethnicity, Contact) | Personality Traits (e.g., Authoritarianism, Fundamentalism, Gender Role Attitudes) | Target Characteristics (e.g., Gender, Gender Conformity, Sexual Orientation, Race, Social Role) | Attitude Issue (e.g. Behavior, Persons, Communities, Civil Rights, Social Cognitive Reasoning) |

FIGURE 17.1. Multidimensional Framework of Attitudes about Sexual Orientation.

described above (e.g., do men, in general, hold more traditional attitudes about gender roles and how does this relate to attitudes about sexual orientation?). Investigating patterns across these different dimensions of sexual prejudice may help us better understand these and other types of connections.

Understanding how differences within each of the four dimensions relate to different types of attitudes is just as important as understanding patterns across the dimensions. For example, more research should examine attitudes toward different types of targets. Although we know something about how attitudes toward gay men and lesbians may differ, we know very little about attitudes toward bisexuality and even less about attitudes toward transgender individuals. Furthermore, within sexual orientation groups, attitudes may differ based on the "type" of individual being described. For example, do attitudes toward gay athletes differ from attitudes toward gay fashion designers? If so, why do they differ? When describing an undifferentiated gay target, what image do people form in their minds and how does this image affect their beliefs and attitudes? Lesbian, gay, bisexual, and transgender people are not all the same. To understand attitudes about sexual orientation, we must begin to investigate how diversity within lesbian, gay, bisexual, and transgender communities is or is not associated with individuals' attitudes and beliefs.

It is also critical for research to move beyond the use of unidimensional measures of attitudes. Although research using these measures has been important in understanding the correlates of attitudes, contemporary attitudes about sexual orientation are complex and multifaceted, requiring similarly complex assessment. Individuals hold different attitudes about same-sex sexual behaviors; lesbian, gay, and bisexual people or communities; and civil liberties and rights afforded to lesbian, gay, and bisexual people. By utilizing measures that result in a single attitude score, research conflates individuals' attitudes about the acceptability of homosexuality or homosexual behavior with their judgments about the treatment of lesbian, gay, and bisexual people and/or their civil liberties or rights. Horn (2006, 2008) provides evidence that individuals hold differing beliefs about these issues. That is, individuals can have the attitude that it is wrong to be lesbian or gay, while also believing that it is wrong to treat an individual unfairly because of her or his sexual orientation. By better understanding different types of attitudes, how they relate to one another, and the different factors that relate to various attitudes we will gain important insights into how best to reduce negative attitudes toward lesbian, gay, and bisexual people and how best to increase respect for sexually diverse people and communities.

We also need to learn more about how attitudes are formed and structured. Simply assessing attitudes does not afford insight into these issues. Assessing individuals' beliefs about the acceptability of homosexuality (is it wrong or not?) may reveal something important about those individuals. Probing into why individuals hold those particular attitudes, however, may lead to understanding about the origins and formation of those attitudes. For example, an individual could hold the belief that homosexuality is wrong for any of several reasons. To begin to understand the complexity of attitudes about sexual orientation, research must go beyond the assessment of individuals' attitudes and begin to investigate cognitive, social cognitive, and affective structures underlying those attitudes.

Finally, although very few studies to date have investigated the role of social and structural context on individuals' attitudes about sexual orientation, it seems that context could be important in at least two different ways. First, the social context could make sexual orientation more or less salient as an issue of focus. For instance, Horn and Nucci (2003) found that adolescents expressed much less comfort interacting with lesbian or gay peers in contexts that called for a high degree of closeness (e.g., sports team, roommate on an overnight class trip) than in contexts that did not require the same degree of intimacy (e.g., classroom). Thus, context may affect the "threat" that individuals experience related to sexual orientation and, in this way, affect negative attitudes. Second, the social and/or cultural context may be related to dimensions within the overall model. For example, in a country in which same-sex sexual orientation is illegal (e.g., Saudi Arabia), it would be difficult for an individual to express positive or accepting attitudes toward lesbian and gay people, even if those attitudes represent his or her actual beliefs. Thus, an additional avenue for future research would be to begin to include context and/or contextual variation into investigations of attitudes about sexual orientation.

CONCLUSIONS

Research on attitudes about sexual orientation provides evidence that, in the past decade, attitudes have changed in some important ways, but also that attitudes and the correlates of these attitudes have remained surprisingly the same. It is clear that contemporary attitudes about sexual orientation are complex and include a number of different dimensions. To better understand attitudes about sexual orientation, researchers need to continue to explore these different attitudinal dimensions, as well as the associations among them.

NOTES

1. Connecticut, 2008; District of Columbia, 2010; Iowa, 2009; Massachusetts, 2004; New Hampshire, 2009; New York, 2011; and Vermont, 2009.
2. Argentina, 2010; Belgium, 2003; Canada, 2005; Denmark, 2012; Iceland, 2010; The Netherlands, 2001; Norway, 2009; Portugal, 2010; South Africa, 2006; Spain, 2005; and Sweden, 2009.
3. Sexual prejudice is defined as "all negative attitudes based on sexual orientation, whether the target is homosexual, bisexual, or heterosexual. Given the current social organization of sexuality, however, such prejudice is almost always directed at people who engage in homosexual behavior or label themselves gay, lesbian, or bisexual" (Herek, 2000b, p. 19).

REFERENCES

Allport, G. (1979). *The nature of prejudice.* Reading, MA. Addison-Wesley Publishing Company.

Altemeyer, B., & Hunsberger, B. (1992). Authoritarianism, religious fundamentalism, quest, and prejudice. *International Journal for the Psychology of Religion, 2,* 113–133.

Anderssen, N. (2002). Does contact with lesbians and gays lead to friendlier attitudes? A two-year longitudinal study. *Journal of Community and Applied Social Psychology, 12,* 124–136.

Bassett, R. L., Baldwin, D., Tammaro, J., Mackmer, D., Mundig, C., Wareing, A., & Tschorke, D. (2001). Reconsidering intrinsic religion as a source of universal compassion. *Journal of Psychology and Theology, 30,* 131–143.

Bassett, R. L., Kirnan, R., Hill, M., & Schultz, A. (2005). SOAP: Validating the Sexual Orientation and Practices Scale. *Journal of the Psychology of Christianity, 25,* 65–175.

Blashill, A., & Powlishta, K. (2009). The impact of sexual orientation and gender role on evaluations of men. *Psychology of Men and Masculinity, 10,* 160–173.

Brown, M. J., & Henriquez, E. (2008). Sociodemographic predictors of Attitudes Towards Gays and Lesbians. *Individual Differences Research, 6,* 193–202.

Cardenas, M., & Barrientos, J. E. (2008). The Attitudes toward Lesbians and Gay Men Scale (ATLG): Adaptation and testing the reliability and validity in Chile. *Journal of Sex Research, 45,* 140–149.

CBS News. (2010). Same-Sex marriage around the world: From criminal prosecution to legal unions. CBS News on-line. Retrieved www.cbs.ca/world/story/2009/05/26/f-same-sex-timeline.html, January 4, 2011.

Church of Jesus Christ of the Latter-Day Saints. (August 13, 2008). The divine institution of marriage. *The News Room: Commentary*. Retrieved, May 24, 2010 from http://www.lds.org/ldsnewsroom/eng/commentary/the-divine-institution-of-marriage.

Cirakoglu, O. C. (2006). Perception of homosexuality among Turkish university students: The roles of labels, gender, and prior contact. *The Journal of Social Psychology, 146*, 293–305.

Dasgupta, N., & Rivera, L. (2008). When social context matters: The influence of long-term contact and short-term exposure to admired out-group members on implicit attitudes and behavioral intentions. *Social Cognition, 26*, 112–123.

Davies, M. (2004). Correlates of negative attitudes toward gay men, sexism, male role norms, and male sexuality. *Journal of Sex Research, 41*, 259–266.

Eliason, M. (2001). BiNegativity: The stigma facing bisexual men. *Journal of Bisexuality, 1*, 137–154.

Fingerhut, A., & Peplau, L. A., (2006). The impact of social roles on stereotypes of gay men. *Sex Roles, 55*, 273–278.

Franklin, K. (2000). Antigay behaviors by young adults: Prevalence, patterns and motivators in a noncriminal population. *Journal of Interpersonal Violence, 15*, 339–362.

Gelbal, S., & Dunyan, V. (2006). Attitudes of university students toward lesbians and gay men in Turkey. *Sex Roles, 55*, 573–579.

Goodman, M. B., & Moradi, B. (2008). Attitudes and behaviors toward lesbian and gay persons: Critical correlates and mediated relations. *Journal of Counseling Psychology, 55*, 371–384.

Haddock, G., & Zanna, M. P. (1998). Authoritarianism, values, and the favorability and structure of anti-gay attitudes. In G. Herek (Ed.), *Stigma and sexual orientation: Understanding prejudice against lesbians, gay men, and bisexuals* (pp. 82–107). Thousand Oaks, CA: Sage.

Haslam, N., & Levy, S. (2006). Essentialist beliefs about homosexuality: Structure and implications for prejudice. *Personality and Social Psychology Bulletin, 32*, 471–485.

Hegarty, P. (2002). "It's not a choice, it's the way we're built": Symbolic beliefs about sexual orientation in the U.S. and Britain. *Journal of Community and Applied Social Psychology, 12*, 153–166.

Hegarty, P., & Pratto, F. (2001). Sexual orientation beliefs: Their relationships to anti-gay attitudes and biological determinist arguments. *Journal of Homosexuality, 41*, 121–135.

Heinze, J., & Horn, S. S. (2009). Intergroup contact and beliefs about homosexuality in adolescence. *Journal of Youth and Adolescence, 38*, 937–951.

Herek, G. (1994). Assessing heterosexuals' attitudes toward lesbians and gay men: A review of empirical research with the ATLG scale. In B. Greene & G. Herek (Eds.), *Lesbian and gay psychology: Theory, research and clinical applications* (pp. 206–228). Thousand Oaks, CA: Sage Publications.

Herek, G. M. (2000a). Sexual prejudice and gender: Do heterosexuals' attitudes toward lesbians and gay men differ? *Journal of Social Issues, 56*, 251–266.

Herek, G. M. (2000b). The psychology of sexual prejudice. *Current Directions in Psychological Science, 9*, 19–22.

Herek, G. M. (2002). Heterosexuals' attitudes toward bisexual men and women in the U.S. *Journal of Sex Research, 39*, 264–274.

Herek, G., & Glunt, E. K. (1993). Interpersonal contact and heterosexuals' attitudes toward gay men: Results from a national survey. *Journal of Sex Research, 30*, 239–244.

Herek, G. M., & Gonzalez-Rivera, M. (2006). Attitudes toward homosexuality among U.S. residents of Mexican descent. *Journal of Sex Research, 43*, 122–135.

Hicks, G. R., & Lee, T. (2006). Public attitudes towards gays and lesbians: Trends and predictors. *Journal of Homosexuality, 51*, 51–77.

Horn, S. S. (2006). Heterosexual students' attitudes and beliefs about same-sex sexuality and the treatment of gay, lesbian, and gender non-conforming youth. *Cognitive Development, 21*, 420–440.

Horn, S. S. (2007). Adolescents' acceptance of same-sex peers based on sexual orientation and gender expression. *Journal of Youth and Adolescence, 36*, 363–371.

Horn, S. S. (2008). The multifaceted nature of sexual prejudice: What we can learn from studying how adolescents reason about sexual orientation and sexual prejudice. In S. Levy & M. Killen (Eds.), *Intergroup attitudes and relations in childhood through adulthood* (pp. 398–437). Oxford: Oxford University Press.

Horn, S. S., & Heinze, J. (2011). She can't help it, she was born that way: Adolescents' beliefs about the origins of homosexuality and sexual prejudice. *Anales de Psicología: Social and Developmental Aspects of Prejudice during Childhood and Adolescence, 27*, 688–697.

Horn, S. S., & Nucci, L. P. (2003). The multidimensionality of adolescents' beliefs about and attitudes toward gay and lesbian peers in school. *Equity and Excellence in Education, Special Issue on LGBTQ issues in K-12 schools, 36*, 1–12.

Israel, T., & Mohr, J. (2004). Attitudes toward bisexual women and men: Current research, future directions. *Journal of Bisexuality, 4*, 117–134.

Kirkpatrick, L. A. (1989). A psychometric analysis of the Allport-Ross and Feagin measures of intrinsic-extrinsic religious orientation. *Research in the Social Scientific Study of Religion, 1*, 1–31.

Kite, M. E., & Whitley, B. E. (1998). Do heterosexual women and men differ in their attitudes toward homosexuality? A conceptual and methodological analysis. In G. Herek (Ed.), *Stigma and sexual orientation: Understanding prejudice against lesbians, gay men, and bisexuals.* (pp. 39–61). Thousand Oaks, CA: Sage.

Lemelle, A. J., & Battle, J. (2004). Black masculinity matters in attitudes toward gay males. *Journal of Homosexuality, 47,* 39–51.

Lemm, K. M. (2006). Positive associations among interpersonal contact, motivation, and implicit and explicit attitudes toward gay men. *Journal of Homosexuality, 51,* 79–99.

Lewis, G. (2003). Black-white differences in attitudes toward homosexuality and gay rights. *Public Opinion Quarterly, 67,* 59–78.

Mak, H. K., & Tsang, J. (2008). Separating the "sinner" from the "sin": Religious orientation and prejudiced behaviors toward sexual orientation and promiscuous sex. *Journal for the Scientific Study of Religion, 47,* 379–392.

Meldrom, A. (2010). Gay rights movement gains momentum around the world. The Huffington Post, www.huffingtonpost.com/2009/10/13/gay-rights-movement-gains_n_319283.html, retrieved January 4, 2011.

Morrison, M., & Morrison, T. G. (2002). Development and validations of a scale measuring modern prejudice toward gay men and lesbians. *Journal of Homosexuality, 43,* 15–37.

National Gay and Lesbian Task Force. (2010). Relationship recognition for same-sex couples within the United States. *Issues Map.* Retrieved from http://www.thetaskforce.org/downloads/reports/issue_maps/rel_recog_6_28_11_color.pdf.

Negy, C., & Eisenman, R. (2005). A comparison of African American and white college students' affective and attitudinal reactions to lesbian, gay, and bisexual individuals: An exploratory study. *Journal of Sex Research, 42,* 291–298.

Newman, B. S. (2002). Lesbians, gays, and religion: Strategies for challenging belief systems. *Journal of Lesbian Studies, 6,* 87–98.

Nierman, A. J., Thompson, S. C., Bryan, A., & Mahafley, A. L. (2007). Gender role beliefs and attitudes toward lesbians and gay men in Chile and the U.S. *Sex Roles, 57,* 61–67.

Nosek, B. A. (2007). Implicit-explicit relations. *Current Directions in Psychological Science, 16,* 65–69.

Olson, L. R., Cadge, W., & Harrison, J. T. (2006). Religion and public opinion about same-sex marriage. *Social Science Quarterly, 87,* 340–360.

Parrott, D. (2009). Aggression toward gay men as gender role enforcement: Effects of male role norms, sexual prejudice, and masculine gender role stress. *Journal of Personality, 77,* 1137–1166.

Polling Report. (2010). Same-sex marriage, gay rights, law, and civil rights. Retrieved from http://pollingreport.com/civil.htm.

Rosik, C. H., Griffith, L. K., & Cruz, Z. (2007). Homophobia and conservative religion: Toward a more nuanced understanding. *American Journal of Orthopsychiatry, 77,* 10–19.

Schope, R., & Eliason, M. J. (2004). Sissies and tomboys: Gender role behaviors and homophobia. *Journal of Gay and Lesbian Social Services, 16,* 73–97.

Schulte, L. J., & Battle, J. (2004). The relative importance of ethnicity and religion in predicting attitudes towards gays and lesbians. *Journal of Homosexuality, 47,* 127–141.

Sheldon, J. P., Pfeffer, C. A., Jayaratne, T. E., Feldbaum, M., & Petty, E. M. (2007). Beliefs about the etiology of homosexuality and about the ramifications of discovering its possible genetic origin. *Journal of Homosexuality, 52,* 11–150.

Steffens, M. C. (2005). Implicit and explicit attitudes toward lesbian and gay men. *Journal of Homosexuality, 49,* 39–66.

Steffens, M. C., & Buchner, A. (2003). Implicit association test: Separating transsituationally stable and variable components of attitudes toward gay men. *Experimental Psychology, 50,* 33–48.

Strand, D. (1998). Civil liberties, civil rights, and stigma: Voter attitudes and behavior in the politics of homosexuality. In G. M. Herek (Ed.), *Stigma and sexual orientation: Understanding prejudice against lesbians, gay men, and bisexuals* (pp. 108–137). Newbury Park, CA: Sage.

Van de Ven, P., Bornholt, L., & Bailey, M. (1996). Measuring cognitive, affective and behavioral components of homophobic reaction. *Archives of Sexual Behavior, 25,* 155–179.

Vonofakou, C., Hewstone, M., & Voci, A. (2007). Contact with out-group friends as a predictor of meta-attitudinal strength and accessibility attitudes toward gay men. *Journal of Personality and Social Psychology, 92,* 804–820.

Weinberg, G. (1972). *Society and the healthy homosexual.* New York: St. Martin's Press.

Wilkinson, W. W. (2004). Religiosity, authoritarianism, and homophobia: A multidimensional approach. *The International Journal for the Psychology of Religion, 14,* 55–67.

Wilkinson, W. W. (2006). Exploring heterosexual women's anti-lesbian attitudes. *Journal of Homosexuality, 51,* 139–155.

Whitley, B. E. (2009). Religiosity and attitudes toward lesbians and gay men: A meta-analysis. *The International Journal for the Psychology of Religion, 19,* 21–38.

18

Minority Stress and the Health of Sexual Minorities

ILAN H. MEYER AND DAVID M. FROST

Minority stress refers to a conceptual model that describes stressors embedded in the social position of sexual minority individuals as causes of health-related conditions, such as mental disorders, psychological distress, physical disorders, health behaviors (e.g., smoking, condom use), and, more generally, a sense of well-being (Meyer, 2003a). The minority stress model suggests that because of stigma, prejudice, and discrimination, lesbian, gay, and bisexual people experience more stress than do heterosexuals and that this stress can lead to mental and physical disorders. We begin with a brief overview of the minority stress model and discuss the domains of health and well-being that are affected by minority stressors, including mental health, physical health, health behaviors, and well-being.

MINORITY STRESS PROCESSES

The minority stress model is based on general stress theory (Dohrenwend, 2000). Meyer (2003a) described minority stress processes that are unique to lesbian, gay, and bisexual populations. The model (Figure 18.1) shows stress and coping and their impact on mental health outcomes (box i). Minority stress emerges from general environmental circumstances (box a), which include advantages and disadvantages related to factors such as socioeconomic status. An important aspect of these circumstances in the environment is the person's minority statuses, for example, being lesbian, gay, or bisexual (box b). These statuses are depicted as overlapping boxes in the figure to indicate associations with other circumstances in the person's environment. For example, minority stress for a gay man who is poor results from both his sexual orientation *and* his poverty. Together these characteristics determine his exposure to stress as well as

to coping resources (Díaz, Ayala, Bein, Henne, & Marin, 2001). Circumstances in the environment lead to exposure to stressors, including general stressors such as job loss or death of an intimate (box c), and stressors unique to minority group members, such as prejudice events (e.g., discrimination in employment) (box d). Similar to their source circumstances, the stressors are depicted as overlapping, representing their interdependence (Pearlin, 1999). For example, an experience of anti-gay violence (box d) is likely to increase vigilance and expectations of rejection (box f).

Prejudice-related stressors include the *structural* exclusion of lesbian, gay, and bisexual individuals from resources and advantages available to heterosexual people (e.g., marriage), as well as *interpersonal* events that disadvantage nonheterosexual people. There are numerous accounts of the widespread exposure of lesbian, gay, and bisexual people to such prejudice events (Herek, 2009a, 2009b; Meyer, Schwartz, & Frost, 2008). In addition to acute major stressful events, such as being a victim of antigay violence or losing a job, nonheterosexual people are exposed to minor incidents and chronic conditions that are related to prejudice. These forms of *everyday discrimination* or *heterosexist daily hassles* also constitute prejudice-related stressors. Verbal harassment and other instances of rejection and disrespect are examples of everyday discrimination (Swim, Johnston, & Pearson, 2009). Such incidents do not qualify as life events because they are minor in magnitude and require relatively little adaptation. But such seemingly minor events can be damaging because of the symbolic message of rejection that they convey, especially when they accumulate over time (Meyer, Ouellette, Haile, & McFarlane, 2011).

Often minority status leads to personal identification with a person's minority status (Figure 18.1,

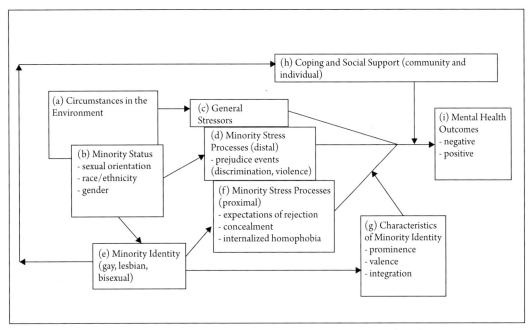

FIGURE 18.1. Minority Stress Processes and Health Outcomes. From Meyer, I. H. (2003). Prejudice, social stress, and mental health in lesbian, gay, and bisexual populations: Conceptual issues and research evidence. *Psychological Bulletin,* *129*(5), 674–697. Published by the American Psychological Association. Reprinted with permission.

box e). This minority identity leads to additional stressors (box f) related to the individual's perception of the self as a stigmatized and devalued minority (Miller & Major, 2000), including expectations of rejection, concealment, and internalized homophobia, which is defined as a lesbian, gay, or bisexual individual's direction of negative social attitudes toward himself or herself.

Internalized homophobia can be a particularly insidious stressor because it is directed by the person toward himself or herself due to years of socialization in a stigmatizing society even when no external stimulus is present (Meyer & Dean, 1998). Indeed, one of the developmental tasks faced by people upon identifying as lesbian, gay, or bisexual is learning to dissociate their sense of self from the negative messages they have learned about homosexuality, even if they are not aware that these messages have been learned (Eliason & Schope, 2007). We demonstrate the workings of internalized homophobia with research in the area of intimacy. In most states of the United States and in most other nations, lesbian, gay, and bisexual people are barred from marrying a person of the same sex. Marriage is an important status and highly valued goal for most people in our society. One of the core

stigmas about homosexuality has been the denial of intimacy for same-sex couples. Because intimacy is a basic human goal, society has built social structures to support the achievement of lasting intimate bonds for heterosexual couples. But the achievement of similar intimacy goals is not available for most lesbian and gay people (Frost, 2011a; Meyer & Dean, 1998). The denial of the right to marry—a structural prejudice with specific legal consequences—is the most fundamental of such barriers. The significance of denial of marriage is three-pronged: It excludes lesbian and gay individuals from full participation in society, given that marriage and family are key components of citizenship (Herdt & Kertzner, 2006); it impedes the development of lasting intimate relationships by same-sex couples by removing the structural support that marriage affords; and it implicitly propagates the stigma that they are undeserving or incapable of attaining satisfying intimate family relations. This stigma can then be internalized by individuals who are in or seek to be in same-sex relationships, potentially resulting in their disengagement from intimate relationships (Frost, 2011a; Frost & Meyer, 2009).

Minority identity is not only a source of stress, but also has positive effects (Riggle, Rostosky, &

Danner, 2009; Meyer, et al., 2011). Characteristics of minority identity can augment or weaken the impact of stress (Figure 18.1, box g). For example, minority stressors may have a greater impact on health outcomes when a lesbian, gay, or bisexual identity is prominent than when it is secondary to the person's self-definition (Thoits, 1999). Nonheterosexual identity may also be a source of strength (box h) when it is associated with opportunities for affiliation, social support, and coping (Riggle, Whitman, Olson, Rostosky, & Strong, 2008), which mitigate the impact of stress (Crocker & Major, 1989; Miller & Major, 2000). In short, the minority stress model articulates how the effect of stressors on health outcomes is the net result of negative (stress) and positive (ameliorative) factors.

The positive effects of feeling connected to or being involved in sexual minority communities on the health of sexual minorities have been demonstrated in various studies. Sexual minority communities vary from specific groups of similar others (e.g., other black lesbians) to neighborhoods to larger geospecific communities (e.g., New York City's lesbian, gay, bisexual, and transgender communities). Engagement with sexual minority communities has been shown to be related to mental health and well-being (Kertzner, Meyer, Frost, & Stirratt, 2009; Ramirez-Valles, Fegus, Reisen, Poppen, & Zea, 2005), safer sex practices (Ramirez-Valles & Brown, 2003), sexual risk (Ramirez-Valles, 2002), medication adherence among HIV-positive men who have sex with men (Wolitski, Pals, Kidder, Courtenay-Quirk, & Holtgrave, 2009), and coping with chronic sorrow among those who are HIV positive (Lichtenstein, Laska, & Clair, 2002).

It is important to note that although some of the positive effects work through individual resources (Masten, 2001), many positive effects can be provided only by the community as a whole—through the person's affiliation and identification with the community. Two functions of coping achieved through minority group affiliations are to allow stigmatized persons to experience social environments in which they are not stigmatized by others, and to provide practical, emotional, and symbolic support for the consequences of external negative evaluation of the stigmatized minority group (Jones et al., 1984).

The distinction between personal and group-level coping may be complicated because even group-level resources (such as the services of a lesbian/gay-affirmative church) are accessed and utilized by individuals. Whether individuals can access and use group-level resources depends upon many factors, including personal strengths and resources. But it is also true that an individual with strong personal coping resources could be lacking minority coping resources. For example, a young lesbian in a rural community will likely have a more difficult time attending events at a lesbian/gay community center (one may not be available in his or her local area and the only available centers require considerable travel) than a similar young lesbian in a major metropolitan area (e.g., Hastings & Hoover-Thompson, 2011). Young people living in a rural area have less access to group-level resources, making them more vulnerable to adverse health outcomes, regardless of their personal coping abilities (D'Augelli & Hart, 1987).

HEALTH OUTCOMES RELATED TO MINORITY STRESS
Mental Health

Minority stress causes serious injury in the form of psychological distress, mental health problems, suicide, and lowered psychological and social well-being. Studies have concluded that minority stress processes are related to an array of mental health problems including depressive symptoms, substance use, and suicide ideation. Studies of mental disorders, as defined by the *Diagnostic and Statistical Manual* (*DSM-IV*) of the American Psychiatric Association, have shown a higher prevalence of disorders among lesbian, gay, and bisexual compared to heterosexual populations (for reviews and meta-analyses, see Cochran & Mays, 2007; Herek & Garnets, 2007; King et al., 2008; Meyer, 2003a; see also Cochran and Mays, Chapter 15, this volume).

Diagnosed mental disorders are not the only measure of psychological distress; subthreshold mental health problems, such as depressed mood, anxiety, suicidal ideation, or substance use problems, that do not meet criteria for a formal psychiatric disorder are indicative of distress. Studies have shown that lesbian, gay, and bisexual individuals score higher than heterosexual people on such distress measures because of minority stress stemming from prevailing cultural stigma (Cochran, Sullivan, & Mays, 2003; Mays & Cochran, 2001).

Also, although less often studied, lesbian, gay, and bisexual individuals have lower levels of psychological and social well-being than heterosexual people because of exposure to minority stress, such as stigma and discrimination experiences (Frable, Wortman, & Joseph, 1997; Kertzner, Meyer, & Dolezal, 2004; Riggle, Rostosky, & Danner, 2009). This is not surprising because well-being, especially *social well-being*, reflects the person's relationship with his or her social environment: "the fit between the individuals and their social worlds" (Kertzner, Meyer et al., 2009, p. 500). Other studies have shown, for example, that stigma leads lesbian, gay, and bisexual persons to experience alienation, lack of integration with the community, and problems with self-acceptance (Frable, Wortman, & Joseph, 1997).

Minority stress is also associated with a higher incidence of reported suicide attempts among non-heterosexual as compared with heterosexual individuals (e.g., Cochran & Mays, 2000; Gilman et al., 2001; Herrell et al., 1999; Marshal et al., 2011; Meyer, Dietrich, & Schwartz, 2008; Safren & Heimberg, 1999). Higher rates of suicide attempts among members of sexual minorities are related to minority stress encountered by youth due to coming out conflicts with family and community (Ryan, Huebler, Diaz, & Sanchez, 2009). Youth is a time that can be particularly stressful, a time when young people realize they are lesbian, gay, or bisexual, and often disclose their sexual minority identities to parents, siblings, and others (Flowers & Buston, 2001).

Although most distal to the individual, minority stressors stemming from social structural discrimination have serious negative consequences for the mental health of sexual minorities. For example, lesbian, gay, and bisexual men and women who live in states without laws that extend protections to sexual minorities (e.g., job discrimination, hate crimes, relationship recognition) demonstrate higher levels of mental health problems compared to those living in states with laws that provide equal protection (Hatzenbuehler, Keyes, & Hasin, 2009). Furthermore, the denial of marriage rights for same-sex couples via U.S. federal and state policies has a demonstrated negative effect on the mental health of sexual minorities, regardless of their relationship status (Riggle, Rostosky, & Horne, 2010; Rostosky, Riggle, Horne, & Miller, 2009). Thus, minority stressors—ranging from distal structural discrimination, to interpersonal microaggressions, to personal

processes such as internalized homophobia—create a toxic everyday environment for lesbian, gay, and bisexual individuals, thereby increasing their risk for many kinds of mental health problems.

Physical Health

A number of studies have also demonstrated links between minority stress factors and physical health. In a recent study, we examined the impact of minority stress on physical health problems (e.g., flu, hypertension, sexually transmitted infections, tendonitis, and cancer) among a diverse group of lesbian, gay, and bisexual men and women (Frost, Lehavot, & Meyer, 2011). We found that lesbian, gay, and bisexual people who had experienced a prejudice-related stressful life event (e.g., assault provoked by known or assumed sexual orientation, being fired from a job because of your sexual minority identity) were about three times more likely than those who did not experience a prejudice-related life event to have suffered a serious physical health problem over a 1-year period. This effect remained statistically significant even after controlling for the experience of other stressful events that did not involve prejudice, as well as other factors known to affect physical health, such as age, gender, socioeconomic status, employment, and lifetime health history. Thus, prejudice-related stressful life events were more damaging to the physical health of lesbian, gay, and bisexual people than general stressful life events that did not involve prejudice.

Most of the research on the relationship between minority stress and physical health has been concerned with HIV/AIDS and has focused on men only. For example, studies examined the impact of concealing your sexual orientation—something unique to members of sexual minorities—as a stressor. Thus, HIV-positive but healthy gay men were followed up for 9 years to assess factors that contributed to progression of HIV (e.g., moving from asymptomatic HIV infection to a diagnosis with an AIDS-defining disease, such as pneumonia). The researchers showed that HIV progressed more rapidly among men who concealed their gay identity than among those who disclosed it. This was true even after the investigators controlled for the effects of other potentially confounding factors, such as health practices, risky sexual behaviors, and medication use (Cole, Kemeny, Taylor, Visscher, & Fahey, 1996). More recent studies, conducted in the context of the availability of more effective HIV medications than were available in 1996, similarly found that concealment of gay identity was associated with lower CD4 counts, which measure the progression of HIV disease (Strachan, Bennett, Russo, & Roy-Byrne, 2007; Ullrich, Lutgendorf, & Stapleton, 2003).

The effects of concealment can be injurious in less medically vulnerable individuals too. In a study of HIV-negative gay men, Cole, Kemeny, Taylor, and Visscher (1996) showed that men who concealed their gay identity experienced a higher incidence of disease—including infectious diseases and cancer—than men who did not conceal their gay identity. As in the research on HIV-positive men, concealment was found to have a deleterious effect on health outcomes even after controlling for the effect of other potentially confounding factors, such as coping styles, health behaviors, and mental health problems. Other studies examined other aspects of the minority stress model. For example, Huebner and Davis (2007) studied the impact of experiences of discrimination on gay and bisexual men's health, and found that exposure to discrimination was related to outcomes such as number of sick days and number of physician visits.

Many other studies assessed the role of minority stressors in promoting risky behavior, especially HIV-related risk. For example, Hatzenbuehler, Nolen-Hoeksema, and Erickson (2008) assessed minority stress processes in a sample of bereaved gay men. They found that minority stressors, including internalized homophobia, discrimination experiences, and expectations of rejection, were associated with HIV risk behavior. Similar findings—assessing various aspects of minority stress processes and sexual risk outcome—were reported in other populations: Latino gay and bisexual men and transgender persons (Bruce, Ramirez-Valles, & Campbell, 2008; Nakamura & Zea, 2010); white and Latino lesbian, gay, and bisexual young adults (Ryan et al., 2009); gay/bisexual/two-spirit American Indian men (Lehavot, Walters, & Simoni, 2009); rural men who have sex with men (Preston, D'Augelli, Kassab, & Starks, 2007); and transgendered women of color (Sugano, Nemoto, & Operario, 2006).

One possible mechanism that explains how minority stressors increase high-risk sexual behaviors may be that they lead to the use of drugs and alcohol during sexual experiences, which reduces condom use (Kashubeck-West & Szymanski, 2008; Nakamura & Zea, 2010). For example, it is possible that drugs and alcohol may be used during sex to reduce the self-reproach associated with internalized homophobia (Meyer & Dean, 1998). Another possible explanation for this association is increased fatalism regarding HIV risk among men with high levels of internalized homophobia. Yi and colleagues found that men with high levels of internalized homophobia demonstrated high levels of fatalism regarding the eventuality of becoming infected with HIV, which were in turn associated with increased HIV risk behavior (Yi, Sandfort, & Shidlo, 2011). In other words, minority stress, in the internalization of the cultural stereotype about gay men as "disease vectors," may produce a self-fulfilling prophecy, increasing HIV risk-taking behavior among gay men. Johnson, Carrico, Chesney, and Morin (2008) extend this pattern of findings to explain further health risk in the form of nonadherence to antiretroviral therapy among HIV-positive gay men. Namely, increased internalized homophobia was associated with more anxiety and substance use, which resulted in increased sexual risk taking and decreased adherence to HIV treatment regimens among gay-identified men. It is important to note that much of this research is cross-sectional, and future research is needed to document the causal directions of these relationships.

Although few studies have examined the relationship between minority stress and physical health outcomes among sexual minority women, evidence suggests a pressing need for such research. Most notably, Cochran and Mays (2007) found more physical health problems among sexual minority women compared to heterosexual women, but sexual orientation differences were attenuated when feelings of distress were controlled for. Further evidence exists with regard to specific physical health conditions and negative health behaviors for which sexual minority women are at greatest risk. For example, rates of smoking are higher among lesbian and bisexual women compared to sexual minority men and heterosexual men and women (Blosnich & Horn, 2011; Hughes, Johnson, & Matthews, 2008). However, despite the higher prevalence of smoking behavior, sexual minorities do not differ from heterosexuals in terms of knowledge of the risks associated with smoking, a common determinant of smoking behavior (Pizacani et al., 2009). This suggests that other factors unique to the experiences of lesbian and bisexual women, including minority stress, may account for this disparity. Additionally, lesbian women tend to more often be overweight compared to heterosexual women (see Bowen, Balsam, & Ender, 2008 for a review). Recent qualitative findings suggest that experiences of minority stress—in the form of concealment, shame, and general feelings of oppression—are major factors in producing this weight-related health disparity (Roberts, Stuart-Shor, & Oppenheimer, 2010). Further research is necessary to adequately understand the connection between minority stress and the physical health of sexual minority women.

INTERPERSONAL RELATIONSHIPS: INTIMACY AND WORK ENVIRONMENT

The discussion of minority stress processes and outcomes above focuses on mental and physical health outcomes. However, there is a growing body of research aimed at extending the minority stress model to explain outcomes in other areas central to the health and well-being of lesbian, gay, and bisexual individuals. These include interpersonal romantic relationships (e.g., Frost, 2011a, 2011b; Frost & Meyer, 2009), parenting (e.g., Bos & van Balen, 2008; Weber, 2008), the workplace (e.g., Fassinger, 2008), and crime and incarceration (e.g., Jones et al., 2008).

Intimate Relationships

Lesbian, gay, and bisexual individuals in interpersonal romantic relationships are subject to minority stressors that are distinctively products of the social, political, and cultural devaluation of same-sex sexualities, relationships, and intimacy (Frost, 2011a, 2011b; Frost & Meyer, 2009; Rostosky, Riggle, Gray, & Halton, 2007; Todosijevic, Rothblum, & Solomon, 2005). Minority stressors may affect lesbian, gay, and bisexual people's experiences within and in pursuit of relationships because of discrimination and stigmatization from other people in their lives. Sexual minority individuals in same-sex relationships experience stigmatization specific to their relationships on an interpersonal level (Diamond, 2006; Green & Mitchell, 2002; Peplau & Fingerhut, 2007). Compared to single lesbian, gay, and bisexual individuals, those in relationships may experience greater stress related to not being accepted, especially by their families (Lewis, Derlega, Berndt, Morris, & Rose, 2001). These types of minority stressors make it difficult for individuals in, or desiring to be in, same-sex relationships to achieve their needs and goals for intimacy (Frost, 2011a), which puts them

at risk not only for poorer well-being and mental health, but also for decreased relationship quality (Caron & Ulin, 1997; Frost & Meyer, 2009; Meyer & Dean, 1998; Otis, Rostosky, Riggle, & Hamrin, 2006; Todosijevic, Rothblum, & Solomon, 2005).

These findings can extend to the sexual domain as well (McClelland, 2010). For example, although similar factors predict sexual satisfaction for heterosexual and sexual minority women, internalized homophobia exerts an additional negative influence on sexual minority women's sexual satisfaction. Although very little research has focused on experiences of intimacy for lesbian, gay, and bisexual individuals not in relationships, preliminary findings suggest experiences of internalized homophobia can have a negative effect on intimacy-related outcomes such as generalized sexual problems, loneliness, and other relational strains (Frost & Meyer, 2009).

In the late 1990s and early 2000s public debate on same-sex marriage was ignited by election campaigns and court decisions that suggested that such marriages may become legal in some states. Such public debate and legal battles about the place of same-sex marriages in American society, which often took overtly hostile tones, exacerbated stress faced by lesbian, gay, and bisexual persons, including those in intimate relationships. Voter initiatives such as California's Proposition 8, which added to California's constitution a definition of marriage as only between a man and a woman, and the Defense of Marriage Act, passed by Congress in 1996, which prohibits the United States from recognizing same-sex marriages performed in states or other nations, add to minority stress for lesbian, gay, and bisexual people by reminding them of social disapproval of their relationships (Herek, 2006; Riggle, et al., 2010; Russell & Richards, 2003). The passage of anti-same-sex marriage policies frustrates and devalues the pursuit of same-sex intimacy (Frost, 2011a). Furthermore, the uncertainty of the legal status of same-sex partnerships creates relational uncertainty regarding couples' lives together, including raising children and property rights. Particularly painful is the effect on end-of-life planning, as uncertainty and hostile laws disrupt the protective functions that relationships serve (de Vries, Mason, Quam, & Acquaviva, 2009).

Minority Stress at the Workplace

Lesbian, gay, and bisexual people face high levels of discrimination and harassment in the workplace when compared with heterosexual people. Analysis of data from the General Social Survey (GSS), a national probability survey representative of the U.S. population, found that, 27% of lesbian, gay, and bisexual respondents had experienced at least one form of sexual orientation-based discrimination during the 5 years prior to the survey (Sears & Mallory, 2011). Research has consistently demonstrated that lesbian, gay, and bisexual people frequently face the challenge of negotiating minority stressors in the workplace (e.g., Fassinger, 2008; Ragins, Singh, & Cornwell, 2007; Huffman, Watrous-Rodriguez, & King, 2008). Waldo (1999) showed a relationship between employers' organizational climate and the experience of heterosexism in the workplace, which was related to adverse psychological, health, and job-related outcomes in lesbian, gay, and bisexual employees. Heterosexual and nonheterosexual individuals do not receive equal protection under the law regarding workplace rights. Although some states in the United States have laws protecting workers' rights, no Federal law exists to protect lesbian, gay, and bisexual workers from employment discrimination. Thus, minority stress persists in many job-related contexts in both structural and interpersonal forms. Structurally, such stress may result from the sense that an employer treats lesbian, gay, and bisexual persons and their families unfairly when, for example, an employer denies health and other benefits to nonheterosexual employees. Stressors may also include being treated with disrespect by supervisors and other employees.

Stigma concealment is a commonly experienced minority stressor for lesbian, gay, and bisexual people within the workplace. Analysis of the 2008 GSS data showed that more than a third of lesbian, gay, and bisexual employees had not disclosed their sexual identities to anyone at work and that only 25% were out to all of their co-workers (Sears & Mallory, 2011). The 2008 GSS data showed that lesbian, gay, and bisexual employees who were more open experienced more discrimination and harassment at work than those who were less open (Sears & Mallory, 2011). Lesbian, gay, and bisexual people who successfully conceal their sexual identity at work do not, however, avoid the harm of minority stress (Pachankis, 2007). The cognitive burden associated with hypervigilance and concealment can have negative effects on various indicators of job performance and satisfaction

(Ragins et al., 2007). Lyons and colleagues found that greater heterosexism in the workplace led to a decreased perceived fit within the workplace, which in turn predicted lower job satisfaction among lesbian, gay, and bisexual employees (Lyons, Brenner, & Fassinger, 2005). It is in many companies' and employers' social and economic best interests to address the needs of nonheterosexual workers (King & Cortina, 2010) because minority stress remains a persistent hindrance to workplace performance and satisfaction for lesbian, gay, and bisexual workers (Fassinger, 2008).

Structural interventions to reduce workplace minority stress would enact laws and regulations that protect lesbian, gay, and bisexual persons at the workplace. At present, some states and localities within the United States have enacted laws against sexual orientation-based workplace discrimination, and some have also enacted laws that protect against discrimination based on gender identity, but there is as yet no national law to prohibit workplace discrimination based on sexual orientation and gender identity in the United States.

DISCUSSION

The minority stress model has guided research in many areas documenting the impact of the social environment on lesbian, gay, and bisexual people's health and well-being (Institute of Medicine, 2011). Minority stress is helpful as an organizing model that can point researchers to the various factors that affect lesbian, gay, and bisexual people's health and well-being, such as trauma, internalized homophobia, or coping. The model can be useful for both research and interventions.

Interventions based on Minority Stress

The minority stress model can be used as a framework to guide multiple forms of interventions targeted at reducing the negative effects of minority stress (Ouellette, 1998). Figure 18.2 shows how elements of the model can point to various interventions sites and delivery methods (in the ovals), such as structural changes or service provision. The minority stress model reminds us that any one intervention site may not suffice and that multiple sites ought to be considered. An organized approach to prevention and intervention that uses the minority stress model would address the various areas impacted by minority stress and do so at various levels of intervention. Interventions

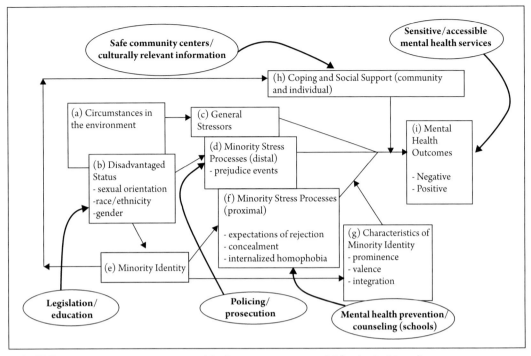

FIGURE 18.2. Intervention Sites Suggested by the Minority Stress Model (in the Oval Boxes).

at the structural level would institute protections from a stressful environment. For example, laws that protect lesbian, gay, and bisexual people from prejudice, discrimination, and violence would help to reduce the occurrence of prejudice-related stressors. Among such structural interventions are laws that respect gay men and lesbians' intimate relationships by providing them access to marriage and the benefits afforded to heterosexual married people and their families. The current version of a federal Employment Non-Discrimination Act (ENDA) would protect lesbian, gay, bisexual, and transgender people from discrimination in the workplace— another example of a legislative intervention that would protect lesbian, gay, bisexual, and transgender people at the structural level.

Other areas for intervention at the personal level would include, for example, culturally competent health and mental health services. The minority stress model points to resources that help members of sexual minorities cope with minority stress. Few researchers have developed and assessed interventions that explicitly address minority stress processes. However, a good example of an intervention that has proven impact in the area of HIV/AIDS prevention is the Mpowerment intervention (Hays, Rebchook, & Kegeles, 2003). By seeking to

empower young gay and bisexual men, this intervention targets some core minority stress processes. Unfortunately, little intervention research has addressed issues other than HIV/AIDS prevention in lesbian, gay, and bisexual populations.

Critiques of Minority Stress Theory

It is important to consider critiques of minority stress theory. By addressing and considering critiques, a theory can be better articulated and, hopefully, improved. One critique of the minority stress model is a general one that notes that there has been much positive change in the social environment of sexual minorities, and that lesbian, gay, and bisexual people—especially sexual minority youth—are no longer exposed to minority stress. Because of social changes over the past few decades in Western societies, with social attitudes becoming more accepting of homosexuality, this critique suggests that lesbian, gay, and bisexual people no longer encounter the minority stressors as described by the model. The critique suggests that the minority stress model is no longer a viable psychological model. As Savin-Williams, one proponent of this view, wrote in *The New Gay Teenager* (2005), "The culture of contemporary teenagers easily incorporates its homoerotic members. It's more than being gay-friendly. It's being gay-blind" (p. 197). He also states, "What if young people with same-sex desires are basically content with modern culture...? Maybe real changes in society's politics, laws and consciousness toward gay people have raised the possibility that sexual orientation is or will soon be irrelevant in all important respects" (p. 194).

This critique is correct to some degree because as a social theory, minority stress assumes the existence of certain stigmatizing social conditions. If these have changed, then the theory would require revision. But any theory should be assessed based on empirical evidence. New evidence would provide a good direction for future research and for elaboration and growth of theory. For example, if this critique is fundamentally correct, research should find no differences among lesbian, gay, bisexual, and heterosexual youth in their levels of stress and related mental health outcomes.

Empirical findings do not support this view. Neither condition outlined above—that lesbian, gay, and bisexual people experience no more stress than heterosexual people, or that they do not have more health and mental health problems—is satisfied. Thus, to conclude that we live in a gay-blind (some say, *postgay*) society that is equally accepting of heterosexual and nonheterosexual people is simply wrong (Herek, 2009b). Even with the many advances in social acceptance of sexual minorities over the past few decades, there is still considerable evidence of pervasive bullying of school children because they are perceived to be lesbian, gay, or bisexual (Blow, 2009; Tharinger, 2008). Surveys of sexual minority youth report that they are more likely than their peers to encounter chronic harassment, such as being called derogatory names, and that such name-calling is in fact commonplace. A survey by the Gay, Lesbian, and Straight Education Network found that as many as 85% of sexual minority students were called names or were threatened at school (Kosciw, Greytak, Diaz, & Bartkiewicz, 2010). Friedman and colleagues (2011) conducted a meta-analysis of studies examining antigay environments in schools. Compared to heterosexual youth, sexual minority youth were 170% more likely to be assaulted at school and 240% more likely to miss school due to fear that they would be unsafe at school or on their way to or from school. In particular, 40% of lesbians, 44% of bisexual females, 43% of gay males, and 50% of bisexual males were assaulted at school and 16% of lesbian females, 23% of bisexual females, 14% of gay males, and 23% of bisexual males missed school because they feared for their safety.

Studies have also shown that unlike other minority groups, rejection can occur at home, and antigay victimization can be perpetrated by family members of sexual minority children and youth (D'Augelli, Hershberger, & Pilkington, 1998; Diamond et al., 2011; Ryan, et al., 2009). For example, in one study, a gay man recalled being raped and brutally beaten to unconsciousness at age 13 by a family member who, in the respondent's words, "raped me because I was gay and to teach me what a faggot goes through" (Gordon & Meyer, 2008, p. 62). There is strong evidence as well of boys and girls who were thrown out of their homes and became homeless because of their family's rejection of their homosexuality (Ryan et al., 2009). In one probability study of high school students conducted in Massachusetts, 16% of sexual minority youth as compared with 3% of heterosexual youth were homeless for various reasons, although not necessarily as a result of being rejected by their families (Fournier et al., 2009). In short, research has found that stigma and discrimination against nonheterosexual youth still exist, and that many lesbian, gay, and bisexual adolescents and young adults suffer from minority stress.

Future Directions

Although researchers have developed many areas of study, there are areas of minority stress research that need to be addressed in the future.

Improved measures. First, researchers need to develop more focused measures of minority stress. For example, one area that has not been well described is the experience of minor stressors, also referred to as daily hassles or everyday discrimination. Such stressors can have a great impact on well-being by reminding the lesbian, gay, or bisexual person of his or her disadvantaged status. Filling out an administrative form that inquires about marital status by asking about "spouse" but does not provide language that accounts for long-term same-sex partners is something that many lesbians and gay men describe as distressing. We do not have well-developed quantitative measures and do not fully understand the impact of such minor events. Are they merely annoyances that can be easily shrugged off, or do they have a more profound and cumulative impact on the well-being of lesbian, gay, and bisexual individuals?

On the other end of the stress continuum, researchers have not yet developed measures that assess the social environment without relying on self-report data. Subjective assessments of exposure to prejudice may be biased both by overreporting and underreporting exposure to negative prejudice-related stress (Meyer, 2003b). For example, Meyer et al., (2008) found that lesbian, gay, and bisexual people experience more minority stress than heterosexual people when stress was assessed objectively by the researchers, but when the researchers assessed subjective experiences of stress, sexual minority individuals did not report greater exposure to stress than did heterosexual people. One example of an objective measure is the categorization of states with and without laws that protect members of sexual minorities (Hatzenbuehler, et al., 2009). The authors found a more pronounced minority stress effect on mental health in states without protections as compared with states with protections for lesbian, gay, and bisexual people (see also Hatzenbuehler, 2011). Another example is research (Heck, Flentje, & Cochran, 2011) that assessed the mental health of youth in schools that have a Gay-Straight Alliance compared with those that do not. These studies found that students in schools with a Gay-Straight Alliance reported lower psychological distress, less alcohol use, and higher self-esteem than did those in schools without these groups.

Minority stress across the life course. Two other areas that are underdeveloped are interrelated. We need to better understand minority stress across the life course, and contextualize minority stress within a continually shifting social environment. Clearly the social environment of lesbian, gay, and bisexual persons has been shifting in many important ways. This is true both in terms of global historical social changes and developmentally during an individual's lifespan. As a person moves across the lifespan he or she can change the social environment significantly. For example, peer environments of young people may be more accepting than the environment they will find as they enter the work force. In contrast, older lesbian, gay, and bisexual people moving to retirement homes and related facilities may find them less accommodating.

The role of identity in minority stress. Another area that is not well understood is how identity dimensions are related to the experience and impact of minority stress. Identity dimensions include prominence (how central a person's sexual minority identity is to their sense of self), valence (how positive or negative the identity is), and integration (how strongly connected to one another are sexual minority and other identities) (Meyer, 2003a; Stirratt, Meyer, Ouellette, & Gara, 2008). There are two questions that need elaboration. First, what is the impact of prominence of identity? Although the model (Figure 18.1) suggests that identity will interact with the effect of stress on health outcomes—for example, the greater a person's identification with a sexual minority identity, the more harm there is from a stressful event in that area—little research has examined this relationship. Moreover, there are conflicting hypotheses and evidence regarding this relationship. One hypothesis suggests that a prominent identity may make someone more sensitive to stress in that realm, and therefore there would be greater impact for a stressor in an identity area. The other hypothesis is that a more prominent identity will generate better coping and resources to ameliorate the impact of stress. Little evidence exists to answer these questions. Models of identity integration have yet to be developed that take into account the complexities of the process. Models of coming out employed relatively simplistic notions of identity, focusing on sexual minority identity alone with little consideration of its relationship to other social identities. A more useful model involves identity hierarchies that encompass various identities and their intersections (Rosenberg, 1997; Eliason & Schope, 2007). Stemming from this recognition is the intersectionality perspective, which suggests that the experience of diverse groups, such as those defined by gender, race/ethnicity, class, and sexual orientation, cannot be easily captured by adding knowledge about each group alone. That is, combining of separate knowledge about black women with knowledge about lesbian women is not sufficient to understanding the unique experiences of black lesbian women (Bowleg, 2008). Other aspects of diversity include bisexual men and women, nongay identified men who have sex with men and women who have sex with women, urban/rural lesbians and gay men, those of varying socioeconomic levels, immigrants, and so forth. Research in this area is growing (e.g., Bowleg, 2008; Purdie-Vaughns & Eibach, 2008; Stirratt et al., 2008). Greater attention to how minority stress processes impact various intersectional groups would, however, help to achieve better understandings of health and well-being within these populations.

CONCLUSIONS

The minority stress model has been a useful and productive model to understand and address disparities in health outcomes among lesbian, gay, bisexual, and heterosexual populations. The model points to social stress processes caused by prejudice and stigma, such as experiences of victimization of different types, ranging from harassment to hate crimes, and the internalization of negative social attitudes. The model also points to the importance of considering resiliency factors—such as social support and coping resources—in considering causes of health outcomes. Ultimately, according to the model, health outcomes are determined by the balance of positive (coping and social support) and negative (stressors) effects. Future work must take this balance into account to better understand and improve the health and well-being of lesbian, gay, and bisexual individuals and communities.

REFERENCES

Blosnich, J. R., & Horn, K. (2011). Associations of discrimination and violence with smoking among emerging adults: Differences by gender and sexual orientation. *Nicotine & Tobacco Research, 13,* 1284–1295. doi: 10.1093/ntr/ntr183.

Blow, C. M. (2009, April 24).Two little boys. *The New York Times.* Retrieved from http://blow.blogs.nytimes.com/2009/04/24/two-little-boys/ (accessed May 11, 2012).

Bos, H. M., & van Balen, F. (2008). Children in planned lesbian families: Stigmatisation, psychological adjustment and protective factors. *Culture, Health & Sexuality, 10*(3), 221–236. doi: 10.1080/13691050701601702.

Bowen, D. J., Balsam, K. F., & Ender, S. R. (2008). A review of obesity issues in sexual minority women. *Obesity, 16,* 221–228. doi: 10.1038/oby.2007.34.

Bowleg, L. (2008). When black + lesbian + woman ≠ black lesbian woman: The methodological challenges of qualitative and quantitative intersectionality research. *Sex Roles, 59,* 312–325. doi: 10.1007/s11199-008-9400-z.

Bruce, D., Ramirez-Valles, J., & Campbell, R. T. (2008). Stigmatization, substance use, and sexual risk behavior among Latino gay and bisexual men and transgender persons. *Journal of Drug Issues, 38,* 235–260.

Caron, S. L., & Ulin, M. (1997). Closeting and the quality of lesbian relationships. *Families in Society, 78,* 413–419.

Cochran, S. D., & Mays, V. M. (2000). Lifetime prevalence of suicide symptoms and affective disorders among men reporting same-sex sexual partners: Results from NHANES III. *American Journal of Public Health, 90,* 573.

Cochran, S. D., & Mays, V. M. (2007). Physical health complaints among lesbians, gay men, and bisexual and homosexually experienced heterosexual individuals: Results from the California quality of life survey. *American Journal of Public Health, 97,* 2048–2055. doi: 10.2105/AJPH.2006.087254.

Cochran, S. D., Sullivan, J. G., & Mays, V. M. (2003). Prevalence of mental disorders, psychological distress, and mental health services use among lesbian, gay, and bisexual adults in the United States. *Journal of Consulting and Clinical Psychology, 71,* 53–61. doi: 10.1037/0022-006X.71.1.53.

Cole, S. W., Kemeny, M. E., Taylor, S. E., & Visscher, B. R. (1996). Accelerated course of human immunodeficiency virus infection in gay men who conceal their homosexual identity. *Psychosomatic Medicine, 58,* 219–231.

Cole, S. W., Kemeny, M. E., Taylor, S. E., Visscher, B. R., & Fahey, J. L. (1996). Accelerated course of human immunodeficiency virus infection in gay men who conceal their homosexual identity. *Psychosomatic Medicine, 58*(3), 219.

Crocker, J., & Major, B. (1989). Social stigma and self-esteem: The self-protective properties of stigma. *Psychological Review, 96,* 608–630.

D'Augelli, A. R., & Hart, M. M. (1987). Gay women, men, and families in rural settings: Toward the development of helping communities. *American Journal of Community Psychology, 15,* 79–93.

D'Augelli, A. R., Hershberger, S. L., & Pilkington, N. W. (1998). Lesbian, gay, and bisexual youths and their families: Disclosure of sexual orientation and its consequences. *American Journal of Orthopsychiatry, 68,* 361–371.

de Vries, B., Mason, A.M., Quam, J., & Acquaviva, K. (2009). State recognition of same-sex relationships and preparation for end of life among lesbian and gay boomers. *Sexuality Research and Social Policy, 6,* 90–101.

Diamond, L. M. (2006). The intimate same-sex relationships of sexual minorities. In A. L. Vangelisti & D. Perlman (Eds.), *The Cambridge handbook of personal relationships* (pp. 293–312). New York: Cambridge University Press.

Diamond, G. M., Shilo, G., Jurgensen, E., D'Augelli, A., Samarova, V., & White, K. (2011). How depressed and suicidal sexual minority adolescents understand the causes of their distress. *Journal of Gay & Lesbian Mental Health, 15,* 130–151.

Díaz, R. M., Ayala, G., Bein, E., Henne, J., & Marin, B. V. (2001). The impact of homophobia, poverty, and racism on the mental health of gay and bisexual Latino men: Findings from 3 US cities. *American Journal of Public Health, 91,* 927–932.

Dohrenwend, B. P. (2000). The role of adversity and stress in psychopathology: Some evidence and its implications for theory and research. *Journal of Health and Social Behavior, 41,* 1–19.

Eliason, M. J., & Schope, R. (2007). Shifting sands or solid foundation? Lesbian, gay, bisexual, and transgender identity formation. In I. H. Meyer & M. E. Northridge (Eds.), *The health of sexual minorities: Public health perspectives on lesbian, gay, bisexual and transgender populations* (pp. 3–26). New York: Springer.

Fassinger, R. E. (2008). Workplace diversity and public policy: Challenges and opportunities for psychology. *American Psychologist, 63,* 252–268.

Flowers, P., & Buston, K. (2001). "I was terrified of being different": Exploring gay men's accounts of growing-up in a heterosexist society. *Journal of Adolescence, 24,* 51–65.

Fournier, M. E., Austin, S. B., Samples, C. L., Goodenow, C. S., Wylie, S. A., & Corliss, H. L. (2009). A comparison of weight-related behaviors among high school students who are homeless and non-homeless. *Journal of School Health, 79,* 466–473.

Frable, D. E., Wortman, C., & Joseph, J. (1997). Predicting self-esteem, well-being, and distress in a cohort of gay men: The importance of cultural stigma, personal visibility, community networks, and positive identity. *Journal of Personality, 65,* 599–624.

Friedman, M. S., Marshal, M. P., Guadamuz, T. E., Wei, C., Wong, C. F., Saewyc, E., & Stall, R. (2011). A meta-analysis of disparities in childhood sexual abuse, parental physical abuse, and peer victimization among sexual minority and sexual nonminority individuals. *American Journal of Public Health, 101*(8), 1481–1494. doi: 10.2105/AJPH.2009.190009.

Frost, D. M. (2011a). Similarities and differences in the pursuit of intimacy among sexual minority and heterosexual individuals: A personal projects analysis. *Journal of Social Issues, 67,* 282–301.

Frost, D. M. (2011b). Stigma and intimacy in same-sex relationships: A narrative approach. *Journal of Family Psychology, 25,* 1–10.

Frost, D. M., Lehavot, K., & Meyer, I. H. (2011, August). *Minority stress and physical health among sexual minorities.* Poster presented at the annual meetings of the American Psychological Association, Washington, DC.

Frost, D. M., & Meyer, I. H. (2009). Internalized homophobia and relationship quality among lesbians, gay men, and bisexuals. *Journal of Counseling Psychology, 56,* 97–109.

Gilman, S. E., Cochran, S. D., Mays, V. M., Hughes, M., Ostrow, D., & Kessler, R. C. (2001). Risk of psychiatric disorders among individuals reporting same-sex sexual partners in the National Comorbidity Survey. *American Journal of Public Health, 91,* 933–939.

Gordon, A. R., & Meyer, I. H. (2008). Gender nonconformity as a target of prejudice, discrimination, and violence against LGB individuals. *Journal of LGBT Health Research, 3,* 55–71. doi: 10.1080.15574090802093562.

Green, R.-J., & Mitchell, V. (2002). Gay and lesbian couples in therapy: Homophobia, relational ambiguity, and social support. In A. S. Gurman & N. S. Jacobson (Eds.), *Clinical handbook of couple therapy* (3rd ed., pp. 546–568). New York: Guilford Press.

Hastings, S. L., & Hoover-Thompson, A. (2011). Effective support for lesbians in rural communities: The role of psychotherapy. *Journal of Lesbian Studies, 15,* 197–204.

Hatzenbuehler, M. L. (2011). The social environment and suicide attempts in lesbian, gay, and bisexual youth. *Pediatrics, 127,* 896–903. doi: 10.1542/peds.2010–3020.

Hatzenbuehler, M. L., Keyes, K. M., & Hasin, D. S. (2009). State-level policies and psychiatric morbidity in lesbian, gay, and bisexual populations. *American Journal of Public Health, 99*(12), 2275–2281. doi: 10.2105/AJPH.2008.153510.

Hatzenbuehler, M. L., Nolen-Hoeksema, S., & Erickson, S. J. (2008). Minority stress predictors of HIV risk behavior, substance use, and depressive symptoms: Results from a prospective study of bereaved gay men. *Health Psychology, 27,* 455–462. doi: 10.1037/0278–6133.27.4.455.

Hays, R. B., Rebchook, G. M., & Kegeles, S. M. (2003). The Mpowerment project: Community-building with young gay and bisexual men to prevent HIV. *American Journal of Community Psychology, 31*(3), 301–312.

Heck, N. C., Flentje, A., & Cochran, B. N. (2011). Offsetting risks: High school gay-straight alliances and sexual minority youth. *School Psychology Quarterly, 26,* 161–174.

Herdt, G., & Kertzner, R. (2006). "I do, but I can't": The impact of marriage denial on the mental health and sexual citizenship of lesbians and gay men in the United States. *Sexuality Research & Social Policy, 3,* 33–49.

Herek, G. M. (2006). Legal recognition of same-sex relationships in the United States: A social science perspective. *American Psychologist, 61,* 607–621.

Herek, G. M. (2009a). Hate crimes and stigma-related experiences among sexual minority adults in the United States: Prevalence estimates from a national probability sample. *Journal of Interpersonal Violence, 24,* 54–74. doi: 10.1177/0886260508316477.

Herek, G. M. (2009b). Sexual stigma and sexual preju-dice in the United States: A conceptual framework. In D. A. Hope (Ed.), *Contemporary perspectives on les-bian, gay, and bisexual Identities* (pp. 65–111): New York: Springer.

Herek, G. M., & Garnets, L. D. (2007). Sexual orien-tation and mental health. *Annual Review of Clinical Psychology, 3*, 353–375.

Herrell, R., Goldberg, J., True, W. R., Ramakrishnam, V., Lyons, M., Eisen, S., et al. (1999). Sexual orientation and suicidality: A co-twin control study in adult men. *Archives of General Psychiatry, 56*, 867–874.

Huebner, D. M., & Davis, M. C. (2007). Perceived anti-gay discrimination and physical health outcomes. *Health Psychology, 26*, 627–634.

Huffman, A. H., Watrous-Rodriguez, K. M., & King, E. B. (2008). Supporting a diverse workforce: What type of support is most meaningful for lesbian and gay employees? *Human Resource Management, 47*, 237–253.

Hughes, T. L., Johnson, T. P., & Matthews, A. K. (2008). Sexual orientation and smoking: Results from a multi-site women's health study. *Substance Use & Misuse, 43*, 1218–1239. doi: 10.1080/10826080801914170.

Institute of Medicine (IOM). (2011). *The health of les-bian, gay, bisexual, and transgender people: Building a foundation for better understanding.* Washington, DC: The National Academies Press.

Johnson, M. O., Carrico, A. W., Chesney, M. A., & Morin, S. F. (2008). Internalized heterosexism among HIV-positive, gay-identified men: Implications for HIV prevention and care. *Journal of Consulting and Clinical Psychology, 76*, 829–839. doi: 10.1037/0022–006X.76.5.829.

Jones, E. E., Farina, A., Hestrof, A. H., Markus, H., Miller, D. T., & Scott, R. A. (1984). *Social stigma: The psy-chology of marked relationships.* New York: W.H. Freeman & Co.

Jones, K. T., Johnson, W. D., Wheeler, D. P., Gray, P., Foust, E., Gaiter, J., & North Carolina Men's Health Initiative Study Team. (2008). Nonsupportive peer norms and incarceration as HIV risk correlates for young black men who have sex with men. *AIDS and Behavior, 12*, 41–50. doi: 10.1007/s10461–007–9228–5.

Kashubeck-West, S., & Szymanski, D. M. (2008). Risky sexual behavior in gay and bisexual men. *The Counseling Psychologist, 36*, 595–614. doi: 10.1177/0011000007309633.

Kertzner, R., Meyer, I., & Dolezal, C. (2004). Psychological well-being in midlife and older gay men. In G. H. Herdt & B. De Vries (Eds.), *Gay and lesbian aging: Research and future directions* (pp. 97–115).New York: Springer.

Kertzner, R. M., Meyer, I. H., Frost, D. M., & Stirratt, M. J. (2009). Social and psychological well-being in lesbians, gay men, and bisexuals: The effects of race, gender, age, and sexual identity. *American Journal*

of Orthopsychiatry, 79, 500–510. doi: 10.1037/a0016848.

King, M., Semlyen, J., Tai, S. S., Killaspy, H., Osborn, D., Popelyuk, D., & Nazareth, I. (2008). A system-atic review of mental disorder, suicide, and deliberate self harm in lesbian, gay and bisexual people. *BMC Psychiatry, 8*, 70. doi: 10.1186/1471–244X-8–70.

King, E. B., & Cortina, J. M. (2010). The social and eco-nomic imperative of lesbian, gay, bisexual, and trans-gendered supportive organizational policies. *Industrial and Organizational Psychology, 3*, 69–78.

Kosciw, J. G., Greytak, E. A., Diaz, E. M., & Bartkiewicz, M. J. (2010). *The 2009 National School Climate Survey: The experiences of lesbian, gay, bisexual and transgender youth in our nation's schools.* New York: GLSEN.

Lehavot, K., Walters, K. L., & Simoni, J. M. (2009). Abuse, mastery, and health among lesbian, bisex-ual, and two-spirit American Indian and Alaska native women. *Cultural Diversity and Ethnic Minority Psychology, 15*, 275–284. doi: 10.1037/a0013458.

Lewis, R. J., Derlega, V. J., Berndt, A., Morris, L. M., & Rose, S. (2001). An empirical analysis of stressors for gay men and lesbians. *Journal of Homosexuality, 42*, 63–88.

Lichtenstein, B., Laska, M. K., & Clair, J. M. (2002). Chronic sorrow in the HIV-positive patient: Issues of race, gender, and social support. *AIDS Patient Care and STDs, 16*, 27–38. doi: 10.1089/108729102753429370.

Lyons, H. Z., Brenner, B. R., & Fassinger, R. E. (2005). A multicultural test of the theory of work adjustment: Investigating the role of heterosexism and fit percep-tions in the job satisfaction of lesbian, gay, and bisex-ual employees. *Journal of Counseling Psychology, 52*, 537–548.

Marshal, M. P., Dietz, L. J., Friedman, M. S., Stall, R., Smith, H. A., McGinley, J., Thoma, B. C., et al. (2011). Suicidality and depression disparities between sex-ual minority and heterosexual youth: A meta-analytic review. *Journal of Adolescent Health, 49*, 115–123. doi: 10.1016/j.jadohealth.2011.02.005.

Masten, A. S. (2001). Ordinary magic: Resilience processes in development. *American Psychologist, 56*, 227–238.

Mays, V. M., & Cochran, S. D. (2001). Mental health correlates of perceived discrimination among lesbian, gay, and bisexual adults in the United States. *American Journal of Public Health, 91*, 1869–1876.

McClelland, S. I. (2010). Intimate justice: A critical analysis of sexual satisfaction. *Social and Personality Psychology Compass, 4*, 663–680.

Meyer, I. H. (2003a). Prejudice, social stress, and men-tal health in lesbian, gay, and bisexual populations: Conceptual issues and research evidence. *Psychological Bulletin, 129*, 674–697.

Meyer, I. H. (2003b). Prejudice as stress: Conceptual and measurement problems. *American Journal of Public Health, 93*, 262–265.

Meyer, I. H., & Dean, L. (1998). Internalized homophobia, intimacy, and sexual behavior among gay and bisexual men. In G. M. Herek (Ed.), *Stigma and sexual orientation: Understanding prejudice against lesbians, gay men, and bisexuals* (pp. 160–186). Thousand Oaks, CA: Sage.

Meyer, I. H., Dietrich, J., & Schwartz, S. (2008). Lifetime prevalence of mental disorders and suicide attempts in diverse lesbian, gay, and bisexual populations. *American Journal of Public Health, 98*, 1004–1006.

Meyer, I. H., Ouellette, S. C., Haile, R., & McFarlane, T. A. (2011). "We'd Be Free": Narratives of life without homophobia, racism, or sexism. *Sexuality Research and Social Policy, 8*, 204–214. doi: 10.1007/s13178-011-0063-0.

Meyer, I. H., Schwartz, S., & Frost, D. M. (2008). Social patterning of stress and coping: Does disadvantaged social statuses confer more stress and fewer coping resources? *Social Science & Medicine, 67*, 368–379. doi: 10.1016/j.socscimed.2008.03.012.

Miller, C. T., & Major, B. (2000). Coping with stigma and prejudice. In T. F. Heatherton, R. E. Kleck, M. R. Hebl, & J. G. Hull (Eds.), *The social psychology of stigma* (pp. 243–272). New York: The Guilford Press.

Nakamura, N., & Cecilia Zea, M. (2010). Experiences of homonegativity and sexual risk behavior in a sample of Latino gay and bisexual men. *Culture, Health & Sexuality, 12*, 73–85.

Otis, M. D., Rostosky, S. S., Riggle, E. D. B., & Hamrin, R. (2006). Stress and relationship quality in same-sex couples. *Journal of Social and Personal Relationships, 23*, 81–99.

Ouellette, S. C. (1998). The value and limitations of stress models in HIV/AIDS. In B. P. Dohrenwend (Ed.), *Adversity, stress, and psychopathology* (pp. 142–160). New York: Oxford University Press.

Pachankis, J. E. (2007). The psychological implications of concealing a stigma: A cognitive-affective-behavioral model. *Psychological Bulletin, 133*, 328–345. doi: 10.1037/0033-2909.133.2.328.

Pearlin, L. (1999). The stress process revisited. In *Handbook of the sociology of mental health* (pp. 395–415). Retrieved from http://dx.doi.org/10.1007/0-387-36223-1_19.

Peplau, L. A., & Fingerhut, A. W. (2007). The close relationships of lesbian and gay men. *Annual Review of Psychology, 58*, 405–424.

Pizacani, B. A., Rohde, K., Bushore, C., Stark, M. J., Maher, J. E., Dilley, J. A., & Boysun, M. J. (2009). Smoking-related knowledge, attitudes and behaviors in the lesbian, gay and bisexual community: A population-based study from the U.S. Pacific Northwest. *Preventive Medicine, 48*, 555-561. doi:10.1016/j.ypmed.2009.03.013.

Preston, D. B., D'Augelli, A. R., Kassab, C. D., & Starks, M. T. (2007). The relationship of stigma to the sexual risk behavior of rural men who have sex with men.

AIDS Education and Prevention, 19, 218–230. doi: 10.1521/aeap.2007.19.3.218.

Purdie-Vaughns, V., & Eibach, R. P. (2008). Intersectional invisibility: The distinctive advantages and disadvantages of multiple subordinate-group identities. *Sex Roles, 59*, 377–391. doi: 10.1007/s11199-008-9424-4.

Ragins, B. R., Singh, R., & Cornwell, J. M. (2007). Making the invisible visible: Fear and disclosure of sexual orientation at work. *Journal of Applied Psychology, 92*, 1103–1118. doi: 10.1037/0021-9010.92.4.1103.

Ramirez-Valles, J. J. (2002). The protective effects of community involvement for HIV risk behavior: A conceptual framework. *Health Education Research, 17*, 389–403.

Ramirez-Valles, J., & Brown, A. (2003). Latinos' community involvement in HIV/AIDS: Organizational and individual perspectives on volunteering. *AIDS Education and Prevention, 15*(Suppl. 1), 90–104.

Ramirez-Valles, J., Fergus, S., Reisen, C. A., Poppen, P. J., & Zea, M. C. (2005). Confronting stigma: Community involvement and psychological well-being among HIV-positive Latino gay men. *Hispanic Journal of Behavioral Sciences, 27*, 101–119.

Riggle, E. B., Rostosky, S. S., & Danner, F. (2009). LGB identity and eudaimonic well being in midlife. *Journal of Homosexuality, 56*, 786–798.

Riggle, E. D. B., Rostosky, S. S., & Horne, S. G. (2010). Psychological distress, well-being, and legal recognition in same-sex couple relationships. *Journal of Family Psychology, 24*, 82–86. doi: 10.1037/a0017942.

Riggle, E. B., Whitman, J. S., Olson, A., Rostosky, S., & Strong, S. (2008). The positive aspects of being a lesbian or gay man. *Professional Psychology: Research and Practice, 39*, 210–217. doi: 10.1037/0735-7028.39.2.210.

Roberts, S. J., Stuart-Shor, E. M., & Oppenheimer, R. A. (2010). Lesbians' attitudes and beliefs regarding overweight and weight reduction. *Journal of Clinical Nursing, 19*, 1986–1994. doi: 10.1111/j.1365-2702.2009.03182.x.

Rosenberg, S. (1997). Multiplicity of selves. In R. D. Ashmore & L. J. Jussim (Eds.), *Self and identity: Fundamental issues* (pp. 23–45). New York: Oxford University Press.

Rostosky, S. S., Riggle, E. D. B., Gray, B. E., & Hatton, R. L. (2007). Minority stress experiences in committed same-sex couple relationships. *Professional Psychology: Research and Practice, 38*, 392–400. doi: 10.1037/0735-7028.38.4.392.

Rostosky, S. S., Riggle, E. D. B., Horne, S. G., & Miller, A. D. (2009). Marriage amendments and psychological distress in lesbian, gay, and bisexual (LGB) adults. *Journal of Counseling Psychology, 56*, 56–66.

Russell, G. M., & Richards, J. A. (2003). Stressor and resilience factors for lesbians, gay men, and bisexuals confronting antigay politics. *American Journal of Community Psychology, 31*, 313–328.

Ryan, C., Huebner, D., Diaz, R. M., & Sanchez, J. (2009). Family rejection as a predictor of negative health outcomes in white and Latino lesbian, gay, and bisexual young adults. *Pediatrics, 123,* 346–352. doi: 10.1542/peds.2007–3524.

Safren, S. A., & Heimberg, R. G. (1999). Depression, hopelessness, suicidality, and related factors in sexual minority and heterosexual adolescents. *Journal of Consulting and Clinical Psychology, 67*(6), 859–866.

Savin-Williams, R. C. (2005). *The new gay teenager.* Cambridge, MA; Harvard University Press.

Sears, B., & Mallory, C. (2011). *Documented evidence of employment discrimination and its effects on LGBT people.* The Williams Institute, UCLA School of Law. Accessed online May 11, 2012 at http://williamsinstitute.law.ucla.edu/wp-content/uploads/Sears-Mallory-Discrimination-July-20111.pdf.

Smart, L., & Wegner, D. M. (1999). Covering up what can't be seen: Concealable stigma and mental control. *Journal of Personality and Social Psychology, 77,* 474–486.

Stirratt, M. J., Meyer, I. H., Ouellette, S. C., & Gara, M. (2008). Assessing the intersectionality of identities through HICLAS analysis. *Self & Identity, 7,* 89–111.

Strachan, E. D., Bennett, W. R., Russo, J., & Roy-Byrne, P. P. (2007). Disclosure of HIV status and sexual orientation independently predicts increased absolute CD4 cell counts over time for psychiatric patients. *Psychosomatic Medicine, 69,* 74–80. doi: 10.1097/01.psy.0000249900.34885.46.

Sugano, E., Nemoto, T., & Operario, D. (2006). The impact of exposure to transphobia on HIV risk behavior in a sample of transgendered women of color in San Francisco. *AIDS and Behavior, 10,* 217–225. doi: 10.1007/s10461–005–9040-z.

Swim, J. K., Johnston, K., & Pearson, N. B. (2009). Daily experiences with heterosexism: Relations between heterosexist hassles and psychological well-being. *Journal of Social and Clinical Psychology, 28,* 597–629.

Tharinger, D. (2008). Maintaining the hegemonic masculinity through selective attachment, homophobia, and gay-bashing in schools: Challenges to intervention. *Social Psychology Review, 37*(2), 221–227.

Thoits, P. (1999). Self, identity, stress, and mental health. In C. S. Aneshensel & J. C. Phelan (Eds.), *Handbook of the sociology of mental health* (pp. 345–368). New York: Kluwer Academic/Plenum Publishers.

Todosijevic, J., Rothblum, E. D., & Solomon, S. E. (2005). Relationship satisfaction, affectivity, and gay-specific stressors in same-sex couples joined in civil unions. *Psychology of Women Quarterly, 29,* 158–166.

Ullrich, P. M., Lutgendorf, S. K., & Stapleton, J. T. (2003). Concealment of homosexual identity, social support and CD4 cell count among HIV-seropositive gay men. *Journal of Psychosomatic Research, 54,* 205–212.

Waldo, C. R. (1999). Working in a majority context: A structural model of heterosexism as minority stress in the workplace. *Journal of Counseling Psychology, 46,* 218–232.

Weber, S. (2008). Parenting, family life, and well-being among sexual minorities: Nursing policy and practice implications. *Issues in Mental Health Nursing, 29,* 601–618.

Wolitski, R. J., Pals, S. L., Kidder, D. P., Courtenay-Quirk, C., & Holtgrave, D. R. (2009). The effects of HIV stigma on health, disclosure of HIV status, and risk behavior of homeless and unstably housed persons living with HIV. *AIDS and Behavior, 13,* 1222–1232. doi: 10.1007/s10461–008–9455–4.

Yi, H., Shidlo, A., & Sandfort, T. (2011). Assessing maladaptive responses to the stress of being at risk of HIV infection among HIV-negative gay men in New York City. *Journal of Sex Research, 48,* 62-73. doi:10.1080/00224490903487570.

19

Sexual Orientation, Victimization, and Hate Crimes

KIMBERLY BALSAM AND TONDA HUGHES

Trauma has increasingly been recognized as playing an important role in the psychology of human experience. Recognition of the importance of such experiences was formalized in the third edition of the *Diagnostic and Statistical Manual* (American Psychiatric Association, 1980), when posttraumatic stress disorder (PTSD) became the first diagnosis to make explicit the connection between external events and internal psychological distress. Although the PTSD diagnosis was initially based on the experiences of combat veterans, researchers have broadened their conceptions of trauma, examining the impact of a wide range of experiences such as natural disasters, medical procedures, sudden death of a loved one, abuse, and criminal victimization.

Over the past two decades, researchers have increasingly focused on interpersonal victimization as a specific subset of trauma. Finkelhor and Kendall-Tackett (1997, p. 2) explain this distinction, defining victimization as "harms that occur to individuals because other human actors behave in ways that violate social norms." A large body of literature documents the occurrence of victimization experiences such as childhood abuse, bullying, intimate partner violence, and sexual and physical assault. Victimization experiences that are perpetrated by another human being are by definition embedded in an interpersonal context and have unique implications for psychological and social functioning. Research findings document the deleterious effects of such victimization experiences on health, including mental health, substance abuse, eating disorders, self-esteem, relationship quality, and sexual risk behaviors (Koenig, Doll, O'Leary, & Pequegnat, 2004; Logan, Walker, Jordan, & Leukefeld, 2006; Ouimette & Brown, 2003).

Although a great deal is known about victimization and its effects on the general population, research on victimization among lesbian, gay, and bisexual people has lagged considerably behind other work in this area. Very few studies of victimization assess sexual orientation. In addition, until recently, the majority of studies of childhood abuse, intimate partner violence, and sexual assault have focused exclusively on women as victims. Although some research has examined the effects of childhood sexual abuse on boys (Holmes & Slap, 1998), few have assessed victimization of adult men of any sexual orientation. Although the body of research on the health, mental health, and life experiences of lesbians, gay men, and bisexual women and men has grown in recent decades, only recently have studies of these population groups assessed victimization in a comprehensive manner.

Nevertheless, research on victimization experiences of sexual minority women and men has increased in the past decade (Friedman, Marshal, Guadamuz, Wei, & Wong, 2011). From these studies, it is clear that sexual minority people are at elevated risk for a wide range of victimization experiences over the lifespan, from childhood abuse in the home, to bullying and victimization at school, to physical and sexual assault in adulthood. The goal of this chapter is to provide an overview of this body of literature, highlighting prevalence and correlates of victimization among sexual minority people as well as implications for future research. We begin, however, by highlighting some methodological challenges of work in this area.

METHODOLOGICAL CHALLENGES

Researchers studying interpersonal victimization in any population face a number of methodological challenges that can influence research outcomes. One such challenge concerns the definition of victimization, which can be assessed behaviorally (e.g., did someone hit you?) or subjectively (e.g., were you physically abused?). Because individuals often do not define their experiences as "abuse," subjective definitions tend to yield lower prevalence rates than behavioral definitions. In addition, behavioral definitions within categories of victimization can vary widely. For example, definitions of "sexual assault" can range from unwanted touching to forced penetration or rape and can vary depending upon the age of the victim (Briere, 1992; Rinehart & Yeater, 2011). The cutoff age at which an unwanted sexual experience is considered "child sexual abuse" varies in the literature from 13 to 18 years of age. Similarly, intimate partner violence has been operationalized variously as including only physical violence, verbal or physical violence, and any behavior that includes an element of power and control. The overlap among various types of abuse (e.g., whether rape within the context of an intimate relationship is considered partner violence or sexual assault) can also confound results. The broad range of operational definitions of victimization has resulted in a wide range of prevalence rates in the literature that must be taken into account when attempting to interpret findings of studies with lesbian, gay, and bisexual people.

In addition to definitional issues, there are particular methodological issues that must be considered when studying victimization among lesbian, gay, and bisexual people, some of which have contributed to the reluctance of researchers to address this topic. For example, sexual minority individuals who have experienced abuse may view this as a double stigma and may be reluctant to participate in research that addresses victimization. This may be particularly true for gay and bisexual men, given that victimization runs counter to stereotypes of masculinity in our culture.

Another methodological consideration arises from stereotypes about the links between victimization and sexual orientation. Such stereotypes include the notion that being molested by a man in childhood causes boys to grow up to be gay, that being abused by men, either in childhood or adulthood, causes women to shun men and become lesbians, and that being gay means being a perpetrator of child sexual abuse. Although there is no empirical evidence for any of these beliefs, they are held by many people, and this may affect both research participants and the researchers themselves. Lesbian, gay, and bisexual participants may be cautious

about reporting experiences of child sexual abuse because they may fear that researchers will interpret their sexual orientation as being "caused" by the abuse. In the Lesbian Wellness Survey (Morris, 1997), several participants who reported a history of childhood sexual abuse wrote in the "comments" section that they wanted to be clear that they were not lesbian "because of" this abuse. Researchers, too, may avoid examining this topic out of fear of perpetuating stereotypes.

CHILDHOOD ABUSE
Childhood Physical Abuse
Definitions of childhood physical abuse (CPA) generally focus on childhood experiences of actions such as punching, beating, kicking, biting, burning, or shaking a child by a parent or adult caretaker. These definitions generally specify that intention to harm must be present, or that the actions caused physical injury. In their review of the literature, Kaplan, Pelcovitz, and Labruna (1999) define physical abuse as including physical injury or risk of injury as a result of physical aggression by a parent or parent substitute.

Researchers examining CPA among sexual minority people have generally found that these groups report higher rates than do their heterosexual counterparts (Austin et al., 2008; Balsam, Rothblum, & Beauchaine, 2005; Corliss, et al., 2002; Saewyc et al., 2006; Stoddard, Dibble, & Fineman, 2009; Tjaden, Thoeness, & Allison, 1999). For instance, using data from the National Survey of Midlife Development, Corliss, Cochran, and Mays (2002) found that both gay/bisexual men and lesbian/bisexual women reported greater major physical maltreatment by their parents or guardians than did heterosexual men and women. Similarly, Tjaden et al. (1999) found that adults who lived with a same-sex partner, a proxy measure for sexual minority status, were more likely to report being physically assaulted as children by adult caretakers than respondents who lived with opposite-sex partners. In recent analyses of data from the National Epidemiologic Survey on Alcohol and Related Conditions (NESARC), Hughes and colleagues (2010) also found higher rates of CPA among nonheterosexual respondents, although only the difference between bisexual and heterosexual women was statistically significant.

Sexual orientation differences in CPA are not due merely to sexual minority people growing up in more violent families. To test the hypothesis that sexual minority people are disproportionately exposed to CPA, even within the same family, Balsam et al. (2005) recruited a large national sample of lesbian, gay, and bisexual adults and their heterosexual siblings. After accounting for between-family variance, sexual minority status was a significant predictor of all childhood abuse experiences assessed, including physical abuse by parents or caretakers. This suggests that even within households, sexual minority siblings are at heightened risk of abuse. Stoddard et al. (2009) used a smaller sample of women in a sibling-matched design and found that 20% of lesbian women reported that they had been physically abused as children (before age 16) compared with 10% of their heterosexual sisters. The severity of physical abuse may also differ among sexual minorities relative to their heterosexual counterparts. For example, using the Nurse's Health Study (NHS II) dataset, Austin and colleagues (2008) found that lesbian and bisexual women experienced more severe, frequent, and persistent physical abuse as children and adolescents than did heterosexual women.

Although the majority of studies have not examined differences in rates of CPA based on lesbian/gay versus bisexual identity, there is some indication that those who identify as bisexual are at greater risk. For example, in a meta-analysis of school-based studies, Friedman et al. (2011) found that bisexual adolescents were 1.4 times as likely as heterosexual adolescents to report parental physical abuse, whereas, gay and lesbian adolescents were only 0.9 times as likely as heterosexual adolescents to report such parental physical abuse. Balsam et al. (2005) did not, however, find significant differences in CPA history between lesbian/gay and bisexual adults, nor have differences in CPA been reported between lesbian and gay respondents.

Childhood Sexual Abuse

In studies of sexual abuse, Finkelhor's (1979) definition of forced sexual behavior and/or sexual contact with someone 5 years or more older than the victim is frequently used. Some definitions include nonphysical contact, such as the perpetrator masturbating in front of the child. The upper age limit for child sexual abuse in published studies ranges from 13 to 18 years of age. Like CPA, prevalence rates for childhood sexual abuse (CSA)

vary substantially depending on whether subjective definitions (i.e., self-perception) or behavioral definitions are used (Hughes, Wilsnack, Kristjanson, & Benson, 2010).

Compared to CPA, there has been relatively more research examining CSA among sexual minority people. Numerous studies have reported high rates of CSA among lesbian and bisexual women. Depending on definitions and measures, studies have found rates ranging from 19% (Austin et al., 2008) to nearly 50% (Balsam et al., 2005) or even higher (Wilsnack et al., 2008). Most studies using community-based samples of lesbian and bisexual women estimate CSA prevalence in the range of 30–40% (Balsam et al., 2005; Hughes, Haas, Razzano, Cassidy, & Matthews, 2000; Matthews, Hughes, Johnson, Razzano, & Cassidy, 2002). Studies that include a heterosexual comparison group consistently show higher rates among sexual minority than among heterosexual people (Austin et al., 2008; Balsam et al., 2005). For example, Austin and colleagues (2008), using data from the population-based NHSII study, found that lesbian and bisexual women were more than twice as likely as heterosexual women to report CSA. Similarly, Hughes, McCabe and colleagues (Hughes, McCabe, et al., 2010) found rates of CSA to be twice as high for lesbian and bisexual women (35% and 39%) as for heterosexual women (10%) in the NESARC. In Balsam and colleagues' (2005) sibling study, lesbian (44%) and bisexual (48%) women were more likely to report a CSA history than heterosexual (30%) women, suggesting that sexual orientation differences may exist even within families.

Gay and bisexual men also report high rates of CSA. In nonclinical, community samples of gay and bisexual men, estimates range from 15% to 19% (Brennan, Hellerstedt, Ross, & Welles, 2007; Heidt, Marx, & Gold, 2005). Among men sampled at clinics, estimates run up to 37% (Doll et al., 1992). Using a more methodologically rigorous probability-based sampling method, Paul and colleagues (2001) found that 21% of the gay and bisexual male respondents in the multisite Urban Men's Health Study reported a history of CSA. Consistent with findings from research on women, studies that include heterosexual comparison groups have reported higher rates among gay and bisexual men. For example, comparing gay/bisexual men recruited from a local gay community event to a sample of predominately heterosexual college students, Tomeo and colleagues (2001) found that 49% of the gay/bisexual men but only 24% of the heterosexual men reported childhood molestation. Gay/bisexual men were also more likely to report CSA by male perpetrators than were heterosexual men, but were not more likely to report CSA by female perpetrators. In a meta-analytic study, Friedman and colleagues (2011) found that compared with male heterosexual adolescents, male gay and bisexual adolescents were almost five times as likely to report CSA. Using NESARC data, Hughes and colleagues (2010) found that gay and bisexual men (15% and 11%, respectively) were more likely than heterosexual men (2%) to report CSA, but only the difference between gay and heterosexual men was statistically significant. In Balsam and colleagues' (2005) study, gay (17%) and bisexual (32%) men were more likely to report a CSA history than were heterosexual (11%) men.

Bullying and Victimization at School

The elevated risk for victimization among sexual minority youth extends beyond the home and community and into school environments. Indeed, a growing body of research indicates that lesbian, gay, and bisexual adolescents are subject to a variety of victimization experiences at school, including verbal harassment, physical abuse, and sexual assault. For example, D'Augelli, Grossman, and Starks (2006) reported that 78% of 528 lesbian, gay, and bisexual adolescent participants had experienced verbal harassment, most of which occurred at school. Research using data from the population-based Growing Up Today Survey (GUTS) (N = 7559) found that sexual minority adolescents were more likely to report being bullied, and less likely to report that they bullied others, than were heterosexual adolescents (Berlan, Corliss, Field, Goodman, & Austin, 2010). Birkett, Espelage, and Koenig (2009) also found higher rates of reporting victimization via bullying and verbal and physical attacks among lesbian, gay, and bisexual youth than among their heterosexual peers. Even when not the target of direct bullying or victimization, sexual minority youth are subject to negative school environments in which homophobic comments are common and minority sexual identities are not affirmed (Kosciw & Greytak, 2009).

The extent to which lesbian, gay, and bisexual youth are vulnerable to school victimization and bullying may vary according to gender and gender expression. Prejudice and stereotypes about lesbian, gay, and bisexual identities are generally more negative with respect to males than females; hence, boys may be more vulnerable to bias-related victimization. For example, D'Augelli et al. (2006) found that gay and bisexual male youth were more likely to report victimization than were lesbian and bisexual female youth. Gender noncomformity may also increase visibility of lesbian, gay, and bisexual identities and evoke greater prejudice. In D'Augelli and his colleagues' (2006) study, youth whose gender expression was atypical were also more likely to experience victimization. Toomey, Ryan, Diaz, Card, and Russell (2010) similarly reported associations between gender nonconformity and school victimization.

Schools are embedded within a social-ecological context and the extent to which antigay bullying and harassment occur can be affected by characteristics of the neighborhood and community. For example, a national survey of 6209 high school students found that lesbian, gay, and bisexual adolescents in rural communities and in communities with lower adult educational attainment were more at risk than adolescents in urban areas (Kosciw & Greytak, 2009). A qualitative study that examined the responses of 307 teachers showed that 97% were aware of instances of general verbal and physical bullying, 82% were aware of homophobic verbal bullying, and 26% were aware of homophobic physical bullying (Warwick, Aggleton, & Douglas, 2001). However, awareness did not always translate into protective action; many teachers and staff lack the skills and knowledge to work effectively with lesbian, gay, and bisexual students. On the other hand, availability of lesbian- and gay-specific or inclusive programs has been shown to be associated with fewer reports of harassment and victimization within schools (Chesir-Teran & Hughes, 2009).

INTIMATE PARTNER VIOLENCE

Definitions of intimate partner violence (IPV) generally include physical aggression, but often also include verbal/psychological aggression, sexual aggression, and exertion of power and control. Koss et al. (1994) define intimate partner violence as "physical, visual, verbal, or sexual acts that are experienced by a woman or girl as a threat, invasion, or assault and that have the effect of hurting her or degrading her and/or taking away her ability to control contact with another individual." Definitions also vary in terms of the boundaries of an "intimate relationship." Some researchers may include couples who are dating or living together, whereas others may include only those who are legally married.

Despite gender stereotypes that explain IPV as a form of violence perpetrated by men against their female partners, research reveals that IPV does occur in same-sex intimate relationships. Some studies with heterosexual comparison groups have reported similar lifetime rates among heterosexual and sexual minority adults (Balsam et al., 2005; Elliott, 1996; Renzetti, 1989; Turell, 2000; Waldner-Haugrud & Gratch, 1997), but others have found higher rates among lesbian, gay, and bisexual people (Greenwood et al., 2002; Tjaden et al., 1999). In a 2010 analysis of data from the California Health Interview Survey, gay and lesbian adults were almost twice as likely as heterosexual adults to report lifetime IPV. Despite variations in the estimates, the findings show that same-sex relationships are not immune to IPV.

Among lesbian, gay, and bisexual people, some gender differences have been found with respect to lifetime prevalence of IPV. Studies using nonprobability samples have yielded rates ranging from 25% to 50% among lesbian and bisexual women (Balsam et al., 2005; Brand & Kidd, 1986; Lie et al., 1991), compared with rates of 12% to 39% among gay and bisexual men (Greenwood et al., 2002; Waldner-Haugrud & Gratch, 1997; Waterman, Dawson, & Bologna, 1989). Given the low rate of IPV victimization reported by heterosexual men it is not surprising that discrepancies between heterosexual and sexual minority people are larger for men than for women (Balsam et al., 2005; Tjaden et al., 1999). It is notable that gay and bisexual men's experiences of IPV more closely mirror those of women rather than those of heterosexual men. Only a few studies have included samples large enough to estimate rates of IPV among bisexual women and men. Using data from the Massachusetts State Behavior Risk Factor Surveillance Survey, Conron, Mimiaga, and Landers (2010) found that bisexual women reported the highest rates of lifetime IPV—higher than bisexual men, gays/lesbians, and heterosexual women and men. Similar results were found in analyses of NESARC data (Hughes, McCabe, et al., 2010).

Findings of comparable or higher rates of IPV in same-sex compared to opposite-sex relationships present a challenge to traditional theories of IPV and the interrelationships among oppression, power, and gender. Indeed, studies of lesbians and bisexual women that assess the gender of the perpetrator (Balsam et al., 2005; Brand & Kidd, 1986; Lie et al., 1991) have dispelled the myth that high rates of lifetime IPV among lesbians are due mostly to experiences with male partners, demonstrating that women can also be perpetrators of IPV. Although there is less research on factors that contribute to IPV among same-sex couples than among opposite-sex couples, power imbalance has been identified as a risk factor in both groups (Burke & Follingstad, 1999; Eaton et al., 2008; Lockhart, White, Causby, & Isaac, 1994; McClennen, 2005; McClennen, Summers, & Daley, 2002). At the same time, same-sex couples live in a social context that stigmatizes their lives and relationships. Minority stress associated with being lesbian, gay, or bisexual in a heterosexist society may also be a contributing factor. Balsam and Szymanski (2005) found that both IPV victimization and perpetration were associated with minority stress among lesbian and bisexual women.

Understanding of IPV in same-sex male couples is complicated by societal assumptions about who can be a victim. Because men are generally presumed to be perpetrators rather than victims of IPV, partner abuse within male same-sex relationships has received little attention (Elliott, 1996; Letellier, 1994; Seelau & Seelau, 2005). In addition, gay men may be reluctant to report IPV or acknowledge being victimized because this may be seen as inconsistent with their views of masculinity (Letellier, 1994).

The relative invisibility of same-sex IPV and the predominance of gender stereotypes of IPV result in a general lack of recognition of this phenomenon among healthcare providers, social service agencies, and law enforcement personnel (Merrill & Wolfe, 2000). Several studies cite disparities in access to domestic violence resources for victims in same-sex relationships (Kuehnle & Sullivan, 2003; McClennen et al., 2002; Merrill & Wolfe, 2000; Potoczniak, Mourot, Crosbie-Burnett, & Potoczniak, 2003). Because victims of same-sex IPV may not perceive formal sources of support (e.g., shelters, doctors, attorneys) to be helpful, they may turn instead to informal sources of support, such as friends (Kuehnle & Sullivan, 2003; McClennen, Summers, & Vaughan, 2002; McClennen, 2005; Merrill & Wolfe, 2000; Potoczniak et al., 2003). Although little research has evaluated the extent to which perceptions of heterosexism among providers are correct, it is important to recognize that many state laws do not extend restraining or protective orders to victims of same-sex IPV.

ADULT SEXUAL ASSAULT

Contemporary definitions of sexual assault focus on nonconsensual sexual penetration, including sexual intercourse, oral–genital contact, anal intercourse, or other bodily intrusions. In addition, some degree of force is usually involved, including physical force, threat of bodily harm, or proceeding with sexual activity when the victim is incapable of giving consent (e.g., he or she is under the influence of alcohol or drugs). The term "rape" is often used to mean penetration, whereas the terms "sexual assault" or "sexual coercion" usually include a broader range of unwanted sexual experiences. The definitional boundaries of sexual assault in adulthood can become blurred with IPV, given that sexual assault may occur within the context of an intimate relationship.

Research on adult sexual assault (ASA) among lesbians has generally found rates similar to or higher than those among heterosexual women. In a study using a community sample of lesbians and a demographically matched sample of heterosexual women, Hughes and colleagues (2001) found similar rates of ASA for lesbians (39%) and heterosexual women (42%). Similarly, analyses of data from the National Epidemiologic Survey on Alcohol and Related Conditions (Hughes, Szalacha, et al., 2010) found no significant differences in ASA among lesbian (8%), bisexual (7%), not sure (9%), and heterosexual (3%) women. In contrast, using samples of lesbian/bisexual women and their heterosexual sisters, Balsam and colleagues (Balsam, Lehavot, & Beadnell, 2011; Balsam et al., 2005) found that lesbian and bisexual women were more likely than their heterosexual sisters to report a history of sexual coercion, coerced intercourse, and rape. Stoddard and colleagues also found higher rates of ASA among lesbians than among their heterosexual sisters (Stoddard et al., 2009). Taken as a whole, these findings suggest that lesbian and bisexual women are at least as likely as their heterosexual peers to experience ASA in their lifetime.

Differences in sexual orientation in ASA among men, in contrast, are more pronounced. Although heterosexual men rarely report experiencing sexual assault in adulthood, gay and bisexual men report such experiences at rates similar to those reported by women. For example, in Balsam and colleagues' study (Balsam et al., 2005, 2011), almost 2% of heterosexual men compared with 13% of bisexual men and 12% of gay men reported rape in adulthood. In general, reports of ASA vary substantially, with rates as low as 5% in a probability-based sample reporting ASA within the context of IPV in the past 5 years (Greenwood et al., 2002) to as high at 18% in a community sample of men who have sex with men reporting ASA in a current or past relationship (Houston & McKirnan, 2007). Tjaden and colleagues (Tjaden et al., 1999) assessed the prevalence of forcible rape and found that almost 11% of same-sex cohabiting men reported rape since age 18, with perpetrators mostly being acquaintances or strangers.

REVICTIMIZATION

The term "revictimization" usually refers to the finding that individuals who experience sexual victimization in childhood are significantly more likely to experience sexual victimization in adulthood. This phenomenon has been well-documented in the empirical literature with women (Cloitre et al., 1996; Wyatt, Guthrie, & Notgrass, 1992) but is typically not studied among men, given men's relatively low risk for sexual assault in adulthood. However, recent research indicates the importance of studying revictimization among gay and bisexual men, whose risk of revictimization parallels that of women. For example, Balsam and colleagues (2011) found that among those who experienced CSA, gay men, lesbians, and heterosexual women were equally likely to be sexually revictimized in adulthood; heterosexual men, on the other hand, very rarely reported ASA, regardless of CSA history. (2005) found that gay men, bisexual men, and bisexual women with a history of CSA were more likely to report sexual revictimization than were lesbian women with a history of CSA. Given the relatively high rates of sexual victimization over the lifespan for sexual minority populations, it is important that revictimization be given attention in future research. It is possible that some of the elevated risk for victimization in adulthood in this population is a function of greater exposure to sexual abuse in childhood.

BIAS-RELATED VICTIMIZATION

Bias-related victimization, sometimes referred to as "hate crimes," is generally defined as crimes that occur because of an individual's minority status. Both heterosexual and sexual minority individuals may be victims of bias-related victimization based on gender, class, nationality, race/ethnicity, and religion, but lesbian, gay, and bisexual individuals are subject to additional bias-related victimization based on their sexual orientation. These experiences are, unfortunately, quite common. A report on bias crime commissioned by the U.S. Department of Justice (Finn & McNeil, 1987, cited in Klinger & Stein, 1994) concluded that lesbians and gay men may be the most frequently victimized group in the United States. In 2008, 17% of all single-incident hate crimes occurred because of the victim's sexual orientation (Justice, 2009). McDevitt, Balboni, Garcia, and Gu (2001) found that lesbian, gay, and bisexual individuals were more likely to be victims of hate crimes (31%) than other forms of crime (6%). A convenience sample of 306 lesbian, gay, and bisexual participants found that 73% had experienced at least one instance of bias-related victimization (Rose & Mechanic, 2002). Results from a national sample indicated 20% of sexual minority individuals had experienced person or property crimes; this proportion increased to 25% when attempted crimes were included (Herek, 2009).

Although bias-related victimization based on sexual orientation shares many features with other types of bias-related victimization, research also suggests some differences. For example, Dunbar (1998) found that physical assault, sexual assault, sexual harassment, and stalking were more frequent components of sexual orientation bias crimes than of other hate crimes. However, similar to other populations, lesbian, gay, and bisexual individuals are more likely to report less severe forms of bias victimization such as verbal harassment than more severe forms such as physical victimization (D'Augelli & Grossman, 2001; Herek, 2009).

Another line of research has focused on the characteristics of hate crimes (Green, Strolovich, Wong, & Bailey, 2001; Herek, Cogan, & Gillis, 2002; McDevitt et al., 2001). Green et al. (2001) found that hate crimes against gay men were more likely to occur in areas of New York City that are densely populated by lesbians and gay men. Herek and colleagues (2002) found that relative to nonbias crimes, crimes related to bias occurred much more frequently in public places (e.g., 60% for bias crimes versus 32% for nonbias crimes), including gay-identified settings (e.g., gay bars), schools, and other public settings (e.g., parks). Bias crimes were also more likely to have multiple perpetrators; 46% of bias crimes had two or more perpetrators, compared to only 17% of nonbias crimes. Other research on the location of hate crimes suggests that hate crime incidents generally occur close to the victim's home (McDevitt et al., 2001).

Compared to other sexual minority groups, gay men are more likely to report criminal victimization (Herek, Gillis, & Cogan, 1999; McDevitt et al., 2001). For example, approximately 59% of hate crimes against sexual minority individuals in 2008 occurred because of bias against gay or bisexual men (Justice, 2009). Both Herek (2009) and D'Augelli and Grossman (2001) reported that gay men were more likely than lesbians and bisexual men and women to report experiences of physical attack. Rothman and colleagues (Rothman, Exner, & Baughman, 2011) reviewed 75 studies on sexual assault among lesbian, gay, and bisexual people and concluded that experiences of bias-related sexual assaults are more common among gay and bisexual men than among lesbian and bisexual women.

RACE/ETHNICITY AND VICTIMIZATION

Although the majority of research studies have focused on predominantly white samples, there is growing evidence that some lesbian, gay, and bisexual ethnic minority individuals may be at heightened risk of abuse during childhood. For example, in a large national survey of lesbians, Morris and Balsam (2003) found especially high rates of CPA among women of color. In a more recent study that included a large national sample of ethnically diverse lesbian, gay, and bisexual adults, Balsam, Lehavot, Beadnell, and Circo (2010) found higher rates of CPA among African-American (51%) and Latina/o (57%) than among white (32%) participants. Even within ethnic or racial groups, lesbian, gay, and bisexual people of color may experience elevated risk of CPA. In a sample of adult American Indians, Balsam, Huang, Fieland, Simoni, and Walters (2004) found that those who identified as members of sexual minorities were more likely to report CPA than were those who identified as heterosexual.

Regarding racial/ethnic differences in childhood sexual abuse, the limited data available suggest that some sexual minority people of color experience elevated risk. In the survey by Balsam and colleagues' (2010), African-American (52%) and Latina/o (63%) participants reported higher rates of CSA compared to white (35%) and Asian-American (29%) participants. Both Doll and colleagues (1992) and Feldman and Meyer (2007) found that African-American and Latino gay men reported higher rates of CSA than white gay men. Although little research has been conducted on racial/ethnic differences in adulthood victimization among lesbian, gay, and bisexual people, there is some evidence that sexual minority people of color may experience additional risk. For example, Comstock (1989) found that ethnic minority lesbian, gay, and bisexual individuals were more likely than whites to report having been hit with objects (31% versus 17%) or physically assaulted (21% versus 18%). At the same time, there is evidence that despite these elevated rates of victimization, lesbian, gay, and bisexual people of color do not report elevated psychological distress or mental health problems compared to those reported by their white counterparts (Balsam et al., 2010). Thus, further research is needed to understand both risk for victimization and resilience among lesbian, gay, and bisexual people of color.

CORRELATES OF SEXUAL ORIENTATION DIFFERENCES IN VICTIMIZATION

As indicated in this review, research over the past two decades has clearly established that lesbian, gay, and bisexual people are at elevated risk for a range of victimization experiences across the lifespan. Such experiences can occur in school or at home, by known or unknown perpetrators, and may or may not involve explicit statements of homophobia on the part of the perpetrator.

By increasing their visibility to homophobic perpetrators, gender nonconformity (e.g., gender atypical appearance or behavior) may be a risk factor for victimization among lesbian, gay, and bisexual people. Gender nonconformity has been found to be associated with parental rejection, harassment, and verbal and physical victimization (Blashill & Powlishta, 2009; D'Augelli et al., 2006; D'Augelli, Hershberger, & Pilkington, 1998; Harry, 1989; Landolt, Bartholomew, Saffrey, Oram, & Perlman, 2004; Smith & Leaper, 2006). In addition, disclosure of sexual orientation, particularly in adolescence, can serve as a risk factor by increasing visibility (D'Augelli & Grossman, 2001; Friedman, Marshal, Stall, Cheong, & Wright, 2008; Lampinen, Chan, & Anema, 2008).

Age is another important correlate of victimization. Unlike lesbian, gay, and bisexual adults, who may have more choice regarding their environment, sexual minority youth are situated within families, schools, and communities that are often hostile to them. Indeed, many sexual minority youth attribute victimization experiences to their sexual orientation (Rivers & D'Augelli, 2001). For all sexual minority youth, regardless of gender expression, disclosure of sexual orientation to family members may confer additional risk. D'Augelli and colleagues (1998) found that youth living at home who disclosed their sexual orientation to their families reported more victimization by family members than did those who did not disclose. Similarly, both early disclosure and gender nonconformity may be associated with greater risk for victimization in school environments (D'Augelli, Pilkington, & Hershberger, 2002). In addition, behavioral risks associated with minority stress, such as alcohol use and running away from home, may further increase exposure of sexual minority youth to perpetrators of victimization (Birkett et al., 2009; Bontempo & D'Augelli, 2002; Kruks, 1991; Noell & Ochs, 2001).

Given that most studies of sexual orientation and victimization are based upon self-report it is possible that higher rates of victimization among lesbian, gay, and bisexual people can be explained, at least in part, by differences in reporting. Sexual minority women and men who participate in research, and who are willing to acknowledge a stigmatized sexual minority identity, may also be more willing to report other potentially stigmatizing information, such as victimization. However, the reverse may also be true. Lesbian, gay, and bisexual women and men who have been victimized may be more likely to disclose sexual minority identities than those who have not been abused because they may already perceive themselves to be social outsiders (Saewyc et al., 2006). For some lesbian, gay, and bisexual people, fear of perpetuating stereotypes about abuse "making people gay" may prompt them to withhold information about victimization, particularly sexual victimization. On the other hand, lesbian, gay, and bisexual adults are more likely than heterosexual adults to have participated in psychotherapy (Hughes et al., 2000; Rothblum, Balsam, & Mickey, 2004), which may lead to greater openness about victimization. More research is needed to produce accurate estimates of rates of victimization and to understand the causes of sexual minority individuals' heightened risk of victimization.

VICTIMIZATION OF LESBIAN, GAY, AND BISEXUAL PEOPLE: HEALTH IMPACT

Victimization has important implications for health and well-being among lesbian, gay, and bisexual people. Indeed, victimization experiences in childhood and adulthood have been linked to a wide range of psychological problems, including depressive and anxiety disorders, suicidality, eating disorders, personality disorders, and substance use disorders (Logan et al., 2006; Ouimette & Brown, 2003). Victimization has also been linked to elevated risk for behaviors such as tobacco use and sexual risk-taking and to a variety of physical health problems (Koenig et al., 2004; Schnurr & Green, 2005). Although many studies on victimization and its impact on health focus on women, recent studies have paid particular attention to the role of victimization in the lives of gay and bisexual men, pointing to the important role of victimization in subsequent HIV-risk behaviors and infection (Jinich et al., 1998; Mimiaga et al., 2009; Paul, Catania, Pollack, & Stall, 2001; Wolitski, Stall, & Valdiserri, 2008). For lesbian, gay, and bisexual people, victimization experiences that are perceived to be associated with sexual orientation may have an even more deleterious effect on mental health than those that are not because they are viewed as a threat to their personal and community identity (Herek et al., 1999). As is true of heterosexual people, sexual minority people who have had more than one victimization experience are at greater risk for mental health and substance use problems compared to those with only one or no victimization experience (Balsam et al., 2011; Heidt et al., 2005; Hughes, McCabe, et al., 2010). Furthermore, the ongoing experience of minority stress and discrimination, theorized as "cultural victimization" (Neisen, 1993) or "insidious trauma" (Root, 1992), may interact with actual victimization experiences to create a greater risk for negative mental health outcomes. Indeed, House,

Van Horn, Coppeans, and Stepleman (2011) found the highest rates of suicidal and nonsuicidal self-injurious behaviors among lesbian, gay, and heterosexual individuals who reported both victimization and discrimination. Further research is needed to understand the extent and mechanisms of this phenomenon.

FUTURE DIRECTIONS IN RESEARCH ON LESBIAN, GAY, AND BISEXUAL VICTIMIZATION

Research to date has provided strong evidence that lesbian, gay, and bisexual people are at elevated risk for victimization over the lifespan. Given the high rates of physical and sexual abuse experienced by sexual minority individuals during both childhood and adulthood, it is essential that future research and scholarship attend to these variables. Recent advances in societal acceptance of sexual minority identities have led to a greater willingness on the part of researchers to study this stigmatized topic. However, additional work is needed to understand the victimization of lesbian, gay, and bisexual people and, most importantly, to inform prevention and intervention strategies.

First, it is important to conduct research to develop explanations for the elevated risk of victimization among lesbian, gay, and bisexual people. To do so, researchers must be willing to address sensitive topics, such as the question of whether acknowledgment of sexual minority identities precedes or follows sexual abuse in childhood or adolescence. Longitudinal designs that follow youth and young adults over time may help to identify factors that are not contained in retrospective, cross-sectional reports. This may be accomplished, in part, by further inclusion of items assessing sexual orientation in large, population-based health surveys and other longitudinal studies. Identification of factors that contribute to risk can guide efforts by policymakers, educators, and clinicians to prevent victimization of lesbian, gay, and bisexual individuals.

Second, mixed-methods designs that combine qualitative and quantitative data collection could help identify risk and resiliency factors that have not previously been assessed in public health surveys. Qualitative methods, such as semistructured interviews with lesbian, gay, and bisexual victims of violence, can be particularly useful for generating hypotheses and may inform the development of new measures and approaches to studying this topic.

Third, models of cumulative stress are needed that add to the understanding of how victimization interacts with minority stressors in the lives of sexual minority persons to create distinctive patterns of risk. The concept of "syndemics" has been used by Stall and colleagues (Stall, Friedman, & Catania, 2008) to refer to the interaction of victimization, mental health problems, substance use, and HIV risk among men who have sex with men. This concept could be applied more broadly to understanding the health profiles of lesbian, gay, and bisexual men and women over the lifespan.

Fourth, greater attention to diversity, in all its forms, is critical to understanding victimization of sexual minority people. This is particularly important with respect to racial and ethnic minority status, which has been largely neglected in this area of research. It is critical that researchers work collaboratively with communities of color to ensure that their voices are represented in victimization research.

Fifth, there is relatively little research on resilience among lesbian, gay, and bisexual people, particularly with respect to victimization. Given the high rates of victimization among this population, it could be argued that compared to heterosexual populations health disparities should be even greater than what has been found in comparative studies. More research is needed to understand how and why some people are able to thrive even in the face of adverse life experiences, and what factors might differentiate these individuals from those who exhibit more negative health outcomes.

Finally, there is a dearth of information about prevention and treatment strategies that can help address victimization and its health consequences among sexual minority populations. Indeed, with the exception of HIV prevention, very little research to date examines any interventions specifically geared toward lesbian, gay, or bisexual people who have experienced victimization. Future research might include needs assessments among lesbian, gay, and bisexual victims, the development of prevention programs to reduce risk behaviors, and interventions to address the psychological sequelae of victimization. Numerous empirically supported approaches to prevention and treatment have been developed for general populations, but little is known about the relative efficacy of these interventions for sexual minority individuals. Data could be gathered by including an item assessing sexual orientation in large-scale clinical trials for trauma-related problems. In addition, researchers could adapt existing interventions to include content relevant to sexual minority individuals, and test the extent to which adapted interventions confer additional benefit. Research on prevention and treatment strategies could improve the lives of many lesbian, gay, and bisexual people.

REFERENCES

American Psychiatric Association. (1980). *Diagnostic and statistical manual of mental disorders (3rd Edition)*. Washington, DC: American Psychiatric Association.

Austin, S. B., Jun, H. J., Jackson, B., Spiegelman, D., Rich-Edwards, J., Corliss, H. L., & Wright, R. J. (2008). Disparities in child abuse victimization in lesbian, bisexual, and heterosexual women in the Nurses' Health Study II. *Journal of Women's Health, 17*, 597–606.

Balsam, K. F., Huang, B., Fieland, K. C., Simoni, J. M., & Walters, K. L. (2004). Culture, trauma, and wellness: A comparison of heterosexual and lesbian, gay, bisexual, and two-spirit Native Americans. *Cultural Diversity & Ethnic Minority Psychology, 10*, 287–301.

Balsam, K. F., Lehavot, K., & Beadnell, B. (2011). Sexual revictimization and mental health: A comparison of lesbians, gay men, and heterosexual women. *Journal of Interpersonal Violence, 26*, 1798–1814.

Balsam, K. F., Lehavot, K., Beadnell, B., & Circo, E. (2010). Childhood abuse and mental health indicators among ethnically diverse lesbian, gay, and bisexual adults. *Journal of Consulting & Clinical Psychology, 78*, 459–468.

Balsam, K. F., Rothblum, E. D., & Beauchaine, T. P. (2005). Victimization over the life span: A comparison of lesbian, gay, bisexual, and heterosexual siblings. *Journal of Consulting & Clinical Psychology, 73*, 477–487.

Balsam, K. F., & Szymanski, D. M. (2005). Relationship quality and domestic violence in women's same-sex relationships: The role of minority stress. *Psychology of Women Quarterly, 29*, 258–269.

Berlan, E. D., Corliss, H. L., Field, A. E., Goodman, E., & Austin, S. (2010). Sexual orientation and bullying among adolescents in the Growing Up Today study. *Journal of Adolescent Health, 46*, 366–371.

Birkett, M., Espelage, D. L., & Koenig, B. (2009). LGB and questioning students in schools: The moderating effects of homophobic bullying and school climate on negative outcomes. *Journal of Youth and Adolescence, 38*, 989–1000.

Blashill, A., & Powlishta, K. (2009). the impact of sexual orientation and gender role on evaluations of men. *Psychology of Men and Masculinity, 10*, 160–173.

Bontempo, D. E., & D'Augelli, A. R. (2002). Effect of at-school victimization and sexual orientation on lesbian, gay, or bisexual youths' health risk behavior. *Journal of Adolescent Health, 30,* 364–374.

Brand, P. A., & Kidd, A. H. (1986). Frequency of physical aggression in heterosexual and female homosexual dyads. *Psychological Reports, 59,* 1307–1313.

Brennan, D. J., Hellerstedt, W. L., Ross, M. W., & Welles, S. L. (2007). History of childhood sexual abuse and HIV risk behaviors in homosexual and bisexual men. *American Journal of Public Health, 97,* 1107–1112.

Briere, J. N. (1992). *Child abuse trauma: Theory and treatment of the lasting effects.* Newbury Park, CA: Sage Publications.

Burke, L. K., & Follingstad, D. R. (1999). Violence in lesbian and gay relationships: Theory, prevalence, and correlational factors. *Clinical Psychology Review, 19,* 487–512.

Chesir-Teran, D., & Hughes, D. (2009). Heterosexism in high school and victimization among lesbian, gay, bisexual, and questioning students. *Journal of Youth and Adolescence, 38,* 963–975.

Cloitre, M., Tardiff, K., Marzuk, P. M., Leon, A. C., et al. (1996). Childhood abuse and subsequent sexual assault among female inpatients. *Journal of Traumatic Stress. 9,* 473–482.

Comstock, G. D. (1989). Victims of anti-gay/lesbian violence. *Journal of Interpersonal Violence, 4,* 101–106.

Conron, K. J., Mimiaga, M. J., & Landers, S. J. (2010). A population-based study of sexual orientation identity and gender differences in adult health. *American Journal of Public Health, 100,* 1953–1960. doi: 10.2105/ajph.2009.174169.

Corliss, H. L., Cochran, S. D., & Mays, V. M. (2002). Reports of parental maltreatment during childhood in a United States population-based survey of homosexual, bisexual, and heterosexual adults. *Child Abuse & Neglect, 26,* 1165–1178.

D'Augelli, A. R., & Grossman, A. H. (2001). Disclosure of sexual orientation, victimization, and mental health among lesbian, gay, and bisexual older adults. *Journal of Interpersonal Violence, 16,* 1008–1027.

D'Augelli, A. R., Grossman, A. H., & Starks, M. T. (2006). Childhood gender atypicality, victimization, and PTSD among lesbian, gay, and bisexual youth. *Journal of Interpersonal Violence, 21,* 1462–1482. doi: 10.1177/0886260506293482.

D'Augelli, A. R., Hershberger, S. L., & Pilkington, N. W. (1998). Lesbian, gay, and bisexual youth and their families: disclosure of sexual orientation and its consequences. *American Journal of Orthopsychiatry, 68,* 361–371; discussion 372–375.

D'Augelli, A. R., Pilkington, N. W., & Hershberger, S. L. (2002). Incidence and mental health impact of sexual orientation victimization of lesbian, gay, and bisexual youths in high school. *School Psychology Quarterly, 17,* 148–167.

Doll, L. S., Joy, D., Bartholow, B. N., Harrison, J. S., et al. (1992). Self-reported childhood and adolescent sexual abuse among adult homosexual and bisexual men. *Child Abuse & Neglect, 16,* 855–864.

Dunbar, E. D. (1998). *Hate Crime Reportage: A comparison of demographic and behavioral characteristics.* Paper presented at the 106th Annual American Psychological Association Convention, San Francisco, CA.

Eaton, L., Kalichman, S., Cain, D., Cherry, C., Pope, H., Fuhrel, A., & Kaufman, M. (2008). Perceived prevalence and risks for human papillomavirus (HPV) infection among women who have sex with women. *Journal of Women's Health, 17,* 75–83.

Elliott, P. (1996). Shattering illusions: Same-sex domestic violence. In C. M. Renzetti & C. H. Miley (Eds.), *Violence in gay and lesbian domestic partnerships* (pp. 107–116). New York: Harrington Park Press.

Feldman, M. B., & Meyer, I. H. (2007). Childhood abuse and eating disorders in gay and bisexual men. *International Journal of Eating Disorders, 40,* 418–423. doi: 10.1002/Eat.20378.

Finkelhor, D. (1979). *Sexually victimized children.* New York: The Free Press.

Finkelhor, D., & Kendall-Tackett, K. (1997). A developmental perspective on the childhood impact of crime, abuse, and violent victimization. In D. Cicchetti & S. L. Toth (Eds.), *Developmental perspectives on trauma: Theory, research, and intervention. Rochester symposium on developmental psychology, Vol. 8* (pp. 1–32). Rochester, NY: University of Rochester Press.

Friedman, M. S., Marshal, M. P., Guadamuz, T. E., Wei, C., & Wong, C. F. (2011). A meta analysis of disparities in childhood sexual abuse, parental physical abuse, and peer victimization among sexual minority and sexual nonminority individuals. *American Journal of Public Health, 191,* 1481–1494.

Friedman, M. S., Marshal, M. P., Stall, R., Cheong, J., & Wright, E. R. (2008). Gay-related development, early abuse and adult health outcomes among gay males. *AIDS and Behavior, 12,* 891–902.

Green, D. P., Strolovich, D. Z., Wong, J. S., & Bailey, R. W. (2001). Measuring gay populations and antigay hate crime. *Social Science Quarterly, 82,* 281–296.

Greenwood, G. L., Relf, M. V., Huang, B., Pollack, L. M., Canchola, J. A., & Catania, J. A. (2002). Battering victimization among a probability-based sample of men who have sex with men. *American Journal of Public Health, 92,* 1964–1969.

Harry, J. (1989). Parental physical abuse and sexual orientation in males. *Archives of Sexual Behavior, 18,* 251–261.

Heidt, J. M., Marx, B. P., & Gold, S. D. (2005). Sexual revictimization among sexual minorities: A preliminary study. *Journal of Traumatic Stress, 18,* 533–540.

Herek, G. M. (2009). Sexual stigma and sexual prejudice in the United States: A conceptual framework. *Nebraska Symposium on Motivation., 54,* 65–112.

Herek, G. M., Cogan, J. C., & Gillis, J. R. (2002). Victim experiences in hate crimes based on sexual orientation. *Journal of Social Issues, 58*, 319–339.

Herek, G. M., Gillis, J. R., & Cogan, J. C. (1999). Psychological sequelae of hate-crime victimization among lesbian, gay, and bisexual adults. *Journal of Consulting & Clinical Psychology, 67*, 945–951.

Holmes, W. C., & Slap, G. E. (1998). Sexual abuse of boys. *Journal of the American Medical Association, 280*, 1855–1862.

House, A. S., Van Horn, E., Coppeans, C., & Stepleman, L. M. (2011). Interpersonal trauma and discriminatory events as predictors of suicidal and non-suicidal self-injury in gay, lesbian, bisexual, and transgender persons. *Traumatology, 17*, 75–85. doi: 10.1177/1534765610395621.

Houston, E., & McKirnan, D. J. (2007). Intimate partner abuse among gay and bisexual men: Risk correlates and health outcomes. *Journal of Urban Health, 84*, 681–690.

Hughes, T. L., Haas, A. P., Razzano, L., Cassidy, R., & Matthews, A. (2000). Comparing lesbians' and heterosexual women's mental health: A multi-site survey. *Journal of Gay and Lesbian Social Services, 11*, 57–76.

Hughes, T. L., Johnson, T., & Wilsnack, S. C. (2001). Sexual assault and alcohol abuse: A comparison of lesbians and heterosexual women. *Journal of Substance Abuse, 13*, 515–532.

Hughes, T., McCabe, S. E., Wilsnack, S. C., West, B. T., & Boyd, C. J. (2010). Victimization and substance use disorders in a national sample of heterosexual and sexual minority women and men. *Addiction, 105*, 2130–2140. doi: 10.1111/j.1360–0443.2010.03088.x.

Hughes, T. L., Szalacha, L. A., Johnson, T. P., Kinnison, K., Wilsnack, S. C., & Young, C. (2010). Sexual victimization and hazardous drinking among heterosexual and sexual minority women. *Addictive Behaviors, 35*, 1152–1156.

Hughes, T. L., Wilsnack, S., Kristjanson, A., & Benson, P. (2010, June). *CSA severity as a risk factor for hazardous drinking: A comparison of lesbian and heterosexual women.* Paper presented at the Kettil Bruun Society for Social and Epidemiological Research on Alcohol, Lausanne, Switzerland.

Jinich, S., Paul, J. P., Stall, R., Acree, M., Kegeles, S., Hoff, C., & Coates, T. J. (1998). Childhood sexual abuse and HIV risk-taking behavior among gay and bisexual men. *AIDS and Behavior, 2*, 41–51. doi: 10.1023/a:1022307323744.

Justice, U. S. D. o. (2009). http://www2.fbi.gov/ucr/hc2008/victims.html. Retrieved October 24, 2011.

Kaplan, S. J., Pelcovitz, D., & Labruna, V. (1999). Child and adolescent abuse and neglect research: A review of the past 10 years. Part I: Physical and emotional abuse and neglect. *Journal of the American Academy of Child & Adolescent Psychiatry, 38*, 1214–1222.

Klinger, R. L., & Stein, T. S. (1994). Impact of violence, childhood sexual abuse, and domestic violence and abuse on lesbians, bisexuals, and gay men. In R. P. Cabaj & T. S. Stein (Eds.), *Textbook of homosexuality and mental health* (pp. 801–817). Washington, DC: American Psychiatric Press.

Koenig, L. J., Doll, L. S., O'Leary, A., & Pequegnat, W. (Eds.). (2004). *From child sexual abuse to adult sexual risk: Trauma, revictimization, and intervention.* Washington, DC: American Psychological Association.

Kosciw, J. G., & Greytak, E. A. (2009). Who, what, where, when, and why: Demographic and ecological factors contributing to hostile school climate for lesbian, gay, bisexual, and transgender youth. *Journal of Youth and Adolescence, 38*, 976–988.

Koss, M. P., Goodman, L. A., Browne, A., Fitzgerald, L. F., Keita, G. P., & Russo, N. F. (1994). *No safe haven: Male violence against women at home, at work, and in the community.* Washington, DC: American Psychological Association.

Kruks, G. (1991). Gay and lesbian homeless/street youth: Special issues and concerns. *Journal of Adolescent Health, 12*, 515–518.

Kuehnle, K., & Sullivan, A. (2003). Gay and lesbian victimization: Reporting factors in domestic violence and bias incidents. *Criminal Justice and Behavior, 30*, 85–96.

Lampinen, T. M., Chan, K., & Anema, A. (2008). Incidence of and risk factors for sexual orientation-related physical assault among young men who have sex with men. *American Journal of Public Health, 98*, 1028–1035.

Landolt, M. A., Bartholomew, K., Saffrey, C., Oram, D., & Perlman, D. (2004). Gender nonconformity, childhood rejection, and adult attachment; a study of gay men. *Archives of Sexual Behavior, 33*, 117–128.

Letellier, P. (1994). Gay and bisexual male domestic violence victimization: Challenges to feminist theory and responses to violence *Violence and Victims, 9*, 95–106.

Lie, G.-y., Schilit, R., Bush, J., Montagne, M., et al. (1991). Lesbians in currently aggressive relationships: How frequently do they report aggressive past relationships? *Violence and Victims, 6*, 121–135.

Lockhart, L. L., White, B. W., Causby, V., & Isaac, A. (1994). Letting out the secret: Violence in lesbian relationships. *Journal of Interpersonal Violence, 9*, 469–492.

Logan, T. K., Walker, R., Jordan, C. E., & Leukefeld, C. G. (2006). *Women and victimization: Contributing factors, interventions, and implications.* Washington DC: American Psychological Association Press.

Matthews, A. K., Hughes, T. L., Johnson, T., Razzano, L. A., & Cassidy, R. (2002). Prediction of depressive distress in a community sample of women: The role of sexual orientation. *American Journal of Public Health, 92*, 1131–1139.

McClennen, J. (2005). Domestic violence between same-gender partners. *Journal of Interpersonal Violence, 20*, 149–154.

McClennen, J. C., Summers, A. B., & Daley, J. G. (2002). The Lesbian Partner Abuse Scale. *Research on Social Work Practice, 12*, 277–292.

McDevitt, J., Balboni, J., Garcia, L., & Gu, J. (2001). Consequences for victims: A comparison of bias- and non-bias-motivated assaults. *American Behavioral Scientist, 45*, 697–713.

Merrill, G. S., & Wolfe, V. A. (2000). Battered gay men: An exploration of abuse, help seeking and why they stay. *Journal of Homosexuality, 39*, 1–30.

Mimiaga, M. J., Noonan, E., Donnell, D., Safren, S., Koenen, K. C., Gortmaker, S., & Mayer, K. H. (2009). Childhood sexual abuse is highly associated with HIV-risk taking behavior and infection among MSM in the EXPLORE study. *Journal of Acquired Immune Deficiency Syndrome, 51*, 340–351.

Morris, J. F. (1997). *Set free: Lesbian mental health and the coming out process.* Unpublished Doctoral Dissertation, Department of Psychology, University of Vermont.

Morris, J. F., & Balsam, K. F. (2003). Lesbian and bisexual women's self-reported experiences of victimization: Mental health and sexual identity development. *Journal of Lesbian Studies, 7*, 67–85.

Neisen, J. H. (1993). Healing from cultural victimization: Recovery from shame due to heterosexism. *Journal of Gay & Lesbian Psychotherapy, 2*, 49–63.

Noell, J. W., & Ochs, L. M. (2001). Relationship of sexual orientation to substance use, suicidal ideation, suicide attempts, and other factors in a population of homeless adolescents. *Journal of Adolescent Health, 29*, 31–36.

Ouimette, P., & Brown, P. J. (Eds.). (2003). *Trauma and Substance Abuse: Causes, Consequences, and Treatment of Comorbid Disorders.* Washington, D. C.: American Psychological Association.

Paul, J. P., Catania, J., Pollack, L., & Stall, R. (2001). Understanding childhood sexual abuse as a predictor of sexual risk-taking among men who have sex with men: The Urban Men's Health Study. *Child Abuse & Neglect, 25*, 557–584.

Potocziak, M. J., Mourot, J. E., Crosbie-Burnett, M., & Potocziak, D. J. (2003). Legal and psychological perspectives on same-sex domestic violence: A multisystemic approach *Journal of Family Psychology, 17*, 252–259.

Renzetti, C. M. (1989). Building a second closet: Third party responses to victims of lesbian partner abuse. *Family Relations, 38*, 157–163.

Rinehart, J. K., & Yeater, E. A. (2011). A qualitative analysis of sexual victimization narratives. *Violence Against Women, 17*, 925–943.

Rivers, I., & D'Augelli, A. R. (2001). The victimization of lesbians, gay, and bisexual youths. In A. R. D'Augelli &

C. J. Patterson (Eds.),*Lesbian, gay, and bisexual identities and youth: Psychological perspectives* (pp. 199–223). New York: Oxford University Press.

Root, M. P. P. (1992). Reconstructing the impact of trauma on personality. In L. S. Brown & M. Ballou (Eds.), *Personality and psychopathology: Feminist reappraisals* (pp. 229–265). New York: Guilford Press.

Rose, S. M., & Mechanic, M. B. (2002). Psychological distress, crime features, and help-seeking behaviors related to homophobic bias incidents. *American Behavioral Scientist, 46*, 14–26. doi: 10.1177/0002764202046001003.

Rothblum, E. D., Balsam, K. F., & Mickey, R. M. (2004). Brothers and sisters of lesbians, gay men, and bisexuals as a demographic comparison group: An innovative research methodology to examine social change. *Journal of Applied Behavioral Science, 40*, 283–301.

Rothman, E. F., Exner, D., & Baughman, A. L. (2011). The prevalence of sexual assault against people who identify as gay, lesbian, or bisexual in the United States: A systematic review. *Trauma, Violence, & Abuse, 12*, 55–66. doi: 10.1177/1524838010390707.

Saewyc, E. M., Skay, C. L., Pettingell, S. L., Reis, E. A., Bearinger, L., Resnick, M., & Combs, L. (2006). Hazards of stigma: The sexual and physical abuse of gay, lesbian, and bisexual adolescents in the United States and Canada. *Child Welfare, 85*, 195–213.

Schnurr, P. P., & Green, B. L. (2005). Understanding relationships among trauma, posttraumatic stress disorder, and health outcomes. In P. P. Schnurr & B. L. Green (Eds.), *Trauma and health: Physical health consequences of exposure to extreme stress* (pp. 247–275). Washington, DC: American Psychological Association Press.

Seelau, S. M., & Seelau, E. P. (2005). Gender-role stereotypes and perceptions of heterosexual, gay and lesbian domestic violence. *Journal of Family Violence, 20*, 363–371.

Smith, T. E., & Leaper, C. (2006). Self-perceived gender typicality and the peer context during adolescence. *Journal of Research on Adolescence, 16*, 91–103.

Stall, R., Friedman, M. S., & Catania, J. A. (2008). Interacting epidemics and gay men's health: A theory of syndemic production among urban gay men. In R. J. Wolitski, R. Stall, & R. O. Valdiserri (Eds.), *Unequal opportunity: Health disparities affecting gay and bisexual men in the United States* (pp. 251–274). New York: Oxford University Press.

Stoddard, J. P., Dibble, S. L., & Fineman, N. (2009). Sexual and physical abuse: A comparison between lesbians and their heterosexual sisters. *Journal of Homosexuality, 56*, 407–420.

Tjaden, P., Thoeness, N., & Allison, C. J. (1999). Comparing violence over the life span in samples of same-sex and opposite-sex cohabitants. *Violence and Victims, 14*, 413–425.

Tomeo, M. E., Templer, D. I., Anderson, S., & Kotler, D. (2001). Comparative data of childhood and adolescence molestation in heterosexual and homosexual persons. *Archives of Sexual Behavior, 30,* 535–541.

Toomey, R. B., Ryan, C., Diaz, R. M., Card, N. A., & Russell, S. T. (2010). Gender-nonconforming lesbian, gay, bisexual, and transgender youth: school victimization and young adult psychosocial adjustment. *Developmental Psychology, 46,* 1580–1589.

Turell, S. C. (2000). A descriptive analysis of same-sex relationship violence for a diverse sample. *Journal of Family Violence, 15,* 281–305.

Waldner-Haugrud, L. K., & Gratch, L. V. (1997). Sexual coercion in gay/lesbian relationships: Descriptives and gender differences. *Violence and Victims, 12,* 87–98.

Warwick, I., Aggleton, P., & Douglas, N. (2001). Playing it safe: Addressing emotional and physical health of lesbian and gay pupils in the UK. *Journal of Adolescence, 24,* 129–140.

Waterman, C. K., Dawson, L. J., & Bologna, M. J. (1989). Sexual coercion in gay male and lesbian relationships: Predictors and implications for support services. *Journal of Sex Research, 26,* 118–124.

Wilsnack, S. C., Hughes, T. L., Johnson, T. P., Bostwick, W. B., Szalacha, L. A., Benson, P., & Kinnison, K. E. (2008). Drinking and drinking-related problems among heterosexual and sexual minority women. *Journal of Studies on Alcohol and Drugs, 69,* 129–139.

Wolitski, R. J., Stall, R., & Valdiserri, R. O. (Eds.) (2008). *Unequal opportunity: Health disparities affecting gay and bisexual men in the United States.* New York: Oxford University Press.

Wyatt, G. E., Guthrie, D., & Notgrass, C. M. (1992). Differential effects of women's child sexual abuse and subsequent sexual revictimization. *Journal of Consulting & Clinical Psychology, 60,* 167–173.

20

Race and Ethnicity among Lesbian, Gay, and Bisexual Communities

BIANCA D. M. WILSON AND GARY W. HARPER

There are longstanding critiques of the field of psychology (as with most of the academy) that assert it is saturated with a patriarchal/androcentric, eurocentric, heteronormative bias. As the field has evolved and incorporated the voices of scholars and communities of color, women, sexual minorities, and other minorities, this has typically progressed with the use of singular lenses that focus on only one type of identity at a time. For example, the body of psychological research on communities of color in the United States is dominated by research focusing on (assumed-to-be) heterosexual populations [e.g., Black racial identity theories (see Yip, Seaton, & Sellers, 2006, for a review) and acculturation theories (see Schwartz, Unger, Zamboanga, & Szapocznik, 2010, for a review)]. Paralleling this trend, research on sexual minority communities is heavily dominated by research on the concerns of White gays and lesbians (and far less so on the concerns of bisexuals). In fact, the original psychological theories regarding the development of a lesbian/gay/bisexual sexual orientation that continue to influence the way lesbian, gay, and bisexual identity development is viewed were developed through retrospective reports of primarily White gay men (e.g., Cass, 1979; Colemen, 1982; Troiden, 1989), and thus may not represent the lived experiences of lesbian, gay, and bisexual people of color.

In essence, the field of psychology generally has lacked what has been called an *intersectional framework*, in which political and social categories are studied with attention to the ways in which all people embody multiple identities and core social statuses. The general concept of intersectionality and what it represents in the United States is rooted in the writings of Black and Chicana feminist activists, many of them lesbian identified (see, e.g., Moraga, & Anzaldúa, 1983; Combahee River Collective Statement, 1977; Smith, 1983). As an academic term, intersectionality was initially coined to refer to the position of Black women in U.S. culture by Crenshaw (1989) in the context of critical race studies, a subfield of legal studies, and has been further explicated by multiple authors outside of psychology (e.g., Battle & Ashley, 2008; Collins, 2008). Within psychology, this construct has been studied primarily using the term "multiple identities," reflecting the more varied ways scholars have examined individuals from multiple (usually minority) groups, from individual identity developmental processes to assessing contexts of intersecting institutionalized oppressions.

This chapter is aimed at reviewing, discussing, and providing an overview of the field's current status concerning the study of one configuration of multiple identities with regard to two core social statuses, race/ethnicity and sexuality. The primary thesis of this review is that although there has been an increase in attention to the intersection of race/ethnicity and sexual minority peoples, most of this research does not explicitly study the influence, significance, or relevance of ethnic/racial statuses and identities in the lives of lesbian, gay, bisexual, and transgender people. Instead, many authors implicitly examine race/ethnicity by studying various topics, particularly sexual identity development and sexual risk behavior, and comparing these concepts as they are experienced similarly or differently among ethnic minority as compared to white lesbian, gay, or bisexual people.

One concern with many comparative studies is that by examining group differences, very little is learned about the mechanisms through which ethnic/racial factors influence the lives of lesbian, gay, and bisexual people of color. For example, knowing that Asian American bisexual women self-identify as "bisexual" at older ages than White bisexual women does not necessarily offer new information regarding the ways in which race/ethnicity influences the sexual orientation identity development and expression of Asian American women. Authors may attempt to offer explanations for such group differences in the discussion sections of their articles, but these conjectures often remain unfounded since the specific sociocultural, historical, and political factors that may influence the phenomena of interest are typically not explored empirically. Another challenge with studies that explore group differences between White and ethnic minority lesbian, gay, and bisexual populations is that they often privilege the experiences of White individuals by using this group as the standard against which other ethnic/racial groups are compared.

Current studies of ethnic/racial issues among lesbian, gay, and bisexual people and communities are also traditionally grounded in psychological research on sexual minorities as opposed to ethnic/racial psychological research, and thus are conducted from a perspective of studying ethnic/racial diversity among lesbian, gay, and bisexual populations, as opposed to studying sexual orientation diversity among ethnic minority populations. Thus researchers may utilize sexual orientation and sexuality models and theories that were developed from a White/eurocentric perspective as the basis for their investigations, and fail to examine constructs that are most relevant for different ethnic/racial groups. In addition, research exploring the intersection of race/ethnicity and sexual orientation has focused almost exclusively on the study of ethnic minority lesbian, gay, and bisexual populations, and neglected the further investigation of the role of European American ethnicity/race or "whiteness" on same-gender sexuality and sexual orientation. Furthermore, we also find that most of the research on race/ethnicity and lesbian, gay, and bisexual populations has centered on the problematization of identity development and sexual behavior, with a primary focus on challenges experienced by sexual minority people of color.

Despite the limitations of this problem-focused approach, the field has nonetheless gained knowledge about the experiences of ethnic minority lesbian, gay, and bisexual people from the body of empirical research with predominantly ethnic minority samples. With regard to identity development, implicitly race-focused lesbian, gay, and bisexual research (i.e., studies that include ethnic

minority populations, but do not empirically test racial or ethnically relevant variables beyond group membership) has demonstrated that, for the most part, sexual identity development and the "coming out" process of ethnic minority lesbian, gay, and bisexual people look markedly similar to that of their White counterparts (see, e.g., Dube & Savin-Williams, 1999). Yet some differences have been revealed. For example, Black and Latino sexual minority men in particular tend to be more likely than White men to identify as bisexual (Doll, Petersen, White, & Johnson, 1992; Muñoz-Laboy & Dodge, 2007; Stokes, McKirnan, & Burzette, 1993; Stokes, Vanable, & McKirnan, 1997); in addition, people who are dually ethnic and sexual minorities are less likely to be out to family members and tend to perceive a high risk of losing an ethnic support system as a consequence of disclosure compared to White sexual minorities (Parks, Hughes, & Matthews, 2004; Rosario, Schrimshaw, & Hunter, 2004).

The field has also documented throughout various studies that Black and Latino sexual minority men in particular are at increased risk for HIV infection (Celentano et al., 2005; Hall et al., 2007; Valleroy et al., 2000), though the pathways to this increased risk are less understood. The area of mental health is another major area in which psychologists, expectedly, have studied the experiences of ethnic minority lesbian, gay, and bisexual people. Generally, they have found similar to elevated levels of depression or other indicators of mental distress among ethnic minority compared to White lesbian, gay, and bisexual people (cf. Cochran, Mays, Ortega, Alegria, & Takeuchi, 2007; Consolacion, Russell, & Sue, 2004; Diaz, Ayala, Bein, Henne, & Marin, 2001; Pinhey & Millman, 2004; Yoshikawa, Wilson, Chae, & Cheng, 2004; Zea, Reisen, & Poppen, 1999; Zea, Reisen, Poppen, Bianchi, & Echeverry, 2005; Kertzner, Meyer, Frost, & Stirratt, 2009), and scholars have noted limitations to current psychotherapy approaches given the lack of intersectional approaches in treatment (Greene, 1997; Milan & Caban, 1996). Other less studied topics covering issues related to race/ethnicity and sexual orientation have included experiences in the academic and employment contexts (see Adams, Cahill, & Ackerlind, 2005; Cruz, 2008; Cheung & Katayama, 1999). In sum, it is clear that ethnic/racial status is an important factor differentiating the experiences of ethnic minority and majority lesbian, gay, and bisexual people. However, why and how these differences develop are less clear, as are the specific areas of resiliency and strength that may exist for various ethnic/racial groups. That is, what makes race and ethnicity an important predictor of psychological and behavioral problems and strengths among sexual minority persons?

Developing theoretical specifications of how and why race/ethnicity (as well as sexuality) matter is important for moving the field beyond a simplistic majority-versus-minority framework and into areas of inquiry in which scholars and activists can best understand how to apply psychological research findings for advancing social justice. In this chapter we will first focus on describing the few theories and conceptual frameworks that psychologists have put forth to explain the ways race and ethnicity influence the varied experiences of lesbian, gay, and bisexual people, as well as empirical research supporting these frameworks. In particular, we examine theoretical frameworks addressing (1) multiple oppressions, (2) cultural contexts, and (3) queer theory, discourse theory, and challenging hegemony. In the second part of the chapter we offer recommendations for how to move the field forward with regard to more sensitive and nuanced explorations of the lived experiences of lesbian, gay, and bisexual people of color. This section explores both conceptual/theoretical issues to examine in future research as well as methodological issues to consider in such explorations.

MULTIPLE OPPRESSIONS

One major set of theories and conceptual frameworks guiding our understanding of the ways racial and ethnic categories create different systems of experiences across lesbian, gay, and bisexual individuals emphasizes the expected variation in behavior and health as a function of experiencing (or not experiencing) "multiple oppressions." Although all sexual minority individuals may share experiences of oppression related to their sexual orientation, their membership in different ethnic/racial groups that possess varying levels of social power and privilege may compound the societal challenges they experience. In addition, the interplay between oppressed and privileged statuses related to gender, race/ethnicity, social class, and sexual orientation has been shown to have differential effects on individuals depending on the composition and visibility of their oppressed and privileged statuses (Croteau, Talbot, Lance, & Evans, 2002). Theory

and research on multiple oppressions constitute the most widely studied area of focus for psychological research on the intersection of race/ethnicity and sexual orientation. The following section will examine the varying ways in which the phenomenon of multiple oppressions among sexual minority people has been explored.

One predominant theoretical framework in this area is Greene's "Triple Jeopardy" (Greene, 1997). Her concept of Triple Jeopardy drew primarily from Black feminist theory from the late 1970s to early 1990s. The primary tenets of this concept are that lesbians of color experience heterosexism, racism, and sexism as a function of the cultural and social systems in mainstream U.S. society; in addition, Black communities create an experience distinct from that of White gays and lesbians, and produce a unique set of mental health risk factors. This concept has been extended to account for the distinct experiences of ethnic minority gay men, where the influence of racism and heterosexism are emphasized (Díaz, Ayala, & Bein, 2004; Wilson, et al., 2010). The focus of this approach has been on the study of the intersection of race and sexuality from the perspectives of lesbian, gay, and bisexual people of color.

Aspects of Greene's (1997) concept of Triple Jeopardy have been described and explicated by others, and background information has been offered to explain why such a phenomenon may exist and the impact that it may have on sexual minority individuals. Theorists have suggested that lesbian, gay, and bisexual people of color often experience nonacceptance and acts of discrimination and marginalization from both communities, leading some to believe that they must choose between being lesbian, gay, or bisexual and being a member of their ethnic/racial group (Bonilla & Porter, 1990; Herek & Capitanio, 1995; Washington, 2001). Members of various ethnic/racial communities may not view being lesbian, gay, or bisexual as acceptable within their community and/or culture and thus may shun a person of color who embodies such an identification. This may be partially based on the belief that participation in same-gender romantic relationships and sexual activity are violations of traditional cultural values or rules, especially those related to gender roles (Bridges, Selvidge, & Matthews, 2003; Chan, 1995; Espin, 1993; Greene, 2000;). People of color also may experience discrimination within the predominantly White mainstream lesbian, gay, and bisexual community, as they may be objectified and eroticized by White sexual minority men and women who are seeking to fulfill an exotic or passionate fantasy (Diaz, 1998; Han, 2009; Martinez & Sullivan, 1998).

This differential treatment in both the ethnic community and the mainstream White lesbian, gay, and bisexual community may lead some sexual minority people of color to conceal aspects of their various identities depending on the context of their interactions with others, thus experiencing varying degrees of visibility and invisibility within their own communities (Crawford, Allison, Zamboni, & Soto, 2002; Fukuyama & Ferguson, 2000; Morales, 1989; Wilson & Miller, 2002; Wilson & Yoshikawa, 2004). Zea, Reisen, and Diaz (2003) have illustrated this by their finding that some Latino men identify as "gay" when they are in the context of a gay bar, but not when they are with their families. Other sexual minority people may make themselves "invisible" within their ethnic cultural group, as was demonstrated by Tremble, Schneider, and Appathurai's (1989) study of lesbian and gay youth of color in Toronto, which revealed that these young people would often exclude themselves from cultural activities in order to avoid bringing shame to their families. Wilson and Miller (2002) identified strategies used by gay and bisexual African American men to manage heterosexism in intolerant contexts, including intentionally altering their actions, dress, and mannerisms to conform to standards of masculinity (including being homoantagonistic toward others), censoring information about their sexuality to others, and avoiding confronting others when they made antigay statements toward others.

However, it is important to note that not all ethnic minority lesbian, gay, and bisexual people manage multiple oppressions by engaging in impression management and becoming invisible. Wilson and Miller (2002) also found that many Black gay and bisexual men in their study openly challenged heterosexist comments within their Black community settings. Similarly, Romo-Carmona and Hidalgo (1995) suggest that for lesbians of color the act of integrating their multiple identities and being visible can be empowering since "'coming out' by the least powerful, most oppressed members of a society challenges the foundation of power, by individuals whom the power structure considers to be the least threatening" (p. 90). She does caution,

however, that this level of visibility may incite retaliation from those in power who perceive lesbian women of color's strong identification as a threat to their attempts at social control.

Greene's (1997) concept of Triple Jeopardy shares some characteristics with Ilan Meyer's conceptualization of minority stress as it is applied to dual or triply oppressed groups. Minority stress is essentially the "psychosocial stress derived from minority status" (Meyer, 1995, p. 38). Within Meyer's framework, using social stress theory as its basis (Meyer & Ouellette, 2009), sexual minority and ethnic/racial statuses are associated with an increased amount of stress due to their subjugated place within society. In turn, the sociological paradigm that Meyer draws from posits that increased stress due to social status affects health, creating a direct and indirect relationship between minority stress and mental and physical health. Both the construct of minority stress and components of Triple Jeopardy emphasize the deleterious effects of oppression through primarily psychological mechanisms—a unique contribution of the field of psychology.

A strong source of empirical support for these theoretical frameworks comes from the body of research documenting correlations between oppression, stress, and coping. Meyer, Schwartz, and Frost (2008) found that Black and Latino lesbian, gay, and bisexual persons experience significantly more stress, in part due to prejudice-specific stress, than their White counterparts. Although not comparative in nature, several additional studies with ethnic minority gay men and lesbians further support the argument that ethnic minority lesbian, gay, and bisexual people are likely to experience high levels of minority stress and need to develop forms of coping and resistance due to a combination of sexual and racial minority statuses (Bowleg, Brooks, & Ritz, 2008; Wilson & Miller, 2002; Wilson & Yoshikawa, 2004). Connecting experienced oppression and minority stress to health among ethnic minority lesbian, gay, and bisexual people, Szymanski and Meyer (2008) explicitly tested the multiplicative effects of two forms of oppression, racism and heterosexism, on the mental health of Black same-gender loving women and found that experiencing both forms independently, but not interactively, predicted poorer mental health. Correlations between heterosexism and racism and sexual risk have also been found, particularly among gay and bisexual men of color (Diaz et al.,

2001; Rosario, Hunter, Maguen, Gwadz, & Smith, 2001). For example, Diaz et al. (2004) tested this relationship directly by examining whether experiencing multiple forms of oppression predicts sexual risk behavior, and further whether this relationship is mediated by participation in difficult sexual situations (e.g., anonymous sex venues or sex driven by negative feelings). They found both a direct and indirect relationship between oppression based on race and sexuality and sexual risk taking.

Examining additional areas of experienced oppression, research has also shown that among Black lesbian and bisexual women, both heterosexism and typically less studied forms of discrimination, such as weight-based oppression, predicted poorer subjective physical health (Wilson, Okwu, & Mills, 2011). Native American lesbian, gay, and bisexual people are rarely included in research studies. One project that studied the relationships between discrimination and health among Native Americans found that heterosexism faced by Native American gay men often isolated them from their tribal communities and led to engaging in risky sexual behavior in gay community contexts (Gilley & Co-Cke, 2005). Among Latinos, Guarnero (2007) found that experienced heterosexism and racism within family and community settings were highly correlated with higher vulnerability to depression and suicide. It is important to note that despite the potential negative and multiplicative effects of dual or triple minority statues on health, there is evidence of great resilience as well (Wilson et al., 2011; Zea et al., 1999). For example, Wilson and colleagues (2010) used path analysis to test the relationships between multiple forms of oppression and health among Black lesbian and bisexual women. They found that although one form of oppression, weight-bias, was negatively associated with subjective health, reported experiences with heterosexism surprisingly predicted higher health scores. This finding seems counter to most research on oppression and health, yet other research has suggested that having an awareness of your vulnerability to oppression is ideal for health in that critical consciousness creates a potential psychological buffer and may lead to seeking out social support for managing oppression (Huebner & Davis, 2007). Given the setting in which the study was conducted (a weekend retreat designed for social support and activism around issues connected to race, sexuality, and gender), these findings demonstrate the

potential protective power of supportive settings and training in oppression resistance, and are evidence of great resilience.

Developmental research, especially research related to identity development during adolescence, has provided additional exploration of the effects of experiencing multiple oppressions among sexual minority people of color. During adolescent development the value and importance of having a strong ethnic identity are clear, and youth establish a more coherent sense of personal identity that includes ethnic identity. For all youth, especially youth of color, integrating a sense of ethnic identity into their overall sense of self is an important developmental task (Phinney, 1990). The unsuccessful resolution of identity development for adolescents has been associated with a host of negative mental health outcomes such as low self-esteem or alienation (Phinney, 1991; Phinney & Chavira, 1992; Rotheram-Borus, 1990), negative affective states (Parham & Helms, 1985), behavioral and adjustment problems (Rotheram-Borus, 1989, 1990), and poorer academic achievement (Bowman & Howard, 1985).

Lesbian, gay, and bisexual youth of color in particular experience unique challenges to ethnic identity formation due to experiences of both individual-level and institutionalized racism and heterosexism, as well as sexism experienced by young lesbians and bisexual girls. Sexual minority youth of color must not only contend with the negative societal reactions to their sexual orientation, but also may experience racial prejudice, limited economic opportunities and resources as a consequence of racism, and limited acceptance of their sexuality within their own ethnic cultural community (Diaz, 1998; Harper, Jernewall, & Zea, 2004; Martinez & Sullivan, 1998). These adolescents often experience negative ethnic cultural messages regarding their sexual orientation, which may lead to confusion, frustration, and potentially increased rates of participation in health risk behaviors.

Sparse literature exists on the intersection of ethnic identity and sexual orientation identity development among adolescents, although some studies have noted the ability of gay/bisexual adolescent males to integrate their sexual identity with their ethnic culture/identity as a resiliency factor (Alfonso, Diaz, Andujar-Bello, & Rosa, 2006; Jamil, Harper, & Fernandez, 2009). Research with adult gay and bisexual men has demonstrated that the ability to achieve a positive integrated identity related to being a sexual minority person of color can result in healthier functioning and improved well-being (Crawford et al., 2002). These researchers demonstrated that among African American gay and bisexual men, those who were able to achieve a positive identity related to both their ethnicity and sexual orientation reported higher levels of self-esteem, stronger social support networks, greater levels of life satisfaction, and lower levels of psychosocial distress than men in all other identity categories (Crawford et al., 2002).

Although theoretical writings have suggested that the process of developing two potentially stigmatized identities simultaneously may present major challenges for adolescents, empirical research has not fully supported this notion. For example, Cheung and Katayama (1999) theorized that gay Asian American adolescents go through a process of developing their sexual and ethnic identities simultaneously, and that their progress in one identity may be impeded by progress in the other. Yet, empirical investigations by both Dube and Savin-Williams (1999) and Rosario et al. (2004) failed to find ethnic differences in the timing of sexual orientation identity development milestones for adolescents, although Rosario et al. (2004) did find ethnic difference with regard to level of disclosure and involvement in gay-related activities. Data from qualitative interviews with African American and Latino gay/bisexual/questioning male adolescents suggest that sexual and ethnic identity development for these youth are very different processes often occurring simultaneously, with ethnic identity being a more "public" process and sexual orientation identity being a more "private" process (Jamil et al., 2009). In opposition to prior theoretical writings that suggested that lesbian, gay, and bisexual youth of color may utilize skills they acquire in combating ethnic/racial-based oppression during childhood to the challenges of experiencing sexual orientation-based oppression as adolescents, youth included in the study by Jamil et al. (2009) reported that the processes of developing their sexual orientation and ethnic/racial identities were very distinct and required different sets of coping skills and social supports.

CULTURAL CONTEXT

The multiple oppressions frameworks described above focus primarily on experiencing more than one type of discrimination due to race, sexuality, and sometimes gender. The authors of those theories often note that these oppressive belief systems are culturally bound—that is rooted in the either/both the eurocentric and ethnic minority cultural context in the United States that perpetuates anti-gay, antiwoman, and antipeople of color beliefs (e.g., Diaz, 1998; Greene, 1997; Wilson & Miller, 2002). Another loose collection of theoretical frameworks that guides the psychological study of race and ethnicity among lesbian, gay, and bisexual individuals posits that there are ethnically specific cultural beliefs and norms that are focused on the culturally prescribed beliefs and expectations for sexual behavior, gender expression, familial responsibilities, and academic achievement (Harper, 2007).

When considering these theoretical approaches, it becomes clear that researchers cannot study race and ethnicity among sexual minority people without actually studying minority sexualities among racial and ethnic groups. That is, individuals' sexualities and beliefs about sex, love, health, adulthood, and relationships are heavily grounded in ethnic/racial cultural teachings. For example, Colon (2001) examined the factors affecting the day-to-day functioning and overall well-being of working class Latino gay and bisexual men, drawing from theories and research on Latino cultures. He asserted that in addition to ethnic-based culturally prescribed beliefs about heterosexuality, ethnic cultural beliefs and norms related to family structure and healthcare behaviors were relevant to understanding how Latino gay and bisexual men navigated social services. With regard to the coming out process, Operario, Han, and Choi (2008) conceptualized dual identity development as a function, in part, of the different ethnic cultural values regarding the prioritization of the individual versus the community in Asian and non-Asian cultures.

The impact of various ethnic cultural constructions of human behavior and their influence on the varied experiences of lesbian, gay, and bisexual people have been most studied in the domains of sexual risk and HIV. Boehmer (2002) found that, at least in the area of lesbian, gay, bisexual, and transgender health, the explicit discussion of race and ethnicity issues has been driven by research on sexually transmitted infections. For example, O'Donnell et al. (2002) noted the likely different cultural values around masculinity and family between Latinos and other groups that have been studied and examined whether varying levels of attachment and identification with ethnic and gay communities predicted unprotected anal intercourse among Latino men who have sex with men. One of their findings highlighted the potential protective effect that involvement and attachment to a person's ethnic community may have against HIV risk for this population. Diaz's (1998) work with adult gay/bisexual Latino men has found that inconsistent condom use was partially attributable to a sense of machismo, which is often diffused into the socialization of Latino youth and may promote risk taking, low sexual control, and sexual activity with multiple sexual partners. Williams, Wyatt, Resell, Peterson, and Asuan-O'Brien's (2004) qualitative study of HIV-positive African American and Latino gay men and other men who have sex with men revealed that cultural beliefs related to the importance of children, particularly sons who would continue the family name, influenced the sexual behavior of these men by encouraging sexual activity with women for the purposes of procreation. Similarly, cultural norms related to gender roles and expectations also influenced the ways in which these men expressed their gender.

Early qualitative investigations with Black gay/bisexual young men demonstrated that internalized negative cultural beliefs related to their sexuality were associated with negative self-perceptions and increased participation in sexual risk behaviors. Beeker and colleagues (1998) conducted qualitative interviews with Black gay/bisexual young men ages 18–29 and found cultural beliefs about masculinity, in addition to high levels of perceived homophobia, were related to low self-esteem, as well as increased substance use behavior and sexual risk-taking. More current investigations with Black gay/bisexual adult men have shown that when these men are also living with HIV, they must contend with additional cultural negativity related to their status and may experience social isolation and rejection from the larger Black community (Harawa, Williams, Ramamurthi, & Bingham, 2006), as well as major black social institutions such as the "Black church" (Miller, 2007). These studies reinforce the need to attend to culturally specific messages related to sexual activity when developing sexual health promotion program for sexual minority people of color, and to analyze the ways in which such cultural messages may either enhance or impede such efforts (Harper, 2007; Wilson & Miller, 2002). What is missing in the extant literature are explorations of nonproblematized culturally influenced behaviors and factors among lesbian, gay, and bisexual individuals from varying ethnic/racial groups that would provide needed information to promote all forms of health among these populations.

QUEER THEORY, DISCOURSE THEORY, AND CHALLENGING HEGEMONY

A smaller subset of theories and research in psychology that examines race and ethnicity among lesbian, gay, and bisexual people frames their work more explicitly in terms of power differentials with an emphasis on the importance of examining public discourse and forms of resistance. Whereas queer theory tends to acknowledge multiple forms of oppression as well as the cultural contexts of behaviors (cf. Cohen, 2005), the greater emphasis is on examining societal and interpersonal discourses in terms of the inherent power dynamics that exist (King, 2008). Specifically, work grounded in queer theory seeks to challenge heteronormativity, the institutionalized normalization of a narrowly defined form of heterosexuality. For example, Yon-Leau and Munoz-Laboy (2010) sought to understand how sexual minority Latino youth asserted cultural and political agency through a study of how they constructed their own sexualities; they found that many youth resisted behaviorally based sexual identity labels and chose other labels or no labels at all to identify their sexual orientation. Specific to the academic setting, the use of queer theory frameworks to create more accepting classroom environments for sexual minority high school students of color has been discussed as a way to guide students in a continual process of reconstructing inclusive notions of sexuality (Jamil & Harper, 2010; McCready, 2004). By focusing on all students regardless of their sexual orientation, educators can attempt to shift negative heteronormative beliefs before they result in negativity toward sexual minority youth of color. In accordance with queer theory, this may be accomplished by creating activities and exercises that encourage students to critically explore and disrupt (hetero)normalizing social discourses about sexuality, and to view sexuality as more of a fluid rather than a binary and fixed concept (Jamil & Harper, 2010).

Related to approaches drawing from queer theory, Phua (2007) drew on similar theories of power and hegemony to examine how Asian American gay men experienced masculinity ideologies and mate selection. He found evidence of varying forms of support for the U.S. hegemonic masculinity frame relegating non-White and non-"straight-acting" men to a subordinate feminine position, as well as evidence of resistance to this cultural framing. Also in the area of gender expression, our studies have drawn on discourse theory, feminist theory, and queer theory to document the complex relationship between ethnic minority lesbian, gay, and bisexual communities and dominant gender ideologies among both Black and Latino gay and bisexual male youth (Wilson et al., 2010) and among Black lesbians (Wilson, 2009). For example, Wilson (2009) used sexual discourse theory (Schifter & Madrigal, 2001) to study sexual culture among a community of Black American lesbians and found that although data highlighted the central role that lesbian gender roles (e.g., femme, stud) play in this community, analyses also revealed a strong resistance to the dominance of this sexual cultural system. Documenting the interplay between assimilation and resistance to both heterosexual and ethnic-specific lesbian community beliefs and norms around gender expression aided in understanding the diversity, resiliency, and agency within the community. The use of theories that emphasize both individual and institutional roles in power dynamics adds greatly to frameworks used more commonly within lesbian, gay, and bisexual psychology, such as the multiple oppression and cultural theories described earlier.

FUTURE DIRECTIONS

The first part of this chapter illustrates that research and theory that fully explore the intersectionality of race/ethnicity and sexual orientation are still emerging within the fields of psychology and related disciplines. Extant literature in this area utilizes several different lenses through which race and ethnicity are explored among lesbian, gay, and bisexual populations, including emphasizing the significance of experiencing multiple forms of oppression, exploring the varying cultural contexts within which sexual behavior and beliefs are developed, and interrogating and resisting racism and heteronormativity. This second part of the chapter offers recommendations for advancing the study of race/ethnicity among lesbian, gay, and bisexual populations, and moving the field forward with regard to more sensitive and nuanced explorations of the lived experiences of lesbian, gay, and bisexual people. We present these recommendations within two major focal areas, including conceptual and theoretical issues to examine in future research, and methodological issues to consider in such explorations.

CONCEPTUAL AND THEORETICAL ISSUES

(Re)defining racial and ethnic groups. Any one or a combination of the three primary theoretical orientations for understanding the relationships between race/ethnicity and sexual orientation that we discussed above has remained useful for documenting the lives of sexual minority people of color and identifying ways to promote health and well-being among these populations. However, the lack of analysis of the meaning of race and ethnicity more broadly, including attention to White and European identities and intraracial diversity, highlights a need for an expansion of these theoretical approaches or for the development of new approaches altogether. The study of ethnic/racial issues among lesbian, gay, and bisexual people has focused almost exclusively on ethnic minorities, much like the general trend within psychology (Riggs, 2004, 2007). This characteristic of the field has likely been driven primarily by both a need to justify research with communities that have historically received little attention in the social sciences and by those of us who identify with ethnic minority lesbian, gay, and bisexual communities and want to work within communities with which we feel connected. Nonetheless, this approach has limited our theoretical development and served to reinforce a discourse that makes "Whiteness" the normal basis from which everything deviates (Dyer, 1997; Wilson & Miller, 2003). Although examining participants' perspectives of their own Whiteness can be challenging because most White people in the United States learn that their racial identities need no exploration, there is evidence that White youth, in general do maintain an ethnoracial identity (Phinney, Cantu, & Kurtz, 1997) and, when asked, white gay male youth perceive their Whiteness as relevant to their experiences as sexual minorities, particularly in conjunction with socioeconomic status (Wilson et al., 2010). Important next steps for those of us who study issues of race and ethnicity should include, for example, analyses of the role of White privilege in the experiences of diverse groups of White lesbian, gay, and bisexual people or studies of European American culture and its relationships to health behaviors.

In addition to expanding the groups with which scholars study racial or ethnicity-related factors explicitly, another important area of intersectional research conceptualization is the analysis of "race" among lesbian, gay, and bisexual people in ways that represent the varied experiences of sexual minority people within the same racial category. For example, Green (2005) drew from critical theory and Goffman's self-presentation theory to examine the multiple subcategories and dimensions along which Black gay men in New York experience social life, particularly in predominantly White gay settings. He found that many men reported both a uniform experience of Blackness but also a nuanced experience of otherness bounded by skin color (i.e., the lighter skin Black gay men received privileges) and physique (i.e., more muscular and thinner men received privileges), rather than determined by simplistic racial identity categories. His findings reinforce the argument made by Helms, Jernigan, and Mascher (2005) to finally heed the decades-old call of some psychologists to abandon the use of race as a variable of importance altogether as it only reinforces racist stereotypes, creates scientific imprecision, and masks many of the meaningful differences between and within racial groups that affect life experiences. The interplay between oppressed and privileged statuses related to gender, race/ethnicity, social class, and sexual orientation has been shown to have differential effects on individuals depending on the composition and visibility of their oppressed and privileged statuses (Croteau, Talbot, Lance, & Evans, 2002). Thus, although lesbian, gay, and bisexual people of color often experience compounded levels of oppression related to their race/ethnicity as compared to their white counterparts, this will likely vary depending on their gender presentation, visibility of their ethnic/racial background, social class, and other social status characteristics.

Reexamining identity development theories. Developmental theories on both ethnic identity development and sexual orientation identity development typically do not account for the intersectionality of multiple identities and thus may not adequately represent the experiences of these young people. For example, many ethnic identity development models assert that part of the development of people's ethnic identity involves an immersion into their respective ethnic community (Phinney, 1989; Cross, 1978; Helms, 1990; Atkinson et al., 1979). However, for ethnic and sexual minorities, total withdrawal from the larger white gay community and subsequent immersion into their ethnic community may be difficult due to heterosexism within their ethnic community (Tremble, et al., 1989; Cheung & Katayama, 1999; Parks, 2001). Similarly traditional theories of sexual orientation identity development include exploration of lesbian, gay, and bisexual communities through personal contacts with publicly identified lesbian or gay individuals (Cass, 1979; Troiden, 1989), as well as dating and romantic/sexual relationships with openly lesbian or gay people (Coleman, 1982). According to these theories, once an individual has had positive contact with members of a sexual minority community and is able to accept and integrate a sexual minority orientation as an element of her or his total identity, the individual has reached the final stage in sexual identity development (Cass, 1979; Coleman, 1982; Troiden, 1989). However, such interactions with the lesbian, gay, and bisexual community and with openly gay or lesbian people may be limited for many ethnic minority lesbian, gay, and bisexual people. Ethnic minority persons may face ethnically based oppression by White lesbian, gay, and bisexual individuals that may prevent acceptance and integration into broader communities (Diaz, 1998; Harper, et al., 2004; Martinez & Sullivan, 1998). Furthermore, youth of color seeking lesbian, gay, or bisexual spaces are likely to have less access to adult-only venues (e.g., bars) and fewer numbers of sexual minority adults of color who are open to others about their sexual orientation as previously referenced.

D'Augelli's (1994) more contemporary model of sexual orientation identity development differs from traditional stage models as it is based on a social constructivist perspective and thus takes a more fluid lifespan development approach to sexual orientation identity. The final phase in D'Augelli's (1994) model is similar to other models as it is focused on entering a sexual minority community, where people engage and participate in social networks and venues for lesbian, gay, and bisexual people. Thus for sexual minority people of color, challenges may still exist with regard to this phase if they are unable to find or become integrated into a lesbian, gay, or bisexual community.

New conceptual frameworks and models regarding sexual orientation identity development are needed that are based in the contemporary experiences of lesbian, gay, and bisexual people of color, and that explore varying ways of conceptualizing sexual orientation. For example, Harper et al. (2010) created a transactional and theoretically integrated model of same-sex sexual orientation identity (SSSOI) development based on empirical qualitative data collected from African American, Latino, and European American gay/bisexual/questioning male youth. The model presents temporal ordering of SSSOI development processes (i.e., awareness of same-sex attraction, evaluation of same-sex attraction, sexual orientation identity-related explorative experiences, and affective, cognitive, and behavioral evaluation of these experiences), but these may occur in a cyclical fashion and do not necessarily result in one definitive moment at which sexual orientation identity is fully achieved. Instead these processes may occur and change over time, with new experiences and changes in proximal and distal sociocultural influences. Proximal influences in the model may include family, peers, influential others, and sexual orientation identity community connections. Distal influences include perceived roles and responsibilities of what it means to be a same-sex-attracted individual, religion, and sociocultural messages regarding same-sex-attracted people that emanate from ethnic/cultural values, perceived gender roles, and societal heterosexism.

Promoting resiliency research and frameworks. Ethnic minority lesbian, gay, and bisexual people throughout history have demonstrated strength and resiliency even when confronted with seemingly insurmountable challenges and multiple oppressive forces. Unfortunately, research on relationships between race/ethnicity and sexual orientation has all too often approached empirical research from a deficit-based framework, typically focusing on negative health/mental health outcomes that are experienced as a result of multiple oppressions or attempting to explain disproportionate rates of health/mental health outcomes. Given that federal funding through major institutes and agencies such as the National Institutes of Health and the Centers for Disease Control and Prevention requires a demonstration that the population-of-focus for funded studies is experiencing negative health/ mental health outcomes, it is not surprising that such deficit-focused studies prevail. Although such

work is needed in varying domains, more studies need to be developed and implemented that utilize resilience-based frameworks and that highlight the multiple strengths and forms of resistance used by communities at the intersections of multiple social identities. In addition, study samples may focus on those individuals who have not experienced negative health/mental health outcomes as opposed to those who possess some type of pathology, and demonstrate the ways in which ethnic minority lesbian, gay, and bisexual people have been able to avoid such negative health outcomes. Even when investigating negative health outcomes and individuals who are exhibiting pathology, researchers can incorporate measures and methodologies that assess resilience-focused factors and constructs among these populations, especially those that highlight strengths-based aspects of various ethnic/ racial groups.

Research on the resiliency of sexual minority people of color may need to interrogate previously held notions regarding areas of deficit and distress for lesbian, gay, and bisexual people of color, and approach empirical inquiry using nonheterosexist and eurocentric methodologies that privilege both the heterosexual and white experiences. Research grounded in phenomenological and constructivist frameworks in which participants provide their own definitional constructs based on their life experiences and perceptions can also reveal areas of resiliency. This was demonstrated in a recent qualitative study this chapter's authors and colleagues conducted with gay, bisexual, and questioning African American and Latino male adolescents in which youth were able to define and describe their various communities of memberships, and describe the ways in which they navigated and negotiated membership in potentially conflicting communities. The narratives of the youth demonstrated that, contrary to prior research and theoretical speculation, these young men remained connected to both their sexual and ethnic communities throughout their multiple identity development processes by embracing the resources that supported their development in each (Jamil et al., 2009). For example, they maintained connections to their ethnic communities through cultural traditions and elements, as well as family and friends; while also remaining connected to their sexual orientation identity through organizations, social events, and the Internet. Youth were able to maintain these connections amid experiences of oppression from both communities, and manage both identities in creative and adaptive ways (Jamil et al., 2009).

Exploring race/ethnicity, sexuality, and sexual health. Research on the sexual lives and communities of lesbian, gay, and bisexual people that is not focused on either negative sexual health concerns or disease outcomes is needed. This need is particularly high within the area of research on race/ethnicity and sexual orientation, in which constructs of race and ethnicity are deemed relevant only when explaining sexual risk and sexually transmitted infections among sexual minority people of color, particularly men. Research could explore the varying ways that ethnic minority lesbian, gay, and bisexual people construct their sexual lives and communities, including investigations of ethnic-specific sexual cultures, sexual partnerships, and positive sexual health (Harper, 2007). In addition, such studies should focus specifically on the sexual lives of lesbian, gay, and bisexual people of color, without pressure to draw comparisons to samples of white sexual minority people.

Psychological explorations of the influence of race/ethnicity on healthy sexuality and sexual cultures among lesbian, gay, and bisexual populations may benefit from work conducted in allied disciplines such as anthropology. Both Herdt's (1997) and Parker's (1990) work in particular are illuminating as they stress the importance of understanding varying *sexual cultures* that exist in societies, which they define as generally accepted models of cultural ideals regarding sexual behavior within a specific group. Sexual cultures include sexual and gender norms, emotions, beliefs, rules, and symbolic meanings attached to the nature and meaning of sexual encounters and other sexualized social interactions. Thus a sexual culture creates a system for categorizing certain sexual acts and behaviors as desirable, whereas others may be viewed as forbidden. As lesbian, gay, and bisexual people explore their sexuality and learn about sexual cultures, they do this within multiple systems of influence including the oppressive forces previously discussed, as well as ethnic/racial group influences. Thus future investigations may explore the role of race/ethnicity in the development of sexual cultures for sexual minority people, as well as the role of intersectionality in the development and maintenance of sexual cultures.

METHODOLOGICAL ISSUES

In addition to theory building challenges, those of us studying lesbian, gay, and bisexual populations from an intersectional approach must also continue to identify methodologies that best capture relationships between multiplicative identities, social statuses, and the human experience. For example, when examining oppression as a factor of mental and physical health, the "multiple oppression" theories and Black feminist literatures remind us that individuals do not experience oppression in a simple additive way, such as Chicana + bisexual + woman. But rather, the experience of multiple oppressions is likely to be simultaneous as in racially specific gender stereotypes that target Chicana women, but not White women or Chicana men. Additionally, regardless of what intersections of subjugated or privileged statuses are targeted in any moment, people also experience these events as whole human beings (i.e., not separated into identity pieces). People and communities that identify with multiple social statuses are unable to say, for example, "I interpret this oppressive experience only as a Latina, but that earlier experience only as a bisexual person."

These complexities result in an inherent tension between the theoretical goal of capturing our experiences as whole human beings, and yet using the current set of scientific tools to understand the unique and interactive effects of multiple forms of oppressions. This is further complicated by the reality that several qualitative studies demonstrate that many ethnic minority lesbian, gay, and bisexual people talk about themselves in both completely intersectional as well as compartmentalized terms, depending on the context and question of the interview/survey (Bowleg, 2008; Wilson, 2009; Wilson et al., 2010). One methodology that several scholars have used (to various degrees) includes qualitative instruments that elicit participants' perspectives on the core identities relevant to their sense of self, followed by questions that encourage respondents to discuss core identities/statuses in relationship to one another (Bowleg, 2008; Jamil et al., 2009; Narváez, Meyer, Kertzner, Ouellette, & Gordon, 2009; Wilson et al., 2010). Although not without its limitations (see, e.g., Nash, 2008 for a critique of intersectional methodologies), this approach simultaneously allows investigators an opportunity to use academic and politically derived frameworks to examine how lesbian, gay, and bisexual people experience their lives at the intersection of multiple identities, but aid in the development of respondent-driven and contextually bound theories of this process.

Community-based participatory research also continues to provide great promise as a methodology for examining the complexities of an intersectional approach. The strength in community-based participatory research for intersectional studies is that the communities with which academic researchers work play an integral role in the research process by codeveloping research questions and methodologies that are relevant to their life experiences (Israel, Schulz, Parker, & Becker, 1998; Wallerstein & Duran, 2006). Community-based participatory research is based in principles such as cooperative and participatory engagement from stakeholders, collaborative and equitable participation and representation from community members and researchers, a focus on community capacity building, and dissemination of findings to stake-holders (Israel, et al., 2006; Wallerstein & Duran, 2006). Using this approach also provides for more effective communication and dissemination of locally relevant research findings to lesbian, gay, and bisexual communities that can benefit most from such inquiries. Community-based participatory research and other collaborative and participatory research methods can also serve as forms of activism specifically for lesbian, gay, and bisexual people of color. They do this by (1) raising awareness within the academy about the issues that confront sexual minority people of color and the need for activism, while also working to elevate the status of ethnic minority lesbian, gay, and bisexual research within these academic institutions; (2) creating safe settings in which lesbian, gay, and bisexual people of color can be affirmed and validated when they engage in self-expression; and (3) improving the capacity of local community organizations to advocate for sexual minority people of color (Harper, Jamil, & Wilson, 2007).

CONCLUSIONS

In the existing research that discusses or directly examines race/ethnicity among lesbian, gay, and bisexual populations, several important theoretical lenses have been used, including those that emphasize the significance of experiencing multiple forms of oppression, the importance of taking into account multiple cultural referent groups impacting behavior and beliefs, and/or the need to examine individual and community resistance to racism and heteronormativity. The extant empirical research among communities that identify with both racial and sexual minority identities has helped the field of psychology to consider diversity within various communities by emphasizing the multiple intersectionalities that they all possess. Useful next steps for the field of psychology will be to continue reconceptualizing and researching the significance of identities such as race, ethnicity, and sexual orientation in ways that serve to dismantle, rather than reify, racial and sexual identities as static concepts. Furthermore, expanding our empirical focus to evaluate the significance and experience of majority statuses, such as Whiteness and heterosexuality, will also aid in our ability to create more accurate theories about multiple social identities and their relevance to well-being.

ACKNOWLEDGMENT

We thank Joseph Benjamin for his dependable and efficient assistance with the references and literature searches.

REFERENCES

Adams, E., Cahill, B., & Ackerlind, S. (2005). A qualitative study of Latino lesbian and gay youths: Experiences with discrimination and the career development process. *Journal of Vocational Behavior, 66,* 199–218. doi: 10.1016/j.jvb.2004.11.002.

Alfonso, J. T., Díaz, N. V., Andújar-Bello, I., & Rosa, L. E. N. (2006). Strengths and vulnerabilities of a sample of gay and bisexual male adolescents in Puerto Rico. *Revista Interamericana de Psicología, 40,* 55–64.

Atkinson, D. R., Morten, G., & Sue, D. W. (1979). *Counseling American minorities: A cross-cultural perspective.* Dubuque, IA: William C. Brown.

Battle, J., & Ashley, C. (2008). Intersectionality, heteronormativity and black lesbian, gay, bisexual, and transgender (LGBT) families. *Black Women, Gender, and Families. 2,* 1–24.

Beeker, C., Guenther-Grey, C., & Raj, A. (1998). Community empowerment paradigm drift and the primary prevention of HIV/AIDS. *Social Science and Medicine, 46*(7), 831–842.

Boehmer, U. (2002). Twenty years of public health research: Inclusion of lesbian, gay, bisexual, and transgender populations. *American Journal of Public Health, 92,* 1125–1130.

Bonilla, L., & Porter, J. (1990). A comparison of Latino, Black, and non-Hispanic white attitudes toward homosexuality. *Hispanic Journal of Behavioral Sciences, 12,* 437–452. doi: 10.1177/07399863900124007.

Bowleg, L. (2008). When Black + lesbian + woman ≠ Black lesbian woman: The methodological challenges of qualitative and quantitative intersectionality research. *Sex Roles, 59,* 312–325. doi: 10.1007/s11199-008-9400-z.

Bowleg, L., Brooks, K., & Ritz, S. F. (2008). Bringing home more than a paycheck: An exploratory analysis of Black lesbians' experiences of stress and coping in the workplace. *Journal of Lesbian Studies, 12,* 69–84.

Bowman, P., & Howard, C. (1985). Race-related socialization, motivation, and academic achievement: A study of Black youths in three-generation families. *Journal of the American Academy of Child Psychiatry, 24*(2), 134–141. doi: 10.1016/S0002-7138(09)60438-6.

Bridges, S. K., Selvidge, M. M. D., & Matthews, C. R. (2003). Lesbian women of color: Therapeutic issues and challenges. *Journal of Multicultural Counseling & Development, 31,* 113–130.

Cass, V. C. (1979). Homosexual identity formation: A theoretical model. *Journal of Homosexuality, 4,* 219–235.

Celentano, D. D., Sifakis, F., Hylton, J., Torian, L. V., Guillin, V., & Koblin, B. A. (2005). Race/ethnic differences in HIV prevalence and risks among adolescent and young adult men who have sex with men. *Journal of Urban Health, 82,* 610–621.

Chan, C. (1995). Issues of sexual identity in an ethnic minority: The case of Chinese American lesbians, gay men, and bisexual people. In A. R. D'Augelli & C. Patterson (Eds.), *Lesbian, gay, and bisexual identities over the lifespan: Psychological perspectives* (pp. 87–101). New York: Oxford University Press.

Cheung, Y. B., & Katayama, M. (1999). Ethnic and sexual identity development of Asian American lesbian and gay adolescents. In K. S. Ng (Ed.), *Counseling Asian families from a systems perspective* (pp. 159–169). Alexandria, VA: American Counseling Association.

Cochran, S. D., Mays, V. M., Ortega, A. N., Alegria, M., & Takeuchi, D. (2007). Mental health and substance use disorders among Latino and Asian American lesbian, gay, and bisexual adults. *Journal of Consulting & Clinical Psychology, 75,* 785–794. doi: 10.1037/0022-006x.75.5.785.

Cohen, C. (2005). Punks, bulldaggers, and welfare queens: The radical potential of queer politics? In E. Johnson & M. Henderson (Eds.), *Black queer studies: A critical anthology* (pp. 21–51). Durham, NC: Duke University Press.

Coleman, E. (1982). Developmental stages of the coming out process. *Journal of Homosexuality, 9,* 105–126.

Collins, P. H. (2008). *Black feminist thought: Knowledge, consciousness, and the politics of empowerment* (3rd ed.). New York: Routledge.

Colon, E. (2001). An ethnographic study of six Latino gay and bisexual men. *Journal of Gay & Lesbian Social Services, 12,* 77–92.

Combahee River Collective Statement. (1977). In B. Smith (Ed.), *Home girls: A Black feminist anthology* (pp. 272–282). New York: Kitchen Table: Women of Color Press.

Consolacion, T., Russell, S., & Sue, S. (2004). Sex, race/ethnicity, and romantic attractions: Multiple minority status adolescents and mental health. *Cultural Diversity and Ethnic Minority Psychology, 10,* 200–214. doi: 10.1037/1099–9809.10.3.200.

Crawford, I., Allison, K. W., Zamboni, B. D., & Soto, T. (2002). The influence of dual-identity development on the psychosocial functioning of African American gay and bisexual men. *Journal of Sex Research, 39,* 179.

Crenshaw, K. (1989). Demarginalizing the intersection of race and sex: A Black feminist critique of antidiscrimination doctrine, feminist theory, and antiracist politics. *University of Chicago Legal Forum, 1989,* 139–167.

Cross, W. (1978). The Thomas and Cross models of psychological nigrescence: A review. *Journal of Black Psychology, 5,* 13–31. doi: 10.1177/009579847800500102.

Croteau, J., Talbot, D., Lance, T., & Evans, N. (2002). A qualitative study of the interplay between privilege and oppression. *Journal of Multicultural Counseling and Development, 30*(4), 239–258.

Cruz, C. (2008). Notes on immigration, youth, and ethnographic silence. *Theory Into Practice, 47,* 67–73. doi: 10.1080/00405840701764797.

D'Augelli, A. R. (1994). Identity development and sexual orientation: Toward a model of lesbian, gay, and bisexual development. In E. J. Trickett & R. J. Watts (Eds.), *Human diversity: Perspectives on people in context* (pp. 312–333). San Francisco, CA: Jossey-Bass.

Díaz, R. M. (1998). *Latino gay men and HIV: Culture, sexuality and risk behavior.* New York: Routledge.

Díaz, R. M., Ayala, G., & Bein, E. (2004). Sexual risk as an outcome of social oppression: Data from a probability sample of Latino gay men in three U.S. cities. *Cultural Diversity and Ethnic Minority Psychology, 10,* 255–267. doi: 10.1037/1099–9809.10.3.255.

Diaz, R. M., Ayala, G., Bein, E., Henne, J., & Marin, B. V. (2001). The impact of homophobia, poverty, and racism on the mental health of gay and bisexual Latino men: Findings from 3 U.S. cities. *American Journal of Public Health, 91,* 927–932.

Doll, L., Petersen, L., White, C., & Johnson, E. (1992). Homosexually and nonhomosexually identified men who have sex with men: A behavioral comparison. *Journal of Sex Research, 29,* 1–14. doi: 10.1080/00224499209551630.

Dubé, E., & Savin-Williams, R. (1999). Sexual identity development among ethnic sexual-minority male youths. *Developmental Psychology, 35,* 1389–1398. doi: 10.1037/0012–1649.35.6.1389.

Dyer, R. (1997). *White.* New York: Routledge.

Espín, O. (1993). Issues of identity in the psychology of Latina lesbians. In L. D. Gamets & D. C. Kimmel

(Eds.), *Psychological perspectives on lesbian and gay male experiences* (pp. 348–363). New York: Columbia University Press.

Fukuyama, M. A., & Ferguson, A. D. (2000). Lesbian, gay, and bisexual people of color: Understanding cultural complexity and managing multiple oppressions. In R. M. Perez, K. A. DeBord, & K. J. Bieschke (Eds.), *Handbook of counseling and psychotherapy with lesbian, gay, and bisexual clients* (pp. 81–105). Washington, DC: American Psychological Association.

Gilley, B. J., & Co-Cké, J. H. (2005). Cultural investment: Providing opportunities to reduce risky behavior among gay American Indian males. *Journal of Psychoactive Drugs, 37,* 293–298.

Green, A. I. (2005). The kind that all White men want: Race and the role of subtle status characteristics in an urban gay setting. *Social Theory & Health, 3,* 206–227. doi: 10.1057/palgrave.sth.8700054.

Greene, B. (1997). Lesbian women of color: Triple jeopardy. *Journal of Lesbian Studies, 1,* 109–147.

Greene, B. (2000). African American lesbian and bisexual women. *Journal of Social Issues, 56,* 239–249. doi: 10.1111/0022–4537.00163.

Guarnero, P. A. (2007). Family and community influences on the social and sexual lives of Latino gay men. *Journal of Transcultural Nursing, 18,* 12–18. doi: 10.1177/1043659606294191.

Hall, H. I., Byers, R. H., Ling, Q., & Espinoza, L. (2007). Racial/ethnic and age disparities in HIV prevalence and disease progression among men who have sex with men in the United States. *American Journal of Public Health, 97,* 1060–1066.

Han, C. (2009). Introduction to the special issue on GLBTQ of color. *Journal of Gay & Lesbian Social Services, 21,* 109–114. doi: 10.1080/10538720902771826.

Harawa, N., Williams, J., Ramamurthi, H. C., & Bingham, T. (2006). Perceptions towards condom use, sexual activity, and HIV disclosure among HIV-positive African American men who have sex with men: Implications for heterosexual transmission. *Journal of Urban Health, 83,* 682–694.

Harper, G. W. (2007). Sex isn't that simple: Culture and context in HIV prevention interventions for gay and bisexual male adolescents. *American Psychologist, 62,* 806–819. doi: 10.1037/0003–066x.62.8.806.

Harper, G. W., Fernandez, M. I., Jamil, O. A., Hidalgo, M. A., Torres, R. S., Bruce, D., et al. (2010). *An empirically-based transactional model of same-sex sexual orientation identity development.* Poster session presented at the annual meeting of the American Psychological Association, San Diego, CA.

Harper, G., Jamil, O., & Wilson, B. (2007). Collaborative community-based research as activism: Giving voice and hope to lesbian, gay, and bisexual youth. *Journal of Gay and Lesbian Psychotherapy, 11,* 99–119.

Harper, G. W., Jernewall, N., & Zea, M. C. (2004). Giving voice to emerging science and theory for

lesbian, gay, and bisexual people of color. *Cultural Diversity and Ethnic Minority Psychology, 10,* 187–199. doi: 10.1037/1099–9809.10.3.187.

Helms, J. (1990). *Black and White racial identity: Theory, research, and practice.* New York: Greenwood Press.

Helms, J., Jernigan, M., & Mascher, J. (2005). The meaning of race in psychology and how to change it: A methodological perspective. *American Psychologist, 60,* 27–36. doi: 10.1037/0003–066X.60.1.27.

Herdt, G. H. (1997). *Same sex, different cultures: Gays and lesbians across cultures.* Boulder, CO: Westview Press.

Herek, G., & Capitanio, J. (1995). Black heterosexuals' attitudes toward lesbians and gay men in the United States. *Journal of Sex Research, 32,* 95–105.

Huebner, D. M., & Davis, M. C. (2007). Perceived anti-gay discrimination and physical health outcomes. *Health Psychology, 26,* 627–634. doi: 10.1037/0278-6133.26.5.627

Israel, B., Schulz, A., Parker, A., & Becker, A. (1998). Review of community-based research: Assessing partnership approaches to improve public health. *Annual Reviews in Public Health, 19,* 173–202.

Jamil, O. B., & Harper, G. W. (2010). School for the self: Examining the role of educational settings for identity development among gay/bisexual/questioning male youth of color. In C. Bertram, M. S. Crowley, & S. Massey (Eds.), *LGBTQ youth in their educational contexts* (pp. 175–202) . New York: Peter Lang.

Jamil, O. B., Harper, G. W., & Fernandez, M. I. (2009). Sexual and ethnic identity development among gay–bisexual-questioning (GBQ) male ethnic minority adolescents. *Cultural Diversity and Ethnic Minority Psychology, 15,* 203–214. doi: 10.1037/a0014795.

Kertzner, R. M., Meyer, I. H., Frost, D. M., & Stirratt, M. J. (2009). Social and psychological well-being in lesbians, gay men, and bisexuals: The effects of race, gender, age, and sexual identity. *American Journal of Orthopsychiatry, 79,* 500–510. doi: 10.1037/a0016848.

King, B. W. (2008). Being gay guy, that is the advantage: Queer Korean language learning and identity construction. *Journal of Language, Identity & Education, 7,* 230–252. doi: 10.1080/15348450802237855.

Martinez, D. G., & Sullivan, S. C. (1998). African American gay men and lesbians: Examining the complexity of gay identity development. In L. A. See (Ed.), *Human behavior in the social environment from an African American perspective* (pp. 243–264). Binghamton, NY: The Haworth Press.

McCready, L. T. (2004). Understanding the marginalization of gay and gender non-conforming Black male students. *Theory Into Practice, 43,* 136–143.

Meyer, I. H. (1995). Minority stress and mental health in gay men. *Journal of Health and Social Behavior, 36,* 38–56.

Meyer, I. H., & Ouellette, S. C. (2009). Unity and purpose at the intersections of racial/ethnic and sexual identities. In P. L. Hammack & B. J. Cohler (Eds.), *The story of sexual identity: Narrative perspectives on the gay and lesbian life course* (pp. 79–106). New York: Oxford University Press.

Meyer, I., Schwartz, S., & Frost, D. (2008). Social patterning of stress and coping: Does disadvantaged social statuses confer more stress and fewer coping resources? *Social Science & Medicine, 67*, 368–379. doi: 10.1016/j.socscimed.2008.03.012.

Miller, R. (2007). Legacy denied: African American gay men, AIDS, and the Black church. *Social Work, 52*, 51–61.

Moraga, C., & Anzaldúa, G. (Eds.). (1983). *This bridge called my back: Writings by radical women of color.* New York: Kitchen Table: Women of Color Press

Morales, E. (1989). Ethnic minority families and minority gays and lesbians. *Marriage & Family Review, 14*, 217–239. doi: 10.1300/J002v14n03_11.

Muñoz-Laboy, M., & Dodge, B. (2007). Bisexual Latino men and HIV and sexually transmitted infections risk: An exploratory analysis. *American Journal of Public Health, 97*, 1102–1106. doi: 10.2105/ajph.2005.078345.

Narváez, R. F., Meyer, I. H., Kertzner, R. M., Ouellette, S. C., & Gordon, A. R. (2009). A qualitative approach to the intersection of sexual, ethnic, and gender identities. *Identity, 9*, 63–86. doi: 10.1080/15283480802579375.

Nash, J. (2008). Re-thinking intersectionality. *Feminist Review*, (89), 1–15.

O'Donnell, L., Argronick, G., San Doval, A., Duran, R., Myint-U, A., & Stueve, A. (2002). Ethnic and gay community attachments and sexual risk: Attachments and sexual risk behaviors among urban Latino young men who have sex with men. *AIDS Education & Prevention, 14*, 457.

Operario, D., Han, C., & Choi, K. (2008). Dual identity among gay Asian Pacific Islander men. *Culture, Health & Sexuality, 10*, 447–461. doi:10.1080/13691050701861454

Parham, T. A., & Helms, J. E. (1985). Attitudes of racial identity and self-esteem of Black students: An exploratory investigation. *Journal of College Student Personnel, 26*, 143–147.

Parker, R. (1990). *Bodies, pleasures, and passions: Sexual culture in contemporary Brazil.* Boston, MA: Beacon Press.

Parks, C. (2001). African-American same-gender-loving youths and families in urban schools. *Journal of Gay & Lesbian Social Services: Issues in Practice, Policy & Research, 13*, 41–56. doi: 10.1300/J041v13n03_03.

Parks, C. A., Hughes, T. L., & Matthews, A. K. (2004). Race/ethnicity and sexual orientation: Intersecting identities. *Cultural Diversity and Ethnic Minority Psychology, 10*, 241–254. doi: 10.1037/1099-9809.10.3.241.

Phinney, J. (1989). Stages of ethnic identity development in minority group adolescents. *Journal of Early Adolescence, 9*(1–2), 34–49. doi: 10.1177/0272431689091004.

Phinney, J. S. (1990). Ethnic identity in adolescents and adults: Review of research. *Psychological Bulletin, 108*, 499–514.

Phinney, J. S. (1991). Ethnic identity and self-esteem: A review and integration. *Hispanic Journal of Behavioral Sciences, 13*, 193–208.

Phinney, J., Cantu, C., & Kurtz, D. (1997). Ethnic and American identity as predictors of self-esteem among African American, Latino, and White adolescents. *Journal of Youth and Adolescence, 26*, 165–185. doi: 10.1023/A:1024500514834.

Phinney, J. S., & Chavira, V. (1992). Ethnic identity and self-esteem: An exploratory longitudinal study. *Journal of Adolescence, 15*, 271–281.

Phua, V. C. (2007). Contesting and maintaining hegemonic masculinities: Gay Asian American men in mate selection. *Sex Roles, 57*, 909–918. doi:10.1007/s11199-007-9318-x

Pinhey, T. K., & Millman, S. R. (2004). Asian/Pacific Islander adolescent sexual orientation and suicide risk in Guam. *American Journal of Public Health, 94*, 1204–1206.

Riggs, D. W. (2004). Challenging the monoculturalism of psychology: Towards a more socially accountable pedagogy and practice. *Australian Psychologist, 39*, 118–126.

Riggs, D. W. (2007). Recognizing race in LGBTQ psychology: Power, privilege and complicity. In V. Clarke & E. Peel (Eds.), *Out in psychology: Lesbian, gay, bisexual, trans and queer perspectives* (pp. 59–76). New York: John Wiley & Sons.

Romo-Carmona, M., & Hidalgo, H. (1995). Lesbian Latinas: Organizational efforts to end oppression. In H. Hidalgo (Ed.), *Lesbians of color: Social and human services* (pp. 85–93). Binghamton, NY: Haworth Press.

Rosario, M., Hunter, J., Maguen, S., Gwadz, M., & Smith, R. (2001). The coming-out process and its adaptational and health-related associations among gay, lesbian, and bisexual youths: Stipulation and exploration of a model. *American Journal of Community Psychology, 29*, 113–160. doi: 10.1023/A:1005205630978.

Rosario, M., Schrimshaw, E. W., & Hunter, J. (2004). Ethnic/racial differences in the coming-out process of lesbian, gay, and bisexual youths: A comparison of sexual identity development over time. *Cultural Diversity & Ethnic Minority Psychology, 10*, 215–228. doi: 10.1037/1099-9809.10.3.2152004–17288–003 [pii].

Rotheram-Borus, M. (1989). Ethnic differences in adolescents' identity status and associated behavior problems. *Journal of Adolescence, 12*, 361–374. doi: 10.1016/0140-1971(89)90060-2.

Rotheram-Borus, M. (1990). Adolescents' reference-group choices, self-esteem, and adjustment. *Journal of*

Personality and Social Psychology, 59, 1075–1081. doi: 10.1037/0022–3514.59.5.1075.

Schifter, J., & Madrigal, J. (2001). *The sexual construction of Latino youth.* New York: The Haworth Hispanic/Latina Press.

Schwartz, S., Unger, J., Zamboanga, B., & Szapocznik, J. (2010). Rethinking the concept of acculturation: Implications for theory and research. *American Psychologist, 65*, 237–251. doi: 10.1037/a0019330.

Smith, B. (1983). Introduction. In B. Smith (Ed.), *Home girls: A Black feminist anthology* (pp. xix–lvi). New York: Kitchen Table: Women of Color Press.

Stokes, J. P., McKirnan, D. J., & Burzette, R. G. (1993). Sexual behavior, condom use, disclosure of sexuality, and stability of sexual orientation in bisexual man. *Journal of Sex Research, 30*, 201–213.

Stokes, J. P., Vanable, P., & McKirnan, D. J. (1997). Comparing gay and bisexual men on sexual behavior, condom use, and psychosocial variables related to HIV/AIDS. *Archives of Sexual Behavior, 26*, 383–397.

Szymanski, D., & Meyer, D. (2008). Racism and heterosexism as correlates of psychological distress in African American sexual minority women. *Journal of LGBT Issues in Counseling, 2*, 94–108.

Tremble, B., Schneider, M., & Appathurai, C. (1989). Growing up gay or lesbian in a multicultural context. *Journal of Homosexuality, 17*, 253–267.

Troiden, R. R. (1989). The formation of homosexual identities. *Journal of Homosexuality, 17*, 43–73.

Valleroy, L. A., MacKellar, D. A., Karon, J. M., Rosen, D. H., McFarland, W., Shehan, D. A., et al. (2000). HIV prevalence and associated risks in young men who have sex with men. *Journal of the American Medical Association, 284*, 198–204.

Wallerstein, N. B., & Duran, B. (2006). Using community-based participatory research to address health disparities. *Health Promotion Practice, 7*, 312–323. doi: 10.1177/1524839906289376

Washington, P. (2001). Who gets to drink from the fountain of freedom? Homophobia in communities of color. *Journal of Gay and Lesbian Social Services, 13*, 117–131.

Williams, J., Wyatt, G., Resell, J., Peterson, J., & Asuan-O'Brien, A. (2004). Psychosocial issues among gay- and non-gay-identifying HIV-seropositive African American and Latino MSM. *Cultural Diversity and Ethnic Minority Psychology, 10*, 268–286.

Wilson, B. D. M. (2009). Black lesbian sexual culture and lesbian gender: Celebration and resistance. *Culture, Health, & Sexuality, 1*, 297–313.

Wilson, B. D. M., Harper, G. W., Hidalgo, M. A., Jamil, O. B., Torres, R. S., & Fernandez, M. I. (2010). Negotiating dominant masculinity ideology: Strategies used by gay, bisexual and questioning male adolescents. *American Journal of Community Psychology, 45*, 169–185. doi: 10.1007/s10464–009–9291–3.

Wilson, B. D. M., & Miller, R. L. (2002). Strategies for managing heterosexism used among African American gay and bisexual men. *Journal of Black Psychology, 28*, 371–391. doi: 10.1177/009579802237543.

Wilson, B. D. M. & Miller, R. L. (2003). Examining strategies for culturally grounding HIV prevention: A review. *AIDS Education and Prevention, 15*, 184–202.

Wilson, B. D. M., Okwu, C., & Mills, S. (2011). Brief report: The relationship between multiple forms of oppression and subjective health among Black lesbian and bisexual women. *Journal of Lesbian Studies, 15*(1), 15–24.

Wilson, P., & Yoshikawa, H. (2004). Experiences of and responses to social discrimination among Asian and Pacific Islander gay men: Their relationship to HIV risk. *AIDS Education and Prevention, 16*, 68–83. doi: 10.1521/aeap.16.1.68.27724.

Yip, T., Seaton, E., & Sellers, R. (2006). African American racial identity across the lifespan: Identity status, identity content, and depressive symptoms. *Child Development, 77*, 1504–1517. doi: 10.1111/j.1467–8624.2006.00950.x.

Yon-Leau, C., & Muñoz-Laboy, M. (2010). I don't like to say that I'm anything: Sexuality politics and cultural critique among sexual-minority Latino youth. *Sexuality Research and Social Policy, 7*, 105–117. doi: 10.1007/s13178–010–0009-y.

Yoshikawa, H., Wilson, P. A., Chae, D. H., & Cheng, J. F. (2004). Do family and friendship networks protect against the influence of discrimination on mental health and HIV risk among Asian and Pacific Islander gay men? *AIDS Education and Prevention, 16*, 84–100.

Zea, M. C., Reisen, C. A., & Díaz, R. M. (2003). Methodological issues in research on sexual behavior with Latino gay and bisexual men. *American Journal of Community Psychology, 31*, 281.

Zea, M. C., Reisen, C. A., & Poppen, P. J. (1999). Psychological well-being among Latino lesbians and gay men. *Cultural Diversity and Ethnic Minority Psychology, 5*, 371–379. doi: 10.1037/1099–9809.5.4.371.

Zea, M. C., Reisen, C. A., Poppen, P. J., Bianchi, F. T., & Echeverry, J. J. (2005). Disclosure of HIV status and psychological well-being among Latino gay and bisexual men. *AIDS and Behavior, 9*(1), 15–26. doi: 10.1007/s10461–005–1678-z.

21

Lesbian, Gay, Bisexual, and Transgender Communities

ESTHER D. ROTHBLUM

...she got the feeling that there were certain rules in this community: like you should be a vegetarian and not like red meat or pork and prefer shopping at the natural foods store. These were people who preferred whole wheat bread, wore Earth Shoes, drove small cars, and didn't use paper products. They believed mostly in triangles, like fidelity in a relationship was almost a negative value. Also you couldn't shave your legs. It was an anti-cigarette culture. You had to go canoeing. You had to know about the moon. (Krieger, 1983, p. 16)

It is common to hear reference to the lesbian, gay, bisexual, or transgender "communities." An Internet search for "gay community" or "lesbian community" lists hundreds of millions of sites. A recent edition of the guidebook *Gayellow Pages* (Green, 2007) alone contains over 500 pages of bars, bookstores, clubs, community centers, inns, and youth groups for lesbian, gay, bisexual, and transgender persons in the United States and Canada. My friends and acquaintances tell me their communities are large or small, inclusive or rejecting, demographically diverse or homogeneous, easy or hard to locate. There is often a sense of disappointment or betrayal about our communities. We would like to come out, or meet a lover, or move to a new town and find a welcoming community.

But what exactly is meant by "community"? Definitions of "community" (e.g., www.bing.com) focus on groups of people who live in the same area, or people with a common background. How does this apply to lesbian, gay, bisexual, and transgender people? As Botnick (2000) stated about the gay male community, "The ephemeral nature of community...fails to lend itself to concrete examination; in

fact, since it lacks geography, homogeneity of class, language, or ideology it can hardly be considered as a sociological entity" (p. 1). This chapter will focus on how community functions as a psychological entity, given that lesbian, gay, bisexual, and transgender people may not live in the same geographic area or have a common background.

There have been several historical descriptions of lesbian, gay, and bisexual localities, such as Newton's (1995) study of Fire Island or Chauncey's (1995) description of gay New York. When social scientists conduct research on these issues, they often conclude with suggestions for lesbian, gay, bisexual, and transgender communities, with no precise explanation of what is meant by the term. For example, Toro-Alfonso (1999) surveyed lesbians and gay men in Puerto Rico about domestic violence and stated that "This effort may be useful for other Latino communities in the mainland and a guide to develop intervention programs" (p. 69). Whittle (1998, p. 389) examined how cyberspace functions as a networking tool for the "transsexual and cross-dressing communities." Glaus (1989, p. 131) indicated that "the prevalence of alcoholism or chemical dependency in the lesbian community is unknown but presumed to be high."

WHAT IS "COMMUNITY"?

There is an enormous social science literature on community and the role of community on health and mental health (cf. Fischer, 1982; Folkman & Lazarus, 1980; Idler & Benyamini, 1997; Leavy, 2006). Sometimes community is assumed to be a region or neighborhood, consisting of many organizations and events. For example, several historians have written about lesbian, gay, bisexual, and transgender communities in U.S. cities or particular areas (Beemyn, 1997; Franzen, 1993; Schneider, 1989). Other times community is envisioned as friends and social supports, who may not reside in a specific geographic area (Woolwine, 2000). Finally, Woolwine (2000, p. 7) described the concept of "imagined community" as developed by the media, by which people are led to believe that they are part of a united national or global community. As D'Augelli and Garnets (1995) stated, "Lesbians, gay men, and bisexual people are perhaps unique in their creation of 'communities' because their invisibility and their oppressed status have hampered their efforts to find each other. Within psychology, the concept of community has represented both the literal environments in which people live and the affiliative links they develop to kindred others without regard to proximity" (p. 293).

Based on my prior research (Rothblum, 2010), I will define lesbian, gay, bisexual, and transgender community as *"Lesbian, gay, bisexual, and transgender individuals or organizations with whom one has perceived similarity due to sexual orientation, and who provide connection with others, recreation, and/ or support."* Community can consist of physical proximity (e.g., a gay neighborhood) as well as virtual communities such as might be found on the Internet.

LESBIAN, GAY, BISEXUAL, AND TRANSGENDER COMMUNITIES IN HISTORICAL CONTEXT

D'Emilio (1992) and Miller (1995) have described factors influencing present-day lesbian, gay, bisexual, and transgender identity. Urbanization and industrialization gave rise to a sense of personal identity and choice outside of the structure of the extended family. Individuals could move to cities where they had more anonymity and where they could find a lesbian/gay subculture. They could decide not to undertake heterosexual marriages, a choice that would have been difficult in nonmetropolitan areas. Nevertheless, Greene (1994) described how the extended family is still an important issue for people who are members of ethnic minority groups, including sexual minority people of color. Members of oppressed groups value the support of their families in a way that more privileged groups do not. Also, African American, Latino, Asian American, and Native-American communities often place a high value on kinship whereas European-American

cultures typically emphasize individuation and separation from families (Greene, 1994).

To form communities, nonheterosexual people had to form identities, so that there was a common language about their group membership. That meant that there had to be awareness that there were others like them. Meeker (2006) described the processes by which people found community in the middle of the last century:

> Seeking and pursuing meant that individuals may have visited doctors, read psychology journals, or browsed the shelves at the local library in order to learn more about their sexual desires; they may have picked up a newspaper or walked the streets looking for something or someone that was different, that was a little queer; they may have asked around and scoured catalogs for books and magazines published on the fringes of society and legality that promised stories about 'twilight men' or 'odd girls'; they may have moved to a city or a particular neighborhood that was rumored to harbor certain kinds of people; or they may have mimeographed their own circulars, written their own newsletters, or formed their own organizations hoping that others would heed the call and join them. (pp. 2–3)

In the 1940s and 1950s, when it was illegal to send "obscene materials" through the mail, including anything that mentioned homosexuality, gay men would use the *Hobby Directory* as a place for coded personal ads. Meeker (2006) stated: "Occupations and the other stated interests of the *Hobby Directory* members provide perhaps the most obvious statements about their different, queer preferences, making it easier for them to slyly self-identify as homosexual and assume other gays would catch on; careful readers of the *Hobby Directory* would encounter more than an average number of 'male nurses,' 'interior decorators,' 'hairdressers,' 'actors,' 'florists,' and so on." Most of the personals included the initials "C.D." that stood for "contacts desired" (pp. 24–25).

Lesbians faced additional challenges in meeting one another in earlier historical eras. Kennedy and Davis (1993) described the environment for working-class lesbians of the 1930s and 1940s. Unmarried women lived with their parents, and unescorted women in public places were often harassed by men. Lesbian bars thus played an important role for women to meet each other. Alan Bérubé (1990) and Lillian Faderman (1991) have described how World War II was a "government-sponsored subculture" (Faderman, 1991, p. 125) in which lesbian, gay, and bisexual people in the military lived in same-sex environments and where talk about sexuality was tolerated in ways it never would have been in their home towns. When the war ended, military personnel returned to the large port cities of New York, San Francisco, Boston, and Los Angeles, and many stayed there, creating large lesbian, gay, and bisexual communities in those cities (Faderman, 1991).

When lesbian, gay, bisexual, and transgender individuals were feeling isolated, they could move to or visit urban centers, or just take solace in the knowledge that such communities existed. New York City became a leading center of sexual minority communities in the 1920s and 1930s, even while police raids were quite frequent (cf. Chauncey, 1995). The Harlem Renaissance was not just important in African American history but also in the history of sexual minority communities. As the result of thousands of African Americans moving from the rural South to the urban North, Harlem became a center for Black music, literature, and politics. Gay parties, balls, and other entertainment flourished in Harlem in the 1920s and 1930s. African American lesbians and gay men had created a gay subculture or community that attracted White lesbian, gay, bisexual, and transgender individuals as well (see Faderman, 1991, and Garber, 1990, for reviews).

SEXUAL MINORITY COMMUNITIES NEED TO BE VISIBLE EVEN IF THEIR MEMBERS ARE NOT

Lesbian, gay, bisexual, and transgender people function in two cultures—the heterosexual "mainstream" society and sexual minority communities. Lukes and Land (1990) described how members of minority groups become bicultural, living in both the mainstream and minority cultures. They point out that lesbians and gay men differ from members of other minority groups in this process. Most minority groups first become acculturated within their own cultural group and are then later socialized (by families, schools, religious organizations, and the media) within the dominant culture.

Members of sexual minority groups, however, are first socialized by the dominant culture and later identify with a minority culture. Lukes and Land (1990, p. 159) state: "Those who do not fit the stereotype held by the majority culture may pass as heterosexual…and assume the advantages and privileges held by members of the dominant culture or other minority culture. However, because sexual minorities are not easily identifiable to those in other cultures, they also are not easily identifiable to each other." Lesbian, gay, bisexual, and transgender communities thus become particularly important as places for members of sexual minorities to find a subculture in order to meet people like themselves, facilitate personal development, and become socially integrated without undue risk.

For lesbian, gay, bisexual, and transgender people who are closeted, socializing with neighbors, co-workers, or even extended family members may feel stressful or inauthentic. Valentine (1993) interviewed 40 lesbians in England about where they first met other lesbians and established social networks. She found that first contacts were often with other lesbians who were similarly isolated and had no contact with the "gay scene" (p. 110). These women met each other through luck or chance, in environments (such as the workplace or a sports event) in which it was risky to disclose their sexual orientation. Many of the women remembered attending their first lesbian or gay event as a major milestone; some were highly anxious or did not know how to behave at a lesbian event. As women became comfortable in lesbian and gay environments, 85% of their current friends were people they had met in lesbian/gay settings (Valentine, 1993).

In a society in which their relationships are not formally recognized, it is not surprising that many lesbian and gay male couples seek social support from their "family of friends" or friendship circle (cf. Weston, 1997). Consequently, families of origin become less important, and friends become more so. Though "community" is usually conceptualized as something we leave our homes to find, Elwood (2000) pointed out how lesbians who want to create a lesbian-visible home space that is comfortable for them and their friendship circles often have to decide which items to remove when heterosexual family or strangers enter the home. The gay male performers Romanovsky and Phillips (1987) describe a similar phenomenon in their song "Straightening up the House."

In the sections that follow, this chapter will focus separately on issues in the lesbian, gay male, bisexual male and female, and transgender communities. Each section will review relevant research on communities, describe characteristics of the group related to community involvement, and present some unique aspects of community.

Lesbian Communities

The women's liberation movement of the 1960s and 1970s focused on women investing their energies in other women, including women-only spaces and culture. As Barnhart (1975) stated, "Among women advocating the beliefs and values of the counter-culture, there is a small minority who, in addition, share a commitment to a lesbian sexual orientation. In Portland, Oregon, some of these counterculture lesbian women have formed groups which band together and call themselves the 'Community'" (p. 90). Barnhart also found The Community to be antimaterialistic, antimale, and committed to lesbianism. By the 1990s, there was less sexism and heterosexism in society, and lesbian communities became more diversified as needs, values, and interests changed, so that lesbians reported a sense of lost commonality (Kline, 2006). Even today, there is nostalgia among older lesbians for the vibrant women's communities of the 1970s, because those communities, in hindsight, are viewed as more feminist than current communities (e.g., Rothblum & Sablove, 2005). Women coming out today find that lesbian communities interface with the queer community, the transgender community, and the gay male community (Kline, 2006).

Despite media focus on lesbians thriving in tightly knit communities (e.g., the cable television show, *The L Word,* and the popular lesbian comic strip, *Dykes to Watch Out For,* Bechdel, 2008), lesbians often report being disappointed with their communities. In 1983, Krieger published *The Mirror Dance,* a qualitative study of a Midwestern lesbian community in the 1970s that had about 60 active members. She described how the lesbian community presented "a basic identity conflict" (p. xii). On the one hand, it promised acceptance, affirmation, and shelter from the homophobic world. On the other hand, there was pressure for lesbians to act and look a certain way, so that women felt the need to hide their unique identities. Although social norms are important for most forms of communities, the lesbian-feminist communities seemed

particularly dogmatic, as the quote at the beginning of this chapter illustrates.

Berberet (2005) conducted a needs assessment to evaluate how a lesbian, gay, bisexual, and transgender community center in a large U.S. urban city could better serve the needs of women. She conducted focus groups and surveyed 368 women, of whom 65% were lesbian, 17% bisexual, 11% heterosexual, and 3% questioning. About half the women were single, about half were parents, and 38% were women of color. The women wanted to belong or feel connected to the community, yet also felt that the community was at times rejecting, cliquish, or fragmented. Reactions ranged from disappointment and sadness to anger and powerlessness; the women felt invisible and neglected. They also perceived that gay men in their city had more community (Berberet, 2005), although there has been no research comparing the quality of communities for lesbians versus gay men. Similar reactions— seeking support from lesbian communities yet feeling somewhat disappointed—were found in Kline's (2006) Australian study.

My research on 762 lesbian, bisexual, and heterosexual sisters (Rothblum & Factor, 2001) and on 1274 brothers and sisters who were lesbian, gay, bisexual, or heterosexual (Rothblum, Balsam, & Mickey, 2004) found a number of ways that lesbians differed demographically from heterosexual sisters in adulthood, with implications for lesbian communities. Lesbians have higher levels of education than their sisters and have attended colleges that were further from their parents than the ones that heterosexual women attended. In fact, the research of Laumann, Gagnon, Michael, and Michaels (1994) indicated that lesbians often continue to live in college towns (the lesbian mecca of Northampton, Massachusetts, is one example of this phenomenon, but there are many others). Lesbians lived further in miles from their parents than their heterosexual sisters. They reported moving to their current location from a greater distance than their heterosexual sisters. Lesbians tended to move for their own education, whereas heterosexual women may move because of husbands' jobs or children's educations (Rothblum et al., 2004). In my research comparing 659 members of same-sex couples in civil unions in Vermont, 466 members of same-sex couples who did not have civil unions, and 413 heterosexual married siblings and spouses (Solomon, Rothblum, & Balsam, 2004), lesbians perceived less support from and had less contact with their families of origin than did heterosexual women. Lesbians were less religious and were more politically liberal than heterosexual women. Both this study and that of Gates, Ost, and Birch (2004) based on U.S. census data found that about one-third of lesbian couples have children, which is less than heterosexual married women. All of these differences make sense if there are few welcoming rural areas, towns, and cities, so that lesbians seek out affirmative locations with strong lesbian communities.

Without longitudinal research, it is difficult to know whether lesbians become different than their heterosexual sisters and move away, or move away and become different. Are there ways in which the daughter who moves away to attend college, or who seeks a higher level of education than her siblings or parents, is already predisposed to be more independent or to seek out novel experiences? Either way, less contact with and support from their families of origin and less engagement with traditional religious institutions make lesbian communities of great importance to lesbians.

I recently conducted a qualitative study of 60 women (lesbians, bisexual women, and heterosexual sisters) on what community means to them and how they find community (Rothblum, 2008). Women across sexual orientations emphasized the role of support, but also mentioned similarity to others and physical proximity as important factors in facilitating social interaction and defining community. The focus on support explains why so many lesbians seem disappointed with community. What the Internet and guidebooks are offering lesbians is a huge range of activities with a focus on social and recreational events. This is in marked contrast to what many lesbians report needing from their communities—support when times are hard. However, when the lesbians in the study conceptualized an ideal community as one that provides support, they rarely considered the fact that they, along with others, will have to provide this support. Thus women's social supports may themselves become sources of stress. Edwards and Riggs (2008) assessed social capital among same-sex-attracted women living in rural communities in South Australia. They found women's networks to provide support, but the networks also put excessive demands on them. My research found that some lesbians, indeed, had assumed "the cost of caring" and consequently felt burned out (Rothblum, 2008, p. 71).

I also categorized women into three groups in relation to community (Rothblum, 2010). *Founders* were those who started their own groups and organizations; these were the women who noticed an absence of community and started one. *Finders* joined organizations and found community; they knew that in order to meet new friends, an active approach was necessary. Finally, *flounderers* did not find or become part of communities; they were closeted, isolated, or felt marginalized by their communities. Over 50% the lesbians in this sample were finders and over 25% were founders, in marked contrast to heterosexual sisters who were more likely to be flounderers (that is, feel isolated and disconnected from community), and who depended on family of origin for support.

There are a number of unique aspects to lesbian communities. One aspect of the lesbian community that spans age groups is a shared interest in women's sporting events. Female athletes, coaches, and sports administrators of all sexual orientations have had to cope with the stereotype that they are lesbian, and it is still rare for elite female athletes to be out as lesbian (Griffin, 1998). Many female athletes project an image of heterosexuality (including a boyfriend or husband) while socializing with other lesbians in very closeted settings (cf. Cayleff, 1996). For amateur athletes, one way to find lesbians is to join the local women's softball league. Dolance (2005) has written about the presence of lesbian fans at Women's National Basketball Association (WNBA) events and how these fans perceive themselves to be a lesbian community. Myrdahl (2009) described how the WNBA is aware of its lesbian fan base, yet these fans are nearly invisible in the media. Instead, the jumbotron screens at the games and the television coverage focus on the children who attend the games.

The annual women's music festivals, most notably the Michigan Womyn's Music Festival founded in 1976, attract thousands of lesbians each year. Women's music festivals often limit attendance to "womyn born womyn," which still causes controversy in the transgender communities (Morris, 2005). Many lesbians also recall feminist bookstores as key places in their coming out process in the 1970s (Liddle, 2005). Feminist bookstores provided safe spaces for women's gatherings in the 1970s and their bulletin boards listed local lesbian events. However, the increasing availability of lesbian books in bookstore chains and on the Internet has led to the decline of feminist bookstores. In the 1970s, some separatist lesbians formed lesbian land collectives, and some of these have lasted to the present day (e.g., Dickie, Cook, Gazda, Martin, & Sturrus, 2005; Ralston & Stoller, 2005). The cohort of lesbians who came of age during the Second Wave of the feminist movement and frequented lesbian bookstores, music festivals, and land collectives is growing older. Not surprisingly, there has been a surge of interest among this age group in lesbian retirement homes (cf. Rabin & Slater, 2005)—a new form of community.

For younger lesbians, blogs, chat rooms, and other Internet sites have replaced physical spaces such as coffee shops, bookstores, and land collectives. Virtual spaces fit younger lesbians, who view their own sexual identity as more fluid and noncategorical compared with older lesbians (Diamond, 2008). Indeed, much of the research reviewed above may be inapplicable to this younger generation of lesbians as they enter adulthood and search for community.

Gay Male Communities

My research on lesbian, gay, and bisexual and heterosexual siblings (Rothblum et al., 2004) found that compared to heterosexual men, gay men had higher educational levels, were less likely to have ever been married, were less likely to be in a current relationship, were less likely to have children, and were more likely to be living in large urban areas. This corresponds with the research based on same-sex couples in U.S. census data (Black, Gates, Sanders, & Taylor, 2002), which found that gay men were overrepresented in large urban areas and were less likely to have children than heterosexual married men. In my research on same-sex couples who had civil unions, their friends in same-sex relationships who had not had civil unions, and their heterosexual married siblings (Solomon et al., 2004), male same-sex couples rated religion as less important, were more likely to live in large urban areas, were less likely to have children, had less contact with family of origin, and perceived more support from friends than did heterosexual married couples. As these results indicate, gay men are likely to seek different communities than their heterosexual brothers or brothers-in-law. Gay men are less likely to receive support from extended family or religious organizations (Laumann et al., 1994). One of the reasons why some gay men perceive more support

from friends may be because they have left rural areas and small towns in favor of large cities with gay communities. Similarly, Crosbie-Burnett and Helmbrecht (1993) found that 48 gay male couples parenting children reported more social support from gay friends than from family members.

Woolwine (2000) interviewed 31 gay men in New York City about their experiences of community. Many of the men had joined local organizations and/or had friendship circles. Woolwine also found evidence of symbolic communities (such as when men strongly identified with gay organizations at the national level, despite not knowing many members personally). LeBeau and Jellison (2009) asked 129 gay and bisexual men about their perceptions of the "gay community." Some respondents mentioned social networks; others listed established organizations. Similarly, some focused on local activities whereas others perceived the community to consist of "all lesbian, gay, bisexual, and transgender people and allies" (p. 9). Two-thirds of the men indicated that the greatest advantage of the gay community was social (e.g., meeting sex partners, lovers, and friends), followed by increased self-understanding, and, for some, activism. Disadvantages of the gay community were reported to be the perceived shallowness of the community, dislike of specific people in the community, and the potential for harassment and prejudice by heterosexual society as the result of being visibly part of the gay community.

Gay male communities are different from lesbian and heterosexual communities in their acceptance of nonmonogamy (Hoff & Beougher, 2010; Hoff et al., 2009). In their large sample of 12,000 U.S. couples that included 957 gay male couples, Blumstein and Schwartz (1983) reported that a high percentage of gay men in couples also had casual sex with strangers or sex outside their relationships. Researchers in the United Kingdom found that the majority of gay male couples had developed a specific agreement about sex outside their relationship (Hickson et al., 1992). Peplau, Cochran, and Mays (1997) found African American gay men to be less monogamous than African American lesbians. In the research of Solomon, Rothblum, and Balsam (2005), nonmonogamy was an accepted part of gay men's relationships in that over 40% of gay men in civil unions and those not in civil unions had an agreement that sex outside their relationship was permissible in some circumstances, whereas 5% or fewer lesbian and heterosexual couples had such an agreement (Solomon et al., 2005). Blasband and Peplau (1985) surveyed 17 monogamous and 23 nonmonogamous gay male couples. The two types of couples did not differ on any variable, including relationship satisfaction.

In sum, it is possible that gay men's greater presence in large urban centers (Laumann et al., 1994) combined with the gay male communities' greater acceptance of social and sexual activities may make it easier for gay men to find community than for lesbians. Certainly the majority of entries in lesbian, gay, and bisexual guides such as the *Gayellow Pages* (Green, 2007) and websites focus on gay men. However, there has been no research comparing lesbians and gay men on community satisfaction.

Bisexual Male and Female Communities

There has been little social science scholarship about bisexual women and men compared with research on lesbians and gay men. Furthermore, bisexuality is hard to define—many people who are not exclusively heterosexual, gay, or lesbian prefer to avoid labels (Rust, 1995). There is also a stereotype that bisexual people are focused on sex (the word "sex" in "bisexuality" is part of the reason some bisexuals do not like using the term to describe themselves).

How then do bisexual women and men negotiate friendships and social networks? Galupo (2007) edited a book of personal stories and research articles about bisexual women's friendships and social organizations. A common theme throughout the book was how difficult it was for bisexual women to form a community based on the fact that their own identities were more fluid. Because bisexuality removes the idea of a dichotomous gender identity by creating a continuum, it also presents a dilemma when bisexual women want to find others like themselves.

In my research on lesbian, gay, and bisexual individuals and their heterosexual siblings (Rothblum et al., 2004), bisexual women were more demographically similar to lesbians than they were to heterosexual women. Both lesbians and bisexual women had higher levels of education than heterosexual women, were less likely to have ever been married, were less likely to have children, and were unlikely to be homemakers. Bisexual women and lesbians were more likely to have spiritual beliefs that did not fit a formal religion, and less likely to attend religious services than heterosexual women.

Thus most bisexual women, like lesbians, will not be looking for community within the traditional categories of extended family and religious organizations that are more typical of heterosexual women (Rothblum, 2010).

Some bisexual women report feeling stigmatized and excluded by lesbian communities. Ault (1996, p. 207) describes how lesbians use "techniques of neutralization" to discount, depoliticize, or negate bisexuality. For example, my research on lesbian, bisexual, and heterosexual sisters' communities found that bisexual women generally mentioned a lack of bisexual organizations, while at the same time feeling ostracized or marginalized by lesbian communities (Rothblum, 2010). I was intrigued that more bisexual women do not start their own specifically bisexual organizations or networks. When I asked about this, some women stated that it was hard to find other women who identify as bisexual, or who are willing to be out as bisexual, because that would make them less welcome in lesbian communities. Women who identify as bisexual tend to be younger than those who identify as lesbian (e.g., Rothblum & Factor, 2001), so it is possible that future cohorts of bisexual women may organize more community activities that are specifically for bisexual women.

On the other hand, my research found that bisexual men were demographically more similar to heterosexual men than to gay men (Rothblum et al., 2004). Bisexual and heterosexual men had lower levels of education than did gay men. Bisexual men were more likely to be currently heterosexually married and have children, compared with gay men. Unlike gay men, they were less likely to be living in large urban areas. These results may explain why surveys of lesbian, gay, and bisexual people often find very small numbers of bisexual men (e.g., Rothblum et al., 2004)—they are not easy to locate via gay organizations or events, or may simply not self-identify as bisexual on surveys. Or they may be more accurately categorized as MSM—men who have sex with men, who may self-identify as heterosexual. The term "down low" or DL is used in African American communities for men who have sex with men, unbeknownst to wives or girlfriends. It is also possible that bisexual men who are not or have never been married are demographically different from bisexual men married to women, though there is no research comparing these two groups. Galupo's (2007) book was intended to be about both bisexual women's and men's friend-ships and social supports; instead, only one of the submissions she received was about bisexual men. Closeted bisexual men, therefore, may survive in heterosexual communities in small towns, but at a psychological cost.

Even though there are about half as many websites for bisexual men's communities as those for bisexual women, the Internet is still an impor-tant way for men to meet each other. It is interest-ing that many websites for bisexual men focus on their need to be discreet and private; one website is named ShyBi-Guys.com. Bi Men Network (bimen. org, accessed March 1, 2010) states its mission as follows: "That bi men need to be private and dis-creet—and generally prefer this—yet do need a place, a forum—to chat, network, ask questions, to seek and offer guidance from and to others." Even when bisexual men join gay community organiza-tions and events, they may feel ostracized (LeBeau & Jellison, 2009).

Transgender Communities

Factor and Rothblum (2008a, 2008b) compared 295 transgender adults and their nontransgen-der siblings on demographic characteristics, per-ceptions of social support, and victimization. All three transgender groups—female-to-male (FTM), male-to-female (MTF), and genderqueer (those who did not identify fully as MTF or FTM)—had higher levels of education and were less conven-tionally religious than nontransgender brothers and sisters. Trans groups were also less likely to have children, to be married, or to identify as hetero-sexual. Trans groups perceived less social support from their families of origin than did nontrans-gender siblings, and FTMs lived further from their parents than did conventionally gendered siblings. MTFs were less likely to disclose their gender iden-tity to their parents than were FTMs. Trans groups were more likely to report harassment or discrimi-nation by co-workers, work supervisors, strangers, members of religious communities, leaders of reli-gious communities, leaders of ethnic communities, healthcare providers, and casual acquaintances than their nontransgender siblings (Factor & Rothblum, 2008a). These results indicate that transgender individuals are less likely to view their families of origin or their religion as important parts of their social networks, so having a community of friends would seem to be important.

We asked the three transgender groups about their connection to the transgender community and also to lesbian, gay, and transgender communities (Factor & Rothblum, 2008b). There was no differ-ence in the extent to which participants in the three trans groups felt connected to the transgender com-munity. There were no differences in the frequency of attending trans social gatherings; the proportion of social gatherings that were trans compared with all social gatherings attended; attending trans politi-cal, professional, or cultural activities; accessing the trans community electronically; or in the extent to which they had transgender friends. There was a significant difference in the extent to which groups felt connected to the lesbian, gay, and transgender community. Genderqueers felt more connected to those communities than did MTFs and FTMs. FTMs and genderqueers reported more lesbian, gay, and transgender individuals among the five people they are closest to than did MTFs (Factor & Rothblum, 2008b).

One phenomenon among some MTF and FTM transgender individuals is hesitancy to dis-close their transgender identity. Gagne, Tewksbury, and McGaughey (1997) interviewed 65 MTFs and concluded: "Only the gender radicals in our sample wished to live and be recognized as trans-gendered....Among transsexuals, because of the internalized identity by others as real women, it was most common to find an aspiration to be seen and identified by others as real women....Often, after learning to pass and completing the transformation process, transsexuals dropped out of the transgen-der community and assumed their place as women in society" (pp. 500–501). This study indicated that there are risks attached to being different for every oppressed group. It also implies that just as bisexual women are demographically different from bisexual men, so MTFs, FTMs, and genderqueers should be viewed as three separate groups with very different needs for community. MTFs, like bisexual men, may be invisible within heterosexual mainstream society and may be less connected to lesbian, gay, and bisexual communities.

CONCLUSIONS

As this chapter has indicated, lesbian, gay, bisexual, and transgender people yearn for communities that are supportive of their needs, and often feel that these needs are not adequately met. For lesbians, bisexual women, gay men, and some transgender people, their geographic and emotional distance from families of origin and their relative disinterest in traditional religious organizations make alternative communities especially vital. For bisexual men who are trying to pass as heterosexual and some transgender people who are trying to pass as conventionally gendered, their relative invisibility may make them especially isolated and lonely.

In addition, there are some other factors relevant to lesbian, gay, bisexual, and transgender communities, which have implications for future research:

Lesbian, gay, and bisexual communities are demographically heterogeneous. Research on heterosexual people indicates that friends are similar in age and socioeconomic class (Valentine, 1993). Not surprisingly, heterosexual married couples too are often similar demographically, a concept known as "assortative mating" (e.g., Adams, 1979). Laumann et al. (1994) described how assortative mating among heterosexual men and women is the norm, given how schools, colleges, neighborhoods, and employment settings may be stratified by factors such as age, social class, race, ethnicity, and religion. They speculated that lesbian, gay, and bisexual people might meet partners in settings (e.g., gay bars, gay pride marches, online dating services) that are less demographically stratified. Based on their research with U.S. census data, Rosenfeld and Kim (2005) found that both interracial couples and same-sex couples are more geographically mobile and more likely to live in urban settings. Laumann et al. (1994) emphasized that the best way to find large samples of gay men for research is to focus on the largest U.S. cities. Rosenfeld and Kim (2005) speculated that this geographic distance frees members of sexual minorities from parental oversight and that urban locations make lesbians and gay men more likely to meet people who are similar in sexual orientation but, compared with heterosexual social settings, more demographically diverse. It would be interesting to focus future research on how lesbians, gay men, and others negotiate demographic diversity in their partners, friends, and community. Perhaps this heterogeneity can serve as a model for heterosexual people in an increasingly diverse U.S. society.

LGBT groups are getting more specialized. Rural and conservative communities may still form networks of the few nonheterosexual women and men, providing support across gender and sexual orientation (e.g., D'Augelli & Hart, 1987).

However, beginning in major urban gay enclaves and now increasingly in many smaller U.S. cities and towns, lesbian, gay, bisexual, and transgender people can choose from many organizations and events: a support group for lesbians who have adopted children from China, the Gay and Lesbian Arab Society in New York, the African Ancestresses Book Club, the Massachusetts Transgender Political Coalition, and the Bay Area Bisexual Network. These are just a few of the thousands of organizations available across the United States today. The consequences of this dizzying selection is that lesbian, gay, and bisexual individuals are increasingly socializing with others who share similar interests, resulting in many specialized microcommunities that might not overlap or associate with each other, and that combine heterosexual and nonheterosexual people (Kline, 2006; Rothblum, 2010). Further research is needed to examine how members of sexual minorities prioritize sexual orientation versus other aspects of their identity and interests.

What about lesbian, gay, bisexual, and transgender (people who are multicultural? This chapter mentioned earlier how lesbian, gay, and bisexual people grow up in mainstream society and need to find their subculture. Those who are members of other racial and ethnic minority groups—African Americans, Latinos/as, Asian Americans, Pacific Islanders, Native Americans, biracial/biethnic people, immigrants, refugees—may be more visible as members of those communities than for being lesbian, gay, bisexual, or transgender. There has been very little research on polycultural communities (e.g., Diaz, Ayala, Bein, Henne, & Marin, 2001; Parks, Hughes, & Matthews, 2004) and how members of sexual minorities feel included or marginalized.

Lesbian, gay, and bisexual communities must negotiate ex-lover relationships. In an early study of a lesbian community in Oregon, Barnhart (1975) stated: "The ideals of honesty, openness, equality, and sisterhood are demonstrated by one of the main rules of the Community...which states that everyone has to be friends with everyone else, including ex-lovers" (p. 105). There may be pressure for ex-lovers to become friends so as not to divide the lesbian communities (see Weinstock & Rothblum, 2004, for a review). Our research on same-sex couples (Solomon et al., 2004) found that both male and female same-sex couples were more likely to have friends who were ex-lovers than were heterosexual married couples. Valentine (1993) found that lesbian networks were more interconnected than networks of heterosexuals. This is because heterosexuals can socialize at multiple venues openly, whereas lesbians tended to meet the same people at gay and lesbian organizations and events. Consequently, when couples break off their relationships, they find it hard to avoid each other at lesbian events, especially in rural areas and small towns. Yet there has been very little research examining networks of ex-lovers among lesbians or bisexual women, much less among gay or bisexual men.

How does queer identity relate to community? As some sexual minority youth have adopted the identity "queer" to describe nonnormative sexual orientation and gender identity, they also tend to see sexuality as more fluid and flexible (Diamond, 2008; Savin-Williams, 2005). It is too early to know how queer identity influences community membership, especially in the age of the Internet. Will it make bisexual and transgender people feel more included? Or will it alienate or not attract people who feel a need to assume a more categorical identity? This is an important avenue for future research.

In sum, in lieu of support and closeness from families of origin, lesbian, gay, bisexual, and transgender communities take on a central role in the lives of sexual minority people. The increased outness and visibility of lesbian and gay communities have made them more accessible, and the Internet has extended this accessibility to people in rural areas and to those who are closeted. At the same time, it is possible that, over time, lesbian, gay, bisexual, and transgender people will become so assimilated that our communities will be subsumed into mainstream society. As more U.S. states and other countries provide legal recognition of same-sex marriage, as more lesbian, gay, bisexual, and transgender people have children via insemination, surrogacy, or adoption, and now that the military has lifted the ban on openly identified lesbians, gay men, and bisexual individuals, will there still be identifiable lesbian and gay communities? It is important to continue to examine the evolving lesbian, gay, bisexual, and transgender communities, and to realize how little we know about factors that make people feel included and supported in the expression of their sexual and gender identities.

REFERENCES

Adams, B. (1979). Mate selection in the United States: A theoretical summarization. In W. Burr, R. Hill, F. Nie, & I. Reiss (Eds.), *Contemporary theories about the family* (Vol. 1, pp. 259–267). New York: Free Press.

Ault, A. (1996). Lesbian feminist stigmatization of bisexual women. In B. Beemyn & M. Eliason (Eds.), *Queer studies: A lesbian, gay, bisexual and transgender anthology* (pp. 204–216). New York: New York University Press.

Barnhart, E. (1975). Friends and lovers in a lesbian counterculture community. In N. Glazer-Malbin (Ed.), *Old family/new family: Interpersonal relationships* (pp. 90–115). New York: Van Nostrand Company.

Bechdel, A. (2008). *The essential dykes to watch out for.* New York: Houghton Mifflin Harcourt.

Beemyn, B. (1997). *Creating a place for ourselves: Lesbian, gay, and bisexual community histories.* New York: Routledge.

Berberet, H. M. (2005). *The San Diego LGBT Community Center: Lesbian, bisexual, transgender women's needs assessment.* Unpublished report, San Diego, CA.

Bérubé, A. (1990). *Coming out under fire: The history of gay men and women in World War II.* New York: The Free Press.

Black, D., Gates, G., Sanders, S., & Taylor, L. (2002). Why do gay men live in San Francisco? *Journal of Urban Economics, 51,* 54–76.

Blasband, D., & Peplau, L. A. (1985). Sexual exclusivity versus openness in gay male couples. *Archives of Sexual Behavior, 14,* 395–412.

Blumstein, P., & Schwartz, P. (1983). *American couples: Money, work, sex.* New York: William Morrow.

Botnick, M. R. (2000). Introduction. *Journal of Homosexuality, 38*(4), 1–4.

Cayleff, S. (1996). *Babe: The life and legend of Babe Didrikson Zaharias.* Urbana, IL: University of Illinois Press.

Chauncey, G. (1995). *Gay New York: Gender, urban culture, and the making of the gay male world, 1890–1940.* New York: Basic Books.

Crosbie-Burnett, M., & Helmbrecht, L. (1993). A descriptive empirical study of gay male stepfamilies. *Family Relations, 42,* 256–262.

D'Augelli, A. R., & Garnets, L. D. (1995). Lesbian, gay, and bisexual communities. In A. R. D'Augelli & C. J. Patterson (Eds.), *Lesbian, gay, and bisexual identities over the lifespan* (pp. 293–319). New York: Oxford University Press.

D'Augelli, A. R., & Hart, M. M. (1987). Gay women, men, and families in rural settings: Toward the development of helping communities. *American Journal of Community Psychology, 15*(1), 79–93.

D'Emilio, J. (1992). *Making trouble.* New York: Routledge.

Diamond, L. M. (2008). *Sexual fluidity: Understanding women's love and desire.* Cambridge, MA: Harvard University Press.

Diaz, R. M., Ayala, G., Bein, E., Henne, J., & Marin, B. V. (2001). The impact of homophobia, poverty, and racism on the mental health of gay and bisexual Latino men: Findings from three U.S. cities. *American Journal of Public Health, 91*, 927–932.

Dickie, J. R., Cook, A., Gazda, R., Martin, B., & Sturrus, E. (2005). The heirs of Aradia, daughters of Diana: Community in the second and third wave. *Journal of Lesbian Studies, 9*(1/2), 95–110.

Dolance, S. (2005). "A whole stadium full": Lesbian community at Women's National Basketball Association games. *The Journal of Sex Research, 42*, 74–83.

Edwards, J., & Riggs, D. W. (2008). Community, family, citizenship and the health of LGBTIQ people. *Health Sociology Review, 17*(3), 222–225.

Elwood, S. A. (2000). Lesbian living spaces: Multiple meanings of home. *Journal of Lesbian Studies, 4*(1), 11–27.

Factor, R. J., & Rothblum, E. D. (2008a). A study of transgender adults and their non-transgender siblings on demographic characteristics, social support, and experiences of violence. *Journal of LGBT Health Research, 3*(3), 11–30.

Factor, R. J., & Rothblum, E. D. (2008b). Exploring gender identity and community among three groups of transgender individuals in the United States: MTFs, FTMs, and genderqueers. *Health Sociology Review, 17*, 241–259.

Faderman, L. (1991). *Odd girls and twilight lovers: A history of lesbian life in twentieth-century America.* New York: Columbia University Press.

Fischer, C. S. (1982). *To dwell among friends: Personal networks in town and city.* Chicago: University of Chicago Press.

Folkman, S., & Lazarus, R. S. (1980). An analysis of coping in a middle-aged community sample. *Journal of Health and Social Behavior, 21*, 219–239.

Franzen, T. (1993). Differences and identities: Feminism and the Albuquerque lesbian community. *Signs: Journal of Women in Culture and Society, 18*, 891–906.

Gagne, P., Tewksbury, R., & McGaughey, D. (1997). Coming out and crossing over: Identity formation and proclamation in a transgender community. *Gender & Society, 11*, 478–508.

Galupo, M. P. (Ed.). (2007). *Bisexual women: Friendship and social organization.* New York: Harrington Park Press.

Garber, E. (1990). A spectacle in color: The lesbian and gay subculture of Jazz Age Harlem. In M. Duberman, M. Vicinus, & G. Chauncey (Eds.), *Hidden from history: Reclaiming the gay and lesbian past* (pp. 318–331). New York: Penguin.

Gates, G. J., Ost, J., & Birch, E. (2004). *Gay & lesbian atlas.* Washington, DC: Urban Institute Press.

Glaus, K. O. (1989). Alcoholism, chemical dependency, and the lesbian client. *Women & Therapy, 8*, 131–144.

Green, F. (2007). *The Gayellow Pages.* New York: Renaissance House.

Greene, B. (1994). Ethnic-minority lesbians and gay men: Mental health and treatment issues. *Journal of Consulting and Clinical Psychology, 62*, 243–251.

Griffin, P. (1998). *Strong women, deep closets: Lesbians and homophobia in sports.* Champaign, IL: Human Kinetics.

Hickson, F. C. I., Davies, P. M., Hunt, A. J., Weatherburn, P., McManus, T. J., & Coxon, A. P. M. (1992). Maintenance of open gay relationships: Some strategies for protection against HIV. *AIDS Care, 4*, 409–419.

Hoff, C. C., & Beougher, S. C. (2010). Sexual agreements among gay male couples. *Archives of Sexual Behavior, 39*, 774–787

Hoff, C. C., Chakravarty, D., Beougher, S. C., Darbes, L. A., Dadasovich, R., & Neilands, T. (2009). Serostatus differences and agreements about outside sex partners among gay male couples. *AIDS Education and Prevention, 21*, 25–38.

Idler, E. L., & Benyamini, Y. (1997). Self-rated health and mortality: A review of twenty-seven community studies. *Journal of Health and Social Behavior, 38*, 21–37.

Kennedy, E. L., & Davis, M. D. (1993). *Boots of leather, slippers of gold: The history of a lesbian community.* New York: Routledge.

Kline, J. (2006). *Discovering lesbian community? An exploration of lesbians' experiences and perceptions of shared community.* Unpublished dissertation, University of Melbourne, Melbourne, Australia.

Krieger, S. (1983). *The mirror dance: Identity in a women's community.* Philadelphia, PA: Temple University Press.

Laumann, E. O., Gagnon, J. H., Michael, R. T., & Michaels, S. (1994). *The social organization of sexuality: Sexual practices in the United States.* Chicago: University of Chicago Press.

Leavy, R. L. (2006). Social support and psychological disorder: A review. *Journal of Community Psychology, 11*, 3–21.

LeBeau, R. T., & Jellison, W. A. (2009). Why get involved? Exploring gay and bisexual men's experience of the gay community. *Journal of Homosexuality, 56*(1), 56–76.

Liddle, K. (2005). More than a bookstore: The continuing relevance of feminist bookstores for the lesbian community. *Journal of Lesbian Studies, 9*, 145–159.

Lukes, C. A., & Land, H. (1990). Biculturality and homosexuality. *Social Work, 35*, 155–161.

Meeker, M. (2006). *Contacts desired: Gay and lesbian communications and community, 1940s–1970s.* Chicago: University of Chicago Press.

Miller, N. (1995). *Out of the past: Gay and lesbian history from 1869 to the present.* New York: Vintage Books.

Morris, B. J. (2005). Negotiating lesbian worlds: The festival communities. *Journal of Lesbian Studies, 9*, 55–62.

Myrdahl, T. K. M. (2009). "Family-friendly" without the double entendre: A spatial analysis of normative game spaces and lesbian fans. *Journal of Lesbian Studies, 13,* 291–305.

Newton, E. (1995). *Cherry Grove, Fire Island: Sixty years in America's first gay and lesbian town.* Boston, MA: Beacon Press.

Parks, C. A., Hughes, T., & Matthews, A. K. (2004). Race/ethnicity and sexual orientation: Intersecting identities. *Cultural Diversity and Ethnic Minority Psychology, 10,* 241–254.

Peplau, L. A., Cochran, S. D., & Mays, V. M. (1997). A national survey of the intimate relationships of African American lesbians and gay men: A look at commitment, satisfaction, sexual behavior, and HIV disease. In B. Greene & G. Herek (Eds.), *Psychological perspectives on lesbian and gay issues: Ethnic and cultural diversity among lesbians and gay men* (pp. 11–38). Newbury Park, CA: Sage.

Rabin, J. S., & Slater, B. R. (2005). Lesbian communities across the United States: Pockets of resistance and resilience. *Journal of Lesbian Studies, 9,* 169–182.

Ralston, L., & Stoller, N. (2005). Hallomas: Longevity in a back-to-the-land women's group in Northern California. *Journal of Lesbian Studies, 9,* 63–72.

Romanovsky, R., & Phillips, P. (1987). Straightening up the house. Song in *Emotional roller coaster.* Santa Fe, NM: Bodacious Music.

Rosenfeld, M. J., & Kim, B. (2005). The independence of young adults and the rise of interracial and same-sex unions. *American Sociological Review, 70,* 541–562.

Rothblum, E. D. (2008). Finding a large and thriving lesbian and bisexual community: The costs and benefits of caring. *Gay & Lesbian Issues and Psychology Review, 4,* 69–79.

Rothblum, E. D. (2010). Where is the "women's community"? Voices of lesbian, bisexual, and queer women and their heterosexual sisters. *Feminism & Psychology, 20*(4), 454–472.

Rothblum, E. D., Balsam, K. F., & Mickey, R. M. (2004). Brothers and sisters of lesbians, gay men, and bisexuals as a demographic comparison group: An innovative research methodology to examine social change. *Journal of Applied Behavioral Science, 40,* 283–301.

Rothblum, E. D., & Factor, R. J. (2001). Lesbians and their sisters as a control group: Demographic and mental health factors. *Psychological Science, 12,* 63–69.

Rothblum, E. D., & Sablove, P. (Eds.). (2005). *Lesbian communities: Festivals, RVs and the Internet.* New York: Harrington Park Press.

Rust, P. (1995). *Bisexuality and the challenge to lesbian politics: Sex, loyalty and revolution.* New York: New York University Press.

Savin-Williams, R. (2005). *The new gay teenager: Adolescent lives.* Cambridge, MA: Harvard University Press.

Schneider, M. (1989). Sappho was a right-on adolescent: Growing up lesbian. *Journal of Homosexuality, 17,* 111–130.

Solomon, S. E., Rothblum, E. D., & Balsam, K. F. (2004). Pioneers in partnership: Lesbian and gay male couples in civil unions compared with those not in civil unions, and heterosexual married siblings. *Journal of Family Psychology, 18,* 275–286.

Solomon, S. E., Rothblum, E. D., & Balsam, K. F. (2005). Money, housework, sex, and conflict: Same-sex couples in civil unions, those not in civil unions, and heterosexual married siblings. *Sex Roles, 52,* 561–575.

Toro-Alfonso, J. (1999). Domestic violence among same sex partners in Puerto Rico: Implications for HIV intervention. *Journal of Gay & Lesbian Social Services, 9,* 69–78.

Valentine, G. (1993). Desperately seeking Susan: A geography of lesbian friendships. *Area, 25,* 109–116.

Weinstock, J. S., & Rothblum, E. D. (2004). *Lesbian ex-lovers: The really long-term relationships.* New York: Harrington Park Press.

Weston, K. (1997). *Families we choose.* New York: Columbia University Press.

Whittle, S. (1998). The trans-cyberian mail way. *Social & Legal Studies, 7,* 389–408.

Woolwine, D. (2000). Community in gay male experience and moral discourse. *Journal of Homosexuality, 38,* 5–37.

INDEX

Page numbers written in italics denote illustrations.